The European Reformations

To Rod, Tina, and Gary

The European Reformations

Carter Lindberg

School of Theology
Boston University

BLACKWELL
Publishers

First published 1996
Reprinted 1996, 1997

Blackwell Publishers Ltd
108 Cowley Road
Oxford OX4 1JF, UK

Blackwell Publishers Inc
350 Main Street
Malden, Massachusetts 02148, USA

British Library Cataloguing in Publication Data
A CIP catalogue record for this book is available from the British Library

Library of Congress Cataloging in Publication Data
Lindberg, Carter, 1937–
The European reformations / Carter Lindberg
p.   cm.
Includes bibliographical references and index.
ISBN 1–55786–574–4 (alk. paper) — ISBN 1–55786–575–2 (pbk: alk. paper)
1. Reformation. 2. Church history – 15th century. 3. Counter-Reformation.
4. Reformation – Great Britain. I. Title.
  BR305.2.L486   1996   95–22971
  274'.06—dc20   CIP

Commissioning Editor: Alison Mudditt
Development Editor: Nathalie Manners
Desk Editor: Gillian Bromley
Production Controller: Lisa Eaton
Picture Researcher: Ginny Stroud-Lewis/Sarah McKean

Typeset in 11 on 13pt Bembo by Photoprint, Torquay, Devon
Printed and bound in Great Britain by Hartnolls Ltd, Bodmin, Cornwall

This book is printed on acid-free paper

Contents

Contents

Illustrations

Preface

Human life without knowledge of history is nothing other than a perpetual childhood, nay, a permanent obscurity and darkness.

Philip Melanchthon

I hope that this textbook will contribute to the perennial discovery of who we are and how we got this way. The "we" here is meant globally. Such a goal of course smacks of delusions of grandeur or at least an overestimation of the influence of the Reformations of the sixteenth century. But no historian of whatever persuasion thinks he or she is an antiquarian studying the past "for its own sake" as if understanding it did not contribute to understanding ourselves. This is illustrated by citing just two major Reformation historians. Steven Ozment (1992: 217) concludes one of his books on the Reformation: "To people of all nationalities the first Protestants bequeathed in spite of themselves a heritage of spiritual freedom and equality, the consequences of which are still working themselves out in the world today." And William Bouwsma (1988:1) begins his study of Calvin with a litany of his influences: "Calvinism has been widely credited – or blamed – for much that is thought to characterize the modern world: for capitalism and modern science, for the discipline and rationalization of the complex societies of the West, for the revolutionary spirit and democracy, for secularization and social activism, for individualism, utilitarianism, and empiricism." If Ozment and Bouwsma are anywhere near the mark, it behoves us to reflect on our roots.

The influence of the Reformations has extended beyond Euro-American cultures to the wider world. Scholars have pursued the influences of Calvinism on social conditions in the Republic of South Africa and of Lutheranism on modern developments in Germany and the course of Judaism; the once Eurocentric International Congress for Luther Research now includes participants from the so-called "Third World" who are concerned not only about the ecclesial applicability of

Luther's theology but its relevance to liberation and human rights. The global nature of Reformation research is evident in the translation of writings of the Reformers into various Asian languages and the existence of scholarly endeavors everywhere, including the People's Republic of China; not to mention the impact on ecumenical dialogues among Christians and with disciples of other world religions. The Reformations continue to be seen as too important to contemporary life to be left to antiquarians and those whom Carlyle termed "dryasdust" historians.

Why one more textbook on the Reformations? There is of course the personal factor: I suspect that nearly every teacher wishes to tell the story his or her own way. I am no different; and have been stimulated in this endeavor by the occasional student question, "Why don't you write your own text?" Such obviously brilliant and insightful students wise to the utilitarian value of such a question should not however be blamed for this project. Rather, the rationale for sacrificing more trees to the textbook trade is to incorporate aspects of the burgeoning field of Reformation studies into a text that interprets these contributions from a historical–theological perspective. Hence major attention will be directed to what the Reformers and those who received their messages believed to be at stake – literally as well as figuratively – for their salvation. The thread – with all its kinks and knots – running throughout this story is their struggle to understand and to apply to society the freedom and authority of the gospel.

What will this orientation bring to this text? I have already suggested the global impact of the Reformations on contemporary identities. Scholarly fascination with the influences of the Reformations has grown to the point where major historiographical studies are devoted to it. The initial chapter on history and historiography will illustrate that it is not only church historians and theologians who have commitments. All historians are also interpreters; thus any and all suggestions that if you can only shed theological (or political, or Marxist, et al.) convictions you will be scientifically "objective" or "value free" are suspect.

The title of this text speaks of "Reformations." I view the Reformation era as a time of plural reform movements. This approach has significance for interpretation and definition that will be explored throughout the text. For now, the use of the plural reminds us that even commonly used terms such as "Reformation" carry within them subtle or not so subtle value judgments.

I will also attempt to incorporate into this text the research that has mushroomed so recently under the general rubric of social history.

Here there is specific attention to the marginalized (the poor, women), minorities, popular culture in terms of context and reception, the development of modern traits (individualism, rationality, the secular), and the world-building process called confessionalization. Every work of synthesis inevitably carries within it seeds (and sometimes full-grown weeds!) of misunderstandings and all too many omissions. I hope the chronology, maps, genealogical tables, bibliography, and suggestions for further reading will ameliorate to some extent the disjointedness of this synthetic narrative and its lack of discussion of the Reformations in Eastern Europe and Scandinavia. Textbook authors have the temerity angels eschew. This being the case, I take heart from Luther's dictum to "sin boldly" as well as from the words of a great English Reformation scholar, A. G. Dickens (1974: 210): "In short, synthesis must involve writing books which form challenges to write better ones, books which will inevitably be replaced, attacked and patronized by others which climb upon their shoulders."

I am pleased to dedicate these efforts to our new sons and daughter who, even after marrying our children, still listen patiently to dinner discourses on the Reformations and provide wry comments. I wish to thank the many students of my "Reformations" course whose lively questions and arguments over the years have frequently redeemed what began as "dryasdust" lectures. My "thorn-in-the-flesh" colleague, J. Paul Sampley, has rendered a similar service in and out of the classroom. Finally, my thanks to Alison Mudditt, Senior Commissioning Editor of Blackwell Publishers, who initiated and shepherded this project to conclusion, to Gillian Bromley, Desk Editor, whose sharp eye caught many an error, and to Sarah McKean, Picture Researcher at Blackwell, for obtaining the illustrations.

Abbreviations

ARG	*Archive for Reformation History/Archiv für Reformationsgeschichte*
CH	*Church History*
CHR	*Catholic Historical Review*
CO	*Ioannis Calvini Opera quae supersunt omnia*, ed. C. Baum, E. Cunitz, and E. Reiss. Brunswick/Berlin: Schwetschke, 1863–1900 (*Corpus Reformatorum*, vols 29–87)
CR	*Corpus Reformatorum*. Berlin/Leipzig, 1811–1911
CTM	The Collected Works of Thomas Müntzer, tr. and ed. Peter Matheson. Edinburgh: T. & T. Clark, 1988
CTQ	*Concordia Theological Quarterly*
HJ	*Historical Journal*
LQ	*Lutheran Quarterly*
LW	*Luther's Works*, ed. Jaroslav Pelikan and Helmut T. Lehmann, 55 vols. St Louis: Concordia/Philadelphia: Fortress, 1955–86 [References in text are to volume and page, thus 31: 318 = vol. 31, p. 318]
MQR	*Mennonite Quarterly Review*
PL	*Patrologia + cursus completus. Series Latina*, ed. J-P. Migne, 221 vols. Paris: Migne, 1844–1900
PP	*Past and Present*
SCJ	*Sixteenth Century Journal*
StA	*Martin Luther: Studienausgabe*, ed. Hans-Ulrich Delius, 5 vols. Berlin: Evangelische Verlagsanstalt, 1979–92
TRE	*Theologische Realenzyklopädie*, ed. G. Krause and G. Muller. Berlin/New York: de Gruyter, 1976–
WA	*D. Martin Luthers Werke: Kritische Gesamtausgabe*, ed. J. K. F. Knaake, G. Kawerau, et al., 58 vols. Weimar: Böhlau, 1883–
WA Br	*D. Martin Luthers Werke: Briefwechsel*, 15 vols. Weimar: Böhlau, 1830
WA TR	*D. Martin Luthers Werke: Tischreden*, 6 vols. Weimar: Böhlau, 1912–21

Z	*Huldreich Zwinglis sämtliche Werke*, ed. F. Egli et al. Berlin/Leipzig, 1905– (*Corpus Reformatorum*, vols 88–101); repr. Zurich: Theologischer Verlag, 1982–
ZKG	*Zeitschrift für Kirchengeschichte*
ZRG	*Zeitschrift der Savigny-Stiftung für Rechtsgeschichte, Kanonische Abteilung*
ZThK	*Zeitschrift für Theologie und Kirche*

1

History, Historiography, and Interpretations of the Reformations

We are like dwarfs standing on the shoulders of giants; thanks to them, we see farther than they. Busying ourselves with the treatises written by the ancients, we take their choice thoughts, buried by age and human neglect, and we raise them, as it were from death to renewed life.

Peter of Blois (d. 1212)

History and Historiography

Peter of Blois penned this famous aphorism almost exactly three centuries before Luther's "Ninety-Five Theses" rocked Europe. A recent major study of the historiography of the Reformation (Dickens and Tonkin 1985: 323) concludes that it is "a window on the West, a major point of access to the developing Western mind through the last five centuries. . . . By any reckoning, the Reformation has proved a giant among the great international movements of modern times." On its shoulders we can look farther and deeper in both directions, that is, we can peer into both the medieval and contemporary worlds.

History provides a horizon for viewing not only the past but also the present and the future. The philosopher Hans-Georg Gadamer (1975: 269, 272) argued that a person without a horizon will overvalue what is immediately present, whereas the horizon enables us to sense the relative significance of what is near or far, great or small. "A horizon means that one learns to look beyond what is close at hand – not in order to look away from it, but to see it better within a larger whole and in truer proportion." In other words, "far away facts – in history as in navigation – are more effective than near ones in giving us true bearings" (Murray 1974: 285). Even novice sailors know it is foolish to navigate by sighting your prow rather than by sighting the stars or land.

Historical distance, by providing a focus beyond what we take for granted, can be a surprising component of contemporary comprehension. The analogy of living in a foreign city illustrates this. If you live in a foreign city for a year, you will not learn a great deal about that city. But when you return home you will be surprised by your increasing comprehension of some of the most profound and individual characteristics of your homeland. You did not previously "see" these characteristics because you were too close to them; you knew them too well. Likewise, a visit to the past provides distance and a vantage point from which to comprehend the present (Braudel 1972; Nygren 1948).

Memory also illustrates this. "Memory is the thread of personal identity, history of public identity" (Hofstadter 1968: 3; Leff 1971: 115). Memory and historical identity are inseparable. Have you ever been asked to introduce someone and suddenly forgotten her name? At worst this common human experience is a temporary embarrassment. But think what life would be like if you had no memory at all. We all have heard how terribly difficult life is for amnesiacs, and about the tragic effects of Alzheimer's disease upon its victims and their families. The loss of memory is not just the absence of "facts;" it is the loss of personal identity, family, friends, indeed, the whole complex of life's meaning. It is very difficult if not impossible to function in society if we do not know who we are and how we got this way. Our memory is the thread of our personal identity; our memory liberates us from what Melanchthon, Luther's colleague, called perpetual childhood. Without our past we have no present and no future.

What about our national and religious community identities? Are we amnesiacs, are we children, when it comes to identifying who we are in relation to our communities? What if we had to identify ourselves as an American or a Christian? Suppose someone asked why we are Protestant or Roman Catholic. Beyond referring to our parents or a move to a new neighborhood, could we explain why we belong to Grace Lutheran by the gas station instead of St Mary's by the grocery store?

I once asked a French friend to explain German–French relations. He began by referring to the ninth-century division of Charlemagne's empire! Most of us do not go that far back to answer contemporary questions, but his response illustrates that if memory is the thread of personal identity, history is the thread of community identity. These tenacious threads of community identity also have a dark side when they are not critically examined. This is painfully evident in the eruption of historical ethnic conflicts such as those in the former Yugoslavia and Soviet Union as well as in the Middle East. If we do not know our personal and community histories we are like children who are easily manipulated by those who would use the past for their own purposes.

Memory and history are crucial to our identity, but they are not easily conceptualized in relation to their origins and goals. Here I take comfort in the comment of the great African theologian, St Augustine (354–430), who in discussing time wrote: "What then is time? If no one asks me, I know; if I wish to explain it to one that asks, I know not" (*Confessions*, Book XI). This most influential western theologian was struggling to relate to his hellenistic–Roman culture the Christian conviction that the identity of the community is rooted in history rather than in philosophy and ethics. This conviction had already been clearly stated in the historical shorthand of the Christian creeds, which confess faith in the historical person of Jesus who was born, suffered, and died. Christians put a unique spin on history when they also confess that this Jesus was raised from the dead and will return to bring history to completion. Thus, from an insider's perspective, the Christian community's identity is formed by both the historical past and the historical future. Without sensitivity to this theological claim, it will be difficult for us to fully realize the power in the Reformations of apocalyptic views of history or such works as John Foxe's *Acts and Monuments*. This sense of the historical past, present, and future identity of the church, expressed in the third article of the creeds by the phrase "communion of saints," was so palpable to the medieval that the English Roman Catholic historian, John Bossy (1985), makes it the theme of his study of the Reformation. As we shall see, the historical identity of the communion of saints became a central controversial issue in the Reformation era.

Sociologists of knowledge make a similar point about historical identity rooted in community. Historical identity is passed on to us through our conversations with the mothers and fathers who have gone before us. In this sense, church historians take seriously the fourth commandment of the decalogue: "Honor your father and mother." We know, of course, from even limited family experience that when we no longer talk to our parents and children we begin to forget who we are. This is not to say that conversation between generations is always pleasant, but to say that it is important for learning how we got this way. Without such conversation we are condemned to "presentism," a fancy term to describe the solipsism of a continuous "me generation." Thus the postwar German phrase *Welt ohne Vater* is shorthand for the loss of roots and the authority crises suffered by the generation whose fathers fell in the war. Lord Acton stated this elegantly: "History must be our deliverer not only from the undue influence of other times, but from the undue influence of our own, from the tyranny of environment and the pressure of the air we breathe. It requires all historic forces to produce their record and submit it to judgment, and it promotes the faculty of resistance to contemporary surroundings by familiarity with other ages and orbits of thought" (Pelikan 1971: 150).

Until recently the collectors and tellers of the family conversations of Christianity were nearly all insiders. Thus the subject matter and the discipline of its telling fell under the rubric of "church history." For a variety of reasons today, persons outside the Christian churches are also interested in presenting the history of Christianity. There is, to paraphrase an old maxim, the sense that the telling of the story of Christian contributions to contemporary identity is too important to be left to the Christians. The field of Reformation studies is a marked example of this recent development.

Awareness of the distinct perspectives of church historians and historians of Christianity will be useful in terms of reading both contemporary textbooks and the historical sources. We shall get to other perspectives later, but for now we may remind ourselves that interpretations of the past are not value free. Indeed, Heisenberg's "indeterminacy principle" applies as much to historical studies as it does to sub-atomic physics: what is observed is influenced by the observer. "It is paradoxical, in fact, that nature seems more unambiguously susceptible to human understanding and control than is history which man makes and in which he is personally and intimately involved" (Spitz 1962: vii). In the words of the eminent English historian, G. R. Elton (1967: 13): "In truth, historians, like other people, tend to judge their world from their own experiences and practice, and it is disturbing to see how narrow in their sympathies even eminent men can be."

Some of the presuppositions which govern an author's collection and interpretation of events leap right off the page at us; others are more subtle. This is exemplified by the work of Eusebius of Caesarea (ca. 260–ca. 340), the "Father of Church History." In the introduction to his *The History of the Church*, Eusebius begins with a "truth in advertising" statement, the candor of which is all too rare in modern historical works. "From the scattered hints dropped by my predecessors I have picked out whatever seems relevant to the task I have undertaken, plucking like flowers in literary pastures the helpful contributions of earlier writers to be embodied in the continuous narrative I have in mind."

Historians are selective in choosing data. Until very recently this selection has been governed by religious and theological commitments.

This is not surprising since church historians traditionally work with a double perspective: the history of the church and the contemporizing of the past as a critical measure of the church's faithfulness. The latter critical point means that the focus of the church historian's work is a community which is already existing but not yet completed. In theological terms, there is an eschatological dimension to church historical work because the community being studied believes it lives between the "now" of the historical activity and promise of Jesus, and the "not yet" of the full realization of the Jesus movement. The problem this poses for modern historical method is how to write a history of that which claims to occur in history but also claims to be the end to history. Such metahistorical claims to privileged insight into the course and goal of history are of course not limited to theologians; they may be seen in such disparate modern expressions as Hegel's idealist conviction of the self-realization of the absolute world spirit, Marx's materialist conviction of the realization of the classless society, and the American belief in the triumph of democracy, to name but a few.

The hegemony of theological and church historical studies of the Reformations of the sixteenth century has only recently been critically questioned, and the implications of this questioning are only beginning to find their way into textbooks. How radical this change is may be seen by a review of the long predominance of the Eusebian model of historical writing which normed the "true" church by the community of the first centuries of the Christian era. The norm of the first centuries led to the rationalization of historical change and development as expressions of the unchanging essence of early Christianity, and idealized the apostolic age, the time of origins. This norm was operative in all parties of the Reformation era, and is easily seen in the various Reformers' appeals to Scripture and the apostolic faith to support their respective claims to be *the* continuation of the early church. Thus in the Leipzig debate (1519) over papal authority, Luther stated that papal claims to superiority are relatively recent. "Against them stand the history of eleven hundred years, the text of divine Scripture, and the decree of the Council of Nicea [325], the most sacred of all councils" (*LW* 31: 318).

Even though the Reformations of the sixteenth century split the church, all parties continued to hold to the Eusebian model of church history by claiming to be *the* faithful recovery or continuation of the early church, and by accusing other churches of innovation, i.e. heresy. The Reformers urged people to judge all doctrines by Scripture; and all the churches turned to history to legitimate and bolster their individual claims to be the faithful community. Those convinced that the medieval church was a total corruption of the early church developed martyrologies to support their view that in spite of corruption there continued to be faithful witnesses to the Jesus movement in history.

The ground for the Reformers' critique of the recent past as degenerate was prepared by the prior generation of humanists. The term "Middle Ages" (*media aetas, medium tempus, medium aevum*) is first encountered in scattered references by fifteenth-century humanists. They considered this segment of time an intermediate period between what they perceived as the ideal and glorified classical period (à la Eusebius) and their own time, which they termed "modern." The humanists aspired and strove for a rebirth (Renaissance) of ancient and classical language, education, science, art, and the church. Humanists regarded the Middle Ages as barbaric; so, for example, its art was called "gothic." This humanist characterization was driven not just by aesthetic and philological criteria but by theological and religious criteria as well. The men and women of the Renaissance projected back into history their own reactions to what they regarded as the super-stitious and narrow-minded orthodoxy and authoritarianism of the church of their day. The influence of this humanist perspective continues to be evident in our use of pejorative labels such as "Dark Ages" and "scholastic."

While it is sometimes said that contemporary culture is fascinated with innovation and the new, the motto of Renaissance culture was *ad fontes*, back to the sources. The Reformers, most of whom were strongly influenced by humanism, echoed this with regard to Scripture and the early church. Melanchthon characterized the Reformation as the age "in which God recalled the church to its origins" (*in qua Deus Ecclesiam iterum ad fontes revocavit*: Ferguson 1948: 52). The sense that "older is better" characterized histories of the church stemming from the Reformations. Under the leadership of the Lutheran, Matthew Flacius Illyricus (1520–75), a group of scholars developed a history of the church from its beginning down to 1400 titled *Historia Ecclesiae Christi*. Since this work divided the history of the church into centuries and was begun in the city of Magdeburg, it is also known as the "Magdeburg Centuries." The Eusebian model remains effective in the "Centuries," for Flacius argued that the Reformation was the resto-ration of the original purity of the early church. Not surprisingly for a Lutheran apologist, the key to the faithfulness of the church was seen to be the doctrine of justification by grace alone. The original purity of the church lasted to about 300, and with some reservations even up to 600, but then there was a fall away from the faith due to the expansion of the papacy. In terms of periodization, the "Magdeburg Centuries" present the three periods now familiar to us: the ancient church or time of origins up to the fourth century, the medieval period of decay up to the fifteenth century, and the new period of recovery of the gospel. The historical reality of this tripartite division into ancient, medieval, and modern was little questioned and passed into the schema of universal history by the end of the seventeenth century as exemplified by the title of Christoph Cellarius's work, *Historia tripartita* (1685).

Not to be outdone, the Roman Catholic church responded to the "Magdeburg Centuries" with the herculean efforts of Caesar Baronius (1538–1607). After years of work in the Vatican archives, Baronius began publishing his study of the history of the church. Baronius proceeded year by year, and hence the title of his work is *Annales Ecclesiastici*; by the time of his death it had reached the year 1198. No less partisan than Flacius, and equally subject to the Eusebian model, Baronius focused his study on the institution of the papacy rather than the doctrine of justification. These two works illustrate the different understandings of Reformation by the Lutheran and Roman Catholic reform movements. The former focused on the reformation of dogma; the latter focused on renewal of the church as institution.

The dissident movements of the Reformation era were more interested in personal renewal than in either dogma or institution. In terms of church historical writing this tendency came to the fore in the so-called "impartial" history by Gottfried Arnold (1666–1714): *Unparteiische Kirchen- und Ketzerhistorie* (the full title translates as "The Impartial History of the Church and of Heretics from the Beginnings of the New Testament to the Year of Christ 1688"). To Arnold, the essence of the Christian faith was not dogmatic, ecclesiastical, juridical, or cultic, but rather the personal piety of individuals. From this point of view those whom the churches (Protestant and Catholic) had persecuted as heretics were now seen as the true Christians who had faithfully followed Jesus in opposing the "Babel" of both the established church and the world. The key to the critical reading of the history of the church was seen to be the "rebirth" of individuals. While Arnold's concept of a "nonpartisan" or "impartial" reading of history should not be equated with more modern attempts at "objectivity," it is sometimes seen as foreshadowing this effort. Furthermore, the concern with individuals and their conversion experiences foreshadows later interest in biographical and psychological studies of historical figures such as Erik H. Erikson's *Young Man Luther* (1958).

But even with these contributions, Arnold and the dissident reform movements before him remained in debt to the Eusebian model of church history. For them the consummate epoch of the church was the first three centuries which they saw as filled with the spirit of freedom, living faith, and holy living. The corruption and decay of the early church began under the first Christian emperor, Constantine the Great (d. 337), with the legitimizing of the church in the Roman empire and its consequent participation in Roman power and wealth. Here, too, the Middle Ages were seen as a long period of decline.

The Eusebian model of church history set the stage for the various Reformers' understandings of their own contexts, and it also illustrates that reflections on history are colored by value judgments. It is all too easy for us today as we stand upon the shoulders of those who went before us to criticize them for being unaware of what now appears self-evident to us. But every age is marked by what it takes to be self-evident, and hence uncritically takes for granted. This is equally true of us. Thus a recent study of twentieth-century medievalists is titled *Inventing the Middle Ages*. The author writes that our own anxieties, hopes, loves, and disappointments interact with our reading and writing of history. "The ideas of the Middle Ages articulated by the master medievalists vary substantially one from another. The libretto and score they are working from – the data of historical fact – are the same. The truth, therefore, is ultimately not in the textual details but in the interpretations" (Cantor 1991: 45).

Interpretations of the Reformations

To cite Cantor (1991: 367) again: "We tend to discover the past we set out to find. This is not because the past is a willfully imagined fiction but because it is such a complicated and mutifaceted reality." Without a perspective, without a horizon, the selection, arrangement, and interpretation of historical data would be helter-skelter. The multiplicity of interpretations may contribute to our understanding as well as to our confusion. Given the existence of varying horizons among historians, it is helpful to both the historian and his or her audience when the horizon is indicated. Mine is that religion and theology are central to understanding the Reformations. I hasten to add that they must be seen in their cultural contexts.

An initial move to control the complicated and multifaceted reality of the Reformation is to define the terms used for it and the era it covers. Until recently that was briefly and simply done. The widely used textbook for undergraduate "Renaissance–Reformation" history courses of the prior generation in America, Harold J. Grimm's *The*

Reformation Era 1500–1650, quickly disposed of the temporal para-
meters and the problem of definition: "In these pages the word
Reformation is used in its conventional sense, that is, involving the rise
of an evangelical Christianity, called Protestantism, that could not
accommodate itself to the old theology and ecclesiastical institutions"
(Grimm 1973: 2; cf. Cameron 1991: 2).

In more recent scholarship this "conventional sense" of the Reformation has given way to recognition that there was a plurality of
Reformations which interacted with each other: Lutheran, Catholic,
Reformed, and dissident movements. These multiple reforming movements are not fully understood if explained *only* in terms of religious
reform without account being taken of their historical, political, social,
and economic contexts and influences. If we lose sight of the Reformations' complex network of historical relationships we may oversimplify
our conception and evaluation of Reformation theology itself. "After
all, this theology had such a great impact in history precisely because it
was intricately interwoven into history" (Moeller 1982: 7).

The word "Reformation" has a long, involved history that on the
one hand goes back to classical times and on the other hand in
contemporary undergraduate curricula is almost always associated with
the "Renaissance," as in "Ren–Ref" courses. The medieval use of
reformatio may generally be understood in terms of the Eusebian rubric
that older is better. Technically, the term was used in relation to the re-
establishing of universities in their original condition, e.g. *reformatio in
pristinum statum*. The fourteenth-century conciliar movement used the
phrase "reformation of the church in head and members" (*reformatio
ecclesiae in capite et in membris*), meaning by this an ethical appeal to self-
reform by individuals. Thus ethical renewal appeared more important
than the reform of the church as an institution. This theme is continued
in the widely circulated *The Reformation of the Emperor Sigismund*
(ca. 1438) which calls for the restoration of the lost proper order of
things through ethical renewal and the re-establishment of God's order.
Similarly, the "Prophecy of Johann Lichtenberger" (1488) spoke of a
new reformation, a new law, a new kingdom, and a change among the
clergy and the common people. The observance of the law of Christ
and of the natural law were to return church and society to their
original God-willed condition. In the sixteenth century "reformation"
developed further meanings of improvement and renewal in both
ecclesiastical and profane usage.

It is of interest that Luther himself seldom used the term "reformation" apart from his successful effort to create a new curriculum at his
own university. The English translation of his significant outline for

reform, *Address to the Christian Nobility of the German Nation Concerning the Reform of the Christian Estate* (1520), suggests Luther's use of the term, but the title in German denotes "improvement" (*Besserung*). When Luther does use the term reformation he gives it a new sense: he ties it to doctrine rather than ethical renewal. The crux of genuine reform, he said in an early sermon, is the proclamation of the gospel of grace alone. This requires the reform of theology and preaching but is ultimately the work of God alone. Here Luther differs from all the so-called "forerunners" of the Reformation. "For Luther man could not be reformed – that is, restored to an earlier condition – but only forgiven" (Bouwsma 1980: 239).

It was not until the end of the seventeenth century that the concept Reformation was applied to the history of the church in Veit Ludwig von Seckendorff's *Commentarius historicus et apologeticus de Lutheranismo sive de reformatione religionis ductu D. Martini Lutheri in magna Germaniae parte aliisque regionibus* (1694). Seckendorff understood "Reformation" as the key word for the clarification of events in Germany in the first half of the sixteenth century. His work is not a history of the Reformation in a comprehensive sense, for it is limited to religion and ends with Luther's death; nevertheless, with his work, Reformation as a concept for an era or epoch entered the vocabulary and concepts of historical studies.

The early characterization of the Reformation as an era or epoch linked it to the career of Luther. The dictionaries and encyclopedias of the eighteenth century characterized the Reformation as an epoch defined by Luther's divinely motivated work of cleansing the church of abuses and doctrinal errors. For all practical purposes the Reformation was identified with Luther. This illustrates Protestantism's paradoxical tendency to make saints of those who rejected the veneration of saints (Bouwsma 1988: 2). Hence the Reformation as an epoch was bracketed by the date of the "Ninety-Five Theses" (1517) as the beginning and the Religious Peace of Augsburg (1555) as the end. "The whole period 1517–1555 was canonized as a self-sufficient phase of history, which tended to make people overlook the Bohemian Reformation of the fifteenth century and to undervalue not only the radical sects, but also the Reformed churches of Switzerland, France, and England" (Dickens and Tonkin 1985: 9). Such periodization also neglects the reforming movements within Catholicism as well as non-ecclesiastical events.

A comprehensive cultural sense of this era was first expressed in Leopold von Ranke's *Deutscher Geschichte im Zeitalter der Reformation* (1839–) which presented the church historical and political events as inseparable and mutually interactive. The "Epoch of the Reformation"

(*Zeitalter der Reformation*) is paradigmatically expressed in the title of the second half of his study, "Die Anfänge Luthers und Karls V," which juxtaposes Luther and the Emperor Charles V.

Ranke also popularized the term Counter-Reformation. He initially used this term in the plural (*Gegenreformationen*, "Counter-Reformations"). Roman Catholic historians took umbrage because this implied – and frequently stated – the historical and theological priority of the Protestant Reformation to which Catholicism then reacted. "The expression seemed to interpret the recovery of the Catholic Church merely as a counteraction to the schism and seemed to imply the use of force in religious matters" (Iserloh et al. 1986: 431). The Catholic scholar John Bossy (1985: 91) would just as soon drop the term Reformation altogether because "it goes along too easily with the notion that a bad form of Christianity was being replaced by a good one." Indeed, earlier Roman Catholic historians generally used the term "religious schism" (*Glaubensspaltung*) rather than Reformation to designate this period. In short, terms are not always innocent of values and problems. Yet without terms and periodizations it would be impossible to provide a coherent drama of complex changes.

More recent terminology, sensitive to contemporary ecumenical relationships as well as to historical accuracy, focuses on "Catholic Reformation" or "Catholic Reform" to indicate that Catholic reform or renewal movements pre- as well as postdated Luther and were not merely reactive. Nevertheless, confessional commitments aside, it is a historical mistake to ignore the reality of a "Catholic Counter-Reformation, which, springing from a preexistent, theologically conservative reformism, arose in force well within Luther's lifetime and set bounds to Protestant expansion" (Dickens and Tonkin 1985: 2; Jedin 1973: 46–81). "Counter-Reformation" thus locates and characterizes much of the Catholic Church's reaction to Protestantism. "But the term Reformation for Catholicism . . . unwittingly implies a substantive reformation of doctrine, which was, in fact, programmatically resisted by the Council of Trent" (Williams 1992: 3, 5). The Jesuit Reformation scholar, John O'Malley (1991: 177–93), argues however that there was far more to Catholicism in this period than the council of Trent. Although "Catholic Reform" and "Counter-Reformation" are coextensive in this period the terms may divert our attention from the more comprehensive reality of sixteenth-century Catholicism concerned with the care of souls beyond reform of abuses and institutions. Perhaps "early modern Catholicism" better designates both change and continuity than the older terms. I shall use the label "Roman Catholicism," although it is anachronistic for this time period, because phrases such as "adherents of the old faith," "adherents of the new faith," and "early modern Catholicism" are awkward. Also, the Reformers believed they were faithfully representing the Catholic church. Technically, the modification of "Catholic" by "Roman" is appropriate only after the council of Trent (1545–63).

The term "Reformation" is frequently modified by "magisterial" and "radical." Magisterial Reformation denotes the evangelical reform movements that were supported and enabled by magistrates, whether on the level of kings, princes, or town councils. Thus, for example, Luther won the support of the prince of Electoral Saxony, Zwingli the support of the town council of Zurich, and Calvin that of the councils of Geneva. Magisterial also refers to the authority of a teacher (*magister*); hence the teaching authority in the Roman Catholic Church, located in the pope and bishops in council, is termed the *Magisterium*. Among Protestants the teaching authority of Luther and Calvin was so great that reforming movements used their names, Lutheranism and Calvinism. "Thus the classical Magisterial Reformation was 'magisterial' not only in the primary sense that it allowed for a large role on the part of the state in implementing Reformation and even in assessing doctrinal, liturgical, and ecclesiological issues but also in the subsidiary sense that it accorded extraordinary authority to an individual teacher" (Williams 1992: 1281).

Those reforming movements which dissented from the so-called magisterial Reformers and stressed autonomy from political authorities have been labeled the "left wing" of the Reformation or, more recently, the "radical Reformation." Although the latter term has been widely used in Reformation studies since George H. Williams's major study, *The Radical Reformation*, "there has prevailed considerable uncertainty about its precise definition" (Hillerbrand 1986: 26). At the very least, it is clear that Luther was "left" of the Catholic establishment, and there is a consensus that Luther's position was "radical" up to the early 1520s. Thus "radical Reformation" is a problematic term associated with theological value judgments which "cannot be adjudicated by scholarly criteria" (Hillerbrand 1993: 416–17). Alternative terms for the so-called radicals are nonconformists and dissidents.

Indeed, it may be argued that "radical" in its fundamental sense of going to the roots (*radix*) equally applies to Luther's conviction that Scripture alone is the norm of Christian faith. This is a sober argument when it is realized that it was the medieval clergy who were custodians of the predominant social myth and hence the legitimators of social structure and political organization, not to mention controllers of a good deal of property and wealth. "A challenge to the clergy thus had to be a radical challenge, calling for a revolutionary change in European society . . . the Protestant Reformation was such a challenge" (Kingdon 1974: 57). "Together with the Italian Renaissance, the German Reformation has traditionally been viewed as the first of the great revolutions that created the modern world" (Ozment 1992: xiv). But, as with the other terms mentioned above, there are also many nuances and outright differences in how "revolution" is understood, including the Marxist view of the Reformation as an "early bourgeois revolution." In so far as the Reformation "can fairly be called . . . an anticlerical revolution" one may speak of "the people's Reformation" or "the Reformation of the common people" (Kingdon 1974: 60; Abray 1985; Blickle 1992).

In this brief survey of the definitions and periodization of the Reformation we have moved from a theological norm that judged sixteenth-century movements in relation to Luther (right – Catholicism; left – radicals) to social history. This latter, recent historiographical development does not necessarily conflict with the earlier approaches of intellectual historians conerned with biography and theology. "Rather, it asserts that the religious changes of the sixteenth century were fundamentally important in shaping the history of Europe and the wider world up to the modern age, and it defines as territory for exploration that area in which religious ideas and rituals impinged upon the structures of everyday life" (Hsia 1988: 8). The period has been extended back into the Middle Ages through increased awareness of the role of Catholic reforming movements and stretched into the eighteenth century in relation to its confessional, economic, and social effects. Some scholars refer heuristically to these centuries as "the long sixteenth century" or the "early modern" period to distinguish it from the modern period associated with the American, French, and Industrial Revolutions. Recent titles suggest this fluidity in characterizing the Reformation (e.g. Ozment 1971, 1980; Bossy 1985). In short, the definitions various scholars give to the word Reformation and its periodization are not merely academic antics with semantics but rather endeavors to clarify and sort out the presuppositions and value judgments that create a kaleidoscope of views of the Reformation, coloring one's perspective according to the turns one makes. It remains for us now to survey the history of these turns.

Interpretations of the Reformations of the sixteenth century are so legion that there are numerous large studies of the history of these interpretations. For the sake of simplicity, interpretations of the Reformation may be grouped under two basic headings: intellectual history and social history. The players in the former are mainly church historians and theologians, whereas the players in the latter are social historians and secular historians.

Until very recently the predominant interpretive position was located in terms of intellectual or cultural history, what the Germans call *Geistesgeschichte*. The major concern in this orientation is with the ideas of the Reformation. In some cases, the pursuit of these ideas was narrowly conceived in terms of Reformation theologies; in other cases the interpretations broadened to biography, psychohistory, political ideology, and, especially after the second Vatican council, ecumenical theology.

The predominant figure in the church historical and theological interpretations of the Reformation continues to be Martin Luther, about whom, it is said, more has been written than about any other figure in the history of the church. Since Luther has long been at center stage, a survey of interpretations of the Reformation is simplified by remaining within the boundaries of the history of Luther interpretation. The historiography of other Reformers and movements will be mentioned in other chapters.

It would seem that the portraits and interpretations of a person about whom we have so much information should be unambiguous and uncomplicated. Not so. As Heinrich Boehmer remarked in 1914: "There are as many Luthers as there are books about Luther." Luther has been called the offspring of the devil, the precursor of Hitler and antisemitism on the one hand, and the "Fifth Evangelist" on the other hand. Such extremes of vilification and glorification were especially rife during the immediate generations following the Reformation but have also echoed down to today. So, for example, the well-known Harvard Law School professor, Alan Dershowitz (1991: 107), continues to blame Luther for setting in motion modern antisemitism: "It is shocking that Luther's ignoble name is still honored rather than forever cursed by mainstream Protestant churches." The opposite extreme is summarized by Hillerbrand's (1993: 418) comment that Reformation scholarship has been dominated "for the better part of our century by Germanophiles disposed to see Germany as the navel of the universe, and by theologians, especially Lutheran theologians, for whom Luther's theology was the epitome of Christian perfection."

The favorable interpretations by Luther's contemporaries viewed him through the biblical parallels of Elijah, Jeremiah, John the Baptist, the angel of Revelation 14, and Moses. The radical Reformers, however, criticized Luther for his authoritarian binding of the Spirit of God to the Bible and also for his personal life of reputed ease, complaining that Luther lived in a handsome room, enjoyed drinking and laughing with his colleagues, wore a golden ring, and was paid for his sermons. The extreme example of Roman Catholic defamation of Luther is the work by his contemporary Johann Cochlaeus (1479–1552) who characterized Luther as a man who falsely set himself up as an evangelist, as the second St John. Furthermore, Cochlaeus claimed, Luther was a person totally without morals; he was arrogant, presumptuous, boastful, deceitful, and a liar. Cochlaeus's "Commentaries on the Acts and Writings of Martin Luther" was published at Mainz in 1549. Cochlaeus appealed to the anxieties of his Catholic contemporaries that Luther's theology, once unleashed, would bring chaos not only to the church but to society at large, just as a century earlier Hus had created trouble for Bohemia. Cochlaeus perceived Luther to be an active promoter of the moral decline of the times. Thus he did not hesitate to pass on some of the legends of the day concerning Luther's "incestuous" marriage with a nun (a monk, i.e. "brother," marrying a nun, i.e. "sister"); Luther's pact with the devil; and that Luther was the offspring of his mother's liaison with the devil (Dickens and Tonkin 1985: 21–5). The view of Luther as a psychopathic "deformer" and rebel to be explained by recourse to his religious psychology continued to influence Roman Catholic scholarship into the twentieth century and received new vitality in the works of Denifle and Grisar (Stauffer 1967; Wiedermann 1983).

The idolizers of Luther shared Cochlaeus's tendency to explain the Reformation by recourse to supernatural explanations. For Luther's champions, it was God who spoke through him; for his detractors, it was the devil; for both, however, the Reformation was the agency of supernatural or spiritual forces. It appears that only Johannes Sleidanus (1506–66) rose above the extremes of confessional partisanship. His "Commentaries on Religion and the State in the Reign of Emperor Charles V" (1555) focused on source materials rather than private inspiration and was a forerunner of the modern approach to history inaugurated by Leopold von Ranke that focused on politics and institutions (Dickens 1982: 537–63).

Between Sleidanus and Ranke, however, the church historians and theologians interpreted the Reformation in light of their respective theological commitments. Orthodox Lutherans were impelled to create truly scholastic systems of dogma designed to be impregnable by enemies of the true faith ranging from Catholics to Calvinists. This edifice complex was ruled by a monomaniacal concern for correct doctrine. Hence it was assumed that this too was Luther's basic concern. What Luther taught was regarded on nearly the same level as the Word of God; and Luther was regarded as the compendium of the truth of salvation and right belief. These convictions found expression in such jingles as "Gottes Wort und Luthers Lehr, wird vergehen nimmermehr" (God's Word and Luther's teaching shall never perish) and "Gross war er in Leben, grösser im Reden, der Grösste aber im Lehren" (He was great in life, greater in speech, but greatest in teaching).

The Pietists of the seventeenth century and later saw the orthodox emphasis upon correct doctrine and its systematic exposition in classroom and pulpit as a rationalistic head trip that shrivelled the hearts of the faithful. To the Pietists, Luther's great contribution was the recovery of faith as trust in God's mercy. Pietism saw itself as the continuation of the Reformation or as the second Reformation, i.e. the reform of life following upon the initial reform of doctrine (Lindberg 1983: 131–78). There was a tendency, however, in the Pietist emphasis upon personal spiritual regeneration or rebirth to associate sin (against which it urged constant battle) with nature or the "world." In this regard Pietists were disturbed by Luther's earthy interpretations of the Bible, not to mention his personal earthiness. The Pietists rationalized his joy as a gift of God, and covered his toleration of dancing with the cloak of his unending merit, but they could not excuse his reputed comment that if God does not have a sense of humor he did not want to go to heaven.

The Enlightenment, in many ways the successor to Pietism, perceived Luther as mainly the great German liberator from authoritarianism, the hero of freedom not only in the area of religion but in all areas of life. The nineteenth-century French sociologist Louis Blanc stated: "Whoever teaches the people to question the pope will irresistibly also lead them to question the king." That Luther's contribution to human liberty is perceived as universal and not just national is seen in the Prussian philosopher Fichte's prayer of 1793 (the year of the Jacobin ascendancy in Paris): "O Jesus and Luther, holy patron saints of liberty, who in your times of humiliation seized and with titanic power smashed the chains of humanity, . . . look down now from your heights upon your descendants, and rejoice at the sprouting grains now waving in the wind" (Brady 1987: 234).

A predominant image in the Enlightenment is that of Luther defying pope and emperor at the diet of Worms in 1521. This displacement of Luther's theology by his person dovetailed the "great man" theory of history which viewed historical developments in terms of pivotal

Figure 1.1 "Dr Martin Luther's Glorification," by Johann E. Hummell, 1806. Luther, walking on the clouds, is followed by the allegorical figure of Religious Freedom carrying a cross on which is perched the so-called "Liberty Cap," symbol of the French Revolution. She is led by female figures carrying the Bible and Luther's catechism. Luther is being offered the palm of victory by the allegory of Mercy, behind whom are women dressed as Greek goddesses symbolizing faith, hope, and love. Border scenes represent major events in Luther's career.
Source: Lutherhalle, Wittenberg.

individuals and the Pietist interest in conversion experience. In our day this has taken the form of psychohistory, a more scientifically sophisticated but formally comparable effort to explain Luther and the Reformation by recourse to his psyche. To a lesser degree psychohistory has also been used with other reformers such as Calvin (Bouwsma 1988; Selinger 1984: 72–91), Karlstadt (Bubenheimer 1981b), and Loyola (Meissner 1992).

The best-known example of psychohistory is Erik H. Erikson's (1958) *Young Man Luther*. For Erikson, the key to understanding a person's development is how he or she resolves fundamental identity crises, in Luther's case those with his father. Since fathers are crucially important (where would we be without them?) and since everyone has one, Erikson proceeds to relate Luther's personal problems to the problems of Luther's society. Both problems participated in the same "ideological crisis." This crisis concerned "the theory and practice, the power and responsibility of the moral authority invested in fathers: on earth and in heaven; at home, in the marketplace, and in politics; in the castles, the capitals, and in Rome" (Erikson 1958: 77). Luther, and consequently the Reformation, is understood as the consequence of personal projection of basic doubts of paternal justice and love upon God. Conversely, Luther's concept of God is inferred from his early psychosocial crises. The difficulty such inferences present to historians is that the historical evidence for them is both meager and contradictory (Johnson 1977; Edwards 1983: 6–9; Scharfenberg 1986: 113–28).

A far more colorful effort to explain the Reformation is the study by Norman O. Brown (1959: 203), which depicts Luther as an anal personality whose experience in the privy "inaugurated Protestant theology." Put more crudely, Luther's conversion experience (located by dubious reference in the medieval outhouse) may be compared to a giant dose of theological laxative that purged Luther of his religious constipation. This neo-Freudian interpetation was given dramatic form in John Osborne's play *Luther*, which opened at the Nottingham Royal Theatre in 1961 and then played Broadway. As Luther prepares for his first mass, he responds to a fellow priest's exhortation to faith by saying, "I wish my bowels would open. I'm blocked like an old crypt." And as he later describes his conversion experience in the privy, Luther says: "And I sat in a heap of pain until the words emerged and opened out. 'The just shall live by faith.' My pain vanished, my bowels flushed and I could get up. I could see the life I'd lost" (Osborne 1963: 32, 76).

Erikson and Brown interpreted the Reformation by reducing it to the pathologies they respectively perceived in its initiator, Martin Luther. Scott Hendrix (1994), an established Reformation scholar and a family therapist, suggests a more constructive and potentially more fruitful psychohistorical approach to Reformation studies through the use of contextual family theory. Hendrix uses contextual family theory to analyse the human behavior of historical figures in terms of historical, political, economic, and family systems and thereby avoids the tendency to reductionist and pathological explanations present in other psychohistorical methods. In his case study of the north German duchy of Lüneburg, Hendrix argues that its ruler, Duke Ernest, adopted the Reformation from a complex of motives which interwove religious and political integrity with loyal affirmation of his family's values and commitments. In short, Duke Ernest's support of the Reformation in his territory may not be reduced to either political opportunism or personal piety alone.

About the same time that some Catholic scholars and analysts were attempting to understand Luther as a rebel with (or without) a cause there began to develop studies that strove to avoid both hagiography and demonology. In the words of one book title, Luther was "neither heretic nor saint" (Geisser et al. 1982), but rather a genuinely religious person. Joseph Lortz led the way among Roman Catholic scholars with a two-volume study on the Reformation in Germany. To Lortz (1968), Luther was a religious genius who initiated the Reformation on the basis of a misunderstanding. This tragic misunderstanding was due both to his training in late medieval nominalism (*via moderna*) rather than in Thomism, and to his association of widespread late medieval corruption in the institutional church with the Catholic faith as a whole. In one of his last essays, Lortz wrote: "Luther's 'No' to the papal Church is both in content and intensity such that one could hardly imagine it more radical. But this 'No' needs sober re-examination. For it was directed against a Church whose sub-Christian reality would deserve the strongest condemnation, if one took the sub-Christian elements as the essence of the Church. This is precisely what Luther did. His religious and pastoral zeal seemed to leave him no other way" (Lortz 1970: 33). Although Lortz initiated a fundamental revision in Roman Catholic Reformation scholarship by forcing attention to historical context and development, he himself continued to retain a metahistorical Catholic theological position that finally displaced historical analysis by a theological norm. Nevertheless, Lortz's legacy includes development of excellent Roman Catholic Reformation scholarship with a commitment to ecumenical dialogue and awareness of the deep medieval roots of the Reformations.

In recent decades the "cutting edge" of Reformation studies has been social history. Like intellectual history, social history covers a multitude of perspectives, but unlike intellectual history it focuses primarily on local histories, social groups, economic and urban history, power relationships, cultural anthropology, and popular culture. The church historical and theological orientation in Reformation studies views European society in terms of its struggles with religious issues which

lead to social and political change. The social historical perspective
reverses this orientation and emphasizes the centrality of communal
political and social goals which stimulated collective behavior. Theology is only one role among others in the social construction of reality.
A leading social historian of the Reformation, Thomas A. Brady, Jr
(1982: 176; 1979: 40–3), suggests that "perhaps the time has come for a
new approach . . . the Reformation as an adaptation of Christianity to
the social evolution of Europe."

Historians of ideas and of the church caution that the emphasis upon
social history may give the impression that religious motivation was
merely a private affair unrelated to the so-called real issues. The
explanation of the Reformation in terms of its perceived political
usefulness to princely or communal powers misses the fact that
religious commitments could clearly be counterproductive to social and
political self-interest. For example, the inheritance practices of Protestant princes were formed by Lutheran teaching on family responsibility to love and care equally for all their children. In dividing their
wealth among all their sons, the Protestant princes fragmented their
lands and power in comparison to Catholic princes who concentrated
their power through primogeniture which conferred all on the eldest
son (Ozment 1992: 28–9; Fichtner 1989: 22–3; Hendrix 1994).

Although the theological and sociological approaches to understanding the Reformations are not mutually exclusive, the practitioners of
each orientation have tended to polemicize the other. This is illustrated
in brief by Lewis W. Spitz's textbook *The Protestant Reformation 1517–
1559*, where he wrote that "social historians who are disdainful of all
but statistical evidence and the condition of the masses are in grave
danger of producing hoministic rather than humanistic history
(reminding one of Disraeli's comment that there are three kinds of lies –
lies, more lies, and statistics)" (1985: 2). The reviewer of this book, a
prominent scholar of the social history persuasion, wrote: "Spitz treats
all social and economic topics like a child gagging on his spinach, which
shows that he stands far outside that broad spectrum of intellectual and
social historians . . . who insist – whatever else they may argue about –
on the complimentarity [*sic*] of events and structures, ideas and social
forces, and theology and popular religion" (Brady 1985: 411). "The
study of the Reformation," as Steven Ozment (1989: 4) remarks, "still
awaits a Moses who can lead it through the sea of contemporary
polemics between social and intellectual historians and into a historiography both mindful and tolerant of all the forces that shape historical
experience."

Figure 1.2 This sign outside the Allstedt Castle where Müntzer delivered his famous "Princes' Sermon" juxtaposes lines from the constitution of the German Democratic Republic and from Müntzer to suggest their direct connection. The former reads: "All political power in the German Democratic Republic is exercised by the workers." The latter reads: "Power shall be given to the common people."
Source: Carter Lindberg.

Such ideological partisanship, sharply illustrated by the title of a volume in the "Problems in European Civilization" series: *The Reformation: Material or Spiritual?* (Spitz 1962), has roots in the stimulus provided by Marxist historiography, which emphasized theology as only a religious cover for the fundamental material and economic causes of the Reformation. Friedrich Engels's *History of the German Peasant War* provided the basic Marxist model of the Reformation as primarily a social phenomenon in which religious attitudes and expressions were arrayed in the struggle of declining feudalism against the new capitalism. Since in this view Luther is seen as a significant voice in the defeat of the revolution's goals in the Peasants' War (1524–6), Marxist historians posited that the radical Reformer, Thomas Müntzer, is the real hero of the period. The Marxist motive was to prove that there was a revolutionary tradition in Germany in spite of the defeats of 1525 and 1848, and that it could be related to the French Revolution of

1789 and the Russian October Revolution of 1917. The more recent thesis (Blickle 1992) of a communal Reformation both replaces Marxist class analysis and continues its interest in a populist–communal Reformation.

The following study of the Reformations does not equate the period with any one particular Reformer, but it does take seriously the religious character of particular persons as well as events and decisions. There is a reciprocity and mutuality between religion and culture, so that we may certainly say that, for example, Luther's discovery of justification by faith occurred under the historical–cultural, linguistic, and personal conditions of his context while yet not being contained by these conditions. In the words of Bouwsma (1988: 4), we are "as much concerned to scrutinize the man in order to understand the time as to scrutinize the time in order to understand the man." Without continuity and mutuality with their age the Reformers would have been providing answers to unasked questions; but without their rephrasing of the questions in at least some discontinuous sense, the Reformers' answers would have been no different from those of their predecessors.

These questions and answers of the Reformers as well as their reception will be pursued over the course of the "long sixteenth century," beginning with its late medieval context and concluding with the process of Protestant and Roman Catholic confessionalization. The story line will set the evangelical movement initiated by Luther in the context of the late medieval challenges to the ancient Augustinian aspiration for a *corpus Christianum*, and then discuss how this evangelical movement differentiated itself through a series of internal crises into various streams, some of which gained specific contours through confessional formulations.

Suggestions for Further Reading

Norman Cantor, *Inventing the Middle Ages: The Lives, Works, and Ideas of the Great Medievalists of the Twentieth Century*, New York: Morrow, 1991

A. G. Dickens and John Tonkin, *The Reformation in Historical Thought*, Cambridge, MA: Harvard University Press, 1985

Wallace K. Ferguson, *The Renaissance in Historical Thought: Five Centuries of Interpretation*, Cambridge, MA: Houghton Mifflin, 1948

Scott Hendrix, "Loyalty, Piety, or Opportunism: German Princes and the Reformation," *Journal of Interdisciplinary History* 25 (Autumn 1994), 211–24

Roger Johnson, ed., *Psychohistory and Religion: The Case of "Young Man Luther"*, Philadelphia: Fortress, 1977

William S. Maltby, ed., *Reformation Europe: A Guide to Research*, II, St. Louis: Center for Reformation Research, 1992

Bruce Mansfield, *Phoenix of His Age: Interpretations of Erasmus, c. 1550–1750*, Toronto: University of Toronto Press, 1979

Bruce Mansfield, *Man on His Own: Interpretations of Erasmus, c. 1750–1920*, Buffalo: University of Toronto Press, 1992

John O'Malley, SJ, ed., *Catholicism in Early Modern Europe: A Guide to Research*, St. Louis: Center for Reformation Research, 1988

Steven Ozment, ed., *Reformation Europe: A Guide to Research*, St Louis: Center for Reformation Research, 1982

R. W. Scribner, *The German Reformation*, Atlantic Highlands: Humanities Press International, 1986

Robert Wilken, *The Myth of Christian Beginnings: History's Impact on Belief*, New York: Doubleday Anchor, 1972

2

The Late Middle Ages:
Threshold and Foothold of
the Reformations

Age of tears, of envy, of torment, . . . Age of decline nigh to the end.

Eustache Deschamps (1346–1406)

Deschamps may be excused for being a bit melancholic since he lived during the Hundred Years War between England and France, the "captivity of the papacy" in Avignon, and the consequent great schism of the church, not to mention outbreaks of the plague. He may have been the leading pessimist of a depressed age (Huizinga 1956: 33; Delumeau 1984: 129, 131), but his depression was not unique. Towards the end of the fifteenth century Jean Meschinot echoed his sentiment: "O miserable and very sad life! . . . We suffer from warfare, death and famine; Cold and heat, day and night, sap our strength; Fleas, scabmites and so much other vermine make war upon us. In short, have mercy, Lord, upon our wicked persons, whose life is very short" (Huizinga 1956: 34). Such "melancholy," depicted in the art of Dürer and Lucas Cranach the Elder among others, continued into the sixteenth century and beyond. Life, according to the English philosopher Thomas Hobbes (1588–1679), is "nasty, brutish, and short."

The pervasive mood of the times, of anxiety and foreboding, found a focus in widespread expectations of divine judgment:

> O World, be ever mindful how in times gone by,
> When thoughtless men did truth and right deny,
> When men were faithless and in spite did wrong,
> God never tarried with his vengeance long. (Strauss 1963: 18)

Sin, death, and the devil loomed large on the stage of late medieval life and mentality. Numerous studies and textbooks speak of this period as an age of crisis. In this chapter, "crisis" will be the heuristic key to the context of the Reformations. Of course, such a broad generalization about the eve of the Reformations risks distortion and loss of nuance and detail. Historians can always find contemporary sources that portray the world as normal in the aftermath of catastrophes; then as now, one may profit as well as suffer in a crisis. Nevertheless, I shall try to present with broad strokes the Reformations as both a part and a child of the late medieval crisis (Oberman 1973: 31). In the lapidary phrase of Steven Ozment (1975: 118), "late medieval developments were a threshold as well as a foothold" for the Reformations of the sixteenth century.

It may appear presumptuous to speak of the late medieval era as an era of crisis because crisis is not the prerogative of any single era. As Ranke said: "Every age is immediate to God." In this sense the Middle Ages have no more of a monopoly on crisis than we do. "Yet there have been few times in which the awareness of crisis has reached and encompassed all social classes, and pervaded . . . such extensive areas of Western Europe." What was being judged and called into account to a hitherto unknown extent was "the sacred basis of existence." This was more than the perennial generational questioning of the received tradition; it was a "crisis of symbols of security" (Oberman 1973: 20, 17). Traditional values and certainties were under fire and new ones had not yet been found.

The crisis of the symbols of security did not arise from an immediate cause or a single event but grew from an accumulation of events and developments, some positive and some negative. This conjuncture of developments eroded confidence and security in the medieval vision of a Christian commonwealth, the *corpus Christianum*, and its guarantor, the church. In a world in which the modern compartmentalization of religion and life was inconceivable, natural catastrophes such as famine and plague, rapid social changes related to economics and urban development, and religious uncertainty stemming from schism and corruption in the church were perceived as part and parcel of a world whose center, the church, no longer held (Graus 1969, 1971, 1993; Lutz 1986).

Agrarian Crisis, Famine, and Plague

Many of the events and developments contributing to the sense of crisis were occurring concurrently. Bearing that in mind, we shall for the sake of convenience begin with an overview of the conjuncture of crises concerned with farming, famine, and the great plague of the mid-fourteenth century. Preceding this conjuncture but also as a consequence of it, there was a remarkable growth of urbanization that drew survivors to the cities. The rise of the cities and a new social mobility were also cause and consequence of the shift from a natural economy to a money economy, commercial production, and techno- logical development. Most of those who flocked to the cities looking for a new life did not find it; excluded from the guilds, most newcomers, if not reduced to begging, became dependent upon jobs that provided little more than a hand-to-mouth existence. New attitudes of individualism fostered by the Renaissance also contributed to the erosion of the sense of a Christian community developed over a thousand years of the *corpus Christianum*.

Increased food production during the twelfth and thirteenth centuries fed a steady population growth. However, the growing population outgrew the agrarian basis that had made it possible. By 1320 nearly all of northern Europe was suffering from widespread famine precipitated by a series of crop failures due to unusually bad weather. Chronicles of the time list a succession of floods, bitter winters, and severe droughts. In southern France, rains inundated Provence in 1307–8 and in 1315. Clergy and laity processed barefoot to appease God for the sins of humankind, but "God was slow to hear their prayers." Rivers seemed to overflow with terrible regularity, sweeping away bridges, harvests, and people. Severe winters froze rivers, vineyards, and animals. In 1355 it snowed for nearly 20 days on Avignon; in 1439 wolves prowled through Carpentras. In summer heat grilled the grain and wells went dry (Chiffoleau 1980: 101–2). In southeast Germany earthquakes and massive locust swarms followed the famine years of 1315–17. Emperor Charles IV wrote of being awakened one morning by a knight with the words, "Lord, arise, the Last Judgment is here for the whole world is full of locusts." Charles set out on horseback to measure the extent of the swarms. After a full day's ride, about 25 kilometers, he had still not come to the edge of the swarm, which devoured all vegetation in its path (Boockmann 1987: 228). Natural disasters were compounded by considerable price inflation, and urban dependence upon the immediate countryside due to lack of long-distance transportation.

Weak and malnourished, the population was hit by outbreaks of typhoid fever and then the terrible Black Death in its forms of bubonic, pneumonic, and septicaemic plague. The spread of the plague to Europe was facilitated by improvements in the Italian merchant fleets which enabled ships to rapidly transport their deadly stowaway cargo of rats carrying plague-ridden fleas. Originating in the Far East, the plague reached Sicily in October 1347 via Genoese ships, traveled rapidly through Italy, and infested southern Germany by the spring of 1348 and England by June of that year. The densely populated and filthy cities were an ideal habitation for the rats which carried the fleas, and thatched roofs and dirty streets provided ideal launching pads for flea-to-person trajectories. Once infected, people transmitted the pneumonic form of the disease by coughs and sneezes inhaled by others. It has been estimated on the basis of modern studies of the plague in twentieth-century Manchuria that these infections were practically 100 percent lethal (McNeill 1976; Ziegler 1969).

It is not possible to estimate accurately the mortality rate due to the plague, but it is supposed that approximately 30 percent of the population succumbed. There were, of course, local variations; some areas were passed over by the plague while others were completely wiped out. The gruesome nature of this disease increased its horror: large painful boils (the term "bubonic" comes from *buba*, Latin for groin, where lymph nodes were often the first to swell since many flea bites were on the legs) accompanied by black spots or blotches due to bleeding under the skin were the prelude to the final stage of violent coughs of blood. A contemporary description is less clinical: "All the matter which exuded from their bodies let off an unbearable stench; sweat, excrement, spittle, breath, so fetid as to be overpowering; urine turbid, thick, black or red" (McKay et al. 1988: 430). As Boccaccio makes clear in his introduction to the *Decameron* (1353), family and friends deserted the sick, leaving them to die alone and in agony.

By the Reformation period the plague had abated but it was still a real danger. The Swiss Reformer, Ulrich Zwingli (1484–1531), nearly succumbed to it, and in 1527 the plague struck Luther's area. In Wittenberg those who could, fled; the others died or were cared for in Luther's home, which he turned into a sort of hospice. This was the occasion for his tract, *Whether One May Flee From a Deadly Plague*. Even love could not close a person's eyes to the omnipresence of death in the midst of life, for by the end of the fifteenth century syphilis appeared on the continent as the other great epidemic disease. Like the plague, syphilis created terror and helplessness in the minds of contemporaries. The shortness of life was never far from people's minds.

It is difficult for us today to realize the profound personal and social impact the plague had upon its survivors. It was an inexplicable and swift disaster. People did not know its whence and wherefore. The plague could strike down a healthy person within days or, in the septicaemic version where the bacillus entered the bloodstream, within hours. The widespread fear of both an imminent and a horrible death broke down customs and norms. Parents deserted their children, and children deserted their parents. The horror extended to the nursery, as suggested by the rhyme, "Ring Around the Rosey." The "rosey" was the reddish "ring" that preceded the skin blotch; the "pocket full of posies" refers to the use of flowers to mask the stench and supposedly ward off infection; "ashes, ashes" is shorthand for "ashes to ashes, dust to dust;" and "we all fall down" is the inevitable result. There was often panic, bizarre behavior, and the projection of guilt and fear upon others.

The plague was widely perceived as God's punishment for humankind's sins. Flagellation movements engaged in bloody penances for the personal and communal sins believed responsible for the plague. The Strasbourg chronicler, Fritsche Closener, reported that in 1349 two hundred flagellants arrived in Strasbourg. They carried costly pennants and candles at the head of their procession, and village and city bells announced their arrival wherever they went. Their ritual included kneeling and singing in the churches followed by throwing themselves three times on the ground in the form of a cross. Twice a day the members flagellated themselves. At the ringing of a bell they assembled in a field, removed their clothes except for a covering of the lower half of their bodies, kneeled in a circle and confessed their sins, and then engaged in spiritual songs and flagellation (Boockmann 1987: 230–1; Cohn 1961: 124–48). Ironically, their processions and the hordes of followers they attracted helped to spread the plague.

Intercession for protection from the plague was also sought from saints, especially Rochus and Sebastian: the former because he had aided plague victims and himself succumbed; the latter because of the

---

Figure 2.1 "The Pilgrimage to the 'Beautiful Mary' in Regensburg," by Michael Ostendorfer, 1520. This woodcut illustrates the excesses of the religious adoration of images on the eve of the Reformations. Pilgrims are beside themselves in ecstasy before the statue, "Beautiful Mary," in the foreground, and streaming into the chapel to view the wonder-working image of the "Beautiful Madonna" (note the huge votive candle carried by the pilgrim on the right). This pilgrimage site originated in direct connection to the 1519 persecution of the Jews in Regensburg. The provisional wooden pilgrimage chapel was erected on the very place where the Jewish synagogue had stood; the ruins of the recently destroyed Jewish quarter are depicted in the background. During the demolition of the synagogue in February 1519 the stonemason Jakob Kern was severely injured, but on the next day miraculously restored to health by petition to Mary. Through the clever management of the cathedral preacher Balthasar Hubmaier, a later Anabaptist leader, whose preaching had fomented the Jewish pogrom, this miracle sparked the pilgrimage site and a lucrative income for the city. Within a month of the erection of this shrine, 50,000 pilgrims had worshipped there. In his 1520 *Address to the Christian Nobility*, Luther recommended that this and similar shrines be leveled (*LW* 44: 185).
Source: © Elke Walford, Hamburger Kunsthalle.

iconography associated with his martyrdom by arrows. Since it was believed that God shot plague arrows at sinful humankind, Sebastian's death by arrows made him an aide to the afflicted. Help was also sought from Mary. A panel of the high altar of the Franciscan church in Göttingen provides a classic image of Mary's protective mantle catching plague arrows. The image of Mary protecting humankind with her cloak became widespread.

The plague was perceived by some as a Jewish plot. Fear stimulated prejudice with the consequence that thousands of Jews were murdered across Europe. In spite of the fact that Jews also contracted the plague, people claimed they had poisoned wells. The Dominican, Heinrich von Herford, provided a brief description: "In this year [1349] the Jews including women and children were cruelly and inhumanly destroyed in Germany and many other lands." Reasonable people and responsible clergy such as Heinrich rejected the charge that Jews caused the plague, and suggested that a more likely cause of these pogroms was greed for Jewish wealth. A contemporary account states: "The money was indeed the thing that killed the Jews. If they had been poor and if the feudal lords had not been in debt to them, they would not have been burnt" (Marcus 1973: 47).

The plague severely tested people's faith. The ensuing pessimism informed literature and art. It is at this time that the French word *macabre* first appeared and summed up a gruesome and dismal vision of death. This was graphically illustrated by the dance of death motif and by tomb inscriptions such as that of Cardinal Jean de Lagrange in Avignon (d. 1402) on the sculpture of his putrefying body: "We [the dead] are a spectacle for the world so that the great and the small may see clearly by our example the condition to which they shall be inexorably reduced whatever their condition, sex, or age. Why then, wretch, are you full of pride? You are ashes, and you shall return to ashes, a fetid corpse, food for vermin." Thousands of epitaphs on lesser graves echoed the *memento mori* theme: "As I am, so you shall be."

These images mirrored the rupture of personal and social life. The old rules of mourning that channeled and reduced the trauma of death rarely held up before the mass deaths of this time. The desertion of family and friends threatened the faith that death was a passage to a new life. The traditional religious rites and customs of death, the funeral procession and meal, which enacted the separation of the dead from the living while symbolically reconstituting the family and the continuity of society, collapsed in the face of the plague. If one was fortunate enough even to have a deathbed, there would be no relatives and friends gathered around it. Nor, after death, would there be rest among

Figure 2.2   "Death and the Maiden" from the Heidelberg Dance of Death series. Death is portrayed as a dancer whom every person will have to follow. The woodcut series portrays persons from every walk of life being caught in the final dance. The maiden here claimed by death confesses her preoccupation with the world's pleasures to the neglect of God's commandments. Frogs and toads symbolized sins; worms and snakes signified the pangs of conscience. Huizinga (1956: 138) wrote: "No other epoch has laid so much stress as the expiring Middle Ages on the thought of death."
Source: Archiv für Kunst und Geschichte.

ancestors in the churchyard. The dead no longer earned continuity with their forebears but only darkness. Survivors more and more understood themselves to be like orphans, and were anguished by the reality of being thrown back upon themselves.

The disturbing discovery of the death of the self in this context was nearly contemporaneous with the development of new funeral practices and the writing of wills or testaments. In the church's hierarchy of contributions to the "price of passage" from this world to the next, concern to endow as many masses as possible for oneself after death now displaced the earlier emphasis upon charity to the poor. Faced by the dissolution of the qualitative boundaries of life, people turned to number and measurement as a means for creating order. The new "book-keeping mentality" substituted quantity for quality in an effort to impose pattern and reduce anxiety before disorder (Bouwsma 1980: 234–8). This "mathematics of salvation" (Chiffoleau 1980) exalted the multiplication of liturgical intercessions to facilitate the passage of the deceased to heaven. "Catholicism at the end of the Middle Ages was in large part a cult of the living in the service of the dead" (Galpern 1974: 149). This shift from the traditional works of mercy to the mass for the dead indicated not only the church's ability to adapt to a new situation but also the growing influence of a market mentality with its orientation toward the calculation of accounts, in this case, as Chiffoleau's (1980) book title suggests, "the account book of the beyond." The mass became the essential preparation for the journey through death to heaven, ritually establishing powerful bonds between this world and the next that would be exploited by the doctrines of purgatory and indulgences.

The development of the doctrine of purgatory complemented the development of masses for the dead. The multiplication of masses for the dead popularized purgatory as a place for those snatched from life without benefit of time to amend their ways or prepare for death. These "orphaned" souls found in purgatory a refuge with a new "family." Purgatory also offered a mitigation of the fear of damnation by its opportunity to purge the offenses occurred during life, and the possibility to benefit from the prayers and intercessions of masses and indulgences bought by the living.

But purgatory was no picnic! Thomas More (1478–1535) described its terrors in grisly detail in his *Supplication of Souls*: "If ye pity any man in pain, never knew ye pain comparable to ours; whose fire as far passeth in heat all the fires that ever burned upon earth . . . If ever ye lay sick and thought the night long and longed sore for day, while every hour seemed longer than five, bethink you then what a long night we silly souls endure, that lie sleepless, restless, burning and broiling in the dark fire one long night . . . of many years together" (Dickens 1991: 29).

As if natural disasters were not enough, the human community managed to create its own plague of wars. The long-term expression of this was the Hundred Years War (1337–1453) between the French and English monarchies. It was both a dynastic and a feudal struggle as the French king, Philip VI (r. 1328–50) sought to absorb the English duchy of Aquitaine. The war, consisting mainly of raids and sieges, dragged on and on. It was fought almost entirely in France, and is popularly remembered as the context of Joan of Arc.

Peasant rebellions also caused much destruction and impeded economic and social life. Most people in the sixteenth century were peasants who toiled on the land from sunrise to sunset or day laborers at the mercy of urban entrepreneurs. Their life of labor found occasional relief in the festivities of major holy days and the ritual breaks occasioned by marriages and funerals. In some areas the peasant was a virtual slave; in other areas, a small landholder. Likewise, peasant diet and housing were sometimes adequate and sometimes inadequate. Diverse conditions make generalization about peasant life difficult. In any case, the life of the peasant was hard, and not infrequently hardening. The upper class frequently depicted the peasant as stupid, coarse, loathsome, untrustworthy, and prone to violence. For the nobles, of course, such self-serving descriptions rationalized and legitimated oppression of the peasants.

Not all writers and lawyers supported such prejudice against the peasants; some reproached lay and ecclesiastical nobility with the adage that true nobility derives from virtue not from blood. Nevertheless, long before the Reformation, the adverse economic and social status of the peasant was legitimated by blaming the victim. It is of interest that the Noah story (Genesis 9: 20–7) was (mis)used in medieval Europe for the same purpose as in slaveholding America: to explain that subjugated people bore the curse of God.

When pushed to extremes, the normally conservative peasant could react violently. Usually peasants acted out their rage against their conditions by turning against each other, but one picture from the period shows four peasants slaughtering an armored knight with axes. Far more serious than individual acts of violence were the outbreaks of communal peasant rebellion against the oppression of their lords. In France, taxation for the Hundred Years War fell as a heavy burden on peasants, who exploded in rage and rampage in 1358. The nobles avenged themselves by vicious suppression of the peasants, slaughtering guilty and innocent alike. The Peasants' Revolt in England in 1381 combined economic and religious grievances against noble and clerical rulers. Its revolutionary sentiment of social equality was immortalized in the famous couplet attributed to the popular preacher John Ball (d. 1381): "When Adam delved and Eve span, who then was the gentleman?" In England, too, the revolt was ferociously crushed. Similar rebellions occurred in Italy, some of the north German cities, and parts of Spain. In the Empire there were peasant uprisings in 1493, 1502, 1513, and 1517, before the great Peasants' War of 1524–6. The nobility believed these were orchestrated conspiracies, but they began as spontaneous revolts generated by much the same kind of rage and frustration as that which stimulated the race riots that swept through

American cities in the 1960s. This long-repressed peasant anger against the lords, including the ecclesiastical lords who were great landholders, helps to explain the enthusiastic reception of Luther's early writings that attacked church authority and extolled Christian liberty.

Population loss through plague and war put at risk the economic holdings of surviving noble and clerical landowners. The decrease in peasant population meant the increased cost of hiring laborers. At the same time, if there was a decent harvest it brought lower returns because there were fewer people to feed. In the towns wages and prices were driven up because of urban labor shortages. The lords sought to stem peasant flight from the land by establishing or intensifying serfdom. In turn, peasant opportunities and social freedoms were radically curtailed. In order to cope with the inflation that was eroding their fixed incomes, noble and clerical lords began to displace the old "divine law," i.e. the common law of the people's tradition, by Roman law based on the tenet of private property which exploited possession. These developments were also to influence the reception of the Reformation by the peasants, who perceived the social and political significance of theological critiques of Roman law.

Towns and Cities: Loci of Ideas and Change

The late medieval city was the locus of change, the "*foyer* of modernity" (Chiffoleau 1980: 430; Greyerz 1985: 6–63) in the double sense of both "home" and "hotbed." With regard to the Reformation this is summarized in the oft-cited phrase of the English scholar A. G. Dickens (1974: 182): "the German Reformation was an urban event at once literary, technological and oratorical."

It is estimated that, at most, about a fifth of the population lived in the cities and towns. However, some areas in Germany and the Netherlands had a higher percentage of urban population, with as much as 20 percent of the population of Saxony, Luther's area, living in its many small towns. By the eve of the Reformation towns and cities were experiencing rapid growth, some even doubling in size. Cologne, the largest German city, had a population of about 40,000, and by 1500 Nuremberg had grown to about 30,000. Other major cities such as Strasbourg, Metz, Augsburg, Vienna, Prague, Lübeck, Magdeburg, and Danzig had between 20,000 and 30,000 inhabitants. Most of the 4,000 or so other German towns were smaller than 3,000 persons.

Elsewhere in Europe the numbers were similar, except for the very large cities of Paris, Milan, and Florence.

The population growth in the urban areas was stimulated by the new money economy and by new ideas. This made urban centers places both of creative change and opportunity, and of social conflict. The feudal economy was being displaced by an early form of capitalism which in turn undermined the traditional idea of society as a sacral corporation, the *corpus Christianum* in miniature, wherein each person was ethically responsible to all others.

There is no doubt today concerning the strong appeal of the Reformation in late medieval towns and cities. *Why* the Reformation appealed to the towns and cities, however, remains controversial. In a provocative study first published in 1972, Bernd Moeller (1982) argued that the appeal of the Reformation in the numerous cities of the continent rested on its support for late medieval communal values under attack from different quarters. On the other hand, Steven Ozment (1975: 9) claimed that the appeal of the Reformation lay not in the reinforcement of the ideal of a sacral community, but precisely the opposite: its desacralization, i.e. liberation "from onerous religious beliefs, practices, and institutions." For Ozment, the Reformers were theological "freedom fighters" whose preaching of justification by faith alone did not reflect social change but stimulated it. Thomas Brady (1978: 9, 12) criticized both Ozment and Moeller: the former for psychologizing the appeal of the Reformation along the lines of Luther's conversion experience, and the latter for a "romantic conception of urban society, the ideal of the sacral corporation." From Brady's perspective, the key to understanding the course of the Reformation in the cities is class struggle in which ruling coalitions related to the Reformation in light of their vested interests. Moeller, in turn, criticized Brady for ignoring the religious dimension of the Reformation, and warned against "sociologizing." And Ozment asks whether this stress on class divisions, economic and demographic conflicts "will come any closer to elucidating human motivation than the much scorned narrow theological treatments of the Reformation and so-called 'airy-fairy' intellectual history" (Moeller 1979; Brady 1979; Ozment 1979). There is no reason to assume that the medieval urban dweller was any less beset by conflicting ideological and social concerns than we are, but there is reason to think that religious concerns played a major role. For the medieval, religion was a public or corporate not a private or individualistic affair. Hence religion was the key to both preservation of the past and liberation from it.

The Printing Press

As the locus for new ideas, cities were concerned with communication and therefore also with expanding lay education. By the eve of the Reformation the number of European universities had risen from 20 to 70 due to the efforts of monarchs, princes, and wealthy merchants. The University of Wittenberg, for example, was founded by Prince Frederick the Wise in 1502. A conservative estimate of literacy suggests that 5 percent of the overall population and 30 percent of the urban population could read by the beginning of the sixteenth century. However, it is important to realize that the communication of ideas was not limited by literacy; those who could read passed ideas on to those who could not. The thousands of published Reformation pamphlets and sermons were thus designed to be read to the illiterate as well as by the literate. "Faith," as Luther stressed, "comes by hearing" (Romans 10: 17).

Prior to the media revolution caused by the invention of printing, the greatest initial expense for books was the material they were written on. Both papyrus (from the swamps of the Nile) and parchment (from the backs of sheep) were expensive. The development of a relatively inexpensive linen rag paper introduced by Marco Polo from China made the development of printing financially feasible. The next step was the development of a good ink, made by mixing carbon with an oily solution. The key invention, as is well known, was moveable metal type in the mid-fifteenth century in the Rhineland area. This durable moveable type could be arranged and rearranged and used again and again. The printing industry was first centered along the Rhine in Germany (Gutenberg at Mainz) and then spread down to Basle and up to the Low Countries. The earliest printing experts were the Germans.

New ideas now spread rapidly and reliably by means of the new technology of printing, a technology Luther deemed a gift from God. Whereas Wyclif's religious ideas spread very slowly through handwritten copies, Luther's ideas blanketed Europe within months. "By the end of the fifteenth century printing presses existed in over two hundred cities and towns. An estimated six million books had been printed and half of the thirty thousand titles were on religious subjects. More books were printed in the forty years between 1460 and 1500 than had been produced by scribes and monks throughout the entire Middle Ages" (Ozment 1980: 199; Chrisman 1982; Eisenstein 1979; Edwards 1994).

The Reformation ignited a tremendous increase in book production and rapidly expanded the book market. This ready market made printers eager to snatch every new work from Luther's hand. In Wittenberg alone there were soon seven print shops devoted to the writings of Luther and his colleagues. By Luther's death in 1546 over 3,400 editions of the Bible in whole or in part had appeared in High German and about 430 editions in Low German. Calculating on the basis of 2,000 copies per edition there appeared at least three-quarters of a million of the former and altogether about a million copies. This number is even more astonishing when it is considered that the price of books was increasing at this time. Although the common attribution of the creation of modern German to Luther's Bible translation is an exaggeration, it is true that his widely used translation contributed to the normalization of the language. His linguistic skill is evident in the continuing popularity in Germany of the Luther Bible.

Thousands of other Reformation writings in the form of brief tracts and pamphlets (*Flugblätter* and *Flugschriften*: literally "flying leaves" and "flying writings") flooded the Empire. This Reformation propaganda was not limited to the printed word but was also visual, incorporating pictures, images, and cartoons. In contrast to the Middle Ages, and even the first printed works which primarily served the preservation and transmission of knowledge, the Reformation gave the printed book a new function: the transmission of opinions. "A handful of copies of a single sixteenth-century pamphlet only a few dozen pages long could prove enormously provocative, help stimulate opponents of a government to heroic resistance, and thus arouse within a government terrible fears of subversion" (Kingdon 1988: 9). And the dominant publicist using this new tool was Martin Luther. According to Edwards (1994: xii), "he dominated to a degree that no other person to my knowledge has ever dominated a major propaganda campaign and mass movement since. Not Lenin, not Mao Tse-tung, not Thomas Jefferson, John Adams, or Patrick Henry."

Of Mines and Militancy

Along with the invention of printing, the technology of mining and weaponry contributed weal and woe to the Reformation context. From 1460 to 1530 there was a mining boom in Germany that centered on Saxony, Luther's home area. Especially important for the context of the Reformation was the mining of silver which was unmatched in quantity until the mid-nineteenth century. This was facilitated by solutions to the technical problems of removing water from the mines and separating the silver from other metals in the ore. The first problem was resolved by the development of ventilation systems and suction pumps allowing deep shafts to be dug; the second by developments in smelting which utilized strong hot furnaces to separate minerals on the basis of their different melting points. This required chemical catalysts, bellows, and the use of coal rather than charcoal to fire the furnaces. The engineers of the time improved the furnaces by using taller chimneys, thus increasing their draft. All these processes were gathered into a primitive factory system.

The social effects of this mining boom were manifold. Most of the silver was used for coinage, which in turn facilitated a monetary revolution. As the economy shifted from barter to money there was a growth in banking in Germany. Thus the great Fugger banking house of Augsburg displaced the Italian papal bankers, the Medici. The Fuggers involved themselves in all areas of culture, including politics, becoming closely allied with the House of Habsburg. As we shall see, their money was involved not only in the indulgence business but also in the imperial election of Charles V. The mining boom directly benefited Frederick the Wise, the elector of Saxony and Luther's future protector. Frederick's wealth not only made him a force to be reckoned with in the Empire, it also allowed him to realize one of his dreams, the founding of the University of Wittenberg, where a bright young monk, Martin Luther, soon joined the faculty. In turn, Luther had been able to obtain the education for this position because his father as a mining engineer earned enough money to send Martin to school.

Another consequence of this mining boom was inflation. The kings and princes who controlled the mines increased their wealth. Their prosperity as well as that of the bankers may still be seen in the great civic buildings and monuments of this time. But nobles dependent upon feudal rents, i.e. fixed incomes, suffered from the rise in prices, as did also the workers and artisans. Economic and social discontent issued in revolts: the Knights' Revolt in 1523 and the Peasants' War in 1524–6.

The developments in metallurgy, along with other technological advances, also found military application. After the discovery that gunpowder could be used to propel missiles, the next advance was to develop reliable cannon. The first cannon cast or wrought of bronze tended to come apart upon firing, which of course made their use somewhat exciting for all involved. Carved stone cannon balls whose rough edges might catch in the barrel were equally problematic to the cannoneer, who, given his primitive working conditions, was exhorted to fear, honor, and love God more than any other soldier.

The first war in which cannon played a major role was the Hundred Years War. The French king engaged the Bureau brothers to set up a department (hence the beginnings of "bureaucracy") to utilize cannon offensively. Cannon were used effectively later by the Hussites, who mounted cannons on wagons as a mobile defense tactic, thus enabling Hussite survival into the Reformation era. By the time of the French–Italian wars (1494–1559) the French had a trained artillery with several hundred horsedrawn bronze cannons. Some of the best minds of the time, including such as Da Vinci, worked on improving artillery. At the battle of Ravenna (1512) the French artillery destroyed the Spanish cavalry. The development of a stable gunpowder and reliable cannons contributed to the destabilization of late medieval society. Indiscriminate death and destruction were now possible beyond the medieval's wildest dreams. When this technology was coupled with national and religious fanaticism the dreams became a devastating reality. But it also became clear that there was money to be made in arms, and so the fledgeling military–industrial complex of the late medieval era grew and bore its deadly fruit. One of the social side effects was to make an entire class – the knights – obsolete. Now anyone with a gun could bring down a knight. One more reason for their revolt.

Social Tensions

The rise of a money economy created new social and religious issues and tensions. By the Reformation period cities were plagued by disunity, factiousness, and mutual suspicion due to increasing size and economic changes which raised social tensions to new levels. The expansion of commerce created both new wealth and new poverty. It became increasingly apparent that the profit economy and political centralization conflicted with the traditional ideal of urban community as a sacred corporation. Medieval towns, in contrast to the feudal vassalage system which bound inferiors to superiors, organized their members horizontally by an egalitarian oath. Each person, irrespective of social status, was ethically responsible to all other members of the body politic. By about 1500, the symbiosis of increasingly widespread literacy and printing along with Renaissance intellectual impulses stimulated an unprecedented development of individuality and the formation of individual consciousness. This, along with the ability of individuals and small groups to attain great wealth and political power by their own initiative, gave rise to new values and political factions and challenged the old ones. Traditional morality was incapable of coping with urban and monetary development. "The received tradition was in fact biased against all the main elements of the new economy: against cities, against money, and against urban professions." The traditional morality could do little more than repeat with more volume the dictum from the early church that had been enshrined in canon law: "A merchant is rarely or never able to please God" (Little 1978: 35, 38).

The new profit economy affected virtually every institution, group, area, and idea of medieval society. It affected the size of communities and the human relationships within them. The increasing size of cities led to changes in the quality of life within them. Money affected the kind of work people did and how they were rewarded for it, often bringing in its wake distress for individuals and institutions alike. The old Christian morality no longer seemed relevant to the new urban realities and their acute social and religious problems involving impersonalism, money, and moral uncertainty. "The psychological boundaries by which the old culture had sought to understand the nature of man and predict his behavior were useless when he was no longer inhibited by the pressures of traditional community . . . He then seemed thrown, disoriented, back into the void from which it was the task of culture to rescue him. [This] . . . is the immediate explanation for the extraordinary anxiety of this period. It was an inevitable response to the growing inability of an inherited culture to invest experience with meaning" (Bouwsma 1980: 230). The new morality of achievement, of accounts, of accumulation, a capitalist not a Protestant ethic, infected both personal and religious relations. This slowly developing individualism stimulated both a heady sense of liberation and a morbid insecurity and terror before the loss of this newly found self in death. The fear of purgatory was nothing compared now to the fear of hell where the damned were portrayed as feeding on their own flesh, and one spark of hellfire was more painful than a thousand years of a woman in childbirth.

Externally, the cities found themselves increasingly involved in battles against royal and princely overlords, both lay and episcopal, who wanted to subject them to higher territorial or national policy as well as benefit from their economy and holdings. There was a rising national consciousness; vernacular literature aided by the printing press displaced Latin; the Augustinian aspiration for the *corpus Christianum* was eroding. The process of nation building had already advanced the farthest in Spain and France; and, although the Holy Roman Empire of the German Nation would continue to lag behind the rest of Europe for centuries, the desire for nation building by the Germans is evident in the popularity of Luther's tract *To the Christian Nobility of the German Nation* (1520).

However, it is difficult to build a nation when its major centers are infected by loss of moral direction, distrust, depersonalization and social fragmentation due to competing selfish interests. Long before Machiavelli, the animal epic of Reynard the Fox expressed cunning and the brutal self-seeking drive for advantage and success. As Reynard says to his nephew, Grimbert the Badger: "Little crooks are hanged; big crooks govern our lands and cities. I grew wise to this long ago, nephew, which is why I seek my own profit in life. Sometimes, I think that, since everybody does it, this is the way it ought to be." Reynard is the master of the big lie and extravagant flattery. The epic ends with the moral:

> He who has not learned Reynard's craft is not made for this world and his advice is not heeded. But with the aid of which Reynard is past master, success and power are within everyone's reach. For this reason our world is full of Reynards, and we find them at the pope's court no less than at the emperor's. Simon [i.e. buying and selling of church offices] is on the throne. Money counts, and nothing else. He who has money to give gets the benefice; he who has not does not get it. Whoever knows Reynard's cunning best is on his way to the top. (Strauss 1971: 91, 95–6)

Luther would later echo this widespread cynicism in the adages "the big crooks hang the little crooks" and "the big fish eat the little fish."

The Crisis of Values

This brings us to the main point of this chapter. The major crisis of the late medieval era was a crisis of values. There were numerous contributing factors, some of which we have already enumerated. But the core of the crisis was the tottering of the symbols of security. The late medieval crisis was not primarily economic or political or feudal, but a crisis of the symbols of security. This crisis came to a head in the crisis of the guarantor of those symbols – the church. "The Middle Ages was primarily concerned with the guarantee of security which the Church offered to believers" (Graus 1971: 98). That is why the full impact of all these factors found expression in the ecclesiastical crisis marked by the western schism and by anticlericalism.

Figure 2.3 "The Big Fish Eat the Little Fish," by Pieter Bruegel the Elder (ca. 1525–69), a copper engraving in the style of Bosch. Note the anthropomorphizing of the fish in the figure at the right which denotes the greed of townsmen preying on each other for self-benefit.
Source: Private collection.

The Western Schism

The roots of the western schism reach deep into the early relationships of the bishop of Rome to the western Empire. Through skillful use of Roman law and creative "documentation" such as the "Donation of Constantine" and its affirmation in the "Donation of Pepin" (756), and the crowning of Charlemagne (800), the papacy legitimated its assertion of the divine right to crown the western emperor; the theory being that if the pope had the right to crown an emperor, he had the right to take the crown away. This papal ideology of political control foundered with the rise of national kings whose political authority, unlike that of the emperor, did not rest on papal crowning. At the beginning of the fourteenth century, Pope Boniface VIII discovered to his dismay that since he had not "made" the French king, he could not control him. The humiliation of Boniface and his immediate successors at the hands of the French led to the so-called "Babylonian captivity of the church" at Avignon (1309–78). Although the papacy bought Avignon, still situated in the German Empire, all of Europe now perceived the papacy as a French satellite.

In this broad context the first critical studies of the church and its theological and legal bases began appearing. The French Dominican, John of Paris (ca. 1250–1306), had already argued in his treatise *On Papal and Royal Power* that secular government was rooted in the natural human community, and that since royal authority was not derived from the papacy, the popes had no authority to depose kings. Marsiglio of Padua's (ca. 1275–1342) *The Defender of the Peace* (1324) was a far more radical expression of such "secularism." Marsiglio, one-time rector of the University of Paris, argued that the papacy was destroying world peace. The solution was to limit the executive authority of the papacy by the laws governing all human institutions, laws which derived from the whole community. Marsiglio not only stressed the principle of popular consent as the basis for legitimate government but also denied that the papacy was divinely established.

These attacks upon the papacy, which went to the heart of its legitimacy as an institution, utilized arguments from Aristotle and Roman law. The Franciscan William of Ockham (ca. 1285–1347) concluded that Pope John XXII was a heretic because of his rejection of the Franciscan theology of poverty. Ockham went beyond reviving older canonistic arguments regarding the possibility of deposing a heretical pope to posit that no ecclesiastical institution, not even a general council, could claim to define with certainty the faith of the church. To claim that the whole church could not err meant, according to Ockham, only that the true faith would survive in unspecified individuals even when popes and councils denied the truth. The Italian poet Dante Alighieri (1265–1321), who had been exiled from Florence in 1301 for supporting the opponents of Boniface VIII, assailed the papacy and popes not only in his *Divine Comedy* but also in his *On Monarchy*. In the latter he argued that the papacy should abandon all temporal authority and possessions, and that temporal peace required a universal monarchy under the emperor. Papal condemnations and excommunications could no longer either control rulers or silence critics. As sharp as these criticisms of the papacy appear, it is important to realize that medieval critics did not want to abolish the papacy but to reform it and to conform the church to the model of the early church.

However, the Avignonese papacy continued to alienate Christians throughout Europe by a building craze that left splendid palaces and monuments in Avignon but severely taxed the faithful to pay for them. The poet Francesco Petrarch (1304–74), who had lived in and around

Avignon, described the luxury and worldliness of the papal court as "the sewer of the world." A bureaucratic mentality and materialism clouded the spiritual vision of the papacy. Instead of responding to the philosophical, theological, and literary critiques against it, the papacy developed increasingly efficient administrative machinery to collect more and more taxes, shuffle its thousands of pages of documents concerned with benefices and indulgences and politics, and administer its webs of patronage. Pastoral work was displaced by work to create greener and greener pastures. Critics began to murmur that Jesus had commanded Peter to "feed my sheep" (John 21: 15–17), not fleece them.

Ebbing papal prestige and authority was noted by many, and calls increased to return the papacy to Rome. Gregory XI (1370–8) heeded these calls in 1377. Ironically, the end of the Babylonian captivity of the church led almost immediately to the western schism. Gregory XI died on 27 March 1378. His body was barely cold when Romans began rioting in the streets, demanding that the papacy remain in Rome and that a Roman or at least an Italian be chosen pope. The cardinals chose Bartolomeo Prignano, the efficient, hard-working administrator of the Avignonese curia. He was neither a Roman nor an Italian nor even a Frenchman, but a Neapolitan (Naples was closely related to France through the House of Anjou). Although a respected administrator, he was essentially a civil servant with no experience in policy-making. He took the title Urban VI (1378–89). In spite of the riotous behavior during the election process, there is no indication that the cardinals were intimidated by the mobs. Indeed, the very choice of Prignano may indicate the cardinals' resistance to threats. It is important to note this, because soon after the enthronement of Urban the cardinals decided they had made a serious mistake and used the supposed pressure of the mobs to claim that the election was invalid. Concluding that Urban was unfit to be pope, the cardinals impugned their own election process on the basis that it had taken place under conditions of duress and fear. One by one they slipped out of Rome and gathered at Anagni, where they declared that Urban had been uncanonically elected and that the papacy was to be considered vacant. In September they elected Cardinal Robert of Geneva, who took the title of Clement VII (1378–94). Urban did not accept the cardinals' request that he abdicate, but instead excommunicated Clement, who returned the favor. The sorry spectacle of pope excommunicating pope, and vice versa, would continue for nearly forty years (1378–1417).

There had been anti-popes before in the history of the church, but this was the first time that the same legitimate college of cardinals had legitimately elected two popes within a few months. Urban VI and his successors remained in Rome. Clement VII and his successor resided in Avignon. It is difficult today to appreciate fully the depth of the religious insecurity and the intensity of institutional criticism this schism caused. If, as decreed by Boniface VIII's bull *Unam sanctam* (1302), salvation itself was contingent upon obedience to the pope, it was crucial to know who was the true vicar of Christ. But how could this be decided? Now, too, not only were there two popes, each claiming to be the sole vicar of Christ, there were also two colleges of cardinals, and so on down the line even to some parishes that had two priests. Europe itself split its allegiance. Clement VII was followed by France, Scotland, Aragon, Castile, and Navarre, while Urban VI was followed by much of Italy, Germany, Hungary, England, Poland, and Scandinavia. Public opinion was hopelessly confused. Even the learned and the holy clashed over who was the true pope. St Catherine of Siena worked tirelessly to secure universal recognition of Urban. She called the cardinals who elected Clement "fools, liars, and devils in human form." On the other hand, the noted Spanish Dominican preacher, Vincent Ferrar, was equally zealous for the Avignon popes and labelled the adherents of Urban as "dupes of the devil and heretics."

In the course of this protracted struggle the prestige of the papacy and the credibility of the church sank to a new low. The rise of renewal movements in England under Wyclif and in Bohemia under Hus further complicated efforts to restore the credibility of the church. John Wyclif (ca. 1330–84) was an English philosopher and theologian whose concern for reform of the church led to his condemnation by synods of the English church and finally by the council of Constance in 1415. He was for a time in the service of the English crown, and his claim that the state could lawfully deprive corrupt clergy of their endowments was certainly of interest to the crown but was condemned by Pope Gregory XI in 1377. He further argued that papal claims to temporal power had no biblical warrant, and he appealed to the English government to reform the whole church in England. The extent to which he was an influence upon the Lollard movement for a biblically based Christianity, which supposedly prepared the soil for the seeds of Reformation in England, remains controversial (Aston 1984; Hudson 1988).

Wyclif's ideas were widespread among the lower English clergy and spread to Bohemia after the marriage in 1382 of Richard II of England to Anne, the sister of King Wenceslaus IV of Bohemia. The Bohemian reformer John Hus (ca. 1372–1415) translated some of Wyclif's writing into Czech. Hus, rector of the University of Prague, was a fiery preacher against the immorality of the papacy and the higher clergy in general, and a champion of the distribution of wine as well as bread to the laity in the Lord's Supper. In spite of a safe conduct from the Emperor Sigismund, Hus was condemned and executed at the council of Constance in 1415. His follower, Jerome of Prague, suffered the same fate.

The Hussite account of Hus's trial provided parallels to the crucifixion of Christ. "On the seventh day of June [1415] – it was the sixth day of the week – in the eleventh hour, there was a total eclipse of the sun so that no mass could be celebrated without candles, thus indicating that Christ, the Sun of Righteousness, was eclipsed in the hearts of many of the prelates, who breathlessly panted for the death of Master John Hus who should be killed as soon as possible by the Council." Falsely accused, the account continues, Hus was led from Constance, bound to a post and burned to death while he serenely sang to the end "Christ, Son of the living God, have mercy on me" (Bujnoch 1988: 45). A century later, Luther would be compared to Hus, and Müntzer would appeal to the Hussites in his "Prague Manifesto." Both Wyclif and Hus were signs of growing national consciousness and criticism of the church. After his execution, Hus was declared a martyr and national hero by the University of Prague. Hus's prophecy that though his enemies were burning a goose at the stake ("Hus" in Czech means "goose") a swan would follow that they could not burn was popularly applied to Luther a century later (Pelikan 1964: 106–46).

Conciliarism

The western schism had to be solved. It was proposed that both popes abdicate in order to allow a new election. Neither the Roman nor the Avignonese line favored this. Other solutions included the establishment of a tribunal, whose verdict would be acknowledged by each pope, and the proposal that government supporters of the popes withdraw allegiance and thus prepare the way for a new election. The universities favored and advanced the recovery of the ancient principle that in an emergency, such as the case of a heretical pope, a general council would decide what to do. This "royal way of the ancient church" was already suggested at the beginning of the schism by two German professors at the University of Paris, Henry of Langenstein (d. 1397) and Conrad of Gelnhausen (d. 1390). Their writings promoting this solution were augmented by the concurrence of others in the many new universities founded at this time.

Finally, in June 1408, cardinals of both popes met and resolved to summon a general council to meet at Pisa. Both popes were invited to attend but they refused. The council of Pisa (March to July 1409) met anyway and was well attended by cardinals, bishops, hundreds of theologians, and representatives of almost every western country. Among the participants were distinguished scholars of conciliarism such as Pierre d'Ailly, chancellor of the university of Paris, and Jean Gerson, his successor. Their argument that supreme ecclesiastical power was located in the council was accepted. The council proceeded to depose both popes as notorious schismatics and heretics, and then elected a new pope, Alexander V (1409–10), archbishop of Milan and a cardinal of the Roman line. But the deposed popes refused to recognize the validity of the Pisan council; thus there were now three popes!

This scandalous situation was further aggravated after the death of Alexander V by the election to this new Pisan papacy of a man reputed to have engaged in piracy during his previous military career. Baldassare Cossa had been such a successful commander of papal troops that Boniface IX had made him a cardinal in 1402, and then a papal legate. Cossa took the title John XXIII and reigned from 1410 until 1415, when he was imprisoned and deposed by the council of Constance. His title and efforts to manipulate the council of Constance were redeemed approximately 450 years later by John XXIII (1958–63) and the "open" council Vatican II. Without being unduly concerned about the means used, John was able to achieve his initial goal of expelling the pope of the Roman obedience from Rome. However, political and military events in central Italy forced him to take shelter with his curia in Florence, and to seek a protector. He turned to the king, later (1433) emperor, of Germany, Sigismund.

Sigismund had already endorsed the Pisan line of popes established at the council of Pisa and thus was a natural source of assistance for John XXIII. However, Sigismund was also greatly concerned for the unity of the church. He had been persuaded by conciliarists, especially Dietrich of Niem (1340–1418), that in an ecclesiastical emergency the emperor should follow the model of the ancient Christian emperors and convoke a general council. Dietrich further argued that a general council had plenary powers, including the rights to depose a pope and to reform the church. Although not yet emperor, Sigismund decided to act on the arguments that a general council is superior to the pope and that the emperor as first prince of Christendom and protector of the church has the duty to call a council when needed. He successfully arranged to organize such a council on German soil at the city of Constance.

The council of Constance (1414–17) was convoked in 1414 by Pope John. The council faced three main issues: the great schism, extirpation of heresy, and reform of the church in "head and members." The active participation of Sigismund not only stimulated a large and representative attendance, but also overcame threats to its validity. By early 1415 the attendance included 29 cardinals, 33 archbishops, 3 patriarchs, over 300 bishops, and numerous abbots, priors, theologians, canonists, and representatives of rulers. The council vindicated conciliarism and defeated the papal hierocratic system.

Pope John hoped that the council would depose the popes of the Roman and Avignonese obediences and legitimize him. He soon discovered there was a consensus that all three popes should resign. John's own plans for the council were further jeopardized by the conciliar decision to vote by nations rather than by persons, with each nation having one vote. This procedure counterbalanced the preponderance of Italian prelates upon whom John depended.

The decision to vote by nations had a significance which extended beyond the immediate politics of John's efforts to win conciliar endorsement. It was a democratizing event, because in the separate deliberations of the nations it was now not only the prelates but also representatives of cathedral chapters and universities, theologians, canonists, and representatives of princes who had a voice. Furthermore, the idea of a nation as a unit, an idea taken over from the universities, contributed to the already developing sense of nationalism that was undermining the old idea of a universal Christian commonwealth under the headship of the papacy. The further consequences of this nationalism will be seen in the rise of national churches and in the Reformation.

The council's famous decree *Haec sancta* (1415) placed the authority of the council over that of the pope and sanctioned conciliar theory as the official teaching of the church. The character of a general council was set forth as a lawful assembly, representing the universal church, whose power was directly from Christ and whose authority therefore extended over every office holder in the church, including the pope. The council deposed the rival popes and on 11 November 1417 Cardinal Odo Colonna was elected pope by the college of cardinals and six representatives of each of the five nations present at the council. He took the title of Martin V in honor of the saint of the day. The great western schism was over.

Concerned that reform of the church would falter without conciliar direction and support, the council passed the decree *Frequens* in 1417. In unmistakable language, the council stated that the holding of frequent meetings of general councils "is a principal means for tilling the Lord's field for it uproots the brambles, thorns and thistles of heresies, errors and schisms, corrects excesses and reforms what is amiss, and restores the vineyard of the Lord to rich and fruitful bearing" (Kidd 1941: 210–11). The decree provided that the next council was to be held in five years, a second in seven years, and thereafter every ten years "in perpetuity." It concluded that it is lawful for the pope to "shorten the period but on no account to put it off."

Martin V closed the council in April 1418. He did not however confirm or approve it, an omission probably little noted because of the profound relief over resolving the schism. His successor Eugene IV (1431–47), however, approved it in 1446 in so far as it was not prejudicial to the rights, dignity, and supremacy of the papacy. However, Pius II (1458–64) in his bull *Execrabilis* (1460) prohibited any and all appeals to a council over the pope, such an appeal to be regarded as heresy and schism. This would later be applied against Luther who called for reform of the church through an ecumenical council.

Some of the decrees of the council of Constance became parts of special agreements between Martin V and particular nations, now for the first time called "concordats." This development further indicates the displacement of the ideal of a universal Christian commonwealth by individual independent nations. The papacy, hitherto claiming sovereignty over all peoples, was now reduced to one government among many national governments which bound itself to them in a contractual manner. This, too, was to have significance a century later in the Reformation.

The immediate aftermath of the council of Constance may perhaps be best described in terms of battle fatigue. The spiritual and physical anxiety and stress occasioned by the long schism and the energy required for its resolution left an inheritance of confusion and uncertainty. The church was now entering a period of transition in which the old hierocratic papal institution had not yet become merely a memory, and the new conciliar orientiation was still an innovation. Was the *corpus Christianum* to be reformed and renewed from below or from above?

Martin V, in accordance with the decree *Frequens*, convoked a council at Basle for 1431. By December only a few participants had arrived, and in February Martin died. His successor, Eugene IV, opposed to the council from the start, dissolved it on the basis of insufficient attendance and the argument that the appropriate setting for reunion discussions with the Greeks was an Italian city. The mutual hostility between Eugene and the council increased when Eugene transferred the council to Ferrara to advance his aim of reunion with the east. A minority of the council acceded to the pope's decision; the majority declared Eugene deposed. In turn, the pope declared those remaining at Basle heretics and schismatics. The election of an anti-pope, Felix V (1439–49) had little significance because he received little or no support from the nations. The French had already embodied no fewer than 23 decrees of Basle into national law in the "pragmatic sanction of Bourges" (7 July 1438), which supported the older claims of the French national church to a privileged position in relation to the papacy. This "Gallicanism," so-called from these *libertés de l'Eglise gallicane*, continued to assert the autonomy of the French church until the definition of papal infallibility at the first Vatican council (1869–70).

Meanwhile, the authority of the council of Basle eroded as its leading spokesmen deserted their own camp and joined the forces of the very papacy they had vigorously attacked. One of these men, the secretary of the council, later became a robust opponent of conciliarism when he was elected as Pius II. These one-time conciliarists now sensed what the representatives of rulers also saw in the conciliar movement – the danger that the governed everywhere would become the masters of their kings and princes as well as of their pope. Now that the papacy had been demoted to the status of one monarchical government among others, it dawned on other monarchs that conciliarism was a two-edged sword. As rulers came to realize that the means developed to control the papacy could become a weapon used against them, they raised gloomy predictions of sedition and anarchy. Thus the papacy and monarchs were now disposed to conclude concordats with each other. The possibility of democracy drove all theocratic monarchs, including the papacy, toward cooperation for the sake of mutual preservation. Hence Felix V was the last anti-pope, and his role was negligible because monarchs saw that any short-term benefit in supporting him would be outweighed by long-term costs.

The papacy's own effort to overcome the challenge of conciliarism and to consolidate its patrimony in Italy diverted its energy and attention from the widespread cry for reform of the church in head and members. In less than a century this cry would become the full-throated roar of the Reformations that blew away the last vestiges of the ideal of the *corpus Christianum* and the papal efforts to realize a universal headship over Christians. That roar included a cacophany of voices: those alienated by poverty, the profit economy, and the stress of urban growth; those made anxious by terrors of famine, plague, and war; those angered by the frustration of the renewal movements of Wyclif and Hus; and those enamored of the individualism of the Renaissance. Altogether, people by the end of the Middle Ages were in one way or another being thrown back upon themselves as the external supports of their Christian commonwealth were undermined. "The Western Schism, with its concatenation of abortive solutions from Pisa and Constance to Basel . . . called the sacred basis of existence into question to an extent hitherto unknown" (Oberman 1973: 17).

The clue to the magnitude of this crisis resides in the fact that the whole of medieval society had striven to attain the Augustinian vision of the City of God. Within this vision the church encompassed the whole of human society subject to the will of God. The church was the ark of salvation in the treacherous and mortal seas of life. "It was membership in the church that gave men a thoroughly intelligible purpose and place in God's universe. So that the church was not only *a* state, it was *the* state; it was not only *a* society, it was *the* society – the human *societas perfecta*" (Southern 1970: 22).

Sociological perspectives shed light on the depth of this crisis. In *The Sacred Canopy* Peter Berger (1969: 28) argues that every human society is involved in the continuous task of structuring a meaningful world for itself. In the face of the precariousness of personal and social life, society strives to shield itself from chaos, formlessness, meaninglessness, and the terror of the void by structuring a meaning which can deal with the marginal situations of life. Faced by the constant possibility of personal and cultural collapse into anomie, humankind has perpetually grounded social structures in the cosmos, and thereby given ontological status to institutions. "Put differently, religion is the audacious attempt to conceive of the universe as being humanly significant."

This theoretical orientation helps us to see that the famous effort by Pope Boniface VIII to subordinate the French king Philip was more than just political aggrandizement gone awry – though that certainly was part of it. The high papology of *Unam sanctam* (1302) "is not novel, but a fine summary of the political consequences of that hierarchy of being where peace and justice in the world are derived from the sacred, from sanctification and legitimation through the sacraments and the jurisdiction of the Church" (Oberman 1973: 27). For medieval society, the church is the "agency through which the divine order is brought into human order, by which divine law becomes positive legal codes" (Wilks 1963: 163–4). That is, human institutions and values have an ontological validity because they are rooted in the mind of God. More succinctly put: "The power of religion depends, in the last resort, upon the credibility of the banners it puts in the hands of men as they stand before death, or more accurately, as they walk, inevitably, toward it" (Berger 1969: 51). By the eve of the Reformations the credibility of these banners was in question as never before.

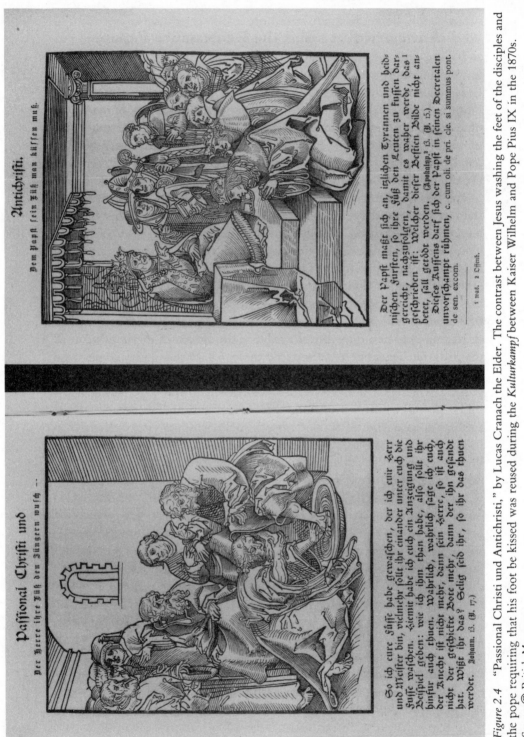

Figure 2.4 "Passional Christi und Antichristi," by Lucas Cranach the Elder. The contrast between Jesus washing the feet of the disciples and the pope requiring that his foot be kissed was reused during the *Kulturkampf* between Kaiser Wilhelm and Pope Pius IX in the 1870s.

Anticlericalism and the Renaissance Papacy

It was not the doctrine emblazoned on the banners of late medieval Christianity that was in question so much as it was the lives of those who bore them. Although the term "anticlericalism" itself is of nineteenth-century coinage, it is a useful designator for the wide range of criticism – oral, literary, and physical – directed against the perceived gap between Jesus and the apostles on the one hand and the contemporary clergy on the other.

The personal characters of the Renaissance papacy raised more issues than they resolved. Sharp and tough-minded, they set out to smash the conciliar movement's strictures on papal authority. Their success in this endeavor may be seen in the fact that, apart from the council of Trent (1545–63), there was not another council until the first Vatican council (1869–70), which in its declaration of papal primacy and infallibility was the final answer to the council of Constance. Late medieval people, of course, could not see that far ahead. What they could see was the great gulf between the biblical image of the shepherd guiding the flock toward the heavenly city and the series of Renaissance popes who exploited the flock for their own advancement in the earthly city. The papacy became an Italian Renaissance court and the pope was increasingly perceived to be nothing more than an Italian prince whose problems and interests were now local and egoistic rather than universal and pastoral. Two particularly notorious popes exemplify the depths to which the papacy sank at this time: Alexander VI (1431–1503, pope from 1492) and Julius II (1443–1513, pope from 1503).

A Spaniard by birth, Rodrigo Borgia was made a cardinal by his uncle, Pope Callistus III, in 1456 and won the papacy largely through bribery. Rooted in nepotism and simony from its beginning, it is no surprise that Alexander VI's reign was determined by continuing familial and financial concerns. He is one pope to whom the title "father," if not "holy," may be literally applied. His many mistresses bore him at least eight known children, the most famous of whom are Cesare Borgia and Lucrezia Borgia. The former is infamous for his ruthless exaction of total obedience as his father's military leader, as well as for his immorality, murders, and possibly the assassination of his brother. He is reputedly the model for Niccolò Machiavelli's *The Prince* (1513). Lucrezia served her father's plans by a series of ambitious political marriages marked by extravagant wedding parties in the Vatican palace. One of her husbands was murdered by order of her brother Cesare. At one point, when absent from Rome for a military campaign, Alexander appointed his daughter regent of the Holy See.

Alexander's own involvement in sexual promiscuity, alleged poisonings, and intrigue made the name Borgia a synonym for corruption. He was denounced in his own time by the influential and fiery Dominican preacher Girolamo Savonarola (1452–98). When Alexander could not persuade Savonarola to discontinue his attacks by offering him a cardinal's hat, he proceeded against him and was at least partly responsible for Savonarola's execution in Florence. Alexander's political efforts to strengthen the papal state abetted French intervention in northern Italy, which helped initiate a new period of power politics with Italy as the focus of international struggles.

Ironically, the worldliness of Alexander's life also included the patronage of great artists whose legacy may still be enjoyed by the visitor to Rome. Cynics of the time, however, played upon the traditional image of the church as the ark of salvation by comparing it to Noah's ark without benefit of shovelled stalls. It was common to suggest that the closer one got to Rome the worse the Christians, and that everything was for sale in Rome. The ambition and avarice of the Renaissance popes was spelled out by arranging the first letters of the saying "avarice is the root of all evil" to spell "Rome" (*Radix Omnia Malorum Avaritia* = ROMA).

Julius II continued patronage of the arts by his support of Raphael, Michelangelo, and Bramante; his enthusiasm for rebuilding St Peter's led to the indulgence which later occasioned Martin Luther's "Ninety-Five Theses." But in his own time, the art by which Julius was primarily known was the art of war; Raphael painted Julius mounted and in armor. Julius continued the political and military efforts of the Borgias to control the Papal States and expel all foreigners from Italy. He himself led his troops with such strength and drive that he became known as *terribilita*, the terrible man. So much of his reign was characterized by warfare that more and more of the laity began to wonder in disgust what this pontiff had to do with the Prince of Peace. The great humanist, Erasmus (1469–1536), who had witnessed Julius's triumphal martial entry into Bologna, angrily criticized and satirized Julius in *The Praise of Folly* (1511), *The Complaint of Peace* (1517), and *Julius Exclusus* (1517). The latter writing, in dialogue form, spread rapidly all over Europe and portrays Julius appearing before the gates of heaven upon his death. For all his threats and bombast, Julius cannot force his way into heaven. In response to Julius's demand that Peter recognize him as the Vicar of Christ, Peter says:

I see the man who wants to be regarded as next to Christ and, in fact equal to Him, submerged in the filthiest of all things by far: money, power, armies, wars, alliances – not to say anything at this point about his vices. But then, although you are as remote as possible from Christ, nevertheless you misuse the name of Christ for your own arrogant purposes; and under the pretext of Him who despised the world, you act the part of a tyrant of the world; and although a true enemy of Christ, you take the honor due Him. You bless others, yourself accursed; to others you open heaven, from which you yourself are locked out and kept far away; you consecrate, and are execrated; you excommunicate, when you have no communion with the saints. (Erasmus 1968: 87–8).

On the eve of the Reformation, the question was not whether the church should be reformed, but when. The successor to Julius II was a son of the famous Florentine political and banking family, the Medici. He took the title Leo X (1513–21) and was pope during the early years of the Reformation. The words with which he reputedly opened his reign indicate how well prepared he was to respond to the widespread desire for reform of the church: "Now that God has given us the papacy, let us enjoy it."

Suggestions for Further Reading

Norman Cohn, *The Pursuit of the Millennium: Revolutionary Messianism in Medieval and Reformation Europe*, New York: Harper Torchbooks, 1961

A. G. Dickens, *The German Nation and Martin Luther*, New York: Harper & Row, 1974

Peter A. Dykema and Heiko A. Oberman, eds, *Anticlericalism in Late Medieval and Early Modern Europe*, Leiden: E. J. Brill, 1993

Mark U. Edwards, Jr, *Printing, Propaganda and Martin Luther*, Berkeley: University of California Press, 1994

Johan Huizinga, *The Waning of the Middle Ages: A Study of the Forms of Life, Thought and Art in France and the Netherlands in the Dawn of the Renaissance*, Garden City: Doubleday Anchor, 1956

Jacques Le Goff, *Medieval Civilization 400–1500*, Oxford: Blackwell, 1988

Joseph H. Lynch, *The Medieval Church: A Brief History*, London: Longman, 1992

Bernd Moeller, *Imperial Cities and the Reformation: Three Essays*, ed. and tr. H. C. Erik Midelfort and Mark U. Edwards, Jr, Durham: Labyrinth, 1982

Heiko A. Oberman, ed., *Forerunners of the Reformation: The Shape of Late Medieval Thought Illustrated by Key Documents*, New York: Holt, Rinehart and Winston, 1966

Steven Ozment, ed., *The Reformation in Medieval Perspective*, Chicago: Quadrangle, 1971

Steven Ozment, *The Reformation in the Cities: The Appeal of Protestantism to Sixteenth-Century Germany and Switzerland*, New Haven: Yale University Press, 1975

R. W. Scribner, *For the Sake of Simple Folk: Popular Propaganda for the German Reformation*, Cambridge: Cambridge University Press, 1981

R. W. Southern, *Western Society and the Church in the Middle Ages*, Baltimore: Penguin, 1970

3

The Dawn of a New Era

It is through living, indeed through dying and being damned that one becomes a theologian, not through understanding, reading, or speculation.

Martin Luther

Little did Leo X know as he was preparing to enjoy his spoils that his papacy would be the lightning rod for a reform movement unleashed by a young student terrified by a lightning bolt in 1505. The thunderstorm that prompted Martin Luther to become a monk was but a foretaste of the storm that would shake late medieval Europe to its foundations and permanently alter western Christianity. Flashes across the horizon of the late medieval sky had already indicated the energy of this coming storm, fed by the highly charged atmosphere of life on the eve of the Reformation. Now the suddenness and speed of its discharges illuminated the dawn of the Reformation. Seeded by Luther's resolution of his personal anxiety over salvation and pastoral concern for his parishioners, the clouds of crisis broke over Europe.

Martin Luther (1483–1546)

Luther came from an upwardly mobile family. His grandfather was a peasant farmer but his ambitious, determined father worked his way up in the mining industry to the position of a small employer. Luther himself was the first of his family to gain a formal education and become an academic. It is striking that other leading Reformers – Melanchthon, Zwingli, Bucer, and Calvin – came from similar backgrounds.

The poor to modest circumstances of Luther's youth were ameliorated as his father's mining ventures prospered. Indeed, as a smelter-master, Hans Luther earned sufficient income to provide Martin with a university education. After the younger Luther's marriage, his prince gave him the Augustinian monastery in Wittenberg for living quarters;

he and his family had meat, fish, and fruit to supplement the medieval staple of life, bread, and Luther's wife – by his account – made the best beer available.

The educational system Luther encountered as a youth was certainly effective, although he did not find it at all edifying. Knowledge was literally beaten into the students. Luther probably started school around the age of seven. The techniques by which he was forced to learn Latin as the basis for later studies included coercion and ridicule. Unprepared students were forced to wear an image of a jackass and addressed as an ass. A student speaking German rather than Latin in class was beaten with a rod. Even music, Luther's favorite subject, was presented in a utilitarian fashion in order to train youths for church choirs. In short, the education of children was at best dull and at worst barbaric. Luther later recalled that one morning he was caned fifteen times for not mastering the tables of Latin grammar.

Those who did master Latin could go on to more advanced education. At fourteen Luther went to Magdeburg, where he lived and studied at a school run by a pious lay religious organization, the Brethren of the Common Life. From there he went on to study in Eisenach. All the students literally sang for their suppers: after classes they roamed the streets in children's choirs to beg for food. Toward the end of his studies in the Eisenach school, Luther was fortunate to find some supportive teachers who recognized his abilities. They introduced him to the Latin classics and history, which made a life-long impression on him and gave him great pleasure. In later life, he translated Aesop's fables into German, and insisted that everyone should study the classics and history. It was a university education, however, that opened doors for commoners to careers in medicine, law, and the church. Like Calvin's father a generation later, Luther's father was eager for Martin to improve the family status and wealth by going to university and becoming a lawyer. Thus Luther attended the University of Erfurt, where he received both his Bachelor of Arts and Master's degrees.

The medieval university consisted of an arts faculty and the three professional faculties of medicine, law, and theology. The language of instruction was Latin, and the method of instruction was detailed study and commentary on texts with particular attention to *the* authority, Aristotle, and his writings on logic. Disputations, an adversarial style of presentation central to this process, not only allowed display of intellectual skill but served the search for the truth. Disputants presented the evidence for their position in the form of theses; opponents then presented alternative evidence to support their own position. Every professor was required to hold public disputations to show how this was done, and both faculty and students were required to attend weekly disputations on selected topics. Disputations educated students in logical thinking. The teacher assigned a set of theses to a student who then defended them according to the rules of logic. This was also the form for the final examination for a degree. Today's oral examination of PhD students in our universities during which they defend their dissertation or thesis is but a pale reflection of the rigorous academic exercises common to the medieval university. The disputation is precisely the form in which Luther cast his "Ninety-Five Theses" as well as many of his other Reformation writings. In this as well as other ways, the Reformation was a movement from within the universities.

As a movement within the universities, the Reformation benefited greatly from the approach known as humanism, which strove to apply the critical intellectual recovery of ancient sources to education, the church, and society as a whole. The significance of humanism as a reforming party is conveyed by Bernd Moeller's (1982: 36) succinct phrase: "No humanism, no Reformation." The sources and norms for humanism included Scripture and the church fathers, whose writings were newly accessible through the recovery and improvement of scholarship in Greek, Hebrew, and Latin. The widespread approval of Luther as "our Martin" by humanists in the years up to the edict of Worms (1521) reflected their view of him as a prominent representative of the new learning who opposed their common enemies of scholastic and ecclesiastical abuses of religion and power (Grane 1994).

Luther's move from the study of law to monastic life and the study of theology occurred in the context of the piety of his day. Chapter 2 presented the late medieval period as a time of crisis and insecurity prompted not only by the physical difficulties of the time but also by the rapid social changes that called into question the values and traditional truths by which people had lived. The church exacerbated these insecurities by promoting a type of pastoral care designed to make people uncertain about their salvation and thus more dependent upon the intercessions of the church. The Christian pilgrimage toward the heavenly city was a balancing act between fear and hope. Visitors to medieval cathedrals and churches can still see representations of Christ on the throne of judgment with a sword and a lily on opposite sides of his mouth. The lily represented the resurrection to heaven, but the sword of judgment to eternal torment was more vivid in the minds of most people. A sandstone relief of this common depiction of Christ seated on a rainbow "graced" the Wittenberg parish churchyard and so terrified Luther that he refused to look at it.

Figure 3.1 Christ as judge seated on the rainbow. Sandstone relief from around 1400 at the Wittenberg parish church; in 1955 it was moved inside the church. The image of the sword refers to Isaiah 49: 2, "He made my mouth like a sharp sword," and Revelation 1: 16, "from his mouth issued a sharp two-edged sword."
Source: Foto Kirsch, Lutherhalle, Wittenberg.

Everywhere in everyday life the medieval person was surrounded by images serving to remind him or her of eternity and how to achieve it. As the early medieval pope, Gregory the Great (d. 604) had said, "images are the books of the laity." Medieval churches presented the

Bible and the lives of the saints in stone, stained glass, and wood. The medieval person did not compartmentalize life into sacred and secular spheres. Thus "the books of the laity" were evident at the town fountain and town hall, carved in the doorways and painted on the walls of homes and public buildings. Where people walked, worked, and gathered for news and gossip, there were religious reminders of their origin and their destination in heaven or hell.

Since hell was not the preferred option, the church and its theologians developed a whole set of practices and exercises to assist people to avoid it. The irony was that in attempting to provide security in an insecure world, the church largely mirrored the new urban and economic developments that exacerbated human insecurity. Suspended between hope and fear, the individual had to achieve his or her goal through a whole system of *quid pro quo* services that reflected the new ledger mentality of the urban burgher absorbed in the developing profit economy. Taken as a whole, Christendom at the end of the Middle Ages appeared as performance-oriented as the new business enterprises of the day.

The very effort of late medieval theology and pastoral practice to provide security only led an insecure world to more insecurity and uncertainty about salvation. One of the key scholastic ideas that led to this uncertainty about salvation was expressed in the phrase *facere quod in se est*: do what lies within you; do your very best. That is, striving to love God to the best of one's ability – however weak that may be – will prompt God to reward one's efforts with the grace to do even better. The Christian's life of pilgrimage toward the heavenly city was increasingly perceived, literally and not just theologically, as an economy of salvation. As mentioned earlier, this "mathematics of salvation" concentrated upon achieving as many good works as possible in order to merit God's reward. In religion as in early capitalism, contracted work merited reward. Individuals were responsible for their own life, society, and world on the basis and within the limits stipulated by God. Pastoral care was intended to provide an avenue to security through human participation in the process of salvation. This theology, however, enhanced the crisis because it threw people back upon their own resources. That is, no matter how grace-assisted their good works, the burden of proof for these works fell back upon the performers, the more sensitive of whom began asking how they could know if they had done their best.

Most people, however, were grateful for whatever help they could get in their quest for salvation. Saints' bones and other relics were avidly collected and venerated with the conviction this was efficacious in reducing sentences to purgatory. Thus the Wittenberg Castle church was dedicated to All Saints; and within it Luther's prince, Frederick the Wise, housed one of the largest relic collections of the area – over 19,000 pieces, worth more than 1,900,000 days' indulgence. This pious intoxication with numbers is also evident in the celebration of masses. In 1517 at the Wittenberg Castle church of All Saints more than 9,000 masses were celebrated which consumed 40,932 candles (over 7,000 pounds of wax!) costing 1,112 gulden (Brecht 1985: 118). Frederick's relic collection included a piece of the burning bush, soot from the fiery furnace, milk from Mary, and a piece of Jesus' crib, to name but a few of his treasures acquired at great cost and lavishly displayed in expensive containers (Hillerbrand 1964: 47–9). Luther's contemporary, Cardinal Albrecht, believed his relic collection was worth 39,245,120 days' indulgence.

The extraordinary prosperity of the indulgence trade was fueled as much by the desires of believers as by the financial interests of the church. If this seems surprising, think of the similar appeal and success of modern media evangelists who promise to satisfy modern desires to control God and conquer insecurity. Late medieval Christendom has been characterized as having "an immense appetite for the divine." Scholars have sometimes puzzled over the great surge of popular piety in the late Middle Ages. No other period celebrated so many religious festivals and processions, nor threw itself so wholeheartedly into church construction. Mass pilgrimages, frequently sparked by some perceived miracle usually associated with the Lord's Supper, caught on like wildfire. The dark side of this devotion erupted in mass attacks upon Jews and persons thought to be witches. Miracles seemed to multiply everywhere in the Empire. The veneration of saints reached its peak and changed its form. Saints were depicted life-size, individualized, and garbed in contemporary dress. Saints were now aligned with the arrangement of society and made patrons for every human exigency. The practice of giving children saints' names became so widespread that the old German names all but disappeared. Insecure about salvation, people attempted to guarantee it by capturing mediators between themselves and God.

Why did people throw themselves into such a piety of achievement? Why was the treadmill of religious performance thought to be the path to security and certainty of salvation? Perhaps because in times of crisis people tend to yearn for the "good old days," and try harder to emulate what they think they were. Hidden behind the late medieval surge in piety there "was an oppressive uncertainty about salvation together with the longing for it. By capturing the mediators between them and

God, men attempted to force a guarantee of salvation. Death seems never to have been more realistically considered than in this era, and hardly ever so anxiously feared" (Moeller 1971: 55). Even today we are still fascinated by the bizarre paintings of Hieronymous Bosch (ca. 1450–1516) with their weird, rapid-breeding hybrid creatures associated with lust and fertility but which in the end symbolize sterility and death. Artistic realism blossomed in popular manuals on the art of dying, depictions of the dance of death, and deeply moving representations of Christ's passion.

Religious and psychological anxiety appears to have been heightened by the imposition upon people of clerical standards of morality and behavior. The place where every real or imagined failure to meet clerical norms was ferreted out was the confessional. The laity were expected to go to confession frequently. There the priest pried into every aspect of their lives, especially their sexual lives. The lists of sexual sins in the confessional manuals of the day were so complete that even sexual thoughts were categorized according to the particular danger of damnation consequent on them. Whether or not sexual relations within marriage were serious sins was debated, but there was agreement that at least in principle they were sins. One catechism from 1494 listed sex for enjoyment rather than procreation as a sin. The other side of this coin was the elevation of celibacy and the cloister as the supreme form of a God-pleasing life. Marriage and family were demeaned as necessary evils for the propagation of the community. It is no wonder that the Reformers' attack upon mandatory celibacy for the clergy, and their renewed appreciation of the joy of sex in marriage, were so well received by the laity (Ozment 1992: 152–3; 1983: 12; Tentler 1977: 162–232).

Everyday life on the eve of the Reformation included elements regarded today as superstitions: belief in witches, magic, and astrology. But before we look too quickly down our collective modern nose at late medieval superstitions, we might recall that most of our daily newspapers include horoscopes, and that the "health and wealth" gospels utilizing contemporary media appeal to the same fears and desires that motivated the medieval person to seek out supernatural healers and diviners of the future.

Luther's reform movement was not initiated by the righteous and moral indignation of a Savonarola or an Erasmus directed against perceived superstitions or the corruption of the Renaissance papacy. Luther's movement was rooted in his own personal anxiety about salvation; an anxiety that, if the popular response to him is any indication, was widespread throughout Europe. This anxiety was an effect of the crises of the late medieval period already sketched, but its root cause was the uncertainty of salvation in the message of the church.

Theological and Pastoral Responses to Insecurity

According to Thomas Aquinas, grace does not do away with nature but completes it. So the famous scholastic phrase *facere quod in se est*, "do what lies within you," means that salvation is a process that takes place *within* us as we perfect ourselves. Put another way, we become righteous before God as we do righteous acts, as we do good works. But to an anxious and insecure age, the question became: "How do I know if I have done my best?"

The answers came primarily from the parish priests, most of whom were unversed in the subtleties of academic theology. The most common answer was "try harder!" This is the clue to that great surge in popular piety mentioned earlier. When in doubt about your salvation, examine yourself to determine if you have done your best, and then put more effort into achieving the best you can. In order to encourage more effort, pastoral practice consciously stimulated anxiety and introspection by citing the church's translation of Ecclesiastes 9:1, "No one knows whether he is worthy of God's love or hate." The church's pastoral theology suspended people between hope and fear – a sort of spiritual carrot-and-stick incentive system.

Catechisms provide a clue to the religious sensibilities of the people and the lower clergy. Priests used these simplified expositions of basic theology, usually in question and answer format, in daily pastoral practice. Widely popular, these catechisms were translated from Latin into the vernaculars, and in this process reflected the spiritual needs of the people. Dietrich Kolde's *Mirror of a Christian Man* indicates the deep religious fear and anxiety of the people up to the eve of the Reformation, and thereby provides a clue for understanding Luther's reform movement.

Kolde's *Mirror* was very popular. First printed in 1470, it appeared in 19 editions before the Reformation and continued to be reprinted after it. Translated into various European vernaculars, Kolde's work was probably the most widely used Catholic catechism before and during the early years of the Reformation. The significant point of this catechism for our purposes is the author's expression of the people's widespread lack of certitude about salvation. Kolde summed up this anxiety when he wrote: "There are three things I know to be true that frequently make my heart heavy. The first troubles my spirit, because I will have to die. The second troubles my heart more, because I do not know when. The third troubles me above all. I do not know where I will go" (Janz 1982: 182).

Luther's first steps on his own quest for certainty about his relationship to God paralleled those of many before him and countless others since: he entered a "seminary." In Luther's case it was the Augustinian monastery in Erfurt. Again, not unlike countless other seminarians past and present, Luther's decision greatly upset his father. Hans Luther was by this time making a decent living. He had sent Martin to Erfurt University with the ambition that he would earn a law degree, return home to the town of Mansfeld, and perhaps eventually become mayor. But Luther had barely begun his law studies when his father's dreams were shattered by the same lightning bolt that knocked Martin to the ground as he walked to Erfurt after a visit home. In terror, Martin implored St Anne, the patron saint of miners, for help, shouting, "I will become a monk."

And become a monk he did. In July 1505 he entered the Black Cloister (so-called because the monks wore black) of the Observant Augustinians in Erfurt. The Black Augustinians were known for their rigorous pursuit of spiritual benefits that more than matched in intensity the pursuit of material benefits practiced by Luther's father and other budding entrepreneurs. It was no less the business of monks to earn spiritual currency for themselves and others than it was the business of the early capitalists to earn material currency.

In the monastery, Luther threw himself wholeheartedly into efforts to achieve salvation. Between the six worship services of each day, which began at 2:00 a.m., Luther sandwiched intense prayer, meditation, and spiritual exercises. But this was just the normal routine, which Luther in his zeal to mortify his flesh and make himself acceptable to God soon surpassed. "I tortured myself with prayers, fasting, vigils, and freezing; the frost alone might have killed me" (*LW* 24: 24). It has been suggested that his long periods of fasting, self-flagellation, and sleepless nights in a stone cell without a blanket all contributed to the continual illness that plagued him for the rest of his life. Later in life, Luther remarked: "I almost fasted myself to death, for again and again I went for three days without taking a drop of water or a morsel of food. I was very serious about it" (*LW* 54: 339–40).

In fact, Luther was so serious about perfecting himself in order to gain God's acceptance that he soon became a burden to his fellow monks. Monastic practice prized introspection and self-examination that probed the conscience: "Have I really done my best for God?" "Have I fully realized my God-given potential?" No sensitive person under such introspective pressure to achieve righteousness before God can answer these questions affirmatively. Luther was in a continual state of anxiety about his righteousness. He constantly sought out spiritual guidance and confessors. Years later Luther remarked about all this: "Sometimes my confessor said to me when I repeatedly discussed silly sins with him, 'You are a fool . . . God is not angry with you, but you are angry with God.' " (*LW* 54: 15). Ironically, Luther entered the monastery to overcome his uncertainty of salvation, but there was confronted by the very introspection, intensified to a fine art, that had caused his very anxiety before God.

Luther's monastic superior, Johann von Staupitz, directed him to continue his theological studies to a doctoral degree. Luther protested he was too ill, unworthy, and inadequate. Staupitz was unimpressed. In 1512, Luther became a "sworn Doctor of the Holy Scripture" and embarked on his life-long career as professor of biblical studies at Wittenberg. Later, in his controversies with the church, he appealed to his doctoral oath in which he vowed to exposit and to defend the Scriptures. He believed he had a mandate from the church, and that his efforts for reform were not just a personal crusade.

At this point a brief description of Luther's Wittenberg context is in order. This small town of about 2,500 was the capital of Electoral Saxony. The duchy of Saxony had divided in the late thirteenth century, and in 1356 the area including the town of Wittenberg was granted electoral dignity by the Golden Bull, the decree regulating imperial elections. The prince of Electoral Saxony when Luther arrived was Frederick III, known as "the Wise" (1463–1525). Frederick was not only wealthy but also politically powerful and astute. Loyal to the Habsburg line, he nevertheless opposed expansion of imperial power as well as the powers of the neighboring states of Ducal Saxony and Brandenburg. Frederick was also well traveled and personally concerned for the well-being of his people, land, church, and education. By the turn of the century, he was engaged in rebuilding the castle and the church of the All Saints Foundation and establishing the university.

The division of Saxony into Ducal and Electoral territories left Electoral Saxony without a university, since Leipzig University was in Ducal Saxony. By 1503 Frederick obtained papal confirmation for a new university for which the All Saints Foundation would serve as chief financial support. Frederick also poured his own resources into the university and in 1508 published its statutes. The establishment in 1502 of the Augustinian monastery in Wittenberg by Staupitz provided the university with many of its faculty. That is how Luther came to be in Wittenberg. At first about 200 students enrolled annually. After Luther's burst into notoriety in 1517, the enrollment mushroomed. A student saying of the time suggested that if you want an education go to Wittenberg, if you are looking for amusement go elsewhere. The university was Frederick's pride and joy; he would be reluctant to allow one of his prize professors to be burned at the stake! Besides, Frederick had invested a good sum in the promotion of Luther to the doctorate on the promise that Luther would serve in the professorship of Bible for life; it would be a poor investment to allow that life to end unnaturally soon.

Luther began lecturing at the university in the winter semester of 1513–14. The exact time-frame for his lectures is uncertain, but the sequence up to the controversy over indulgences included lectures on the Psalms (1513–15), Romans (1515–16), Galatians (1516–17), and Hebrews (1517). There is nothing quite like having to explain a text to others to intensify one's own study of the material. Luther had at his disposal a good library of biblical commentaries, various biblical translations, and, after 1516, the new edition of the Greek New Testament by Erasmus. But Luther's intellectual focus was further sharpened by his own personal religious quest for certainty of salvation, the resolution of which occurred in this academic context. His conversion experience was, in the words of Gerhard Ebeling (1970), a *Sprachereignis*, a language event.

Luther's intense study of the language and grammar of the Bible, assisted by the linguistic tools provided by the Renaissance humanists, radically changed his understanding of salvation. He learned that the righteousness of God is not a demand to be met by achievement but a gift to be accepted by faith. Luther's conversion experience set medieval piety on its head. He came to see that salvation is no longer the goal of life but rather its foundation. On the basis of this discovery the theology faculty at the University of Wittenberg instituted a curriculum reform that replaced scholastic theology by biblical studies. In the spring of 1517, Luther wrote to a friend in Erfurt: "Our theology and St Augustine are progressing well, and with God's help rule at our University. Aristotle is gradually falling from his throne, and his final doom is only a matter of time. . . . Indeed no one can expect to have any students if he does not want to teach this theology, that is, lecture on the Bible or on St Augustine or another teacher of ecclesiastical eminence" (*LW* 48: 42). The authority of Aristotle was displaced by the authority of the Bible.

What Luther discovered, and what so moved his faculty colleagues and students, was an understanding of God and salvation that overthrew the anxiety-ridden catechetical teachings of priests like Kolde. Luther's biblical study led him to the conviction that the crisis of human life is not overcome by striving to achieve security by what we do, but by the certainty of God's acceptance of us in spite of what we do. The gospel, Luther argued, repudiates "the wicked idea of the entire kingdom of the pope, the teaching that a Christian man must be uncertain about the grace of God toward him. If this opinion stands, then Christ is completely useless. . . . Therefore the papacy is a veritable torture chamber of consciences and the very kingdom of the devil." Luther now never tired of proclaiming that the burden of proof for salvation rests not upon a person's deeds but upon God's action. This conviction delivered Luther from what he called "the monster of uncertainty" that left consciences in doubt of their salvation. For Luther theology is certain when "it snatches us away from ourselves and places us outside ourselves, so that we do not depend on our own strength, conscience, experience, person, or works but depend on that which is outside ourselves, that is, on the promise and truth of God, which cannot deceive" (*LW* 26: 386–7).

Medieval theology and pastoral care had attempted to provide religious security by what we may call a covenantal theology which said that if we do our best then God will not deny us grace. Although theologians employed numerous and subtle qualifications, the gist of the universal theme *facere quod in se est* ("do your best") was that people could at least initiate their salvation. That is, if you strive to love God to the best of your ability, weak as that may be, God will reward you with the grace to do even better. God, the medieval theologians claimed, has made a covenant to be our contractual partner in creation and salvation. In religion, as in the rest of life, work merited reward. Individuals were to be responsible for their own life, society, and world on the basis and within the limits of the covenant God stipulated. The theological and pastoral concern here was to provide an avenue of security through participation in the process of salvation. The consequence of this theology, however, was to enhance insecurity and uncertainty because it threw individuals back on their own resources.

Perhaps an analogy will help clarify this covenant theology. Parents are often reluctant to make absolute demands on their children. After all, popular literature warns against asking so much that children become stifled and "uptight." Parents are supposed to help children "realize themselves." On the other hand, parents also recognize that without any limits and expectations everyone's life will be frustrating. So, one common course parents follow is to tell their child: "We do not expect you to excel in everything. Just do the best you can, and we will love you even though you do not get straight As, become class president, star athlete, or prom queen." The intention is to provide guidelines without excessive pressure. For some people such an approach may work just fine. But such a relativization of expectations throws the burden of proof for achievement back on the person. The introspective question is: "How do I know when I have done my best?" No matter what is accomplished, one may think more could have been achieved with just some more effort. Whether you are an A student or an F student you can always do more. "Do what lies within you," "do the best you can." This approach is not uniquely medieval or Aristotelian; it is equally modern, certainly American. Realize your own potential; anyone can be a success if he or she only tries hard enough; you can better yourself. But how did this idea enter medieval theology and worship?

The concept came from Aristotle. If we look briefly at how medieval theologians applied just two of Aristotle's ideas, we can see how influential he was. In logic Aristotle posited that like is known by like. Applied to theology, this meant that fellowship with God can only take place when the sinner is raised to likeness with God. The sinner must become holy because God is holy and does not associate with the unholy. To the question of where fellowship with God may be achieved, the answer could only be: on God's level. The sinner must become "like" God, that is, perfected and raised to where God is. Hence the popularity of ladder imagery in medieval theology.

The widespread imagery of a ladder to heaven graphically depicted the idea that salvation requires ascent to God. Thus the twelfth-century *Hortus deliciarum* ("Garden of Delights") includes the picture of the "ladder of virtues" leading from earth to heaven. The top of the ladder enters a cloud from which the hand of God extends offering the crown of life to the climber who reaches the top. The rungs of the ladder correspond to the virtues the climber must acquire. At the foot and side of the ladder are demons who try to hinder human ascent. Angels with swords fight these demons. The persons on the rungs represent various social and religious roles: a soldier and a laywoman, a cleric, a nun and a mendicant monk, a monk from an enclosed cloister, a hermit, and, at the top, "charity," who alone reaches the goal. All the others fall off the ladder as they reach for their respective temptations below them. The hermit is attracted by his garden, the monk by his bed, the mendicant and nun by money, the cleric by food and friends, the soldier and laywoman by the goods of the world. On the ladder itself is inscribed: "Whoever falls can start climbing again thanks to the remedy of penance."

But how is the sinner to accomplish this feat? Aristotle's other idea comes into play at this point. Aristotle spoke of self-improvement in terms of what he called a *habitus*, a personal modification through habitual activity, through practice. People acquire skills through practice. A person becomes a guitarist by practicing the guitar, a good citizen by practicing civic virtues, ethical by practicing moral virtues, and so on. Through such habits or practices ethics becomes a kind of second nature.

Medieval theologians took this basically commonsense idea and applied it to achieving righteousness before God. They "baptized" Aristotle's philosophy by saying that God through the sacraments infuses a supernatural "habit" in us. On the basis of this habitual grace, we are responsible to actualize it; to do what now lies within us. In so far as we perfect the gifts God has given us, we merit more grace. Thomas Aquinas (1225–74) stated that grace does not do away with nature but perfects it. Thus, the famous scholastic phrase "do what lies within you" means that salvation is a process that occurs *within* us as we perfect ourselves. Put another way, we become righteous before God as we do righteous acts, as we do good works. But again the question becomes: "How do I know if I have done enough good works to merit salvation?"

Luther could not believe that God was placated by his efforts to do his best for his salvation. Toward the end of his life Luther reflected on his struggles with this covenantal theology. He wrote: "Though I lived as a monk without reproach, I felt that I was a sinner before God with an extremely disturbed conscience. . . . I hated the righteous God who punishes sinners . . . Nevertheless, I beat importunately upon Paul at that place, most ardently desiring to know what St Paul wanted" (*LW* 34: 336–7).

"That place" is the passage in Romans 1: 17, "For in it [the gospel] the righteousness of God is revealed through faith for faith; as it is written, 'He who through faith is righteous shall live.' " Up to this point Luther, like so many of his contemporaries, had heard the gospel as the threat of God's righteous wrath because medieval theology and pastoral care presented the righteousness of God as the standard that sinners had to meet in order to achieve salvation. Luther now came to realize that we are not to think of the righteousness of God in the active sense (that we must become righteous like God) but rather in the passive sense (that God gives us his righteousness). The good news, Luther discovered, is that justification is not what the sinner achieves but what the sinner receives. That is, it is not the sinner who is changed, but rather the sinner's situation before God. In short, the term "to be justified" means that God considers the sinner righteous (*LW* 34: 167). "God does not want to redeem us through our own, but through external, righteousness and wisdom, not through one that comes from us and grows in us, but through one that comes from outside; not through one that originates here on earth, but through one that comes from heaven. Therefore, we must be taught a righteousness that comes from the outside and is foreign" (*LW* 25: 136).

So Luther turned the medieval piety of achievement on its head. We do not do good works in order to become accceptable to God; rather, because God accepts us we do good works. Justification by grace alone through faith alone thus is a metatheological proclamation. That is, it changes the language of theology from an "if . . . then" structure to a "because . . . therefore" structure; from a language of conditions to be fulfilled in order to receive whatever is promised, to a language of unconditional promise (Gritsch and Jenson 1976: 42).

This radical shift is clearly expressed by Luther's move from a theology of covenant and contract to a theology of testament, as in a person's last will and testament. If a person is named in a will as an heir then the only condition necessary for inheritance is the death of the one who made the will. In his discussion of Hebrews 9:17, Luther wrote: "You would have to spend a long time polishing your shoes, preening and primping to attain an inheritance, if you had no letter and seal with which you could prove your right to it. But if you have a letter and seal, and believe, desire, and seek it, it must be given to you, even though you were scaly, scabby, and most filthy" (*LW* 35: 88; see Hagen 1974).

The language of testament is unconditional promise. God has named us in his will, and with his death on the cross the will is in effect. The "language event" of Luther's biblical study presented "a totally other face of the Scriptures" to him. "Thereupon I ran through the Scriptures from memory. I also found in other terms an analogy, as, the work of God, that is, what God does in us, the power of God, with which he makes us strong, the wisdom of God, with which he makes us wise, the strength of God, the salvation of God, the glory of God" (*LW* 34: 337).

Theological Implications

I have belabored Luther's understanding of the sinner's righteousness before God because it is at the heart of everything Luther said and did after his conversion. At this point we need to take a moment to sketch the difference this made in other areas of Luther's theology.

The Reformation is sometimes described in terms of the watchwords "grace alone," "Scripture alone," and "faith alone." We have already seen what Luther meant by grace alone. But what did he mean by the other two *solas*? He did not mean by these battle cries what some modern Protestants mean by them. According to Luther, the Word of God is primarily Christ. Secondarily, the Word of God is the preached or spoken Word. He was fond of emphasizing that faith comes by hearing the promise of God because he was aware that we can look away from written words but have more difficulty closing our ears to spoken words. Only on a third level did Luther relate the Word of God to the written words of the Bible. The Bible is rather "the swaddling clothes and the manger in which Christ lies . . . Simple and lowly are these swaddling clothes, but dear is the treasure, Christ, who lies in them" (*LW* 35: 236).

Faith is trust and confidence in God's promise of acceptance in spite of being unacceptable. Faith is not belief in particular doctrines. Faith is a relationship with God based on trust in God. The tendency among Protestants to speak of "salvation by faith alone" can lead to the misunderstanding that faith itself is an achievement. The confusion of faith with intellectual belief in particular doctrines or in biblical stories may lead to a kind of "can you top this" contest in which the person who believes the most unbelievable things is considered the most Christian. Then faith becomes the intellectual or psychological equivalent of medieval good works. This is far afield from Luther's understanding. "Faith is not a paltry and petty matter . . . ; but it is a heartfelt confidence in God through Christ that Christ's suffering and death pertain to you and should belong to you" (*LW* 22: 369).

Luther's radical understanding of justification brought with it a radical understanding of the person before God. Luther departed from all religious anthropologies that divide the person, whether it be into body and soul; body, soul, and spirit; flesh and spirit; or inner and outer. For Luther, the person is always the whole person. Luther could use traditional terminology, but he redefined it. Thus the distinction between flesh and spirit is no longer dualistic and anthropological but biblical and theological. Flesh and spirit do not designate parts of the person but refer to the whole person's relationship to God. Living according to the flesh means the whole person in rebellion against God. Living according to the spirit means the whole person in confidence in God's grace. "Flesh and spirit you must not understand as though flesh is only that which has to do with unchastity and spirit is only that which has to do with what is inwardly in the heart. . . . Thus you should learn to call him 'fleshly' too who thinks, teaches, and talks a great deal about lofty spiritual matters, yet does so without grace" (*LW* 35: 371–2).

Human beings have no intrinsic capacity that entitles them to a relationship with God. The whole person, not just some "lower" aspect, is a sinner. Luther understood sin theologically rather than ethically. Sin is not doing bad things but rather it is not trusting God. "Unbelief is the root, the sap, and the chief power of all sin" (*LW* 35: 369). In other words, the serpent's question to Eve is whispered in everyone's ears. Sin is the egocentric compulsion to assert self-righteousness against God; it is the refusal to allow God to be God.

Acknowledgement of sin and the acceptance of God's judgment enable the sinner to live as righteous in spite of sin. By "letting God be God," that is by ceasing one's efforts to be like God, the sinner is allowed to be what he or she is intended to be – human. The sinner is not called to deny his or her humanity and to seek "likeness" to God. Rather, the forgiveness of sin occurs in the midst of life. The Christian before God is therefore at one and the same time both sinner and righteous; "a sinner in fact, but a righteous man by the sure imputation and promise of God that He will continue to deliver him from sin until He has completely cured him. And thus he is entirely healthy in hope, but in fact he is still a sinner" (*LW* 25: 260).

The theological motif that relates justification and anthropology is the dialectical distinction of law and gospel. To Luther this is the essential nerve of theological thinking; it is what makes a theologian a theologian. "Nearly the entire Scripture and the knowledge of all theology depends upon the correct understanding of law and gospel" (*WA* 7: 502). Throughout his career Luther never tired of emphasizing the distinction between law and gospel as the key to correct theology. He believed that without this distinction the Word of God will be confused with human judgment.

The distinction between law and gospel is the distinction between two fundamental kinds of speech. The law is the communication of demands and conditions; it is the language of covenant. The law imposes an "if . . . then" structure on life. All law-type communication presents a future contingent upon human achievement: "If you hold up your end of the bargain, then I will hold up mine." The gospel however is the communication of promise. It is the language of testament with the pattern of "because . . . therefore." "Because I love you I will commit myself to you." But even in the best of human relationships this analogy breaks down. There are all sorts of contingencies over which we have no control. Death is the clearest example. We may be committed to our children but death may take us away just when they need us the most. But Luther's point is that we are not the gospel. The gospel is the unconditional promise of God. It is unconditional because God has already satisfied all conditions, including death. In this sense, then, justification is not just a particular doctrine among others. Rather, justification is *the* language that is always unconditional promise.

Indulgences: The Purchase of Paradise

At the same time as Luther was reaching a radical theological reversal of his received tradition in the context of his biblical lectures, he was also carrying out pastoral responsibilities in the Wittenberg parishes. It is important to remember that while the form of the "Ninety-Five Theses" was that of an academic disputation, the context of this disputation was pastoral. Luther was propelled into the public arena by concern for his parishioners, who believed they could purchase paradise if they bought letters of indulgence. "I am," Luther later wrote, "a sworn doctor of Holy Scripture, and beyond that a preacher each weekday whose duty it is on account of his name, station, oath, and office, to destroy or at least ward off false, corrupt, unchristian doctrine" (*LW* 31: 383).

Indulgences grew from the sacrament of penance. Baptism incorporated a person into the pilgrim community of the church which was always in process of traveling to its true home with God in the heavenly city, and the eucharist nourished the pilgrims during their trip. However, pilgrims continually faced the danger of shipwreck on earthly delights. The church's response to this danger was to offer what the early church called the "second plank after shipwreck," the sacrament of penance.

The sacrament of penance was the subjective side of the objective sacrament of the mass. Through the sacrament of penance, the church provided not only the absolution of guilt but also the means for satisfying the socially disruptive and religiously offensive actions of persons. It has been suggested that the idea of atoning for crimes by rendering commensurate satisfaction has Germanic and feudal roots. Secular penal practice allowed the "redemption" of a punishment for money. Applied to religious practice this meant that a fast could be replaced by the cost of the meal or a pilgrimage by the cost of the journey.

The significance of penance for medieval life and religion cannot be overrated. The term itself derives from the Latin *poena*, which means not only punishment but also compensation, satisfaction, expiation, and penalty. St Augustine had spoken of the necessity of punishment for sin that will be satisfied either here through human acts or hereafter by God. From this perspective there developed the doctrine of purgatory and its purifying fire, the pastoral and disciplinary life of the church, and the indulgence system for commuting penitential impositions too severe for completion outside the monastic regimen. Thus when the austere eleventh-century reformer, Cardinal Peter Damian (1007–72) imposed a 100-year penance on the archbishop of Milan for simony, he also indicated how much money would commute each year of penance. Although the intent of the indulgence system was to adjust satisfaction for sins to changing social conditions (a developing urban environment made certain penances difficult), by the late Middle Ages it was becoming an abused instrument for clerical social control and revenue raising.

By the twelfth century, the norm was a private penance before a priest that consisted of contrition (a heartfelt repentance), confession, and satisfaction. By the eve of the Reformation some wags spoke of contrition, confession, and compensation! A development that eased the sacrament of penance substituted attrition (fear of punishment) for contrition. Theoretical justification for remission of the ecclesiastical satisfaction imposed on the penitent rested on the thirteenth-century theological development of the treasury of grace available to the church. This treasury of the church contained the accumulated merits of Christ and the saints (mainly the works of monastics) which, since they were superfluous for those who originally achieved them, were available for ordinary sinners in the church. Here again, we see a ledger mentality, a calculating frame of mind concerned with "the account books of the beyond." An indulgence, then, drew on the treasure of the church to pay off the debt of the penitent sinner who would otherwise be obliged to pay off the penance by works of satisfaction. The possibility of a capitalist interpretation of this system may be seen in the story of the nobleman who decided to invest in futures. The story goes that after Tetzel made a large sum of money from indulgences in Leipzig, a nobleman approached him and asked if he could buy an indulgence for a future sin. Tetzel agreed upon the basis of an immediate payment. When Tetzel departed from Leipzig, the noble-man attacked and robbed him with the comment that this was the future sin he had in mind (Hillerbrand 1964: 44–5).

The popular mind, abetted by some preachers, twisted the meaning of indulgence from that of the church's remission of a temporal penalty imposed because of sin to that of a ticket to heaven. The hard-sell medieval indulgence sellers such as Tetzel, whom Luther attacked, offered direct access to heaven even for those who were already dead and in purgatory. One of Tetzel's sales jingles was, "As soon as the coin into the box rings, a soul from purgatory to heaven springs." Would you buy a used car from this man? Well, crowds of anxious contempor-aries believed they could buy salvation from him. He was good at his job, but then he was also rewarded handsomely.

Tetzel's routine would have been the envy of Madison Avenue, had it existed. His advance men announced his arrival some weeks before he came to town. They also compiled a special directory of the town that listed the financial resources of its citizens so they would know how much they could charge. Tetzel's entrance into the town was accompanied by a fanfare of trumpets and drums and a procession complete with the flags and symbols of the papacy. After a vivid sermon on hell and its terrors in the town square, he proceeded to the largest church and gave an equally vivid sermon on purgatory and the sufferings not only awaiting the audience but presently endured by their dead relatives and loved ones. "Do you not hear the voices of your dead parents and other people, screaming and saying: 'Have pity on me, have pity on me . . . for the hand of God hath touched me' [Job 19: 21]? We are suffering severe punishments and pain, from which you could rescue us with a few alms, if only you would.' Open your ears, because the father is calling to the son and the mother to the daughter" (Oberman 1989b: 188). After the next sermon picturing heaven, his audience was sufficiently prepared and eager to buy indulgences. There was always something for everyone because he had a sliding scale of prices depending upon the person's financial resources.

Tetzel was not allowed in Wittenberg because Frederick the Wise did not want competition for his own relic collection with its associated indulgences. But Luther's parishioners overcame this inconvenience by going out to Tetzel. Luther was appalled when they returned and said they no longer needed confession, penance, and the mass because now they had tickets to heaven. Indeed, it was said that a papal indulgence "could absolve a man even if he had done the impossible and had violated the mother of God" (LW 31: 32). As a priest responsible before

God for his parishioners, Luther had to warn them against spiritual pitfalls.

This is the immediate context for the "Ninety-Five Theses" of 31 October 1517, the traditional date of the beginning of the Reformation. But that was not Luther's first criticism of current indulgence practice. As early as 1514 Luther had denounced the abuse of indulgences and in sermons in 1516 had criticized his own prince's relic collection. Frederick was not amused. Luther was not only questioning his prince's devout piety but also undermining a source of revenue for his own university: indulgences, "the bingo of the sixteenth century" (Bainton 1957: 54), were a source of revenue for construction projects ranging from bridges to cathedrals.

The "Ninety-Five Theses" were a typical academic proposition for a university debate. They were written in Latin, and most Wittenbergers could not even read German. Thus the popular image of Luther the angry young man pounding incendiary theses to the church door is far more romantic fiction than reality. In fact there has been intensive historical discussion about whether they were posted or posted, i.e. nailed or mailed (Iserloh 1968; Aland 1965). How, then, did this document for debate cause such an uproar? Luther sent it to Tetzel's superior, Albrecht, the archbishop of Mainz, with the naïve thought that Albrecht did not know that his hireling was abusing the authority of the church. The document was then sent on to Rome. The result was an explosion that startled and frightened Luther as much as anyone else. Luther had unknowingly touched some very sensitive nerves concerning papal authority and far-reaching political and ecclesiastical intrigue.

The Squeaky Mouse

Although Pope Leo X reputedly first dismissed Luther as another drunken monk, envious of the Dominicans, the case was given to the papal theologian Sylvester Mazzolini, known as Prierias after his birthplace, Prierio. Prierias, a Dominican, was the first literary opponent of Luther (Lindberg 1972; Bagchi 1991: 17–44; Hendrix 1981: 46–52). He had already played a role in the infamous trial of Reuchlin, the famous humanist Hebraist charged with heresy by another Dominican, Pfefferkorn. That long trial was the occasion for the humanist satire against the clergy, *Letters of Obscure Men*. The Dominicans, still smarting from the Reuchlin affair, saw the indulgence controversy and the attack on the Dominican Tetzel in the context of university reform, Dominican–Augustinian rivalry, and their own role as champions of

Figure 3.2 "A Question to a Minter," by Jörg Breu, ca. 1530. This woodcut illustrates the answer of a minter to the question where all the money goes that is daily minted. The minter names three drains of the money supply: the pope with his bulls and indulgences (at the right), merchants with false measures and weights (at the left), and minters making debased coinage (center). The proclamation of papal indulgences takes the most prominent place among these three enemies of the common good. In the foreground a bishop reads aloud an indulgence. Behind him an indulgence letter complete with seals is borne on a cross. The mounted cardinal and monk illustrate the opulent lifestyle of the papacy. The text compares the Catholic clergy with a merchant for whom everything is for sale, including salvation. A fool at the right margin, unnoticed by the clergy, ridicules them.
Source: Photo Jörg P. Anders. Staatliche Museen zu Berlin-Preussischer Kulturbesitz Kupferstich-kabinett.

the papacy. The curricular reform at the University of Wittenberg had displaced Thomistic and scholastic studies by Augustine and biblical studies. The Dominicans understood themselves to be the appointed guardians of Catholic doctrine and, since the mid-fifteenth century, the champions of papal primacy and authority. Under Leo X the curia included a number of Dominicans. Thus Luther's attack on indulgences appeared as an attack on Thomistic–scholastic theology, papal authority, and Dominican (curial) jurisdiction over heretics. Luther, on the other hand, understood his questioning of indulgences as an academic dispute to which he was entitled under his doctoral oath (*LW* 34: 103). From this understanding of his position as a servant of the church in the office of doctor, Luther insisted on proof of his error by a convincing refutation of his teaching. This was both shocking and infuriating to the Dominicans.

Prierias quickly formulated a response to Luther: *Dialogue Against the Arrogant Theses of Martin Luther Concerning the Power of the Pope*. This "dialogue" accused Luther of heresy by framing the indulgence controversy in terms of papal authority. To be sure, Luther's theses raised a number of questions concerning the pope (Why doesn't he empty purgatory for love rather than money? Why doesn't he build St Peter's with his own money?) and pointed out that the true treasure of the church is the gospel, but Prierias's perspective was basically formed by an anticonciliarist papalism. His four fundamentals of the papacy, already essentially formed before the "Ninety-Five Theses," ended dialogue before it could begin. These fundamentals stated that "virtually it is the pope who is head of the church, though in another manner than Christ;" that "the pope cannot err when he in his capacity as pope comes to a decision;" that "he who does not hold to the teaching of the Roman Church and the pope as an infallible rule of faith, from which even Holy Scripture draws its power and authority, is a heretic;" and that "the Roman Church can establish something with regard to faith and ethics not only through word but also through deed. . . . In this same sense custom acquires the power of law, . . . And it follows [that he is] a heretic who wrongly interprets the teaching and actions of the church in so far as they relate to faith and ethics." In case Luther does not get the point, Prierias concludes: "He who says in regard to indulgences that the Roman Church cannot do what she has actually done is a heretic."

Luther's initial reaction to the *Dialogue* was shock and fear. "Then I thought, 'Good God, has it come to this that the matter will go before the pope?' However, our Lord God was gracious to me, and the stupid dolt wrote such wretched stuff that I had to laugh. Since then I've never been frightened" (*LW* 54: 83). Although Luther later said that Prierias as the first to come forth against him "squeaked like a mouse and then perished," this "squeak" was such that, echoing in the successive attacks by Cajetan and Eck, it shaped the future discussion.

It is, I think, no accident that during these days (1518–21) Luther's existential epistemology is so clearly expressed in the words from his second series of lectures on the Psalms: "It is through living, indeed through dying and being damned that one becomes a theologian, not through understanding, reading, or speculation" (*WA* 5: 163, 28–9).

Luther was now forced to recognize that a particular "abuse," indulgences, could not be reformed without addressing the larger context of the church's self-understanding and theology. In this sense, the original issue of the Reformation appears to be papal authority, not justification (Bagchi 1991; Lindberg 1972; Headley 1987). The ensuing conflict clarified and sharpened Luther's thought, driving him to study church history and preparing him for future confrontations with Cajetan and Eck. This conflict is also the context for Luther's 1520 appeal to the German nobility for a council and for his suspicion that the papacy was the Antichrist.

Politics and Piety

Prierias's *Dialogue* formed the basis for the citation summoning Luther to appear in Rome within 60 days of its receipt. Both documents reached Wittenberg on 7 August 1518. But before the grace period had expired Rome decided that Luther was a heretic and should be delivered to the authorities. That Luther did not suffer the fate of Hus owes much to the peculiar mix of local and imperial politics with piety. This larger context had two main foci: political jockeying for the impending imperial election in 1519; and Pope Leo X's desire to impress his secular rivals by completing the building of St Peter's, begun by Julius II. Luther escaped the normal fate of a heretic through the loopholes left by the interweaving of these concerns.

Religion and politics had been inextricably intertwined since the emperor Constantine had called the council of Nicea in 325. By the Middle Ages the papacy exercised direct temporal power and the imperial ideal included the mandate to protect the church and the true faith. Although there were open as well as latent tensions between the papacy and the German emperors in the late Middle Ages, Habsburgs such as Maximilian and Charles V took their religious duty seriously. Indeed, Charles V's reign was marked by his striving to achieve hegemony in Europe on the one hand and to combat heresy on the other. Charles's profound attachment to the Catholic church supported his perceived duty to preserve it against the Reformation. But this gets ahead of our story.

Since 1257 certain princes had claimed the right of electing the emperor. This group consisted of the duke of Saxony, margrave of Brandenburg, king of Bohemia, count palatinate of the Rhine, and the archbishops of Cologne, Trier, and Mainz. This tradition was codified in the Golden Bull of 1356, the so-called Magna Carta of German particularism, which provided an orderly procedure for an imperial regime on a federative basis, exempted the seven electors from imperial jurisdiction, and excluded papal participation in the election. The Habsburgs had been emperors since 1438 but that did not mean their election would be automatic. The dynastic rivalry of the time was between the Habsburgs and the Hohenzollerns. Since 1517 the Emperor Maximilian had tried to line up the electors in favor of his grandson, Charles of Spain. On the eve of both the Reformation and the election of a new emperor, the elector of Brandenburg, Joachim, was a Hohenzollern. In 1513 three important church positions were vacant: the archbishoprics of Magdeburg, Halberstadt, and Mainz. The last of these, see of the primate of Germany, carried a vote in the electoral college. Elector Joachim saw this situation as an opportunity to strengthen the Hohenzollern house and to influence the imperial election by having two of the seven votes in his pocket. Joachim therefore determined to acquire these positions for his younger brother Albrecht.

The difficulty with Joachim's plan was that Albrecht, under canonical age for an archbishop, was not even a priest, and it was illegal to hold more than one church office. It was, of course, possible to get papal dispensations for these impediments; but dispensations for matters of this importance were very expensive. But, as Reynard the Fox said, money talks. Albrecht negotiated a price with Rome for the archbishopric of 29,000 Rhenish gold gulden. This was clearly more than the credit lines of both Joachim and Albrecht. Leo, however, was a reasonable man and willing to work out a financial arrangement. The curia proposed that Albrecht take a loan from the Fugger banking house. Leo demanded a down payment of about 25 percent in cash, and granted Albrecht the right to sell indulgences to raise the rest of the money. As the money came in, half of it was to go to the papacy to finance the building of St Peter's, and the rest to repay the enormous Fugger loan and its interest. It is not surprising that Albrecht would hire the best indulgence salesman he could find in order to pay off his debt as quickly as possible.

The imperial election which took place in Frankfurt am Main on 28 June 1519 was one of the most hotly contested and significant political events of sixteenth-century Germany. The traditional three-cornered power struggle between the Empire, France, and the papacy was sharpened as both France and the papacy realized the immense world holdings that would be brought together under the Habsburgs if Charles were elected. Charles was already duke of Burgundy, king of Spain and Naples–Sicily, and, with his brother Ferdinand, heir to the lands of Austria. The search for alternative candidates and funds for propaganda and bribery began before the death of Maximilian. Even Henry VIII of England was briefly considered, although it was clear that Francis I of France had a more credible position. One candidate significant for Luther's personal well-being and for the course of the Reformation was his prince, Frederick the Wise, elector of Saxony. Papal efforts to persuade Frederick to be a candidate in order to counter Habsburg power rendered the papacy hesitant to proceed with full force against Luther, Frederick's prize professor; and the Habsburg effort to garner Frederick's support to the extent of a marriage alliance between Charles's sister, Catherine, and Frederick's nephew, John Frederick, meant the imperial desire to root out heresy also had to be tempered.

Charles was elected, but the machinations engaged in to achieve this result left political and financial impediments in their wake. Politically, Charles accepted the so-called "capitulation of election" as a precondition of his election. Its intent was to confirm existing constitutional order and maintain the laws and customs of the Empire. Important imperial decisions were not to be made without consultation with the German estates, German and Latin were to be the official languages, foreigners were to be excluded from German imperial offices, foreign troops were not permitted in Germany, and imperial resources were not to be used for dynastic interests. Financially, the Habsburg investment in this election approached a million gulden. The Fugger banking house supplied so much of this capital that later Jacob Fugger could brazenly request repayment with the reminder that "It is known and thus need not be emphasized that your Majesty could not have obtained the Roman crown without my help" (Hillerbrand 1964: 87). Charles V became emperor, but not with a totally free hand. His empire was geographically at least close to the medieval aspiration for a *corpus Christianum*, but he himself was forced to recognize German "liberties;" emperor and empire were no longer a unity but an opposition. His chancellor, Gattinara, argued for an imperial ideology to stabilize the empire. But imperial hegemony was a perpetual problem, now intensified by the rise of nations and the opposing powers of France and the papacy. Charles faced numerous problems with his huge empire. He had inherited everything but conquered nothing. He had to deal everywhere with the complex structures and institutions of the late phase of medieval feudalism with all their complicated privileges, precedents, and exemptions. The person of the monarch held it all together, but in a pre-jet age it took him months to get around. In all this Germany played a secondary role. Charles

himself knew little German and resided mainly outside the Empire.
The politics of the time were in Luther's favor as he was impelled
toward confrontation with pope and emperor at the diet of Worms.

From the Diet of Worms to the Land of the Birds

Events accelerated rapidly after the publication of the "Ninety-Five
Theses." Luther received significant support from his prince, Frederick
the Wise, the founder and proud patron of the University of Wittenberg. Frederick had earlier prohibited indulgence selling in his lands not
only because of his own relic collection but as a measure against his
rivals, the Hohenzollerns of Brandenburg, especially the archbishop
Albrecht. Also, Frederick's university was in the process of a significant
curriculum reform, led by Luther and his colleagues, that displaced
scholasticism with biblical and patristic studies. Frederick knew that the
Dominicans opposed this new theological orientation in Wittenberg
and moved to protect his talented professor of Scripture against
opponents in the arenas of both politics (archbishop Albrecht) and
education (the Dominicans), whom he suspected of fomenting heresy
charges in order to discredit Wittenberg and its university. If Frederick
had doubts concerning Luther they seem to have been dispelled by
Erasmus's clever reply to Frederick's question of what he thought of
the Luther affair: "He has committed great sin – he has hit the monks in
their belly, and the Pope in his crown!"

As a professor, Luther had the status of a state official of Electoral
Saxony. On this basis, Frederick "allowed" Luther to attend his order's
chapter meeting in Heidelberg. There, rather than being silenced by his
superior, he was encouraged to set forth his theology. The famous
Heidelberg disputation took the younger theologians by storm, some
of whom, such as Martin Bucer (1491–1551), went on to become major
Reformers in their own right. In the meantime, Prierias's report on
Luther served as the basis for a formal indictment before an ecclesiastical judge, and Luther was cited to appear in Rome within 60 days to
answer the charge of heresy against him.

When Luther received the citation to Rome, he wrote to Frederick,
who was at the imperial diet at Augsburg, requesting the prince to
intervene on his behalf with the pope. The request was for a hearing in
Germany before an impartial judge or group of university theologians.
This was not a unique request in this period, when rulers often
expressed concern that their subjects in matters of ecclesiastical dispute

were too often taken to Rome. Also, coupled with the German national pride in this matter was the ostensible claim that the issue was an academic matter that affected the good name of the University of Wittenberg.

Frederick could count on a sympathetic hearing from Leo X because Leo was at this time urging the members of the diet to mount – at great cost to themselves – a crusade against the Turk. The papal legate, Cardinal Cajetan (a Dominican) had been sent to address the diet, arguing that not only the future of religion but that of humanity itself was threatened if Croatia and Hungary fell to Turkish advances. The German estates were dubious about this enterprise, which would entail a tax of up to 20 percent, and they gave an evasive answer to the pope.

In this context Frederick arranged Luther's meeting in Augsburg with Cajetan. Meanwhile Cajetan received a papal letter instructing the summary trial and imprisonment of Luther unless Luther recanted and requested forgiveness. Another papal letter, sent to Frederick at the same time, voiced a much more subtle request for assistance because the pope did not want to offend such a powerful prince at the very moment he needed his support. The prince, the pope wrote, should think of his good family name, although of course the pope did not believe all the ugly rumors that Frederick was supporting a heretic.

Frederick insisted upon Luther's safety if he were to meet with Cajetan. Furthermore, there was to be full examination and proof of charges; Luther would be given the opportunity to defend himself; and no definitive judgment was to issue from this meeting.

The first interview with Cajetan quickly relieved Luther of any illusion of dialogue. The cardinal told Luther to do three things: repent and revoke his errors; promise not to teach them again; and refrain from future disruptive activity. Three further interviews did nothing but escalate tempers and fray nerves, for Luther insisted on a theological discussion of the issues. Cajetan cut short the last interview, telling Luther not to come back unless he were ready to recant. Days passed in silence and rumors spread that Luther was to be seized and sent to Rome in chains. Luther's friends panicked and hustled him out of town. He later learned he had escaped just in the nick of time.

The furious Cajetan complained to the elector of Luther's insolence. Frederick passed this complaint on to Luther, who responded that Cajetan had broken his promise of discussion and ended by saying he would be willing to leave Electoral Saxony. He then made preparations to leave. At the farewell dinner Luther was giving on 1 December, two letters dramatically arrived. The first expressed Frederick's surprise that Luther was still around; the second said Luther must remain. The latter was probably prompted by the arrival of the papal emissary, Miltitz, on a mission concerning the imminent imperial election. On 18 December, Frederick made up his mind that Luther would not go to Rome or into exile unless he was first duly heard and properly convicted. On 12 January 1519 Emperor Maximilian died, and papal and imperial politics superseded the supposed peril of heresy.

Enter Dr Johann Eck of Ingolstadt. Eck had struck up a friendship with Luther in 1517, so Luther was hurt and angered when Eck now attacked Luther's theses. Eck did not attack Luther directly, instead challenging Luther's faculty colleague, Andreas Bodenstein von Karlstadt (ca. 1480–1541), to a public disputation; but it was clear that he was after Luther. The disputation negotiations dragged on for months, and in the process led to a small pamphlet war. Karlstadt got his artist friend, Lucas Cranach, to draw a cartoon showing two wagons, one bearing the cross on the way to heaven, and the other loaded with scholastic writings on the way to hell. The Leipzig theologians and clerics were furious, and even went to the extent of questioning people in the confessional whether they had laughed at the "wagon cartoon."

Luther now suggested that at the time of Gregory I (d. 604), the Roman church was not above all other churches. Eck chose this for the focal point of his attack (recall that the Catholic controversialists saw the issue to be that of papal authority). In response to Prierias and now Eck, Luther turned to an intensive study of church history and canon law. In his thirteenth thesis against Eck, Luther wrote: "That the Roman Church is superior to all churches is indeed proved by the far-fetched decrees put out by the Roman pontiffs in the last 400 years. But this ecclesiastical dogma is contrary to the approved histories of 1100 years, the plain teaching of Scripture, and the decrees of the Council of Nicea, the most sacred of all councils." Luther frequently scared his friends as much as his enemies, and Karlstadt and Spalatin expressed their concern that he had gone too far. Luther responded that their caution almost made him sick to his stomach.

The Leipzig debate began in early July 1519. The Wittenbergers arrived in wagons flanked by numerous armed students on 24 June. The first wagon contained Karlstadt and all his precious books. The second wagon included Luther, Melanchthon, and the rector of the University of Wittenberg. As the procession reached the city gate of Leipzig, Karlstadt's wagon crashed, flinging Karlstadt into the muck. The Leipzigers were delighted. This was undoubtedly a good omen, for Eck to have the perpetrator of the infamous "wagon cartoon" hurled from his wagon. Karlstadt lost more than his pride in this incident; badly shaken, he was given medical treatment and bled twice. Altogether, the debate was a bad scene for Karlstadt. He had had a tiring trip from Wittenberg, a public humiliation, and two bleedings as prelude to facing a vicious and clever debater already licking his lips in anticipation of an upcoming roasting – literal as well as intellectual – of Karlstadt and Luther. Furthermore, Karlstadt was not good at thinking and speaking on his feet; he needed his reference works, which was why he brought all his books with him.

Duke George placed his castle at the disposal of Leipzig University for the debate. But the duke himself was not about to let a little theological fracas intrude on his vision of reality. He grumbled that they should finish soon because he had a hunting party coming; and he said to Luther: "God's law or man's law, what does it matter? The pope is the pope!" Luther's immediate problem, however, was obtaining permission to join the debate since he was not originally invited; permission was granted only after much ranting and cajoling.

The debate itself had a long wind-up, beginning at 7 a.m. with a mass written for the occasion, followed by a lengthy and tedious harangue in Latin on the procedure of the debate, then more music, and finally lunch. The debate itself began after lunch. Eck and Karlstadt spent the first week on grace and free will. Eck played to the audience and won their approval, while Karlstadt searched for references in his many texts. But since the debate would be judged by faculties from other universities on the basis of the written record, Eck finally persuaded the referee to prohibit Karlstadt from entering data into the transcript from his books.

It soon became apparent to the laity that disputations were not the most fun to watch. Indeed, even the theologians were falling asleep as they sat through the hot afternoons following big lunches. On the other hand, it has been suggested that it was safer to feign sleep because if you were later asked about volatile issues you could always plead ignorance due to a nap. The livelier debates were carried on by students in the taverns.

On 4 July Luther came into the debate. Eck prodded him with charges of being a "Hussite" and a "Bohemian." This was tantamount to being labeled a communist in the 1950s, because this area still recalled the numbers of Germans expelled from Bohemia during the Hussite revolt. Luther protested Eck's charges but finally went to the library and looked up Hus's teachings. When he returned, he stated that many of the condemned Hussite articles were truly Christian and evangelical, and ought not to be condemned by the church. After a moment of shocked silence, there was uproar. Eck pressed on and got

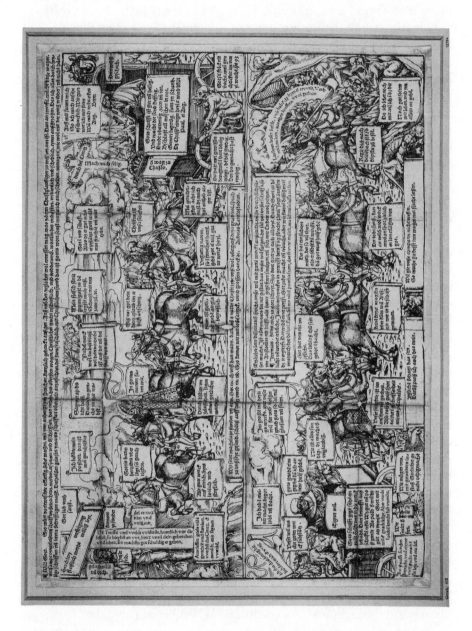

Luther to state that both the papacy and councils may err. This was an immediate triumph for Eck. After this, Karlstadt returned to take up the debate again, but Duke George was anxious to bring the whole thing to a close.

Eck spent the following weeks gloating about his success and fantasizing about receiving a cardinal's hat. Luther was now fully face to face with the implications of his Ninety-Five Theses. His opponents had put questions to him that led him farther than he at first thought he would go. Ironically, the debate had not pursued Luther's more radical attack on scholastic authorities. That was now taken up by scholastic theologians who began writing that "having arrogantly abandoned holy teachers and basic philosophy and having decided to interpret Scripture according to their own minority methods, Luther and Carlstadt had not only thrown away any chance they might have had of making their views appear reasonable but had also cut themselves off from the historic faith of the church." The Italian controversialists such as Prierias "identified the source of all Luther's errors as his rejection of Aristotle and thus of Aquinas" (Bagchi 1991: 73, 76). The faculties of Paris and Erfurt had been chosen as judges of the debate, but they stalled on giving their opinion.

The Leipzig debate was of great significance to Luther's development because here he publicly stated his evangelical conception of the church in unmistakable terms, and revealed that in the last analysis his sole authority in matters of faith was Scripture. He stated without reservation that not only the papacy but also church councils could err. This made reconciliation with the Roman church virtually impossible, and led to his excommunication.

After the Leipzig debate, Eck went to Rome to help prepare the condemnation of Luther, the papal bull *Exsurge Domine* (15 June 1520). Eck was further honored with the responsibility of disseminating the bull in Germany. He and the papal nuncio, Aleander, however, soon discovered that while they might be heroes in Rome, they were intensely disliked in Germany as respectively a traitor and a foreigner.

Figure 3.3 "The Fuhrwagon," by Lucas Cranach the Elder, 1519. This cartoon is one of the first significant expressions of Reformation propaganda. Prepared shortly before the Leipzig Disputation of 1519, it ridicules scholastic theologians and their theology. The top frame presents the wagon of the evangelical moving "in God's name" toward Christ in spite of the demon attempting to brake the wheels. The bottom frame shows the wagon of the scholastics proceeding to hell, its wheels greased by the theology of "doing one's best."
Source: © Elke Walford, Hamburger Kunsthalle.

The bull, "Arise, O Lord, judge thine own cause," listed and condemned 41 errors in Luther's writings. Luther was enjoined to return to
mother church within 60 days of its posting. If Luther failed to recant,
then his very memory was to be wiped out. But this was easier said
than done, for by now much of Germany was rallying to Luther's side.
Not only were many humanists supporting his cause, so were nobles,
such as Sylvester von Schaumburg, who offered Luther the protection
of 100 Franconian nobles; and Franz von Sickengen and Ulrich Hutten,
who later led the Knights' Revolt, hailed Luther as the potential
liberator of Germany. When the bull was posted in Germany, it was
frequently defaced. When inquisitors went about with orders to burn
Luther's writings they often encountered students who gleefully
substituted the writings of scholastics for those of Luther. Eck himself
added more fuel to the fire by adding names of his personal enemies to
the list of those condemned by the bull.

On the 60th day of grace granted Luther, 10 December 1520,
Melanchthon led the Wittenberg faculty and students out to the banks
of the nearby Elbe river for their own book-burning ritual. There,
along with classic scholastic and legal texts, and some of Eck's
writings, Luther consigned to the flames both the papal bull, *Exsurge
Domine*, and a copy of the *Corpus iuris canonica*, the legal foundation for
the medieval *corpus Christianum*. This was clearly a revolutionary act,
comparable to burning the United States Constitution. Luther was
quite aware of the significance of what he had done, and spoke of it in
class (*LW* 31: 381–95). After singing the Te Deum and the De
Profundis, the faculty returned to the university. The students, however, continued demonstrating against the pope until after two days the
town authorities put a stop to it. On 3 January 1521, the final bull of
excommunication, *Decet Romanum Pontificem*, appeared.

The Diet of Worms

Aleander urged the new emperor, Charles V, to issue a mandate against
Luther in Germany. But Charles had agreed in his coronation oath that
no German should be condemned unless his case was heard in Germany
by an impartial panel of judges. In this context, Charles V had three
basic options. He could yield to Rome and condemn Luther by imperial
mandate, since he was already under the papal ban; try private
negotiations to attempt to persuade Luther to bow to Rome; or permit
Luther to appear before the imminent diet of Worms for an investigation. Charles chose the last course, partially because of the arguments

of Frederick the Wise, and partially for political leverage against Rome, promising that Luther would not be condemned unheard, and would be given a safe conduct to Worms.

Luther's popularity is indicated by the fact that when the papal nuncio Aleander arrived in Worms he could not find a comfortable room, even though he had plenty of money; when he walked in the streets people threatened him, and when he looked in bookshops he found them full of Luther's writings. Aleander wrote to the pope: "Nine-tenths of the people are shouting 'Luther,' and the other tenth shouts, 'Down with the Pope!' " When Aleander heard of Luther's rebellious burning of the bull and the canon law, he persuaded Charles to revoke the permission to come to Worms. However, other voices counter-persuaded Charles to compromise and maintain the safe conduct, although limiting Luther's hearing to the question of whether or not he would recant.

Luther's journey to Worms became a spectacle of cheering mobs in town after town. His preaching services were so jammed that in one place the church balcony threatened to collapse. Although Luther's friends warned him of the fate of Hus, who also had had a safe conduct, Luther vowed he would go to Worms even if all the tiles of the roofs became devils. Such bravado escaped him when he was ushered into the hall to face the leadership of the world. Asked whether he would recant the pile of his writings placed before him, he begged leave to consider his response for an extra day. Luther was brought back the next day. There, before the emperor, princes, and lords – a whole world away from his monastic cell and dingy classroom – Luther did not receive the hearing he had hoped for. Rather, he was presented with a pile of his writings and asked to recant their errors. Luther's brief answer included the memorable lines: "Unless I am convinced by the testimony of the Scriptures or by clear reason . . . I am bound by the Scriptures I have quoted and my conscience is captive to the Word of God. I cannot and I will not retract anything, since it is neither safe nor right to go against conscience. I cannot do otherwise, here I stand, may God help me. Amen" (*LW* 32: 112–13).

The German princes were in general impressed by this skinny monk standing up to the powers of the world; such courage they could understand, even if the theological issues might escape them. A lasting impression was made on the young duke of Schleswig-Holstein who when he became King Christian III of Denmark immediately decreed that his subjects (including Norway and Iceland) should become Lutherans. The Spanish soldiers, however, shouted: "Into the fire!" And the emperor declared: "He will not make a heretic out of me!"

After Luther's political supporters left the diet, a rump diet voted to place Luther under the imperial ban. The edict of Worms outlawed Luther and all who gave him support. All subjects were forbidden to assist or even communicate with Luther on pain of arrest and confiscation of their property. All his writings were condemned as heretical and ordered burned. Now outlawed by the state as well as excommunicated by the church, Luther was compelled by his conscience and faith to defy both church and state. Deprived of help by the great medieval authorities, Luther now relied upon his prince and also appealed directly to the people. The latter move had already been noted by the Catholic controversialists as a rebellious stance that could only lead to insurrection. In short, Luther was now the leader of a religious movement that in effect had become a revolution.

On Luther's way back to Wittenberg he was kidnapped by order of his own prince, and taken in secret to Frederick's Wartburg Castle where he was kept in protective custody, disguised as a knight, for nearly a year (early May 1521 to early March 1522). There, high above the surrounding hills, Luther said, he was ensconced in the land of the birds. It was a fitting respite for one whom the Nuremberg Mastersinger, Hans Sachs, called "the Wittenberg nightingale."

Suggestions for Further Reading

David V. N. Bagchi, *Luther's Earliest Opponents: Catholic Controversialists 1518–1525*, Minneapolis: Fortress, 1991

Martin Brecht, *Martin Luther*, 3 vols, Minneapolis: Fortress, 1985–93

Mark U. Edwards, Jr, *Luther and the False Brethren*, Stanford: Stanford University Press, 1975

Mark U. Edwards, Jr, *Luther's Last Battles: Politics and Polemics 1531–1546*, Ithaca: Cornell University Press, 1983

Leif Grane, *Martinus Noster: Luther in the German Reform Movement 1518–1521*, Mainz: Zabern, 1994

H. G. Haile, *Luther: An Experiment in Biography*, Princeton: Princeton University Press, 1983

James M. Kittelson, *Luther the Reformer: The Story of the Man and His Career*, Minneapolis: Augsburg, 1986

Jacques Le Goff, *Intellectuals in the Middle Ages*, Oxford: Blackwell, 1993

Heiko A. Oberman, *The Dawn of the Reformation: Essays in Late Medieval and Early Reformation Thought*, Edinburgh: T. and T. Clark, 1986

Heiko A. Oberman, *Luther: Man between God and the Devil*, New Haven: Yale University Press, 1989

Thomas N. Tentler, *Sin and Confession on the Eve of the Reformation*, Princeton: Princeton University Press, 1977

Jared Wicks, SJ, *Cajetan Responds: A Reader in Reformation Controversy*, Washington, DC: Catholic University of America Press, 1978

4

Wait for No One:
Implementation of Reforms
in Wittenberg

*Every congregation, however little or great it may be, should see for itself
that it acts properly and well and waits for no one.*

Andreas Bodenstein von Karlstadt

In the Land of the Birds

Safely perched in the Wartburg Castle overlooking his "land of the
birds," Luther began work on making the new song of the gospel
accessible to the people. His German translation of the New Testament, though an intensely academic labor, was potentially as revolutionary as his burning of the papal bull and canon law. Both actions
were public affirmations of reform. Luther's provision of a readable and
accurate translation of the Bible was a stimulus toward universal
education – everyone should be able to read in order to read God's
Word. More immediately, his translation deprived the elite, the priestly
class, of their exclusive control over words as well as the Word. Even
today scholars, the "priestly classes," of all disciplines, the natural
sciences as well as the humanities, like to develop exclusive languages
for their specialties. Luther would have none of this penchant for the
arcane that makes the uninitiated dependent on "experts." His translation of the New Testament – completed within three months! – was
printed in Wittenberg in September 1522, and hence is known as the
Septembertestament. This first printing of 3,000 copies quickly sold out
and a new printing was done in December, the *Dezembertestament*.

Luther's translation of the Bible into German was not the first. There
were over a dozen translations before his, but their German was poor
and they were translations of the Vulgate, that is translations of a
translation, rather than translations from the Hebrew and Greek texts.
Luther's concern was to get as close to the original text as possible.
Philologically and stylistically his translation is superior to prior

translations, and indeed to many since then. Some of the leading literary lights of Germany, such as Herder, Goethe, and Nietzsche, "accorded Luther's Bible the highest praise" (Bluhm 1983: 178). His translation influenced the English translations by Tyndale and Coverdale as well as translations in Scandinavia and the Netherlands. Throughout his life, Luther worked continually to make the Bible more accessible to the laity through translations, explanatory prefaces, and even plans for a large print version for those with failing eyesight.

Luther's sense of evangelical freedom was evident in his concern to translate "not word for word but sense for sense." Hence his famous addition of the word "alone" in the translation of Romans 3: 28: ". . . justified without the works of the law, by faith alone" (*allein durch den Glauben*). In his treatise *On Translating: An Open Letter* (1530; *LW* 35: 188–9), Luther explained that he wanted to speak clear and vigorous German, not Latin or Greek. Thus his translation was guided by how people speak in the home, on the street, and in the marketplace. Luther further argued that the theological point of the text supersedes the nature of language alone. The meaning of justification by faith in Christ without any works of the law is "the main point of Christian doctrine. . . . Whoever would speak plainly and clearly about this cutting away of works will have to say, 'Faith alone justifies us, and not works.' The matter itself, as well as the nature of language, demands it" (*LW* 35: 195).

During Luther's enforced "sabbatical" at the Wartburg, winds of confusion and pressure to implement reforms buffeted his colleagues in Wittenberg. A new theology had been proclaimed; now, some cried, it should be enacted. But Luther had disappeared. Was he dead? In hiding? Had he deserted the cause? Who would lead reform of the church in his absence? Leadership logically fell on two of Luther's closest colleagues in the reform of the university: Philip Melanchthon (1497–1560) and Andreas Bodenstein von Karlstadt (ca. 1480–1541). Both would soon be involved in the efforts to implement the new understanding of the gospel. But as they picked their ways through the personal and political minefields of reform, it would be Karlstadt who would receive the ministerial equivalent of a battlefield commission.

Melanchthon: Teacher of Germany

Melanchthon, grandnephew of the famous humanist Johann Reuchlin, became a famous humanist and theologian in his own right as well as Luther's close life-long collaborator. A precocious youth, Melanchthon finished his BA in less than two years at the University of Heidelberg at the ripe old age of 14, and received his MA from the University of Tübingen in 1514. His enthusiasm for humanism and Greek studies is evident in the graecizing of his German family name (from Schwarzerd to Melanchthon: "black earth" in Greek does have a certain cachet lacking in the German!), a practice common among the humanists of the time. By the age of 21 he had published a Greek grammar textbook that remained in demand for decades. His contributions to German pedagogy led to the appellation *Praeceptor Germaniae*, "the teacher of Germany." His many contributions to the Reformation included the first systematic theology textbook, *Loci communes rerum theologicarum* ("Fundamental Theological Themes," 1521) and the confessional statement read before the emperor at the diet of Augsburg (1530) that remains foundational for Lutheran churches up to today, the Augsburg confession.

With the shift from scholastic to biblical theology at the university, the faculty wanted to add Greek and Hebrew to the curriculum in order to develop the ability to read the Bible in its original languages. The "regularization" of Luther's "language event" would require a learned ministry. This was the context for Melanchthon's appointment in 1518 as the first professor of Greek. Luther was so impressed by Melanchthon's language skills that he soon had Melanchthon delivering the lectures on Romans. On his part, Melanchthon was soon an enthusiastic supporter of Luther. The two men differed on various points and certainly in temperament. Although there were times when Luther became impatient with Melanchthon's cautiousness, his so-called "pussy-footing," and times when Melanchthon was upset by Luther's rages, their personality differences did not separate them. The same cannot be said for Luther's other colleague, Karlstadt.

Karlstadt and Proto-Puritanism

Karlstadt received his BA from the University of Erfurt in 1502; he also studied Thomism at Cologne. He went to Wittenberg in 1505, and there received his doctorate in 1510. Supported by Martin Pollich, the vice-chancellor of the university who was also a Thomist, Karlstadt's career rapidly progressed. By the time Luther arrived in 1512, Karlstadt was regarded as a theologian of promise. He had produced two studies in Thomist logic, been promoted to archdeacon of All Saints, professor of theology, and dean of the faculty. As a young professor on the make, his ambition directed him also to the study of law. Perhaps he had his eye on the position of provost, usually the preserve of the lawyers. At any rate, he contrived a leave and went to Italy in the fall of 1515. On his return in May 1516 he ostentatiously sported doctorates in canon and civil law. This did not sit well with faculty colleagues who had covered his responsibilities in his absence and who had been told he was only going on a brief pilgrimage to Italy to fulfill a vow. Perhaps too much should not be made of this, since faculties are renowned for petty jealousies; but it does seem that Karlstadt did not relate well with his colleagues. He has been described as a volatile, exasperating, scheming, fiery-tempered man suffering from an inferiority complex. It has been suggested that his later falling-out with Luther had elements of "sibling rivalry" and jealousy of his fellow theologian's growing fame (Sider 1974: 11–15; Bubenheimer 1981a: 110).

Some scholars have argued that the conflict that developed between Karlstadt and Luther was rooted in differences over strategies and tactics concerning the pace and direction of reform in Wittenberg, and/or Luther's insistence on personal ownership of the reform movement. These pertinent observations should not obscure the theological differences between the two men. The developments in Wittenberg following the diet of Worms foreshadow alternative theologies of reform that were soon also to swirl around Zwingli in Zurich and dog reform movements throughout the period. The question faced everywhere was the relationship between Christian freedom and authority in the implementation of reforms. Already, the Reformation initiated by Luther had become the Reformations. The application of this interpretation to the story of the reform movement in Wittenberg requires a brief excursus into Karlstadt's theology and its difference from Luther's.

When Karlstadt returned to Wittenberg in June of 1516, he discovered that the university had undergone marked change in orientation and curriculum due to Luther's impact. When Luther declared in a disputation that September that the scholastics understood neither Scripture nor Augustine, Karlstadt angrily opposed him and confidently took up Luther's challenge to check the primary sources. After buying a new edition of Augustine's works, Karlstadt set about to refute Luther. In the process he discovered to his amazement that Luther was correct and that he, Karlstadt, had been "deceived by a thousand scholastic opinions." With surprising rapidity Karlstadt's reading of Augustine brought him to the side of Luther against scholastic theology. Within months Karlstadt had a theological conversion that found expression in 151 theses on nature, law, and grace that were predominantly excerpts from Augustine. With Luther, he rejected scholasticism's piety of achievement that rested on human freedom to cooperate in its own salvation. Karlstadt now argued that persons can contribute nothing to their salvation; the human will is in this regard passive, only receptive; God alone is active. By the summer of 1517 he had followed up these theses with a series of lectures on Augustine's treatise *On the Spirit and the Letter*.

Luther was overjoyed by Karlstadt's move to the reforming camp; but by the time of the Leipzig debate with Eck tensions were already arising between the two reformers. These tensions were rooted in alternative readings of the Bible and Augustine. Luther understood God's favor to the sinner as a Word of promise, a Word that addressed the sinner from outside the self. Luther emphasized that this promise from "outside us" (*extra nos*) is "for us" (*pro nobis*). To Luther the Christian always remained simultaneously sinner and righteous, unable to fulfill God's law from himself but rather accepting Christ's fulfillment through faith.

In contrast, Karlstadt's theology seems to have been more determined by a theological shift from Thomist to Augustinian thought. This was certainly personally and religiously significant to Karlstadt. His "theological" conversion meant not only a major turn in his theology but also the repudiation of ten years of scholarly labor and publications. Few professors are ever willing to change this radically! In contrast to Luther's theological motif of the dialectic of law and gospel, Karlstadt emphasized the contrast of letter and spirit; in contrast to Luther's empasis on the Christian as simultaneously sinner and righteous (*simul iustus et peccator*), Karlstadt spoke in more ethical terms of the Christian as simultaneously good and evil (*simul bonus et malus*). Hence Karlstadt emphasized inner renewal in contrast to outer acceptance, regeneration over justification, obedience to the Christ "in us" (*in nobis*). Karlstadt, like Luther, saw forgiveness through Christ's atonement as central, but unlike Luther he focused on self-mortification and inner regeneration. This led Karlstadt in the direction of conceiving of the Scriptures as divine law that governs church and individual, demanding perfection. So Karlstadt's major twentieth-century biographer, Hermann Barge (1968), referred to Karlstadt as "the champion" or "pioneer" of "lay Christian puritanism." And Ulrich Bubenheimer (1989: 62–3) has traced the influence of Karlstadt's theology of rebirth and sanctification on the development of Pietism into the eighteenth century.

Along with Karlstadt's discovery of the theology of Augustine came discovery of the German mystics. The latter especially contributed to his emphasis upon regeneration and a spiritualist interpretation of the

Bible. This mystical influence is evident in his 1520 tract *Missive von der aller hochsten tugent gelassenheit* ("Open Letter on the Very Highest Virtue of Resignation"). The development of the concept of *Gelassenheit* will become central in Karlstadt's theology. Here too is the beginning of a new hermeneutic, a shift from the outer word to an inner, unmediated word of God. "In the *gelassenen* person as the temple of Christ the word of Christ rings out, and thus is God born" (Bubenheimer 1977: 177).

The term *Gelassenheit* has been variously defined as "resignation," "yieldedness," "abandon," "a way of renunciation for the soul seeking union with God," "detachment of the soul from creatures," and "joyful endurance and patience in the face of adversity." For Karlstadt this is the beginning of the Christian life as one overcomes self-will and merges with the will of God conforming to Christ in suffering. The outer person is to be mortified for the sake of inner regeneration.

The potential conflict between Luther's emphasis on justification and Karlstadt's emphasis on regeneration became an actual conflict in the respective models of ministry developed by the two reformers.

Bishops, Clerical Marriage, and Strategies for Reform

Between Luther's journey to the diet of Worms in April 1521 and his return from the Wartburg in March 1522, there developed in Wittenberg a fateful and paradigmatic power struggle for the further course of the Reformation. From the Wartburg, Luther entrusted the implementation of the reform to his Wittenberg friends. In early May he wrote to Melanchthon of his concern that their work not end like the fig tree of Matthew 21: 19, all leaves and no fruit. "The truth is indeed that it is only foliage and words as long as we do not act in accordance with our teaching" (*LW* 48: 214).

But how should the Reformers act in accord with their teaching? This first city Reformation confronted its participants with political, legal, and theological problems which had no precedents. Who will direct the course through these uncharted waters? Who has competence for church law? New legislation for church and society must be developed and carried out; pastors and preachers will have to be trained, provided for, and supervised; church property will have to be managed; and church discipline will have to be administered.

The question of leadership had to be resolved because of the competing possibilities for carrying out reform. Who had the authority to implement reform: the prince? the town council? or the commune itself? Furthermore, the university with its local relationships was also an institution that could, in relation to one of the above authorities, take over some of the functions in directing a new, evangelical church. The criticism and then elimination of papal and episcopal authority and jurisdiction over not only spiritual but also political and legal structures introduced open and unclear relationships. This in turn led to a power vacuum and social instability so long as new ecclesiastical structures had not replaced the old, discredited ones. In medieval culture church and community were not separate but rather coextensive, and power struggles between the church and various authorities were character-istic whenever one or the other party was weak. In Wittenberg each interested party – prince, town council, and commune – wished to expand its influence on the governance of the church in accord with its own values and needs. Hence conflicts arose involving the relations and goals of individual theologians as well as the theologians as a whole *vis-à-vis* other interest groups.

After the publication of the bull *Exsurge Domini*, papal authority markedly diminished for the Wittenbergers. The authority of the episcopal office was also severely eroded by events, and with the publication of the bull of excommunication and the edict of Worms was extensively destroyed in Electoral Saxony. The territorial lords were ready to step into the breach and create a territorial church, and their hands were strengthened by the disturbances about to break out in Wittenberg in late 1521 and early 1522.

Prior to this, the confrontation with the bishops had two foci: the continuing promotion of indulgences by Albrecht of Mainz, now cardinal, and clerical marriage. In the fall of 1521 Albrecht announced a campaign to sell indulgences to visitors to his relic collection in Halle. When Luther, in the Wartburg, got wind of this he wrote a strong letter to Albrecht demanding he stop this abuse. If Albrecht did not cease, Luther threatened to publish a treatise against him that would "show all the world the difference between a bishop and a wolf" (*LW* 48: 342). Within weeks the cardinal apologized and told Luther it would stop. This was a remarkable about-face considering that Luther had been condemned by pope and emperor and was now concealed in the Wartburg. This was not just an echo of the earlier indulgence controversy but rather a direct challenge to the spiritual authority of Cardinal Archbishop Albrecht and hence all bishops; and the Reformer seemed to have more power than the cardinal!

Clerical marriage especially challenged episcopal spiritual and legal jurisdiction and forced a clarification of whether episcopal claims could still be realized. Luther had criticized celibacy in his *Address To the Christian Nobility* (1520). Every priest should be free to marry because "before God and the Holy Scriptures marriage of the clergy is no offense." Clerical celibacy is not God's law but the pope's, and "Christ has set us free from all man-made laws, especially when they are opposed to God and the salvation of souls. . ." Thus the pope has no more power to command celibacy than "he has to forbid eating, drinking, the natural movement of the bowels, or growing fat."

Luther's tract was liberating for many clergy who suffered anguish over their failure to remain celibate, an anguish that led many to self-hatred. Anticlerical writings such as the *Letters of Obscure Men* had long exploited the sexual meanderings of the clergy, and it was not uncommon for priests' concubines and children to be maligned as whores and bastards. A contemporary described the dilemma in these words: "I cannot be without a wife. If I am not permitted to have a wife, then I am forced to lead publicly a disgraceful life, which damages my soul and honor and leads other people, who are offended by me, to damnation. How can I preach about chastity and unchastity, adultery and depravity, when my whore comes openly to church and my bastards sit right in front of me? How shall I conduct mass in this state?" (Hendrix 1993: 456). The evangelical endorsement of clerical marriage offered conscience-stricken priests "a resolution especially to their personal dilemmas, thus enabling the self-hating cleric to attain a new dignity freed from the causes of self-hatred" (Scribner 1993: 153–4).

In May 1521 three priests, one of them Luther's student Bartholomew Bernhardi, drew the practical consequences from Luther's treatise. Other priests followed suit. These were courageous acts, for they entailed persecution and imprisonment because the obligation to clerical celibacy was also embodied in imperial law. Bernhardi's bishop, none other than Albrecht, demanded Elector Frederick turn him over for trial. Frederick refused and referred the case to a commission of jurists for decision. Melanchthon's brief for the defense argued that both Scripture and the practice of the early church supported clerical marriage, and that frailty of the flesh impeded observance of the vow of celibacy.

These events sparked a lively debate and prompted Karlstadt to propose an academic disputation on celibacy. In Karlstadt's theses and his tract *On Celibacy* he argued on the bases of 1 Timothy 3: 2 and 5: 9 that all priests should be married; anyone under 60 should not enter a monastery; and monks and nuns under 60 should be given the freedom to live in wedlock in the monasteries. When Luther received Karlstadt's arguments he was disappointed in the exegetical bases for them and by November had begun his own tract, *On Monastic Vows*. Not only, Luther argued, are vows not commanded by God, they are counter to God's word. Here Luther attacked the medieval distinction between commands and counsels which claimed that while all Christians are to fulfill the commandments of God there is extra merit in keeping the counsels of poverty, celibacy, and obedience. These counsels were the special province of monasticism and their salvatory merit contributed to the treasury of grace. Another significant point is Luther's rejection of the claim that only those who kept the counsels, i.e. monastics, have a religious vocation. To Luther, the only difference between the "religious" life and the "secular" life is the form, not the content. Luther's abolition of distinctions among Christians opened the way for his view of the priesthood of all the baptized and of all Christians as having a divine calling, a vocation in the world. Luther did not advocate the abolition of monastic life altogether, only of its compulsion. If one wished to be a monk, the choice must be as free as other human vocational choices, and it should be clear that that choice is in no way superior to the choice to be, say, a farmer or a teacher. Faith is the "great equalizer" which frees the clergy as well as the laity for service to the neighbor. Monastic vows conflict with faith because they embrace works rather than God's promise of mercy. Thus vows are against evangelical freedom, because what is not necessary for salvation is free. In baptism God made a vow to us; we do not become acceptable to God by making vows to him. Baptism frees one from dependence on works for salvation; any human commandments that encroach on this freedom are contrary to God. This tract, according to Brecht (1990: 24), "is one of Luther's most beautiful writings on evangelical freedom." On 6 January the Augustinians held their chapter meeting in Wittenberg and decreed that those who wished to leave the monastery might do so.

The intensive propaganda and activity of the Wittenberg theologians in favor of clerical marriage now rebounded on themselves. They had encouraged other priests to marry but had not themselves taken this step, and thus their own credibility was on the line. In November of 1521 Karlstadt proposed to set an example. The day after Christmas he became engaged to Anna von Mochau, the young daughter of a poor nobleman of a nearby village. Karlstadt's marriage on 19 January 1522 was an act of propaganda. The public invitation to the wedding expressly stated that his marriage was to serve as a model to other priests to marry their "cooks." He also sent a personal invitation to the elector and invited the entire university faculty and the town council. He expected a big party and spent more than 50 florins for sausage and drink! More to the point, his guest list also included the bishops of Magdeburg, Brandenburg, and Meissen. These invitations indicate Karlstadt's self-confidence regarding clerical marriage, underscored the programmatic and political significance of his wedding, and treated the bishops as equals in spiritual authority. The elector played the better part of valor and did not attend, although the Wittenberg theologians were confident of his positive disposition on this matter. For political purposes Frederick wanted to keep his distance from his married priests. Thus when Bugenhagen married, the court provided the venison for the wedding feast but had it listed as the gift of Spalatin, privy councilor to the Elector (Brecht 1990: 92).

Karlstadt's marriage created a sensation. It was praised by the evangelicals and condemned by the establishment. Within months a large number of priests followed suit. According to Ozment, "No institutional change brought about by the Reformation was more visible, responsive to late medieval pleas for reform, and conducive to new social attitudes than the marriage of Protestant clergy. Nor was there another point in the Protestant program where theology and practice corresponded more closely" (Ozment 1980: 381). The first clerical marriages were a public rejection of contemporary ecclesiastical order. In the face of the papal ban and proscription, the Reformers' courage to implement the implications of their theology was an important demonstration of the reform movement. Not only were other priests given a model, but their congregations were also drawn into the process. Bernhardi had obtained the agreement of his parish for his marriage; and the parish of Seidler interceded for him after his arrest by Duke George. Written defenses of clerical marriage also addressed the laity with respect to Christian freedom and vocation as well as marriage. Clerical marriage was popular with the laity and also moved clergy toward the obligations of citizenship.

The self-confidence of the priests and theologians in advocating and enacting clerical marriage over against the bishops and in some cases the secular authorities is astonishing. In the process the Wittenberg theologians and other pastors and preachers claimed for themselves a spiritual authority hitherto reserved for the bishops. Archbishop Albrecht refused to engage in substantive discussion of the issue, claiming that he had the right to judge matters on the basis of canon law and legal praxis. But for the Reformers the only norm was the Bible.

Wherever territorial lords refused to provide support for the bishop, as in the case of Bernhardi, the crisis of spiritual jurisdiction became public. While Frederick's position may be attributed to his personal sympathy for his married priests or to religious uncertainty, it is equally reasonable to see here the tendency on the part of territorial rulers to expand their influence over the church. By hindering the execution of the bishops' judgments the princes intruded upon episcopal jurisdiction not theoretically but practically. This was not new to the Reformation but it was a further challenge to the power of Rome and strengthened secular authority, thereby contributing to the development of the Protestant territorial church.

Luther himself did not marry until 1525. Luther met his Katy (Katherine von Bora, 1499–1552) when she arrived in Wittenberg in April 1523 with other nuns who had escaped a nearby monastery. The Reformers were soon able to place or marry off all these nuns except Katherine (there were few possibilities for a single woman in the Middle Ages). A strong-willed personality, she let it be known that she was not pleased with the match proposed for her, but that Luther would do just fine. In the meantime Luther himself was under continual pressure from others to marry: his supporters wanted a practical expression of Luther's support for married priests, and his father wanted grandchildren. On 13 June 1525 Luther married his Katy, to please his father and to spite the pope (*LW* 29: 21).

Now Luther affirmed marriage from experience as well as theory. It is, he claimed, a glimpse of what the lost Eden must have been like. Certainly he knew married life was not one long honeymoon, and commented that if we knew what lay in store for us, we probably would not get married. But celibacy, he believed, removed men and women from service to the neighbor, contravened the divine order, and denied the goodness of sexual relations. Marriage created a new awareness of human community. "Marriage does not consist only of sleeping with a woman – everybody can do that! – but keeping house and bringing up children" (*LW* 54: 441). The father washing smelly diapers may be ridiculed by fools, but "God, with all his angels and creatures, is smiling – not because the father is washing diapers, but because he is doing so in Christian faith" (*LW* 45: 40).

For Luther the companionship of husband and wife is a marvelous thing. But the Luthers also knew firsthand the pain of the loss of children. Elizabeth died in infancy, and Magdelene died in his arms when she was only thirteen. "It's strange to know that she is surely at peace . . . and yet to grieve so much" (*LW* 54: 432). Altogether Martin and Katy had six children whom they loved dearly. Katy nurtured and scolded her husband through more than 25 years of what certainly must have been one of the most eventful marriages in history. Luther was convinced that God had come to his aid by giving them to each other. His marriage was an influence upon his theology of human relations, especially in terms of the mutuality and reciprocity of love, and contributed to new perspectives on the dignity and responsibility of women (Scharffenorth 1983).

The Gospel and Social Order

Concomitant with the agenda of clerical marriage was that of reform of the mass, the abolition of images, and the reform of poor relief (the last of these will be discussed in the next chapter). We shall discuss the mass at greater length later, but for now we need to recall that the eucharist was the central symbol and reality for late medieval culture. The eucharist was presented by the church as the foremost sacrament which supported the whole sacramental system and clerical power. The mass was the central element in church life. To change the mass was bound to shock and shock profoundly the Wittenberg congregation.

From the Wartburg, Luther requested Melanchthon be appointed preacher in his stead in the city church. But the town council, although affirming Melanchthon's theological qualifications, would not appoint this married layman to the position. Whether Melanchthon could have provided stability in this tumultuous period is questionable.

In July of 1521 Karlstadt argued with regard to the mass that "those who partake of the bread and wine are not Bohemians but true Christians. He who receives only the bread, in my opinion, commits sin" (Barge 1968: I, 291). Luther had already spoken his mind against withholding the wine from the laity at communion, but he could not claim that reception of both kinds was a necessity on pain of sin. Luther's fellow Augustinian, Gabriel Zwilling, now attacked the private mass in his sermons and preached against veneration of the consecrated host. When the monastery prior forbade changes in the mass, masses in the monastery ceased entirely. When the hermits of St Anthony appeared in early October for their annual round of begging, students interrupted their sermons and pelted them with dung and stones. The elector rejected any changes in the mass; Wittenberg was not to innovate on its own. This of course got the students even more exercised and prompted stronger steps by Zwilling, who led an exodus of monks from the Augustinian monastery. Anticlerical violence began to build during the weeks of December. The crisis was at hand. Karlstadt at first counseled caution but then advocated mandatory reforms. In the next weeks a commission to the elector submitted a report favoring immediate reform in practice in line with the new theology. In December a petition to the town council requested amnesty for the rioters and reforms in liturgy and ethics. The elector again expressed his view that this was not the time for innovation.

On 22 December Karlstadt announced that at his next mass, scheduled for 1 January, he intended to celebrate in line with the new theology. The elector sent word that Karlstadt was to do no such thing. Karlstadt responded that in that case he would do it on Christmas Day. This may have been less bull-headedness on Karlstadt's part than an attempt to forestall another riot. Also, when events begin to take on a momentum of their own it is sometimes necessary for leaders to run fast in order to get out ahead of the crowd. Certainly what was most important for Karlstadt was that the mandates of God take precedence over the concerns of others, whether they be a prince's concern for maintaining order or a pastor's that his congregation not be scandalized. To Karlstadt, grace was costly, for it meant keeping in step with Jesus and scriptural norms rather than with the prevailing culture.

Christmas Eve was neither silent nor holy: gangs roamed the streets, threatened priests, and disrupted services. The next day Karlstadt celebrated communion in the castle church without vestments; dressed as a layman, he pronounced the consecration in German and distributed communion in both kinds. Karlstadt did publicly what Melanchthon had done privately with his students some months earlier. This was the "sign language" of anticlericalism, and the public break with a millennium of tradition. The congregation, including both community and church leaders, communed without having previously fasted or gone to confession. The fact that those communing took the chalice in their own hands, and that a host was dropped on the floor, deeply offended contemporary sensitivities. Karlstadt announced that the next evangelical celebration of the Lord's Supper would be New Year's Day in the city church, a parish not under his jurisdiction. To say the least, the Christmas mass was a sensation and a public rejection of tradition. It was a hard act to follow, but in his zeal to translate theory into practice, he at least equaled it. The next day he was betrothed.

In the meantime more tinder was added to this already volatile mix by the arrival of the so-called "Zwickau prophets." Zwickau, a city in the southern part of the electorate known for trade and its cloth industry, had a history of social tension between its wealthy upper class and the poor journeymen of the cloth industry. Waldensian and Hussite influences prior to the Reformation abetted these tensions and also prepared the ground for widespread sympathy for Luther. Thomas Müntzer (see Chapter 6) had since May 1520 been preaching there to the socially discontented from his pulpit in St Catherine's church, in the parish where most of the lesser artisans belonged. His critical preaching led to his expulsion from the town in April 1521. During his brief ministry in Zwickau Müntzer met and encouraged the religious ideas of Nicholas Storch, a master clothier, Thomas Drechsel, a weaver, and Marcus Thomae, a former Wittenberg student known as Stübner. These three men, "the Zwickau prophets," were themselves forced out of the city because of their radical religious ideas, which included the rejection of infant baptism and convictions of immediate divine revelations by the Spirit of God. They arrived in Wittenberg soon after Christmas claiming divinely inspired dreams and visions of a great Turkish invasion, the elimination of all priests, and the imminent end of the world. They further claimed that people are to be taught by God's Spirit alone who has no connection to Christ and the Bible. Melanchthon was unnerved by them and urged the elector to allow Luther to return. Karlstadt did not seem to be taken by them, and the elector did not think it wise to recall Luther. The Zwickau prophets soon moved on in search of greener pastures, their main contribution having been to undermine Melanchthon's leadership.

On 24 January the town council endorsed the changes in the mass as well as another of Karlstadt's causes, the elimination of images. Two weeks earlier Zwilling had led the monks remaining in the Augustinian monastery in removing its images, smashing the statues and burning whatever was combustible, including the consecrated oil used for extreme unction. Karlstadt had been preaching that Old Testament law forbade images, and he kept up the pressure until the council named a day for the removal of images. The result was more violence and disorder.

The widespread destruction of the images and symbols of the old faith that accompanied the introduction of reform movements was not mere vandalism but rather a ritual action that both deconstructed Catholicism and contributed to the construction of Protestantism, and was all the more powerful because the image-breakers had only recently been the image-makers. The "ritual process" of the Reformation was a metaphysical shaping of the world according to new convictions. Destroying images, or degrading them by unusual placement or by urinating or defecating on them, drove "the pope and papal religion out of the minds and hearts of those who took part." The iconoclasts viewed images as "voracious idols" which devoured resources but produced nothing in return. Icons and altars represented the displacement of charity from the poor to lifeless objects (Scribner 1987: 103–22; Eire 1986; Wandel 1995).

This understanding helps to explain the influence of Karlstadt's tract, *On the Abolition of Images*. On page after page he emphasized that images are against the first commandment. There is no excuse, he argued, in the claim that an image – even the crucifix – points beyond itself to God. Christians are to abolish images, just as in the Old Testament the altars to idols were smashed and overturned; for Christ is the continuation of Old Testament law, and God forbids images no less than murder, robbery, adultery, and the like. Karlstadt may well have been motivated by more than just his understanding of the gospel as a new law. Trained as a Thomist, he had imbibed a metaphysics that gave reality to images. The physics of vision of the time reinforced the metaphysics by holding that the eye was passive and acted upon by images (Scribner 1987: 106; Wandel 1995: 27). "My heart was trained and reared from my youth up to offer honor and worship to images, and a destructive fear was produced in me which I desire eagerly to rid myself of, but cannot. Thus I stand in fear that I burn no idols. . . . Although I have and know the Scripture that images do not have influence . . . nevertheless . . . fear held me and made me stand in fear of a painted devil" (Karlstadt 1522: 19).

Since, Karlstadt argued, the priests have perverted God's law and thereby hindered the faithful, the magistrates should follow the example of King Josiah and forcibly reform the church. Only days earlier, on 20 January, the imperial diet, meeting in Nuremberg, had issued a mandate that criticized Electoral Saxony for innovation and demanded that all innovations concerning religious practice be nullified under threat of punishment. Needless to say, Elector Frederick was not about to begin emulating King Josiah. Melanchthon was told to silence Zwilling, and Karlstadt was directly requested to stop preaching. The town council was forced to compromise its program to implement reform. By now Melanchthon was having a bad case of nerves; he appealed to Luther to return from the Wartburg and restore order.

News of Luther's intention to leave the safety of the Wartburg for the upheaval of Wittenberg did little for the elector's peace of mind. He wanted his rambunctious professors to keep a low profile. Thus, soon after he had ensconced Luther in the Wartburg, he sent Karlstadt off to Denmark to get him out of town too; but Karlstadt had returned to Wittenberg in only two weeks and had since thoroughly stirred the pot. Frederick wrote Luther to stay put. Luther's replies reflected his faith and confidence, as well as making a dig at Frederick's relic collection. "To my most gracious Lord, Duke Frederick, elector of Saxony . . . Grace and joy from the God the Father on the acquisition of a new relic! I put this greeting in place of my assurances of respect. For many years Your Grace has been acquiring relics in every land, but God has now heard Your Grace's request and has sent Your Grace without cost or

(a)

(b)

effort a whole cross, together with nails, spears, and scourges" (*LW* 48: 389). Soon after this letter, Luther informed the elector he would return to Wittenberg in spite of the elector's wishes because he must obey God rather than any secular government. "The sword ought not and cannot help a matter of this kind. God alone must do it" (*LW* 48: 391). We shall have occasion later to refer to Luther's rejection of the use of force or government for support of religion. For now, it is important to call attention to Luther's conviction, a conviction he was to hold consistently throughout his career, that to enforce the gospel by law is to change the gospel into law and thereby pervert the Reformation. What is free cannot be compelled.

Luther arrived in Wittenberg on Friday, 6 March 1522. The following Sunday he began a series of sermons known as the "Invocavit Sermons" after the liturgical name of that Sunday, Invocavit, the first Sunday in Lent. The theme of these sermons was the distinction between an evangelical "may" and a legalistic "must." Luther emphasized the centrality of the gospel which frees persons from sin and makes them children of God. He then spoke of the inseparability of faith and love. Faith active in love gives patience for the neighbor who may not yet be equally strong in the faith. Some of the Wittenbergers were not yet ready for the implementation of reforms, for they saw these liturgical innovations as ungodly. Luther's concern was not with the reforms initiated but rather with their haste and compulsion. "The cause is good, but there has been too much haste. For there are still brothers and sisters on the other side who belong to us and must still be won" (*LW* 51: 72).

Figure 4.1 (a) "Lament of the Poor Persecuted Idols and Temple Images," ca. 1530, ascribed to Erhard Schön. This is one of the earliest renditions of the iconoclasm that followed in the wake of the Reformation. To the left is a church "cleansed" of images, which are being burned to the right. The remaining bare altar with only two candles burning on it reflects the Swiss Reformed rejection of ecclesiastical artwork. Above the fire is a man whose wealth is indicated by his large sack of money and the large wine flask. He gestures towards the iconoclasts and has a large beam in his eye that illustrates the parable of seeing a splinter in someone else's eye but not noticing the beam in one's own (Matthew 7: 3; Luke 6: 42). The point is that removal of images does not remove idolatry, in this case that of wealth, and reflects Luther's point that idolatry is not located in images but in people's hearts. This satirical critique of iconoclasm is also seen in the man who takes up the cross – for vandalism. (b) Rage against the gods who fail the people, a reaction not limited to narrow religious contexts, was widely seen in the destruction of the symbols of communism after the dissolution of the USSR.
Sources: (a) Germanisches Nationalmuseum, Nürnberg, (b) Associated Press.

In Luther's perspective, Karlstadt has been preaching "must-y" sermons. That is, the sacrifice of order and the consequent offense to the weak resulted from making a "must" out of what is free. Faith is a free gift to which no one can be constrained. Luther opposed the papists but only, he said, with God's Word, not with force. Indeed, according to Luther, God's Word did everything "while I slept or drank Wittenberg beer with my friends Philip and Amsdorf." Luther is well aware that he could have fomented a revolt within the Empire, but to do so would have been "mere fool's play" (*LW* 51: 77).

Luther argued that forced reform changed the good news into bad news, that is, gospel into law. The history of the church shows, he said, that one law quickly leads to thousands of laws. Furthermore, rushing about smashing altars and destroying images is counterproductive, for it only sets images more firmly in people's hearts. Compulsive zeal not only offends the weak, it creates the suspicion that Christian liberty is being flaunted in order to prove that one is a better Christian than others. "For if you desire to be regarded as better Christians than others just because you take the sacrament into your own hands and receive it in both kinds, you are bad Christians as far as I am concerned" (*LW* 51: 91).

The sermons differentiated reformism from puritanism. The abolition of abuse and the forcible implementation of reform, no matter how correct the theology, does violence to ignorant and unconvinced consciences. The weak need to be started on pablum and then gradually led to the strong meat of Christian freedom. To do otherwise is to be concerned only for outward things and external change. Even worse, in Luther's view, is that it substitutes exhortation for proclamation, the very criticism he had of the medieval piety of achievement. For Luther, the first word will always be what God has done for humankind; only the second word speaks of what humankind ought to do in response. The effect of these sermons was an almost immediate restoration of order. Innovations ceased for the time being and so did the violence.

Throughout the sermons Luther never referred to Karlstadt by name, but it was obvious from the context as well as the content that the two Reformers had divergent models of ministry. Each derived his model from the historical and theological resources of the church in an effort to respond constructively to social, political, and religious unrest; and each believed his model was incompatible with that of the other. This tension led in the coming years to an angry parting of the ways, Karlstadt's expulsion from Electoral Saxony, and Luther's vehement attack on him in the treatise *Against the Heavenly Prophets* (1525). However, it also needs to be said that in the aftermath of the Peasants'

War, Luther saved Karlstadt from disaster by taking him and his family into his own home and obtaining permission for Karlstadt to remain in Electoral Saxony if he would only keep quiet.

There has been a persistent tendency in Reformation studies to equate the initiation of the Reformation with Luther. However, it was Karlstadt who tried to implement the new theology while Luther was in the Wartburg. Karlstadt lived out his theology of regeneration in the face of tremendous pressures, the greatest of which to him was the Spirit of God. Luther later remarked that Karlstadt seemed to have swallowed the Holy Spirit feathers and all (*LW* 40: 83). But Karlstadt's impatience with the slowness of implementing reform had biblical roots (e.g. Matthew 7: 21; 10: 34–8), and that impatience was to become evident in other centers of the reform, such as Zurich. Wherever the Reformation was introduced there was tension between those who advocated rapid, radical reform and those who insisted on gradual reform. In his later tract *Whether One Should Proceed Slowly* (1524), Karlstadt gave the following analogy to clarify his drive to implement reforms and his opposition to gradualism: "If I should see that a little innocent child holds a sharp, pointed knife in his hand and wants to keep it, will I show him brotherly love when I let him keep the dreadful knife . . . or when I break his will and take the knife? . . . When you take from the child what injures him, you do a fatherly or brotherly, Christlike deed (Sider 1978: 65; Baylor 1991: 49–73). To Karlstadt, genuine brotherly love "would forcibly break the will of fools." Hence, in the context of the recovery of the gospel, "each congregation, however little or great it may be, should see for itself that it acts properly and well and waits for no one" (Sider 1978: 65, 56).

The events in Wittenberg raised the perennial questions of every reform movement. Once reform is underway should it be gradual or radical? How will it be controlled? Who will guide it? Where will it lead? Where will it stop? With the unfolding of events in Wittenberg the Reformation became a social and political movement. As a social movement involving the elector, the town council, and the commune as a whole, it was no longer coterminous with Luther's personal breakthrough to the gospel. The Reformation had already become Reformations. Luther's sense of this is reflected in a passage of his *A Sincere Admonition by Martin Luther to All Christians to Guard against Insurrection and Rebellion*, written from the Wartburg after a secret visit to Wittenberg in early December, 1521.

> I ask that men make no reference to my name; let them call themselves Christians, not Lutherans. What is Luther? After all the teaching is not

mine [John 7: 16]. Neither was I crucified for anyone [1 Corinthians 1: 13]. St Paul, in 1 Corinthians 3, would not allow the Christians to call themselves Pauline or Petrine, but Christian. How then should I – poor stinking maggot-fodder that I am – come to have men call the children of Christ by my wretched name? Not so, my dear friends; let us abolish all party names and call ourselves Christians, after him whose teaching we hold. (*LW* 45: 70–1).

It was a fine appeal, but it would not inhibit people from reading and hearing Luther's precious Scriptures differently from how he did. And so Luther came to identify with St Paul and to embrace the view that those who differed from him were, like those who had differed from St Paul, "false brethren" (Edwards 1975: 112–26).

Suggestions for Further Reading

Mark U. Edwards, Jr, *Luther and the False Brethren*, Stanford: Stanford University Press, 1975

Carlos M. N. Eire, *War Against the Idols: The Reformation of Worship from Erasmus to Calvin*, Cambridge: Cambridge University Press, 1986

Calvin Pater, *Karlstadt as the Father of the Baptist Movements: The Emergence of Lay Protestantism*, Toronto: University of Toronto Press, 1984

James S. Preus, *Carlstadt's "Ordinaciones" and Luther's Liberty: A Study of the Wittenberg Movement 1521–22*, Cambridge, MA: Harvard University Press, 1974

Ronald J. Sider, *Andreas Bodenstein von Karlstadt: The Development of his Thought 1517–1525*, Leiden: E. J. Brill, 1974

Ronald J. Sider, *Karlstadt's Battle with Luther: Documents in a Liberal–Radical Debate*, Philadelphia: Fortress, 1978

Lee Palmer Wandel, *Voracious Idols and Violent Hands: Iconoclasm in Reformation Zurich, Strasbourg, and Basel*, Cambridge: Cambridge University Press, 1995

5

Fruits of the Fig Tree: Social Welfare and Education

Nobody ought to go begging among Christians.

Martin Luther

The Wittenberg Church Order of 22 January 1522 included in its agenda the reform of poor relief. The enormity of this task was due not only to the social consequences of the contemporary transition from feudalism to capitalism but to the church's ancient endorsement of poverty as the preferred path to salvation. Lowliness – not cleanliness – was next to godliness. In response to feudal glorification of honor in strength and combat the Benedictines emphasized spiritual poverty or humility on the basis of Matthew 5: 3: "Blessed are the poor in spirit, for theirs is the kingdom of heaven." Later, in response to the profit economy's glorification of material achievement, the Franciscans emphasized material poverty on the basis of Luke 6: 20: "Blessed are you poor, for yours is the kingdom of God." Most people, however, would prefer to admire virtue in someone else than practice it themselves. Thus giving alms to the poor allowed vicarious participation in their closeness to God. For over a millennium preachers had proclaimed the salvatory virtue of giving alms, and remarkable ascetics such as St Francis had embodied holy poverty and modeled almsgiving for the laity. As the alter egos of the poor, the Franciscans became intermediaries between the wealthy and the poor, thereby justifying the rich and dispensing charity while maintaining the poor in their poverty (Little 1994). In this context almsgiving was believed to be a salvatory work; indeed, medieval theology spoke of "faith formed by charity." By the late Middle Ages, however, poverty was clearly a growing social problem that the medieval tradition of almsgiving and personal charity was incapable of addressing constructively in spite of monastic charity, church-supported hospices, and low-interest loan banks established by the Franciscans and other mendicants.

The Wittenberg Reformers' shift of the locus of the relationship to God from charity to faith enabled them to envision a new social ethic in relation to poverty. Reform of society flowed from reform of the mass. The impact of this linkage may be seen against the background of late medieval social welfare. The following brief description of the Reformation's contribution to early modern social welfare focuses on the Wittenberg Reformers since they are chronologically consonant with the present narrative. It should be noted, however, that the other major Reformers as well as humanists and Roman Catholic theologians were equally engaged in efforts to respond to the growing social problem of poverty on the bases of their respective theologies (Lindberg 1993).

Late Medieval Poor Relief

Late medieval poor relief was marked by struggles between the urban laity and the clergy over the administration of its designated funds, properties, and institutions, all of which were church-related. The contentious debate "was not between state or church over charity, but between public or private, centralized or decentralized relief" (Jütte 1994: 105). The struggle to rationalize and centralize early modern social welfare by placing it in public hands received a new framework for articulation and legitimation by the Reformation. Luther, the first major Reformer to address the theory and praxis of early modern poor relief and social welfare, did so from the standpoint of his theology. His theology not only undercut the medieval idealization of poverty, it also provided a theological rationale for social welfare that was translated into legislation. Luther "created, as it were, a *discursive field* in which to bring together in imaginative ways the practical realities of institutional life on the one hand and the ideas evident in Scripture on the other" (Wuthnow 1989: 134). This constructive resource for the development of social welfare was rooted in worship. As such, social welfare for Luther was a specific example of liturgy after the liturgy, a work of the people flowing from worship, service to others continuing after the formal worship service. In short, the reform of worship entailed the renewal of social life (Strohm 1989: 183).

By the eve of the Reformation, worship and welfare were no longer the inseparable expression of the community that "holds all in common" (Acts 4: 32), but became distinct avenues, paved by money, for the achievement of salvation. Concern for personal salvation found expression in material contributions to ecclesiastical institutions, masses, confraternities, and almsgiving. The mass was no longer communion but the easily multipliable means to meet the "price of passage" from this world to the next. The most evident sign of change in religion and piety in the late Middle Ages is "without doubt the penetration of mathematics, numbers, bookkeeping and cumulative logic in devotional practices" (Chiffoleau 1980: 434). The business of salvation was the big business of the time, whose income was not limited to indulgences but included all the support services of ritual redemption. "The splendor of medieval worship . . . , the riches of innumerable cloisters and foundations, the support of thousands of simple priests saying mass . . . , all this stemmed to a very great extent from endeavors to aid souls in purgatory. Before the Reformation there was hardly a testament which did not include considerable sums for the holding of masses and other services for the dead" (Meyer 1965: 131).

Likewise, poor relief was perceived under the much overworked rubric from Ecclesiasticus 3: 30 that "almsgiving atones for sin." Thus bishops and theologians quoted approvingly the old rationale that God could have made all persons rich but he willed that there be poor in the world so that the rich would have an opportunity to atone for their sins. Medieval preachers did not hesitate to refer to this relationship as a commercial transaction: the poor carry the riches of the wealthy on their backs to heaven. An early fourteenth-century vernacular sermon by the Italian Dominican, Giordano da Pisa, similarly explains the divine rationale behind inequality: "God has ordered that there be rich and poor so that the rich may be served by the poor and the poor may be taken care of by the rich. And this is a common organization among all peoples. Why are the poor given their station? So that the rich might earn eternal life through them" (Lesnick 1989: 126, 151). The primary purpose of charity was therefore not to alleviate the plight of the recipient but to achieve merit before God (Chatellier 1989: 133). The ancient tradition of the poor as intercessors with God was supplemented by a theology that presented the poor as objects for good works and thereby a means to salvation. On the eve of the Reformation, the "piety of achievement" permeated all aspects of worship and welfare.

By the fifteenth century, however, poverty was no longer only a theological virtue and an opportunity for the salvatory works of the rich; it was also a major social problem comprising a complex of issues involved with the developing profit economy, work, idleness, begging, and poor relief. Statistical studies of the tax registers of the time indicate that in the cities the portion of the populace who were without property, the so-called "have-nots," ranged from 30 to 75 percent. Furthermore, there were major fluctuations in this widespread poverty because large number of day laborers survived at a subsistence level without any reserves for times of crisis; thus they were always on the verge of mendicancy. Practical efforts to restrain begging were frustrated by a theology that legitimated begging and valued almsgiving, and by a church whose own mendicant monks compounded the social problems of poverty. Sermonic and literary exposés of false beggars, such as the *Liber vagatorum*, were not directed against poverty and begging as such; rather, they were designed to assist the charitable citizen concerned about the "embezzlement of heaven" because alms given to frauds went to the devil instead of God (Assion 1971/2: 87). In religious terms, begging continued to be valued as a vocation; the poor had an important soteriological function as intercessors for almsgivers. At the same time, the poor were a cheap labor pool for an expanding profit economy.

Beyond Charity

Luther undercut this medieval religious ideology of poverty with his doctrine of justification by grace alone apart from human works. Since righteousness before God is gained by grace alone, and since salvation is the source of life rather than the achievement of life, poverty and the plight of the poor cannot be rationalized as a peculiar form of blessedness. There is no salvific value in being poor or in giving alms. This new theology de-ideologized the medieval approach to the poor, which had both obscured the social and economic problems of poverty and obstructed the development of social welfare. In other words: "The role of a clear discursive field such as that enunciated by the reformers was to alter the framework in which specific conflicts and grievances were expressed" (Wuthnow 1989: 138).

In the "Ninety-Five Theses" (1517) Luther grounded his critique of the sacrament of penance in Jesus' words, "Repent and believe in the gospel" (Mark 1: 15; thesis 1). Penance is thus not a discrete act such as almsgiving but rather applies to "the entire life of believers" (*LW* 31: 25). This struck directly at the heart of the contemporary church's power, because according to church doctrine the priest determined the steps and conditions of penance necessary for the sinner to obtain God's grace. The anxiety before death and God's judgment was met by the necessity of good works. Thus it may be argued that alms to begging cripples, hungry children, and the poor, as well as to the mendicant monks, appeared as welcome aids in the endeavors for eternal salvation, but did little to liberate the conscience of the almsgiver or to alleviate the conditions of poverty.

Figure 5.1 "All Kinds of Beggars' Tricks," by Hieronymous Bosch (also known as "Cripples and Beggars"). Bosch's sketches of beggars show the bodily contortions assumed by "professional" beggars to inspire pity and alms. Bosch here reflects the widespread late medieval attitude expressed by Sebastian Brant in his poem *The Ship of Fools*: "Bold begging charms many a fool / For begging has become the rule / And ranks among our best professions."
Source: Albertina, Vienna.

Luther understood the preaching office to be responsible both for the liberation of consciences and for raising and commenting upon issues of worldly government such as poor relief. The preacher is "to unmask *hidden* injustice, thus saving the souls of duped Christians and opening the eyes of the secular authorities for their mandate to establish *civil* justice" (Oberman 1988: 444). Furthermore, not only was the preacher obligated to social–ethical instruction and action; so too was the Christian community, whose worship activity was the source and resource for service to the neighbor. In the "Ninety-Five Theses" Luther stated: "Christians are to be taught that he who gives to the poor or lends to the needy does a better deed than he who buys indulgences" (thesis 43). Also, "he who sees a needy man and passes him by, yet gives his money for indulgences, does not buy papal indulgences but God's wrath" (thesis 45).

By 1519 Luther had amplified this connection between theology, worship, and social ethics in a number of tracts and sermons. In his *Short Sermon on Usury* he contrasted God's command to serve the neighbor with the self-chosen "worship" that concentrated on building churches and endowing masses, to the detriment of the needy. In his treatise *The Blessed Sacrament of the Holy and True Body of Christ, and the Brotherhoods*, written in German and addressed to the laity, he specifically related reform of the mass to social ethics. "The *significance* or effect of this sacrament is fellowship of all the saints. . . . Hence it is that Christ and all saints are one spiritual body, just as the inhabitants of a city are one community and body, each citizen being a member of the other and of the entire city" (*LW* 35: 50).

Luther's analogy of the relationship of sacrament and social ethics to the benefits and responsibilities of citizenship is noteworthy with regard to the relationship of the Reformation and the cities. The right use of the sacrament builds up community. Thus the person in need is enjoined to "go joyfully to the sacrament of the altar and lay down his woe in the midst of the community . . . and seek help from the entire company," just as a citizen would ask the authorities and fellow citizens for help (*LW* 35: 53–4).

In short, Luther argued, this is a sacrament of love that shares "the misfortunes of the fellowship." "As love and support are given you, you in turn must render love and support to Christ in his needy ones." Indeed, on the basis of the sacrament, the Christian "must fight, work, pray" for the needy. From Luther's perspective the late medieval church had broken this connection between worship and welfare to the detriment of each. "So we at present see to our sorrow that many masses are held and yet the Christian fellowship which should be preached, practiced, and kept before us by Christ's example has virtually perished." Referring to the early church, Luther continued: "But in times past this sacrament was so properly used, and the people were taught to understand this fellowship so well, that they even gathered food and material goods in the church, and there . . . distributed among those who were in need." To emphasize his point, Luther interpreted the origin of the "collect" in the mass as a general collection and fund gathered to be given to the poor (*LW* 35: 53–7).

The extent to which the mass had degenerated from this service to God in the neighbor to self-service was evident, Luther claimed, in "the evil practices of the brotherhoods." By the sixteenth century brotherhoods or confraternities, which had originally been lay associations for devotional and charitable purposes, had largely declined into vehicles for salvation. Each brotherhood had its own priests, altars, chapels, and festivals. An example is the Brotherhood of 11,000 Virgins in Cologne, which assured participants of the merits of 6,455 masses, 3,550 entire Psalters, 200,000 rosaries, 200,000 Te Deums, etc. The merits of one brotherhood were multiplied through "cartel" arrangements with other brotherhoods. This ledger mentality is evident also in the new synonyms for confraternities, "societies" and "consortiums," terms with the commercial significance of pooling investments for profit-seeking ventures (Little 1988: 68–9). Thus by the time of his death in 1519 the Electoral Saxon councilor Degenhard Pfeffinger belonged to eight brotherhoods in Wittenberg and through them enjoyed the salvatory achievements of 27 foreign associations. In 1520 there were 21 such brotherhoods in Wittenberg.

Since these brotherhoods were based upon the multiplication of masses and other religious practices to achieve merit for salvation, Luther's critique of them was linked to his exposition of the sacrament. These supposed convocations of good works had become occasions for debauchery. "What have the names of Our Lady, St Anne, St Sebastian, or other saints to do with your brotherhoods, in which you have nothing but gluttony, drunkenness, useless squandering of money, howling, chattering, dancing, and wasting of time? If a sow were made the patron saint of such a brotherhood she would not consent" (*LW* 35: 68).

Real Christian brotherhood, Luther argued, would serve the poor. His initial elaboration of this point foreshadowed the development of institutionalized social welfare in the evangelical church orders. "If men desire to maintain a brotherhood, . . . they should gather the money which they intend to squander for drink, and collect it into a common treasury, each craft for itself. Then in cases of hardship, needy fellow workmen might be helped to get started, and be lent money, or a young couple of the same craft might be fitted out respectably from this common treasury" (*LW* 35: 68–9).

These suggestions are futher elaborated in Luther's 1520 writings: the *Long Sermon on Usury*, the *Treatise on Good Works*, and the *Address to the Christian Nobility of the German Nation*. The last of these in particular presents an explicit and forceful expression of social welfare relief based upon Luther's doctrine of justification. Here he urged that every city and place should take care of its poor, and that all begging should be forbidden. He conceived of securing a minimal existence for those unable to work but also stressed that those who were able to work had a responsibility to do so. By this time Luther was already arguing that the source of contemporary impoverishment was not the feudal system but the new profit economy. "Therefore, I beg and pray at this point that everyone open his eyes and see the ruin of his children and heirs. Ruin is not just at the door, it is already in the house. I pray and beseech emperor, princes, lords, and city councilors to condemn this trade as speedily as possible and prevent it from now on . . . In this connection, we must put a bit in the mouth of the Fuggers and similar companies" (*LW* 44: 213). This was easier said than done, for, as noted earlier, the Fugger bankrolling of Charles V precluded effective imperial legislation and control of interest rates. Nevertheless, throughout his career Luther attacked the profit-taking of his day as a major source of social injustice and suffering. He even went so far as to exhort pastors to excommunicate those who charged excessive interest.

The Institutionalization of Social Welfare

The first effort to institutionalize welfare in Wittenberg, known as the *Beutelordnung*, was passed by the town council with Luther's assistance sometime in late 1520 or early 1521. The next major step was the council's Wittenberg Order of January 1522, influenced by both Luther and Karlstadt. The focus of this legislation was the reform of worship and welfare. Of the 17 articles in this measure, all but three were concerned with alleviating the plight of the poor. A common chest was established for poor relief, low-interest loans were provided for workers and artisans, and education and training for children of the poor was subsidized. Funding was provided from the endowments of the discontinued religious institutions and church properties. Were funding to be insufficient, article 11 provides for a sort of graduated tax

Figure 5.2 The original Wittenberg common chest, Lutherhalle, Wittenberg. This heavy iron strongbox, fitted with three independent locks and with one handle removed to prevent its being carried off, was kept in the church as the town depository for social welfare funds.
Source: Lutherhalle, Wittenberg.

on the clergy and citizens "for the maintenance of the multitude of the poor." Begging, including that of monks and mendicants, was prohibited. Artisans and craftsmen unable to repay loans would be excused from repayment for God's sake. Daughters of the poor would be provided with appropriate dowries and given in marriage.

The next major legislative expression of the relationship between the reform of worship and the institutionalization of welfare was the Leisnig Order of 1523. In his "Preface" Luther explicitly tied worship and welfare together. "Now there is no greater service of God [*gottis dienst*, i.e. worship] than Christian love which helps and serves the needy, as Christ himself will judge and testify at the Last Day, Matthew 25 [: 31–46]" (*LW* 45: 172). The term *Gottesdienst* links service to God and to the neighbor with worship.

In September 1522 Luther responded to the appeal of the Leisnig town council and spent a week there assisting the parish in developing a comprehensive evangelical church order which included a common chest for poor relief. In January 1523 the town council and the congregation sent two representatives to Wittenberg with a formal letter requesting his further advice on their proposed ordinance. The letter notes the establishment of a common chest "to the honor of God and for the love of fellow Christians," and requests Luther to provide the community with a biblical rationale for the calling of evangelical pastors and an evangelical order of worship. Luther responded to the town council on 29 January 1523 with a letter expressing his great joy and pleasure over their ordinance. He hopes that their order "shall both honor God and present a good example of Christian faith and love to many people" (*WA Br* 3: 23). By early summer Luther responded in print to the request for biblical warrants for Leisnig's plans in the following writings: *Ordinance of a Common Chest: Preface. Suggestions on How to Deal with Ecclesiastical Property, That a Christian Assembly or Congregation has the Right and Power to Judge all Teaching and to Call, Appoint, Dismiss Teachers, Established and Proven by Scripture*, and *Concerning the Order of Public Worship*.

The Leisnig parish proceeded to reform the order of worship and to set up their common chest for social welfare on the basis of Luther's advice and his theological legitimation of their concern through his doctrine of the universal priesthood of all the baptized. The organization and principles of the common chest included the election of ten directors or trustees by the community every year on the first Sunday after 13 January: "two from the nobility, two from the incumbent city council, three from among the common citizens of the town, and three from the rural peasantry." The three important and detailed record books were to be kept in the chest, itself locked with four different locks, and kept in a secure place in the church. The different locks had keys assigned to the representatives of the different groups involved. The directors were to give triennial reports to the whole community. The funds from the common chest were also to be used for mainten-ance of buildings, pastors' salaries, and schools – including a special school for girls. This inclusiveness proved to be a strain on resources, and Johann Bugenhagen (1485–1558), the great Wittenberg formulator of church orders, later separated the common chest funds from the funds for church maintenance and education.

The Leisnig Order, like its predecessor in Wittenberg, prohibited all begging. This was a departure from the late medieval begging orders whose purpose was to control rather than eliminate begging and which were motivated by political economics rather than the religiously motivated social ethics of the Reformation orders. The Reformation church orders mandated that only the truly needy should be supported; all others must either leave or work – a theme to be repeated in countless later pamphlets under the overworked motto that he who does not work shall not eat (2 Thessalonians 3: 6–13).

The initial funding for the common chest came from the expropriated church properties and endowments that the medieval church had cultivated as works contributing to salvation. Luther hoped that as a result of the Leisnig example there would "be a great decline in the existing foundations, monastic houses, chapels, and those horrible dregs which have until now fattened on the wealth of the whole world under the pretense of serving God" (*LW* 45: 169). But Luther was also concerned about the possibility of plundering the church. "There is need of great care lest there be a mad scramble for the assets of such vacated foundations, and everyone makes off with whatever he can lay his hands on" (*LW* 45: 170). Luther advised placing all the ecclesiastical assets in the common chest after providing for those who wished to remain in the cloisters, giving transitional support to those who wished to leave the monastic life, and partially restoring funds to the needy families of donors. The remaining capital was still a major financial resource, but with foresight for potential insufficiency in the future, the community decreed that each person in the parish "according to his ability and means, [annually] remit in taxes" what the general assembly deems necessary (*LW* 45: 192).

In terms of direct relief to the poor, the order regulated disbursements of loans and gifts to newcomers to help them get settled; to the housepoor, who, impoverished by circumstances beyond their control, lived in their own dwellings and did not beg in public, to help them get established in a trade or occupation; and to orphans, dependants, the infirm, and the aged for daily support. The order concluded on behalf of all the inhabitants that all its articles and provisions "shall at all times be applied, used, and administered faithfully and without fraud by the parish here in Leisnig for no other purpose than the honor of God, the love of our fellow Christians, and hence for the common good" (*LW* 45: 194).

In a remarkably short period of time these reforms of worship and welfare became models for similar efforts throughout the empire. Luther, of course, did not stand alone in this development. His

Wittenberg colleague Karlstadt utilized Luther's early writings to develop his own position. In late January 1522 Karlstadt published his own perception of the relationship of worship and social welfare: *Von abtuhung der Bylder und das keyn Bedtler unther den Christen seyn sollen* (*On the Abolition of Images and That There Shall Be no Beggars among Christians*). However, Karlstadt's removal of himself from the Wittenberg scene, and his falling-out with Luther, precluded any further contributions he might have made to the translation of theology into social welfare legislation.

The Reformation conviction that the liturgy could stimulate social change motivated the widely effective church orders penned by Bugenhagen and others. The reform of worship included the renewal of community life. In the words of the title of the 1523 tract by the Strasbourg reformer Martin Bucer (1491–1551): *One Should Not Live for Oneself Alone but for Others, and How to Go About It*. The attempt to resolve social problems in the cities was a constitutive component of the early Reformation initiated also by Zwingli and Calvin; the decisive theoretical breakthrough for it goes back to Luther (Laube 1983: 1003ff). The effort to communalize social welfare had counterparts in Catholic areas. "But there can be no doubt that the discussion of Luther's principles of relief and their effects in the sixteenth century shaped the centralized poor relief system not only in early modern Germany but also elsewhere in Europe. The Reformation paved the way for the development of a new social policy which favoured secular systems of poor relief" (Jütte 1994: 108).

Bugenhagen and the Spread of Evangelical Social Welfare

The contributions of Karlstadt and Luther to the translation of theology into social legislation were most fully realized by Johann Bugenhagen. A priest and educator in his home country of Pomerania, hence later called Pomeranus and Dr Pommer, Bugenhagen moved to Wittenberg and enrolled in the university in April 1521 after reading some of Luther's writings. He soon became a friend and colleague of both Luther and Melanchthon. His exegetical lectures were highly regarded but initially there was no funded faculty position available for him; this was the context for his election as pastor of the city church in 1523. In this position Bugenhagen served as Luther's pastor as well as spiritual advisor. He became a doctor of theology in 1533, and a professor in 1535. He published a number of biblical commentaries, theological tracts, a Low German translation of the entire Bible, and a very popular harmony of the four Gospels.

Although in histories of the Reformation Bugenhagen has been overshadowed by his friend and colleague Luther, his organizational genius was highly esteemed by his evangelical contemporaries. Upon becoming pastor of the Wittenberg city church he was instrumental in the reconstruction of the church in Wittenberg after the disturbances of 1522. Soon cities, areas, and countries throughout northern Europe requested his help in instituting the Reformation. He himself wrote or edited church orders for Braunschweig (1528), Hamburg (1529), Lübeck (1531), Pomerania (1535), Denmark (1537), Schleswig-Holstein (1542), Braunschweig-Wolfenbüttel (1543), and Hildesheim (1544).

Bugenhagen's activity in Denmark was signficant for the spread of the Reformation in Scandinavia. He crowned the new king and queen, introduced evangelical reform in the University of Copenhagen, and deliberately broke with the tradition of apostolic succession in ordaining seven new evangelical superindendents (equivalent to bishops) for the churches of Denmark and Norway.

The "Reformer of the North," as Bugenhagen is sometimes called, ranked after Luther as a theologian and after Melanchthon as an educator. His specific genius was to bind theology to exegesis and ecclesiastical praxis to the application of Scripture. In his originality and historical effect he must be ranked with the great south German reformers, Zwingli, Bucer, Osiander, and Brenz.

Bugenhagen was so effective in translating Reformation theology into legislation that until recently most research has focused on his practical accomplishments to the neglect of their theological foundation. It is equally important to emphasize that Bugenhagen's contributions to poor relief legislation and its enactment were embedded in the doctrine he learned from Luther. For Bugenhagen, Reformation doctrine and its institutionalization were inseparable constitutive factors for the progress of the Reformation.

Bugenhagen's fundamental theological orientation received clear and programmatic articulation in the long open letter he wrote to the city of Hamburg. In 1525 he was called to become the pastor of the St Nicholas church in Hamburg; however, his Wittenberg congregation's reluctance to let him go, and a shift in the Hamburg city council's attitude to the evangelical movement in the city, made acceptance impossible. Thus, in the manner of the apostles and Luther, Bugenhagen wrote an epistle to Hamburg titled: "To the Honorable City of Hamburg Concerning the Christian Faith and True Good Works in

Opposition to False Faith and Imaginary Good Works, Thereto, How This Shall Be Prepared by Good Preachers, In Order That Such [True] Faith and Works Be Preached."

The Scriptures make it clear, Bugenhagen affirmed, that salvation is by God's grace alone apart from all works and merit; indeed, apart from faith, all human works are sins. Care of the poor is an expression of faith active in love. Thus in his letter to Hamburg he evangelically recast the medieval perspective on Matthew 25: 40: good works are done not to merit the kingdom of God but to honor Christ and to serve the neighbor. Bugenhagen repeatedly emphasized that salvation is solely by the grace of God, and that service to the neighbor is the human response to the gift of salvation.

With regard to poor relief, Bugenhagen echoed the suggestions Luther had been advancing since 1519: "Combine together all the goods such as those from benefices and other charitable foundations . . . [With these resources] establish a common chest for dependent widows, orphans, the poor, the sick, the needy house-poor, poor maidens, and the like to whom honest citizens can determine on the basis of their need what is to be given or loaned, and how it is to be appropriately sent to them" (Vogt 1867: 261).

Bugenhagen's 1526 epistle to Hamburg was the theological basis for his 1528 Braunschweig church order, the formative model for his later church orders. To him, a responsible church order cannot be independent of its theological substance, and thus the introduction to the Braunschweig order repeats the theme of his earlier tract:

> If we wish to be Christians we must be aware of the consequences. We must avoid monkish charades and penitential liturgies lest God despise us. God has not commanded us to perform any of these. We must carry out the true worship of God, that is, true good works of faith which were first commanded us by Christ. This is primarily that we bear the burden of our neighbors' needs as Jesus said [John 13: 35]: "So will all people know that you are my followers if you always love one another." (Lietzmann 1912: 135)

Bugenhagen emphasized that good works are not the prerequisite but rather the consequence of salvation. Thus the description of Christian social ethics as the "liturgy after the liturgy" is as applicable to Bugenhagen as it is to Luther. Bugenhagen contrasted the Reformation recovery of the gospel to its use in the late medieval church, in which he believed worship was falsified by efforts to acquire merit through charity. Such false worship and "good works" of exchanging money for merit are to be displaced by true worship and the good works of serving the poor.

Bugenhagen's 1529 Hamburg church order, influenced by Luther's Leisnig Order, also presents the evangelical commandment to love the neighbor in place of salvation by works. The new relief system raised poor relief from a vehicle of individual salvation to a Christian responsibility of the parish for all the needy, without distinction. Bugenhagen believed effort to help the needy stand on their own feet both corresponded to evangelical teaching (Matthew 10: 10, 20: 1–16, 25: 14–30; Luke 10: 7; Ephesians 4: 28; 1 Thessalonians 4: 11–12; 2 Thessalonians 3: 6–12; 1 Timothy 5: 18) and made economic sense. But above all it presupposed that those who were supported were to be seen not as impersonal objects of good works, but rather as independent members of the parish. This new poor relief thus had a communal aspect.

Bugenhagen's church order for Lübeck (1531) followed the form of his earlier work. He began by stating that Christians are to support themselves and their families according to Paul's injunction in 1 Timothy 5: 8, 16. Those who are able should also assist their poor servants, relatives, neighbors, and other poor people who are known to them (1 Timothy 6: 9, 17; Mathew 6: 24). Preachers are to exhort not only the rich but also craftsmen blessed by good fortune to help the worthy poor, as Paul teaches (Ephesians 4: 28). "We will no longer tolerate money-preachers who do not preach the gospel and saving doctrine, but rather preach such doctrine as is advantageous to themselves. For these are the fellows who held purgatory masses and sold us indulgences, etc." (Hauschild 1981: 10*). The preachers can boldly appeal for social welfare because people will know they are not lining their own pockets now that they are honorably supported by salaries. In this regard, Bugenhagen's genius was to separate the fund for poor relief from the fund for schools, pastors' salaries, and the maintenance of the church. A further advantage of this arrangement was to establish the independent financing of the church, and thereby make an effort to preserve the independence of the preacher with regard to the political authorities.

Bugenhagen acknowledged, too, that there are decent, honorable people who through misfortune, unemployment, or underemployment suffer demonstrable need through no fault of their own. "We are to care for the worthy poor just as we would have others come to our aid in our need. . . . Christ will indeed remember these things on the last day even if we have already forgotten them, . . . This may be read in Matthew 25 (: 31–46)" (Hauschild 1981: 12*).

Bugenhagen's point is that up to now everyone has been taken in by the many beautiful objects in the churches and the numerous other means for acquiring merit before God, such as indulgences, masses, special pilgrimages, brotherhoods, and ways to participate in all the good works taking place in the cloisters and in the monastic orders. All these efforts to find something special to help one's own blessedness were not only without God's Word, Bugenhagen argued, but even against God's Word. Now, in light of the gospel "we must diligently care for the worthy poor and thus aspire to true worship of God, the worship that Christ deems of value at the day of judgment. No Christian can disapprove of this unless he or she would forget all integrity, and no pope and council may make this otherwise" (Hauschild 1981: 15*).

That such preaching was not without social effect is suggested by the testament of Anna Büring, the aged and wealthy widow of the Hamburg mayor. In 1535 she changed the will she had drafted in 1503. In her earlier testament, she declared, she had left her money to purchase vigils, masses for her soul, and numerous other good works in order to avoid the pain of purgatory. Now, however, having heard God's Word and his holy gospel, she renounces this earlier orientation. Since she now believes she is saved by grace alone, she decides to provide for her family and then to leave the rest of her fortune for the sick, the poor, and the needy. This included establishing housing for the poor, and a five-year scholarship at a Christian university. Smaller bequests were received by the church for construction, and by the city for the common good. "Testaments give particularly serious and heartfelt witness to personal convictions. The relatively broad tradition shows that Anna Büring is representative for the change which occurred with the Reformation. At the same time it demonstrates some of its social-historical dimensions" (Postel 1980: 63–4). Nevertheless, by itself this account gives a one-sided picture: back in Wittenberg Luther was bitterly complaining of the community's lack of support for social welfare, ministry, and education. On more than one occasion Luther vowed he would no longer be their pastor unless the people reformed their lives.

Bugenhagen's basic principle for formulating church orders was to link theological argumentation and its practical and legal consequences. His theological basis was expressed in a sermonic style intended to make the order plausible to the community. To Bugenhagen, the reform of the church was not just to be a legal decree from above, but the engagement of the whole urban community in the reform of worship, the development of schools, and the creation of a new social welfare program. All of this was perceived to be central to Christian responsibility, and the duty of the entire city. Bugenhagen applied the writings of Luther to the totality of daily life. This exploded the late medieval concentration on the cultic as expressly Christian. The church was no longer defined and organized by the priestly office but as the assembled community under God's Word and around Christ's sacrament. Poor relief expressed this community solidarity through faith active in love; it was, in fact, an act of worship, of divine service.

Education for Service to God and Service to the Neighbor

The reorganization of the church included the development of schools. Medieval education was closely linked to monastic and cathedral schools, and scholarships came primarily from ecclesiastical benefices. By the eve of the Reformation this ecclesiastical grip on education had fostered two basic attitudes. One was that the church contributed to social inequality by limiting access to education to those entering the church or the professions. There was a sense that society was divided between the learned and the "common man." The other attitude was that education was a waste of time unless one went into the church or the professions of law or medicine. This attitude was summarized in the popular phrase *die Gelehrte sind verkehrte* ("the learned are daft"). Luther opposed both attitudes, and argued that service to both God and the neighbor required an educated population.

Already in his *Address to the Christian Nobility* (1520) Luther appealed for universal education for boys and girls. This was explicitly developed in his *To the Councilmen of all Cities in Germany that they Establish and Maintain Christian Schools* (1524). To the perennial complaint that education is expensive, Luther replied: "My dear sirs, if we have to spend such large sums every year on guns, roads, bridges, dams, and countless similar items to insure the temporal peace and prosperity of a city, why should not much more be devoted to our poor neglected youth – at least enough to engage one or two competent men to teach school?" (*LW* 45: 350). Government and society cannot continue without educated leaders and citizens. The young must be trained in history, the arts, languages, mathematics, and sciences to be able to benefit and serve the world. "The devil very much prefers coarse blockheads and ne'er-do-wells, lest men get along too well on earth" (*LW* 45: 371). Schools should be supplemented by publicly maintained libraries. "For if the gospel and all the arts are to be preserved, they must be set down and held fast in books and writings" (*LW* 45: 373).

This appeal had some success in establishing schools through the church orders in a number of cities and territories. The problem now became that of convincing parents of the value of educating their children. In *A Sermon on Keeping Children in School* (1530) Luther argued that an evangelical church requires a learned ministry. God did not give children so that parents could train them just to get ahead in the world. "You have been earnestly commanded to raise them for God's service . . . But how will you raise them for God's service if the office of preaching and the spiritual estate have fallen into oblivion?" (*LW* 46: 222).

This is not to say that all children should be directed to the ministry, for the world also needs capable leaders. "If there were no worldly government, one man could not stand before another; each would necessarily devour the other, as irrational beasts devour one another. Therefore as it is the function and honor of the office of preaching to make sinners saints, dead men live, damned men saved, and the devil's children God's children, so it is the function and honor of worldly government to make men out of wild beasts and to prevent men from becoming wild beasts." Without a capable and wise government, society would devolve to the survival of the fittest. "For if men were to rule solely by the fist, the end result would surely be a bestial kind of existence: whoever could get the better of another would simply toss him into the discard pile." Wisdom, not might, should rule. "All experience proves this and in all the histories we find that force, without reason or wisdom, has never accomplished anything" (*LW* 46: 237–8). Thus "it is the duty of the temporal authority to compel its subjects to keep their children in school . . . so that there will always be preachers, jurists, pastors, writers, physicians, schoolmasters, and the like, for we cannot do without them" (*LW* 46: 256–7). Education, then, has the double goal of serving the worship of God and serving the needs of the neighbor.

The Catechisms and Christian Vocation

Education for responsible Christian citizenship in the church and in society is the purpose of Luther's catechisms or "lay bible." His dismay over the ignorance of those he encountered when visiting parishes in Saxony impressed on him the need for simple instruction in the faith addressed to daily life. The purpose of the catechism is to present the fundamentals of the Christian faith in simple language. Daily life is viewed in light of the last judgment: "The summons of death comes to us all, and no one can die for another. Every one must fight his own battle with death by himself, alone. We can shout into another's ears, but every one must himself be prepared for the time of death, for I will not be with you then, nor you with me. Therefore every one must himself know and be armed with the chief things which concern a Christian" (*LW* 51: 70). These "chief things" included the ten commandments, the creed, and the Lord's Prayer. Also included in the catechisms were brief expositions of baptism and the Lord's Supper, instruction for confession, morning and evening prayers, and grace for meals. The Small Catechism was intended for use in the home, while the Large Catechism was addressed to the clergy for use in the church. Both were published in 1529.

As might be expected, the catechism is governed by the motif of justification by grace alone. Thus in the creed the first article of creation is explained by saying that God's creation of me and all that exists is done "out of his pure, fatherly, and divine goodnesss and mercy, without any merit or worthiness on my part." The second article explains redemption as the redemption of "a lost and condemned creature;" and the third article confesses: "I believe that by my own reason or strength I cannot believe in Jesus Christ . . . But the Holy Spirit has called me through the Gospel . . ."

Luther's pedagogical method is clear in the catechism's question-and-answer format and in his instructions to those who use it as a teaching tool. In this format he attempted to give guidance to everyday life. Thus the ten commandments are presented not only as prohibitions but also as positive exhortations. For example: " 'You shall not steal.' What does this mean? Answer: We should fear and love God, and so we should not rob our neighbor of his money or property, not bring them into our possession by dishonest trade or by dealing in shoddy wares, but help him to improve and protect his income and property" (Tappert 1959: 343).

The Small Catechism in particular attempted to make fruitful for daily life the basic elements of the Christian faith. Luther introduced his manifesto of Christian freedom, *The Freedom of a Christian* (1520), with two theses that capture his sense of the essence of Christian life: "A Christian is a perfectly free lord of all, subject to none. A Christian is a perfectly dutiful servant of all, subject to all" (*LW* 31: 344). The Christian life is a vocation. The term "vocation" is derived from a Latin word that means to call, to invite, to welcome, to call by name. Thus to

Luther, Christian vocation is not understood as a meritorious work for salvation but rather as being called by name and welcomed by God in the ongoing work of creation.

Luther's approach to vocation was a major break from medieval tradition. Prior to Luther the word "vocation" was reserved for the specific religious life of priest, monk, or nun. Luther's emphasis that every Christian belongs to the priesthood of believers freed vocation from its narrow religious definition. Vocation is not outside the sphere of everyday life but precisely in the midst of everyday life. Christians are not called to other-worldly but rather this-worldly service. Since, Luther proclaimed, our worth as persons is not dependent on what we do but on who we are, all the energy that the medieval Christian directed to religion is now freed to worldly activity for the sake of others. The liberating power of this message for the medieval may be grasped by analogy to modern culture. Just as the medieval attributed self-worth to achievement of religious works, so the modern attributes self-worth to the achievement of material works, e.g. "you are what you eat," "you are what you do/wear/appear," etc. Imagine what human and material resources would be liberated if the contemporary diet industry ceased to exist.

Luther, and in the next generation Calvin, claimed that God does not call the Christian out of the world but into it. Because God's acceptance occurs on the human level, persons are not called to extraordinary tasks but to mundane ones. This led to a religious revaluation of ordinary work which is perhaps more easily grasped in German than in English. In German the vocabulary of religion and the mundane are related. The words for "gift" and "word" are incorporated in the words for "duty" and "responsibility." *Gabe* means gift and *Aufgabe* means duty. Thus duty carries within it the element of gift; vocation in the world reflects God's gift. The same is true in the relations of the German words *Wort* (word), *Antwort* (answer), and *Verantwortung* (responsibility). In all three, "word" is present. The Word of God calls forth the human answer which encompasses everyday responsibilities. Hence theologians like to play with German! In short, faith is to be active in love.

The contribution of the Reformation understanding of vocation was to break the hold of the religious elite upon vocation and to democratize it and imbue all of life with religion. Vocation encompasses all human relationships at once in the sense that a person may be a daughter, mother, wife, citizen, worker, student, etc., at the same time. For Luther, human life is a web of relationships, the many strands of which are anchored in the center of the forgiveness of sins. Vocation is practiced in these relationships of life; and this means that there is a

"God-givenness" to life specific to the particular relationships and talents of each person.

The perennial human tendency to devalue what is close at hand and seek to do something extraordinary is precisely what Luther attacked in the medieval understanding of vocational (i.e. religious) vows. People did not want to fulfill mundane God-given tasks such as being a parent, but rather devised their own tasks, such as celibacy, which they thought would please God and make them holy. This goal-orientation led to neglect of the tasks at hand. That is why Luther always chose examples of vocation from daily life: the father washing smelly diapers, the maid sweeping the floor, the brewer making good beer. These activities are concrete forms of serving the neighbor. Luther's point is that people are not called beyond their talents but only to be faithful to what is given to them.

Luther never advocated that Christians withdraw from the world. The very point of his understanding of the gospel was that since salvation is the foundation rather than the goal of life, the Christian is free to redirect the time and energy previously expended on achieving salvation to service to the neighbor. Boldly expressed, Luther was advocating a "religionless Christianity."

Because the Christian is "called" to serve in the world, Luther vigorously distinguished between the kingdom of God and the kingdom of the world. He hammered incessantly upon this distinction because he wanted to call Christians to political action in an age that conceived of religion primarily as withdrawal from the world. Even kings, including the Emperor Charles V, preferred to spend their last days in a monastery so they could be buried in a religious habit. The medieval could not conceive of having a vocation in the world, because vocation had a narrow religious meaning and politics was "dirty." Luther hoped to free Christians for service in a world that is always shrouded in political and ethical ambiguity by distinguishing between the righteousness of human, civil laws, that demanded achievement, and the righteousness before God, that is a free gift.

Was the Early Reformation a Failure?

Luther was convinced that the church must take seriously its educational and moral responsibilities if it was to have any credibility. We have already noted that Luther was motivated to write his catechisms after his shock and disappointment at the low level of Christian life he witnessed when visiting parishes. Wittenberg, too, disappointed

Luther. The people were not contributing regularly to the common chest, or to support of the clergy, or to support of the schools. Luther ranted in sermons that the people were "unthankful beasts, unworthy of the gospel; if you do not repent I will stop preaching to you." Evangelical preaching was not producing the desired fruit. Too many people were abusing Christian freedom, and Luther no longer wanted to be "the shepherd of such pigs." Indeed, for a while he even went on a preaching strike. Visitations of other parishes indicated similar problems (Brecht 1990: 287–90).

Recent scholarship, in particular that of Gerald Strauss (1978: 307), has argued that the Lutheran efforts to implant reform through education basically failed. On the basis of his painstaking examination of visitation records, Strauss concluded that if the central purpose of the Reformation was "to make people – all people – think, feel, and act as Christians, to imbue them with a Christian mind-set, motivational drive, and way of life, it failed." Another historian, James Kittelson (1985: 100), dissents from this evaluation on the basis of a study of the local conditions of Strasbourg. He concludes that "Protestant pastors were remarkably successful in creating precisely the religious culture they sought to create, at least in so far as it can be certainly documented." Noting that those not intimately acquainted with the sources will have difficulty in ascertaining the validity of either position, Kittelson suggests that general evaluations of popular religious culture will be problematic unless the Reformers' own goals are kept in mind and evaluated in their historical and local contexts.

From Luther's theological perspective the very question of success or failure, especially in terms of the ethical regeneration of society, is the wrong question. To be sure, Luther had bouts of depression over the conditions of the reformed churches. But the very point of justification by grace alone is that discipleship is not dependent upon its results. The Christian was called to be faithful, not successful. Luther knew quite well that the gospel is the proclamation of God's promise, not the exhortation to the moral regeneration of society. This conviction is what distinguished Luther from Wyclif and Hus.

> Doctrine and life are to be distinguished. Life is as bad among us as among the papists. Hence we do not fight and damn them because of their bad lives. Wyclif and Hus, who fought over the moral quality of life, failed to understand this. . . . When the Word of God remains pure, even if the quality of life fails us, life is placed in a position to become what it ought to be. That is why everything hinges on the purity of the Word. I have succeeded only if I have taught correctly. (*WA TR* 1: 624; *LW* 54: 110)

The outcome of every human venture, including reform of the church, rests in God's hands. So Luther explained the petition "your kingdom come": "To be sure, the kingdom of God comes of itself, without our prayer, but we pray in this petition that it may also come to us" (Tappert 1959: 346). It is this perspective that distinguishes Luther from Müntzer (see Chapter 6).

Luther's conviction that God alone works everything did not lead him into personal or social quietism, as may be seen on a number of levels. For example, his concern for poor relief led to his involvement in changing social structures; and his commitment to good works led to his final journey in poor health and old age to mediate a quarrel between the counts of Mansfeld. It is of interest that in his great controversy with Erasmus over the human will, Luther, who emphasized Christian liberty, argued for the bondage of the will, and Erasmus, who argued for the freedom of the will, emphasized moralism.

The modern effort to understand the Reformers' success or failure probably founders most of all on their sense of eschatology. Luther, among others, was convinced that the world was near its end. He had no optimism with regard to the world, and longed for the day of judgment. This longing was informed by his doctrine of justification, and thus was no longer the medieval angst before the day of wrath (*dies irae*) but rather the joyous expectation of the coming Redeemer who will create a new heaven and a new earth. At the same time, this is not only a historical but also an existential view: judgment and grace are present as well as future realities. There is a double perspective here: readiness for the end of history is the readiness for the end of every failure and self-disappointment and thereby creates freedom for action. Paradoxically, Luther's certainty of completion and fulfillment at the last day leads to enjoyment of creation and the praxis of grateful and responsible use of the old creation, which is decaying but through which the new creation is already evident. This eschatological stamp on the creation is expressed in the saying attributed to Luther: "If I knew that tomorrow the world would be destroyed, I would still plant an apple tree today."

Suggestions for Further Reading

Robert Jütte, *Poverty and Deviance in Early Modern Europe*, Cambridge: Cambridge University Press, 1994

James Kittelson, "Luther the Educational Reformer" in Marilyn J. Harran, ed., *Luther and Learning: The Wittenberg University Luther Symposium*, 95–114, Selinsgrove: Susquehanna University Press, 1985

Carter Lindberg, *Beyond Charity: Reformation Initiatives for the Poor*, Minneapolis: Fortress, 1993

Lester K. Little, *Religious Poverty and the Profit Economy in Medieval Europe*, Ithaca: Cornell University Press, 1978

Elsie Anne McKee, *John Calvin on the Diaconate and Liturgical Almsgiving*, Geneva: Droz, 1984

Michel Mollat, *The Poor in the Middle Ages: An Essay in Social History*, trans. Arthur Goldhammer, New Haven: Yale University Press, 1986

Jeannine Olson, *Calvin and Social Welfare: Deacons and the "Bourse française"*, Selinsgrove: Susquehanna University Press, 1989

Brian Pullan, *Rich and Poor in Renaissance Venice: The Social Institutions of a Catholic State to 1620*, Cambridge, MA: Harvard University Press, 1971

Lee Palmer Wandel, *Always Among Us: Images of the Poor in Zwingli's Zurich*, Cambridge: Cambridge University Press, 1990

6

The Reformation of the Common Man

The people will go free and God alone will be their Lord.

Thomas Müntzer

"Brother Andy"

Luther's return to Wittenberg from the Wartburg halted Karlstadt's rapid implementation of reform and displaced his leadership. Karlstadt expressed his anger over this turn of events by displacing it toward Catholic refusal of communion in both kinds to the laity, the use of Latin in the liturgy, and all the other aspects of Catholic ritual he had overturned during Luther's absence. The fact that this attack also covered the recent events following Luther's "Invocavit Sermons" was not lost on Luther and the university, which seized Karlstadt's writing and forbade its publication. Although Melanchthon feared Karlstadt would jeopardize the evangelical cause out of personal pique, Karlstadt initially contained his resentment.

Whether or not Karlstadt had an inferiority complex that motivated his aspiration for success and status, he interpreted the rejection of his reform efforts as divine chastisement of his desire for honor and status. In a dramatic move that would warm the heart of any radical student, Karlstadt renounced his academic achievements and announced he would no longer participate in the granting of academic degrees. That was no small feat for a man who had acquired doctoral degrees in theology, civil law, and canon law, and become a full professor and archdeacon. The occasion was the promotion of two of his students on 3 February 1523, after which he made his announcement with an appeal to Matthew 23: 10, "Neither be called masters, for you have one master, the Christ." This was one time when Luther, rarely at a loss for words, was too stunned to comment.

Shortly after this Karlstadt wrote that formerly he had studied and written for acclaim, but now he realized how egocentric he had been

and indeed how arrogant and self-serving the whole academic enterprise was with its degrees, intellectual elitism, and quests for glory.
Henceforth, he said, he would be a simple layman. He signed his works
"Andreas Karlstadt, a new layman" and replaced his academic garb
with that of a peasant. As if clothes made the man – did Christ deck
himself in finery? – he asked to be addressed as "brother Andy" and, it
seems, he tried farming. He later explained his preference for the honest
labor that brings dirty hands over the professional privilege that lives
off the labor of others, of which he too was once guilty: a peasant or
craftsman lives according to God's law by the sweat of his brow, while
the academics and other big shots exploit them. But Luther has
forgotten this true mortification of the flesh. "What think you Luther,
are not blisters on the hands more honorable than golden rings?"
(Hertzsch 1957: II, 95–6).

Faithful to his convictions, Karlstadt left Wittenberg in the early
summer of 1523 for the life of a parish pastor in Orlamünde, a small
town not far away on the river Saale. The story of this move and its
consequences is complicated and historically controversial because it
involved financial and legal matters as well as Karlstadt's conscience.
Unlike Luther and Melanchthon, who received salaries, Karlstadt was
still financially dependent on the benefices and mass endowments all the
Reformers had condemned. Included in his income was the benefice
from the Orlamünde parish which Karlstadt received as archdeacon of
All Saints. By becoming pastor at Orlamünde, Karlstadt would free
himself from the strongly criticized ecclesiastical abuses which
provided his income in Wittenberg. Also, the present pastor, Glitzsch,
had failed to pay the stipend due All Saints that provided Karlstadt's
income, and had also let the local parish go to rack and ruin. When
Glitzsch was legally told to leave for failure to maintain his responsibilities, Karlstadt requested permission to take his place. Prince Frederick
granted his request. However, there were potential complications
beause as archdeacon Karlstadt was obligated to teach at the university
for part of his income, and the university had the right to nominate the
vicar of Orlamünde.

These potential problems were actualized when Karlstadt proceeded
to institute the changes in Orlamünde which had been quenched in
Wittenberg. Images were removed from the church, infant baptism
was discontinued, the Lord's Supper was interpreted as a memorial of
Christ's death, and Karlstadt began publishing his ideas for reform of
the church. The divisive ramifications of the sacramental changes will
be treated in the next chapters, but it should be clear that Luther and his

Wittenberg colleagues did not approve. They now started legal moves to evict Karlstadt from his parish on the basis that he was not legally called there and was not fulfilling his university assignments. The effort to silence Karlstadt was also motivated both by the diet of Nuremberg's injunction against innovation and by peasant unrest spreading through the Saale valley, stimulated by the revolutionary preaching of Thomas Müntzer, with whom Karlstadt was now – unfairly – associated. The response of the Orlamünde parish, which appreciated Karlstadt, was clever and ironic. They elected him their pastor – a congregational right that Luther had just emphasized in a tract written for the parish in Leisnig (*LW* 39: 303–14).

By July 1524 Luther was convinced that Karlstadt was supporting the violence preached by Müntzer (in March Müntzer's followers had burned a chapel outside the gates of Allstedt). Müntzer had indeed approached Karlstadt for political support; but he and his parish rejected violent reform on the basis of its biblical prohibition: "We cannot help you with armed resistance . . . We have not been commanded to do this, for Christ ordered Peter to sheath his sword" (Baylor 1991: 33–4). "Karlstadt was trapped between the radical Müntzer and the complex Luther whose conservative fear of social disorder was at least equal to his desire for religious change" (Sider 1974: 196). The Electoral Saxon princes now sent Luther on a tour of the Saale valley to assess the situation and to counter what they perceived to be a rising tide of violence.

Luther's reception through the area and its towns of Jena, Kahla, Neustadt, and Orlamünde was warm – too warm: he was often greeted by abuse and at times stones; at Kahla, where the pastor supported Karlstadt, Luther had to step over a smashed crucifix to get to the pulpit to preach his sermon on tolerating images. On 22 August Luther preached at Jena against the destruction of images, the cessation of both infant baptism and the Lord's Supper, and the evil fruits of the spiritualist theology that led to insurrection. At the rear of the church slouched Karlstadt under a felt hat pulled forward to prevent recognition. Though Luther mentioned no one by name, Karlstadt was incensed by the sermon and convinced that Luther was attacking him personally. After the sermon Karlstadt sent Luther a note asking for a meeting. That afternoon the two Reformers met at Luther's place of lodging, the Black Bear Inn in Jena. There was an unpleasant exchange of accusations and charges, both theological and personal, which concluded when Luther challenged Karlstadt to write against him and gave him a gulden in pledge of his willingness to engage in polemical battle. All in all it was a declaration of theological war.

Luther's encounter two days later with the parish in Orlamünde went no better. The congregation wanted Karlstadt as their pastor, and supported their election of him on the basis of Luther's own writings. Luther rejected this with the argument that Karlstadt had broken his commitments to All Saints and the university. In the argument over the removal of images the congregation would not retract their claim that Luther's toleration of images was unbiblical and jeopardized his own membership in the body of Christ. Luther then broke off the conversation, such as it was. Soon thereafter Karlstadt preached against Luther, calling him an unfaithful servant of God and a perverter of the Scriptures.

Karlstadt soon obliged Luther's challenge with a series of tracts on the Lord's Supper as well as a polemic against Luther's concern for the weak in faith. The five tracts on the Lord's Supper illustrate his adaptation of a mystical terminology, spiritualist leanings, and a vigorous concern for a regenerate life of obedience to the Lord. These eucharistic tracts, which were both direct attacks upon Luther and the first expressions of a purely symbolic understanding of the Lord's Supper, were sent to Switzerland via Karlstadt's brother-in-law, Dr Gerhard Westerburg of Cologne, in the fall of 1524. By now Karlstadt was banished from Electoral Saxony. He complained that he had been driven out without benefit of trial or sentence at the instigation of a Luther who now wished to defend the gospel with force.

The bone of contention between Luther and Karlstadt was not the timetable of reform but the understanding of reform itself. In retrospect scholars have contrasted Luther's theology of justification with Karlstadt's theology of regeneration. There were hints of this difference already in Wittenberg, but these hints blossomed into public differences with the publication of Karlstadt's eucharistic tracts. His emphasis upon the inner testimony of the Spirit of God is what led Luther to draw the connection between Müntzer and Karlstadt. This spiritualism was perhaps most clearly articulated in Karlstadt's "Dialogue" on the Lord's Supper. Here Karlstadt provides via his protaganist, Peter the layman, the following testimony to the inward witness of the Spirit: "I do not need the external witness for my own sake, for I desire to have my testimony of the Spirit inwardly as Christ has promised." When asked who taught him his interpretation, Peter responds, "He whose voice I heard yet did not see; I also knew not how he came and went from me . . . Our Father in heaven." When further pressed as to why he had not explained his views earlier, Peter says, "The Spirit did not impel me quickly enough . . . At times one must conceal the Spirit for the sake of his honor, and sometimes fight with externally received testimony. I knew quite well that you and the whole world, especially the 'Scripture-wise,' would have laughed at me and said, 'He raves,' if I had burst forth earlier" (Lindberg 1979: 50–1).

The inner witness of the Spirit, in contrast to Luther's emphasis on the external word of God's promise, is according to Karlstadt the agency which makes the uneducated laity independent of the learned theologians. Here is Karlstadt's model for the social structure of the congregation and thus communal reform: the laity are to be "Peter the layman." Karlstadt strove to realize this model of renewal in Orlamünde by fostering a democratic–synodal communal polity, an evangelical mass, abolition of images, oral confession, fasting, and the development of an evangelical poor relief. Through the internal witness of the Spirit, power is given to the people. Although Karlstadt refused Müntzer's exhortation to forced reform, he and his congregation at Orlamünde had achieved a passive disobedience. For him churchly reforms belonged in the jurisdiction of the congregational or city authority. Thus he opposed the Lutheran model of the territorial church with the model of a congregational or city church. In terms of ecclesiology he was a proto-congregationalist. That this tendency, even without overt revolutionary political actions, had to lead to conflicts with the territorial lords, who on their part sought to exploit the Reformation upheaval to expand their power, was inevitable.

After Karlstadt's expulsion from Electoral Saxony in September 1524 he traveled through southwest Germany. The following sketch of Karlstadt's travels and contacts will suggest how widespread his influence became. In Strasbourg he gained a certain amount of support from the Reformer Wolfgang Capito, and also was able to publish his defense, *Ursachen derhalben Andreas Karlstadt aus den Landen zu Sachsen vertreiben* ("Reasons Why Andreas Karlstadt Was Expelled from Saxony"). In Zurich and Basle he had contact with Anabaptist circles, and in Basle his brother-in-law Westerburg, expelled from Jena, and Felix Manz, from Zurich, tried to get his tracts on infant baptism and the (now lost) writing "On the Living Voice of God" published. Johannes Oecolampadius hindered the printing of the dialogue on infant baptism in Basle; however it was published anonymously in 1527. In this tract Karlstadt rejected infant baptism because he both denied Luther's teaching of the representative faith of the sponsors and affirmed the precedence of the baptism of the Spirit over that of water. Karlstadt did not, however, raise the demand for rebaptism.

In Basle seven writings by Karlstadt were published, of which five were directed against Luther's doctrine of the Lord's Supper. In Nuremberg Karlstadt had a following which included among others

Hans Greifenberger, Hans Denck, and the so-called "three godless painters;" also, two of Karlstadt's writings were circulated here in 1524 by the printer Hieronymous Höltzel. In his five eucharistic tracts Karlstadt attacked Luther's doctrine of the real presence of Christ in the bread and wine. The bread and wine are rather signs of the spiritual presence of the Lord. In his "Dialogue" Karlstadt advanced the exegetical argument that with the words "this is my body" Jesus pointed to himself, not the bread. This was an argument that had been advanced since the thirteenth century and apparently mediated by the Bohemian Waldensians. It also had been advanced a half year before Karlstadt's tract by the circle of dissidents in Zwickau. For Karlstadt the center of his understanding of the eucharist is the remembrance of the cross of Jesus.

After traveling through Heidelberg, Schweinfurt, and Kitzingen, Karlstadt arrived in Rothenburg on the Tauber in December 1524 and settled there for a while, striving to influence the reform movement. After the outbreak of the Peasants' War he left the city around the end of May 1525.

Karlstadt was on friendly terms with the Thuringian leader of the Peasants' War, Thomas Müntzer, and they had influenced each other. However, already in his *Ursachen, dass Andreas Karlstadt ein Zeit stillgeschwiegen* (1523: "Reasons Why Andreas Karlstadt Was Temporarily Silent"), Karlstadt had cautiously drawn back from Müntzer's understanding of revelation in which dreams and visions played an important role. Yet in spite of Karlstadt's clear rejection of Müntzer's revolutionary efforts, Karlstadt found himself caught between two fronts during the Peasants' War. On the one hand, Luther unfairly smelled revolution in Karlstadt; and on the other, Karlstadt sought without success to influence the Frankish peasants toward nonaggression. After a week's refuge with his mother during Pentecost of 1525, he fled to Luther's protection. Luther exacted Karlstadt's promise to desist writing. In the preface to Karlstadt's *Entschuldigung des falschen Namens des Aufruhrs* (June 1525: "Apology Regarding the False Charge of Insurrection"), Luther retracted the imputation that Karlstadt was a rebel. However, Karlstadt's retraction of his eucharistic teaching was a forced compromise which held the seeds of further controversies. At first Karlstadt was given asylum in the towns around Wittenberg, where he eked out a living as a farmer and then as a shopkeeper. However, his influence was not broken and, albeit with great difficulty, he maintained contacts through letters and visits. An intercepted letter to Kasper Schwenkfeld revealed his unchanged convictions regarding the eucharist. He refused to write against Ulrich Zwingli. At the beginning of 1529 he fled his oppressive situation to Kiel at the call of the lay preacher and furrier, Melchior Hoffman. Karlstadt helped Hoffman prepare for the Flensburg (Denmark) disputation on the Lord's Supper (April 1529) but did not himself participate in it, although he did co-author the report on it. Nevertheless Karlstadt was not comfortable with Hoffman's visionary–apocalyptic ideas.

After expulsion from Kiel in April 1529 and a period of existence as a wandering preacher in East Friesland, Karlstadt was in the area around Oldersum south of Emden from around August 1529 to January 1530. After his flight from Oldersum he sought positions from Strasbourg to Basle to Zurich, where with Zwingli's help he became a deacon at the Great Minster and hospital chaplain. In a foreword of 10 December 1530 to Leo Jud's edition of Zwingli's lectures on Philippians, Karlstadt identified himself publicly with the Zurich Reformation. The one-time second man of the Wittenberg Reformation now found eleven creative years among the fathers of Swiss Reformed Protestantism.

During these years his disputes with the Wittenbergers continued. In early 1530 he responded to Melanchthon and in 1532 he answered Luther's charge that the fates of Müntzer, Zwingli, and Karlstadt were the punishments of God. In 1534 he became professor of Old Testament and pastor of St Peter's in Basle. There he strove with his Basle colleagues and with Martin Bucer of Strasbourg to develop harmony among the Reformers. He was a member of the Basle delegation that discussed with Bucer the Wittenberg Concord on the Lord's Supper, which he supported. In Basle he and the lawyer Bonifazius Amerbach worked together on reform of the university, and reintroduced promotions and disputations in the theological faculty. He himself gave in January 1535 an inaugural disputation that provided a systematic presentation of his theology.

Karlstadt's humanistic interests also now came to the fore, including his high valuation of history and nature, which he held to be an important precondition for the understanding of Scripture. In connection with his lectures on the Old Testament he began instruction in Hebrew. For a while he also gave lectures in New Testament and philosophy. He planned a major encyclopedia of theology to integrate into a pansophical understanding of theology the various influences he had experienced during his career; but he died of the plague on 24 December 1541, having before his death intentionally destroyed the unprinted manuscript which he had only just begun.

With some 90 printed writings in about 213 editions, Karlstadt was among the more prolific writers of the Reformation. For the period 1518–25 he was second only to Luther in the number of publications in

German. During his journey from Wittenberg to Basle, Karlstadt influenced the most varied reforming groups at the times of their formations – Lutherans, Anabaptists, Spiritualists, and the Swiss Reformers. On the one hand he had a broad intellectual influence; but on the other hand, precisely because of the changing fronts he addressed, he was denied an abiding influence on ecclesial formation. His effective influence on the whole course of the Reformation came from his battle against images and against Luther's doctrine of the Lord's Supper. The elimination of images forthwith became an external sign of the Reformation in the cities, even in the many cities that pursued a more Lutheran type of reform. The Lord's Supper controversy with Luther became through its reception and continuation in Zwingli a church-dividing dimension of the Reformation.

The movement of students and followers characterized for a time as "Karlstadtians" reached its high point between 1523 and 1530. Karlstadt's influence centered on the areas of Thuringia, Franken, and the upper German cities; but his influence was felt from Reval to East Friesland and from Holstein to the Tyrol. In social perspective his followers came from contexts similar to his own among the educated urban burghers. On the other hand, since Orlamünde he spoke of aiming at the circle of craftsmen and peasants, to whom he identified himself as a "new layman" or "brother Andy." Karlstadt's external adjustment to the confessional line of the Swiss cities robbed the radical Karlstadtians of their model, and excluded him as a possible coalition partner of the Anabaptists. Nevertheless, later Lutheran polemical writings indicate his continuing influence. Also, significant Spiritualists of the time such as Hoffmann, Denck, Schwenkfeld, and Sebastian Franck, adopted and mediated in many different ways Karlstadt's opinions, above all his strongly mystically stamped writings of 1523–5.

Karlstadt's path led into crypto-dissidentism. Many of his followers appear, like himself, to have taken the path of external accommodation and internal emigration. The praxis derived from the priesthood of all believers and home Bible study supported a clandestine continuation of the Karlstadtian spirit along with the heritage of other Reformation dissidents. Karlstadt's writings continued to be read in secret.

With his theology of rebirth and sanctification Karlstadt was a forerunner of Pietism. There are not only material agreements between him and Pietism but also historical lines of connection. Most significant for the transmission of Karlstadt's heritage between the Reformation and Pietism was the mystic and crypto-dissident Valentin Weigel (1533–88).

Thomas Müntzer

Far more than Karlstadt, Thomas Müntzer (ca. 1489–1525) developed the political as well as religious consequences of Spiritualism. With Müntzer the inner order of the Spirit led directly to change of the outer order of the world; mysticism became the theological basis for revolution.

Müntzer initially viewed Luther as a comrade-in-arms but then believed he was a lackey of the princes after learning of Luther's role in reversing Karlstadt's innovations in Wittenberg. In his *A Highly Provoked Vindication and a Refutation of the Unspiritual Soft-Living Flesh in Wittenberg whose Robbery and Distortion of Scripture has so Grievously Polluted our Wretched Christian Church* (1524) Müntzer denounced Luther as a carrion crow, Father Pussyfoot, Dr Liar, the Wittenberg Pope, the chaste Babylonian virgin, archdevil, and a rabid fox. The better part of valor was never Müntzer's strong point! But Luther himself was also no slouch at invective. He labeled Müntzer a bloodthirsty rioter possessed by the devil who was hellbent on destroying both church and state, "a man born for heresies and schisms." Thus began the Protestant historiography of Müntzer, and by association all the so-called "radical" Reformers. Luther's theological suspicion of all theologies of inner change and regeneration was sharpened and hardened by his experiences with Karlstadt and Müntzer and thereby became a vehement rejection of any person or group which appeared to hold Spiritualist views. To Luther, Müntzer became *the* symbol of dissent and heresy that logically led to the horrors of the Peasants' War and the later disaster at the city of Münster (1534–5).

The modern stimulus for Müntzer research has come from Marxist historians who took their cue from Friedrich Engels' reinterpretation of Müntzer as a theologian of liberation from social and political oppression. In a pamphlet prepared for the 1989 quincentenary of his birth, a committee in the former East Germany wrote: "The GDR [German Democratic Republic] . . . has understood itself as a state living up to the idea of Thomas Müntzer's that 'power shall be given to the common folk.' As a man who fought with dedicated self-sacrifice for the goal of building a new society in the interests of the common people, Müntzer's example demonstrates ethical and moral values that . . . still bear fruit in creating the foundations of socialism."

Archdevil or socialist hero? Revolutionary or servant of God? Bloodthirsty killer or spiritual pastor? Will the real Thomas Müntzer stand up! Unlike Luther, Müntzer's reforming activity was compressed into the few years between 1521 and 1525, a period marked by polemical and physical violence and culminating with his execution. The events of this time-frame, which also include the Peasants' War, all associated with the controversial nature of his person and work, make Müntzer a difficult person to assess.

Müntzer's Origins and Theology

Scholarly efforts to find the "real" Müntzer have to deal not only with a centuries-long polemical historiography but also with an almost complete lack of sources and studies of his origins and ideas. There are practically no sources for his childhood and school years. Claims for his birthdate have ranged between 1470 and 1495, though the present consensus is around 1489. It seems clear that his parents were from an urban milieu, and the family name suggests that at some point they were engaged in minting. Müntzer identified his home as Stolberg, and the family name is recorded there and also in the nearby towns of Quedlinburg, Aschersleben, and Halberstadt. Since a direct analysis of his family origins is not possible, Ulrich Bubenheimer has recently explored Müntzer's social relationships for clues to his origins. The sources from his time in Braunschweig (1514–17) and his later contacts there up to 1522 indicate he associated with people from the professional strata of international merchants, goldsmiths, and minters. His connections with these people suggest that he came from a relatively well-to-do social milieu that in the larger cities was an educated and politically influential citizenry. Müntzer's origins and personal relationships were in the circles of the early capitalist mining economy of the Harz and Thuringian area, and thus were similar to Luther's (Bubenheimer 1989: 11–40).

Müntzer studied at Leipzig, Frankfurt an der Oder, Wittenberg (1517–18, 1519), and perhaps at other universities. He received the degrees of Bachelor and Master of Arts, and Bachelor of Scripture. He was probably ordained before his acceptance on 6 May 1514 of a prebend at St Michael's church in Braunschweig. His service as chaplain to a nunnery at Frose is dated by correspondence in July 1515 and August 1516. The foundation church there was dedicated to the martyr St Cyriacus, and thus occasioned his early liturgical work on the office of St Cyriacus. His *Officium Sancti Cyriaci* shows that no later than 1515–16 he possessed the liturgical and musical training expected of his educational and vocational development. The liturgy of the martyr Cyriacus not only indicates Müntzer's early liturgical interest but also reflects his esteem for martyrdom that later became a characteristic of his piety. Discipleship to Christ leads to martyrdom. One of the favorite citations of Müntzer and his followers was Matthew 10: 24: "A disciple is not above his master." This was interpreted in light of John 15: 20: "A servant is not greater than his master. If they persecuted me, they will also persecute you" (Bubenheimer 1989: 94). The conviction that reform of the church will require martyrdom is the leitmotif of Müntzer's career.

Müntzer's religious development at this time is further suggested by a letter to him signed "in the passionate love of purity." There is a mystical element in this formula which seeks identification with Christ and his passion. The letter addresses Müntzer with the title "Persecutor of Injustice." This title seems to have a programmatic character but unfortunately the historical context is difficult to determine. Nevertheless, this formulation suggests that Müntzer critically confronted his environment, and that the establishment of "justice," whatever he may have meant by it, was integral to Müntzer's goals from the beginning. The concern for justice appears two years later in a request for Müntzer's opinion of indulgences in Braunschweig. Bubenheimer (1989: 96, 106) suggests that Müntzer's possible involvement in this pre-"Ninety-Five Theses" indulgence controversy indicates that his development as a critic of the church was not initially stimulated by Luther but rather has pre-Reformation roots.

Müntzer's Braunschweig circle of relatives and friends were not only interested in humanism; some were also involved in a kind of self-renunciation characteristic of early capitalists concerned that their worldly success would dull their hearing for the voice of God. Müntzer's demand for an ascetic structure of life developed in this social–economic context keyed to growth, expansion, and capital accumulation.

Müntzer remained bound not only biographically but also spiritually to those dedicated to his anti-feudal struggle. His close relationship to the circle of merchants is reflected in his *Highly Provoked Vindication*, where he rejects Luther's abuse of merchants expressed in the summer 1524 tract *Trade and Usury*. In this writing Luther sharply criticized early capitalist business practices as well as the international trade he saw developing from the Frankfurt Fair. According to Luther, the merchants, with few honorable exceptions, were equivalent to thieves in their tendency to maximize profit; and he recommended the worldly authorities restrain their usury. But according to Müntzer, the essential authors of usury, thievery, and robbery were the princes who oppressed the merchants. Müntzer held that Luther should rather preach judgment against the princes, who merited condemnation more than any others. Müntzer's partisanship and implicit courtship of the merchants has concrete biographical background in the fact that at the time he was having the *Highly Provoked Vindication* printed in Nuremberg he was in communication with Christoph Fürer, a participant in the leading Nuremberg mining society. Luther had totally rejected exactly such societies, which he perceived as monopolies.

Müntzer's support of merchant entrepreneurs against Luther conveys an important insight: his struggle since the fall of 1524 was against feudalism, against the "godless rulers." The urban population involved in early capitalist economic forms did not, after all, exclude the desire for an ascetic standard of living. Müntzer was certainly able to recognize forms of exploitation also in early capitalist entrepreneurship, but his Braunschweig relationships led him to seek a coalition rather than a confrontation with the economically leading urban class in the struggle against the feudal lords.

Müntzer's period of study in Wittenberg cannot be definitively attributed to a desire to become acquainted with Luther's theology, for it is not known whether he arrived there before or after the indulgence controversy. Furthermore, at this time in Wittenberg there was a complex mix of humanistic and theological studies from which the early Reformation theology had not yet been distilled. Certainly, however, Müntzer must have had some acquaintance at this time with Luther, Karlstadt, and Melanchthon, and he did later attend the Leipzig debate in 1519. While in Wittenberg for part of the winter semester of 1517–18, he attended lectures on St Jerome by the humanist Johannes Rhagius Aesticampanius. Müntzer's notes indicate he attended these lectures with the intention to pursue humanistic studies. It is evident that Rhagius' interest in rhetoric and the ethical education of his students with regard to an ascetic lifestyle, especially in the area of sexuality, intrigued Müntzer. The notes also indicate Müntzer's interest in St Jerome's emphasis upon having a teacher for the living voice as more effective than the written word. Müntzer was also influenced by the humanist emphasis upon travel not only as a way of increasing learning but as a pedagogy of suffering. This humanist form of monastic asceticism included celibacy and the lack of a fixed abode. Its phenomenological closeness to Müntzer's theology of suffering is evident, and may also be the source of his criticism of the Wittenberg advocacy of clerical marriage. For Müntzer, the only justification of sexual intercourse within marriage was the divine instruction for the generation of elect descendants (*CTM* 44–5).

Humanist influences came not just from his contemporaries such as Erasmus and Ficino, in particular the latter's edition of Plato, but also from the classics of the faith by the church fathers. He studied Jerome, Augustine, Cyprian, Eusebius, Tertullian, Cassiodorus, and Basil, among others. From Cyprian he got the notion of "nothing without the consent of the people" that later developed into the claim that the worldly authorities are dependent upon the decision of the people. From Eusebius, Müntzer imbibed the theme that the virgin church of the apostolic period had fallen. To Müntzer, the once pure church had become a whore and prostitute through the spiritual adultery introduced by self-serving scholars and faithless priests. Thus the laity, the common folk, must become the new priests. The community must be purified until it consists only of the elect separated from the godless (*CTM* 377–8).

In the spring of 1519 Müntzer visited Orlamünde for about a month, probably at the invitation of Karlstadt with whom Müntzer was now well acquainted. It was here that Müntzer immersed himself in the study of the medieval German mystic, Tauler, whose emphasis upon reception of the Holy Spirit in the abyss of the soul became fundamental to Müntzer's mature theology. It is also of interest that Müntzer's study of Tauler at this time took place with the Orlamünde parish cook, a simple pious woman. He may already have begun studying Tauler with Karlstadt in Wittenberg, but this study in Orlamünde again suggests Müntzer's orientation toward the wisdom of the unlearned over that of the "scribes."

Humanist rhetoric also provided Müntzer with the category of "the order of things" (*ordo rerum*) by which he structured his theology. This rhetorical concept with its emphasis upon the right relationship between "beginning" and "end" functioned in Müntzer's theology as a fundamental hermeneutical category. It comprehends rhetorically a revelation process from the immanent order of creation to the structure of the Creator's speech. The knowledge of God is not teachable, it may be conferred only in connection with a spirit-worked faith saturated with experience. The catastrophic inability of the church to mediate this spiritual renewal is related to its loss of the right "order of things" in God and in all creatures. Thus Müntzer called for reversal from the traditional movement from the external order to the internal order. The living Word of God must be heard from God's own mouth and not from books, even the Bible. The mystical tradition as well as the humanist expressions of neoplatonism served his effort to express the priority of an inner-oriented hearing by humankind that will lead persons to turn from their bondage to creatures to the process of divinization in God.

Theologically, God's living spoken Word of creation is present in every period, and the creation is analogous to a rhetorical construction. Holy Scripture is thus a historically limited precipitate of this revelation process, a "part" of the "whole" revelation. Beyond Scripture there are other realms of divine revelation: the living speech of God, nature, and history. Theologians who limit revelation to Scripture are nothing but scribes.

The particularity of Müntzer's reception of ancient rhetoric can be more sharply seen by a comparison to Luther, who also was influenced by the humanist recovery of classical rhetoric. For Luther, however, the role of rhetoric is to serve the text as a philological tool, as an exegetical aid to understanding the language of the Bible. For Müntzer the import of rhetoric goes beyond its function as an aide to exegesis. Sharply put, Luther is interested in an exegetical–hermeneutical sense mainly for the "order of the words" (*ordo verborum*) of the interpreted texts, whereas Müntzer's concern is the systematic–hermeneutical sense of the "order of things" (*ordo rerum*). This finds in the *ordo verborum* of the written text of the Bible only *an* expression next to which the actual address of the living God is to be heard in the here and now. Once again, for Müntzer, the Holy Scripture is a prominent but historically limited expression of the process of revelation, one part of the whole of revelation.

Müntzer's Historical Development

In May of 1520 Müntzer was called to stand in for Johannes Egranus, the preacher of St Mary's, the most important church in Zwickau. Zwickau was a thriving town of about 7,500 inhabitants whose work in textiles and mining created wealthy patricians, merchants, and artisans. Elector Frederick called Zwickau the "pearl" of Saxony. The prosperity of the city supported numerous institutions including eight churches, six chapels, a large Franciscan cloister, and Carthusian, Dominican, and Beguine communities as well as numerous religious brotherhoods. This prosperity however brought in its wake new social tensions as the merchants and manufacturers broke the power of the guilds and markedly increased the economic and social gap between themselves and the lower ranks of citizens. The city council gravitated toward the wealthy and distanced itself from traditional communal principles, thus alienating the "common man" of the city. By the time of Müntzer's arrival there were also increasing ecclesiastical conflicts and anticlerical anger, especially among the lower ranks. In 1516 the weavers' guild challenged the rule of the magistrates and in 1521 was the locus of support for Müntzer.

Müntzer no sooner arrived than he leaped into the social fray with vehement sermons against the Franciscans for their exploitation of the poor. He not only rang the changes on the customary themes of anticlericalism (clerical and monastic avarice, hypocrisy, external ritualism instead of preaching the gospel), but spiced his message with *bon mots* such as that you could cut a pound of flesh from the mouths of the monks and they would still have too much mouth.

The Franciscans were not amused. The monks not only denounced Müntzer to the bishop of Naumberg and the Franciscan Provincial but took to the streets to foment the citizens against him. The town council asked him to seek Luther's advice, for it was Luther who had recommended him to the town. In his letter to Luther, Müntzer reviews the charges against him and appeals for Luther's support and advice: "You are my advocate in the Lord Jesus. I beg you not to lend your ears to those who are defaming me. . . . It is not my work I am doing, but that of the Lord." He refers to Luther as the one who "brought [him] to birth by the gospel" and as a "model and beacon to the friends of God" (*CTM* 18–22). Müntzer's strong identification of himself with the will of God continues throughout his ministry; his deference to Luther soon ceased.

The town council was obviously not too disturbed by events, for upon the return of Egranus, Müntzer was provided the preaching position at St Catherine's. But a bitter controversy soon arose between Egranus and Müntzer. Egranus was more interested in humanistic studies than in theology and pastoral care; Luther described him as "a man most unlearned in theological matters." Müntzer attacked Egranus for his lack of commitment, and advanced in contrast his conviction that it is not the learned but the experienced in faith who are saved. By experience in faith Müntzer meant being led by God through despair and suffering to true experiential faith formed and filled by the Holy Spirit. In terms of the history of theology this debate foreshadows the debate between Luther and Erasmus over freedom of the will, and the later development of the hermeneutic of experience in both Pietism and Protestant liberalism. Müntzer's emphasis on the suffering experience of God found a positive reception among the poor weavers and day laborers of St Catherine's whose piety related to their socio-economic conditions. This piety perceived material and spiritual suffering as the precondition to faith, and spoke of the mystical illumination of unlearned laity. Among these parishioners was Nicholas Storch, one of the Zwickau prophets who contributed to the unrest in Wittenberg in early 1522.

Müntzer continued to preach against Egranus and, more forcefully, those priests and monks who still adhered to Catholicism. Anticlerical actions similar to those that took place in Wittenberg and elsewhere began to occur. In return Müntzer himself began to receive abuse, and public disorder on a major scale appeared more and more likely. On 16 April 1521, the very day Luther was entering Worms to face the emperor, Müntzer was dismissed by the council from his office. A large group of armed weavers came to his defense, but 50 of them were promptly arrested. Müntzer later claimed he did not engineer this uprising because he was taking a bath at the time. That night he fled the town.

On to the Land of Hus

From Zwickau, Müntzer made his way to Prague, where he would stay until December of 1521. In his self-perception, the experience in Zwickau did not undermine but rather confirmed his theology of experiential suffering. He wrote to Nicholas Hausmann, the preacher called to Zwickau to continue the reform along moderate lines: "I desire nothing else but my own persecution, so that all may profit and be converted through me" (*CTM* 35). With Müntzer and soon also with the Anabaptists who professed that the true church is always a persecuted church, the authorities, both Protestant and Catholic, were confronted by a seemingly intractable problem: toleration allowed such perceived heresy to spread, and persecution confirmed and stimulated it. For Müntzer the travail of the last days had begun and persecution was necessary for credible preaching.

It appeared that Prague "was to be Müntzer's Jerusalem" (*CTM* 352). He seems to have gone there as much in the expectation of martyrdom as in hope of a favorable reception. He may have recalled Luther's words at the Leipzig debate that all true Christians are Hussites. At any rate, even though he continued to present himself as a follower of Luther, the so-called *Prague Manifesto* of November broke with him.

After an initially warm welcome by many Bohemians who apparently thought Müntzer was representing the Wittenberg reform movement, the reception became increasingly chilly in response to his inflammatory sermons. The *Prague Manifesto* was Müntzer's tirade against the godless clergy who had seduced the people and blocked reform. The Bohemians, he asserted, are not called to a human, created theology but rather to a direct living Word of God from God's own mouth:

> At no time in my life (God knows I am not lying) did I learn anything about the true exercise of the faith from any monk or priest, or about the edifying time of trial which clarifies faith in the spirit of the fear of God, showing the need for an elect man to have the seven-fold gift of the holy spirit. I have not heard from a single scholar about the order of God implanted in all creatures, not the tiniest word about it; while as to understanding the whole as a unity of all the parts those who claim to be Christians have not caught the least whiff of it – least of all the accursed priests . . . For anyone who does not feel the spirit of Christ within him, or is not quite sure of having it, is not a member of Christ, but of the devil. (*CTM* 357–8)

Müntzer concluded by proclaiming that God would create the new church right here in Bohemia, and it would be "a mirror for the whole world." He called on the Bohemians to help defend God's word and claimed that if they did not they would be overrun by the Turks in the coming year.

The theological difference between Müntzer and Luther was becoming clear. *Sola scriptura* is displaced by *sola experientia*. Scriptural faith is a dead faith which worships a mute God. The God who speaks is the God who is experienced directly in the heart. In a letter to Melanchthon dated 29 March 1522, Müntzer wrote: "What I disapprove of is this: that it is a dumb God whom you adore . . . Man does not live by bread alone but by every word which proceeds from the mouth of God; note that it proceeds from the mouth of God and not from books." Müntzer concludes that Luther's "Invocavit Sermons" were a mistake: "Our brother Martin acts ignorantly because he does not want to offend the little ones . . . But the tribulation of Christians is already at the door; why you should consider that it is still to come, I do not know" (*CTM* 43–6).

By early December it appears that Müntzer was under some sort of house arrest; shortly thereafter he was expelled from Prague. The following months were for him a time of wandering through Germany. By this time his friends the Zwickau prophets had left their mark on Wittenberg, and his acquaintances in Wittenberg were leery of giving him much support. Karlstadt had written a somewhat curious letter to him in December that expressed both hesitation and a willingness to help him find a new post. He is pleased by Müntzer's "zeal to climb into the abyss of the divine will" but cautions him to "come alone" to visit him. "Then I can say the things which I am unwilling to commit to writing." Karlstadt ends with a reference that suggests his own Spiritualism: "God is the master of my heart; I have learnt his power and his strong hand by experience. Hence I have said more about visions and dreams than any of the professors" (*CTM* 52–3).

The misery of Müntzer's exile ended when he obtained the post of preacher in the parish church of St John in Allstedt in Electoral Saxony. It is not clear how he obtained this post, but the town council acted on its own authority and bypassed the elector who had sole authority to award it. "With a sleep-walker's certainty he had found his way to the one town which unlike any other was to give him the opportunity to reflect once more upon his reform programme and put it step-by-step into practice" (Goertz 1993b: 97–8).

"The Prophet of Allstedt" was incredibly busy. He developed the first thoroughgoing liturgical experiments in Saxony. "Not only was he among the creative pioneers, but his stresses . . . were strikingly modern, and not least in his emphasis on worship as the common action of the whole People of God" (Rupp 1969: 305). He translated Psalms into the vernacular and wrote hymns. Between his new liturgy and his preaching Müntzer began attracting crowds, large enough to disturb the nearby Count Ernest of Mansfeld. The count's attempt to prohibit his subjects from listening to Müntzer aroused the preacher's wrath to such a degree that he challenged the count to bring the bishop and theologians to test his teaching. This request was fulfilled a year later. In the meantime Müntzer's tongue and pen remained active. In his tract *Of False Faith* he emphasized the necessity of the true faith that experiences suffering and the "bitter Christ." In his *Protestation or Defence of Thomas Müntzer* and in his *Exposition of Psalm Nineteen* he made it clear that the Wittenberg theology of justification by faith alone was an "invented doctrine." Christ had come to fulfill the law, and the sinner is to be converted to God's willing instrument to do likewise. Müntzer was now referring to himself as the hammer and the sickle of God against the godless. He proceeded to put his views into action by organizing a secret military league which on 24 March 1524 destroyed the small Mallerbach chapel just outside the town.

The subsequent investigation of this incident by Duke John, the elector's brother, was indecisive. For, while insisting on the punishment of the guilty, both Frederick and John also heeded Luther's underestimation of Müntzer's influence. Luther did not "perceive any particular fruit of the Allstedt spirit [Müntzer] except that he wants to do violence and destroy wood and stone; love, peace, patience,

goodness, gentleness, have been very little in evidence so far."
However, Luther still thought that this was a battle of the Word, not
princely force, and was convinced that "the Antichrist shall be
vanquished without human hand" (*LW* 40: 56–8).

Duke John decided to visit Allstedt to find out for himself about
Müntzer. This is the context for the famous "Princes' Sermon" (13 July
1524). Preaching to Duke John and his advisors in the electoral
castle near Allstedt, Müntzer used King Nebuchadnezzar just as
Karlstadt had used King Josiah as a model for the conduct of rulers. As
Nebuchadnezzar made Daniel his advisor, so the Saxon princes should
place him, Müntzer, in charge of ushering in the new order. "Therefore
a new Daniel must arise and expound your dreams to you and . . . he
must be in the vanguard, leading the way" (*CTM* 246). In his appeal to
the rulers, Müntzer remained within the classic framework of civil
obedience in requesting protection and support. But his unique twist
was to focus on verse 4 of Romans 13 (the ruler "is the servant of God
to execute his wrath on the wrongdoer"). In contrast, Luther focused
on verse 1 ("Let every person be subject to the governing authorities.
For there is no authority except from God"), a classic text of all
magisterial Reformers. Müntzer preached:

> Do not, therefore, allow the evil-doers, who turn us away from God, to
> continue living, Deut. 13, for a godless man has no right to live if he is
> hindering the pious. . . . I suspect, though, that our scholars will reprove
> me at this point by referring to the clemency of Christ, which they drag
> in to cover their hypocrisy. . . . But our scholars come and – in their
> godless, fraudulent way – understand Daniel to say that the Antichrist
> should be destroyed without human hands. . . . To ensure, however,
> that this now proceeds in a fair and orderly manner, our revered fathers,
> the princes, who with us confess Christ, should carry it out. But if they
> do not carry it out the sword will be taken from them. . . . For the
> godless have no right to live, unless by the sufferance of the elect. (*CTM*
> 248–51).

For Müntzer, revelation is the source for a revolutionary transformation of society. "With this sermon Müntzer destroyed all 'customary
conceptions' and exploded the 'oral and legal systems of his time', and
moreover proclaimed a religiously motivated right of intervention
against the Old Church regimes, 'which clashed with the rule of law
and the laws of public peace'. Müntzer had demanded that his princes
adopt a revolutionary standpoint" (Goertz 1993b: 129).

There is no evidence of this remarkable sermon's immediate effect
upon the princes, but it was not long before Müntzer and some of his

followers were summoned to Weimar. Within a week of his return, Müntzer fled Allstedt. It was clear to him that Luther's "false faith" promoted and supported princely tyranny. To Müntzer, Luther was a preacher of a "honey-sweet Christ" who called for belief without works. This "cheap grace" avoids the "bitter Christ" and the disciple-ship of the cross (*CTM* 191, 200–1). Müntzer was now in his final stage of development. His desire to christianize the world, to realize the medieval aspiration of a *corpus Christianum* with a vengeance, had led him to become a "Reformer without a church." In August he secretly left Allstedt.

Luther's conviction that Müntzer's preaching would ultimately lead to violence is clear in his vigorous call to the princes in the July 1524 *Letter to the Princes of Saxony Concerning the Rebellious Spirit* to intervene at the first sign of violence. Appealing to Romans 13: 4, Luther reminds the princes that their duty is to maintain order, prevent rebellion, and preserve the peace. This is the civil responsibility of the secular authorities; they are not to enforce doctrine.

> As far as doctrine is concerned, time will tell. For the present, your Graces ought not to stand in the way of the ministry of the Word. Let them preach as confidently and boldly as they are able and against whomever they wish. . . . But when they want to do more than fight with the Word, and begin to destroy and use force, then your Graces must intervene, whether it be ourselves or they who are guilty, and banish them from the country. You can say, "We are willing to endure and permit you to fight with the Word, in order that true doctrine may prevail. But don't use your fist, for that is our business, else get yourselves out of the country." For we who are engaged in the ministry of the Word are not allowed to use force. (*LW* 40: 57)

Müntzer reacted to this with his *Vindication and Refutation*, in which he vented his rage against Luther. Luther has entered an unholy, self-serving alliance with princes and with them tyrannizes the people. Luther and his followers are nothing but Pharisees who preach for money, love the soft life, and refuse to live out the law of God. They support princely oppression but demand punishment of the poor who commit the pettiest crime. "There is no greater abomination on earth than the fact that no one is prepared to take up the cause of the needy. The great do whatever they please . . . And Doctor Liar responds, Amen. It is the lords themselves who make the poor man their enemy. If they refuse to do away with the causes of insurrection how can trouble be avoided in the long run? If saying that makes me an inciter to insurrection, so be it!" He concludes that Luther has "strengthened the power of the godless evil-doers, so that they could continue in their old way. Therefore your fate will be that of the fox that has been hunted down; the people will go free and God alone will be their Lord" (*CTM* 335, 350). The coarseness and rage in this tract can only be appreciated by a full reading, but what is of interest here is Müntzer's sense of how theology could be used to legitimate the status quo. With this sense of "ideology critique" Müntzer is passing out of the circle of the magisterial Reformers and into that of social revolutionaries. The rule of God must be instituted on earth!

Müntzer next attempted to join with Heinrich Pfeiffer in initiating radical reform in Mühlhausen, but both had to flee. Müntzer went to Nuremberg and then on into the Black Forest region at the beginning of the peasant revolts, where he may have influenced some of their writings as well as Balthasar Hubmaier. As the rebellion spread northward Müntzer returned to Mühlhausen and participated with a new council in organizing for the great confrontation he foresaw between the children of light and the children of darkness. The "Eternal Covenant" drawn up in Mühlhausen was no longer the defensive alliance of Allstedt but an offensive alliance against the godless, an active instrument for the coming great judgment. Müntzer now believed that the common man everywhere has received the truth. The sword is to be taken from the godless rulers, for their tyranny has prevented the people from learning the will of God. "All evil-doers who, although members of the Christian community, perpetuate the original transgression of Adam must, as Paul says, be justified by the law, so that the godless Christians who resist the wholesome teaching of Christ can be swept out of the way by the sternness of the father, and so that the just can have time and space to learn the will of God" (*CTM* 336).

The Peasants' War would have occurred without Müntzer, but it did provide him with what he saw as the context for the coming separation of the elect and the godless. It was the eschatological sign, the *kairos*. In his famous appeal (ca. 26 April 1525) to his old disciples at Allstedt he relayed news of the rebellion's progress and exhorted them to action:

> At Fulda four abbeys were laid waste during Easter week, the peasants in the Klettgau and the Hegau in the Black Forest have risen, three thousand strong, and the size of the peasant host is growing all the time . . . Go to it, go to it, go to it! Show no pity . . . Pay no attention to the cries of the godless . . . Alert the villages and towns and especially the mineworkers and other good fellows who will be of use. We cannot slumber any longer . . . Go to it, go to it, while the fire is hot! Don't let

your sword grow cold, don't let it hang down limply! Hammer away ding-dong on the anvils of Nimrod [the princes], cast their tower to the ground! As long as they live it is impossible for you to rid yourselves of the fear of men. One cannot say anything to you about God as long as they rule over you. Go to it, go to it, while it is day! God goes before you; follow, follow! (*CTM* 141–2)

He signed the letter: "Thomas Müntzer, a servant of God against the godless."

The tocsin was sounded, and Müntzer provided the faithful with a flag to march under: a rainbow, symbol of God's covenant after the flood, stood forth on a white field with the motto, "May the word of God last eternally." On 12 May 1525 Müntzer and his troops joined the peasant force of about 7,000 in Frankenhausen which had already taken control of a large area. Here Müntzer had his moment in the sun. He claimed leadership and proclaimed that God was on their side and hence no one could prevail against them. Müntzer filled all roles, including that of judge in conferring the death penalty upon three prisoners.

But this was a fleeting moment of glory, for within days a combined force of Hessian and Saxon troops were confronting the rebels. As the princes' forces encircled the town and drew ever closer, opinion in the camp divided over whether to negotiate. While the peasants conferred over the princes' demand that Müntzer and his followers be surrendered, he continued to preach that God would come to their aid. Then – in a scene any Hollywood special effects crew would envy – a halo appeared around the sun similar to the rainbow symbol of the alliance. Müntzer himself could not have wished for a better omen. Infused with this sign of victory, the peasants looked up to find the armies of the princes upon them. In the horrible slaughter that ensued over 6,000 rebels were killed; the armies of the princes lost six men. So much for omens!

Müntzer fled to an attic in the town where, when discovered, he feigned a disguise and illness. But the soldiers identified him by the correspondence he had with him. In the next days he was interrogated rigorously and tortured. His *Confession* and his letter to Mühlhausen had to be dictated because torture impaired his ability to write. Müntzer was taken back to Mühlhausen, which had surrendered on 25 May without a fight. There he and Pfeiffer were executed by the sword, and their impaled heads and bodies displayed as a warning for all to see.

In light of later portrayals of Müntzer as a forerunner of the revolution of the proletariat it is important to note that his goals were not identical to those of the peasants. Oppression and social misery were to be combated from Müntzer's point of view because they hindered the common man from reading the Bible and coming to faith. Müntzer also was not looking for a better day – the *Besserung* ("improvement") in the title of Luther's address to the German nobility – but rather for the end of all days. His theology is not the ideology of a social revolutionary in the Marxist sense. Although he confessed at his trial that everything was to be ordered according to the maxim that "all things are to be held in common" (*omnia sunt communia*: *CTM* 437), that statement was extracted under torture. It does accord with his biblical or spiritual utopianism, but "it was more than questionable whether the peasants would follow their preacher in this direction" (Goertz 1993b: 184). Furthermore, Müntzer used the terms "poor" and "needy" in a spiritual rather than a material, social sense. As Müntzer himself was to realize, the bread which interested the peasants was not that of the Word of God. After the defeat at Frankenhausen he realized that the people had not understood him properly; "they sought only their own interests and the divine truth was defeated as a result" (*CTM* 160). Müntzer had not been able to free the revolutionaries from their creatureliness and to form them spiritually for their battle against the godless. It turned out that there were unbelievers not only among the rulers but also among the ruled. But an unbeliever, whatever his social standing, is not fit to fight the great battle of God.

We are reminded once again how the early years of the Reformation were marked by proliferating division among the Reformers and their followers. To a great extent this was due to the breakdown of the medieval synthesis, the *corpus Christianum*. This is not to imply that all medieval people were faithful Christians or that prior to 1517 conflict between state and church was unknown. It does mean that the social order, the major institutions and their political structures, could no longer be explained and justified by the traditional religious legitimation. Müntzer's response was to re-establish religious legitimation of social order in light of his convictions about the "order of creation" (*ordo rerum*). For him, society is only possible when governed and populated by the elect. As he had said in the "Princes' Sermon," the godless have no right to live except as the elect wish to grant it to them. By no means did Müntzer intend to spiritualize this analysis and retreat into a community withdrawn from the larger world. Rather, he intended to legitimate society by patterning it after his understanding of the kingdom of God. In this he is a medieval not a modern; he attempted to go back – albeit with a vengeance – to the medieval sense of the universal Christian community. He was "not able to break through and overcome the medieval conception of the *corpus Christianum*" but only to intensify it. "He is the trustee of the old, not a herald of the new" (Goertz 1967: 149).

The Revolution of the Common Man, 1524–1526

The German Peasants' War, the traditional label for the upheavals of 1524–6, was, to echo Voltaire's judgment about the Holy Roman Empire, none of these things. Recent scholarship has shown these events encompassed far more than Germany, included more levels of society than the peasants, and originated long before the Reformation began. It was not just peasants in the literal sense who were involved but rather, to use the term current in sixteenth-century sources, the "common man." The common man was always the person subject to the noble and ecclesiastical lords. It was the politically powerless – the peasant, the miner, townsfolk without voice and vote – who were the "common man."

Before examining the interpretive questions of the relationship of the Reformation to the Revolution of the Common Man, for which I shall use the shorthand of Peasants' War, a brief review of its origins and progress is in order.

For over two centuries prior to the Reformation social unrest and the agitation for a better life on the part of the so-called "simple folk" or "common man" found expression in rebellions in Italy (1304–7), Flanders (1323–8), France (1356), England (1381), Bohemia (1419–34), northern Spain (1437), and Hungary (1514). The line of conflict beginning with Wyclif in England stretched through the Hussite movement in Bohemia and began to focus in the German areas with the religiously motivated anticlericalism of Hans Böheim of Niklashausen in the Tauber valley. The movement started in 1476 by this lay preacher, who as a shepherd and musician is known as "the Piper of Niklashausen," was put down by the bishop of Würzburg. In his two years of activity, however, he attracted adherents from all over south Germany.

Within two decades the *Bundschuh* movement, so-called because its logo was the peasant shoe with its long laces that symbolized peasant solidarity, arose in the area of Alsace. The uprisings at Slestat in 1493 and elsewhere later in the upper Rhine valley failed, but its leader, Joss Fritz, survived to reappear in the Black Forest rebellion in 1524. Fritz provided religious legitimation to these rebellions against economic and social oppression by his appeal to "godly law." The "Poor Conrad" revolt of 1514 in Württemberg, east of the Black Forest, was similarly crushed by the authorities. These and other lesser rebellions throughout south Germany up to 1517 were characterized by participation of urban commoners as well as rural peasants and by the religious principle of godly law as justification for the revolts. Also, these "simple folk" were not so simple, for they published a number of pamphlets which expressed their demands for reform of church and state, often couched in apocalyptic language that forecast disaster if reform did not occur.

The great rebellion associated with the Reformation began in Stühlingen, northwest of Schaffhausen. Here there was the added stimulus of the Zwinglian Reformation centered on Zurich (see Chapter 7). Zurich, the first city in Switzerland and the south German area to institutionalize the Reformation, vigorously promoted the reform of society on the basis of Scripture. "Indeed, the evangelical preachers who spread Zwinglian ideas in the countryside aroused expectations among the peasantry that acceptance of the Word of God would lead to a just redress of their secular grievances. The thoroughness of Zwinglian religious reform . . . easily provoked its adherents to direct action" (Scott and Scribner 1993: 24).

The rebels, led by a mercenary soldier, Hans Müller of Bulgenbach, formed an alliance with the town of Waldshut, whose radical preacher, Balthasar Hubmaier, will be discussed later. At the same time the peasants around Nuremberg emphasized their refusal to pay their tithes by burning the tithe grain in the fields. By the fall of 1524 rebellions were breaking out all around Lake Constance; by winter there were rent strikes throughout the area between the Rhine and the Danube. As the rebels widened their grievances beyond specific abuses to the feudal order itself, the slogan of the godly law was effectively utilized throughout the Black Forest area, given added bite by Thomas Müntzer's presence there in the winter months.

The Swabian League, the great alliance of south Germany, would normally have been able to proceed at once against these rebellions, but at this time suffered a scarcity of troops because of Charles V's Italian campaign against Francis I of France. With the defeat and capture of Francis at the battle of Pavia on 24 February 1525 this situation changed.

The main phase of the revolution occurred between February and May 1525 in south and central Germany. As already suggested by Müntzer's letters cited above, the forces of "the common man" were not limited to peasants but also included miners, townsmen, and some nobles. What did limit their forces, however, was the tendency of the rebellion to be fragmented into local configurations. This was true both militarily and geographically. Militarily the rebel armies were divided into companies varying from 2,000 to up to 15,000 men. Each company consisted of men from a particular locale, a town or a district, normally headed by a local man, and the company organization reflected that of the *Landsknechte* (German mercenary infantry) armies of the time. These rebel armies were well organized and in some cases even better armed with cannon than their opposition. Their failure was not due to lack of weapons and martial ineptitude – though, to be sure, peasant prowess was not a match for the skill of a *Landsknecht* – but to social and strategic reasons. The contingents operated in a rotation system, so that peasants could return to work their farms and miners could return to produce silver to hire mercenaries. Under these conditions individuals were unable to gain much military experience. Strategically, the rebels were deficient in both experienced artillerymen and cavalry; the latter partly by intent because under the rubric of social equality all should be foot soldiers. The social model of equality within the contingents was also a deficit when it led to stalemates between radicals and moderates over the course of action. In the few cases when the rebels did score major military successes over the nobles they did not press their advantage by going beyond their own territory. In contrast to the nobles' transregional lines of communication which enabled their cooperative use of resources against the rebels, the rebels did not establish a solidarity of purpose or a single fighting force beyond their own traditional locales. The professionalization of war put "weekend soldiers" at a severe disadvantage.

The Role of Anticlericalism

The question remains: What was the connection between "the most significant revolutionary mass movement of the Geman people until the November Revolution of 1918" (Scribner and Benecke 1979: 9) and the Reformation? This has long been a controversial historiographical question, most recently debated between those, in particular but not solely Marxist historians, who propound socio–economic causes for the rebellion, and those who maintain the significance of religious values and ideas on the rebels. But monocausal explanations are suspect; the impulses for revolutions do not arise from empty stomachs alone nor from full heads alone, but from their union. The socio–economic grievances of the common folk were rife before the Reformation; they were also more complex than usually portrayed. There was, to be sure, widespread resentment against the imposition of new regulations and the curtailment of old rights. But the rebellion was also fueled by the frustration of the rising expectations of ambitious lords and prosperous peasants pinched between ecclesiastical and secular princes above and the growing mass of rural poor below. "The essential elements which the social scientists have taught us to expect in an insurrection are here: confidence, hope, 'rising expectations', confronted by formidable threats to those expectations" (Scribner and Benecke 1979: 37).

Heiko Oberman (1986: 172, 153) argues that this impulse for reform, which he calls the "Gospel of Social Unrest," was radicalized by the Reformation concepts of freedom and the priesthood of all believers. "In its initial thrust and program, the so-called Peasants' War for both its moderate critics and its radical leaders is basically a religious movement." With the rise of the Reformation as a popular movement, the common man saw the removal of oppression and misery as integral to salvation and blessedness. However, the powerful impetus for this removal was not primarily the doctrine of justification by grace alone but rather the sharpened anticlerical focus provided by the concepts of Christian freedom and the priesthood of all believers, "slogans that electrified and mobilized the peasants everywhere."

It has long been a historical commonplace to posit that lay antagonism towards clerical corruption on the eve of the Reformation was so volatile that all that was needed to explode the medieval church was the spark of Luther's theses against indulgences. To be sure, there was, if you will, widespread cognitive dissonance in the late medieval period concerning the gap between clerical ideal and clerical reality. And there was no lack of criticism of the clergy, which, like the appeal to the "old law," was intended to bring about conformity between priestly ideal and praxis. Recent studies (e.g. Goertz 1987) however have persuasively argued that the Reformation cannot be explained simply in terms of a theological response to medieval anticlericalism. Rather, the anticlericalism of the Reformation was not merely occasional criticism and the effort to remove various abuses but a sustained violent attack upon the clerical estate itself that permeated the whole social atmosphere. This was a fight against the clerical estate which intended, in the words of Goertz (1987: 260), "to break off the top of the medieval pyramid of estates."

Anticlericalism, then, was intimately related to social issues and the very structure of society. The antagonism to church and clergy had to do with oppressive financial burdens such as tithes and rents on peasant land, economic competition to tradesmen from the cloisters, clerical resistance to taxation and civic responsibilities, and the drain of German money into the coffers of Rome. These legal and economic aspects

Figure 6.1 "Ständebaum," ca. 1520. This woodcut by an unknown Augsburg artist on the eve of the Peasants' War reverses the traditional understanding of estates or social class relations. Here the oppressed peasants are presented as both the foundation, the "roots," and the crown of society. All the social estates rest upon the nourishing work of the peasants. The nobility of their work also places them above citizens, doctors, princes, kings, and even the pope. Note how the peasant with his manure fork rests his foot on the crown of the emperor while his companion playing the bagpipe stands on the shoulder of the pope. *Source*: Private collection.

were intertwined with moral–religious ones because people encountered the clergy and their fees in every aspect of life from the cradle to the grave. The explosive power of anticlericalism was due to the fact that it was a critique of society as a whole, not just of the clergy. That is, in the mind of the common man the clergy represented all the oppressive elements of the whole society.

The value of the concept of anticlericalism for historical interpretation is that it provides a wide bed for the various reforming streams (magisterial, radical, urban, communal) flowing toward the revolution of 1525. There are scholars, however, who are dubious about the suitability of the phenomenon of anticlericalism for explaining the Reformation. Their concern is that from this perspective the Reformation would be reduced to simple social history. They also argue that the early Reformation was more nuanced than those who advance the anticlericalism argument acknowledge, and also that an anticlerical desire to abolish the clergy was not part of Luther's early theology. There is, however, agreement that Goertz's (1987) argument for the pivotal role of anticlericalism in the course of the early Reformation does offer an important key to an understanding of the volatile growth of the Reformation after the posting of Luther's theses.

Luther and the Peasants' War

In freeing the Word of God from captivity to the church, Luther also freed words from captivity to the elite. The rapid growth of evangelical preaching by laity as well as by converted priests and theologians testifies to the power of Luther's emphasis upon the Bible and the priesthood of all believers. Of course, Luther soon discovered to his dismay that not everyone read the Bible the way he did. We have seen his conflicts with Karlstadt and Müntzer; now Luther would be in conflict with the tracts of the common man. All parties understood that control of the word was vital. This was because religious discourse in the sixteenth century was not the private affair it became in our time but rather directly addressed the socio-political situation. "We may distinguish, on an analytical basis, between the problems of salvation and those of society, but they were bound together by more than rational deduction because religion served as the general reference for social discourse" (Rublack 1988: 105). From the point of view of the common man the arguments and claims of the Reformation had clear economic, social, and political relevance. Concerns of the common man were unmistakably bound up with the arguments and elements of the Reformation. As Blickle (1981: 156), points out,

economic relief, justice, legal order, and political order were inseparable from the common good, Christian brotherly love, and reliance on
the community.

These slogans and ideals were published in numerous pamphlets, the
best known of which was *The Twelve Articles: The Just and Fundamental
Articles of all the Peasantry and Tenants of Spiritual and Temporal Powers by
Whom They Think Themselves Oppressed* (late February or early March
1525). *The Twelve Articles* was written by Sebastian Lotzer, a tanner
and lay reformer, and Christoph Schappeler, the evangelical pastor of
St Martin's church in the imperial city of Memmingen. The authors
abstracted and summarized the various lists of peasant grievances and
supported them with biblical citations. *The Twelve Articles*, the manifesto of the Upper Swabian peasants, provided the ideology that
informed the revolution of 1525. Within two months there were 25
editions, whose some 25,000 copies blanketed the Empire. One's
allegiance to the cause was sealed by an oath to uphold the articles.

The Twelve Articles is a remarkably moderate document that clearly
evidences the evangelical influence on the movement. It begins by
rejecting the charge that the gospel causes revolution and claims the
Christian justice of the rebellion. To desire the gospel is not revolutionary. In a series of bold rhetorical questions, the authors associate the
gospel and God's justice with the peasants' cause: "For if God deigns to
hear the peasants' earnest plea that they be permitted to live according
to his Word, who will dare deny his will? . . . Did he not hear the
children of Israel crying to him and deliver them out of Pharoah's hand?
And can he not save his own today as well? Yes, he will save them, and
soon!"

Addressed to the "Christian reader," the articles present such themes
as the godly people wanting only their legitimate rights as community
authority to choose, appoint, and, if necessary, depose their pastor;
proper and biblically regulated taxation; abolition of serfdom; common
access to game and fish; free firewood and lumber from the forests;
release from excessive services; cessation of oppression by the lords;
equitable rents; return to the old laws of custom in place of the new
imposition of Roman law; the return of the meadows and fields which
once belonged to the community; and the abolition of the death tax that
oppresses widows and orphans. A list of acceptable judges which
included Luther and Melanchthon but not Karlstadt and Müntzer was
appended.

Luther received the *Twelve Articles* about mid–April and replied with
his *Admonition to Peace: A Reply to the Twelve Articles of the Peasants in
Swabia* (printed 6 May). In three sections Luther addressed the rulers,

the peasants, and then all parties "in a friendly and Christian spirit, as a duty of brotherly love," but also without mincing words. He first called upon the ecclesiastical and secular rulers to amend their ways before a rebellion arose that would destroy all Germany. He excoriated the authorities, lay and ecclesiastical, whose hard hearts have created the conditions for rebellion. Their self-serving oppression of the powerless is no longer bearable. "The sword is already at your throats, but you think you sit so firm in the saddle that no one can unhorse you. This false security and stubborn perversity will break your necks, as you will discover . . . Well, then, since you are the cause of this wrath of God, it will undoubtedly come upon you, unless you mend your ways in time" (*LW* 46: 19).

Luther went on to blame "murder-prophets," that is, those like Müntzer who were preaching religious revolution, and to exonerate the gospel and his own teaching from responsibility for the rebellion. The articles requesting the right to hear the gospel cannot be rejected, he claims, and those articles which protest economic injustice are right, for rulers are to be concerned for the welfare not the exploitation of their subjects. Thus, Luther exhorts the rulers to "try kindness" and negotiate.

The peasants, on the other hand, are warned of the many false prophets in the land. Certainly many of their demands are just; but that does not justify taking up the sword. Since the Wittenberg disturbances, Luther had consistently opposed the defense or promulgation of the gospel by force, because that changes the gospel into a new law and makes mandatory what is free. Furthermore, Luther also consistently denied the right of revolt, which he believed would always makes things worse and bring suffering to the innocent. (Contemporary accounts estimate 100,000 peasants were killed in the war.) Luther held firmly to the legal principle that no one may judge his own case, and that therefore to take justice into one's own hands would lead to the breakdown of all established law. Hence Luther rebuked the peasants for associating their cause with the gospel: "Stop claiming that you have the Christian law on your side." The peasants should be clear, he argued, that they are fighting for justice on the basis of natural law not on the basis of the gospel. "You should use that name, and let the name of Christ alone, for that is the kind of works that you are doing" (*LW* 46: 31–2). Finally, Luther advised both sides to settle their dispute peacefully through negotiations lest they end up destroying themselves.

Unfortunately, by the time Luther had composed this tract events had far outrun any contribution it might have made to the situation.

The unrest spread in the Thuringian area, and Luther encountered it at first hand during a preaching tour during which he was heckled and interrupted. By now numerous castles and monasteries had been destroyed, Erfurt and other towns had surrendered, and reports of atrocities were being conveyed to Luther. This was the context for the infamous exhortation in his tract *Against the Robbing and Murdering Hordes of Peasants* to "smite, slay, and stab" the rebellious. The rulers may slay the peasants in good conscience, for the upholding of social order is a divine mandate.

> For rebellion is not just simple murder; it is like a great fire, which attacks and devastates a whole land. Thus rebellion brings with it a land filled with murder and bloodshed; it makes widows and orphans, and turns everything upside down, like the worst disaster. Therefore let everyone who can, smite, slay, and stab, secretly or openly, remembering that nothing can be more poisonous, hurtful, or devilish than a rebel. It is just as when one must kill a mad dog; if you do not strike him, he will strike you, and a whole land with you. (*LW* 46: 50).

Not a few among the common man who had looked to Luther as the great symbol of liberation from oppression were embittered by this turn against them. But here too events outran Luther's intention. He had written the tract against the peasants in response to the news of the rebellious juggernaut that was laying waste to the country. And he had added the treatise to his prior work with the combined title *Admonition to Peace and Also Against the Robbing and Murdering Hordes of the Other Peasants*. His point was that the *Admonition* was addressed to the "good" peasants and the second half was addressed to the "other" peasants. The printers however split the work and dropped "Other" from the title of the second half, which appeared in print just as the horrible slaughter at Frankenhausen took place. These circumstances made it appear that Luther had totally turned against the common man when in fact he had not. Even in this second work he had urged the rulers first to try reconciliation; only if that failed should they proceed with force to put down the rebellion. These circumstances were not known at the time, and have usually been ignored ever since in historical judgments that Luther was more concerned for his reform program than for the lives of the oppressed.

Criticism of Luther and the bloody suppression of the peasants came from many quarters. The Nuremberg artist Dürer made a woodcut of a proposed "triumphal column" that ironically indicted the victors for their inhumanity: atop the column, consisting of captured peasant "weapons" of shovel, hoe, manure fork, and flail, sits a peasant in the melancholy style of the Man of Sorrows with a sword stuck in his back. Luther's friends urged him to explain his position, which he did in late June or early July in *An Open Letter on the Harsh Book Against the Peasants*. The tract is as much an attack on his critics as an explanation of his earlier work. He reiterated that mercy should be shown those who surrendered or who were coerced into the rebellion, and he emphasized the intent of his writing. "I made it plain that I was speaking of those who were first approached in a friendly way, and would not respond. All my words were directed against the obdurate, hardened, blinded peasants, . . . and yet you say that I advocate the merciless slaughter of the poor captured peasants." Those who are now calling for mercy on the rebels are confusing God's kingdom with the kingdom of the world. In the former there is mercy, but in the world there must be justice enforced with punishment. In fact, severity and wrath in the world are a form of God's mercy. "Suppose I had a wife and children, a house, servants, and property, and a thief or murderer fell upon me, killed me in my own house, ravished my wife and children, took all I had, and went unpunished so that he could do the same thing again, when he wished . . . What a fine mercy to me it would be, to have mercy on the thief and murderer, and let him kill, abuse, and rob me! True mercy would be to restrain and punish the thief" (*LW* 46: 73, 71). By restraining evil and promoting good the secular world served God and the neighbor.

Luther's encounters with Karlstadt, Müntzer, and then the revolution strengthened his conviction that the world must be governed not by any religious ideology, including the gospel, but by reason and law. From Luther's perspective, all efforts to govern the world by the gospel of free forgiveness would lead either to unrestrained chaos and destruction or to a demonic crusade against all perceived "evil empires." To Luther, the identification of any political program, regardless of its intrinsic merit, with the will of God subverts both politics and the gospel. The political process is subverted because the claim to absolute righteousness precludes the ambiguity present in all social life as well as the art of compromise necessary in social relations. Group and national self-righteousness leads people to see political opponents as followers of the devil, that is, as the "ungodly" who have no right to live. The gospel is subverted when identified with a political program because then all citizens are forced to conform to a religious norm, and salvation is made dependent upon a particular political affiliation and program, a political form of good works. For Luther, faith alone granted the security to live within the human insecurity of relative political structures and to avoid the defensive sanctification of past, present, or future goods and values. For Luther, faith alone was the enabling ground of the person content to be human and to let God be God. Luther attempted to de-ideologize politics by declaring that God, not the party and not the church, is sovereign in history.

Suggestions for Further Reading

Michael B. Baylor, ed., *The Radical Reformation*, Cambridge: Cambridge University Press, 1991

Peter Blickle, *The Revolution of 1525: The German Peasants' War from a New Perspective*, Baltimore: Johns Hopkins University Press, 1981

Peter Blickle, *Communal Reformation: The Quest for Salvation in Sixteenth-Century Germany*, Atlantic Highlands: Humanities, 1992

Hans-Jürgen Goertz, ed., *Profiles of Radical Reformers: Biographical Sketches from Thomas Müntzer to Paracelsus*, Kitchener: Herald, 1982

Hans-Jürgen Goertz, *Thomas Müntzer: Apocalyptic Mystic and Revolutionary*, Edinburgh: T. & T. Clark, 1993

Tom Scott and Bob Scribner, eds, *The German Peasants' War: A History in Documents*, Atlantic Highlands: Humanities, 1991

James M. Stayer, *The German Peasants' War and Anabaptist Community of Goods*, Montreal: McGill-Queen's University Press, 1991

7

The Swiss Connection:
Zwingli and the Reformation
in Zurich

The Christian man is nothing else but a faithful and good citizen and the
Christian city nothing other than the Christian church.

Ulrich Zwingli

The Affair of the Sausages

Whereas the German Reformation was sparked by Luther's academic
theological disputation over the sacrament of penance and indulgences,
the Swiss Reformation went public with the so-called "Affair of the
Sausages."

During Lent of 1522, Zwingli was at the house of Christoph
Froschauer, a printer who was laboring over the preparation of a new
edition of the epistles of Paul. In order to refresh his dozen tired
workers, Froschauer served sausages. Was it just a coincidence that the
number of participants and the manner of distribution recalled the
Lord's Supper? This public breaking of the Lenten fast flouted both
medieval piety and ecclesiastical and public authority. The Zurich town
council arrested Froschauer, but not Zwingli, who himself had not
eaten the meat. Zwingli, who held the eminent post of people's priest at
the Great Minster church in Zurich, could have smoothed everything
out. Instead, he made a public issue out of the incident by preaching a
sermon, "On the Choice and Freedom of Foods" (23 March 1522), that
was soon enlarged into a printed pamphlet (16 April 1522). Almost
certainly influenced by Luther's earlier (1520) treatise on Christian
freedom, Zwingli argued that Christians are free to fast or not to fast
because the Bible does not prohibit the eating of meat during Lent. "In
a word, if you will fast, do so; if you do not wish to eat meat, eat it not;
but leave Christians a free choice in the matter" (Jackson 1987: 87).

Zwingli's Beginnings

How had Zwingli reached this point of public opposition to ecclesiastical and political authority? Ulrich Zwingli (1484–1531) was born into a
well-to-do peasant family in Wildhaus, a village high in the alps of the
Toggenburg, a duchy allied with the Swiss Confederacy. His grandfather and then his father served as the local magistrate, an elected
position usually filled by one of the wealthier farmers. A precocious
farmboy from an alpine village with politics in his blood, Zwingli was
already studying Latin and the classics in Basle at the age of ten. After
continuing his Latin studies in Bern, he then went on in 1498, at the age
of fourteen, to the University of Vienna, where he was introduced to
the humanist movement. At the time the poet laureate of the Empire,
Conrad Celtis, was lecturing there, but it is not known whether
Zwingli attended his lectures. Zwingli continued his education at Basle
where he studied theology, philosophy, and the new humanistic
studies, receiving his BA in 1504 and MA in 1506. At Basle he appears
to have been most influenced by the *via antiqua*, that is, Thomistic
theology. Two of his fellow students, Leo Jud and Conrad Pellican,
later became his colleagues in Zurich Reform.

Upon finishing his studies, Zwingli was called to become the parish
priest at Glarus in the Swiss canton of the same name. During his
decade (1506–16) of ministry in Glarus, he found time to pursue his
passionate interests in the classics, the church fathers, and the Bible
with enough time left over for his avocational interest in women. He
also learned Greek and was introduced to Erasmus and the humanist
circle at Basle. Zwingli's fascination with humanism did not precipitate
a break with scholastic theology but rather stimulated his interest in the
primary sources of the Christian faith and provided the philological
resources to understand them. With Erasmus' Greek New Testament
and his own linguistic ability he was able to concentrate on the text
without subservience to traditional interpretations. From Erasmus
Zwingli learned to seek the simple meaning of the biblical text and to
present Jesus as the model for the Christian life. This hardly seems
radical today, but the simplified Christianity of deeds was liberating in
the context of the medieval religious life, complicated and burdened as
it was by numerous church laws and rituals.

The controversy that soon encompassed Zwingli's ministry was not
a result of his humanistically developing theology and preaching.
Rather, his growing tensions with the magistrates of Glarus stemmed
from his political orientation and his public denunciation of the

mainstay of the Swiss export business – the mercenary trade in professional soldiers. Swiss pikemen, renowned for their skill and ferocity, were sought after by the French, Spanish, and papal armies fighting over control of Italy. As chaplain to the Glarus contingent of soldiers in Italy, Zwingli witnessed the carnage of battle at first hand during campaigns in 1513 and 1515: in the latter year he saw thousands of Swiss killed by the French at Marignano. He also experienced the pain of informing families of the dead upon his return. Both Zwingli's pastoral concern and his patriotic nationalism motivated him to oppose the mercenary practices he believed were eroding the moral and social fabric of the Swiss, not to mention their very existence as a people as they killed each other in the pay of opposing armies.

Already in 1510 in his patriotic allegorical poem, *The Ox*, Zwingli attacked foreign use of Swiss soldiers. The legitimate exception, in Zwingli's eyes also a patriotic duty of the Swiss, was defense of the pope; and, it should be noted, he did receive a pension from the Holy See for his service as military chaplain. His enthusiasm for the papal alliance waned however in direct proportion to the mounting body count of the Swiss. His abhorrence of the mercenary business was clearly expressed in his poem *The Labyrinth* (1516), in which his politics now take on a religious tone: "Whoever commits crime and murder is considered a bold man. Did Christ teach us that?" (Jackson 1987: 54).

It should be noted that Zwingli was by no means a pacifist; his criticism was directed against Swiss entanglement with foreign powers and the Swiss eagerness to serve as "hired guns." He was never for peace at any price and he always promoted national self-defense; a stance that cost him his life at the second battle of Kappel in 1531. Zwingli's patriotism is graphically represented by his statue in Zurich which portrays him with a Bible in one hand and a sword in the other. "With such opinions, Zwingli was one of the originators of the Swiss policy of armed neutrality which has played an important role in safeguarding the independence of the nation throughout subsequent history" (Courvoisier 1963: 15).

The opposition to Zwingli's anti-mercenary stance was twofold: economic and political. Economically, in the sixteenth century the Swiss did not yet have income from chocolate, watches, and numbered accounts; they did however have a surplus population and insufficient foreign exchange to feed it. Hence any serious effort to prohibit soldiers for hire "would have meant an economic disaster for the overpopulated forest cantons" (Walton 1984: 82). Politically, Zwingli's position was seen as opposition to the pro-French orientation of Glarus and most of the Swiss Confederacy. The view of Zwingli as an anti-French agent of the papacy led to his departure from Glarus and also to his eventual move to Zurich, the center of his reforming activity.

The magistrates of Glarus willingly granted Zwingli's request to transfer to the nearby parish of Einsiedeln in April 1516. In Einsiedeln, Zwingli functioned as a chaplain to the many pilgrims, including hundreds from Zurich, who flocked to its shrine of the Black Virgin. In his off hours he studied the newly published Greek New Testament compiled by Erasmus. Zwingli soon became a celebrity for his expositions of the Bible in worship and sermon. His Erasmian erudition and biblical fervor served him well in his denunciation of the Franciscan indulgence seller, Bernard Samson, the Swiss counterpart to Tetzel. Zwingli "preached" Samson right out of town. However, in contrast to Tetzel, there were no vested interests aligned with Samson and hence no ecclesiastical reactions against Zwingli.

Zwingli's reputation for biblical preaching led to his nomination for the post of people's priest at the Great Minster in Zurich in 1518. Detractors raised the issue of Zwingli's womanizing. Zwingli responded to the rumor that he had seduced the daughter of an influential citizen by admitting his struggle with sexual temptations but denying both the woman's "purity" and her father's influence. "Some three years ago I firmly resolved not to touch any woman, . . . I succeeded poorly in this, however. In Glarus I kept my resolution about six months, in Einsiedeln about a year, . . . That girl was a 'virgin' during the day and a 'woman' at night. She was such a 'day' virgin, however, that everyone in Einsiedeln knew exactly her role. . . . She had had affairs with many men, finally with me. Or let me say it better: she seduced me with more than flattering words" (Hillerbrand 1964: 115–16). The charge of immorality was finally ineffective since the other priest vying for the post lived openly in concubinage and had six children.

In light of this specific example and the generally widespread practice of priestly concubinage in the late Middle Ages, it is not surprising that one of the first reforms initiated in the Swiss Reformation was the right of the clergy to marry. We have already seen that the Wittenberg endorsement of clerical marriage eroded episcopal authority; it should be noted that clerical marriage also eroded episcopal income. In the bishopric of Constance which included the canton of Zurich, a fixed annual fee of four gulden payable to the bishop "licensed" clerical concubinage. An additional fee of four gulden was due for each child born of such unions. Since it is estimated that about 1,500 children were born in this situation annually, it is easy to appreciate the non-doctrinal reason for the bishop's opposition to clerical marriage. In fact, only months after the "Affair of the Sausages," Zwingli, then living with the widow Anna Reinhart, led ten other Swiss priests in a petition to the bishop of Constance *To Allow Priests to Marry, or at Least Wink at their Marriages* (July 1522). The priests signing this petition declared that chastity is a rare gift of God, and that they hadn't received it (Jackson 1987: 156). Zwingli married Anna in a public ceremony in 1524 shortly before the birth of their child. In 1525 the Zurich magistrates instituted a marriage ordinance mandating clergy living in concubinage either to end the relationship or to marry. A marriage court was also established that clarified marital relationships by expanding grounds for divorce to include extreme incompatibility, desertion, physical and mental illness, and fraud.

But we are getting ahead of our story. Before discussing Zwingli's Reformation of Zurich, it is necessary to discuss in more detail the context of his appointment, because it sheds some light on the symbiotic relationship of Zwingli and the town council that facilitated the reform movement.

Magistracy and Church in Zurich

The Swiss Confederacy, which included Zurich as one of its cantons, had effectively gained independence from the Holy Roman Empire in the Peace of Basle (1499). The city of Zurich, situated on the banks of the Limmat river at the mouth of Lake Zurich, went back to Roman times. By the Reformation period it had a population of about 6,000. Governance of the city was through two councils. The Great Council had 162 members: 12 members from each of the 12 craft guilds, and 18 members from the constables (a body of nobles, property owners, and merchants). The Small Council, in effect a cabinet or executive body, had 50 members. The Small Council also had representatives from the guilds and constables. Since half of the Small Council rotated every six months there was a regular possibility for changing policy in this complicated structure. The two councils together made up the Council of the Two Hundred (actually 212) that concerned itself primarily with foreign policy issues. The canton of Zurich had a population of about 50,000.

The Zurich church belonged to one of the largest dioceses in the Empire, the diocese of Constance. The bishop of Constance, Hugo von Hohenlandberg, had oversight of some 1,800 parishes and over 15,000 priests, 200 of whom were in the city of Zurich. The two major churches of Zurich were the Great Minster and the Minster of Our

Lady, both dating back to the ninth century. Mendicant orders in the city included the Dominicans, Franciscans, and Augustinians. By the sixteenth century, the town council had expanded its role in church affairs and had the right to appoint clergy to the Great Minster and the Minster of Our Lady.

The political process involved in Zwingli's appointment to the Great Minster provided a significant context for the development of the reform of Zurich. Although all parties involved may not have initially recognized the political dynamics of this appointment, it created a symbiotic relationship between Zwingli and the city government. Both parties came to realize that their respective goals were interwoven and mutually dependent; hence neither wished the other to fail. Here we see an important difference from Luther's context. Whereas Luther depended on a supportive prince, Zwingli depended on persuading the civic government. Zwingli's ability to move the city away from its pro-papal sympathies to pro-Reformation activity reflects his political acumen in utilizing the support of the political faction that had supported his appointment as well as that faction's sense that reform would further diminish the power of their opponents, the old pro-papal patrician families.

Zwingli's Reform Program

On 1 January 1519 Zwingli preached and celebrated mass at the Great Minster. His address marked a new departure, for instead of preaching from the traditional text assigned in the church's calendar, he began a series of sermons that went *seriatim* through the whole gospel of Matthew. He then chose other New Testament books on the basis of what he perceived to be the need of the people and proceeded to expound each as a whole. This was not only scriptural preaching; it was education in the Bible. Beginning in 1525, Zwingli instituted the practice of weekly Bible studies known as "prophesyings." The name, taken from 1 Corinthians 14, meant biblical instruction. The goal was theologically to inform and mold the ministers and advanced students of the Latin school. A similar practice was instituted in Geneva around 1536 by Calvin and Farel under the name of "congregations." The centrality of biblical instruction was basic to Zwingli's conception of reform: all of life, personal and communal, is to be normed by Scripture.

The reform principle that Zwingli was formulating on the basis of his humanist and biblical studies was that everything was to be judged by Scripture. What did not conform to biblical teaching did not command obedience. The test was whether traditional ceremonies and teachings promoted the gospel of redemption by Christ. This test, of course, quickly raised questions about all areas of life beyond sex and sausages. The effort to provide biblical norms for all of life also eventually led to "neighborly" spying and court-enforced attempts to oversee the city's moral life.

But was this biblical preaching an indication that Zwingli had broken with the Roman church? Had the banner of *sola scriptura* displaced the authority of the church? Or was this preaching rather an expression of typical humanist concern for biblical exposition? The question of when Zwingli became a Reformer and the related question of when Zurich embraced reform are controversial. If abolition of the mass is to be the criterion, then the definitive step did not occur until 13 April 1525 when an evangelical communion service replaced the mass. If the town council's endorsement of Zwingli's first public disputation is the criterion, then the Zurich Reformation may be dated to 29 January 1523. But if the crucial issue was the recognition of biblical authority over the church's claims to authority, then the reform movement got under way with the beginning of Zwingli's preaching ministry and was formally recognized with the judgment of the first Zurich disputation in January 1523.

The process was not smooth. In the first year of his ministry, Zwingli stirred many a heart – both pro and con – with his biblical preaching, attacks on indulgences, criticism of the honoring of saints and images, and assaults on scholastic theology. He was thrilled when he learned of Luther's July debate with Eck at Leipzig. But although Zwingli could now hail Luther as a new Elijah and began reading Luther's writings, he did not seem to see in Luther any more than a comrade-in-arms in a struggle he was already engaged in. There is little evidence of deep theological influence from Luther, and later Zwingli was to assert that he developed independently of Luther. Luther himself affirmed this later when he asserted that Zwingli "is of a different spirit."

Comparison of Zwingli with Luther and also with Calvin is inevitable, but ought not to subordinate Zwingli. In the comparisons that follow the intention is not to present Luther as the norm of reform by which all others are to be judged. Zwingli's own claim to independence should be respected. But that does not mean that it ought not to be examined in its varying contexts as to whether it was more tactical than substantive, for the name "Lutheran" became a synonym for heresy in the early 1520s. In this regard figure 7.1 is an interesting

Das hond zwen sch=
weytzer bauren gemacht. Fürwar
sy hond es wol betracht.

Figure 7.1 "The Godly Mill," 1521.
Source: Berlin Staatliche Museen.

illustration of Zwingli's sense of reform. "The Godly Mill" was the title woodcut for a pamphlet printed by Froschauer in Zurich in the spring of 1521: *Beschribung der götlichen müly so durch die gnad gottes angelassen* ("Description of the Godly Mill which Operates by the Grace of God"). The traditional allegory of the mill is reinterpreted as an allegory or symbol for the Reformation dissemination of the pure Word of God. The flame of the Holy Spirit descends from God the

Father and propels the mill wheel by grace. Christ pours the four evangelists and Paul (with the sword) into the hopper as the material to be ground. Erasmus, whose edition of the New Testament was so helpful to Luther and whose humanism was influential upon Zwingli, is the miller. Erasmus shovels the meal, marked by the banners of the biblical virtues of hope, love, faith, and strength, into the sack. Behind Erasmus stands Luther as an Augustinian monk at the kneading trough, kneading the dough. The bread of evangelical teaching is distributed as books by an unnamed figure in academic garb. The representatives of the ecclesiastical hierarchy who stand at the right of the woodcut (from left to right: a Dominican monk, cardinal, bishop, and pope) refuse the gospel and let it fall to the ground. Above their heads is a flapping bird croaking out "ban, ban" (Luther was banned on 3 January 1521). The symbol of the peasantry and the "common man," "Hans the Hoeman" (*Karsthans*), looms large with his flail, protecting the proclamation of the gospel and threatening the enemies of the Reformation. It is presumed that the figure distributing the gospel, the only figure without a label or specific attribute, is Zwingli. A letter by Zwingli of 25 May 1521 states that he not only worked on the text of this pamphlet but also assisted in the devising of the woodcut. It is noteworthy, given Zwingli's stated independence of Luther, how freely and impartially he presents Luther as the mediator of the evangelical message, as the "baker of the Reformation" (Hamm 1988: vi–vii).

How did Zwingli come to reform? It appears that biblical humanism was the predominant influence. As Erasmus commented after reading one of Zwingli's writings: "O good Zwingli! What have you written which I have not already written earlier?" Indeed, Büsser (1989: 192) remarks that a point-by-point comparison of Erasmus and Zwingli could suggest Erasmus became "the secret reformer of Zurich, if not the father of Reformed theology generally." Certainly Zwingli had his own existential crisis; but unlike Luther's encounter with lightning, this was an encounter with the plague. In August 1519 the plague struck Zurich and did not run its course until February 1520. Nearly a fourth of the population succumbed, including Zwingli's brother, Andreas. Zwingli himself nearly died of it after contracting it carrying out pastoral care for the sick and dying. His poem *The Plague Song* testifies both to the profound impact this near-death experience had on his faith in God, and his renewed dedication to serve God that came with recovery.

Thus by the time of the "Affair of the Sausages," Zwingli had personally and theologically matured. Luther had been publicly condemned, yet Zurich was still relatively calm. Zwingli had gained the

confidence and support of Zurich's common folk through his exposition of the text of the Bible and his separation of the chaff of ritual
externalization from the wheat of an internally appropriated gospel.
Recall that his preaching ministry in Zurich began with the exposition
of Matthew, a text that powerfully indicts the dead tradition of the
Pharisees and scribes. Well before the conflict over fasting, Zwingli
would have preached on Matthew 15: 10–11: "Hear and understand:
not what goes into the mouth defiles a man, but what comes out of the
mouth, this defiles a man." In Zurich people took their esteemed
priest's preaching very seriously and began to put it into practice.
Discussion of Zwingli's more radical followers will be reserved to the
next chapter, but we may note that by 1522 Zurich was experiencing
nearly simultaneously and substantively the same issues of theory and
praxis encountered in Wittenberg. Zwingli, too, now found himself
between those who wished to proceed more radically with reform
without waiting for anyone and those siding with the bishop against
reform.

   Bishop Hugo admonished Zwingli and his followers to remain
obedient to the church, for no one can be saved outside the church.
Here the battle of tradition and Scripture, ecclesiastical authority and
gospel authority was joined. Now the intercession of the saints was
added to the issues of fasting and clerical celibacy. Here too an appeal to
the Word of God against human words and ordinances challenged the
authority of the church. The theme of the authority of Scripture
interpreted by Scripture ran through all the debates. On 21 July 1522
the Great Council took a significant step toward the introduction of
reform and endorsed Zwingli and preaching from Scripture rather than
from scholastic theology.

   Growing controversy over the church and scriptural authority led
the town magistrates to call a public disputation between the advocates
and opponents of reform in the Zurich town hall for 29 January 1523.
Zwingli himself may have requested this opportunity, but it is also
clear that the city government felt compelled to defend its honor
against the charges of heresy and to develop a principle for regulating
evangelical preaching in the city. An invitation was sent to the other
cantons of the Swiss Confederacy but, in light of their disapproval of
events in Zurich, none of them sent delegates. An announcement was
also sent to the bishop of Constance so that he might be represented at
the disputation. The magistrates referred to "dissension and disagreement" about the gospel, and requested debate on the Bible in German
in order to determine the content of preaching. "If anyone disregards
our regulation and does not cite the Holy Scriptures we will proceed

against him according to our knowledge, in a way from which we would gladly be relieved" (Hillerbrand 1964: 131–2).

The invitation was clearly weighted in favor of Zwingli's position: the discussion was to be in German not Latin, and the basis for judgment was to be Scripture. The boldness of the council's assumption that it could serve as a local council of the church is evident in that it only informed the bishop of its action, and in its prejudgment of the outcome by positing Scripture as the only norm. The council designated itself formally and juridically as judge for both parties, but it must not be forgotten that *the* issue for the evangelical side was whether God's Word or human tradition would be the authority in the church.

This "disputation" was the occasion for Zwingli's preparation of his Sixty-Seven Articles (Cochrane 1966: 3–44), the charter of the Zurich Reformation. The articles affirmed salvation by grace alone, insisted upon the full and final authority of Scripture, and rejected the pope, the mass, good works for salvation, the intercession of the saints, monastic orders, a celibate clergy, penance, and purgatory. Zwingli's proposals meant nothing less than the dismantling of medieval ecclesiology. From the outset the church is made dependent upon Scripture rather than vice versa: "All who say that the Gospel is nothing without the approbation of the Church err and slander God" (Article 1). Here is an instant replay of the Prierias–Luther debate.

Six hundred people crammed the town hall for the debate. After a brief welcome and the sharing of formal pleasantries, Zwingli was permitted to speak. Zwingli declared he was willing to defend his preaching and his theses. Johann Faber, representative of the bishop and a doctor of theology, replied in conciliatory terms that the episcopal delegation was there to hear the causes of dissension, not engage in substantive debate over matters that properly belonged to the impending ecumenical council promised by the recent diet of Nuremberg. "For, as I think, such matters are to be settled by a general Christian assembly of all nations, or by a council of bishops and other scholars as are found at universities." When Faber suggested as judges the universities of Paris, Louvain, or Cologne, all bastions of orthodoxy, Zwingli suggested instead, to the audience's amusement, Erfurt or Wittenberg. Faber supposedly responded that these were too close to Luther, and that "all bad things come from the north" (a reference to Jeremiah 6: 1). But Zwingli's basic point in response was that those presently assembled constituted a Christian council whose only judge was the infallible Scripture. "There are in this assembly many Christian hearts, taught doubtless by the Holy Spirit, and possessing such upright understanding, that in accordance with God's spirit they can judge and decide which party produces Scripture on its side, right or wrong, or otherwise does violence to Scripture contrary to proper understanding" (Jackson 1972: 51, 56–7).

Zwingli carried the day against the old order, and the Zurich clergy were ordered by the council to confine their preaching to Scripture. "What took place on 29 January 1523 in the town hall on the Limmat before the opened Bible was a profound religious communal experience, comparable in the highest degree, psychologically as well as sociologically to the medieval sense of fellowship: the renewal of the catholicity of the church in the small territory of Zurich" (Locher 1979: 115; Goertz 1987: 140). A second disputation held in October, directed to those in the reform party who wanted more radical reform, will be discussed below in chapter 8 in the section on the Anabaptists.

Zwingli's reform movement now began to spread rapidly throughout Switzerland and south Germany. Congregations in Constance, Ulm, Frankfurt, Augsburg, Lindau, Memmingen, and Strasbourg were won over to the Zurich Reformation. The conversion of the Swiss canton of Bern in 1528 to the Zwinglian cause was particularly important not only for the immediate establishment of Zwinglianism in the Swiss Confederacy but also for the future reform of Geneva under the auspices of William Farel and John Calvin. Basle, also of political importance, followed Bern into the Zwinglian fold.

In the meantime, however, internal and external tensions were approaching the breaking point. Tensions within Zurich concerning the pace and extent of the reform, and the control of iconoclastic and other anti–authoritarian activities, will be treated in the next chapter. Outside Zurich the rural and conservative Catholic cantons of Switzerland were allying to oppose the Reformation. The threat of Zwinglian expansion pushed the Catholic cantons of Uri, Schwyz, Unterwalden, Zug, Lucerne, and Fribourg into an alliance with the ancient enemy of the Swiss Confederacy, Habsburg Austria, in 1529. The execution of a Zwinglian preacher as a heretic in Schwyz led to a military confrontation at Kappel. The obvious strength of the Zurich forces, however, and the common Swiss distaste for Habsburg meddling in the affairs of the Confederacy prompted an armistice in June 1529. Swiss nationalism, at least temporarily, superseded religious differences.

But religious friction continued, and Zwingli was convinced that the southern cantons were still allied with Austria. At the same time, the German Lutherans were also menaced by Charles V, who had by now greatly reduced the French and Turkish threats and felt free once again to turn his attention to the "Luther affair." He intended to eliminate heresy from his lands. Thus, at the diet of Speyer in April 1529 the emperor demanded that the previous diet's (1526) allowance of territorial and urban discretion regarding the Lutheran question be rescinded. This in turn prompted four evangelical states and fourteen free imperial cities to submit a formal *protestatio* (hence the name "Protestant") that decreed that the 1526 religious agreement be maintained until a national assembly and ecumenical council could be convoked to settle the religious issues. The signatories to this *protestatio* included Lutheran (e.g. Electoral Saxony), and Zwinglian (e.g. Strasbourg) areas; hence the German Lutheran prince, Philip of Hesse (1504–67), was convinced that the time was ripe to create an international political and military alliance between the Lutherans and the Zwinglians for their mutual protection against the emperor, and for the spread of the Reformation.

Philip, a convinced evangelical who was more concerned for the Christian faith than for theological party labels, understood that his dream of a Protestant alliance was unrealizable unless the mutual antagonisms of Luther and Zwingli over their respective understandings of the Lord's Supper could be reconciled. This is the context for Philip's invitation to the two sides to meet for a religious colloquy at his Marburg castle in October 1529. In order to grasp the volatility of the issue joined at Marburg, it is important to realize that the Reformers were arguing not just over a particular ritual but over the entire western theological heritage in which this sacrament was embedded and from which it took its meaning. Before tracing the Luther–Zwingli debate, a brief excursion into this heritage may shed some light on what Luther and Zwingli believed to be at stake in their argument over the Lord's Supper.

Excursus: Medieval Sacramental Theology

Reformation controversies over the sacraments were rooted in a common medieval heritage of theology and liturgy. The diversity in this heritage became church-dividing as each reform movement reread the tradition in light of its own theological and pastoral commitments. Thus Reformation understandings of the sacraments cannot be isolated from the complex interplay of the received tradition with theology, Renaissance philosophy and philology, pastoral care and liturgy, and the social, political, and economic culture of the late medieval and early modern period. The received sacramental theology included the trinitarian and christological dogmas of the early church. The former developed in response to the position of Arianism that God's nature is unchanging and thus the incarnation must be a lesser form of divinity than God. The latter involved the controversy between Nestorius (d. ca. 451) and Cyril of Alexandria (d. 444) concerning the person and natures of Christ. Nestorianism denied that the incarnate Christ is both fully human and fully divine in one single person with the sacramental consequence being the claim that the human nature of Christ cannot leave heaven. Cyril's formula of the *communicatio idiomatum* (communication of natures) asserted against Nestorius that the divine and human natures are shared in the one person of Christ. Luther applied this christological teaching to understanding of the Lord's Supper.

Throughout these complicated early church controversies the guiding motifs for the orthodox were that salvation is not achieved but received, and that in Jesus humankind is definitively confronted by God. In terms of sacramental theology this meant that the sacraments are primarily God's gifts of himself and not human works. What made the sixteenth-century controversies so bitter was the universal conviction that to be right about the sacraments was to be right about God and salvation. Hence Reformation understandings of the sacraments included not only the vocabulary of theology but the vocabulary of theological actions. In the words of R. W. Scribner (1987: 122): "The Reformation was in this sense fundamentally a ritual process."

The early Christian community initiated members through baptism and centered its worship on the celebration of the eucharist (Greek *eucharistia*, "thanksgiving"), but only gradually classified these and other ritual activities under the general concept of sacrament. The concept of sacrament developed from the Latin translation of the Greek *mysterion* ("mystery") by *sacramentum*. In classical Latin this meant a soldier's oath of allegiance (*sacramentum militare*) accompanied by the concrete symbol (*signum*) of a tattoo. Hence Tertullian (d. ca. 225) spoke of baptism as the beginning of the *militia Christi*, and the early church referred to baptism as the "Lord's seal." From Augustine through Aquinas (d. 1274) the particular sacraments of baptism, confirmation, and ordination were understood to imprint an indelible character (a divine tattoo, so to speak) on the soul. Since this character remains in spite of the gravest sins, these sacraments are received only once.

The liturgical activity of the worshipping community, the context for the sacraments as signs of holy things, stimulated the theological drive to define the sacraments. The relation of praxis to theory is indicated already in the fifth-century axiom that prayer establishes belief (*lex orandi lex credendi*).

Augustine provided two important premises to western sacramental theology: that Christian rituals are forms of God's word of promise

("The word comes to the element; and so there is a sacrament, that is, a sort of visible word"); and that the validity of the sacrament does not depend upon the administrant. The latter countered the claim of the Donatists (a north African renewal movement of Augustine's time) that sacraments administered by unworthy priests were invalid. Augustine emphasized that the grace of God is independent of the subjective attitudes and holiness of the minister. Luther was to echo this position in his vigorous emphasis on the objective reality of the sacraments. Renewal movements throughout the history of the church have tended toward Donatism, a tendency also evident in some movements during the Reformation. By the early thirteenth century the objective action of the sacraments would be expressed in the phrase *ex opera operato*, i.e. the sacraments are effective through the operation of the rite itself, and not dependent upon the character of the administrant. From a pastoral perspective, later shared by Luther, this indicates the certainty of sacramental grace in spite of the communicant's doubts of worthiness.

The understanding of sacraments as "signs of holy things" included a number of ritual actions which the medieval church gradually reduced to seven sacraments. As late as the twelfth century there were varying lists of sacraments. The Gregorian reformer Peter Damian (d. 1072) counted 12 (baptism, confirmation, anointing of the sick, consecration of bishops, anointing of kings, consecration of churches, confession, marriage, and the consecrations of canonists, monks, hermits, and nuns), but omitted eucharist and penance. Hugh of St Victor (d. 1142), author of a major work on the sacraments, listed as many as 30. Peter Lombard (d. 1160), author of what became the standard textbook of theology through the sixteenth century, the *Four Books of Sentences*, fixed the number of sacraments at the seven still recognized within the Roman Catholic communion. His list of baptism, confirmation, eucharist, penance, extreme unction, orders, and marriage, accepted by Aquinas from the perspective that they reflect the stages of life, was formally affirmed in the "Instruction for the Armenians" (council of Florence, 1439). It was reaffirmed at the council of Trent (1545–63) from the perspective that these seven had been divinely instituted by Christ.

Medieval life and doctrine consistently focused on the sacraments of baptism, penance, and the eucharist. All three became controversial to the extent of church-dividing in the Reformation, but during the medieval period it was the eucharist that sparked controversies. These controversies were intertwined with diverse theologies from the early church and developing liturgical practices.

Augustine defined a sacrament as the "visible word." In relation to baptism, he said: "Take away the word, and the water is neither more nor less than water." In the eucharist, the word was the institution attributed to Jesus in the New Testament accounts of the Last Supper, while the elements were the bread and wine. Influenced by neoplatonic philosophy, Augustine could refer to the bread as the "sign" or "image" of the body of Christ. This symbolic theology of the sacrament was influential in the development of the Roman liturgy, and was later emphasized by Zwingli.

Realist or "metabolic" (Greek *metabolé*, "transmutation") theology stemming from Ambrose (d. 397), was influential in the liturgical developments in Spain and Gaul. Ambrose wrote of the "transmutation" of the elements of bread and wine into the flesh and blood of Christ by virtue of the words of consecration. This foreshadowed later scholastic developments toward the doctrine of transubstantiation. Since Isadore of Seville (d. 636), the understanding of the eucharist shifted from community in union with Christ giving thanks to the Father for salvation to the real presence of Christ in the eucharist who in the consecration descends from heaven. The focus upon the real presence was burdened by the tension between the metabolism of Ambrose and the symbolism of Augustine. This tension increased as Germanic thinking was less and less able to understand the platonic relation between symbol and reality, and as the dramatic action *of* the congregation was being displaced by a dramatic spectacle *for* the congregation.

The Carolingian introduction of the Roman liturgy into the Frankish kingdom, and the imperial interest in liturgical uniformity and education, raised awareness of tensions between the liturgies influenced by the theologies of Augustine and Ambrose. The first doctrinal treatment of the eucharist in this context was by the Benedictine monk, Paschasius Radbertus (d. 865) of Corbie. A version of his *De corpore et sanguine Domini* (831) was presented to Emperor Charles the Bald in 844. Paschasius emphasized the identity of the body and blood of the Lord in the sacrament with the earthly and risen body of Christ.

Charles then requested another monk of Corbie, Ratramnus (d. 868), for an interpretation. Ratramnus took the more Augustinian emphasis of the eucharist as an effective sign of Christ's presence and did not identify the elements of bread and wine with the risen, earthly body of Christ. Indeed, Ratramnus foreshadowed the "sacramentarian" (i.e. metaphorical or symbolic understanding) and Zwinglian concerns of the sixteenth century when he contested the corporeal eating with the arguments that Christ has ascended to heaven, and that it is the Spirit not the flesh that gives life (John 6: 63). His Latin treatise influenced Berengar of Tours (d. 1088), and was reprinted under the name of "Bertram" by Swiss and English Reformers of Zwinglian and Calvinist persuasion (Bakhuizen 1965: 54–77).

The controversy that erupted over the eucharistic theology of Berengar provided the framework for subsequent medieval and Reformation discussions of the sacrament. Berengar's claim that the reception of Christ in the eucharist can only be a spiritual reception, a faithful recollection of the mystery of Christ's passion and resurrection, is similar to the later memorial theologies of the sacrament advanced by Karlstadt, Zwingli, and the sacramentarians.

Berengar's position was widely opposed and condemned. At Rome (1059) he was forced to sign a formula that "the bread and wine placed on the altar are, after consecration, not only a sacrament, but also the true body and blood of our Lord Jesus Christ, . . . are sensibly, not only sacramentally but in truth, handled and broken by the hands of the priests and crushed by the teeth of the faithful."

The opposition to Berengar was not only led by the most powerful theologians and ecclesiastics of the time, but also reflected popular piety and liturgical practice. Theologically, Berengar's view that Christ was not substantially present in the eucharist was perceived to undermine salvation. Furthermore, Berengar's understanding of the eucharist as a symbolic meal in which the believer through willful memory of Christ's passion unites with Christ was the sacramental analogy to the Arian heresy that Christ unites with the Father through his will. Against this it was affirmed that the believer is united with Christ because Christ's substantial presence is mediated in the eucharist. The imagery used here has been termed "metabolic" because, as Paschasius stated, "we become part of Christ because we eat him."

The Berengar controversy raised the question of how the bread and wine become the actual body and blood of Christ. Efforts to resolve this question led to the doctrine of transubstantiation (fourth Lateran council, 1215). The doctrine of transubstantiation rests on the Greek metaphysical claim that the "substance" or "essence" of a thing is always more real than its "accidental" sense data. Sense data may be deceiving, but the mind is able to grasp the substance of a thing and thus know it. For example, in spite of accidents of size, shape, and color of individual cows, we know the substance of the cow. "According to this theory, when a priest consecrates the elements of bread and wine, the accidents of bread remain the same but the substance is miraculously changed by the power of God into the body and blood of Christ.

The bread and wine still feel, smell, taste, and look like bread and wine, but appearances in this case are deceiving. The reality which is present is Christ himself" (Steinmetz 1986: 73). The intention of this doctrine is to affirm the priority and reality of God's grace; Christ is really present in the Lord's Supper in spite of appearances.

The Berengar controversy also focused the theology of the eucharist increasingly on Christ; and encouraged the view that the sacrament contained grace as a bottle contains medicine. These developments contributed to the phenomenon beginning in the twelfth century of popular devotion to Christ in the eucharist.

Visions and miracle stories surrounding the sacrament proliferated, especially concerning its misuse; e.g. the host (Latin *hostia*, "a sacrificial victim") became bloody flesh to terrify one who stole it, or paralysed the woman who used it on her cabbage patch (Rubin 1991: 341). Christ as he existed in the sacrament became the greatest of all relics. Popular piety influenced liturgical practices such as burning a perpetual light before the reserved species, altar crosses and candles, elaboration of priestly vestments and actions, and ringing bells to signal the conse-cration and elevation of the host. "The climax of such multiplication and intensification of all that was sensuous in the liturgy of the Mass was the Elevation of the Host . . . Their [the faithful's] insistence upon actually seeing the elements is, perhaps, the supreme expression of the medieval drive for visualizing the sacred" (Garside 1966: 176). The intense desire to see God on the altar increased the power of the priest who alone could do this. "The elevation was perceived as the essence of the clerical office, the focus of the liturgy, the epitome and justification of clerical privilege" (Rubin 1991: 132). In 1264 the Feast of Corpus Christi, the commemoration of the institution of the eucharist, was commanded by Pope Urban IV largely due to the influence of the visions of Juliana (d. 1258), a nun of Liège. By the eve of the Reformation, Corpus Christi processions had become popular ritual reaffirmations of community solidarity to the extent of displacing the early church's sense of communion in the eucharist. The violent anti-sacramental spiritualism of the Reformation period is not so surprising when seen against the background of the late medieval drive to concretize and bind the spiritual to the material, and the use of this drive to justify clerical privilege.

People adored the host and brought their petitions to it. The sacrament was so revered that frequency of reception declined drasti-cally; the sight of the host alone was a devotional substitute for reception. In response to the laity's fears of spilling God's blood, the doctrine of concomitance (council of Constance, 1415) legitimated lay communion with only the bread by affirming the presence of the whole Christ in one specie. (Since the bread is Christ's flesh, and since flesh contains blood, therefore the consecrated bread is both the body and blood of Christ.) The Hussite movement's protest against this practice was reiterated by the sixteenth-century Reformers. Since Latin was of little use to the laity, they no longer "heard" the mass but saw the elevation of the host as the re-enactment of the passion which the priest, by virtue of the sacrament of orders, "offered" to God. Such sacerdotal offerings increased in value as they increased in number; this reflects the "mathematics of salvation" discussed earlier. The English Reformer, Thomas Cranmer (d. 1556), described people running about from altar to altar in order to see and worship God in the host. But well before Cranmer, the Augustinian monk Gottschalk Hollen (d. 1481) had complained that when people hear the bell they come in to see the host "and then run out as if they had seen the devil" (*TRE* 1: 98). These practices were scathingly denounced by the sixteenth-century Reformers as superstitious at best and idolatrous at worst.

Aquinas emphasized that the sacraments contain grace. He introduced Aristotelian causality and its corresponding concepts of matter and form into reflection on the sacraments (the word is the form of the sacrament, and the material elements are the matter) as well as the concepts of *opus operatum* and *opus operantis*. The former affirmed that the sacraments are effective independently of the piety and morality of the recipient or the priest when he intends to do what the church does. The latter affirmed that the right disposition of the recipient is necessary if the received grace is to be really effectual.

The medieval preoccupation with relating the eucharist to the passion of Christ led to the sixteenth-century controversy over whether the mass is a repetition or a remembrance of the passion. If the church is to enter into the past action of the passion, it can do so either by the willful mental activity of remembering it; or, if there is to be an objective reality outside the mind, by some sort of repetition of the redeeming act of Christ. In the sixteenth century these would become church-dividing alternatives which in the polemics of the time were presented, respectively, as the spiritual dissolution of sacramental means of grace into mental voluntarism or as the mechanistic manipulation of sacramental grace. "The eucharist could never really be reformed; it could only be wholly accepted or negated outright" (Rubin 1991: 352). This claim is an adequate description for the Roman Catholic Reformers (acceptance) and the Protestant Reformers such as Karlstadt, Zwingli, Oecolampadius, and the Anabaptists (negation), but it is inadequate for those aligned with Luther and Calvin.

The Reformation was initiated by Luther's attack on the abuse of indulgences in relation to the sacrament of penance. Luther's critique of penance, based on his theology of justification by grace alone, expanded into an attack on the entire medieval understanding of sacraments. God's promise of salvation, he insisted, is unconditional because it is not based on an inner change in the hearer but on a change outside the person (*extra nos*) in his or her standing before God. Recall Luther's emphasis on testament in contrast to covenant as the only adequate expression of God's promise of salvation. A covenant is an agreement between living partners that requires the fulfillment of stipulated conditions to be effective. As discussed earlier, covenant language is always an "if . . . then" construction. A testament, however, only requires the death of the testator to be effective; its language structure is "because . . . therefore." The Lord's Supper, Luther never tired of proclaiming, is a testament: Christ is the testator who makes the testament; the bequest is expressed in Christ's words at the Last Supper; Christ provided his testamentary words with a "seal or emblem" which is the sacramental signs of bread and wine under which are his true body and blood; the bequest received through this distribution is the forgiveness of sin and eternal life; the obligation assigned to the heirs is the command to remember Christ. For Luther, the reality of Word and sacraments, as God's self-communication, does not depend on faith. "Everything depends upon the Word and commandment of God. . . . Baptism is simply water and God's Word in and with each other; that is, when the Word accompanies the water, Baptism is valid, even though faith be lacking. For my faith does not constitute Baptism but receives it. Baptism . . . is bound not to our faith but to the Word" (Tappert 1959: 443). Like Augustine, Luther coordinated word (*sacramentum audibile*, the audible sacrament) and sacrament (*verbum visibile*, the visible word); their focus is God's action instead of human actions.

A consequence of the Reformation focus on God's promise was to reduce the number of sacraments from seven to two. Augustine had defined a sacrament as the word added to the element. Since only baptism and eucharist have dominical institution in the New Testament, the other sacraments are eliminated. All the Protestant Reformers accepted this, although Luther continued to view confession as a means of grace.

In reducing the number of sacraments, the Reformers claimed the church did not have authority to institute sacraments without biblical warrant. The Reformation displacement of the church as hierarchical institution (*Kirche*) by the church as community (*Gemeinde*) was expressed by the view of the eucharist as a "communion," a communal meal of the congregation celebrating God's promise, instead of a meritorious sacrifice offered by the priest to God. Since communion involves communication and participation, the Reformers translated the mass into the vernacular and distributed communion in both kinds (bread and wine); they rejected transubstantiation, withholding the cup from the laity, the mass as a sacrifice, and private masses. Furthermore, all the Reformers, in spite of their differences, understood that communion has social ethical significance for community.

To the Reformers, transubstantiation shifted the focus from the proclamation *that* God communicates himself in the eucharist to speculation about *how* that communication takes place. Luther's point versus Thomas is that extra miracles are not necessary. "The real miracle of the eucharist is that Christ is present, not that the substance of bread and wine are absent" (Steinmetz 1986: 73). Theologically, transubstantiation appears to give priests power to make Christ in the mass, thereby usurping Christ and positing the infallibility of grace upon correct performance of the rite (*ex opere operato*). Salvation thus appeared as a human work dependent upon a clerical class, rather than as a divine gift. Sociologically, this orientation permeated every aspect of the late medieval Christianity so trenchantly described as "a cult of the living in the service of the dead." "The devotion, theology, liturgy, architecture, finances, social structure and institutions of late medieval Christianity are inconceivable without the assumption that friends and relatives of the souls in purgatory had an absolute obligation to procure their release, above all by having masses said for them" (Bossy 1983: 42). The Reformers rejected the medieval interpretation of the mass as a propitiatory sacrifice and its concomitant practice of private masses because these practices separated Word and sacrament. In a private mass there is no community to hear the words of the gospel and thus the elements of bread and wine lose their meaning and become objects, "holy things," to be offered to appease God.

Unhappy with the perceived papist remnant in Luther's emphasis upon the real presence of Christ in the Lord's Supper, and aided by linguistic tools borrowed from the humanists, Zwingli insisted that the "is" in "this is my body" means "signify." Thus when Jesus says "this is my body," he means "this signifies my body," just as a wedding ring signifies a marriage but is not the relationship itself. A favorite biblical verse for this symbolic understanding was John 6: 63: "It is the spirit that gives life, the flesh is of no avail." This text was read in light of Augustine's well-known comment on spiritual eating in his *Exposition of the Gospel of John*, "Believe, and you have already eaten." The more radical Reformers questioned and, in extreme cases such as Caspar Schwenkfeld (d. 1561), even rejected the need for sacraments altogether (McLaughlin 1986a). This is the logical consequence of the sacramentarians' divorce of the reception of the Holy Spirit from external means such as the sacraments. In contrast, Luther insisted that God "deals with us in a twofold manner, first outwardly, then inwardly. . . . The inward experience follows and is effected by the outward. God has determined to give the inward to no one except through the outward [Word and sign instituted by him]" (*LW* 40: 146).

The sacramentarians argued that the sacraments do not give faith but presume it. Thus water baptism and participation in the Lord's Supper are outer expressions or disclosures of an inner change. Zwingli, for example, retained the sacraments of baptism and eucharist, but as signs and symbols aiding the believer's spiritual exercise of recalling God's grace. The focus is therefore not so much God's self-communication but the spiritual–psychological activity of the believers. From Luther's perspective this could be interpreted as a kind of reverse Donatism; that is, the validity of the sacrament depends upon the faith of the recipient. According to B. A. Gerrish (1992: 250) this perspective continued in Zwingli's successor, Heinrich Bullinger (d. 1575): "Believers therefore bring Christ *to* the Supper in their hearts; they do not receive him *in* the Supper." In Zwingli's theology and liturgy the focus is on the community of those who confess their faith in Christ and commit themselves to discipleship. Zwingli's emphasis on the corporate life (a reflection of Swiss communalism) leads to the view of the eucharist as the action *of* the congregation rather than *to* the congregation. The body of Christ is the church. This is why "modern Zwingli scholarship has spoken of a transubstantiation of the worshipping congregation into the body of Christ through the invisible activity of the Spirit" (Steinmetz 1986: 76–7).

To Luther, Zwingli's understanding of the sacraments vitiated the gospel by making it dependent upon faith and personal piety, thereby releasing once more all the medieval insecurities attendant upon introspection as the prerequisite for the sacrament. The "because . . . therefore" grammar of God's promise shifted to the "if . . . then" grammar of human achievement: *if* you have a heartfelt remembrance of Christ's passion, *then* you may participate in the eucharist as an outward and visible sign of an inward and spiritual grace already present. Beyond such a commemorative view of the Lord's Supper as a devotional exercise, both Luther and Calvin asserted divine self-communication in the sacrament.

In the polemical exchanges over the eucharist at the Marburg colloquy (1529), Luther and Zwingli rang all the historical and theological changes available to them. Luther accused Zwingli of a Nestorian separation of the natures of Christ (since Christ's body has ascended to heaven it cannot be in the eucharist) and took up Cyril of Alexandria's *communicatio idiomatum* (the communication of natures) as an affirmation that where Christ's divine nature is so also is his human nature. In other words, the finite is capable of the infinite (*finitum capax infiniti est*). The practical consequences of these differing christologies are evident in Luther's opposition to iconoclasm and his preservation of art in the church, and Zwingli's denuding of the church of art and organ music. The ecclesiastical and political consequences were evident in the subsequent divisions among the Reformers.

The Marburg Colloquy, 1529

It is a tragic irony that the Lord's Supper, the sacrament of Christian unity, has served in various periods of the history of Christianity to divide rather than to unite Christians. This was especially the case in the sixteenth century: to be right about the sacrament was to be right about God and salvation. Neither Luther nor Zwingli thought the other was right about the sacrament. While they agreed in rejecting both the mass as a sacrifice and the doctrine of transubstantiation; they disagreed – vehemently – over their understanding of what the Lord's Supper is.

By 1524 Zwingli had begun to interpret the "is" of "this is my body" as "signifies." This interpretation was influenced by the platonic dualism of flesh and spirit earlier advanced in connection with the sacrament by Zwingli's humanist hero, Erasmus. In his 1503 *Enchiridion*, which went through numerous editions and translations, Erasmus developed a spiritual or memorial understanding of the Lord's Supper that strongly influenced Luther's former colleague, Karlstadt, and through Karlstadt supported Zwingli. One of their favorite biblical verses was John 6: 63, "It is the spirit that gives life, the flesh is of no avail." Karlstadt and those he influenced used this verse to justify differentiating between the bread eaten by the communicant and the Christ received by faith. Indeed, Karlstadt's interpretation of the words of institution of the Lord's Supper posited that when Jesus said "This is my body" he was pointing at himself. This led one contemporary wag to suggest that when Jesus said "This is my blood," he must have had a nosebleed.

After the falling-out between Luther and Karlstadt, Karlstadt not only had his tracts on the Lord's Supper printed in Switzerland, but also visited Zwingli. Erasmus, too, had attacked Luther in 1524. Thus Luther's view of Zwingli was strongly colored by his controversies with Karlstadt and Erasmus. Conversely, Luther's insistence that Christ is really present in the sacrament appeared to Zwingli to be a relapse into the Catholic doctrine of transubstantiation. A further sense of the magnitude of Philip's task in reconciling these two Reformers is provided by an overview of their writings on the subject prior to 1529.

By 1525 the mass had been discontinued in Zurich. Discussions about the Lord's Supper were heatedly carried on throughout the German and Swiss lands. As the divergence between Luther and Zwingli became more apparent, each Reformer was anxious to convince the world that he had not read the other's writings. With the common Protestant rejection of transubstantiation, innumerable theologians (among them Karlstadt, Oecolampadius, Bucer, Schwenkfeld, Althamer, Billican, Stigler, Bugenhagen, Brenz, to name only the better-known) were floating alternative theories and analyses of this central sacrament of the church. It became apparent then that Wittenberg and Zurich were competing for the spiritual – and therefore political – allegiance of the south German cities such as Basle, Strasbourg, Augsburg, Nördlingen, Biberach, Memmingen, Ulm, Isny, Kempten, Lindau, and Constance. Without them Zurich would be isolated. But with the help and allegiance of these cities, the German lands might be won over to Zwingli's movement. Thus the Luther–Zwingli debate was not merely personal or conceptual.

In 1525 Zwingli published a major statement of his position, *Subsidium sive coronis de eucharistia*. Here he developed his distinctions between the natural body of Christ before the crucifixion, the glorified body of Christ ascended to heaven, and the mystical body of the church. In this writing, Zwingli's humanist linguistic work comes to the fore. Only recognition, he argued, of the Bible's figurative use of words, in particular the metaphorical explanation of the Last Supper, could make the Bible plain, reasonable, and humanly intelligible. Christ's own words were intelligible only if the bread and wine were symbols to which the recipient brought faith and hope in God. To Luther this meant that Zwingli had shifted the focus of the Lord's Supper from God's promise of salvation present in the eucharistic action to the active memory of the congregation. Luther saw this shift as another expression of putting the burden of proof for salvation upon the believer rather than upon God.

In the summer of 1525, Oecolampadius, Zwingli's colleague in Basle, published his *De genuine verborum Domini*, which was clearly an attack on Luther. Oecolampadius dedicated his writing to the "beloved brethren in Schwabia" with the intent to win them over to his position. Since these pastors had been his students in Heidelberg, it was natural for Oecolampadius to assume they would harken to his appeal. He did not reckon with Luther's lasting impact upon them made during the Heidelberg disputation in 1518. Led by the young disciple of Luther, Johannes Brenz, 14 south German Lutheran pastors subscribed to a basically Lutheran confession of faith, the *Suevian Syngramma*. Luther was delighted by this affirmation of the real presence of Christ in the eucharist. Zwingli's response in 1526 was that Luther had taken the "simple words of Christ" and made them obscure and incomprehensible, thereby allowing the reintroduction of extreme papal claims. Here Zwingli raised what would become a central theme: the ubiquity (omnipresence) of Christ. Launching into a discussion of the early church's doctrine of the two natures of Christ, Zwingli asserted that Christ's divine nature never left heaven because, being one with God, the divine nature could not ascend to heaven as Christ's human nature did. The divinity of Christ is and always has been everywhere, but after the ascension the bodily Christ remains in heaven at the right hand of God until the last day. Those who claimed that Christ's body was eaten in the Last Supper must believe that Christ was not sensible of his sufferings on the cross or that the disciples did not eat in human fashion since Christ had not yet risen when he instituted this meal. Thus, Zwingli argued, "this is" can only mean "this signifies."

Luther saw in Zwingli's theology the reappearance of the Nestorian heresy of the early church that had separated the divine and human natures of Christ, and thereby denied the full reality of the incarnation. To Luther this clearly meant that how one understood the Lord's Supper was related intimately to how one understood salvation and God's activity in the world. Thus, in a parallel to the early church's controversy over the person of Christ, Luther advocated the position set forth by Cyril of Alexandria that emphasized a personal union in Christ of the divine and human natures known as the *communicatio idomatum* (communication of natures). The council of Chalcedon in 451 had asserted that "the divine and human in Christ are united unchanged and unmixed, but undivided and unseparated." In advancing this doctrine against Zwingli, Luther emphasized that in the incarnation God had genuinely condescended into the depths of human existence (Luther was fond of saying that Christ cannot be dragged too deeply into the flesh), and that in Christ there is a genuine transmission of God's full divinity and majesty.

Luther responded specifically to Zwingli's arguments that Christ's ascension physically removed him from the world, and that "the flesh is of no avail" (John 6: 63) in his lengthy 1527 tract *That These Words of Christ, "This Is My Body," etc., Still Stand Firm Against the Fanatics*. On the basis of the classic doctrines of the trinity and christology, Luther argued that the ascension of Christ to the right hand of God does not denote a spiritual geography but rather Christ's sharing the ubiquity (omnipresence) of God. As creator, God is everywhere upholding the continuous creation of the world; the crucial point is that in the bread and wine of the Lord's Supper God promises to be present *for us* (*pro nobis*). Luther is here struggling to overcome the western metaphysical view of space in his affirmation that space is not restrictive for God. Since, Luther argues, Christians confess in the first article of the creed God's presence in heaven and earth as creator, they should also recognize God's presence in the sacrament as redeemer. God's real presence in the eucharist is his condescension of personal availability. "Why? Because it is one thing if God is present, and another if he is present for you. He is there for you when he adds his Word and binds himself, saying, 'Here you are to find me' " (*LW* 37: 68–9).

Luther responded to the argument that the flesh is of no avail by rejecting the platonic dualism of flesh and spirit as nonbiblical. He argued that biblical anthropology uses the terms flesh and spirit to refer to personal orientation, not being. What is done in faith is spiritual; what is done in unbelief is fleshly. "Nothing can be so material, fleshly, or outward, but it becomes spiritual when it is done in the Word and in faith. 'Spiritual' is nothing else than what is done in us and by us through the Spirit and faith, whether the object with which we are dealing is physical or spiritual. Thus, Spirit consists in the use, not in the object, be it seeing, hearing, speaking, touching, begetting, bearing, eating, drinking, or anything else" (*LW* 37: 92).

Luther's argument against Zwingli found expression in the phrase that "the finite is capable of bearing the infinite." To Zwingli, who like Karlstadt had the sound pastoral intuition that the externalization of religion put God at human disposal, this suggested idolatry. But to Luther this meant not only that ordinary bread and wine may communicate the presence and promise of God, but that all creation may serve the creator. This is the theological foundation for Luther's profound appreciation of nature and art as vehicles for communicating the gospel. Luther's love and use of music in worship, for example, continued to be expressed among his theological descendants, among whom Johann Sebastian Bach is well-known. In contrast, Zwingli, himself an accomplished musician, prohibited music in worship.

Those Reformers who so emphasized the transcendence of God that they denied that the finite is capable of the infinite began the process toward the modern world's exclusion of the sacred altogether. The first steps in this process may be seen in the iconoclastic reactions of Reformers from Karlstadt to Zwingli and in part on into Calvin, who strove to purify the church by removing as much art as possible. They stripped the churches of all images and color, and in Zurich literally nailed shut the organs. This trend will later be expressed by the word "puritan." Some think that these Reformers struggled so successfully against the possibility of idolatry that the holy was transformed into the morally good, and righteousness was given ascetic connotations; all of which was finally banalized in the phrase "cleanliness is next to godliness."

In early 1527 Zwingli completed his *Amica exegesis* ("Friendly Exposition") in which he tried to combine independence and concilia-tion. This tract, which Zwingli sent to Luther, warned that Luther was perilously close to the Catholic doctrine of transubstantiation. But let the conflict end, wrote Zwingli, for the future could be bright if Luther would only recognize his mistakes. It was clear that Zwingli would not give an inch, but expected Luther to surrender. Thus Luther's response that Zwingli is an "insolent Swiss" is not surprising. In his April 1527 tract, *That These Words of Christ, "This Is My Body", etc., Still Stand Firm against the Fanatics*, Luther made a comprehensive response to Zwingli. His opponents, Luther wrote, were both crazy and possessed by the devil, not to mention blasphemous in their appeal to reason and common sense. In May, Zwingli responded in his "Friendly Answer" that among other things Luther had incorrectly read the Scripture and had conceded too much to Rome, and that God had not revealed to him the meaning of the Lord's Supper.

The antagonism between Zwingli and Luther was aggravated by what we may call nondoctrinal factors. One was Zwingli's humanistic fascination with classical figures of speech. Luther was convinced that Zwingli's biblical interpretation suffered from his use of such figures of speech deriving from classical studies as trope, allegory, ellipsis, metathesis, aposiopesis, hyperbole, prolepsis, synecdoche, and allo-eosis. The last of these, one of Zwingli's favorite ways of alluding to the transposition of attributes, allowed him to argue that Christ's humanity could sometimes imply his divinity, and vice versa.

Another nondoctrinal factor that contributed to mutual misunder-standing was the fact that Luther lived under a benevolent and sympathetic prince, whereas Zwingli lived in a city governed by a representative style of government. This meant that for Zwingli to carry out his desired reforms he had to persuade and convince the people and the magistrates. Therefore, with regard to the Lord's Supper, Zwingli had to explain his position in a way that would be intelligible to people. This, along with Zwingli's humanistic leanings, helps to explain why Luther saw him as a rationalist. On the other hand, for Zwingli to agree with Luther's understanding of the Lord's Supper, which many Catholics saw as basically orthodox, would have been a political disaster. Finally, Luther's opinion of the Swiss as a whole was not very complimentary; he was convinced that the Swiss were a belligerent and coarse people.

The Marburg colloquy opened on 1 October 1529. The disputation between Luther and Zwingli began the following morning at 6 a.m. before an audience of about 50. Luther posited that discussion of the Lord's Supper apart from other doctrines such as the trinity, christology, justification, etc. would be fruitless, but Zwingli wished to proceed directly to the Lord's Supper discussion. Luther began by asserting that the words "this is my body" cannot be understood in any other way than as written in the text. If Zwingli is to claim otherwise he must prove it by Scripture, not by reason. For emphasis, Luther wrote in chalk on the table for all to see: *hoc est corpus meum*. When Luther claimed that the use of John 6: 63 was not applicable to the Lord's Supper, the Zurich party responded that this passage would break Luther's neck. In turn, Luther said they should not be so quick to boast about breaking necks for "you are now in Hesse not Switzerland." In spite of all the heat of the discussions, the debate ended with polite phrases and promises of charitable relations. By 4 October the Lutherans and the Zwinglians had agreed to 14 of 15 articles prepared by Luther. They could not agree on the Lord's Supper. Both sides repudiated transubstantiation as well as the belief that the eucharist is a sacrifice for the living and the dead, and they insisted upon communion in both kinds. But the Lutherans continued to hold that Christ is really present in the eucharist for all recipients, whereas the Zwinglians maintained Christ's presence is only in the hearts of believers. Here was their profound difference: for Zwingli the Lord's Supper was an act of thanksgiving for the gospel; for Luther it was a concrete offer of the gospel. Although the two parties left Marburg with the avowed intention to practice Christian charity toward each other, they failed to achieve either a confessional or a military alliance.

In less than a year, the imperial diet met at Augsburg where the Lutherans presented their confession of faith, the Augsburg confession.

The Zwinglian confession, written mainly by the Strasbourg reformer Martin Bucer and known as the Tetrapolitan confession because it was subscribed to by the four cities of Strasbourg, Constance, Memmingen, and Lindau, was also presented at Augsburg. Zwingli, himself not invited to Augsburg, was determined to be heard and thus sent his hastily composed *Fidei ratio*. Since this writing had no effect on Charles V, Zwingli composed a pamphlet, *Fidei expositio*, for Francis I in the hope of winning the French king's support against the Emperor and Rome. There is no evidence that Francis ever read this more impressive defense of Zwingli's faith, and the pamphlet had no influence upon the course of events.

A Zurich-inspired economic blockade of the Catholic cantons that refused to admit Protestant preachers increased Protestant–Catholic tensions in the Swiss Confederacy. In retaliation, the Catholic cantons surprised Zurich with a vastly superior military force. Zwingli, himself armed, accompanied the Zurich forces into this second battle of Kappel in 1531. During the rout of the Zurich forces, Zwingli was seriously wounded and left on the battlefield. Later recognized by the Catholic forces, he was given a mortal blow; the next day he was quartered (the punishment for traitors), and then the parts of his body were burned with dung so that nothing of Zwingli would be left to inspire other Protestants. The story soon circulated that his heart was found intact in the ashes of his body.

Unlike Zwingli, the Swiss Reformation was not exterminated, but where established was allowed to remain. Catholic minorities were not to be disturbed in Protestant lands, whereas Protestant minorities were not to be tolerated in Catholic lands. The division of Switzerland offered a foretaste of the fate of Europe. Almost a quarter century later, in 1555, the Peace of Augsburg legally ratified the confessional divisions of the empire by aligning the religion of an area with that of its ruler. Later this would be described by the motto *cuius regio, eius religio*, "whose reign, his religion." This included the safety valve of allowing persons to emigrate to territories amenable to their confession of faith.

Suggestions for Further Reading

Martin Brecht, *Martin Luther*, vol. 2: *Shaping and Defining the Reformation 1521–1532*, Minneapolis: Fortress, 1990

Mark U. Edwards, Jr, *Luther and the False Brethren*, Stanford: Stanford University Press, 1975

Ulrich Gäbler, *Huldrych Zwingli: His Life and Work*, Philadelphia: Fortress, 1986

Brian A. Gerrish, "The Lord's Supper in the Reformed Confessions" in Donald
  K. McKim, ed., *Major Themes in the Reformed Tradition*, 245–58, Grand Rapids:
  Eerdmans, 1992
Gary Macy, *The Banquet's Wisdom: A Short History of the Theologies of the Lord's Supper*,
  New York: Paulist, 1992
W. P. Stephens, *The Theology of Huldrych Zwingli*, Oxford: Clarendon, 1986
W. P. Stephens, *Zwingli: An Introduction to his Thought*, Oxford: Clarendon, 1992

8

The Sheep against the Shepherds: The Radical Reformations

They are the children of peace who have beaten their swords into plowshares and their spears into pruning hooks, and know war no more.

Menno Simons

The love of enemies and the rejection of violence, understood as New Testament absolutes which characterize the historic peace churches, including the Mennonites, developed from some of the most violent episodes of the Reformation period. The transition from dissonance and revolution to pacifist dissent is one of the more complicated chapters in the story of efforts to relate force and faith, coercion and ethics, society and church in the Reformations. We saw the beginning of this story in the tensions between Karlstadt's "must" and Luther's "may" in Wittenberg. The parallels to this in Zurich are striking. It is common – although somewhat misleading – to lump the protagonists of the dissident groups under the general rubric of "radical Reformers." This convention may be criticized, but the third edition of George H. Williams' magisterial study, *The Radical Reformation* (1992) assures its continuing use.

The radical Reformers were and continue to be a difficult group to define and describe. "The boundaries and origins, to say nothing of the evaluation, of the Anabaptist movement have never been objects of scholarly consensus" (Stayer 1972: 7). From the beginning these Reformers and their adherents have been lumped together under labels that nearly always are pejorative. Their contemporaries called them enthusiasts (from *en theos*, "God-withinism"), spiritualists, fanatics, and Anabaptists (rebaptists [*Wiedertäufer*] and baptists [*Täufer*] are other terms in some of the more recent literature). Luther's pejorative label *Schwärmer* with its onomatopoetic sense of swarms of raving visionaries and fanatics – "too many bees chasing too few bonnets" (Hillerbrand 1986: 25) – may still be found in some studies of the radicals. We need to remember that in the upheavals of the Reformations the differences among theologies were not always so apparent as they sometimes seem today from the vantage point of time and relative stability. The Anabaptist label was applied to those who believed that only adults able to make a profession of faith may be baptized. Since the first generation of these Reformers had been baptized as infants, an adult baptism was literally a rebaptism. Discussion of the radical Reformers or Anabaptists is complicated by their heterogeneous origins, leaders, and visions of Reformation. Under the above labels such disparate groups and persons have been lumped together as the Zwickau prophets who apparently rejected infant baptism and who initiated the Wittenberg disturbances of 1521–2; Karlstadt; Müntzer, who called for the execution of the godless; the equally if not more disruptive leaders who took over the city of Münster in 1534–5 and precipitated a bloody debacle there; the dissenters in Zurich who were a thorn in Zwingli's side; and such men as Menno Simons, whose heirs form the still-existing peace church known as the Mennonites.

There were a number of outstanding Anabaptist leaders who contributed substantially to the vitality of the movement. But none of them – partly because most were executed before 1530 – enjoyed the widely acknowledged leadership positions of Reformers like Luther, Zwingli, and Calvin. The Anabaptist groups also lacked a clear confessional norm or statement, aside from the brief Schleitheim Articles of 1527 which were not generally accepted by all of them. Luther confessed that he was not sure what they believed. "The Anabaptists agree with the foes of the sacrament that only bread and wine are in the Lord's Supper. Yet the sacramentarians disagree with the Anabaptists on baptism. Also, the sacramentarians are not agreed among themselves nor the Anabaptists among themselves. They are at one only in regard to and in opposition to us" (*LW* 40: 261). Zwingli, too, found their demands contradictory (Walton 1967: 153). The modern scholar of Anabaptism, Hans-Jürgen Goertz (1988: 153), recently wrote: "The question of who among the many Anabaptist groups were the 'genuine' Anabaptists cannot be answered in historical terms." The ambiguity surrounding the Anabaptist groups both dismayed and delighted their contemporaries (and modern historians), who picked and chose among the multiplicity of opinions, groupings, divisions, and leaders to form their own judgments. These judgments, whether formed by Lutheran, Zwinglian, Calvinist, or Catholic, at least agreed in perceiving the Anabaptist groups as a threat to sixteenth-century society.

The Anabaptists

A major locus of the Anabaptist development was Zwingli's Zurich. However, recent scholarship has made it clear that this was not the only root of Anabaptism (Deppermann et al. 1975). The diversity of the Anabaptist movement also stemmed from the radical reform of Thomas Müntzer in central Germany, which was implemented under different conditions in south Germany by Hans Hut, and from the charismatic–apocalyptic milieu of Strasbourg under the influence of Melchior Hoffman, whose spiritualistic–eschatological ideas influenced developments in the Netherlands–north Germany area. The differences among these movements are illustrated by the claim of Balthasar Hubmaier, Anabaptist Reformer of Waldshut (Black Forest) and Nikolsburg (Moravia), who stated that the baptism he taught differed from that of Hut "like heaven and earth, East and West, Christ and Belial" (Goertz 1988: 15).

We have already seen that Zwingli's reform program depended upon persuasion of the authorities, and existed in the face of the threats of Catholic cantons. In the sixteenth century it was obvious to nearly everyone that a community without a common ideology was not only at the mercy of one that was united, e.g. the Turks, but was also subject to a civil war that could imperil the very existence of the state. In Zwingli's eyes the rise of the Zurich Anabaptists was therefore a clear and present danger. He regarded these evangelicals as quarrelsome, envious, back-biting, and hypocritical extremists who lacked charity and undermined the government. Their opposition to infant baptism, their open-air preaching, and their constant street discussions and harangues were bringing the gospel into disrepute. Indeed, Zwingli saw these people as social revolutionaries whose teaching would overthrow society and religion alike.

The immediate controversy centered on infant baptism, but behind it lay a very different view of Christianity. Other Reformers such as Luther and Calvin agreed that there was but one catholic (i.e. universal) church with one creed. They understood that the visible church is coextensive with the local community wherein the people must live and worship in harmony. The Anabaptists initially shared this vision but could not actualize it (one of the rare exceptions was Waldshut in the Black Forest under the leadership of Hubmaier). It may be argued that the Anabaptist withdrawal from the larger society was a consequence of their failure to achieve a *corpus Christianum* in their own image. In other words, formally Zwingli and the Zurich radicals were both striving for a Christian commonwealth; convex is but the other side of concave. However, failing to convince the whole community, the Anabaptists turned to local congregations of voluntary members who regarded themselves as altogether set apart from the state. This radical break from all Christian establishments has been characterized as "a steepleless Christianity" – a Christianity "with corporate loyalties and internal disciplines transcending any earthly state and never to be subsumed under one, a people characterized by the pursuit of holiness, separated from the world" (Williams 1992: 1279, 1286–7). For them, the one true church consisted only of true believers. The true believers could be ascertained by tests of conduct and belief. Those not meeting the standards for church membership were to be expelled and banned. The Anabaptists posed a radical alternative to the "state churches" of Lutherans, Zwinglians, and Catholics who believed that the visible church embraced all professing Christians. The alternative communities of the Anabaptists scrutinized members to eliminate the unworthy, and worshipped and associated in separate, voluntary communities.

The Anabaptist development in Zurich is instructive for understanding the widely held perception of this reform movement. Zwingli and the Zurich magistrates perceived a threefold danger in the Anabaptist movement. First, the Anabaptists were seen to be deliberately and consciously disruptive of the social and religious tenets of Zurich and its villages, and thereby a danger to both Swiss unity and the success of Zwingli's reform. In Zurich, as elsewhere, the success of the reform movement was seen to be dependent upon the support of the government. Fearful of possible aggression from the Catholic cantons, Zurich and other reformed cantons believed that only a community united in religion could defend itself and maintain its freedom. Thus, in so far as the Anabaptists hindered this union they were seen as abetting the Counter-Reformation.

Second, the Anabaptists turned Zwingli's own weapon, Scripture, against him, much as Karlstadt and Müntzer had against Luther. To their chagrin, the Reformers were beginning to discover that the lay assertiveness and independence they encouraged against the Roman church could be turned against them as well. The dissidents insisted that they were only carrying Zwingli's own commitment to the Bible as the norm for faith and life to its logical conclusions. When the Anabaptists read the Bible they could find no warrant in it for infant baptism, but only for baptism as a sign of adult faith and regeneration. Nor could they find any warrant in the Bible for the union of church and state. When these dissidents read the Sermon on the Mount, they believed it literally meant believers must separate from the world.

Zwingli, like Luther, experienced the shock of having his own followers read very differently the biblical text he had so labored to make available to them. Both Zwingli and the Anabaptists accepted the same Bible and agreed that tradition and human authorities must give way before the Word of God. And they agreed that the Bible was perfectly clear if read under the guidance of the Holy Spirit in faith and love. Of course, when their followers did not agree with them, Luther and Zwingli insisted that this was precisely what the "fanatics" did not do. So Zwingli viewed the Anabaptists' alternative reading of Scripture as the expression of ignorance, malice, and contentiousness. On the other hand, from the perspective of the Roman Catholics this dissonance and then dissidence was the can of worms opened by the Reformers themselves. The Catholic controversialist Johann Eck derided Zwingli's claim to oppose the Anabaptists since he was in fact their origin: "How near is Zwingli now to the Anabaptists whom nevertheless . . . he torments to death . . . and tortures limb by limb" (Gerrish 1992: 253). There was a widespread perception that the Anabaptists were essentially Zwinglians or at least the logical result of Zwingli's interpretation of the sacraments as an act of public confession of faith. Zwingli himself admitted that "they went out from us, but they were not of us" (1 John 2: 19; Locher 1979: 261).

Third, the Anabaptists were viewed as politically as well as religiously exclusivistic, and thus a civic liability. In refusing to accept the normal obligations of citizenship – oaths, taxes (the tithe), military service – the Anabaptists were seen to be forming a state within the state. Their refusal to take oaths was a serious element in this perception because for late medieval society the oath was a major part of the "glue" that held the society together. Citizens swore oaths to the common good and defense of the town, to the guilds to which they belonged, and to the truth. Perjury, with its assumed certainty of divine punishment, was abhorred. Without the public oath, indispensable in any court of justice, the ordinary daily administration of public life was in danger of breaking down. The refusal to render an oath was tantamount to political separatism. The Swiss Confederacy itself was traditionally dated from an oath-swearing in 1291, and annually renewed by its repetition.

"Early Anabaptism was a religious and social-revolutionary movement" (Wohlfeil and Goertz 1980: 43) which was not opposed to using the sword for its cause (Stayer 1972). However, after the Schleitheim Articles (1527) they refused to bear arms. Pacifism was a serious stance. In sixteenth-century Switzerland there was no standing army. Every man was responsible for defense, and was expected to appear armed and ready when called upon by the government. The citizen-soldier was the support and guarantor of public order and independence. The walls of the towns were to be guarded according to a set pattern. The towns had their own cannon and armory, and held regular crossbow and shooting matches. Every male was liable for military service, and military preparation was a normal, expected masculine duty for which boys were trained from an early age. For a man to refuse military service was, in effect, to renounce citizenship. Townsmen resented Anabaptist pacifism as a shirking of indispensable duty, and as a placing of extra burdens upon themselves. A further fear was that if the Anabaptist movement spread, there would be no one to shoulder arms for defense.

The Anabaptist refusal to pay tithes and interest was similarly seen as a rejection of civic responsibility. The early church had regularized lay support for its work through canonical legislation of the Old Testament tithe. This became a particular imposition on rural areas in the Middle Ages because it exacted one-tenth of the produce of the land, including animals and profits. With the Reformation rejection of the papal use of the Old Testament regulations and canon law, the tithe was widely called into question. The Anabaptists made it clear that the tithe was refused not primarily because it was an economic imposition but because it was perceived as an instrument of control by the Zurich government over the parishes within its jurisdiction. For Zwingli, the tithe was a key to the centralized territorial church which he wanted to reform but not to dissolve. The refusal of tithes, like iconoclasm and attacks upon the mass, represented the disintegration of the old religious order. To some at least, this rejection of tithes and taxes appeared very similar to the Catholic church's unpopular insistence upon exemption from taxation and from civil law courts. Similarly, the Anabaptist insistence upon a church of true believers, and thus the instituting of excommunication and the ban, also led people to associate the Anabaptists with elements of Catholicism.

Since all these concerns were included under the pejorative heading "Anabaptist," it will be useful to explore what the various reforming parties believed to be at stake in their alternative understandings of baptism.

Excursus: Reformation Understandings of Baptism

As already suggested, the radicals' stance on baptism included far more than a change in ritual. In medieval Christianity baptism expressed an understanding both of the gospel and of society. The implications for the latter have been sketched above and will be further delineated below. The focus of this section will be on baptism as an expression of the gospel.

As with their convictions concerning the Lord's Supper, so too with baptism all the Reformers were convinced that a false understanding of baptism falsified the gospel. This is not a simple topic because its scope includes understandings of sin, faith, the Christian life, and the church.

The theological rationale for infant baptism developed in the early church in relation to the doctrine of original sin. Once again, the theologian influential upon western doctrine was Augustine. Augustine posited that the human race inherited sin from Adam. In German the term for this original or inherited sin is *Erbsünde*. How did and does this occur? Augustine explained that Adam fell from grace when he refused to obey God. Adam's body was the instrument, not the source, for his perverted will; but once the fall had occurred, the body also became the bearer and transmitter of sin. Given Augustine's pre-conversion obsession with sexual pleasures and his post-conversion renunciation of them, it is not hard to imagine how he came to view the transmission of sin through the sexual act. "With the fatal ease of a man who believes he can explain a complex phenomenon, simply by reducing it to its historical origins, Augustine will remind his congregation of the exact circumstances of the Fall of Adam and Eve. When they disobeyed God by eating the forbidden fruit, they had been 'ashamed': they had covered their genitals with fig-leaves. That was enough for Augustine: 'Ecce unde. That's the place! That's the place where the first sin is passed on' " (Brown 1975: 388). In short, original sin is the first sexually transmitted disease! Sadly, this interpretation bequeathed to western culture a perennial confusion and guilt about sexual relations. Hence today the Augustinian terms for sin, cupidity and concupiscence, are defined in our dictionaries as lust and ardent sexual desire. One of the more interesting responses in the Reformation period was the view of some of the radicals that sex without lust would create children without sin, children of light and innocence (see Williams 1992: 782, 784).

Augustine's textual reference for his interpretation of sin was Romans 5: 12: "Therefore, just as sin came into the world through one man, and death came through sin, so death spread to all because all have sinned." Augustine read this text in its Latin Vulgate translation. The Latin translated the Greek phrase "because all have sinned" as "in whom all have sinned" (*in quo omnes peccaverunt*). Since *in quo* was read in the masculine by Augustine it supported his doctrine of sin inherited from Adam.

Augustine's textual support for the doctrine of original sin was undermined by linguistic biblical studies in the Reformation. Erasmus, for example, understood Romans 5: 12 "as referring not necessarily to original sin . . . but to sin by imitation of the example of Adam" (Payne 1970: 42, 251). Erasmus uses the word "sin" for actual sins. In so far as sin is inherited it is inherited as the tendency to sin which then is later actualized. In following this reduction of original sin to merely an inclination to sin, Zwingli will use the term *Erbbresten*, signifying a residual impulse to sin, instead of the term *Erbsünde* (hereditary sin). Thus sin is shifted from an ontological condition of human existence to a volitional action, and thereby the rationale for infant baptism is undercut. If persons are not born in sin, the washing away of sin by baptism is not necessary. Erasmus's "catechetical and voluntaristic principles militate against infant baptism" (Payne 1970: 177). Erasmus was a strong influence not only upon Zwingli but also upon the radical Reformers. But while Erasmus could voice a radical theology, he could not himself take radical steps. If the church had done something for centuries, it was not up to him to depart from that tradition. "I cannot depart from the consensus of the Church, nor have I ever departed" (Payne 1970: 153). Zwingli and his radical followers had no such scruples.

Zwingli himself initiated the discussion of infant baptism among his friends and perhaps even from the pulpit. We have already discussed above the rudiments of Zwingli's sacramental theology. Baptism, like the Lord's Supper, is not understood as the expression of God's promise, the gift of God's grace, but rather as a testimony by the community that it is the people of God. Here again we see Zwingli's emphasis upon covenant theology and also the influence upon him of a platonic anthropology that divides spirit from matter. The influence of the latter on sacramental theology leads to the position that the Spirit of God does not need outward means for self-communication. Baptism, then, does not wash away sin, but is only an external sign of initiation into the church and a pledge to lead a life of discipleship to Christ. "Baptism with water was an outward sign. Only when the baptized was granted faith did baptism with the Spirit, which initiated him into the Church universal, accompany the outward sign . . . Zwingli spoke of baptism as an outward sign before the question of rebaptism was raised by the *Täufer*" (Walton 1967: 171) The implication of Zwingli's position was that baptism is only applicable to adults who can consciously commit themselves to Christ. The realization of this

implication by his radical followers forced Zwingli to revise his earlier
doubts about infant baptism and to defend it with a variety of
arguments. What was at stake here for Zwingli was first his opposition
to what he believed was the externalization and mechanization of the
gospel by the sacramental theology of both Roman Catholic and
Lutheran theology, and then his opposition to what he believed was the
sectarianism of the Anabaptists, whom he saw trivializing the weight of
sin with their assumption of the possibility of a pure church.

For their part, the Anabaptists viewed the doctrine that baptism
removed original sin as a papist distortion of Scripture designed to
perpetuate the power to dispense grace which the Roman church had
arrogated to itself from God. The Anabaptist critique of the Lutheran
retention of infant baptism as a sacrament was that not only did this
remain stuck in papism, it also promoted "cheap grace" because it did
not stress faith and discipleship as its precondition. Thus Endres Keller
stated in his confession: "You will have to admit that the popes are
responsible for this wretched situation. One can plainly see it, and no
one can deny that there was no infant baptism in the time of the
apostles, and that they baptized no children. Had they baptized
children, it would be recorded in Scripture. Infant baptism cannot be
defended from Scripture even if Luther and the pope say so" (Klaasen
1981: 178).

The motivation and goal of the Anabaptist movements was to
restore the true Christianity of the biblical community in the face of its
degeneration in the *corpus Christianum* advocated by Roman Catholics,
Lutherans, and Zwinglians. The Anabaptists were acutely sensitive to
the dissonance between water baptism and baptism by the Holy Spirit.
Müntzer had written that "true baptism is not understood, therefore
the entrance into Christendom has become a crude monkey business"
(*CTM* 191). Or, as that great Dane of the nineteenth century, Søren
Kierkegaard, would later acidly comment on establishment Christianity: Where everyone is a Christian, no one is a Christian. The
Anabaptist concern was primarily ecclesiological not sacramental. True
disciples of Jesus are in the world, but not *of* the world; the contemporary church only "aped" the world with its aspiration for the *corpus
Christianum*. The Anabaptists could not rationalize or excuse the gap
between what the church ought to be and what it is. It is in this sense
that Anabaptism blossomed in an anticlerical milieu. That is why it was
not uncommon for Anabaptists to refer to infant baptism as the
baptism of the Antichrist. Grebel expressed this anticlerical connection
with the polemic against infant baptism when he stated that it allowed
people to remain stuck in their own vices.

Anabaptist ecclesiology led to the teaching of a threefold baptism. Baptism is to be the sign of a renewed community, the community as the body of Christ. Admission to the community is only open to Christ's disciples. Discipleship is possible only by the grace of God communicated by the Holy Spirit that leads to repentance. True baptism is first the inner baptism by the Spirit. When a person can confess this, then water baptism is administered as the sign of this faith and a renewed life. Because, however, disciples are not of this world, they will be rejected and persecuted; this is the third baptism, the baptism of blood, that is, martyrdom. Williams (1992: 218) observes that for the Anabaptists, baptism took the place of the medieval sacrament of penance. "The initial call to believers' baptism stressed, over against pedobaptism [infant baptism], not only the adult's capacity to believe but rather to repent. . . . To the worn-out sacrament of Baptism had been restored the experiential significance of the now displaced sacrament of penance."

To Luther this all appeared as the reintroduction of the Donatist heresy and salvation by works. The Anabaptist position, Luther argued in his *Concerning Rebaptism* (1528), displaces God's grace by the work of faith, and thus brings back the uncertainty of salvation prevalent under the papacy. To say that faith and renewal of life is the precondition for baptism leads to either uncertainty or presumption. "I must say that they are guilty of a great presumption. For if they follow this principle they cannot venture to baptize before they are certain that the one to be baptized believes. How and when can they ever know that for certain? Have they now become gods so that they can discern the hearts of men and know whether or not they believe?" "For faith doesn't exist for the sake of baptism, but baptism for the sake of faith" (*LW* 40: 239, 246). For Luther the good news of the sacrament of baptism is that God chooses the sinner, not vice versa. In the Large Catechism (1529) Luther addressed the Anabaptist challenge that infant baptism is invalid because infants do not have faith. The issue, Luther argued, is not personal faith but the promise of God. "Baptism is valid, even though faith be lacking. For my faith does not constitute Baptism but receives it. Baptism does not become invalid even if it is wrongly received or used, for it is bound not to our faith but to the Word" (Tappert 1959: 443). Here again we see Luther's insistence that God's promise of salvation is unconditional because it is based not on an inner change in the person but on a change outside the person (*extra nos*) in his or her standing before God.

In contrast, the Anabaptists emphasized personal change. "The Anabaptists . . . were essentially doers, . . . One finds their insistence on action as against deliberation expressed in their treatment of Christ as Example to be followed rather than Saviour to be explained. Christ meant *Nachfolge* [discipleship] rather than systematic Christology to them" (Oyer 1977: 71). The Grebel circle claimed that infant baptism had created a church of "Mr Everyman" where people remain in their old vices. If a degenerate Christendom is to be restored, baptism must be a sign that the faithful obligate themselves to better their lives. Believer's baptism marked an exclusive church in contrast to the inclusive church signified by infant baptism.

The key issue between Luther on the one hand and Zwingli and the Anabaptists on the other hand was whether the sacrament itself conveys grace or is a sign confirming grace already given in the Word. Once again, as in the debate over the Lord's Supper, the controversy revolved around the ancient metaphysical question of the relationship of inner and outer reality, spirit and matter, reality and sign. The more radical Reformers such as Schwenckfeld developed the logical inference of the independence of the spiritual from the material by rejecting the use of sacraments altogether.

In his attack on Karlstadt, Luther emphasized that inner personal experience of the gospel is effected by the outer proclamation of the Word and administration of the sacraments. Karlstadt has "set up a contrary order." "Instead of the outward order of God in the material sign of baptism and the oral proclamation of the Word of God he wants to teach you, not how the Spirit comes to you but how you come to the Spirit. They would have you learn how to journey on the clouds and ride on the wind. They do not tell you how or when, whither or what, but you are to experience what they do" (*LW* 40: 147). For Luther the Anabaptist position was the other side of the medieval coin of works righteousness, only now the works were located primarily in the sphere of religious experience rather than ethics. In both cases the focus is on human achievement rather than divine action.

Zwingli's response was not so easily set forth as Luther's. For one thing, Zwingli was enmeshed with his own former followers on his home turf; for another, Zwingli continued to view baptism as a covenant sign rather than in Luther's sense of a testament. In a series of tracts from 1524 on, Zwingli defended infant baptism by arguing a covenantal continuity between the peoples of God in the Old Testament and the New. He posited his argument on the analogy between circumcision and infant baptism; the baptism of John the Baptist to whom Jesus himself submitted; and that while the New Testament does not expressly command infant baptism, it can be inferred from Christ's blessing of the children (Luke 18: 15–17) and the accounts of baptisms of whole households in Acts and the Epistles. For Zwingli (as well as for the Anabaptists) baptism was integral to understanding the church. But Zwingli's view of the church is inclusive not exclusive: "The root of the trouble is that the Anabaptists will not recognize any Christians except themselves or any Church except their own. And that is always the way with sectarians who separate themselves on their own authority" (Bromily 1953: 158).

We referred earlier to Zwingli's statement that "A Christian city is nothing other than a Christian church." This Christian community or commonwealth is a mixed community of sheep and goats, believers and unbelievers, known only to God; "but it could not be a company of the baptized and unbaptized lest the civic order itself, and the proclamation of the gospel which depended upon it, be imperiled. It is ironic that water baptism which played at best an adiaphorous role in Zwingli's soteriology became the basis for his defense of the visible church" (George 1988: 144).

Zurich Beginnings

In 1522 a group of future Anabaptists, some of whom had participated in the original Lenten "Affair of the Sausages" protest, began to meet in the home of Klaus Hottinger for Bible study. The most attractive and influential member of this group was Conrad Grebel (1498–1526), the reputed founder of Anabaptism. Grebel came from a patrician family and was educated at Basle and Vienna. In Vienna he became close to the great Swiss humanist and later lay reformer of St Gall, Joachim Vadian (Watt). Vadian married Grebel's sister in 1519. In 1518 Grebel was able to study in Paris thanks to a royal scholarship for Swiss students funded by Francis I. There Grebel's interest in humanism was further stimulated by LeFèvre d'Etaples (a biblical scholar), William Budé, and Nicolas Cop (also Swiss, later involved with the beginnings of the French Reformation). However, Grebel's involvement in riotous living in Paris caused his father to withhold most of the scholarship money, thereby forcing Grebel to return home. Back in Zurich in June 1520, Grebel found kindred humanist souls in Felix Mantz (ca. 1500–27) and Zwingli, with whom he studied Greek and Hebrew. Grebel's conversion seems to have been related to his marriage to a woman below his class, which led to a falling-out with his father in 1522, and to the influence of Zwingli's exposition of the gospel from the Greek text. From 1522 to 1523 Grebel actively supported Zwingli in Zurich, exhibiting his partisanship by interrupting sermons that defended the old faith. But Grebel soon reached the conclusion that Zwingli was more solicitous of the government than of the gospel, and became one of his ablest and bitterest critics.

The split from Zwingli on the part of Grebel and his circle parallels that of the conflict between Karlstadt and Luther in Wittenberg. The issue in both cases was whether reform should be coerced or free. This is not surprising in light of the options posed to religious practice by the new emphasis upon Scripture as the sole norm of theology and praxis. The direct influence of Karlstadt also ought not be ignored: "The Baptists of Zurich immersed themselves in Karlstadt's writings and supported the printing of Karlstadt's most radical works in the fall of 1524" (Pater 1984a: 117).

From the beginning of his ministry at the Great Minster Zwingli had fanned the fires of iconoclasm and rejection of the mass by his sermons and tracts. Nor was he alone in the vehement attack on all forms of externalization of religion. Already in 1521, the exposé of idolatry *On the Old and the New God*, attributed to Vadian, addressed idolatry as the corruption of worship. Christians should forsake the externalization of religion characteristic of Catholic worship and return to the biblical practice of the early church.

Louis Haetzer (ca. 1500–29), taking his cue from Karlstadt's attack on images, intensified iconoclasm with his tract *The Judgment of God Our Spouse as to How One Should Hold Oneself toward All Idols and Images* (1523). There are numerous indications that iconoclastic sentiment and violence were widespread among the Zurich parishes in the early 1520s. On 1 September 1523 Leo Jud, Zwingli's successor at Einsiedeln and now pastor at St Peter's in Zurich, delivered an impassioned sermon against images and demanded their removal from the churches. In the Zurich suburb of Zollikon, Jacob Hottinger followed Jud's advice and interrupted the mass with a diatribe against idolatry which led to the chopping up of a large crucifix as firewood for the poor. The consequent uproar and the jailing of a number of iconoclasts prompted the Zurich magistrates to schedule a disputation (known as the second Zurich disputation) to clarify the issues on the basis of Scripture.

The second Zurich disputation (26–8 October 1523), involving some 900 citizens, theologians, magistrates, and priests, was held in the council hall. Again, other cantons were invited to send ecclesial representatives, but only two (St Gall and Schaffhausen) responded. The debate focused on images and the sacraments. There was agreement to the arguments presented by Zwingli and Jud among others that images should be removed from the churches and that the mass should be replaced by a memorial Lord's Supper. Grebel then stood up and said these changes should be instituted forthwith, and thus sparked again the conflict over implementation of reform. Zwingli left this decision to the council: "My lords will decide the appropriate manner in which the Mass is to be practiced in the future" (Zuck 1975: 51–4). The iconoclast Simon Stumpf, pastor at Höngg since 1522 and a participant in Zwingli's scholarly circle, heatedly replied: "Master Ulrich! You do not have the power to reserve judgment to my lords, for judgment has already been given: The Spirit of God decides. If my lords were to arrive at some decision contrary to the judgment of God, I would implore Christ for the guidance of his spirit and would teach and act in opposition."

The next day Grebel requested discussion of other abuses. Zwingli agreed that other abuses existed by defining abuse as "everything not instituted by Christ." However, Zwingli went on to espouse the same position noted earlier in Luther: "Since, however, one cannot abolish such additions all at once, it is necessary to combat them by preaching the word of God persistently and firmly!" Zwingli's pastoral–theological concern to bring reform by proclamation rather than coercion was endorsed at the end of the disputation by Conrad Schmid, spokesman for the village of Küssnacht: "Yet some people are so precipitous as to believe that we should take action on the articles and effect changes immediately. In my view, it would not be advisable to abolish things of this nature so hastily." Why? The people are not yet ready for such change. Zwingli did not believe that the council had jurisdiction over doctrinal matters, but it was responsible for maintaining the peace and guarding consciences. Thus for Zwingli the practical implementation of the new church order was a matter for the magistrates.

Grebel was deeply disappointed by Zwingli and the magistrates' slowness in "cleansing" the churches, and by the fact that the mass was still being said. Certainly Zwingli had pointed the way to reform, but now he was a false prophet because of his program of compromise and his "hastening slowly" in instituting change. In December 1523 Grebel wrote to his brother-in-law Vadian that "whoever thinks, believes, or says that Zwingli acts as a true shepherd, thinks, believes and speaks wickedly" (Furcha 1985: 86). In Grebel's eyes Zwingli, who began reform through preaching the Word of God, had now oppressed the free course of the Word by subverting it to his own ends. For the radicals a magisterial reform was no longer possible: the church must be free from the state (hence the appellation "free church").

After Christmas 1523 the free church movement began to take form. The changes in society and religion called for by Grebel included a new church consisting only of true believers, a voluntary church independent of the state. Rebuffed by Zwingli, the Grebel circle wrote their famous letter to Thomas Müntzer that expressed their self-understanding as an ecclesiastical minority apart from society. The 5 September 1524 *Letter to Thomas Müntzer* (*CTM* 121–32) is known as the earliest document of the Protestant free church. The Zurich radicals greeted Müntzer as one who shared their convictions, and who like them was fighting against traditional ecclesiology, including baptismal praxis. They were aware of Müntzer's writings and liturgical reforms, and they agreed with Müntzer and Karlstadt, "the purest proclaimers and preachers," that Luther's and Zwingli's false forebearance for the weak had perverted reform. "We are similarly rejected by our learned pastors, . . . ; everyone hangs on their words. They achieve this by preaching a sinful, sweet Christ and by their lack of proper discrimination, as you point out in your books, which for . . . us . . . have been an almost overwhelming source of instruction and strength." Unfortunately, it is not known whether Müntzer received this letter or even whether it was sent.

The *Letter* suggests that the Grebel circle had already developed the major positions that would characterize the Anabaptist movement. What is not biblically commanded should be prohibited in the church; the Lord's Supper is "not a Mass or a sacrament" but a symbol of the covenant with God; baptism is a sign of faith and should not be administered to infants ("the baptism of children is a senseless, idolatrous abomination contrary to all Scripture"); the church is a gathered community identified by the righteous living of its members; those who do not improve their lives to conform to the gospel are to be banned; neither the gospel nor its adherents are to be protected by the sword; the true church is the persecuted church ("True believing Christians are sheep in the midst of wolves, . . . and must be baptized into anxiety and dereliction, tribulation, persecution, suffering and dying, must be tried in the fire and find the fatherland of eternal rest"); true Christians also do not bear the sword, "for among them killing has been done away with altogether." The letter ends with the list of its seven signers, "your brothers and, for Luther, seven new little Müntzers."

The dissidents continued to interrupt sermons, became involved in iconoclasm, and ended up smashing the baptismal font in the Zollikon church – a rather unsymbolic rejection of infant baptism. In the countryside the issue of tithes was as important as the issue of infant baptism. Simon Stumpf (a radical priest from the village of Höngg who, among others, suggested killing priests to advance reform),

Johannes Brötli (a former priest and co-signer of the letter to Müntzer), and Wilhelm Reublin (priest in the village of Witikon, known as the "peasants' revolt in the pulpit") raised the claim that the tithe was not simply an economic and social problem but a political and religious problem as well. Their point was that the entire medieval church benefice system rested upon the tithe. The tithe itself was based upon the church's distribution of grace. But now in light of evangelical preaching it should be clear that grace is free and the church is voluntary. Thus the radicals' biblical principle led to their conclusion that the tithe must be abolished. To the radicals the tithe was not religiously peripheral but of central significance for the reform of the church. They had learned from Zwingli that even externals have spiritual significance. This early "congregationalism" was manifest in the Zurich canton parishes of Höngg, Grüninger, Wynigen, Hallau, and especially in Waldshut in the Black Forest where Balthasar Hubmaier had taken over. The break with Zwingli was over both baptism and the tithe.

Dissonance led to dissidence. The council called for another public disputation for 17 January 1524. Both sides were now hardened in their positions. Zwingli dominated the discussion and the radicals felt cornered. The outcome was that the majority in Zurich thought Zwingli had answered the dissidents' charges and objections. An order was given to baptize all unbaptized children within the next eight days under penalty of expulsion from Zurich. Furthermore, all unauthorized preaching was to cease, and the broken baptismal font was to be repaired.

In response to these orders, a small group of dissenters gathered on 21 January at the house of Felix Mantz. Among them were Grebel and George Blaurock, a married former priest who was executed in Innsbruck in 1529. The company joined in prayer and then Blaurock called upon Grebel to baptize him. After this, Grebel and Blaurock baptized 15 others at the first recorded adult baptism. At this very time the city was drawing up an order requiring Grebel and Mantz to abstain from further propaganda for their cause. A couple of days later, Grebel followed his continued preaching by distributing bread and wine. This was a clear act of defiance, since no town decision had yet been made concerning the mass. These incidents multiplied in the following days so that by the end of January it was reported that 80 adults had been baptized. The emphasis in these early rebaptisms was not on the human capability to believe but rather on that to repent. "Rebaptism had taken the place of the sacrament of penance, long debased by the indulgence traffic, while the eucharistic elements were becoming the sacramental cement, giving coherence to the brotherhood of would-be saints" (Williams 1992: 218).

It should be noted that in terms of imperial law the refusal of infant baptism was heretical and rebellious, a capital offense since the days of Roman law under the emperors Theodosius and Justinian. The mandate against rebaptism in the Theodosian code of 412 was directed against the Donatists of North Africa, who rebaptized their recruits from the Catholic church. In the Middle Ages these codes were endorsed by the Inquisition and severely carried out against the Cathari. The diet of Speyer (1529) renewed the ancient law and stricture against rebaptism. Ironically, the diet has been termed a milestone on the way to freedom of conscience because of the protest there against the enforcement of the edict of Worms. But if the diet of Speyer may be called the moment of the birth of Protestantism, it ought not to be forgotten that it was also the moment of death for Anabaptism (Wohlfeil and Goertz 1980: 25). Zurich had already mandated the death penalty prior to this imperial law. Infant baptism was not only a rule of the church but a law of the state. A voluntary or free church founded on believer's baptism thus was in opposition to both church and state in late medieval Europe. Believer's baptism therefore manifested an explosive power that had to call into question the traditional Christian order of society. Grebel's *Letter* to Müntzer indicates the Anabaptists were quite clear about the consequences of their action.

The authorities took this drastic measure because they feared that Anabaptism would spread like wildfire and stimulate a new uprising of the common man as experienced in the Peasants' War. The rise of the Anabaptist movement in the strongholds of the 1524–6 rebellion was not lost on the authorities, and they saw – not without reason – the criticism of infant baptism as an act of solidarity with the peasants. Persecution of the Anabaptists was one point on which Protestant and Roman Catholic authorities agreed, a kind of perverse early ecumenism. The mandate was most vigorously enforced in the Habsburg (Catholic) lands, whereas evangelical territories and cities tended to milder punishments such as exile. In so far as theology did not lead to rebellion, Luther thought persecution was wrong. "It is not right, and I truly grieve, that these miserable folk should be so lamentably murdered, burned, and tormented to death. We should allow everyone to believe what he wills. If his faith is false, he will be sufficiently punished in eternal hell-fire. Why then should we martyr these people . . . if . . . they are not guilty of rebellion or opposition to the government? . . . By fire we accomplish little" (*LW* 40: 230).

Zwingli and the Zurich magistrates warned and threatened the dissenters, and then proceeded to imprison a few and expel some others. Nevertheless, the new teachings spread with remarkable rapidity. Soon a small group was parading through Zurich with ropes around their waists and willow rods in their hands, crying, "Woe to you, Zurich," and "Freedom to Jerusalem," and calling Zwingli "the old dragon." These new prophets proclaimed that only 40 days remained for Zurich to repent. Blaurock went so far as to call Zwingli the Antichrist. In early November a debate was held on baptism during which Grebel, Mantz, and Blaurock were confronted by Zwingli and others. The debate soon degenerated into a shouting match that ended with the only humorous exchange of the day. A farmer shouted out: "Zwingli, I adjure you by the true and living God, tell me but one truth;" to which Zwingli responded: "You are the worst speciman of a trouble-making, discontented farmer that we've got in the neighborhood" (Potter 1976: 185–6).

The town magistrates now decided to deal more severely with what they regarded as "the wild men in the streets." Hubmaier was arrested, tortured, and allowed to leave upon recanting. Others were imprisoned. Grebel, Blaurock, and Mantz reappeared in March 1526 to renew their attacks upon Zwingli as a false prophet and to demand separatist worship. Since threats did not silence them, they were imprisoned. They were soon free, however, due to the "carelessness" of the prison guards.

At this same time, Zwingli's dream of a reformed Swiss Confederacy was evaporating before the advances of Catholic opponents. Convinced that the Anabaptists were weakening the cause of the reform, Zwingli and the magistrates moved against the dissidents with new severity. Grebel missed martyrdom by dying of the plague in August 1526. His father, Jakob Grebel, a town councilor, who symbolized both the Catholic opposition to Zwingli and the patrician resistance to the more democratic guilds upon which Zwingli depended, was less fortunate: on 30 October 1526, he was beheaded on charges of treason. By mid-December, Mantz and Blaurock had been recaptured and delivered to Zurich. By this time, rebaptism was mandated punishable by death by drowning – a grim parody of believer's baptism. Mantz and Blaurock were steadfast during their hearings, and professed the divine ordinance of adult baptism. Since Blaurock was not a citizen of Zurich, he was whipped out of town. Mantz was executed by drowning on the day he was condemned, 5 January 1527, thus becoming the first "Protestant" martyr at the hands of Protestants. The Anabaptists' understanding of themselves as the continuation of the early suffering church led them to rejoice in martyrdom, and to neglect or refuse opportunities to leave quietly when possible.

Anabaptist Multiplicity

Zwingli may have been one of the first, but he was certainly not the last to learn that the sparks of dissident evangelicalism could not be extinguished by drowning people. Both Protestant and Catholic authorities soon were confronted by a variety of Anabaptist movements in Switzerland, Austria, the Netherlands, and Germany. Popular Anabaptist preachers and leaders continued to arise from both evangelical and Catholic clergy and laity. Their professions in word and deed of brotherhood and egalitarianism appealed to the oppressed both during and after the Peasants' War. The Peasants' War was a formative experience for many leaders of Anabaptism (Stayer 1991). They touched a neuralgic nerve of late medieval life not only by their communal lifestyles but also by their millennial prophecies rooted in the biblical books of Daniel and Revelation. Occasional excesses provided a notoriety to Anabaptism that opponents could exploit. The legalism of the St Gall Anabaptists was one thing, but antinomianism and charismatic excesses were quite another. On the basis of the text that "the letter kills," some burned the Bible. "Glossolalia broke out. There was lewdness and unchastity and the extraordinary declaration of a deranged woman that she was predestined to give birth to the Antichrist, and there was a shocking fratricide by decapitation, perpetrated as God-willed by the killer and earnestly sought by the victim" (Williams 1992: 228). These notorious aspects of the dissident movement reflected radically different expressions of the ideal of restoring the early church that ranged from an absolute pacifism to an apocalyptic crusade to usher in the kingdom of God. In every case, however, the establishment authorities perceived the Anabaptists as seditionists, underminers of social order.

It is easy to understand the nervousness of the authorities when confronted by those radical dissident movements and persons like Thomas Müntzer and the Anabaptists at Waldshut under Hubmaier who linked up with local expressions of the Peasants' War, and who appeared to be able to stimulate mass revolutionary loyalties. But the teeth of the authorities were put on edge even by the more representative Anabaptist teachings expressed by Michael Sattler (ca. 1490–1527).

Sattler was an exemplary leader of the Swiss and south German Anabaptist movements who moved from being prior of a Benedictine monastery in Breisgau to become an Anabaptist in Zurich. After his expulsion from Zurich he took refuge in Strasbourg, and then moved to the Black Forest to continue missionary work. He was so esteemed by the dissidents that he was chosen to preside at the 1527 conference at Schleitheim on the German–Swiss border that developed perhaps the most representative statement of Anabaptist principles, "The Brotherly Agreement of Some Children of God Concerning Seven Articles," known as the Schleitheim Articles. These seven articles set forth a consensus on baptism contingent upon repentance and amendment of life; the ban or excommunication of brethren who do not keep the commandments; the Lord's Supper as a memorial meal expressing Christian community; a radical separation of believers from the evil world, for "truly all creatures are in but two classes, good and bad, . . . and none can have part with the other;" the "shepherd," as the model of the godly life, to be elected by the community; absolute rejection of bearing arms and holding civic offices because the Christians' citizenship is in heaven and their weapons are spiritual; and the prohibition of oaths.

The vision here is of the restoration of the primitive Christian community according to the so-called "rule of Christ" (Matthew 18: 15ff). Central to this vision is separation from the "world" and the formation of a "counter-culture" as the prototype of a better society. The authors at Schleitheim strove to make clear that their Reformation was neither a Reformation from "above" dependent on magisterial authority nor a Reformation from "below" assisted by revolutionary powers. They sought a third way. Their reform program was no longer focused on the expurgation of existing Christendom, but rather on radical separation from the world. As children of the light they refused even to greet the children of darkness; they wore simple clothes, shunned worship services, and supported one another. They were now reading the Bible from the standpoint of the powerless; a very different perspective from that of the powerful. Thus they concluded that the community of Jesus Christ is a small, indeed voluntary but also suffering, separated and defenseless community. The birth of the free church may be explained by the connection of anticlerical aggressiveness, church-political impotence, and biblical study. The free church was a radical alternative to the church of Rome and to the churches of Wittenberg and Zurich. "They sought to save a remnant of the communal Reformation by withdrawing from the realm of this world; but the rulers mercilessly exterminated them" (Blickle 1981: 185).

Das erste Capitel von der vereude
rung aller stende der Christenheyt/ die mag bewert
werden auß den sichtbarn zeychen des himels.

¶ Nach dem die menschlich schwacheyt mag von der dick
en wolcken wegen der fleyschlichen begirligkeyten/ vnnd des
tieffen werfels der laster/ die verborgen maiestet gottes nit er
kennen / noch die heymlichen/ vnd von der sundligkeyt abge
scheyden/ werck der natur begriffen / dem nach will ich den

Figure 8.1 "The World Turned Upside Down." Numerous late medieval images depict the theme of the great reversal of the first and the last, the wealthy and poor, the powerful and the weak that is present in the New Testament (e.g. Matthew 19: 30; Luke 1: 47–55). Luther powerfully expressed this theme in identifying the papacy with the Antichrist. The lines at the top of this illustration read: "The first chapter concerning the transformation of all estates of Christendom which may be proved by the visible signs of heaven." Not only is the church upside down but the clergy and monks are doing the work of the laity and the laity that of the clergy.
Source: J. Grünpeck, "Spiegel der natürlichen himlischen . . ." (Leipzig, 1522), © British Library.

Although at first glance the Schleitheim Articles appear apolitical, they are the effort to continue the revolutionary concerns of the peasants by other means. For example, the peasants demanded free choice of pastors and their support by the tithe; the Anabaptists elected their "shepherds" from their midst and expected to support them in need. The peasants refused oaths to magistrates opposed to them; the Anabaptists provided biblical foundations for a universal refusal of oaths. The peasants chose the form of "articles" to express their revolutionary program; the Anabaptists presented their program in articles. The peasants demonstrated militant solidarity in their forms of address and relations, e.g. the Black Forest "Christian Union and Brotherhood;" the Anabaptists called one another brother and sister and expressed their unity in Schleitheim's "Brotherly Agreement." The peasants employed the ban and disassociation from those unwilling to join them; the Anabaptists employed a "churchly" ban, shunning the "children of darkness." The Anabaptists rejected the military means of the peasants but preserved their solidarity. The Anabaptists also accepted the consequences of persecution and death.

For his leading role in developing these articles, Sattler was arrested, tried, horribly tortured, and executed by the Austrian authorities. The historical context of this Austrian Catholic tribunal does not excuse their action but does provide some insight into the rulers' anxieties about the spread of Anabaptism. At this time Austria was confronted by a Turkish advance which threatened to enter the whole Empire through the gates of Vienna. At his trial, Sattler stated: "If the Turks should come, we ought not to resist them. For it is written [Matthew 5: 21]: Thou shalt not kill. We must not defend ourselves against the Turks and others of our persecutors, . . . If warring *were* right, I would rather take the field against so-called Christians who persecute, capture, and kill pious Christians than against the Turks" (Williams and Mergal 1957: 141).

The suspicion that even the pacifist Anabaptists were really only wolves in sheep's clothing, and potentially radical revolutionaries, was confirmed, if it ever needed confirmation, in the minds of the authorities by the wild events at Münster in 1533–5.

The Münster Debacle

The conjunction of Anabaptist aspirations for the restitution of the pure church they found in the Bible and the social unrest epitomized by the

Peasants' War found explosive expression in the episcopal city of Münster. Located in Westphalia near the Dutch border, this major city of a large prince-bishopric had a population of about 15,000. There was already a widespread religious dissident movement in the Netherlands. Influenced by the extravagant visions and prophecies of Melchior Hoffman (ca. 1495–1543), these people were known as Melchiorites. Sometimes called "the father of Dutch Anabaptism," Hoffman, a furrier by trade and a lay preacher by conviction who was influenced by Karlstadt, preached that everyone should accept baptism into the pure church of Christ in preparation for the return of Christ and the end of the world in 1533. Proclaiming himself to be the prophet Elijah, Hoffman went to the city of Strasbourg, which he prophesied would be the New Jerusalem. The magistrates of Strasbourg declined the honor of being the locus for the end of the world and imprisoned Hoffman until his death in 1543. Nevertheless, Hoffman's preachings and writings continued to influence people in the Netherlands, some of whom transposed his prophecy of the New Jerusalem from Strasbourg to Münster. Hoffman's central ideas about the triumph of the godly were written down while he was in prison, and smuggled out in his tract *Concerning the Pure Fear of God* (1533). His vision was that the ungodly would be exterminated *before* the end of the world, that *before* the return of Christ the saints would rule the earth through cooperation between the prophet (the second Jonah) and a pious ruler (the second Solomon), and that the "apostolic messengers" could not be hurt or defeated. In one way or another, these themes found expression in the Anabaptist takeover of Münster.

By 1532 Münster itself had focused its own social and religious unrest against the prince-bishop of the city and, under the fiery leadership of Bernard Rothmann, a priest who went through Lutheran and Zwinglian phases before becoming a radical, had become an "evangelical city." This news stimulated thousands of Anabaptist refugees to flock to the city in search of haven from persecution in the Netherlands and areas surrounding Münster. The townspeople divided into three factions: a small number of Catholics who still supported the expelled bishop, conservative Lutherans who were initially the majority in the town council, and the Melchiorites who won the backing of the town guilds. In the summer of 1533 simmering tensions in the alliance of the guilds with the magistrates boiled over. Rothmann, under the influence of the Melchiorites, was becoming increasingly radical in politics and religion and both opposed infant baptism and innovated at the celebration of the Lord's Supper with unconsecrated bread. The strength of the radicals was such that the town council no longer had sufficient authority to expel or even discipline Rothmann. Alarmed Catholic and Lutheran families began to flee the city, but this population loss was more than made up by the influx of Anabaptists.

In the February 1534 elections the radical party won the town council. Münster had already been declared the New Jerusalem by Jan Mathijs, a baker from Haarlem, who believed, as had Müntzer, that the godless had no right to live. On 25 February Mathijs announced his intention to put to death "the godless," that is, all who refused to join the new rebaptismal covenant. A colleague, sensitive to the impression this would make on the princes of neighboring areas, persuaded Mathijs to allow people to leave rather than be executed. Mathijs explained this shift in policy by announcing he had received another revelation allowing the expulsion rather than the death of the godless. All who remained were forcibly rebaptized in the marketplace. A blacksmith who dared to challenge Mathijs was killed instantly by Mathijs himself. Not too long after this, Mathijs himself was killed when he led a sortie against the army assembled by the bishop besieging the city. It seems that he had received a vision that God would make him invulnerable to the weapons of the godless. Williams (1992: 567) suggests that his successor "may have encouraged him in this fatuous expectation."

During the six weeks Mathijs ruled Münster he instituted the ideal of a society based on the life of the primitive church as recorded in Acts and an early church writing, the pseudo-Clementine Epistle IV, which claimed that all things should be held in common. The property of the expelled citizens was confiscated; food was made public property; real property was declared to be in common, although people could continue using what was theirs with the stipulation that all house doors had to be kept open day and night; the use of money was outlawed; and 12 elders were appointed to oversee the stockpiling of goods and their distribution to the needy.

After Mathijs' death, the prophetic mantle was assumed by Jan of Leiden, who claimed he was the voice of the Lord. After repelling a major attack by the bishop's army upon the city in May, there was a strong feeling among the Anabaptists of being God's chosen people. After another major victory in August, Jan had himself anointed and crowned "king of righteousness" and "the ruler of the new Zion." He not only stated that to oppose him was to oppose the divine order, but enforced his statement by ruthlessly crushing his, and thus the Lord's, opposition. Church, state, and community were now to be one and the same regenerated body. The regenerate church could consist only of the righteous; sinners were to be punished by death. Sinners were identified by their blasphemy, seditious language, disobedience to parents and masters, adultery, lewd conduct, backbiting, spreading scandal, and complaining!

Jan's most controversial and notorious innovation was the introduction of polygamy. Some 50 townsmen were killed or executed for resisting Jan's vision of the New Jerusalem rationalized as an emulation of the Old Testament patriarchs. Jan found justification for his mandate of polygamy in the Old Testament example of the patriarchs and the divine command to "be fruitful and multiply" (Genesis 1: 22), as well as in the pseudo-Clementine letter that urged all things in common including wives. With ingenious exegesis, Rothmann interpreted the Pauline mandate that a bishop be the husband of one wife (1 Timothy 3: 2) to mean that non-bishops were permitted more than one. But there were also nonbiblical factors operative in his decision. Although already married, Jan hankered for the beautiful young widow of Mathijs and apparently thought marrying her would bolster his own claim to leadership. Furthermore, there was a disproportionate number of women to men in the city due to male attrition from battle and expulsion. Polygamy provided not only the means of increasing the population in preparation for the return of Christ (the eschatological number of the saints, according to Revelation 7: 4, was to be 144,000), but also the means of subjugating all women to male authority. In his book on the restoration of the primitive church, *Restitution* (1534), Rothmann added that sexual dependence upon one woman lets her lead a man about "like a bear on a rope." The world is such a mess, Rothmann argued, because "nowadays, too many women seem to wear the trousers. The husband is the head of the wife, and as the husband is obedient to Christ, so also should the wife be obedient to her husband, without murmuring and contradiction" (Zuck 1975: 101). Feminist consciousness was not one of Rothmann's strong points! In political perspective, what Jan was doing was ensuring control over the majority of the population. As might be expected, many women did not respond warmly to this new state of affairs. Those women who dissented from the new rule of polygamy were imprisoned. Jan himself beheaded and trampled the body of one of his wives in the marketplace in front of the rest of them. That seems to have quieted their murmurings.

In spite of Jan's proclamation of the New Jerusalem and his accompanying revelations, the siege of the city inexorably took its toll of the bodies and spirits of its inhabitants. Appeal after appeal to Anabaptists outside the city to bring armed relief were frustrated by the besiegers. The people in Münster were reduced by famine, and in June

1535 the city was betrayed by two deserters who revealed to the army the weakest gate. After a fierce battle the city was taken on 25 June and nearly all the inhabitants were slaughtered. Rothmann was apparently killed in the battle, but the other three leaders, including Jan of Leiden, were condemned and then tortured with red-hot irons. Their tortured bodies were suspended in an iron cage from the tower of St Lambert's church as an example to all.

The Anabaptist kingdom of Münster was materially destroyed, but it lived on in the minds of religious and political authorities as the logical consequence of Anabaptist dissent. The tragedy of Münster was a consequence not only of the leaders' megalomania but also of the followers' conviction that the Bible as interpreted by their leaders was to be literally followed. In the minds of the establishment, both Protestant and Catholic, it was now clear that there was a revolutionary continuum from Thomas Müntzer to the city of Münster.

The Anabaptists aspired to communal solidarity as a holy people defined by believer's baptism and celebrated by the community-constituting act of consensus in the Lord's Supper. The effort to expand this theocratic ideal to the limits of the urban space in Münster led, however, not to the peaceable kingdom but the annihilation of the community itself. The result was the discrediting of militant millenarian communalism. After this there was not another Anabaptist attempt to restore the world to primitive Christianity. Rather, future Anabaptist developments were marked by withdrawal from the world. Under the leadership of the former priest Menno Simons (1496–1561), whose brother was killed in violence related to the Münster debacle, the Anabaptist remnants were gathered into voluntary communities separate from the established civic and religious world.

What Menno did for the Dutch and north German Anabaptists, Jacob Hutter (d. 1536) did for the disparate Anabaptist refugees in Moravia who had "sold house and goods" to form communistic colonies. Hutter was able to develop and stabilize the faltering communalism expressed by the Anabaptists in Zurich, Münster, and elsewhere into a Christian communism that shared goods and production. In this development we may see a certain continuity with the aspirations of medieval monasticism as well as an advance beyond it. Medieval monasticism was marked by an ascetic contempt for the world that until the Franciscan movement contrasted with the corporate wealth of monasticism itself. Furthermore, although the monastic movement shared a common life and a common goal, each monk was primarily concerned for his own salvation. The Mennonite and Hutterite Anabaptist advance beyond medieval religious asceticism and individualism consisted in developing a covenanted community of families that claimed to be *the* church itself, outside of which there is no salvation. This household of faith was marked by a communism of love and production; pacifistic and suffering separation from the world; trust in their ultimate vindication as the true household of faith; and confidence that until the final end of the world, human freedom and fulfillment are only possible in the brotherly love of evangelical communism.

Persecuted throughout Europe, the Mennonite and Hutterite Anabaptists eventually found homes in North America. Their faithfulness and perseverance under dreadful tortures and oppression contributed to the gradual development of the idea of religious toleration and liberty. And their insistence upon a voluntary, separate church contributed to the modern development of religious pluralism and constitutional separation of church and state.

The Subversive Piety of the Spiritualists

The mix of anticlericalism and reform which formed the milieu of developing Anabaptism was also influential for the development of a disparate group often labeled "Spiritualists," a concept as inexact as some of their ideas. The Spiritualists criticized the clergy for displacing true Christian living and spirituality by external ritual at best and venality at worst. We already encountered this radical critique of the externalization of Christianity in Karlstadt and Müntzer. Their spiritualist descendants rejected all authority but the inward work of the Holy Spirit. Here are the first contours of the modern subjectivity that was to shake traditional Christianity to its foundations in the Enlightenment of the eighteenth century.

The historical roots of this movement can be traced back to Greek philosophical dualism and the Augustinian contrast between the spirit and the letter. The latter became an interpretive approach to difficult biblical texts. When the words of a text, the "letter," were difficult to understand, medieval exegetes appealed to the "spirit" behind the words. The problem was that especially difficult texts received various spiritual interpretations, especially by use of allegory. The confusing variety of interpretations prompted the church to set up a means to control interpretations: the *Magisterium* or teaching authority of the church. One of the concerns of the Reformers was to wrest this control of Scripture away from ecclesiastical authoritarianism. But as Luther and Zwingli among others discovered, a consequence of *sola scriptura* was again a myriad of interpretations which they in turn would attempt to control.

Philosophical dualism influenced western theology through August- ine by the division between God and matter. The puzzle of the connection between divine reality and the material signs of it posed many theological problems, including understanding the eucharist. The general point of the Spiritualists was that there is no connection between God and creatures; indeed, there is an "ontological barrier" between the creaturely and the divine. Salvation is only possible when God's Spirit breaks through this barrier in the interiority of persons and spiritually changes them from inside. The philosophical anthropology that made this theology possible divided the person into body, soul, and spirit. Body and soul were captive to sin, but while the spirit may be distorted by sin, it still retained an undamaged image of God. The divine Spirit relates to the human spirit and thereby creates a new creature.

The Spiritualists, disappointed by the ethical ineffectiveness of the Reformation, saw in Luther's doctrine of justification only a forensic act, a "cheap grace," that led neither to personal rebirth nor to ethical renewal. Numerous radical Reformers shared this view, but two who most thoroughly carried through the Spiritualist dualism and devalua- tion of the external means of salvation were Caspar Schwenkfeld (1489–1561) and Sebastian Franck (1499–1542).

Schwenkfeld came from lower Silesian nobility in Liegnitz. He studied in Cologne and Frankfurt an der Oder and then entered the service of the Silesian court, becoming a counselor to Friedrich II of Liegnitz. Around 1519 he was influenced by Lutheran ideas and began to work for the renewal of the church. By 1524 he had won over his prince and area to the Reformation, but was now himself having doubts about Reformation doctrine. He came to see Luther's doctrine of the Lord's Supper as a regression to works righteousness because it suggested the bread and wine could work salvation. Schwenckfeld became convinced that the Lutheran conviction of the forgiveness of sin communicated in, with, and under the Lord's Supper was the source of immorality and lack of religious fervor. After all, had not Judas also participated in the Lord's Supper? Thus Schwenckfeld emphasized that the outer word of Scripture and the external sacraments must be distinguished from the Spirit. "God's direct intervention must occur before any external ministrations. Internal must precede external. The external never mediates the spirit" (McLaughlin 1986a: 190). Schwenckfeld then developed his own position which affirmed the spiritual presence of Christ. Only the inner person can commune with the heavenly divine Christ. The Lord's Supper in its external manifestation is only a ritual reference to the preceding spiritual event. On this basis he argued that to prevent misunderstanding and hinder misuse of the Lord's Supper, the church should declare a moratorium on it. It may be celebrated again when the people have received intensive instruction leading to spiritual communion with Christ and a reborn life. Schwenckfeld himself no longer participated in the Lord's Supper after 1526. His efforts to convince Luther were strongly rebuffed.

Schwenckfeld's personal situation came to a head in 1529 when the Catholic opponent of the Reformation, Archduke Ferdinand of Austria, took over the Bohemian crown which included Silesia. Schwenckfeld left for Strasbourg, where he was generally well liked and where he further developed his thought in conversation with many of the radicals finding shelter in the city. The last decade of his life was spent wandering from place to place.

The other great Spiritualist of this period, Sebastian Franck, influenced German cultural life more than the church. He is especially known for his 1531 *Chronica, Zeitbuch und Geschichtsbibel* (Chronicle and History) which contained a chronicle of heretics. He was educated at Ingolstadt, where he heard Eck and Hubmaier, and at the Dominican College in Heidelberg. After his studies he served as priest in the bishopric of Augsburg. In 1524 he appeared in Nuremberg where the Reformation was already underway and joined the evangelical ministry. He finally came to a Spiritualist position that Christ rules in the soul of persons through the Holy Spirit. All externalism of religion he saw to be the work of the devil. Francke did not join or lead any community but remained a loner.

The radical Reformation was not a unified movement, but rather a chorus of protest against the clergy, secular authorities, and Reformers such as Luther and Zwingli. It was a reservoir for uncompromising protest that could well up in the most varied social circles. The protest of these varied "radical Reformers" was often sparked by disappointment over the apparent or actual ineffectiveness of the Reformation movements, or by the timidity or slowness in implementing reforms. The radicals were often the first ones to press for the praxis of Reformation ideals. Williams (1992: 1290) sums this up in vivid imagery: "The Radical Reformation drained the brackish pools and opened the sluices for innumerable religious currents long impounded in the interstices of late medieval Christendom . . . Within the turmoiled flood of radical reform or restitution the fresh vitalities of the Reformation . . . were borne along swiftly to radical extremes."

Suggestions for Further Reading

Carlos M. N. Eire, *War against the Idols: The Reformation of Worship from Erasmus to Calvin*, Cambridge: Cambridge University Press, 1986

Hans-Jürgen Goertz, ed., *Profiles of Radical Reformers: Biographical Sketches from Thomas Müntzer to Paracelsus*, Kitchener: Herald, 1982

Walter Klaasen, ed., *Anabaptism in Outline: Selected Primary Sources*, Waterloo: Herald, 1981

Calvin Pater, *Karlstadt as the Father of the Baptist Movements: The Emergence of Lay Protestantism*, Toronto: University of Toronto Press, 1984

John D. Rempel, *The Lord's Supper in Anabaptism: A Study in the Christology of Balthasar Hubmaier, Pilgram Marpeck, and Dirk Philips*, Waterloo: Herald, 1993

James M. Stayer, *The German Peasants' War and Anabaptist Community of Goods*, Montreal: McGill-Queen's University Press, 1991

James M. Stayer and Werner O. Packull, eds, *The Anabaptists and Thomas Müntzer*, Dubuque/Toronto: Kendall/Hunt, 1980

Lee Palmer Wandel, *Voracious Idols and Violent Hands: Iconoclasm in Reformation Zurich, Strasbourg, and Basel*, Cambridge: Cambridge University Press, 1995

George H. Williams, *The Radical Reformation*, 3rd edn, Kirksville: Sixteenth Century Journal Publishers, 1992

9

Augsburg 1530 to Augsburg 1555: Reforms and Politics

It is also taught among us that one holy Christian church will be and remain forever. This is the assembly of all believers among whom the Gospel is preached in its purity and the holy sacraments are administered according to the Gospel.

The Augsburg confession (1530)

It is not unusual to hear the comment that preachers should stick to religion and leave politics out of their sermons. What is meant, of course, is that preachers should not criticize *my* political positions. That the relationship of religion and politics has always been a neuralgic one is clear from even a cursory glance at the Hebrew prophets. In the Reformation period it was a nerve that when touched – and it was touched constantly – radiated pain and anxiety throughout the whole body of society. We have repeatedly referred to the medieval social self-understanding encapsulated in the phrase *corpus Christianum*, meaning the universal consensus that society, including politics, was defined by the Christian religion. "Because salvation was of central importance, any redefinition of religious truth had an automatic bearing on socioreligious authority. As the new definition of religious thought generated sociopolitical action, control of the word was vital. . . . In order to protect the social system, a stricter control of the word was essential" (Rublack 1988: 105). Everyone agreed on this principle; the problem was that the non-negotiable content of one party rarely agreed with that of other parties. We have surveyed this dilemma in the relations between the early Reformers; in this chapter we turn to the relations between the Reformers and the political authority of the Empire.

The Trail of Worms

The edict of Worms (1521) remained the legal basis in the Empire for the treatment of the Reformations up to the Peace of Augsburg in 1555.

However, political considerations both within and without the Empire continually stymied enforcement of this ban on Luther and his followers. Charles V believed the Reformation should be extirpated, and Roman Catholicism and the unity of the Empire restored. The complicated story of Charles's inability to achieve this goal includes various factors. The drive of the imperial princes for their own liberties and aggrandizement at times overrode their own theological commitments, whether Catholic or evangelical. Charles, a non-German (his mother tongue was French), was considered an outsider. But even before Charles's election the formula of *Kaiser und Reich* had shifted its meaning from the unity of "Emperor and Empire" to the rivalry between the princes, who claimed to represent the Empire, and the emperor. Outside the Empire, the continual conflict and oft-shifting alliances between the Holy Roman Empire, France, and the papacy distracted Charles from his religious agenda. The Habsburg–Valois rivalry continued throughout the reigns of Charles and Francis I of France, and the perpetual wars with France were not settled until the Peace of Cateau-Cambrésis (1559). The continual threat of Turkish invasion throughout this period influenced imperial concessions to the evangelical princes to gain their support. All of these events conspired to ensure the emperor's frequent and prolonged absences from Germany.

For nearly 25 years, up to the summer of 1542, Charles was rarely in Germany, and then only for short periods of time. He was present for almost a year in 1520–1 and for two and a half years in 1530–2, but then returned again only in 1541 for a few months. Soon after his election Charles delegated the administration of the German territories to his brother, Archduke Ferdinand of Austria (1503–64), who succeeded him as Emperor Ferdinand I in 1558. Ferdinand, however, was unable to prevent the princes from moving to consolidate their territorial powers. Benefiting from the emperor's worldwide responsibilities and Ferdinand's preoccupation with the Turkish menace in the east, the princes strengthened their own positions and dealt in their own ways with the issues of the Reformation. The initial configuration of the Reformation as communal, the so-called *Gemeindereformation*, began to give way to what historians have termed the "Princes' Reformation" (*Fürstenreformation*). This expression of the Reformation was characterized by the determination of reforming options by the territorial lords and their consequent hierarchical and bureaucratic organization of the church.

Among the evangelical princes, Philip of Hesse (1504–67) took prominent leadership next to the Elector of Saxony. He strove to reconcile the Wittenberg and Zurich Reformers at the Marburg colloquy (1529) with the goal of developing a united evangelical front against the emperor. In 1527 he founded the first evangelical university in Marburg in order to secure the formation of loyal lawyers and theologians whom he deemed necessary for the development of his "state."

Other princes also moved quickly to consolidate their power and build up their territories into early modern states. These moves included placing ecclesiastical responsibilities and institutions under secular authority. It is of interest that the princes of both the old and the new faith proceeded to change medieval institutions on the basis of the medieval doctrine of the *cura religionis*, that is, the care or jurisdiction of the church. Medieval theologians had warmly recommended princes be concerned for religion in their territories. Many of the German lords of the fifteenth century agreed with the phrase coined by the duke of Jülich: *Dux Cliviae est papa in territoriis suis* – "the Duke of Clives is the pope in his territory." The humanist optimism about good government was also a factor supporting the German lords. The pre-Reformation regulation of the church by the princes was quickly confirmed by Protestants and Catholics in the sixteenth century. Theological legitimacy of government "care" of the church was of particular importance to the evangelical princes who were concerned to claim legality for their actions. When Roman Catholic church authorities opposed such reforms, evangelical theologians and lawyers supplied the princes with legitimation in terms of emergency episcopal powers. The evangelical prince became an "emergency bishop" (*Notbischof*). Luther argued that when faced by lack of episcopal leadership in reform, the princes should exercise oversight until ecclesiastical affairs were normalized. Already in 1520 he had appealed to the Christian nobility to carry out reforms in the church by virtue of their baptism (*LW* 44: 127–31). There was also medieval precedent for secular authorities to act as temporary bishops if there were a breakdown of order in the church. In 1525 Luther requested the elector to carry out a visitation, that is examination, of the churches. Because of the Peasants' War this was not carried out in Electoral Saxony until 1527. Melanchthon and Luther wrote the instructions for this process and Luther wrote its preface. Luther desired the retention of an episcopal form of church government but the upheaval of the Reformation made this difficult. The prince, on the model of Constantine, "is not obligated to teach and rule in spiritual affairs, he is obligated as temporal sovereign to so order things that strife, rioting, and rebellion do not arise among his subjects" (*LW* 40: 273). This provisional arrangement solidified into the form of a territorial or "state" church for which government retained responsibility in Germany until 1918. Other territories followed Electoral Saxony's example, including the Catholic territory of Jülich-Cleves where the government implemented an Erasmian reform program. The princes' desire for political liberty and the Reformers' emphasis on Christian freedom mutually strengthened each other in an interplay of understanding and interest.

The governmental consolidation of the Reformation in the German territories developed through the three decisive imperial diets in the 1520s: Worms (1521), Speyer (1526), and Speyer (1529).

The Diet of Worms

We have already sketched Luther's development to the diet of Worms. From the perspective of imperial responsibility it was understood that the imperial ban of a heretic would follow the ecclesiastical ban. However, the election capitulation that accompanied the election of Charles V in 1519 stated that no German could be declared under the ban of the Empire without a hearing and the agreement of the imperial estates. The Luther affair was therefore immediately drawn into the contemporary political struggles between the emperor and the estates; its outcome would be an index of the strength or weakness of the emperor with respect to the princes. Faced by the potential conflict between the claims of the papacy on the Empire and the chances of carrying out these claims in the Empire, Charles as well as the princes sought a compromise. It was thought that a formal retraction by Luther which did not have to be understood as a renunciation of his theology would satisfy all parties. This of course ran aground when Luther refused to recant, and led to the proclamation of the imperial ban against Luther.

But already a broad front of evangelical princes had arisen in the Empire. Until there is more research on these princes it is difficult to generalize about their motives. It cannot be gainsaid that faith convictions played a role in their decisions; at the same time there is little doubt that Luther was perceived as an important piece on the political chessboard. There was also sensitivity to the possibility of a mass uprising of the commoners if Luther were prosecuted. In any case, in 1521 the princes were inclined to leave the religious issue in the balance with the hope for its resolution in either a general or a national council. A national council was the preference of the princes, reflecting their anti-Roman feelings already expressed in their lists of grievances against the Roman church presented at Worms as well as at previous diets.

Charles V, supported by the Habsburg and Wittelsbach territiories, opposed a national council. The Peasants' War convinced the Catholic princes that Luther's movement was responsible for social revolution and that it should be exterminated. The Catholic princes of north Germany (George of Ducal Saxony, Albrecht of Mainz and Magdeburg, Joachim of Brandenburg, Henry of Braunschweig-Wolfenbüttel, and Erich of Braunschweig) formed an alliance in July 1525 to do just that. On the evangelical side the political initiative was exercised by Philip of Hesse, who was won over to the Reformation by Melanchthon in 1524. At approximately the same time the Grand Master of the Teutonic Order, Albrecht, left his clerical calling upon the advice of Luther and made himself a duke of Prussia. Electoral Saxony after the death of Frederick remained firmly supportive of Luther. Between 1524 and 1526 the reform movement spread to a number of cities. Finally, in the winter of 1525–6 Philip of Hesse concluded an agreement with Electoral Saxony that they would act in concert to defend the Reformation at the forthcoming diet to meet in Speyer in 1526.

The Diet of Speyer, 1526

The diet of Speyer occurred in a changing landscape of religious loyalties. In addition, the French King Francis I had escaped his captivity after the battle of Pavia and joined with Pope Clement VII to wage war once again against Charles, and Turkish armies had invaded Hungary. At Speyer the princes again called for a national council of the Empire with the right to make binding regulations on the religious issue. Charles, obviously occupied abroad, instructed Ferdinand not to tolerate moves for a national assembly. The result was the diet's consensus that the edict of Worms could not be executed in the Empire, and that until a general council convened the estates "with their subjects, would live, govern, and act in such a way as everyone trusted to justify before God and the Imperial Majesty" (Holborn 1961: 205). In short, this was an agreement that agreement could not be reached, and that in reality each territory and city was a free agent. The evangelical estates gained even more breathing space by the events that occurred soon after the diet. The death of King Ludwig II of Hungary and Bohemia in the battle of Mohács against the Turks drew Ferdinand into succession struggles in southern and eastern Europe. Charles's intention to rally Europe against the Turks was stalled by his conflict with the League of Cognac (1526: France, Venice, Florence, and the papacy). The battleground was Italy. There the imperial troops wreaked vengeance upon Pope Clement VII with the horrific sack of Rome (1527). The pope fled to his castle San Angelo and became a virtual prisoner and then subservient client to Charles. The infamous *sacco di Roma* marked the end of the Renaissance in Rome and cost Clement his prestige. Luther remarked: "Christ reigns in such a way that the emperor who persecutes Luther for the pope is forced to destroy the pope for Luther" (*LW* 49: 169).

Evangelical authorities seized upon the compromise of Speyer to implement changes in worship and ecclesiastical institutions. To these leaders it seemed clear that Speyer had established a *ius reformandi*, a "right of Reformation," that legitimated their claims to authority in the religious question. Again, the princes were interested not only in establishing the Reformation but also in establishing control over the Reformation. Blickle (1981: 190) argues that this transition from communal to princely reform reflected the concern of the authorities to stabilize change and neutralize revolutionary elements. "The Reformation, therefore, had to be shorn of its power to create social and political disruption, something the rulers achieved by taking the Reformation away from the communities and making it a matter of state."

The church visitation process was the instrument for carrying out the goal of establishing and directing reform of the church. The visitation process included simplification of the cultus by elimination of the practices which had accumulated and were regarded as unevangelical, displacement of unqualified clergy by those approved by the Reformers, the subordination of church property – often as much as a third of the property within a territory – to government administration, and the assigning of clerical jurisdiction to secular courts. This "nationalization" of the Reformation meant a marked increase in power and authority for the territorial princes.

The Diet of Speyer, 1529

At Speyer in 1529, Ferdinand tried to regain imperial control of the religious issue. He categorically demanded the nullification of the 1526 article which had led to such shocking growth of new doctrines and sects. The edict of Worms must be enforced and the old faith protected. All religious innovation must be halted and the jurisdiction of bishops restored. Supported by a majority of Catholic princes and bishops, and buoyed by the emperor's victory over the pope in Italy, Ferdinand led the way to the reinstatement of the edict of Worms.

In response, a minority of Lutherans presented an official *protestatio*, a "protestation," from which the evangelicals were henceforth pejoratively labeled "Protestants." The argument of the minority was that they were bound by the Speyer resolution of 1526. The legal rationale was based on the traditional constitutional *protestatio* principle that protected a minority against an unjust majority position. The point of the "protesting" princes was that since the edict of Worms could only be enforced by war, enforcement would lead to a condition of lawlessness. The religious basis of their protest was an appeal to conscience paralleling Luther's stance at Worms: "In matters concerning God's honor and our soul's salvation everyone must stand before God and answer by himself, nobody can excuse himself in that place by the actions or decisions of others, whether they be a minority or majority" (Holborn 1961: 208). The magistrates' conviction that their consciences are bound to the Word of God was decisive for early Protestantism. The protest was signed by five imperial princes (John of Electoral Saxony, Philip of Hesse, George of Brandenburg-Ansbach, Wolfgang of Anhalt, Ernst of Braunschweig-Lüneburg) and fourteen imperial cities (Strasbourg, Nuremberg, Ulm, Constance, Lindau, Memmingen, Kempton, Nördlingen, Heilbronn, Reutlingen, Isny, St Gall, Weissenburg in Franken, and Windesheim). The Speyer protestation created a separation that would not be overcome.

Historical evaluation of the 1529 diet was stylized in the nineteenth century along with the Ninety-Five Theses as a great event of national liberation and the moment of the birth of the modern conscience. However, "freedom of conscience and reliance upon conscience are not one and the same;" *the* authority for the princes was not their conscience but their conscience captive to the Word of God (Wohlfeil and Goertz 1980: 19). Also, at most, freedom of conscience was a reality only for princes and cities. One could look at this from the other side and read the diet as the protest of the emperor and Catholic parties for freedom for their faith, which should have an equal right to exist in the evangelical territories. From the imperial perspective the Lutheran princes were guilty of abrogating the law with their secularization of church property and suspension of clerical courts. Furthermore, as we have already seen, the role of "conscience" was not in principle or practice to be extended to Anabaptists and Zwinglians. On the contrary, the Anabaptists were condemned to death at this diet.

While the Speyer "protest" should be understood in terms of these historical limitations, it should also be noted that the conviction voiced there that obedience to God comes before obedience to government had political and theological reverberations into the modern world. We shall discuss below its political development as the right of resistance. Theologically this became a motif of the influential modern theologian Paul Tillich (1886–1965), who spoke eloquently of the "Protestant principle." "The Protestant principle, in name derived from the protest of the 'protestants' against decisions of the Catholic majority, contains the divine and human protest against any absolute claim made for a relative reality, even if this claim is made by a Protestant church. The Protestant principle is the judge of every religious and cultural reality, including the religion and culture which calls itself 'Protestant' " (Tillich 1960: 163).

The Diet of Augsburg, 1530, and the Augsburg Confession

The evangelical protest at Speyer was a wake-up call to the emperor to move decisively on the religious question. The improvement of his political fortunes provided Charles with an opportunity to move against the Protestants. He was back in Germany for the first time since 1521; the pope was duly impressed by Charles's victory in Italy and the sack of Rome; there was peace with the Valois; and the Turks had withdrawn from the gates of Vienna. In this context and in a conciliatory mood, Charles resolved to settle the religious issue at the diet of Augsburg in 1530. In January he requested the Protestants to present an account of their faith at the diet.

In response the elector of Saxony called together the leading Lutheran theologians to prepare a brief for presentation at Augsburg. The full story of the development of this presentation, known as the *Confessio Augustana* or Augsburg confession, is too complicated to present here. In brief, a series of drafts were prepared in the weeks prior to the diet. At the end of April the elector and the Wittenberg theologians traveled to Augsburg, leaving Luther at the elector's castle in Coburg at the Saxon border because as an outlaw he could not travel through Catholic territory.

Upon arrival in Augsburg, Melanchthon learned that Eck had prepared 404 articles that condemned as heretical the writings of the Reformers. Melanchthon immediately began to rework the material he had brought with him in order to respond to this attack. The evangelicals strove to demonstrate their true catholicity, to play down or soften controversial issues, and to distance themselves from "heretics" such as the Anabaptists. The primary author of the Augsburg confession was Melanchthon. Luther's influence was limited to preparatory documents, correspondence that took three to four days to arrive, and fervent prayer. With a boldness characteristic of the biblical prophets, Luther prayed for hours on end for God's defense: "This affair is altogether yours [God's]; we have been forced to become involved in it; defend us then!" From this confidence Luther wrote encouragement to an anxious Melanchthon: "Christ knows whether it comes from stupidity or the Spirit, but I for my part am not very much troubled about our cause. . . . God who is able to raise the dead, is also able to uphold his cause when it is falling. . . . If we are not worthy instruments to acomplish his purpose, he will find others" (Fischer 1983: 86–7). Luther's evaluation of Melanchthon's irenic efforts to emphasize the catholicity of the reform movement is well known. "I have read Master Philip's Apologia [the Augsburg confession] and it pleases me very much. I know of nothing to improve or change in it and that would not be appropriate anyway, for I cannot tread so softly and gently as he" (*WA Br* 5: 319–20). Ever since, those who have not appreciated Melanchthon's diplomatic efforts for union have disparaged him as a "soft-stepper."

A sense of panic engulfed Melanchthon and his colleagues when it became clear from imperial directives that Charles did not intend to arbitrate between parties in religious conflict but rather to enforce Catholicism. Evangelical preaching was forbidden in Augsburg, and the evangelicals were commanded to participate in the Corpus Christi procession in Augsburg. Melanchthon was willing to compromise many evangelical positions to avoid the danger of a religious conflict he feared would quickly engulf Germany in civil war. His fear later came to pass as the Thirty Years War (1618–48).

But upon the emperor's arrival in Augsburg on 15 June, the tone once again markedly changed. Charles expressed his willingness to hear both parties. The Lutheran document was again reworked, with special attention to the preface and conclusion which provide the framework for understanding its 28 articles. The preface states that, in obedience to the emperor, "we offer and present a confession of our pastors' and preachers' teaching and of our own faith, setting forth how and in what manner, on the basis of Holy Scriptures, these things are preached, taught, communicated, and embraced in our lands, principalities, dominions, cities, and territories." The preface reminds Charles that he had earlier and repeatedly given assurance not to render decisions in matters of faith but to work for a general council. It is now hoped that since the emperor and the pope are on better terms such a general council may be called at the earliest opportunity. Accordingly, "we offer in full obedience, even beyond what is required, to participate in such a general, free, and Christian council as the electors, princes, and estates have with the highest and best motives requested in all the diets of the empire which have been held during Your Imperial Majesty's reign." We may note, in anticipation of discussion of the council of Trent which finally met 15 years later, that the Lutheran qualification of a general council as "free" and "Christian" was unacceptable to the papal party because "free" meant free from papal domination, and "Christian" meant using Scripture as the norm for deliberations and decisions.

The conclusion reasserts a theme running through the confession that the Lutherans in these chief articles have not introduced anything "either in doctrine or in ceremonies, that is contrary to Holy Scripture or the universal Christian church." The confession was signed by Duke John, elector of Saxony; George, margrave of Brandenburg; Ernest, duke of Lüneburg; Philip, landgrave of Hesse; John Frederick, duke of Saxony; Francis, duke of Lüneburg; Wolfgang, prince of Anhalt; the mayor and council of Nuremberg; and the mayor and council of Reutlingen. All the signatories were secular rulers and magistrates. They risked everything by signing; but, as Elector John Frederick wrote to Count William of Nassau: "Better an ungracious Emperor than an ungracious God." This was not a light comment, for John Frederick would eventually be forced to forfeit his electoral dignity and his freedom.

Their signatures make clear that the origin and development of the Augsburg confession were political as well as religious. While the theologians focused on the content of the proclamation, the rulers focused on legal considerations. It was crucial for the princes that the reforms implemented in their lands be understood in legal terms. The princes had to preserve their legitimacy as estates of the Empire. Thus the confession clearly states that it does not intend to depart from the Catholic faith nor to create any new doctrines. It clearly condemns what the Lutherans regarded as the innovations and heresies of the Anabaptists. Its irenic tone toward the Catholic faith is the work of Melanchthon, which Luther recognized he would not have been able to accomplish. Luther, concerned that Melanchthon was too anxious about the potential political repercussions of the Reformation, was adamant that the confession of the gospel not be compromised by political considerations. In the end the gospel was clearly articulated both in the Psalm verse before the preface (119: 46: "I will also speak of thy testimonies before kings, and shall not be put to shame") and in the last article (28: "All this is to be done not by human power but by God's Word alone"). At the same time the understanding of justification and the church is succinctly and clearly expressed in articles 4 and 7. "It is also taught among us that we cannot obtain forgiveness of sin and righteousness before God by our own merits, works, or satisfactions, but that we receive forgiveness of sin and become righteous before God by grace, for Christ's sake, through faith"; "for it is sufficient for the true unity of the Christian church that the Gospel be preached in conformity with a pure understanding of it and that the sacraments be administered according to the divine Word. It is not necessary for the true unity of the Christian church that ceremonies, instituted by men, should be observed uniformly in all places."

The confession was read in German to the emperor on 25 June – a reading that took over two hours! After receipt of the confession, Charles appointed papal theologians to examine and refute it. Their first responses were not acceptable to Charles because they were too lengthy and polemical. After returning to the drawing board, Eck and his colleagues presented the *confutatio*, which was read aloud on 3 August. Charles then demanded that the Protestants acknowledge they were refuted, and refused to give them a copy of the confutation until they did so. Melanchthon's extensive defense of the Augsburg confession, known as the apology, was written on the basis of notes hastily taken during the reading of the confutation. Charles, however, declared the issue closed with the confutation, and refused to accept the apology.

With Charles's endorsement of the confutation he clearly shifted from the role of mediator to partisan of the papal party, and thus aligned his political struggle with the Roman position which was essentially oriented to conflict. Pope Clement VII wanted neither reform nor a general council; he wanted only the preservation of the papal status quo and, if possible, the extermination of the Protestants.

Charles had already debated the alternatives of a council and a religious war with Rome. As Charles now consulted the Catholic princes in Augsburg with respect to a war against the Protestants he encountered their refusal. The concern of the Catholic princes was not the well-being of the Protestant estates but rather the potential increase of imperial power that would ensue if the Protestants were defeated. When Charles returned to demanding a general council from Rome to negotiate reform and reunion he once again met refusal. The option of a national council in Germany was equally unacceptable to Charles, for it would have meant the foundation of a German national church. This was not without precedent: 15 years earlier the pope had bowed to French pressure for the establishment of a French national church by a concordat of 1516; and by 1530 the English church was also moving in this direction. But a German national church threatened the Habsburg pretensions to world rule. The universal Habsburg empire needed a universal church. Charles could not free himself from the medieval ideal of the emperor as patron of the universal church. And the pope whose predecessors had fought such medieval imperial pretensions was not about to disabuse Charles of this idea; a general council appeared far more dangerous to the pope than did the emperor.

On the Protestant side the differences over the Lord's Supper precluded a common pan-Protestant confession. The Zwinglian orientation of the Swiss cantons and the south German cities prevented them from subscribing to the Augsburg confession. This was the origin of the confession of the four imperial cities of Strasbourg, Constance, Memmingen, and Lindau: the *Confessio Tetrapolitana*. Written by the Strasbourg Reformer Bucer and his colleagues, it was a ponderous and long-winded argumentation that biblically grounded its differences from the old faith and presented a Zwinglian understanding of the Lord's Supper. It was not read before the diet and received hardly any attention. It was an attempt to mediate between the positions of Luther and Zwingli, and also to present the first confession of the Reformed (that is, Zwinglian and, later, Calvinist) churches in Germany. Zwingli sent his own personal confession, *Fidei ratio ad Carolum Imperatorem*, but Charles rejected it and it was never presented to the diet.

At Augsburg it became clear that the Empire would have to live with two confessions. The Augsburg confession soon became the foundational document of the Lutheran churches and remains so today. Melanchthon's original ecumenical intentionality and expression has been rediscovered in the improved ecumenical climate of the late twentieth century. There was even discussion during its 450th anniversary in 1980 about Roman Catholic recognition of it (see e.g. Burgess 1980).

The Right of Resistance to the Emperor

At Augsburg, Charles's carrot-and-stick diplomacy had failed. He had been unable to cajole or coerce both the papacy and the Protestants into overcoming their differences. Guided by the politically astute chancellor of Electoral Saxony, Gregor Brück, the Protestants had avoided submitting to the emperor's demand to return to the old faith. But they were unable to avert a majority of the diet from supporting the edict of Worms and declaring every opposition to it a breaking of the peace in the Empire. The Protestants were given until 15 April 1531 to unite with the old faith. Until then no further innovations were to be introduced, nor were evangelical writings to be permitted.

With Charles's rejection of the Augsburg confession and his commitment to carrying out the edict of Worms, the Protestants were on notice of imminent war. The Protestant estates and princes began preparing for this danger immediately after the close of the diet. In February 1531 a formal defensive league was formed in Schmalkalden. Led by Electoral Saxony and Hesse, it included other signatories of the Augsburg confession as well as a number of imperial cities, including some from south Germany. The issue of resistance to the emperor had long been discussed by lawyers and theologians. Luther in particular was initially opposed. His opposition was consistent with his stance that the gospel could not be made into a new law, and forced upon people. He had argued this position against Karlstadt, Müntzer, Zwingli, the Knights' Revolt, the Peasants' War, and, most recently, proposals for a crusade against the Turks. "One could not trust in political might to preserve the gospel, but could only put one's faith in God" (Brecht 1990: 363). The lawyers and politicians argued the legitimacy of a defensive league on the basis that the rulers were not only subjects of the emperor, they were also rulers politically and spiritually responsible for their own subjects. Furthermore, the lawyers argued, imperial law itself allowed resistance if the emperor acted unjustly and illegally.

Luther's growing conviction that the emperor would use force to reimpose the old faith impelled him to warn against collaboration in such an action. Luther, himself a living example of civil disobedience, now faced the potential political consequences of adherence to the Augsburg confession. In *Dr Martin Luther's Warning to his Dear German People* (probably composed in October 1530, published in April 1531), Luther sanctioned armed resistance to the emperor. Defensive action for protection of the gospel is understood as a case of "just war." The pertinence of this treatise is reflected in its numerous printings, especially during the Schmalkaldic War and the Thirty Years War.

The Schmalkaldic League was a military federation led on a semi-annual rotation by Electoral Saxony and Hesse. As the symbol of their unity and faith the princes and cities in the League subscribed to the Augsburg confession. The League rapidly expanded in response to events. On 11 October 1531 Zwingli was killed at the battle of Kappel, and the south German imperial cities oriented toward Zurich lost political and military support. If they wished to stand up to the emperor they had to seek protection from the Schmalkaldic League.

Meanwhile the Turks were again on the march and the emperor needed the military and financial help of the Protestant estates. To secure such support the emperor in July 1532 declared a truce between the two religious parties – the Nuremberg "Standstill." This legal toleration was renewed for over a decade, and thereby became an umbrella for Protestant expansion. Protected by the religious peace, Philip of Hesse and the city of Strasbourg assisted the Lutheran Duke Ulrich to regain his duchy of Württemberg which had been under Habsburg administration since 1519. Ulrich's return meant a strengthening of the Protestant party in the German southwest. A narrowing of Lutheran and Zwinglian differences over the Lord's Supper by the Wittenberg concord of 1536 allowed further imperial cities to join the League, and displaced the Zwinglian Reformation from the Empire. Joining the League after Württemberg were Pomerania and Anhalt, the imperial cities of Augsburg, Frankfurt, Hanover, and Hamburg, and then the margravate of Brandenburg and the duchy of Saxony. The reforms instituted by these authorities were one-sided governmental introductions of the Augsburg confession.

Catholicism remained supported only in the Habsburg and Wittelsbach territories. For the Habsburgs a confessional change was out of the question so long as the dynasty wished to retain its hold on the office of emperor. The Wittelsbach territory in south Germany had already advanced in its process of "nationalizing" clerical institutions so that further secularization of church property and elimination of clerical courts would have brought only an insignificant increase in power. Episcopal and monastic lands were characterized as "foundations" of the nobility, and hence there was energetic opposition to their reform because it would have been at the expense of the nobles.

Up to the outbreak of the Schmalkaldic War in 1546, the entire area of the east German colonization and the larger part of northern Germany was won for Lutheranism. The advance of reform in these areas formed the bridgehead for Lutheran expansion into the Scandinavian lands and influence in England.

Reformation Ecumenism, War, and the Peace of Augsburg

Charles V's response to the expansion of Protestantism began by enlisting diplomatic activity in favor of calling a general council. But the emperor's interest in church unity was stymied by the suspicions of both parties and by politics. The papacy opposed a council as proposed by the Protestants because the memory of the conciliarist movement and especially the council of Constance was too fresh to agree to a "free and Christian" council. The European kings obstructed a general council because they feared it would become a vehicle for the increase of Habsburg power. The Lutherans were dubious about sending representatives to a general council because they feared this would provide recognition of the papacy as the highest authority in the church. The failure of Charles's endeavors to call a council led him to seek to restore the unity of the Empire through religious dialogues within the Empire. In 1540 and 1541 there were religious colloquies in Hagenau, Worms, and Regensburg that achieved some ecumenical convergence in theological issues concerned with original sin and justification. However, the compromises reached in these colloquies were rejected by both Rome and Luther.

The failures to call a council and to achieve convergence through dialogue moved the religious conflict toward war. By 1546 Charles was in a favorable position to advance against the Lutherans. There was peace with France; the papacy promised to help finance the war against the Schmalkaldic League; and the League was weakened both by Charles's successful effort to bribe Maurice of Saxony to his side and by Philip of Hesse's bigamy. The latter was a personal and political disaster for Philip and the League, and an embarrassment for Luther, Melanchthon, and Bucer who had provided him with pastoral counsel. Since bigamy was punishable by death in imperial law, Philip's position was seriously compromised and he promised support to Charles to avoid the consequences of the law (see Brecht 1993: 205–8, 210–15).

The formal ground for war was enforcement of the edict against Saxony and Hesse. Together these two powers had driven the emperor's supporter Heinrich of Braunschweig from his lands and introduced the Reformation there. The Schmalkaldic League possessed military and strategic advantages over Charles but squandered them. Maurice of Saxony, the "German Machiavelli," pursued his interest in gaining the electoral dignity of Saxony by shifting from the League to Charles. By April 1547 the emperor had won the day and destroyed the Schmalkaldic League at the battle of Mühlberg near Wittenberg. John Frederick was captured, and Philip of Hesse soon was also Charles's prisoner. Maurice of Saxony, known as the "Judas of Meissen," received the electoral dignity from Charles. Luther had died just before the war began. It is said that as Charles stood in the Castle church in Wittenberg where Luther was buried, he was urged to dig up Luther's body and burn it as a heretic, but replied: "I do not make war against dead men" (Kittelson 1986: 299).

Charles now sought to re-establish a unified Empire by the imposition of a temporal settlement at the 1548 diet of Augsburg to be in effect until the council of Trent finished its work. The settlement, known as the Augsburg Interim, allowed the provisional continuation in Protestant lands of married clergy, communion in both kinds, and a form of the doctrine of justification. The Interim was vehemently denounced by most Protestants as an imposition of the old faith. Some theologians, most notoriously Melanchthon, rationalized the reintroduction of elements of the Catholic cultus and theology as "matters of indifference" (*adiaphora*). Other Protestant leaders argued, however, that nothing was "indifferent" if it was forced. Strong opposition to the Interim in Luther's home territory led Maurice, now elector, to promote his own version which allowed many Catholic externals while protecting core Protestant doctrines. Maurice's effort to avoid alienating too many of his new subjects is known as the Leipzig Interim. A remarkable example of the failure of this policy is the city of Magdeburg.

The Protestant leadership in Magdeburg denounced the Interim as the work of the devil and the Antichrist. The city's refusal to accept the Interim provoked the ban of the Empire and a siege. In defense of its position the city produced the first Protestant justification of religious resistance to authority, the "Magdeburg confession." The pastors, led by Nicholas Gallus, Nicholas Amsdorf, and Matthew Flacius Illyricus (of the "Magdeburg Centuries" fame), issued *A Confession of the Magdeburg Pastors Concerning Resistance to the Superior Magistrate* (13 April 1550). A torrent of political propaganda in tracts, satirical cartoons, and ditties against the Interim poured from the presses of Magdeburg and fired public opinion throughout Germany. Taking their cue from Luther's *Warning to his Dear German People* that "God can easily raise up a Judas Maccabeus . . . who will smash Antiochus with his army and teach him real warfare," the Magdeburg confession compares the city's resistance to that of the Maccabees. Their defending troops sang: "Do as the Maccabees did and strive for God's Word. Attack the land's betrayer; Avenge the gross murder done in the German land" (Olson 1972: 69–70).

The Lutheran doctrine of resistance, contrary to the widespread view popularized by William Shirer in his *The Rise and Fall of the Third Reich* (1960), was active and not just passive (Olson 1972; Schoenberger 1977; Benert 1988). The Magdeburg confession was directly influential on the development of Calvinist resistance theories in France, the Nether-lands, and England. A good case can be made that it was also influential in the resistance to Hitler, epitomized by the Confessing Church of Germany and in particular by the famous pastor executed for involve-ment in the attempt to kill Hitler, Dietrich Bonhoeffer. Bonhoeffer's cousin and close confidant, Hans Christoph von Hase, was a Flacius scholar and wrote on the resistance to the Interim (Siemon–Netto 1995). Bonhoeffer continued the point made by Luther and Flacius that certain ethical issues so impinge on faith that they have a confessional status (*casus* or *status confessionis*). An example in Bonhoeffer's context was Nazi treatment of the Jews; a later example is apartheid. The point learned from Flacius and the controversy over the Augsburg Interim is that *nihil est adiaphoron in casu confessionis et scandali* ("nothing is a matter of indifference in the case of confession and scandal"). In more colorful language both Luther and Bonhoeffer answered the question of what to do in the case of perverted institutions quite clearly: "If the coachdriver is drunk, we have to put a spoke in the wheel" (Duchrow 1987: 34).

The city of Magdeburg was no military match for the forces of Maurice, who took the city in November 1551 with the assurance of allowing its religion in return for acceptance of his lordship. But new circumstances led to a reversal of recent Protestant ill fortune. The long called-for general council had indeed begun in Trent in 1545, but its configuration and dogmatic course dealt the final blow to Protestant hopes, which had already reached a nadir after nearly a generation of waiting (see chapter 13 below). What justification there had been to accept the Interim as a temporary settlement prior to a council now evaporated with the hopes of the Protestants. The Interim itself proved to be unworkable on a number of levels, not least of which was clerical refusal to cooperate. Since the beginning of the Reformation a whole new generation of clergy had displaced those of the old faith, so that even if rulers wished to replace rebellious evangelical clergy they would be hard pressed to find replacements suitable to the needs of the Interim. "The Interim was doomed at the grassroots level, and it was as little satisfactory to Catholics as to Protestants" (Scribner 1990: 192).

At the peak of the political hierarchy things were going no better. The imperial brothers were at odds over their differing political interests. Ferdinand's focus was on central and eastern Europe, where he had faced the Turk during most of this period without much help from Charles. Furthermore, while Charles pursued his Spanish inter-ests and wars with the Valois, Ferdinand had been saddled with dealing with the Protestants, but without the final authority to resolve issues one way or another. The tension between the Austrian and Spanish houses of the Habsburgs was sibling rivalry on a grand scale. It even extended to their sons: Charles thought his son Philip should succeed Ferdinand as emperor, while Ferdinand thought his son Maximilian, rather than Philip, should get the hand of Mary Tudor. Thus when the Protestant princes rebelled in 1552, Ferdinand was not enthusiastic about coming to the aid of Charles.

Maurice of Saxony led the revolt of the Protestant princes under the transconfessional banner of preserving princely liberties. The perennial concern of the princes had taken on an added edge, both with the imperial imprisonment of John Frederick of Saxony and Philip of Hesse, and with Charles's proposal that the imperial dignity should alternate between his and Ferdinand's heirs. The latter seemed to make the electoral college superfluous and hence undermine the rights of the prince-electors.

Maurice enlisted the help of Henry II, king of France, by promising him the imperial bishoprics of Metz, Toul, and Verdun in return for support. Charles was forced to flee across the Alps for safety, and would never return to German soil. Charles relinquished to Ferdinand the resolution of the religious division at the 1555 diet of Augsburg. The diet, meeting from March to September, settled the religious conflict independently of the traditional medieval powers of pope and emperor. The papacy had no representative at the diet because of both a rapid succession of popes and papal intransigence. Pope Julius III died in March and his successor, Marcellus II, died in May; the new pope, Paul IV, refused to recognize any competence to resolve religious issues other than that of the papacy. Charles V shared this papal rigidity and thus both pope and emperor were effectively sidelined.

The Peace of Augsburg (1555) was also influenced by the concern of both Protestant and Catholic princes to increase their particularist powers. The Protestant electors sought recognition of their right to reform and control the church; other princes sought security against imperial control; and cities sought their own protection. The result was a provisional "public peace" constituted on political compromises that recognized, at least for the moment, the futility of forcing a religious settlement but still assumed the validity of the medieval vision of a *corpus Christianum*: one church and one empire. The peace was dictated by political reality and insight; it was not a consequence of any sense of tolerance.

The provisions of the Peace of Augsburg included the guarantee of personal and legal security to the imperial estates of both parties, which included rights of worship and church polity for the adherents of the Augsburg confession; the recognition of princely sovereignty over religion on the principle that "where there is one ruler, there should be only one religion" (*ubi unus dominus, ibi una sit religio*), which received classic formulation about 1600 as *cuius regio, eius religio*, "whose reign, his religion;" the right of emigration (*ius emigrandi*) for subjects unwilling to accept their prince's religion; the so-called "ecclesiastical reservation" which deprived an ecclesiastical prince of his office and possessions should he become Lutheran; the retention of the confessional status quo in the imperial cities where both confessions were established; and the right of secular princes to retain church property they had seized up to 1552, excluding that which was directly subject to the Empire.

The Peace of Augsburg was advantageous to the adherents of the Augsburg confession, but the legalization this party received did not extend to other Protestants such as the Anabaptists and the adherents of the Swiss Reformation, whose center of gravity had by this time shifted to Geneva under the influence of John Calvin. The Peace did recognize that an alternative confessional commitment did not in itself mean disloyalty to the Empire, a point which Luther and Melanchthon among others had vociferously argued in 1530.

The provision for emigration has sometimes been seen as the beginning of the struggle for human rights with regard to religious freedom and freedom of movement. But it should be recalled that emigration required paying off one's debts to the prince, which could be economically impossible. In this light the development of crypto-Protestantism and crypto-Catholicism is not surprising. The story of the eighteenth-century expulsion of the Salzburg Protestants illustrates that the migration passage of 1555 could also become a rationale for expulsion.

The medieval principle of one truth gave way to a minimal pluralism with the legal abolition of heresy with regard to the Lutherans. In having to recognize both confessional parties the emperor lost at least in theory the claim to be the second head of Christendom after the pope. Charles was conscious of this problem, and as the parity between confessions began to emerge as a legal solution, he informed his brother that after the diet he would remove his crown. In October 1555 Charles ceded the Netherlands, and in January 1556 Spain and Sicily, to his son Philip II. A consequence of this was to shift the Habsburg–Valois conflict to a conflict between Spain and France. In conformity with medieval ideals, Charles V retired to a monastery at Juste in Spain for his health and his salvation; there he died in 1558. The transfer of the imperial title to Ferdinand of Austria was officially confirmed in 1558. The claim that there is only one religious truth collapsed at Augsburg

1555, and with it went both Charles's vision of Habsburg domination of Europe and the essential Reformation goal to reform the church, not split it.

Suggestions for Further Reading

Thomas A. Brady, Jr, *Protestant Politics: Jacob Sturm (1489–1553) and the German Reformation*, Atlantic Highlands: Humanities, 1995

Bernd Moeller, *Imperial Cities and the Reformation: Three Essays*, ed. and trans. H. C. Erik Midelfort and Mark U. Edwards, Jr, Durham: Labyrinth, 1982

Steven Ozment, *The Reformation in the Cities: The Appeal of the Reformation to Sixteenth-Century Germany and Switzerland*, New Haven: Yale University Press, 1975

R. W. Scribner, "Politics and the Institutionalization of Reform in Germany," in G. R. Elton, ed., *The Reformation 1520–1559*, 2nd edn (New Cambridge Modern History, II), 172–97, Cambridge: Cambridge University Press, 1990

James D. Tracy, ed., *Luther and the Modern State in Germany*, Kirksville: Sixteenth Century Journal Publishers, 1986

10

"The Most Perfect School of Christ": The Genevan Reformation

Geneva is the most perfect school of Christ that ever was in this earth since the days of the Apostles. In other places I confess Christ to be truly preached; but manners and religion to be so sincerely reformed, I have not seen in any other place.

John Knox (1513–72)

In 1556, at the time of uttering the above praise, the fiery Scottish Reformer John Knox was a refugee in Geneva due to Mary Tudor's campaign against Protestants. Knox was neither the only refugee nor the only admirer in Calvin's Geneva. About the same time, another Marian refugee in Geneva wrote: "Geneva seems to me to be the wonderful miracle of the whole world . . . Is it not wonderful that Spaniards, Italians, Scots, Englishmen, Frenchmen, Germans, disagreeing in manners, speech, and apparel . . . being coupled with only the yoke of Christ, should live so lovingly . . . like a spiritual and Christian congregation" (McNeill 1967: 178).

The extravagant praise of Geneva as a "holy city" guarded by "legions of angels" indicates that this "new Rome" of the Reformation was not only a refuge for Protestants expelled from other lands for their faith, but was also a mecca for adherents to the new faith. As we shall see, Geneva as the model of a Christian commonwealth was not "built in a day," but was the result of a long and often bitter struggle. Furthermore, in this process, Geneva not only welcomed refugees, it created them. At the center of all the praise and blame that swirled through and around Geneva stood John Calvin, himself a displaced person from France.

John Calvin (1509–1564) *26 years younger than Luther*

John Calvin (Jean Cauvin), 26 years younger than Luther, was a second-generation Reformer. As the most important Reformer outside

Germany (some would argue *the* most important Reformer of all), Calvin's work and personality place him in that "elect" group of leading figures in the church about whom there are few if any nonpartisan judgments. He has been portrayed as both a narrow dogmatist and an ecumenical churchperson; a ruthless inquisitor and a sensitive, caring pastor; an ascetic, cold authoritarian and a compassionate humanist; a rigorous individualist and a social thinker; a plodding systematizer and the theologians' theologian who finally completed the doctrine of the trinity; a man dominated by logic and a man of contradictory traits and inconsistencies; a theoretician of capitalism and of socialism; the tyrant of Geneva and a defender of freedom; a dictator and a revolutionary. With regard to his theology, some hold that its center is predestination; others claim its center is the forgiveness of sin; and still others argue it has no center at all! In short, few have been neutral about Calvin. The history of the interpretation of Calvin has yet to reach the exhaustive scope of that of Luther, but there is no doubt it will be as colorful. Calvin even had his own "Cochlaeus" in Jerome Bolsec, whose 1577 biography of Calvin was a major achievement in the art of defamation.

Calvin was born in Noyon, a cathedral city about 60 miles northeast of Paris. His mother died when Calvin was about five or six. His father, an attorney for the cathedral chapter and a secretary to the bishop, obtained a modest church benefice for John which subsidized his education. At fourteen, Calvin set out for Paris where he engaged in general studies at the Collège de la Marche and then theological studies at the Collège de Montaigu where Erasmus and Rabelais had preceded him and Loyola was to follow. In 1528, at eighteen, Calvin received his Master of Arts degree. Calvin's mastery and skill in the prevalent forms of Latin argumentation as well as his religious and ethical seriousness may be behind the legend that his classmates nicknamed him "the accusative case." A somewhat more humane description of Calvin's student days comes from his friend and biographer, Theodore Beza (1519–1605), who explained Calvin's penchant for lying in bed in the mornings as time for reflecting on his diligent late-night studies.

In 1528 Calvin moved from Paris to the famous law schools in Orleans and then Bourges, where he completed a degree in law in 1532. This shift from preparatory theological studies to law was at the insistence of his father who had become involved in a controversy with the clergy of Noyon, and who may well have believed that law would provide a better career. At Bourges, Calvin had the opportunity to pursue his lively interest in the classics, including the study of Greek. That Calvin's pursuit of law was largely a matter of filial obedience is evident in the fact that upon the death of his father Calvin returned to Paris to study humanism. In 1532 he published his first work, a learned commentary on Seneca's *On Clemency*. Although apparently a publishing failure, it shows Calvin's early linguistic ability and deep knowledge of the classics. This commentary, contrary to some suggestions, is not a source for Calvin's move toward the Reformation or a plea for religious toleration but rather an expression of his response to the volatile political context of the early Reformation in France confronted by royal absolutism. As a young lawyer Calvin is proposing the "golden mean" of clemency between tyranny and revolt. As such, this commentary is a clue both to his later address to Francis I that prefaces the *Institutes* and to his perennial concern for order in the course of reform.

In fact, Calvin himself provided scant autobiographical information regarding his conversion to "Protestantism." He was, as he said in his reply to Cardinal Sadoleto's appeal to the Genevans to return to the Roman faith, "unwilling to speak of myself" (Olin 1966: 54). This personal reticence is striking when compared to Luther who, it often seems, rarely had a thought or emotion he did not write down. "Whereas Luther's persona looms large on every page of his work, Calvin inclined to be so 'private' that it is difficult to discern the person behind the pen and to discover the emotional heartbeat behind his intellectual drive to grasp the mysteries of God and the world" (Oberman 1994: 114). He certainly shared the humanists' desire to return *ad fontes*, to the sources of culture, including the Scriptures. But recent Calvin scholarship has become sensitive to the many ways sixteenth-century humanism may be defined. Hence some would limit Calvin's humanism to his use of its methodology, while others would include his acceptance of some of its substantive views of human nature and history. What Calvin did share with the French evangelical humanists in the decade prior to his conversion was the existential fear and spiritual anxiety in the face of both the near-annihilation of the French "Lutherans" and the break from Roman Catholicism. Bouwsma (1988) and Oberman (1994) both point to Calvin's use of "labyrinth" and "abyss" as central expressions of the confusion and anxiety of the time. In this context the young Calvin was assisted in developing his own biblical theology by Luther's writings in Latin and in French translation. A master of French, Latin, Greek, and Hebrew, Calvin did not understand German, a fact some Zwinglian theologians suggested accounted for his admiration of Luther. "The young Calvin is theologically not an Erasmian, but – in view of his different understanding of the *iustitia Dei* – to a remarkable extent in experience and at times even in expression a disciple of Luther" (Oberman 1994: 134).

Late in life, Calvin did speak of his "unexpected conversion" that scholars posit took place sometime in 1533–4. In the preface to his 1557 Psalms commentary Calvin referred to God's providence in changing the direction of his life. "What happened first was that by an unexpected conversion he tamed to teachableness a mind too stubborn for its years – for I was so strongly devoted to the superstitions of the papacy that nothing less could draw me from the depths of mire. . . . Before a year slipped by anybody who longed for a purer doctrine kept on coming to learn from me, still a beginner, a raw recruit" (Bouwsma 1988: 10). In his reply to Sadoleto, Calvin further described his conversion in terms similar to Luther's experience of liberation by the mercy of God from the burdens of the confessional and a piety of achievement. In his *Institutes of the Christian Religion* Calvin accused the Roman church of enslaving consciences by many laws that cause extreme anguish and terror and uncertainty of salvation. Here the person "will always doubt whether he has a merciful God; he will always be troubled, and always tremble." "On the contrary, justified by faith is he who, excluded from the righteousness of works, grasps the righteousness of Christ through faith, and clothed in it, appears in God's sight not as a sinner but as a righteous man. . . . Therefore, 'to justify' means nothing else than to acquit of guilt him who was accused, as if his innocence were confirmed" (McNeill and Battles 1960: 1180, 653–4, 726–8).

Calvin's conversion was publicly attested by his return to Noyon in May 1534 to surrender the ecclesiastical benefices he had held since he was twelve. Unlike many French reform-minded humanists who remained publicly in the Roman church, Calvin made a clean break. Throughout the rest of his ministry Calvin would sharply criticize these "Nicodemites" (so-called after Nicodemus in John 3: 1–17) who could not bring themselves to live publicly what they believed inwardly.

Although Calvin referred to being mired in papal superstitions, it is important to note that, unlike most of the first-generation Reformers, Calvin was neither a monk nor a priest. Indeed, it is not clear whether even during his pastoral career in Strasbourg and in Geneva he was ever ordained. Bouwsma (1988: 20) states that Calvin became a preacher and pastor not by ordination but by action of the Geneva town council. In his reply to Sadoleto Calvin refers to his holding the offices of teacher and pastor in Geneva, and his assurance that his ministry "is supported and sanctioned by a call from God" (Olin 1966: 50). Yet Calvin never received the formal training in theology characteristic of the first generation; he was a self-taught theologian.

Calvin also markedly differed in context from the first-generation Reformers. He was neither German nor Swiss, but French. Unlike the Holy Roman Empire, France was progressing toward a centralized and absolute monarchy. It was not at all in the political, let alone religious, interest of the king, Francis I, to tolerate reform movements incompatible with his drive to create political and national unity. Reformers in France could find no cover, as in Germany, behind the magistrates of estates and cities or the protection of princes. Here each was exposed by public confession to the police power of the national state. This helps to explain the "Nicodemite" phenomenon Calvin opposed. The Reformation in France created a church "in the wilderness" watered by the blood of its martyrs in opposition to the power of a central authority which the court lawyers formulated in terms of *un roi, une loi, une foi!* – "one king, one law, one faith!"

Journey to Geneva

Calvin left Paris because of the "Cop affair." Calvin's friend from their days together at the Collège de Montaigu, Nicholas Cop, professor of medicine, was elected rector of the Sorbonne. In his inaugural speech, delivered on 1 November 1533 (All Saints' Day), Cop addressed the gathered professors of the Sorbonne on the Sermon on the Mount, and challenged them to obey God in spite of persecution and slander. His address cited not only the works of French humanists and Erasmus but also a sermon of Luther's, and identified the biblical poor in spirit with persecuted evangelicals. Some theologians responded by charging that Cop was a Lutheran propagandist, and the king called for the arrest of the "Lutherans." Calvin, suspected of being a co-author of the address because of his close association with Cop, fled. Cop managed to escape to Basle. Calvin found security at a friend's home in Angoulême where he began to write what would soon become the most significant single statement of Protestantism, the *Institutes of the Christian Religion.*

Calvin completed and published the first edition of the *Institutes* in 1536 in Basle, where he had sought refuge in January 1535 from the intensifying French persecution of Protestants. Originally intended as an evangelical catechism for the education and reformation of the churches, this work quickly earned Calvin an international reputation. The catechetical form is no accident, for before Calvin began his first edition he knew Luther's Small Catechism. Furthermore, at this time *institutio* was a synonym for *catechismus.* "Luther had been a great influence on the *Institutes,* and Calvin both acknowledged him as the father of the movement with which he had now identified himself and admired his theological insight" (Bouwsma 1988: 18; see Watanabe 1994). Indeed, it has been claimed that Calvin was Luther's best and greatest disciple (Spijker 1993: I, 466; Gerrish 1968; Selinger 1984: 11–56). Analogous to Luther's catechisms, the first edition of the *Institutes* consisted of six chapters on the Law, the creed, the Lord's Prayer, the sacraments of baptism and the Lord's Supper, arguments against the remaining Roman sacraments, and a discussion of Christian liberty. In great demand, the *Institutes* was repeatedly republished, expanded, and also translated into French. By the 1539 edition, Calvin conceived of the work as a text for the training of ministerial candidates. Calvin's final revision of 1559 extends to over 1,500 pages in modern English translation. The *Institutes* was prefaced with a letter to king Francis I of France, pleading for a fair hearing of the evangelical faith, and informing the king that a rule apart from service to God is nothing but banditry. This letter is a defense attorney's masterpiece of vindication for French Protestantism, and clearly exhibited Calvin's leadership qualities to Protestants everywhere. It is of interest that Calvin retained this dedicatory letter in all later editions after the death of Francis. His point is that whoever fills that office "is accountable before God for the well-being of the people, and whoever neglects or betrays his trust will not long remain king" (Willis-Watkins 1989: 117).

But this letter did not prompt a change of heart in Francis. His brief general amnesty for French religious exiles was prompted rather by his need for support on the eve of his third war with the emperor, Charles V. Taking advantage of this opportunity for a safe return, Calvin made his way back home to settle family affairs; it was his last visit to his homeland. Then, with his brother Antoine and his sister Marie, Calvin set out for the free imperial city of Strasbourg where he intended to settle down to a life of scholarship. On the way to Strasbourg they were forced by imperial troop movements to divert via Geneva. It turned out to be one of history's most remarkable detours.

Calvin arrived in Geneva in July 1536. He planned to stay only overnight before continuing his trip to Strasbourg. But someone recognized Calvin and tipped off an old acquaintance of his from Paris, William (Guillaume) Farel (1489–1565). Farel, a fiery preacher, had been laboring for some months to bring Geneva to the Protestantism already espoused by Bern, Basle, and Zurich. Farel saw Calvin as literally a Godsend to the cause, and exhorted him to stay and join in the work of reforming Geneva. Calvin refused, explaining that he was a scholar not an administrator or preacher, and that he lacked the temperament for such a task because he generally did not get along well with people. As Calvin later wrote of himself: "Being of a rather unsociable and shy disposition, I have always loved retirement and peace. So I began to look for some hideout where I could escape from people. . . . My aim was always to live in private without being known" (Gerrish 1967a: 151).

Undeterred by Calvin's refusal, Farel thundered out an angry denunciation of Calvin's selfish plans, and proclaimed that God would curse Calvin's scholarly life if he did not stay in Geneva and carry out God's assignment. Calvin was overcome by this pronouncement. As he said of this event: "Farel kept me at Geneva not so much by advice and entreaty as by a dreadful adjuration, as if God had stretched forth his hand upon me from on high to arrest me" (Walker 1969: 158). Thus Calvin yielded to a responsibility he had neither sought nor wanted. "In spite of my disposition [God] has brought me into the light and made me get involved, as they say" (*CO* 31: 22). This "God-frustrated scholar," as Calvin has been called, devoted the rest of his life to Geneva, except for a short exile in Strasbourg.

The Reformation in Geneva

The Reformation in Geneva was intimately allied with the political emancipation of the town. Geneva more than many other Reformation areas exemplified the revolutionary potential of the Reformation. This fact was not lost on the mind of the French crown, which later always suspected Protestants of political subversion.

In the early sixteenth century Geneva was struggling for independence from the House of Savoy, the dominant power south of Geneva between France and Italy. The traditional ruler of Geneva was a prince-bishop who by this time was little more than an extension of the House of Savoy. To the north of Geneva were the powerful Swiss cantons of Catholic Fribourg and Protestant Bern, both of whom for political reasons wanted to draw Geneva into a Swiss alliance. In 1525 Savoy lost its satellite Lausanne to an alliance with Bern and correctly surmised that Geneva might follow suit. Although Duke Charles III of Savoy coerced reaffirmation of Genevan allegiance to their bishop and the House of Savoy, Genevan exiles negotiated a treaty with Fribourg and Bern which brought Geneva into the Swiss orbit in February 1526. The Genevan supporters of the Swiss Confederacy were called Eidgue-nots (*Eid* = oath; *Genosse* = associate) and it has been suggested that this name was conflated with that of a Genevan exile leader, Besançon Hugues, to form the name "Huguenot" later applied to French Protestants and refugees. The origin of the term "Huguenot" has long been debated. Another explanation attributes it to early French Calvin-ist gatherings near the Hugon Gate in the city of Tours. The derisive diminutive "little Hughes" (Huguenot) was then accepted as a badge of honor (Ozment 1980: 359; Gray 1983).

In 1527 the Genevan Council of Two Hundred was instituted and formally assumed the legislative and judicial powers previously exer-cised by the duke of Savoy. Executive functions were exercised by the Little Council which consisted of 25 members, 16 of whom were appointed by the Council of Two Hundred and the others (four syndics, the city treasurer, and four from the previous year's Little Council) elected annually by the General Council of the citizenry.

Geneva was attacked by Savoy in 1530 but rescued by the interven-tion of Bern and Fribourg. But by now Bern and Fribourg were at religious odds. Bern had embraced the Reformation in 1528 but Fribourg remained rigorously Roman Catholic. In 1533 Bern energet-ically missionized Geneva for Protestantism, and the resultant religious riots, iconoclasm, and rise of "heresy" in the city collapsed its alliance with Catholic Fribourg. Through public disputations and fiery sermons, Farel led the vanguard of Protestants against the old church. He gained the pulpit of the cathedral, and persuaded the Council of Two Hundred to suppress the mass on 10 August 1535. By December 1535, the magistrates gave the Catholic clergy the choice of conversion or exile. In May 1536 a general assembly of citizens ratified reform measures and affirmed their will "to live according to the gospel and the Word of God." Bern had defended and liberated Geneva from Savoy, but Geneva resisted Bernese attempts to substitute itself for the ousted prince-bishop and the House of Savoy. Genevan sovereignty was formally recognized by Bern in August 1536, although Bern continued to be a power for Geneva to respect.

Thus when Calvin arrived in Geneva at the ripe old age of twenty-seven, Farel and his colleagues were just beginning to try to implement the recent mandate for the Reformation. The Roman clergy had been expelled, but a new Protestant structure was yet to be created. It was for this task of firmly establishing and consolidating Protestantism that Farel believed Calvin had been divinely sent to Geneva. Apparently not everyone was privy to Farel's insight, for in formalizing Calvin's appointment as reader in Holy Scripture, the secretary of the Little Council missed his name and wrote down, "that Frenchman" (*ille Gallus*).

Calvin's first attempts to reform Geneva not only failed but led to his expulsion from the city. It was axiomatic to him that church worship and discipline belonged in the hands of the leaders of the church, not the hands of the politicians. This was a departure from the polity of other Swiss Protestant cities including that of Bern, Geneva's defender. The citizenry, which still included a large population of Catholics, was not pleased with the discipline and doctrinal uniformity that Calvin and Farel sought to impose. In November 1537 the General Council refused to enforce the confession of faith to which Calvin insisted the whole population must adhere. The council apparently feared that the church's oversight of the city's morals challenged its own authority, a fear which other cities shared and one which would continue to be a source of tension in Geneva. Thus the Council of Two Hundred denied Calvin and Farel the right to excommunicate. The town had not gotten rid of a Catholic prince-bishop in order to replace him with Protestant ones! In February 1538 the annual election put syndics in office who were hostile to Farel and Calvin. In mid-March the Council of Two Hundred warned Calvin and Farel not to meddle in politics but to stick to religion. The magistrates' understanding of religion included the liturgical practice sanctioned by Bern that unleavened bread must be used in the Lord's Supper.

On Easter Sunday 1538, Calvin and Farel preached in the two main Geneva churches but refused to administer communion, in defiance of the order of the magistrates. In short, they excommunicated their entire congregations! They were not against the use of unleavened bread *per se* but against the right of the civic authorities to dictate in ecclesiastical matters. Calvin saw the crisis in terms of pastoral freedom; the Genevan authorities saw it in terms of independence from Bernese interference. "It was in the interests of Geneva to appease and conform to Berne in as many ways as possible in order to guarantee Bernese military support and to remove or reduce possible points of conflict while maintaining a maximum amount of internal independence" (Naphy 1994: 26). There was an uproar and the Genevan Council immediately dismissed Farel and Calvin and gave them three days to leave Geneva. Informed of the decision, Calvin responded: "Well and good, if we had served men we would be ill rewarded, but we serve a great Master who will reward us" (Monter 1967: 66–7).

Sojourn in Strasbourg

Farel settled in Neuchâtel, and Calvin went to Strasbourg at the urging of the Farel-like threats of Martin Bucer (1491–1551), the leading Reformer there: "Don't think that you can leave the ministry even for a short time without offending God, if another ministry is offered you" Bouwsma 1988: 21–2). Having finally arrived at his original destination, Calvin spent three of his happiest years (1538–41) as a university lecturer and pastor to a French refugee congregation. While in Strasbourg, Calvin learned a great deal about church organization from Martin Bucer (Spijker 1994), a former Dominican, who himself had received his initiation into the evangelical movement from Luther at the Heidelberg disputation in 1518.

The influence of Bucer and Strasbourg on Calvin and the French Reformation was expressed in 1605 by the Catholic judge and friend of Montaigne, Florimond de Raemond:

> Strassburg, they called it the New Jerusalem, . . . was where the Hydra-Headed Heresy drew up its Arsenal . . . . Here was the retreat and rendezvous for Lutherans and Zwinglians under the leadership of Martin Bucer, the great enemy to catholics. This was the receptacle for those banished from France and the host to him who has given his name to calvinism. It was here that he constructed the Talmud of the new heresy, that instrument of our ruin. In short, this was where the first French church, as they call it, was drawn up to serve as a model and patron for those we have since seen everywhere in France. (Greengrass 1987: 21)

From Bucer, Calvin learned and experienced how to integrate civic and religious life through the church offices of doctor or teacher, pastor, lay elder, and lay deacon. By this time Strasbourg had become signatory not only to the semi-Zwinglian Tetrapolitan confession but also to the Lutheran Augsburg confession. Bucer's irenic and ecumenical leadership included Calvin in international Protestant–Catholic ecumenical efforts to avoid the division of Christendom that finally happened with the council of Trent.

As a Strasbourg delegate to the Frankfurt conference (1539), Calvin met representatives from Catholic and Protestant countries, including Melanchthon with whom he remained a life-long friend and shared the desire to overcome the Lutheran–Swiss division over the Lord's Supper. Calvin also participated in the religious colloquies at Worms (1540–1) and Regensburg (1541). At the latter meetings he subscribed to the altered Augsburg confession (the *Variata*). Melanchthon had altered the article on the Lord's Supper (article 10) to facilitate agreement with the south Germans and the Swiss. The original reads: "Our churches teach that the body and blood of Christ are *truly present and are distributed* [*vere adsint et distribuantur*] to those who eat in the Supper of the Lord. They disapprove of those who teach otherwise." The emphasized phrase was changed to "truly exhibited" [*vere exhibeantur*], and the condemnation of divergent opinions was dropped (Bekenntnisschriften 1963: 64–5). This new formulation approached Calvin's point of view, but of course in the process further diverged from the old faith. The original states that everyone who partakes receives Christ's body and blood, whereas the altered article concedes the possibility that unbelievers receive only bread and wine, not Christ's body and blood. Although this was more amenable to Calvin, it should be noted that as pastor of the French congregation in Strasbourg he had already recognized the unaltered Augsburg confession to which the city had subscribed when joining the Schmalkaldic League. Furthermore, already in 1536 there was an agreement on the Lord's Supper negotiated with Luther by Bucer, the Wittenberg concord, to which Calvin was subject. Calvin recognized that in intention and substance the Augsburg confession was not a "Lutheran" document but a witness to the catholicity of the one, holy, catholic, and apostolic church based on the creeds and Scripture.

Calvin also learned from the humanist Jean Sturm (1507–89), whose educational labors made Strasbourg one of the foremost educational centers in Europe, and whose *Gymnasium* (a secondary school to prepare students for advanced studies) continues to this day under his name. Sturm's humanist ideals, which included acquiring Greek, Latin, and the classics as well as religious and moral education, informed Calvin's own later educational efforts in Geneva.

But not least of Calvin's joys in this marvelous reformed city was his marriage to Idelette de Bure, the widow of an Anabaptist he had been instrumental in converting. In response to the efforts of Farel and Bucer to push him toward marriage, Calvin made it clear that his model of womanhood focused on modesty, thrift, and patience with his ill-health rather than on a "fine figure." But Farel, whose priorities in such matters did not exactly coincide with Calvin's, mentions that she was also beautiful. Farel himself married a young refugee widow when he was sixty-nine, much to Calvin's disapproval. In any case, Idelette remained Calvin's faithful companion until her death in 1549. She gave Calvin an instant family, for she brought into the marriage her two children. Together they had at least three children, all of whom died in infancy. Idelette's son lived with them in Geneva for only a short time; her daughter, Judith, lived in Geneva and married in 1554. But there was no lack of small children around the Calvins because his brother's family – eight children! – shared the household. In that context it is hard to imagine Calvin was as dour as detractors suggest. We know little, however, about Calvin's marriage and family life. Unlike Luther, who spoke often in glowing terms about his Katie whom he would not trade for the whole world, Calvin gives few clues to his feelings about Idelette until his poignant lament after her death that he had lost "the best companion of my life."

During his stay in Strasbourg, Calvin reworked his *Institutes* and expanded the original six chapters to seventeen. He also compiled a book of French Psalms and a liturgy for his congregation, and wrote an exposition of Paul's letter to the Romans as well as a treatise on the Lord's Supper. Most important of all, he responded to Cardinal Jacopo Sadoleto's appeal to the people of Geneva to return to the Roman church.

The expulsion of Farel and Calvin from Geneva had created disarray in the evangelical community of Geneva. Factions arose among the evangelicals, and the numerous Catholics still in the city had hope that the reform could be overthrown. Sadoleto was a humanist and a distinguished cardinal who had participated in the drafting of a famous Catholic report calling for thorough moral reform of the church in preparation for a reform council. He took advantage of the unstable situation in Geneva to affirm Roman authority and tradition against Reformation innovations. Sadoleto's long entreaty was addressed to the Little Council. The magistrates could find no one capable of making a suitable reply to this dangerous challenge to Geneva, and thus appealed to Calvin. Calvin responded to Sadoleto with one of the most noteworthy defenses of the evangelical faith. On the two major issues of the Reformation, Calvin fully sided with Luther in arguing that the ultimate authority in the Christian life and community is Scripture not the church, and that justification is by faith and trust in a merciful God alone apart from human achievements.

Calvin's eloquent defense of the evangelical faith won him new respect in the city. This, plus internal political developments concerning concessions to Bern, the ouster of the anti-Calvin party among the magistrates, and the departures of the ministers Morand and Marcourt who had replaced Calvin and Farel, prompted Geneva to recall Calvin. In mid-1540 the new magistrates pleaded with Calvin to return to Geneva and resume his work of Reformation there. Calvin's response was that he would rather die a hundred times than go back to Geneva.

Once again, Farel, who was not invited back, threatened God's wrath on Calvin if he did not accept this call. Bucer also said he should return. Calvin yielded and was back in Geneva in September 1541. This time the secretary noted not only his name but that he was "to be forever the servant of Geneva." He was appointed the pastor of the ancient cathedral of St Peter, provided with a decent salary, a large house, and annual portions of 12 measures of wheat and 250 gallons of wine. On the Sunday after his return Calvin mounted the pulpit in St Peter's and began with the very chapter and verse of the Bible where he had left off preaching three years earlier. "Nothing could have been less dramatic or more effective. . . . In this way Calvin signaled that he intended his life and his theology to be, not a device of his own making, but a responsible witness to the Word of God" (George 1988: 185).

Geneva under Calvin, 1541–1564

In spite of the fact that it was the Geneva government that implored Calvin to return, Calvin's progress in winning the town to his vision of the church rightly constituted and truly reformed was neither smooth nor rapid. His eventual triumph by 1555 over numerous opponents and his creation of a model of Protestantism that continues to influence churches the world over is remarkable because he worked solely by moral suasion. In fact, he did not become a citizen until 1559. Calvin never enjoyed the political power and material resources of the deposed Catholic bishop of Geneva. Nor did Calvin have at his side the hundreds of priests, monks, and canons available to the old church; by Calvin's death there were only 19 pastors in Geneva, all employees of the municipal government. To an astute observer of Geneva in 1541, it would have appeared highly unlikely that Calvin could carry out a thorough reform of the city. Yet Calvin's reform of this recalcitrant city was so thorough it may legitimately be called a revolution (Kingdon 1974: 97–103). How did he accomplish this reform?

The clue to Calvin's success in Geneva is that he wrote the rules for the city's political and ecclesiastical games. He had not been trained as a lawyer for nothing! As one of the conditions for his return from exile he had bargained the right to draft the institutional and legal form of the church. Within six weeks of his return he submitted to the magistrates his Ecclesiastical Ordinances. With a few minor amendments, the government enacted these ordinances into law. Within the next two years, two further sets of laws regarding justice and political offices were enacted that further formed the constitution of the Geneva city-

state. Whether or not Calvin was the author of these later laws as some
scholars believe, there is no doubt that the magistrates looked to Calvin
as a legal and moral resource for the drafting of these laws. In short,
Calvin's success in Geneva was related to his firsthand and intimate
knowledge of who made decisions and how these decisions were made.

The Ecclesiastical Ordinances organized the Genevan church by
setting forth four categories of ministry – doctors, pastors, deacons,
and elders – and creating institutions for the work of each. The doctors
were to study Scripture and to teach. Their theological scholarship was
to serve the maintenance of doctrinal purity and the preparation of
ministers. Pastors were to preach the Word of God, administer the
sacraments, and instruct and admonish. Candidates for the office of
pastor were examined in doctrine and conduct, and had to be approved
by the ministers and the Little Council. The pastors of Geneva and its
dependent villages met weekly for discussion of theology and doctrine.
The deacons were responsible for the supervision of charity, including
relief of the poor and overseeing the hospitals. They were elected once a
year in the same manner as the elders. There is some controversy in
recent scholarship over whether Calvin's idea for this double diaconate
("administering the affairs of the poor" and "caring for the poor
themselves") derived from his knowledge of already existing welfare
institutions in Geneva or from his biblical theology. Whatever the
source, it was clear to Calvin that appeal to Scripture was paramount
for the development of that society which so impressed John Knox.

The doctors and the pastors together constituted the Geneva Company of Pastors, also known as the "Venerable Company." The
Company of Pastors met quarterly for purposes of administration and
mutual discipline. Although of limited legal authority, the Venerable
Company held a notable place in the moral structure of Geneva.

The elders were laymen whose function was to maintain discipline
within the community. Against Calvin's wishes, the elders were
political appointees chosen from and by the magistrates. In all, there
were 12 elders. Two were chosen from the Little Council, four were
chosen from the Council of Sixty, and six were chosen from the
Council of Two Hundred. Selected for their wisdom and piety, they
represented different parts of the city. They were to watch over the
lives of the people, to admonish the disorderly, and when necessary
report erring people to the Consistory.

The Consistory, a kind of ecclesiastical court, was the principal
organ of church discipline; it included the 12 elders and the pastors. Its
presiding officer was ordinarily one of the syndics. The main concern
of the Consistory was the systematic supervision of the morals of the

people of Geneva, including the enforcement of the moral laws. This was the source of Geneva's reputation for austerity and "puritanism." The Consistory had the power to excommunicate those who in its eyes had commited serious offenses. Such offenses included adultery, illicit marriages, cursing, unauthorized luxury, disrespect in church, and comportment bearing traces of the old faith such as regarding the Virgin Mary as a patroness. Scholars have so far only sampled the many cases handled by the Consistory (see Kingdon 1994: 23). Therefore the following list should be viewed as suggestive of about 5 percent of the total cases: relapses to Catholicism (39 instances); blasphemy (28); general disrespect and complaining about Calvin and his rule (62); games of chance (36); immorality (13); insulting French immigrants (9); dancing and unseemly singing (12); absence from worship and catechetical instruction (10); issues of faith (7); suicide attempt (1). It is this effort at the control of morals normed by Scripture that has led some to call Geneva a "bibliocracy" (*TRE* 7: 573; Kingdon 1972; Baker 1988). "No other institution deserves more credit for shaping in Geneva that particularly austere style of life we have come to label Puritan" (Kingdon 1993a: 531).

It is not surprising that the Consistory was the most controversial institution of the Reformation in Geneva. It soon became the focal point for the opposition to Calvin, but it was also for Calvin a crucial vehicle for expressing his authority. This latter point warrants emphasis because those living in contemporary pluralistic and secular societies easily forget how threatening the charge of unauthorized innovation was to the Reformers. In fact, from the early church to the early modern period, innovation was equivalent to heresy. The very reason Calvin had been implored to return to Geneva was Sadoleto's accusation of innovation and his appeal to traditional authority which threatened the Genevans. The Consistory thus was Calvin's means for instilling respect for his authority, even if at times this approximated a moral reign of terror. So, for example, included along with punishable offences relating to infractions of theology and worship are games and dances. "Anyone who sings indecent, dissolute, or outrageous songs or dances the fling or some other similar dance shall be imprisoned for three days and shall then be sent before the consistory" (Hughes 1966: 58). It is, of course, easy to focus on such cases in order to argue that the Consistory's primary role was social and political control of human behavior. Without gainsaying that important task, an effort should also be directed to understand discipline as an expression of social concern. As intrusive and oppressive as the Consistory was, it "was also designed to display social concern, to see to it that every resident of

Geneva was integrated into a caring community." In Geneva, contrary to our contemporary urban anonymity and anomie, "there were real networks of caring" (Kingdon 1993b: 666, 679). Calvin strove to construct a Consistory that would provide education in the Christian faith and a counseling service designed for reconciliation. "Discipline to these early Genevans meant more than social control. It also meant social help. . . . [The Consistory] really tried to assist everyone in its city-state to live the kind of life it thought God intended people to live" (Kingdon 1994: 34).

Calvin's Consolidation of his Authority

Opposition to the not-so-secret ecclesiastical police in Geneva crossed class and economic lines to include magistrates as well as common citizens. In turn, the Consistory did not shrink from judging prominent citizens, including deposing a pastor for alleged sexual harassment. In January of 1546 Pierre Ameaux, a member of the Little Council, publicly criticized Calvin. His motives were both political and personal. Politically, Ameaux was concerned that Calvin's apparent refusal to open the ministry to native Genevans would create undue French influence through the Company of Pastors. Personally, Ameaux, whose family playing-cards business lost out to the new discipline, had also had a drawn-out process with the Consistory over his divorce case against his adulterous wife. When Ameaux asserted Calvin was teaching false doctrine, Calvin perceived this not as a personal attack but as an attack upon his authority as a minister. He persuaded the Council of Two Hundred to impose on Ameaux the punishment of a public penance that included a walk around the town dressed only in a penitential shirt, begging for mercy on his knees at three public squares. Calvin's prescription was "rough halters for rough donkeys" (Monter 1967: 74; Naphy 1994: 66–7, 94–6). The effect was a public proclamation of Calvin's authority. Public outcry against the humiliation of Ameaux was quelled by erecting a gibbet in Ameaux's neighborhood.

More serious threats to Calvin's authority came from the patrician families of the Perrins and Favres. These respected Genevan families had been among the strongest advocates for bringing Calvin back to Geneva; but neither Ami Perrin nor François Favre, his father-in-law, was in favor of the Consistory's inquisitorial practices. When Calvin censured François' wife for lewd dancing at a wedding and excluded François himself from the sacrament for immoral behavior, Ami Perrin publicly questioned the competence of the Consistory. The Favres fled town, and Ami left on a diplomatic mission to France. Upon their respective returns to Geneva both François and Ami were imprisoned, the latter because he was also suspected of being in collusion with France to invade Geneva. Bernese intervention obtained the release of Favre, and Perrin was acquitted. Calvin now labeled Perrin and his followers "libertines," alleging that they did not want discipline because it would expose their loose living and faithless lives.

One of these "libertines," Jacques Gruet, who was also from an old Genevan family, not only criticized Calvin but was found to have appealed to the French king to intervene in Geneva. He was also suspected of posting a placard on the pulpit of St Peter's that declared, "When too much has been endured revenge is taken." Believing Gruet to be part of an international plot against Geneva, the magistrates tortured and then beheaded him with the consent of Calvin. In December a "libertine" mob gathered to intimidate the Council of Two Hundred. Calvin himself ran into their midst, proclaiming: "If you must shed blood, let mine be first." Unnerved, the mob subsided. Less dangerous opposition was expressed by citizens who named their dogs for Calvin and composed ditties that ridiculed him (Walker 1969: 295–312).

One source of hope and comfort came from outside. The continuing influx of religious refugees into Geneva provided a source of political support for Calvin, for they were generally of high social and intellectual status and were obviously grateful for the haven Calvin provided them. Between 1550 and 1562 Geneva received approximately 7,000 immigrants – this in a city whose total population at the time of Calvin's arrival was about 10,000. The vast majority of these refugees were from France, although there were also substantial English and Italian colonies in Geneva. And of course not all refugees remained in Geneva. Thus, for example, when Elizabeth succeeded Mary Tudor on the English throne, many English refugees returned home. The impact of all these newcomers is hard to measure beyond their obvious strain on local resources and their support for Calvin with its frequent lyrical descriptions of Geneva as a holy city. To them Geneva was not just a shelter, it was as close to the city of God as earthly pilgrims could get.

On the other hand, not all of these newcomers agreed with Calvin's theology. A famous example of doctrinal opposition was Jerome Bolsec, who although generally sympathetic to Reformed theology

sharply criticized Calvin's doctrine of predestination. Bolsec was an ex-
Carmelite friar who embraced the Reformed faith in Paris, left his
order, married, and settled near Geneva where he served as a physician.
He frequently visited Geneva and often argued theology with the
pastors. In October 1551 he publicly attacked Calvin's understanding
of predestination as unbiblical (1 Timothy 2: 4 states that God desires all
to be saved) and pagan (portraying God as an unjust tyrant and the
ultimate source of evil). He was immediately imprisoned, tried,
publicly condemned, and banished for life; he later returned to the old
faith. Bolsec's revenge was to publish in 1577 a scurrilous biography of
Calvin, accusing him among other things of sodomy, which continued
to be an arsenal for anti-Calvinist polemics for the next two centuries.

The significance of Bolsec's challenge, not just to Calvin but to the
entire Geneva Company of Pastors, was that he criticized their doctrine
by reference to Scripture, and that he did so in a way that aroused more
interest in the general populace than any other theological debate. This
stimulated Calvin to give his doctrine of predestination a far more
elaborate and prominent place in succeeding editions of his *Institutes*.
Calvin also correctly perceived that popular interest in Bolsec's argument was far more of a danger than more rarefied theological
controversies over the Lord's Supper or the Trinity. "For Calvin's
Reformation was fundamentally dependent upon popular support. If
that support was eroded, he feared that all his life's work for the
advancement of God's kingdom would fade away. And so he hammered out an extreme position that has been identified with his name
and his followers ever since" (Kingdon 1991: 145).

Explication of Calvin's doctrine of predestination and its historical
impact is too large an endeavor to take on here. But in light of the
popular identification of Calvin and Calvinism with the dogma of
predestination, it is important to provide some guidance to Calvin's
intention. Predestination is not the major doctrine from which other
doctrines flow but rather the outcome of the central Reformation
conviction of salvation by grace alone. It is Calvin's emphasis on
"Christ's statement to his disciples, 'You did not choose me, but I
chose you' [John 15: 16]" (McNeill and Battles 1960: 935). Every
theology which focuses on salvation as the sole work of God brings
some form of election and predestination in its wake. "It [the doctrine
of predestination] is the negation of all merit and places salvation solely
in the mercy of God. It means that salvation is rescue and not
achievement" (Leith 1989: 122; Dowey 1994: 218–20).

The doctrine of predestination therefore is not an effort to probe and
map the mind of God, but an expression of pastoral care. On the

personal level it is the proclamation that salvation is God's gift and choice of the person in spite of his or her doubts, unbelief, and external circumstances. On the communal ecclesiastical level it is the proclamation that in spite of conditions and events, God's church will prevail. This was crucially important to the early Reformation churches suffering persecution; and it was precisely to them that Calvin addressed the comfort of predestination. What Bolsec – and too many later Calvinists! – missed was that in doctrinal terms "unconditional election is another way of saying unconditional grace" (Torrance 1994: 19). The practical sense in the preaching of election in these years was in strengthening the persecuted Reformed communities in France. The importance of this is illustrated by the concern of the martyrs of Lyon who, upon learning in prison of the predestination debate in Geneva, feared they would lose the doctrine that enabled them to endure their persecution: God's elect cannot be lost (Wiley 1990: 109).

It is also important to note that for Calvin God's choice of his people is not a matter of speculation but of confession and adoration: "God's hidden decree is not to be searched out but obediently marveled at" (McNeill and Battles 1960: 952–3). Furthermore, this is the affirmation that the universe is not ruled by fate or by chance but rather by God, the God who reveals himself in Christ. First and last for Calvin, God is not a celestial tyrant but a loving parent whom Calvin describes in images of a nurse, a mother who cannot forget her nursing child, and a father who gives good things to his children. "Free adoption is the citadel of Calvin's faith; double predestination is a defensive outwork, and it has not proved a very effective one. He does not seem to have realized how the proof might place in question what he wanted to prove. Predestination, he supposed, would be the final guarantee of both humility and security. But it has guaranteed neither one, as the history of later Calvinism makes painfully clear" (Gerrish 1993: 170).

The Servetus Case

The growing opposition to Calvin was the context for the infamous Servetus case. Michael Servetus (ca. 1511–53) was born in Aragon and became a public figure with the publication of his *Seven Books on the Errors of the Trinity* in Strasbourg in 1531. Protestant and Catholic theologians alike joined in condemning Servetus's attack on the fundamental doctrine of the trinity. In the lapidary phrasing of Roland Bainton (1960: 3), "Michael Servetus has the singular distinction of having been burned by the Catholics in effigy and by the Protestants in actuality." In 1532 Servetus published his *Two Dialogues on the Trinity*, which maintained that in its doctrinal development the church had fallen away from Jesus. Although Servetus was not renowned for his discretion, he did at this time realize that the better part of valor included anonymity and a different profession. Thus he went to Paris where he studied medicine and anatomy. In the annals of medicine he has a certain fame for being one of the first to discover the pulmonary circulation of the blood, a discovery perhaps prompted by his concern to show that the Holy Spirit entered the blood system through the nostrils. Respiration is inspiration; the soul is in the blood (Genesis 9: 4; Leviticus 17: 11).

But Servetus could not abstain from theological publication and controversy. He began a pseudonymous correspondence with Calvin, who recognized him from his writings. When Servetus sent Calvin his newest endeavor, *The Restitution of Christianity* (*restitutio* is the counterpoint to Calvin's *institutio*), Calvin sent back his own *Institutes*, which Servetus promptly returned filled with insulting marginal comments. Calvin then sent all this correspondence to a friend in Vienne who passed it on to the Inquisition in Lyon to assist the capture of Servetus. In August 1553 Servetus managed to escape from his imprisonment by the Catholic Inquisition and fled toward Italy. On the way to seeking asylum in Naples, he stopped in Geneva, apparently drawn there like a moth to a flame.

In his writings and in his correspondence with Calvin, Servetus had presented infant baptism as diabolical, denied original sin, and likened the trinity to a three-headed Cerberus. Jesus was not the eternal son of God but a human become divine. Servetus presented himself as another archangel Michael, leading an angelic host against the Antichrist. To Calvin, this was the "impious ravings of all the ages," and he wrote that should Servetus ever appear in Geneva he would not leave alive. Servetus arrived in Geneva on a Saturday and attended Calvin's church on Sunday! Lest this be interpreted as a death wish, it should be noted that absence from church would have attracted attention. Unfortunately for Servetus his disguise was not sufficient; he was recognized in church by refugees from Lyon, and immediately arrested. In accord with the law, his accuser, Calvin, was also to be held in custody until the conclusion of the trial. Calvin's secretary stood surety for him.

The claim that the "libertines" used the heresy trial of Servetus to embarrass Calvin, who was the expert witness for the prosecution, probably "springs solely from sources supportive of Calvin and desirous of discrediting Calvin's opponents" (Naphy 1994: 184). But Servetus's fate was sealed by the Genevan magistracy even before the unanimous denunciations of him poured in from Basle, Bern, Schaff-hausen, and Zurich. Melanchthon also concurred in the judgment; and Bucer had demanded the death penalty already in 1531 after the appearance of Servetus's first tract on the trinity. Servetus was found guilty of spreading heresy and sentenced to death by burning. The penalty accorded with the law against blasphemers in article 106 of Charles V's criminal code, *Constitutio criminalis Carolina*. On the morning of 27 October 1553, Servetus was burned to death. He died uttering the prayer, "Jesus, Son of the Eternal God, have mercy on me." To the end, Servetus would not pray in trinitarian language to "the eternal Son of God." In that time a misplaced adjective could be fatal.

Calvin had sought, in an unsuccessful humanitarian gesture, to commute the punishment from burning to beheading; Farel rebuked Calvin for such undue leniency. Following the execution of Servetus, Calvin wrote his *Defense of the Orthodox Faith*, in which he declared that in cases of heresy the glory of God must be maintained regardless of all feelings of humanity. Calvin made plain his view in his commentary on Deuteronomy 13 which demands the stoning of false prophets: "God makes plain that the false prophet is to be stoned without mercy. We are to crush beneath our heel all affections of nature when his honor is involved" (Bainton 1951: 70).

But Sebastian Castellio, the Genevan schoolmaster forced out of town in 1544 by Calvin after continuous disputes with the magistracy, published in response a plea for religious toleration and opposition to capital punishment for heretics: *Concerning Heretics, Whether They Are to be Persecuted* (1554). The book does not mention the Servetus affair, but consists of a compilation of citations from ancient and contemporary authors against persecution. One of Castellio's main sources was Sebastian Franck's *Chronicle*. In his later response to Calvin's defense, Castellio wrote the famous line: "To burn a heretic is not to defend a doctrine, but to kill a man" (Bainton 1965: 271). In this Castellio was far ahead of his time, for Calvin and Geneva received congratulations and applause from all quarters for execution of the arch-heretic. On the other hand, Castellio also shared the common concept of the *corpus Christianum*, for after admitting he had not read Servetus's writings he said if he were indeed a blasphemer he deserved to die (Nijenhuis 1972: 128). In our modern world of religious and ethical relativism, the sixteenth-century concern for truth appears strange even as we perse-cute others for political deviance. Well before the infamous words "We destroyed the city to save it" were uttered by an American military leader in the Vietnam War, Bainton (1951: 94; 1960: 215) commented:

"We are today horrified that Geneva should have burned a man for the glory of God, yet we incinerate whole cities for the saving of democracy."

Castellio, by the way, after leaving Geneva moved to Basle where he served as professor of Greek. His continuing concern for peace and toleration found eloquent expression in his pleas against forcing consciences occasioned by the French Wars of Religion: *Advice to a Desolate France*. To his dying day Castellio was attacked for various heresies. Ironically, the last attack came from a physician living in Strasbourg, Adam Bodenstein von Karlstadt, who with his father Andreas had had his own share of hounding! Castellio died in Basle on 29 December 1563 and, to the indignation of the Genevans, was buried with honors in the cloister of the Basle cathedral.

In 1903 Calvin's heirs erected a monument of atonement at the place of Servetus's execution which reads: "We, devout and grateful sons of Calvin, our great reformer, yet condemning an error which was the error of his century, and firmly devoted to the freedom of conscience according to the true principles of the Reformation and the Gospel, have erected this monument of atonement on October 27th 1903" (Nijenhuis 1972: 122). In a certain sense this is curious because Zurich had been drowning Anabaptists since the 1520s and at the very time Servetus was executed so were Calvin's followers in France. And in the decades after Servetus, the streets and fields of France would be soaked with Calvinist blood. The modern toleration of religious pluralism is anachronistic for the sixteenth century. Thanks to Castellio the Servetus case has remained a notorious case of religious persecution. Interestingly, it seems Servetus had contemplated America as a refuge for religious exiles.

The Servetus affair was a turning point for Calvin. His opponents were unable to use the Servetus case against him. Soon Geneva was firmly in Calvin's control. As a consequence, restrictive and disciplinary elements in the city were enhanced; the Consistory became more of an ecclesiastical court; and the ministers were now consulted on the choice of elders. The later years were not without personal trials for Calvin. In 1557 his sister-in-law was discovered in adultery with his own servant and banished from Geneva (see Kingdon 1994: 32–3); and in the same year his step-daughter Judith was also found guilty of adultery. Nevertheless, Calvin's influence continued to grow with the combined circumstances of the defeat of his enemies and the continuing influx of religious refugees. In 1559 Calvin founded the Geneva Academy, now the University of Geneva, which attracted students from all areas of Europe, and became the training ground for Protestant leadership influential throughout Europe. In the same year, Calvin was made a citizen of Geneva.

It is a mistake to conclude that Calvin turned Geneva into a theocratic police state. For most of Calvin's career he had to struggle to maintain authority. His edge in this struggle was his control of the public media through constant preaching and teaching, but there were times when Calvin's authority remained very fragile. Calvin, in common with other Reformers, recognized that the success of his reform movement rested in no small part upon respect for his leadership and authority. What is remarkable is not his efforts to consolidate authority but that in this process he did not succumb to favoritism to win support. Neither prominent citizens nor his own family were allowed to be above the law. In this, Calvin provided a model of democratic equality under the law that modern states would do well to emulate.

Calvin died on 27 May 1564 at the age of fifty-five. Beza reported on Calvin's death at sundown: "Thus in the same moment, that day, the sun set and the greatest light which was in this world, for the direction of the Church of God, was withdrawn to Heaven. We can well say that with this single man it has pleased God in our time, to teach us the way both to live well and to die well" (Kingdon 1967: 13). Like Luther, Calvin had long suffered a variety of ailments that caused severe pain and breathing difficulties, including arthritis, kidney stones, pulmonary tuberculosis, intestinal parasites, hemorrhoids, bowel problems, and migraine headaches. Bouwsma (1988: 30) suggests that "even more erosive" than these physical ailments was Calvin's internal tension between his trust in God and his own need to control and to achieve. At the end he confessed his deficiency in everything: "Truly, even the grace of forgiveness he [God] has given me only renders me all the more guilty, so that my only recourse can be this, that being the father of mercy, he will show himself the father of so miserable a sinner." Whether Calvin was a neurotic overachiever is for psychiatrists to evaluate; but both Calvin and Luther were convinced that only divine therapy can provide more than amelioration of symptoms and begin a cure. Just before his death Luther scribbled the lines, "No one can think he has tasted the Holy Scriptures thoroughly until he has ruled over the churches with the prophets for a hundred years. . . . We are beggars. That is true" (*LW* 54: 476). Both Calvin and Luther "suffered through the conflict – unavoidable for medieval and modern alike – between the conscience and Evangelical reliance on God. . . . This is the sickness unto death which Luther uncovered: we cling to our achievements and cannot shake the need to prove ourselves before God and man, in life and death. Luther's 'neurosis' proves to be part and parcel of the

Reformation discovery: we are beggars – that is true!" (Oberman 1989b: 324). At his own request Calvin was buried in an unmarked grave.

Protestant Mission and Evangelism: The "International Conspiracy"

Nearly 7,000 religious refugees had flocked to Geneva, attracted by the stature of Calvin and driven by persecutions of Protestantism in their homelands. These refugees came from nearly every province in France as well as from England, Scotland, Holland, Italy, Spain, Germany, Poland, and Bohemia. When they returned home, they took Calvinism with them.

The Academy in Geneva trained missionaries for work in other countries. The French crown viewed this activity as subversive and punished those caught by death. Hence these pastors traveled in disguise, frequently as merchants, into countries where Calvinism was outlawed, and established churches patterned after the church in Geneva. As indicated by the figures from 1555 to 1562 (see Monter 1967: 135; Kingdon 1956: 145), their numbers were impressive:

1555	5 (4 to Piedmont)	1559	32 (all to France)
1556	5 (2 to Piedmont, 2 to Brazil)	1560	13 (1 to London)
1557	16 (4 to Piedmont, 1 to Antwerp)	1561	12 (all to France)
1558	23 (1 to Turin)	1562	12 (all to France)

The Geneva church functioned as the international headquarters for this missionary movement, a kind of Protestant Vatican. Foreign theological disputes and questions were sent to Geneva for resolution and clarification. The missionary churches were also served by an extensive news bureau and communications network centered on Geneva. Calvinism ultimately prevailed in England and Scotland, whereas it survived only in a minority status in France. In all this, Calvin "regarded himself as a soldier stationed in Geneva, but at the same time as an officer directing a European army. . . . His parish was as wide as Europe and his vision was directed to France at its center" (Oberman 1992: 102, 109).

It is this vision of the reform of the whole of Europe that contributes to Calvin's reputation as an ecumenical churchman. His active involvement in the major religious colloquies during his years in Strasbourg has been mentioned. He continued to promote his relationship with the Lutherans through his friendship and correspondence with Melanchthon and by publishing some of Melanchthon's major writings in French translation. Calvin's goal of unifying Swiss Protestants and then the Swiss and German Protestants involved him in the ongoing controversies over the Lord's Supper. He realized that union of the Reformed and Lutheran churches was unrealizable unless the stumbling block of the Marburg colloquy (1529) could be overcome. To that end he strove with Zwingli's successor, Heinrich Bullinger (1504–75), to reach a consensus. The Zurich consensus, known as the *Consensus Tigurinus*, was achieved in 1549. The story of Calvin's energetic effort to overcome Bullinger's self-conscious defense of Zwingli's memory and the Zurich suspicion that he, Calvin, was too "Lutheran" is ably told and analysed in recent studies by Paul Rorem (1988; 1994). The key issue for Calvin, as for Luther, was to safeguard the gift character of the sacrament. Unfortunately and ironically, Calvin's ecumenical advance in Switzerland was read with suspicion by second-generation Lutherans as a move more toward Zwingli than toward Luther (Steinmetz 1990).

Thus the Reformed and Lutheran churches entered a long period of controversy in Germany. Elsewhere in Europe Calvin's work received warm responses – in some cases, such as France, too warm! Since Calvin had left France to evangelize it from without, it is to these efforts that we now turn.

Suggestions for Further Reading

William J. Bouwsma, *John Calvin: A Sixteenth Century Portrait*, New York: Oxford University Press, 1988

Edward A. Dowey, Jr, *The Knowledge of God in Calvin's Theology*, 3rd expanded edn, Grand Rapids: Eerdmans, 1994

B. A. Gerrish, *Grace and Gratitude: The Eucharistic Theology of John Calvin*, Minneapolis: Fortress, 1993

Wulfert de Greef, *The Writings of John Calvin: An Introductory Guide*, Grand Rapids: Baker Books, 1993

Robert M. Kingdon, "Was the Protestant Reformation a Revolution? The Case of Geneva," in Robert M. Kingdon, ed., *Transition and Revolution: Problems and Issues of European Renaissance and Reformation History*, 53–107, Minneapolis: Burgess, 1974

Robert M. Kingdon, "Social Control and Political Control in Calvin's Geneva," and "Calvinist Discipline in the Old World and the New," in Hans R. Guggisberg and Gottfried G. Krodel, eds, *The Reformation in Germany and Europe: Interpretations and Issues* (ARG special volume), 521–32, 665–79, Gütersloh: Gütersloher Verlagshaus, 1993

Robert M. Kingdon, "The Genevan Consistory in the Time of Calvin," in Andrew Pettegree, Alastair Duke, and Gillian Lewis, eds, *Calvinism in Europe 1540–1620*, 21–34, Cambridge: Cambridge University Press, 1994

William G. Naphy, *Calvin and the Consolidation of the Genevan Reformation*, Manchester: Manchester University Press, 1994

Wilhelm H. Neuser, ed., *Calvinus Sacrae Scripturae Professor: Calvin as Confessor of Holy Scripture*, Grand Rapids: Eerdmans, 1994

Menna Prestwich, ed., *International Calvinism 1541–1715*, Oxford: Clarendon Press, 1985

11

Refuge in the Shadow of God's Wings: The Reformation in France

If God sometimes allows the blood of his faithful to be spilled, he nevertheless carefully collects their precious tears.

Calvin to the church in Paris (1557)

The story of the Reformation in France is marred by incredible violence and saturated with the blood of thousands of martyrs. The Reformed church in France was a church under the cross whose solace and encouragement to take shelter "in the shadow of the wings of God" (see Diefendorf 1991: 138) came from Calvin and the French Psalms he provided them. Persecuted by crown and commoner, often more viciously by the latter than the former, the Huguenots took refuge in their conviction of election as a chosen people whom God protects as well as chastises.

The Shield of Humanism

Until the late 1520s, Reformers and reform-minded humanists in France were shielded from ecclesiastical censure and punishment by the king, Francis I. Francis himself was quite taken by the Renaissance. He encouraged study of the classics; set up the royal printer Estienne, who printed classics and the Bible; and established royal professorships in Paris. These proclivities and activities were a fertile breeding ground for Reformation ideas which soon had extensive influence.

However, the king had no motivation to introduce Reformation ideas. Since the thirteenth century, French theologians and conciliarists had argued that the French church held a privileged position in relation to the papacy. The supposed liberties of *l'Eglise gallicane* (hence the term "Gallicanism") were reinforced in 1516 by the concordat of Bologna between the king and Pope Leo X. This treaty increased the already considerable power of the crown over the church by, among other things, conceding the nomination of bishops and other ecclesiastics to the king and also the right to levy tithes on the clergy. The latter was both an important source of revenue for the interminable wars with the Habsburgs, and a financial reason for the crown to oppose Protestant reform. In effect, this meant that 10 archbishops, 82 bishops, and over 500 lesser clergy owed their appointments to the king. This assured the fidelity of the higher clergy to the crown, to which they swore a loyalty oath. And the presence of prelates in the provincial and national estates also furthered royal influence. By 1516 Francis I had everything from the church that Henry VIII and German princes broke with the church to get. Furthermore, Francis did not have either Henry VIII's strong personal reasons or the German rulers' outrage at papal financial exactions to motivate a state endorsement of reform.

Another distinguishing political factor regarding the Reformations in Germany and France was the different courses of self-aggrandizement taken by their respective high nobility. We have already seen how the high nobility in Germany were more concerned for their own independence than for national unity. In France the high nobility saw their best advantage in the pursuit of dynastic policies and hence supported the king. In simple terms: the centrifugal political forces in Germany aided the Reformation, whereas the centripetal political forces in France hindered it.

That Reformation ideas were abroad in France quite early is evident in the dissemination in France by 1519 of a collection of Luther's Latin writings printed by John Froben of Basle; French translations of Luther's writings, hymns, and prayers soon followed (Moeller 1987; Higman 1984). Some 600 books, Froben wrote Luther, were on the way to France and Spain: "They are sold in Paris, and even read and approved by the doctors of the Sorbonne" (*WA Br* 1: 332; Hillerbrand 1964: 76). The Paris theologians were reading but certainly not approving. Entrusted with the University of Erfurt to decide the victor of the Leipzig debate, the Sorbonne condemned Luther in April 1521 as an enemy of the church of Christ who "vomited up a doctrine of pestilence." The censoring of religious books was instituted in June.

A more amenable context than Paris for the early stirring of reform in France was Meaux, a small town of weavers some 30 miles east of Paris. The bishop of Meaux, Guillaume Briçonnet (1470–1534), had earlier served as the king's ambassador in negotiating the concordat of Bologna. On return to his diocese he engaged in efforts to reform preaching and the religious life. Preaching had been the nearly exclusive reserve of the mendicant orders, especially the Franciscans, who resented the bishop's encroachment on their preserve and, not incidentally, the consequent diminishment of their financial rewards. To aid his reforming work Briçonnet invited the noted humanist biblical scholar Jacques Lefèvre d'Etaples (ca. 1450–1536) to join him. Lefèvre's *Fivefold Psalter* (1509) and his commentary on the Epistles of Paul (1512, reprinted in 1516) with their emphasis on Christ and the "literal" sense of the text, were influential on Luther's developing biblical interpretation. Lefèvre also contributed to reform in France through his anonymously published French translation of the church lectionary accompanied by evangelical glosses. The *Epistres et evangiles pour les 52 dimanches de l'année* (1525) was intended to facilitate clerical preaching and the reading of the gospels and epistles in French (Higman 1992: 38–9; Hughes 1984). A French translation of the Bible by Pierre Olivétan (Calvin's cousin) appeared in 1535 with a Latin foreword by Calvin promoting the availability of vernacular Scripture so that all may directly know the Bible.

Soon other evangelicals, including William Farel, arrived to make up the Meaux circle. These Reformers advanced an Erasmian style of reform that focused on Bible studies and spiritual and moral renewal. Initially they were shielded from Franciscan complaints to Paris about "Lutheran" preaching by Briçonnet's relationship to the crown and the patronage of Marguerite of Angoulême, queen of Navarre. Marguerite, the king's sister, was a significant humanist in her own right whose Reformation inclination is clear from the Protestant catechism she commissioned in French (Orth 1993).

Evangelical ideas were increasingly taking root among the populace. When the king was in captivity after the battle of Pavia (1525) the parlement of Paris moved quickly to accuse the Meaux group of heresy. Many of these evangelicals fled the country. In 1523 Briçonnet promulgated a decree against Luther and his works, "lest so venomous a plant should extend its roots into the field which has been entrusted to us" (Hughes 1984: 134–5). The Reformers of Meaux were, with the exception of Farel, not of Calvin's mettle. Their concern was really renewal and revitalization of episcopal authority, not reformation of the church. To do more invited the fate of Louis de Berquin, the humanist translator of Luther and convinced evangelical, who was burned in Paris in 1529 after condemnation by the parlement. To be sure, three other evangelical preachers had already been burned for heresy in 1525; but they were not so close to home (Hughes 1984: 148–52; Nicholls 1992: 123–5). Also, by this time unorthodox ideas were finding iconoclastic expression.

The execution of Berquin and the Cop affair made it clear that Francis I's tolerance for reform turned to hostility when radicals indulged in violence and iconoclasm. Both ecclesiastical and royal authorities blamed the teachings of Reformers for the actions of radicals. The results were that men like Calvin fled abroad or went underground. Francis's response to the evangelicals vacillated between persecution by imprisonment and execution on the one hand and moderation on the other. The former was stimulated by outrages such as the "affair of the placards" when posters attacking the "horrible abuse of the papal mass" were posted in Paris, Blois, and Amboise during the night of 17–18 October 1534. The king was particularly outraged to discover a placard had been tacked to his bedroom door in Amboise. Francis instituted a swift and violent persecution of suspected evangelicals. Confident of the success of his repressive measures against perceived sedition, he celebrated a Te Deum at Notre Dame in December 1537. Thus he was even more outraged when the same placards reappeared on 6 January, accompanied this time by a brief tract by Marcourt on the eucharist.

Marcourt argued that (1) the perfect sacrifice of Jesus need not be repeated; (2) the mass induces idolatry through adoration of the consecrated elements; (3) transubstantiation is an invented doctrine without biblical foundation; and (4) the Lord's Supper is a public proclamation of faith and confidence in salvation that expresses the unity of the church (Higman 1992: 69–70, 72–6; Berthoud 1973). The king's violent reaction to the placards initiated such serious repression of the Reformation that it appeared more and more hopeless.

On the other hand, the king was moved to moderation when he desired alliances with German Lutheran princes to assist him against the emperor. So, for example, in this connection there was an unsuccessful attempt that same year to bring Melanchthon and other German Lutherans to Paris to debate religious unity.

Evangelical Progress and Persecution

Unlike the German and Swiss contexts, where reform and its course were supported and guided by public authorities, Reformation movements in France were soon under fire – at times literally. Thus to an extent not present in the German and Swiss territories Protestantism in France had to lead a covert life. Also unlike Germany, where political fragmentation facilitated a "free" press (by 1519 Luther's writings had been printed by 22 different publishers in 11 towns), publication in France was essentially concentrated, and therefore controlled, in only two centers: Paris and Lyon. Protestant writings and vernacular Bibles were however available from the border towns of Basle, Strasbourg, and Anvers. The last of these was a large commercial port technically under the control of the emperor. It had commercial lines to the Low Countries, Spain, England, and Scandinavia, and thereby served as a conduit for English, Dutch, and Danish translations of Luther's writings as well as for French Bibles.

Assessment of the appeal of Protestantism is difficult. It may safely be assumed that late medieval popular criticism of clerical venality and immorality probably played some part. No less a personage than Marguerite, the king's sister, made this clear in the biting anticlericalism of her *Heptaméron*, a collection of stories supposedly told by nobility isolated at an abbey by a flood. Seventeen of the 72 stories depict venality and sexual exploitation by clerics, especially Franciscans. "A storyteller declares that the clerics' lack of opportunity for love of an honest woman renders them unspiritual, never loving anything but good wine and filthy chambermaids" (Douglass 1993: 250). Marguerite sheltered humanists accused of Protestantism and had her own brush with the Inquisition over the publication of her mystical writing, *The Mirror of the Sinful Soul*.

Along with anticlericalism went criticism of religious works righteousness increasingly tied to a money economy. But beyond the criticism of clerical immorality and of religious practice as idolatrous and superstitious, criticism widespread in the late medieval era, there was also the positive embrace of the doctrine of justification by faith. Already in 1524, Farel published in Basle a French translation of the Lord's Prayer and the apostles' creed with a "Lutheran" slant. The accompanying introduction emphasized the biblical basis for faith, that comprehension of the prayer is as important as fervor in praying, and that the negligence of the pastors has obstructed development of true faith. The expositions themselves echoed Luther's emphasis on justification by grace alone, faith as the free gift of God, complete human dependence on God, and the scriptural basis for these evangelical positions. This small "pocket book," designed for common folk, was easy to carry and conceal. Revised and published in 1528 as *The Book of True and Perfect Prayer*, it became "the most popular book of evangelical piety in France . . . reprinted no less than 14 times between 1528 and 1545" (Greengrass 1987: 13; Higman 1992: 26–31).

The wills of Paris Protestants provide "ample evidence that the doctrine of justification by faith was at the heart of their belief. . . .

Protestant testators eliminated the references Catholics traditionally made to the intercession of the Virgin Mary and the saints and expressed their desire for their sins to be forgiven in the direct context of the 'merit' acquired by the death of Christ" (Diefendorf 1991: 113–14). This bedrock Reformation theology found public expression in rejection of the mass and the Roman doctrine of the eucharist.

To attack the mass was to attack the heart of medieval religion and therefore was believed not only to entail the eternal condemnation of the heretic but also to jeopardize the health and salvation of the whole community. Quite simply put, heresy was perceived to be a cancer in the body of society; if society was to be saved, the cancer had to be cut out and destroyed. This was also held to be true for capital crimes; heresy was the capital crime par excellence because it was not merely against the head of the society but against the head of the universe; not just against the king, but against the King of kings. Hence the execution of heretics was ritual action, a liturgy in which the process of degradation of heretics proceeded from symbolic actions to an incineration intended to expunge their memory forever. "The purpose of executing heretics was total obliteration: heresy had to be driven out of society like disease from the body and the social body completely cleansed of all impurities" (Nicholls 1988: 50).

However, this liturgy of purification could also be counterproductive; it could spread the "disease" as well as eliminate it. So, to mention only two specific examples, the execution of an Anabaptist in the Netherlands in 1531 was a turning point for Menno Simons (Williams 1992: 591), and the burning of Servetus in Geneva had a disproportionate impact due to the response of Castellio. The eternal damnation of the heretic symbolized in his or her execution was obscured, even reversed, when the person went to death with convictions unshaken. Indeed, this was almost guaranteed by the authorities who normally chose for execution those who were most adamant in their faith. If they were really instruments of the devil they should have broken. Executions then became a theater of martyrdom in the original sense of the word "martyr" as witness. Executions reinforced the Huguenot conviction that their faith was a return to that of the primitive church when the popular saying arose that "the blood of the martyrs is the seed of the church." Such a "good death" witnessed to genuine faith and consequently impressed at least some of the onlookers. In their suffering, the Calvinist martyrs drew courage and legitimation from Old Testament models of a persecuted chosen people. Like the children of Israel, the Huguenots hoped for divine deliverance from and then victory over the "Caananites" of their homeland (Parker 1993).

Ironically, the Protestant utilization of martyrdom as witness to the truth of their position reflected the ancient and medieval Catholic appreciation of the saints. Thus the Jesuits turned the Protestant tables and accused Beza of the very idolatry the Reformers condemned in their attacks on images and saints (Coats 1994: 20, 27).

The universal embrace of the witness of the martyrs is evident in the numerous martyrologies coming from every Reformation position. For the Huguenots there was Jean Crespin, *Histoire des martyrs persecutez et mis à mort pour la verité de l'evangile, depuis le temps des apostres jusques à present* (Geneva, 1564, 1619) and Simon Goulart, *Mémoires de l'estat de France sous Charles IX* (1576). For the English Protestants there was John Foxe's *Book of Martyrs or the Acts and Monuments of the Christian Church; being a Complete History of the Lives, Sufferings, and Deaths of the Christian Martyrs; from the Commencement of Christianity to the Present Period* (Latin edition Strasbourg, 1554; English edition 1563). For the Anabaptists there were *The Bloody Theater or Martyr's Mirror* (1570) and *The Chronicle of the Hutterian Brethren* (1581) among others. Even the Lutherans developed their own perceptions of martyrdom (Kolb 1987).

As the religious divisions within France hardened, the execution of heretics in the frame of "ritual as containment" broke down. The "cancer" in society was now too widespread to be excised by the deaths of individuals. "Ritual could not compensate for divisions within the social and spiritual 'community' of which it was meant to be an expression" (Nicholls 1988: 71). By the late 1550s Huguenot acceptance of martyrdom was being displaced by resistance which would lead to the religious wars.

Calvin's Influence in France

By the mid-1530s it was clear that evangelical reform of the French church could not be carried out from within France but would need external support. The source of this support was the Reformed church of Geneva. Once Calvin's leadership was firmly established in Geneva in 1555, he and other French exiles set up a very effective propaganda machine directed at France. Calvin was soon besieged by requests from French towns and noble families to provide them with pastors trained in Geneva. The astonishing growth of the Reformed congregations at this time sorely taxed the abilities and energies of the pastors sent from Geneva. In that pre-television day, people could sit – or stand! – for hours to listen to preachers. Their demand for solid and numerous sermons could not always be satisfied. Thus Nicholas Parent, who organized churches in Dauphiné, wrote: "Although I preach for two hours, this seems very little to them, so hungry are they for the Word" (Nicholls 1992: 134).

As noted, the first evangelical congregations in France were called Huguenot, but the French Calvinists preferred the term *Réformés*, the Reformed. Catholic satires of the time called them *la Religion Déformée*. Early congregations at Meaux (1546) and Nîmes (1547) were dispersed by persecution. The martyrdom of the "Fourteen of Meaux" for celebration of an evangelical communion was particularly vicious. All underwent extraordinary torture but refused to reveal the names of other Protestants. At the stake six did submit to confessing to a priest in order to escape the penalty of having their tongues cut out, but the others remained firm even before this last mutilation.

The son of Francis I, Henry II (1547–59), unbiased by humanist sympathies or the need to conciliate German Protestant allies, was even more severe than his father. He issued edicts decreeing harsh punishment for such heretical practices as eating meat during Lent and attending unauthorized assemblies. He also instituted a special court for heresy cases appropriately named *la chambre ardente*, the burning chamber. Clerical resentment of this development was related not to its goal but to its displacement of their jurisdiction over heresy cases. Those accused of disseminating heresy through books or preaching were often sentenced to cruel deaths such as being drawn and quartered while still alive. Thus before Genevan pastors were smuggled into France, they frequently signed their property over to their families since they probably would not live to return.

By 1567 Geneva had sent at least 120 pastors into France to organize congregations, which because of persecution usually led a covert existence. Nevertheless, the Reformed church spread rapidly throughout France. A key to its success was the organizational genius it borrowed from Calvin's Genevan church. The first national synod of the Reformed church in France met in Paris in 1559. It set forth a confession of faith, the Gallican confession, the first draft of which was written by Calvin. An interesting aspect of this confession is its insistence on absolute equality among ministers and churches, i.e. a presbyterial polity. This is a departure from Calvin's openness to a purified episcopacy and a break with the historical polity which was adopted by the other national Reformed churches of western Europe (Sunshine 1994). A modified form of this confession of faith containing 40 articles, ratified at the synod of La Rochelle in 1571, continues to serve the French Reformed church to this day. By 1561 the national synod of France represented more than 2,000 congregations.

The synod of La Rochelle is also known as the "synod of princes" due to the presence of all the secular leaders of the French Protestant movement. The presence of two leaders from the Netherlands, Louis of Nassau and William of Orange, who were to lead Dutch resistance to the Spanish occupation of the Netherlands, was significant for later developments in both countries. "We can be fairly certain that the provisions of an informal alliance between the aristocratic leaders of the Protestant parties in France and in the Netherlands were discussed at La Rochelle. This alliance led to the Protestant attempts to push all of France into a war against Spain in the Netherlands, which in turn helped provoke the St. Bartholomew's massacres" (Kingdon 1988: 185).

Calvinism in France appealed to particular social groups, notably skilled artisans, independent shopkeepers, and middle-class business-men such as bankers. It is this phenomenon that has led some scholars to associate "the Protestant ethic" with "the spirit of capitalism" (usually under the heading of the "Weber thesis"). There is no doubt that the Calvinist virtues of hard work and thrift motivated by a theology of vocation dovetailed nicely with a profit economy; but, as with similar theories about the Jews, there are also a variety of other historical factors involved in Calvinist business success.

The popular appeal of Calvinism came not only from its preaching but also from its rousing songs. The Psalms, set in metrical French by Clement Marot (1497–1544) who fled to Geneva for refuge, became the marching songs and battle hymns of Calvinism in France and then in other countries. Although suspect after the affair of the placards, Marot's versions of some of the Psalms were popular even in the court. "Diane of Poitiers, the mistress of Henry II, for instance, favored the 130th which was appropriately a penitential psalm" (Reid 1971: 40–1). From his refuge in Geneva Marot published an expanded collection of his original "Thirty Psalms of David" (Paris, 1541) which included 49 Psalms and a preface by Calvin. This ran through some 28 editions. By 1560 Beza had expanded this to include the whole Psalter, some of which continues to be included in modern hymnals. The printing of the Huguenot Psalms has been described as the largest printing venture of the time; Geneva alone printed some 27,000 copies (Monter 1967: 181).

The singing of the Psalms was soon a characteristic of Huguenot worship, and provided identity, unity, and courage in persecution and battle. Psalm 68, one of the most popular in the Huguenot armies, has been called the "Marseillaise" of the Huguenots (Reid 1971: 41, 47): "Let God arise, let his enemies be scattered . . . The Lord gives the command; great is the host of those who bore the tidings; 'The kings of the armies, they flee, they flee!' . . . But God will shatter the heads of his enemies, the hairy crown of him who walks in his guilty ways." The Psalms not only inspired Huguenot armies and unnerved their opponents – imagine thousands of armed troops singing "bathe your feet in blood, that the tongues of your dogs may have their portion from the foe" (Psalm 68: 23) – they also strengthened martyrs. The 14 martyred at Meaux sang Psalm 79: "Let the groans of the prisoners come before thee; according to thy great power preserve those doomed to die! Return sevenfold into the bosom of our neighbors the taunts with which they have taunted thee, O Lord!" (Psalm 79: 11–12). The five martyred at Lyon sang Psalm 9: "The Lord is a stronghold for the oppressed, a stronghold in times of trouble. . . . For he who avenges blood is mindful of them; he does not forget the cry of the afflicted." The authorities sought to stop such witness by stuffing the mouths or cutting out the tongues of those about to be put to death.

The social group that was most significant for the Reformation in France was the nobility, especially the houses of Bourbon (after the Valois, next in line for the throne) and Montmorency. Gaspard de Coligny (1519–72, Montmorency), the admiral of France and an influence upon the young king Charles IX, became an outstanding Huguenot leader. The nobility were the "coping stone" of the Reformed church in France; as patrons of the church they provided influence, representation at court, and military strength. The spade-work for this development of the Reformed church into a national political party had been done by noblewomen. "These women fre-quently took the lead in 'the cause', and acted as intermediaries and negotiators between leaders of the rival Catholic and Protestant factions at court" (Blaisdell 1982: 68). Marguerite of Angoulême's early protec-tion of Reformers was paralleled by others such as Louise de Montmor-ency, sister of the constable, and by Jacqueline de Longwy, duchess of Montpensier. Marguerite's daughter, Jeanne d'Albret, created a virtual Protestant kingdom in Navarre. All of these women carried on extensive correspondence with Calvin (Nicholls 1992: 136; Douglass 1985; Roelker 1968, 1972a, 1972b). Other important noble families in the west and southwest of France also joined the Reformed church, and lesser nobles and peasants followed their lead, with the consequence that this area of France became the military bastion of the reform movement.

The north and east part of France was in the control of an ultra-Catholic faction of the nobility led by the Guise-Lorraine family. This powerful dynasty held a strong position under Henry II, and included cardinals who pressed for setting up a Spanish-style inquisition to exterminate all Calvinists. In response a military and political Huguenot party arose to defend their power and privileges as well as their faith. The rivalry between noble families was sharply escalated by their opposing religious commitments. The genealogies of the Valois and Bourbon houses, both descended from the sainted King Louis IX, provide the familial chart for some of the intricate religious–political struggles of the French Reformation.

Although Henry II and his wife Catherine de' Medici, niece of Pope Clement VII, detested Protestants, their major energies were preoccupied with perpetual rivalry with Charles V in the Habsburg–Valois wars. Furthermore, Henry did not seem to realize until the end of his reign how extensive the religious defection of his people had become. With the treaty of Cateau-Cambrésis (1559) which ended the Habsburg–Valois wars, the king was finally free to direct his attention to eliminating heresy in his lands. But within the year Henry died of a wound suffered during a tournament joust. His accidental death created a crisis in royal authority that set the stage for a rapid growth of Protestantism and a long, bitter, religious and political conflict. The crown passed to a succession of three weak Valois kings, the first two of whom were children at their accession, and the last of whom had no children. The devolution of royal authority to minors and women was a source of crisis. A minor or a woman, especially if the latter were only a regent, could not command the loyalty and obedience of such as the Guises and Montmorencys as could an adult male.

The eldest of the four Valois princes was Francis II, who was only fifteen at the death of his father. During his brief eighteen-month reign (1559–60) the ultra-Catholic party came to the fore through the domination of the government by the Guise uncles of Francis's wife, Mary Queen of Scots. Their repressive measures against the Protestants caused such widespread resentment that more nobles joined those already committed to the Reformation because they both hated the Guises and had designs on the wealth of the Catholic church. The queen mother, Catherine, also sought ways to weaken the Guise faction, which not only treated her disdainfully but was trying to displace her sons in its effort to establish its own dynasty to rule France.

The intensity of anti-Guise feeling was evident in the Amboise conspiracy (1560), a bungled attempt by a group of Huguenot nobility to remove the king by force from the influence of the Guises. The fact that some of the conspirators were Geneva residents was an embarrassment to the city and to Calvin. Theodore Beza, Calvin's eventual successor in Geneva and a member of the French lower nobility, had provided some encouragement for this plot but Calvin was consistently against political revolution. Some of these nobles were executed. The Bourbon prince Louis de Condé was implicated in the plot and sentenced to death, but released after the death of Francis. The Amboise conspiracy foreshadowed the coming Wars of Religion which had the nature of civil wars (Kingdon 1956: 68–78). Different groups, including some Calvinist pastors, were beginning to come together in common opposition to the government. But such a negative basis for agreement was an unstable foundation for cooperation and led to confusion and failure. The suggestions by some Reformed leaders such as Knox and Bullinger (the successor to Zwingli) that subjects had the right to revolt against idolatrous, i.e. Catholic, rulers was firmly rejected by Calvin who wrote to dissociate himself from the Amboise conspiracy. The involvement of Calvinist pastors in the plot has been nicely phrased by N. M. Sutherland (1967: 19): "faced with a choice between resistance and extermination, they desired some solution less sublime than that of prayer alone."

Calvin and Beza greeted the death of Francis II (1560) by an ear infection as divine deliverance. Beza even composed a little ditty in celebration.

> Tool of bad men, Henry, thy thirst for blood
> Fit retribution found,
> From thy pierced eyeball gushed a purple flood
> Which crimsoned all the ground.

> Following thy unhappy father in his mad career,
> Francis, unhappy youth,
> Thou felt'st God's arrow cleave thy guilty ear
> Fast closed against God's truth.

> Ye crafty, foolish, dull-eared kings, to you
> These awful warning cry,
> Or now prepare your evil deeds to rue,
> Or in your blindness die. (Duke et al. 1992: 81)

Catherine's second son, Charles IX (r. 1560–74) succeeded as a minor at the age of ten. Legally the regency could go either to the queen mother or to the first prince of the blood, i.e. the first in line to the throne after the reigning king's sons. The first prince of the blood was

Anthony of Bourbon, king of Navarre, a leader of the Huguenots. His wife Jeanne d'Albret, a convinced Calvinist, was a leader of the Huguenots who corresponded with Calvin and participated in the national synod of La Rochelle. Catherine was able to outmaneuver Anthony in the struggle for the regency, but that triumph entailed developing a policy favorable to the Huguenot party as a counter-weight to the Guise faction.

The Colloquy of Poissy, 1561

Catherine, assisted by her chancellor, Michel de L'Hôpital, created a policy of moderation toward the Protestants that involved suspending persecution, releasing Condé and other Huguenot prisoners, allowing Huguenot nobles at court to have their own services, and appointing new, liberal-leaning Catholic tutors for the young king. Anthony of Bourbon renounced his claim to the regency and accepted the title of lieutenant-general of France. As a further effort to pacify her lands and, not incidentally, to provide a Gallican alternative to the council of Trent, Catherine called for a public Protestant–Catholic debate and dialogue. The colloquy of Poissy, engineered by the chancellor Michel de L'Hôpital whose prime concern was the unity of France, met in September–October 1561. The colloquy was a significant royal recognition of the reality and growth of Protestantism.

The colloquy of Poissy was the high-water mark of the Protestant Reformation in France. Chancellor de L'Hôpital opened the colloquy with a speech concerning the king's gracious purpose to resolve the religious crisis by summoning this national council. It was the royal hope that a mutually respectful exchange of theological views between the Catholic and Huguenot representatives might preserve peace in the Gallican church. The colloquy, he went on to state, was not a place of judgment but of dialogue.

In immediate response, the archbishop of Lyons and primate of France, Cardinal Tournon, leaped to his feet to protest the very nature of this assembly. The some 50 bishops present, for all their Gallican-ism, despised a government-imposed assembly that raised heretics to their level. Heretics were to be judged, not debated!

But Catherine was not interested in ultimatums and anathemas; her new policy was accommodation. At her motherly prompting the king indicated, to the chagrin of the bishops, that the meeting would go on as scheduled. The signal was given and the Huguenot delegation – 11 ministers in their black Genevan robes and 20 lay representatives from various Calvinist congregations in France – was ushered into the assembly hall. Cardinal Tournon broke the tense silence with his stage whisper, "Voici ces chiens genevois!" – "Here are those Genevan dogs!"

The "Genevan dog" who now stepped forth to present the Huguenot position immediately impressed his audience as a "purebred." Theodore Beza (1519–1605), born to an established Burgundian family, was a Calvinist's Calvinist and a scholar's scholar. During his 13-year exile in Switzerland he had become Calvin's close friend, confidant, heir apparent, and professor of biblical studies at the new Genevan Academy. His work on the Greek New Testament is still remembered by the naming of the fifth-century Graeco-Latin manuscript of the gospels he discovered and presented to the University of Cambridge in 1581, the Codex Bezae, and by the first critical edition of the Greek New Testament which he published in 1565. His background of family wealth and position, similar to that of his audience, and his years of theological reflection and writing precluded any sense of intimidation from this assembly of royal and ecclesiastical dignitaries. To the astonishment of all, he opened his remarks with a prayer at which his delegation fell to their knees: "Lord God, Father eternal and all-powerful, we confess before your majesty that we are poor and miserable sinners" (O'Connell 1974: 121).

Then for the next hour Beza eloquently and learnedly presented the Calvinist position. The queen mother was filled with hope and even the bishops were not unmoved as Beza pledged himself to concord and elegantly surveyed doctrinal agreements between the antagonistic churches on matters such as the trinity and the incarnation. He discussed matters of disagreement such as authority with a sweet reasonableness. Only at the end of his speech did he make the fateful slip of stating that in the eucharist Christ's body "is as far removed from the bread and wine as is heaven from earth" (Nugent 1974: 100). The hitherto polite reception of Beza's address was now shattered by shouts from the prelates – "He blasphemes!" Catherine later called Beza's simile "absurd and offensive."

The colloquy went on for another month but the neuralgic nerve that had already sent waves of pain through previous colloquies at Marburg (1529) and Regensburg (1541) had been inelegantly exposed by Beza. The mode of Christ's presence in the eucharist was the rock that shattered accommodation. For the Catholic theologians, the mass was the Christian community's supreme good work of offering and receiving the corporeal Christ; whereas for the Calvinist theologians, the mass was an idolatrous and blasphemous denial of the true gospel.

Furthermore, the Calvinists knew as did other Protestants that the mass was only the tip of the Catholic iceberg. The mass was upheld by a whole hierarchical priesthood whose ability to perform the sacrament was linked to an ordination process rooted in the succession to St Peter, and whose caste was endowed with special powers and prerogatives. From Luther on, the mass was the focal point of the Protestant Reformers' attacks on the establishment because they knew that if the mass went the whole papal church would crumble. Throughout Europe a generation of iconoclasts had desecrated churches and trampled and urinated on holy objects including the consecrated sacramental bread in ritualistic reversals of Catholic ritual.

Thus the Catholic laity did not need refined theological rebuttals of Calvinist heresy in order to recognize it. They saw it in the actions of those who refused to honor a Corpus Christi procession and defaced sacred objects. When the Spanish Jesuit theologian Diego Lainez obtained permission to speak, he made it clear to the queen mother that her intentions for conciliation failed to understand that the Calvinists are "serpents, wolves in sheep's clothing, and foxes." The remedy against Calvinist "venom" was not this national council of dubious ecclesiastical legality, but rather the council of Trent already in session and presided over by the pope, not the crown. Lest she did not get the point, Lainez insinuated that her crown as well as her soul was at stake in these matters.

The Wars of Religion, 1562–1598

The colloquy of Poissy failed to create religious accommodation, but it did prepare the way for the first edict of toleration (January 1562) which provided a measure of freedom to the Huguenots. Huguenot leaders like Beza continued to have access to the court and strove for the conversion of the royal family. Huguenot public worship was allowed in private homes in towns and outside the towns' walls. This was the watershed for French Protestantism. It seemed that at the least, France might go the way of England under Henry VIII a generation earlier and adopt a national church under the control of the state.

But within a month of the edict of toleration the situation for the Calvinists was radically altered. By mid-February Catherine was fully cognizant of the wrath of the Guise family and of the Spanish. She now came to believe that the unity of the nation and the royal future of her sons was more threatened by the hostility of the Spanish than by the Huguenots and their allies. Her balance-of-power policy therefore

tilted toward the Catholic faction. Anthony of Bourbon sensed the shift
in the wind and defected from the Huguenot party for the sake of his
own personal and dynastic ambitions. The Huguenot political and
military resources were not sufficient to bring France into Protestantism, but they were strong enough to ensure their existence as a
rebellious minority. Under these conditions civil war was inevitable.

On 1 March 1562 the duke of Guise went on a hunting trip with 200
armed men. At Vassy in Champagne they came across a large
congregation of Huguenots gathered in a barn for worship and set upon
them. Some 70 Huguenots were killed and many more wounded. The
incident sparked more massacres, and the religious wars were on. To
Anthony of Bourbon, king of Navarre, Calvin wrote concerning
Vassy: "It is in truth for God's Church, in whose name I speak, to
endure blows and not to strike them. Remember, though, that this is an
anvil which has broken many a hammer before now" (Greengrass 1987:
vii).

When the Huguenots took up arms they lost the image of a
persecuted church. And when in September 1562 they looked to
English Protestants for assistance (under the Hampton Court Treaty),
they lost their patriotic credibility. They were attacked in sermons as
heretics and traitors. The intensity of Catholic hatred of Protestants,
especially in the area of Paris, is illustrated by the hero's welcome given
the duke of Guise when he entered Paris after the Vassy massacre.
Catholic hatred of Protestants was inflamed by Catholic preaching that
ominously echoed Thomas Müntzer's earlier declaration that the
godless have no right to live, the "godless" in this case being the
Huguenots. The violent sacrilegious activity of Calvinists only confirmed the eschatological terrors of Catholics who, fearing the coming
last judgment, were convinced the social and ecclesiastical body had to
be purified before the end. The parish pulpits of Paris taught hatred of
heretics and suspicion of those – including the magistracy and
monarchy – who allowed their continuing existence. Catholic
preachers goaded people into a frenzy of fear and hatred of the religious
and moral depravity of the "Deformed" that would undermine royal
efforts for toleration and produce deadly fruit. Such preaching was also
seditious in exhorting punishment of heretics in spite of royal edicts to
the contrary (see Diefendorf 1991: ch. 9). For over the next 30 years
Huguenots and Catholics murdered and assassinated each other with
increasing barbarity. In some regions, e.g. the southwest, the war was
endemic; elsewhere it was sporadic or almost non-existent, punctuated
by truces. The most infamous event of all this bloodshed was the St
Bartholomew's Day massacre of 24 August 1572.

The St Bartholomew's Day Massacre

During one of her shifts from repression to moderation, Catherine received the Huguenot leader Coligny at court, where he was welcome into the summer of 1572. Coligny's presence at court, in the wider context of Catholic fear and hatred, aroused Catholic anxiety that he would soon be a strong influence upon Charles IX who was now of age. People believed that Coligny had convinced Charles to reverse traditional foreign policy to support Calvinist resistance to Spain in the Netherlands, thus risking a disastrous war. This aroused both the political and maternal anxieties of Catherine, and was the context for the decision that Coligny must go (Sutherland 1980: ch. 6).

Catherine is most often indicted for the plan to assassinate Coligny on the basis that she believed him an impenitent rebel and a bad influence on the king who had to be killed for the peace, if not the glory, of France. Ever since, Catherine has been depicted as the epitome of evil (Sutherland 1978; Kingdon 1988: 200–13). More recent scholarship questions this and suggests the Guise family as the most likely perpetrators. In 1563 Coligny had condoned the assassination of Duke Francis of Guise. The Guise family, convinced that Coligny had ordered this deed, had long demanded revenge. Whoever wanted Coligny out of the way for whatever reasons was initially disappointed for the assassin only wounded him.

It is said that for the first time in her life, Catherine panicked. All her concerns were now in jeopardy – the interests of state, her passion for power, and the safety of her other son, Henry, who may have participated in the attack. The way out of her dilemma came with the accusation that Coligny was now plotting with the Huguenots to kill the queen and her children. Whether or not the accusation was true, and whether or not Catherine believed it, is not known; what is known is that here was the means for influencing Charles to take steps to thwart a new Amboise conspiracy.

Catherine's argument to Charles was that rebels had to be executed. The crown must act quickly before the Huguenot forces were ready to strike the crown; and, more importantly regarding Catherine's position, before the inquiry into the attempted murder of Coligny discovered anything. Catherine perceived Coligny to be the king's master and believed that if she did not strike first, she would be executed and Catholic France would rise up against her son whom they believed was allied with the Protestants. It was kill or be killed. The Spanish ambassador summed up the situation: "As the musket shot was badly aimed and as the Admiral knew whence it came, they determined to do what they did" (Héritier 1967: 51).

The context for the murder of Coligny and the massacre of his "rebels" was the marriage of Marguerite of Valois, Catherine's daughter, and Henry of Navarre, first prince of the blood since the death of his father. This marriage, negotiated as a means for creating peace between the warring religious factions by uniting the royal princess and the titular leader of the Protestants, took place in Paris on 18 August. The marriage festivities had filled Paris with prominent nobility, including most of the Huguenot leadership. Coligny had been shot on 22 August. The completion of this botched assassination was planned for the early morning of 24 August.

Charles now had the opportunity to prove himself to his mother and brother. To maintain order the gates of Paris were closed, locking the Huguenot troops outside the city in the suburbs. The king's militia was deployed in the city. One of the militia leaders, however, was Claude Marcel, a fanatical Catholic and one of Guise's men. Either he or the duke of Guise proclaimed in the hearing of the militia that the king's orders were to kill all heretics. Lists of heretics were provided to facilitate a methodical massacre. At the signal given by the king, the unsuspecting Huguenots were slaughtered in their beds, beginning with the finishing off of Coligny whose body was tossed from the window of his apartment, mutilated, and disgraced for days by the Catholic mobs.

A conflagration of savagery fueled by religious hatred was now unleashed. In the description by a contemporary: "The streets were covered with dead bodies, the rivers stained, the doors and gates of the palace bespattered with blood. Wagon loads of corpses, men, women, girls, even infants, were thrown into the Seine, while streams of blood ran in many quarters of the city. . . . One little girl was bathed in the blood of her butchered father and mother, and threatened with the same fate if she ever became a Huguenot" (Manschreck 1965: 144). Although the magnitude of the massacres cannot be known with any exactitude, it has been estimated that about 6,000 people were killed in Paris, and thousands in lesser cities as the massacre spread through the land. By the time the frenzy subsided about 20,000 in all France had been murdered. Catherine and the king had unleashed state terrorism.

The French Wars of Religion and even the St Bartholomew's Day massacre have traditionally been interpreted in terms of personal and political conflicts among the nobility and crown. Barbara Diefendorf (1991: 178) has forcefully recalled attention to the religious content of these conflicts. Far more than land, economics, and politics, what was

Figure 11.1 "St Bartholomew's Night," painting by François Dubois d'Amiens. Note Coligny being pushed through window in the center building and the king inspecting his decapitated and mutilated body on the street below.
Source: Bibliothèque Nationale, Paris.

at stake in this extended conflict was "the very bases on which civil society was built and the accustomed relationships that linked the individual to the collectivity and to God. . . . The religious wars represented a crusade against heresy, a crusade that had to be won if civil society was to be preserved and salvation to be assured. The people had a stake in these wars that they did not have in the dynastic squabbles of their kings, and as a consequence, the Wars of Religion had broad repercussions at the popular level." Heresy was no mere intellectual deviation; it was the pollution of the whole community, indeed nation. The Catholics of Paris "were ridding the community of a pollution and pouring out their wrath on a faction of people arrogant enough to defy the deeply felt religious convictions of the majority" (Kingdon 1988: 41). It is an Enlightenment anachronism to assume the fundamental reasons for conflict are always political and economic. The ancient Augustinian usage of Luke 14: 23 ("compel people to come in") to legitimize coercion against heresy and heterodoxy was taken very seriously in the sixteenth century (Repgen 1987: 311).

The martyrdom of Coligny and the atrocities of the St Bartholomew's Day massacre are living memories which continue to be commemorated among French Protestants. In 1972 – 400 years after the event – the city of Paris renamed a street after Coligny near the one where he was shot. The French government also issued a medal in commemoration of his heroic death. "The memory of the massacres keeps alive among French Protestants a sense of being members of a minority that over the centuries has often suffered persecution in its own country. It also reminds other Frenchmen of the significant cost to their homeland of past intolerance and fanaticism" (Kingdon 1988: 217).

European reactions to the massacre were mixed. Within France the extreme Catholic position was one of relief that royal policy was at last conforming to the demands coming from their pulpits. Moderate Catholics preferred to sweep the whole affair under a royal carpet, either denying royal responsibility or excusing it as a pre-emptive strike to avoid a Huguenot revolt. Calvinist polemicists now increased the boldness with which they had already begun to question the religious tyranny of the crown, and in the process developed the first modern arguments for constitutionalism. François Hotman's *Franco-Gallia* (1573) argued from medieval French history that royal authority is derived from the people and thus their representatives in the Estates-General could withdraw it. Hotman hoped thereby to undermine a persecuting monarchy and increase the importance of the Estates-General through which the nobles could assist the Huguenots. Theodore Beza's *Du Droit des magistrats* ("The Right of Magistrates over their Subjects," 1574) also claimed the king had been granted his power by the people and that therefore his violation of it released the people from obedience. If the king is a tyrant, the lower magistrates or the Estates may resist him. The anonymous *Political Discourses* (1578) suggested rebellion and tyrannicide, as did the *Vindiciae contra tyrannos* (1579) attributed to the Huguenot statesman Philippe du Plessis-Mornay. The crown itself was in the awkward position of self-justification since, after all, tradition and theology had always asserted that the king was divinely appointed to uphold law and protect his subjects, not kill them. In what may possibly be the most inflated blame-the-victim defense in history, the crown advanced the innocence of Charles IX and claimed the Huguenots had to be attacked before they attacked the king (see Kingdon 1988: 136–82).

Outside of France Protestant leaders and royalty mourned, but took no major steps against France. In fact, Queen Elizabeth of England accepted the invitation to be a godmother to the newborn French princess. Protestant propagandists did attempt to exploit the massacres with the goal of generating support against Catholicism (Nischan 1994: 190–1). Charles IX sent ambassadors out to defend his view of things. The Polish diet, which included Protestants, was apparently convinced and elected Charles's brother, Duke Henry of Anjou, their king. Pope Gregory XIII prescribed an annual Te Deum as a special thanksgiving service that was celebrated for many years. Gregory also had a special commemorative medal struck, *Ugonatorum stranges*, 1572, that depicted an angel bearing a sword and upholding the cross as prostrate Protestants are being slain. The pope also commissioned frescos of the massacre for the walls of the Sala Regia adjacent to the Sistine Chapel. It was said that the Spanish king, Philip II, laughed publicly for the first time in his life, and ordered his bishops to celebrate the event with Te Deums and other ceremonies. Many prominent Protestants including preachers and the young princes of Navarre and Condé, faced with the choice of the mass or death, chose Catholicism. Others fled to refuge in foreign Protestant communities. The princes later returned to Calvinism (Kingdon 1988: 45–8).

"Paris is Worth a Mass"

Charles IX died less than two years later and was succeeded by his brother, now king of Poland, as Henry III, who reigned 1574–89. Henry III was the last of the Valois line since his brother Francis, duke of Alençon, died in 1584. He refused to side with either Catholics or Protestants, and moved towards a third party, the *politiques*, so-called because they placed national unity over religious uniformity. In response to this moderate party, the Catholic League (formed in 1576) sought to restrain the crown from granting an advantageous peace to the Huguenots and to prevent the Huguenot Henry of Navarre from succeeding Henry III. These conflicts with the Bourbons and Guises are known as the "war of the three Henrys" because each leader had that name. In 1588 Henry of Guise directly challenged the king when he entered Paris by stimulating a popular uprising that expelled the king from the city. In response Henry III arrested the leading League deputies to the Estates-General, and had Guise and his brother the cardinal assassinated. The murders of the Guises, heroes of the extreme Catholics and leaders of the Catholic League, created widespread antipathy to Henry III. The Sorbonne declared Henry III's subjects absolved from their oath of allegiance. Popular opinion against Henry

III was mobilized on every level down to punishment by effigy and masses combined with rituals that stuck pins in his wax image (Ranum 1980: 68). Faced with revolt, Henry III allied himself with the Huguenot leader Henry of Navarre. In 1589 a friar named Jacques Clément, believing he would inaugurate the Second Coming by assassinating the king, plunged a knife into Henry's chest. The immediate consequence, however, was to bring the Bourbon, Henry of Navarre (1553–1610), to the throne as a Huguenot (Wolfe 1993: 43).

The League, led by Henry of Guise's brother, Charles the duke of Mayenne, worked to propose a rival candidate but their first choice, the cardinal of Bourbon, was now dead. It took Henry IV five years to subdue the Catholic League and its Spanish allies. In 1593 he converted to Catholicism under pressure from the Catholic League threatening to declare his succession invalid. On 22 March 1594 he triumphantly entered Paris. The popular story is that Henry said, "Paris is worth a mass." What Henry IV understood was the *politique* view that religion would have to be separated from politics and that only a strong monarchy could guarantee peace and the state. Henry IV thus became an ardent defender of royal absolutism. One of the consequences of the Wars of Religion was that the earlier moves toward constitutionalism had become tainted with violence and treason; the crown now moved to fill this vacuum. Henry's conversion had the desired effect of securing both the legitimacy of the Bourbon succession and the unity of the nation. Since Pope Clement VIII did not insist that the decrees of the council of Trent be enforced in France, Henry responded to the anxieties of his former coreligionists by setting forth a policy of limited toleration, the edict of Nantes, in 1598.

The edict of Nantes made the Catholic church the offical state church with its former rights, income, and possessions. The Huguenots, about 15 percent of the population, were granted rights to worship on Protestant estates and in many areas but not within five leagues of Paris. They were also granted civil rights, such as their own courts for legal protection and eligibility to hold offices, as well as political rights, including 200 fortified places. The edict did not work perfectly but it did bring to an end the religious wars. Calvinism did not triumph in France, but it did survive under the shadows of at least the king's wings. In the end the ancient Gallican tradition of "one king, one law, one faith" endured. To be a good Frenchman meant being a good Catholic. After his assassination in Paris (1610), "Henry IV's conversion entered the annals of royal historiography as infallible proof of God's eternal tutelage over France and its kings" (Wolfe 1993: 158). The edict of Nantes was revoked by Louis XIV in 1685.

Suggestions for Further Reading

Bernard Chevalier, "France from Charles VII to Henry IV," in Thomas A. Brady, Jr, Heiko A. Oberman, and James D. Tracy, eds, *Handbook of European History 1400–1600: Late Middle Ages, Renaissance and Reformation*, vol. 1, 369–401, Leiden: E. J. Brill, 1994

Barbara Diefendorf, *Beneath the Cross: Catholics and Huguenots in Sixteenth-Century Paris*, New York: Oxford University Press, 1991

Mark Greengrass, *The French Reformation*, Oxford: Blackwell, 1987

Robert M. Kingdon, *Myths about the St Bartholomew's Day Massacres, 1572–1576*, Cambridge, MA: Harvard University Press, 1988

David Nicholls, "France," in Andrew Pettegree, ed., *The Early Reformation in Europe*, 120–41, Cambridge: Cambridge University Press, 1992

Donald Nugent, *Ecumenism in the Age of the Reformation: The Colloquy of Poissy*, Cambridge, MA: Harvard University Press, 1974

F. C. Spooner, "The Reformation in France, 1515–1559," in G. R. Elton, ed., *The Reformation 1520–1559*, 2nd edn (New Cambridge Modern History, II), 223–61, Cambridge: Cambridge University Press, 1990

N. M. Sutherland, *The Huguenot Struggle for Recognition*, New Haven: Yale University Press, 1980

Michael Wolfe, *The Conversion of Henri IV: Politics, Power, and Religious Belief in Early Modern France*, Cambridge, MA: Harvard University Press, 1993

12

The Blood of the Martyrs:
The Reformation in the
Netherlands

*The faithful and elect shall be crowned with glory and honor; and the Son
of God will confess their names before God and his elect angels; all tears
shall be wiped from their eyes; and their cause, which is now condemned
by many judges and magistrates as heretical and impious, will then be
known to be the cause of the Son of God.*

The Belgic confession (1561)

If, as the ancient church believed, the blood of the martyrs is the seed of
the church, the Reformation in the Netherlands had an auspicious
beginning. It has been said that there were more martyrs for the
Reformation faiths in the Netherlands than in any other country
(Cochrane, 1966: 185). And in the eyes of contemporaries, pro and con,
martyrdom did seed reform. In 1555 Charles V received word that
"simple people, seeing the public execution of such heretics with firm
constancy and hearing their resolutions and the prayers which they
address to God before dying, fall into vacillation and doubt of their
faith." An example is the address to the crowd by the Reformed pastor
Gilles Verdickt at the moment of his execution: "Do you think
Messieurs, that you can expel and extirpate these poor Christians by
killing and burning them? . . . you delude yourselves greatly; the ashes
of my body will make the Christians multiply" (Crew 1978: 76).

The first martyrs of the Reformation came from the Augustinian
monastery in Antwerp. Many of these monks had studied in Wittenberg and returned as enthusiastic supporters of Luther, whose works
began appearing in the Netherlands as early as 1518, with more than 80
editions and translations by 1525 (Spruyt, 1991: 730, 747–51). As early
as 1519 the prior of the Antwerp Augustinians, Jakob Propst, was
defending Luther's teachings. The Netherlands, however, was Charles
V's home territory and his reaction was swift. The Augustinian

monastery in Antwerp was leveled and all the monks imprisoned with the choice of recantation or the stake. Three maintained their new faith and were condemned to death. Heinrich Voes and Johann Esch met their death at the stake in July 1523 in the marketplace in Brussels; the third monk, Lambert Thorn, was not executed until 1528.

Their executions occasioned the first Reformation martyrology in the form of Luther's ballad, "A New Song Here Shall Be Begun" (August, 1523; *LW* 53: 211–16), which celebrated the victory of the martyrs' faith and witness. This first hymn of the Reformation appeared initially as a broadsheet and then in hymnals. It later served as the pattern for countless Anabaptist hymns celebrating their martyrs. Luther soon had the unhappy occasion for a second martyrology, "The Burning of Brother Henry" (1525; *LW* 32: 263–86), which recounted the witness of the Augustinian, Henry of Zütphen, who escaped Amsterdam only to be lynched in Ditmarschen (northeast of Hamburg) after a brief, successful ministry in Bremen.

Charles V's determination to root out heresy might be frustrated in Germany, but in his hereditary Netherlands the evangelicals had no powerful patrons to intercede for them. By 1555 the Habsburg Netherlands had the dubious distinction of creating more martyrs for Reformation convictions than any other country in Europe: 63 executed in Mons, Tournai, Lille, and Valenciennes, 100 in Flanders, and 384 in the county of Holland. The Reformation was not a live option in the provinces of Brabant, Flanders, Holland, Zeeland, and the Walloon towns in the face of the religious repression exerted from Brussels, the seat of the Spanish administration for the Netherlands (Duke, 1992: 146). The uneven match of the defenseless evangelical witness against the concentrated powers of the emperor and then Catholic Spain stoked the image of Dutch Protestantism as an early modern David facing Goliath (Spitz, 1971: 510). However stirring such a simple contrast may be, it belies the context and complexity of the Reformations in the Netherlands, which consisted of successive waves of Lutheran, Anabaptist, and Calvinist movements (Williams, 1992: 1177).

The area which came to be known as the Netherlands only in the 1530s included the duchies of Luxemburg and Brabant, the counties of Hainault, Artois, Flanders, Zeeland, and Holland, and other smaller counties and lordships which by 1543 under the political organization of Charles V comprised 17 provinces in all. The southern provinces (roughly modern Belgium), the Walloon area, was mainly French-speaking, whereas the people in the larger area to the north (roughly the modern Netherlands) spoke a Low German dialect. Provincial, not to mention local, differences make generalizations difficult. With that caveat in mind, the following minimal sketch of the Netherlands will provide a context for the developing Reformation movements. Political unity among the provinces was fragile and rested to a large degree upon the person of Charles V. There was a central bureaucracy but throughout his reign the provincial governments were quite willing to obstruct government policies for the sake of their own customs and privileges. Furthermore, the efforts to finance imperial policy, such as wars with France, through increased taxation on the Low Countries contributed to such discontent that the regent Margaret of Austria feared rebellion in 1522 and 1525.

By the end of Charles V's reign the Netherlanders were near revolt. They complained of exorbitant taxation to finance imperial campaigns in France and Italy, the oppressive presence of Spanish troops to hold down the people, the trampling of rights and liberties by the Inquisition, inflation, the decline of once-successful centers such as Ghent and Leiden, and the loss of local influence in government and the courts. By the time Charles announced his abdication in Brussels, the Habsburg political system in the Netherlands was on the brink of collapse. Within a few more years the nexus of religious, social, and political issues pushed the Netherlands over the brink into 80 years of civil, religious, and national war (Koenigsberger, 1990: 355–8). The independence of the northern provinces as the Republic of the United Provinces was recognized by the Treaty of Westphalia in 1648.

Netherlandish obedience to Charles V was not due primarily to his being emperor and king of Spain but to the perception of him as their own territorial duke. Personal loyalty to Charles and his failure to establish a true monarchy in this small, diverse territory under Spanish suzerainty are significant reasons for the difficulties encountered in the next generation by his Spanish son, Philip II, whom the Netherlanders regarded as a foreigner (he did not speak French or Flemish). In France the Huguenots could be depicted as renders of national unity and fomenters of civil war because their opposition to religious repression often related to the crown. In contrast, the Dutch Calvinists, in opposing religious repression stemming from a foreign occupying power, Spain, could be perceived as patriots because Spain was also politically and economically repressive.

Charles V's sincere desire to root out heresy was never in doubt but it was difficult to realize with thoroughness and consistency. Provincial and local authorities, for the most part devout Catholics, balked at anti-heresy legislation which might override the rights and privileges of their customs. The merchant and maritime cities had commercial relations with German and Baltic areas which had accepted the

Reformation, and hence opposed measures against Protestant merchants from those areas. Access to the freedom of the seas also meant extended contact with Reformation influences in England and France.

"La secte Lutheriane"

The Antwerp Augustinians were referred to as "the Lutheran sect" as early as 1522. Variations of this description thereafter occurred frequently in government documents and thereby suggested, mistakenly, a unified movement. The government's perception of an organized Lutheran movement may have been in the eye of the beholder, but it nevertheless led to repressive activities designed to enforce the edict of Worms. The laity were forbidden to attend unauthorized sermons, and "secret assemblies" were strictly prohibited. As a result the early evangelicals in the Netherlands were forced underground; they met in small groups in "safe houses" and in fields outside the towns. These clandestine meetings were described as "schools," perhaps because outsiders perceived them as places where heresy was taught. The activities at these meetings included Bible study, doctrinal instruction, and at times preaching. In the Flemish countryside interested villagers and sometimes also clerics met after mass at local taverns to discuss biblical texts. It is not surprising that in this context a certain conviviality developed which could prompt ditties mocking the pope, mass, and purgatory. Anna Bijns, a Catholic poet, complained that "Scripture is read in the tavern, the Gospel in one hand and the tankard in the other" (Duke 1992: 152).

The quandary for the early evangelicals was how to maintain their understanding of the public proclamation of the gospel without recourse to separatism. They were well aware of Luther's opposition to sectarianism, but it was clear that it was impossible to install evangelical clergy in the churches and the Inquisition was making evangelical existence itself precarious. The Dutch evangelicals were being driven by persecution toward separatism.

Dissident Movements

Prevented from implementing reform of the established church, there were evangelicals who now found attractive the proclamation of Melchior Hoffmann that true believers should separate from the world and embrace Christ through believer's baptism. In the summer of 1530

Hoffmann returned to East Friesland and was soon baptizing adults in Emden. His followers spread his teachings and apocalyptic expectation (Deppermann, 1987: 74–75) through the Low Countries in the following, year gaining two future leaders in the process: Obbe Philips of Leeuwarden and Jan Mathijs of Haarlem.

Mathijs's role in the Münster disaster has already been discussed (see chapter 8). It is of interest to note that Mathijs's activity in Amsterdam in late 1533 appears to have been stimulated by Rothmann's writing *Confession of the Two Sacraments*. It seems that, rather than the Dutch prophets stimulating Anabaptism in Münster, "it is more precise to say that the radical turn of the Münster Reformation ignited Anabaptism in the Netherlands" (Stayer, 1990: 136). The attempts at mass migration from the Netherlands to Münster occurred in the context of interpreting the social and religious misery of the Netherlands as signs of the world's end and Mathijs's proclamation of Münster as the New Jerusalem. Most of the thousands who set out for Münster were disbanded by the authorities, who confiscated their possessions but did not slaughter them. Münster's militantism was increasingly questioned by Dutch Anabaptists, led in particular by Obbe Philips whose followers embraced non-violence. The Münster legacy lived on, however, in the violent activities of the "Batenburgers" who, under the leadership of Jan van Batenburg (1495–1538), the "new David," plundered and destroyed churches and monasteries in the northeastern Netherlands. At the beginning the Batenburgers believed in the destruction of the godless in preparation for the imminent establishment of God's reign on earth. After Jan's execution this sect degenerated into a robber band which was more criminal than religious.

The disarray of Dutch Anabaptism was addressed by Menno Simons (1496–1561). A parish priest from West Frisia influenced by evangelical ideas about Scripture and the sacraments, Menno was motivated by the tragedy of Münster to abandon his parish in 1536 and devote his energies to leading the Anabaptists. His *Foundation Book* (1540) outlined his communitarian creed for a church under the cross. He worked in Holland (1541–3) and then in East Frisia around Emden. The name "Mennonites" was coined in 1544 for his followers by the Polish Reformer Jan Laski, pastor of the Lutheran church at Emden. Laski thought these quietist Anabaptists should be spared harsh persecution. After Menno's death his followers split over the degree of discipline required for discipleship. By now the emphasis had shifted from eschatological expectation to the holiness of the community exemplified by strict morality. The stress on church discipline which resulted provoked divisive controversies such as that over whether a spouse is required to shun an excommunicated husband or wife. The discipline designed to preserve the separatist Anabaptist congregations as exemplars of the invisible church of the elect contributed to schism as elders excommunicated each other. In the years following the independence of the northern provinces, the Mennonites adjusted successfully to the commercial culture. "Former gestures of hostility to the broader society, like not carrying arms and not swearing oaths, became the harmless sectarian distinctives of tolerated nonconformists" (Stayer, 1990: 142).

The Rise of Calvinism and the Spanish Reaction

In the 1540s religious repression was stepped up and reinvigorated by Catholic progress in the Counter-Reformation. The Catholic theologians at Louvain issued a brief statement of orthodox faith (1544) and then a detailed list of forbidden books (1546). The central government bolstered the Inquisition and increased the severity of its edicts. A decree of 1550 stated: "No one was to print, transcribe, reproduce, keep, conceal, sell, buy, or give any book or writing of Martin Luther, Johannes Oecolampadius, Ulrich Zwingli, Martin Bucer, Jean Calvin, or any other heretic condemned by Holy Church" (Iserloh et al. 1986: 398). The emperor forbade any gathering which allowed a follower of such heretics to speak and decreed that any man found guilty of doing so be killed by the sword. Guilty women were to be burned at the stake unless they recanted, in which case they were to be buried alive. The majority – at least 1,500 – of those executed between 1540 and 1570 were Anabaptists (Stayer 1990: 141). The intent of the imperial decree was equally to root out Calvinism which was just beginning to spread into the Netherlands in spite of severe persecution.

The incursion of Calvinism into the Netherlands focused in the commercial area of Amsterdam and the Flemish area influenced by French congregations. The southern center of the Reformed movement was Antwerp. The northern center was the East Frisian harbor town of Emden, which became known as the "Geneva of the north" and the "mother church" of Dutch Calvinism (Schilling 1991: 46). Some of these early Calvinists clearly lacked the better part of valor and paid the ultimate price. At the Tournai cathedral on Christmas 1554, Bertrand Le Blas grabbed the eucharistic host from the hands of the priest in protest against "papist idolatry." Before being burned, both his hands were struck off. At Ghent, Georges Kathelyne was executed in 1555 for interrupting a Dominican preacher and calling him a false prophet.

That most people attracted to Calvinism were far more circumspect is indicated by the numerous printings in Dutch of anti-Nicodemite tracts including Calvin's treatises (Marnef 1994: 148). Many of those attracted to Calvinism who eschewed both Nicodemism and martyrdom fled abroad, finding asylum in Geneva, Strasbourg, Frankfurt, and London as well as Wesel and Emden.

The refugee church in London submitted a statement of their faith (*Compendium doctrinae*) to Edward VI in 1551 which was translated into Dutch for use in the Netherlands. This was soon replaced by the Belgic confession of 1561. The main author of the Belgic confession was Guy de Bray (1523–67), known as the "Reformer of the Netherlands." Converted through reading the Bible, he joined the exiles in London in 1548. In 1552 he returned to lead the Calvinist churches. Like the earlier Lutherans in Germany and the Huguenots in France, he and his colleagues hoped to convince the authorities that Calvinism was neither seditious nor fanatical. To this end he composed a confession of faith (1559) which closely followed the French confession of that year. Virtually all of its first printing, done in Rouen in 1561, was destroyed. Another printing at Lille was translated into Dutch and printed in Emden in 1562. The original French version, accompanied by an address to the king, was presented to Philip II in 1562. Affirming loyalty to the govenment, the address also clearly stated that rather than deny Christ they would "offer our backs to be beaten, our tongues to be cut out, our mouths to be bridled, and our whole bodies to be burned, because we know that whoever will follow Christ must take up his cross and deny himself" (Cochrane 1966: 186). Philip was only too pleased to oblige. As he assured the pope in 1566, "rather than suffer the least damage to religion and the service of God, I would lose all my states and a hundred lives, if I had them: for I do not propose nor desire to be ruler of heretics" (Koenigsberger 1994: 180–1). When Valenciennes, where de Bray was preacher, was captured in 1567 he was executed. By then, however, the religious solidarity of the Calvinists had been secured by the Belgic confession, accepted by a synod at Antwerp in 1566.

The Belgic confession facilitated the development of an alliance between the nobles and the Reformed church of the Netherlands against Spanish Catholicism. The nobles desired independence from Spain, and the Reformed desired independence from the papacy. Thus article 36 affirmed the duty of citizens to obey the magistrates "in all things which are not repugnant to the Word of God," and the duty of magistrates to "protect the sacred ministry, and . . . prevent all idolatry and false worship" (read Roman Catholicism!). The article ends with a condemnation of the errors of the Anabaptists and all others "who reject the higher powers and magistrates" (Cochrane 1966: 217–18).

The confession also made an addition to the Calvinist understanding of the church (Kingdon 1994: 21) which later proved troublesome: discipline. Article 29 added church discipline to the preaching of the gospel and the administration of the sacraments as a third mark of identification of the true church. Crew (1978: 58) argues that discipline, embodied by the pastors and the people, was not merely a means for the coherent organization of the Reformed churches. Discipline, especially of the pastors, was a witness against both the magical aura of the Catholic priest and the bizarre and charismatic attraction of the sectarian preachers. "The new pastors were to act as educators, administrators and organizers; but most of all they were to be witnesses to the purity of Reformed worship in the face of Catholic paganism and sectarian Protestantism." The new church was to be authenticated by preaching and exemplary morality. The Belgic confession was adopted by the synod of Wesel (1568) and the synod of Emden (1571). Since 1619 it has been the doctrinal standard of the Dutch Reformed churches in Holland, Belgium, and America.

Political resistance to Spanish rule coalesced around William of Nassau and Orange (1533–84), the governor of Holland, Zeeland, and Utrecht. In 1565 a league of 300 nobles petitioned Philip's regent, his sister Margaret of Parma, to end the Inquisition and soften the harsh religious edicts. Their disdainful dismissal as "beggars," an epithet quickly embraced by the resistance, prompted widespread iconclastic rebellions and destruction of churches. In response Philip sent in the duke of Alva (1508–82) and 20,000 troops. Alva, the "Iron Duke," entered Brussels on 22 August 1567 convinced that only a reign of terror would subjugate the Netherlanders. In short order Alva's "Council of Troubles," known as the "Council of Blood" to the Netherlanders, arrested hundreds, executed thousands including nobles suspected of heresy, and levied excessive taxation.

The resistance garnered sympathy and some funds but no effective help from the English Queen Elizabeth, nor was their appeal to the German princes successful; potential Huguenot support discussed among the French Protestant princes at La Rochelle (1571) with Louis of Nassau (Kingdon 1988: 185) was rendered moot by the St Bartholomew's Day massacre. William of Orange and his brother Louis thus depended upon his northern provinces where Calvinism was making great gains. From there the famous "Sea Beggars" raided Spanish commerce, seized coastal cities, and even defeated the Spanish fleet in the Zuiderzee. The determination of the northern provinces to resist the Spanish was indicated by their willingness to open the dikes against Spanish soldiers. It was during this struggle that Dutch patriotism and Calvinism merged.

The military struggle waged back and forth. In 1580 Philip declared William an outlaw and offered a reward for his capture dead or alive. This had the effect of endearing William even more to his people. At the meeting of the Estates-General in Delft in December 1580, William vindicated his honor in the face of Philip's personal attack by publicly renouncing the overlordship of the Spanish king. It was the first practical application of the argument of the Huguenot tract *Vindicae contra tyrannos* (1579) that people have the moral right and obligation to remove a sovereign derelict in his royal duties (Grimm 1973: 363; Garnett 1994: lxx, 137–8). The consequent Union of Utrecht included the seven northern provinces of Holland, Zeeland, Utrecht, Gelderland, Groningen, Friesland, and Overyssel.

William of Orange was assassinated by a supporter of Philip in July 1584. William had been unable to maintain the unity of the southern and northern provinces; his son, Maurice of Nassau, continued to lead the revolt of the northern provinces. The economic strength of the northern provinces, based on their seafaring skills, was supplemented by the personal and financial capital of numerous religious refugees from the south. It is estimated that upwards of 100,000 people fled the southern provinces during the Spanish reconquest and re-Catholization. This was a series of emigrations that had economic as well as religious motivation. But whatever the mix of motivations the experience "can only have served to reinforce the Reformed faith of those who undertook it." The religious refugees understood themselves in terms of the election and exodus imagery of the Hebrew Bible, and viewed their successes as evidence of God's providence and their participation in the New Covenant. The social experience of exodus and diaspora which Reformed merchants and ministers "endured to an even greater extent than most of their coreligionists, was of paramount importance in providing Calvinism with an international character" (Grell 1994: 257–8, 273). It has been suggested that the Calvinist form of the Reformation was more amenable to the endemic sacramentism of the pre-Reformation Netherlands than the Lutheran form with its emphasis on the real presence in the Lord's Supper (Williams 1992: 96–9). Probably more important was Calvinism's greater dynamism and versatility rooted in sound organization and an international solidarity that transcended national and regional boundaries (Marnef 1994: 158).

In 1601 the Estates-General chartered the Dutch East India Company, the basis for the development of the United Provinces as a great colonial power. The Twelve Years' Truce in 1609 enabled the north to further establish its political and economic independence. When Spain resumed the war, it had already suffered the disastrous defeat of its Great Armada (1588) and the Dutch were now well able to hold their own. In 1648 at the Treaty of Westphalia the independence of the Republic of the United Provinces was internationally recognized.

A Godly Society?

Compared to the fate of the Huguenot brethren in France, the Calvinist Reformation in the Dutch Republic was certainly successful. The Reformers had won a providential victory over great odds. In the 1576 treaty uniting the provinces of Holland and Zeeland, William of Orange received the mandate to "maintain and preserve the exercise of the Reformed evangelical religion, causing to cease and desist the exercise of other religions, which are contrary to the Gospel" (Tracy 1993: 487). The former "church under the cross" was now the public church with aspiration to be the new establishment. Success, however, is sometimes more difficult to manage than persecution. If faith is vindicated by suffering (Calvin, *Institutes* III, 8: 7; 1: 707), what is the effect of prosperity?

The answer for the ministers was to form a godly society through church discipline, the third mark of the church. The core of church discipline was denial of access to the sacrament of communion. Here the ministers soon discovered they did not have a free hand. William of Orange had resisted turning the revolt against Spain into a religious crusade, and he strove to create a tolerant environment in the Dutch Republic. As a consequence, Lutherans, Mennonites, various sects, and even Catholics all managed to provide their own religious services. Church discipline is difficult to carry out in a pluralist context.

Even worse in the eyes of the ministers was the fact that a large segment of the population did not become communing members of the Reformed church even though they attended services. These "libertines," as the Calvinists called them, clearly lacked enthusiasm for the newly established religious institutions. Indeed, the "libertines" did not hesitate to use Reformation slogans of "Scripture alone," "faith alone," and "evangelical freedom" against the disciplinary concerns of the Calvinists. The "libertines" associated church discipline with Catholicism and resented this "remnant of the papal yoke." They had not fought to remove the Spanish Inquisition in order to have it replaced by a Genevan one (Kaplan 1994; Pettegree 1994).

Freedom from oppression also allowed various theological controversies within Calvinism to bloom, most notably that between the
Gomarists and the Arminians over predestination which raged for years
until settled at the synod of Dort (1618–19). All these thorns in the flesh
of the Reformed church were nourished by the persistent attachment
not only to provincial but even local and urban autonomies. National
and religious unity was less a conviction than a necessity when survival
demanded it (Rowan and Harline 1994: 78–9; Tracy 1993: 489, 508).
The 1591 proposal of a church order was not approved by the
provincial states. As a consequence an unusual degree of religious
liberty developed in the Dutch Republic, not by design but by the
failure of church and state "to agree on new premises for unity, despite
the best efforts of both" (Tracy 1993: 490).

Suggestions for Further Reading

Phyllis Mack Crew, *Calvinist Preaching and Iconoclasm in the Netherlands, 1544–1569*,
   Cambridge: Cambridge University Press, 1978
Alastair Duke, *Reformation and Revolt in the Low Countries*, London: Hambledon, 1990
Alastair Duke, "The Netherlands," in Andrew Pettegree, ed., *The Early Reformation in
   Europe*, 142–65, Cambridge: Cambridge University Press, 1992
Irwin Horst, ed., *The Dutch Dissenters: A Critical Companion to their History and Ideas*,
   Leiden: E. J. Brill, 1986
Geoffrey Parker, *The Dutch Revolt*, Harmondsworth, 1990
Andrew Pettegree, *Emden and the Dutch Revolt. Exile and the Development of Reformed
   Protestantism*, Oxford, 1992
Heinz Schilling, *Civic Calvinism in Northwestern Germany and The Netherlands*, Kirks-
   ville: Sixteenth Century Journal Publishers, 1991

13

The Reformations in England and Scotland

Be of good cheer, Ridley; and play the man. We shall this day, by God's grace, light up such a candle in England, as, I trust, will never be put out.

Latimer to Ridley at the stake

Not so long ago historians (e.g. Powicke 1965: 1; Parker 1963: 7; Haigh 1993: 21) portrayed the English Reformation as an act of state: "The one definite thing which can be said about the Reformation in England is that it was an act of State." Contemporary scholarship continues to recognize the crucial role of the Tudors in revolutionizing ecclesiastical authority "by statute" (Brigdon 1992: 216), but corrects the one-sidedness of former political interpretations with social and religious studies. Sources other than state records illustrate that neither England nor Scotland was isolated from the Reformations on the European continent, and that the initiation and advance of Reformation ideas and convictions did not begin with nor completely depend on royal actions. "In essentials the early English Protestants of the 1520s and 1530s were Lutherans, led by Tyndale, Barnes and Cranmer, by the young Cambridge scholars of the early twenties, by Coverdale and the lesser bible-translators, and by a host of other publicists and pamphleteers with strong continental affinities. . . . Even Thomas Cromwell, the first great executive of the state-reformation, displayed a cool but unmistakable affinity with the Lutherans" (Dickens 1991: 13, 82; Clebsch 1964). These conflicting views of the respective priority of politics and religion in the English Reformation continue to foment lively scholarly controversy which undoubtedly will color interpretive studies for some time to come (O'Day 1986; Seaver 1982; Dickens 1987; Haigh 1993: 335–42).

Anticlericalism and Lutheran Beginnings

One of the controversial issues concerns the condition of the English church and the extent and intensity of anticlericalism on the eve of the

Reformation. In keeping with England's maritime tradition, A. G. Dickens provides a colorful description:

> Altogether, the English Church during the period 1500–30 stood poorly equipped to weather the storms of the new age. It was a grandiose but unseaworthy hulk, its timbers rotted and barnacled, its superstructure riddled by the fire of its enemies, its crew grudging, divided, in some cases mutinous, its watchmen near-sighted and far from weather-wise, its officers lacking in navigational skill. If in this situation the King decided to take personal command, most Englishmen – even most churchmen – would be likely to applaud rather than object. And few would stop to consider that the kings of England bore not a little of the responsibility for the problems of the Church! (Hurstfield 1965: 48)

While the following narrative will follow the historiographical consensus led by Dickens, vigorous opposition to it should be noted. Specifically Haigh (1987, 1993), Scarisbrick (1984), and Duffy (1992) contend that Catholicism was not in decay but in bloom on the eve of the Reformation. This argument returns with variations on the theme to the claim that the Reformation was imposed on the people from the top down and did not have strong popular roots. The question remains, however: If Catholicism was so popular, how was the crown able to carry out its program? Why was there so little effective enthusiasm for the old faith (Loades 1992: 3–5)?

Dickens's "storms of the new age" included an endemic anticlericalism rooted in the indigenous heretical tradition of Lollardy stemming from John Wyclif (ca. 1330–84) and fed by anger over the corruption and sexual lapses of the clergy. The Lollards were a shadowy community (Cosgrove 1993: 573); they met in homes and survived as a kind of underground church focused on Bible reading. Their emphasis on knowledge of the Bible and in particular an obsession with the Bible in English led to the outlawing of the English Bible altogether in 1409. To the Lollards Catholic worship, especially the mass, was superstition and idolatry (Hudson 1988; Aston 1984; Brigdon 1992: 86–106).

Anticlericalism was of course not the sole preserve of the Lollards. On the eve of the Reformation, the humanist dean of St Paul's, John Colet, used his convocation sermon (6 February 1512) to attack both parish clergy and prelates. The former "seke none other thynge in the people than foule lucre" and the latter are marked by "gredynes and appetite of honour and dignitie" (Dickens 1987: 385). The prime exemplar of the greed for dignities was Thomas Wolsey (ca. 1474–1530), whose offices included bishop of Lincoln, archbishop of York, cardinal, papal legate, and lord chancellor of England, and who seemed to monopolize all ecclesiastical and civil power in the realm. Popular hatred of Wolsey's exactions, pride, tyranny, wealth, and ambition spilled over into anticlericalism toward all clergy. The more sensationalist charges are illustrated by the tabloid journalism of the notorious *Supplication for Beggars* (1529) by the London lawyer Simon Fish, who argued that the clergy were rich beggars who deprived poor beggars. This charge of economic aggrandizement was spiced up by charges of sexual aggrandizement: The clergy "truly [do] nothing more but apply themselves . . . to have to do with every man's wife, every man's daughter, and every man's maid, that cuckoldry and bawdry should reign over all . . . These be they that have made a hundred thousand idle whores in your realm" (Hillerbrand 1964: 307–8). Fish concluded that the king and the country would prosper if ecclesiastical property were confiscated and priests forced to work. In short, there was a good deal of anticlerical material by the eve of the Reformation which the early Protestants did not hesitate to use for their advantage. Informed by Luther among others, the early Protestants drew the explicit conclusion that "a defective priesthood had inevitably developed out of a defective theology" (Dickens 1987: 399). Given this analysis the solution lay not in moral improvement but in theological reform.

These endemic English resentments, coupled with enthusiasm for the new learning promoted by Colet and Erasmus among others, were fertile ground for Lutheran preaching and doctrine which entered England about 1520 (Hall 1979). Luther and his writings were anathematized on 12 May 1521. On that day Cardinal Wolsey, surrounded by assembled bishops and nobility at London's St Paul's, pronounced Luther's excommunication and ritually burned his books in an ostentatious ceremony. Wolsey then issued an order for the confiscation of all Luther's writings. By this time the first group of Lutheran sympathizers were meeting at the White Horse Inn in Cambridge, soon nicknamed "Little Germany." Cambridge University itself would provide most of the future leaders of English Protestantism, nearly all of whom would be martyred. This circle included prominent classical scholars such as Robert Barnes, John Lambert, and John Frith; the future archbishops Cranmer, Heath, Parker, and May; and the future bishops Latimer, Ridley, Sampson, Shaxton, Bale, Foxe, and Day (Rupp 1966: 15–46).

Robert Barnes (ca. 1495–1540: Rupp 1966; Anderson 1968; Clebsch 1964), an Augustinian prior with a doctorate from Louvain and the usual leader of the Cambridge circle, first ran afoul of Wolsey through his Christmas Eve sermon of 1525. Although ostensibly tried for heresy, Barnes's real offense was ridiculing lawyers and Wolsey.

Wolsey was not interested in burning Barnes as a heretic; he only wanted submission to his authority. When Barnes, under "house arrest" in the London Augustinian house for nearly three years, learned he was to be executed he faked suicide by drowning. By the time the authorities had dragged the river for a week, Barnes had escaped to the Netherlands. From there he made his way to Wittenberg in 1530 where he stayed with Bugenhagen and worked with Luther and Melanchthon. His first Latin publication in Wittenberg consisted of patristic citations supporting evangelical theology as expressed by the recent Augsburg confession and included a preface by Bugenhagen. His next publication, *Supplication to Henry VIII*, was published in 1531 in Antwerp. Here he eloquently protested his loyalty to the king and attacked the secular exercise of papal and ecclesiastical authority. The rest of this book consists of essays in Lutheran theology. It is of interest that Thomas More thought the most dangerous article in this book was that challenging the authority of the papal church. Like Prierias decades earlier, the neuralgic nerve for the establishment was not so much justification by grace alone as it was its corollary – the undermining of ecclesiastical absolutism.

Barnes briefly returned to England under protection of a royal safe conduct – to the anger of Thomas More. There he delivered to the king Luther's negative opinion on Henry's proposed divorce from Catherine: "At the risk of losing his salvation, and under the threat of eternal damnation, therefore the King is to be held responsible for retaining the Queen to whom he is married" (*LW* 50: 39). Luther had not endeared himself to Henry by earlier correspondence either, and it would not be surprising if Henry now blamed the messenger for another unwelcome message. At any rate, Barnes returned to Germany in January 1532. From August 1534 to January 1535 Barnes was again in London as a negotiator with Henry VIII for the cities of Hamburg and Lübeck. The occasion was Henry's effort to establish alliances with the German Lutheran cities and princes since his relations with Spain, Charles V, and France were now broken over both his divorce and Protestant tendencies in England. By late 1538 the pope had excommunicated Henry and called upon Francis I and Charles V to mount a crusade against England. This is the context for Henry's interest in joining the Schmalkaldic League and a marriage alliance with the Lutheran duke of Cleves through his sister Anne. Frantic missions to Germany ensued. Although Barnes served Henry loyally in this mission, the proposed alliance did not occur. To be sure, Henry's effort to forge an alliance with the German Lutherans provided an unprecedented breathing space to Protestantism in England. The hope that

Melanchthon would visit England (*LW* 50: 97–106) was unrealized, as was the alliance itself. The German Lutherans demanded financial support and insisted that membership in the Schmalkaldic League depended upon subscription to the Augsburg confession. This was too high a price for Henry, who hinted he might consider the Augsburg confession if he were first admitted to the Schmalkaldic League. The discussions did result in the "Thirteen Articles" (Bray 1994: 184–221) which closely follow the Augsburg confession and were later influential on the development of the "Forty-Two Articles" under Edward VI and the "Thirty-Nine Articles" under Elizabeth I. Henry set them aside after the breakdown of negotiations with the Germans (Hall 1979: 118). As the negotiations dragged on and the international threat diminished, Henry decided it was time to create religious unity in England. His determination to stamp out nonconformity led to the Six Articles Act (1539) which reaffirmed Roman Catholic dogma and enforced it with penalties more severe than those meted out by prior church courts. Denial of transubstantiation incurred an automatic penalty of burning, total loss of property, and no allowance for recantation. With this end to Henry's flirtation with the Lutherans and the collapse of negotiations, Barnes was dispensable. The occasion for Barnes' demise was once again a sermon contest with a prelate, this time Bishop Gardiner of Winchester. Barnes was burned at the stake along with two other leading English Lutherans as heretics. At the same time three Catholic theologians who had defended Catherine in the divorce proceedings were hanged as traitors for alleged papism. In his drive for supremacy, Henry VIII was an equal opportunity executioner.

From Cambridge the early Protestant movement spread to Oxford. Lutheran ideas were also influencing London merchants and their colleagues in the English business colony in Antwerp as well as the German merchants in London who received Luther's tracts from home. On the one hand this facilitated the importation of Protestant books and ideas into England through international merchants, but on the other hand Catholic propagandists could play on English xenophobia by portraying Protestantism as foreign. Nevertheless, in the Netherlands and elsewhere outside the control of the English king and his bishops, Protestant Bible translators and publicists worked with enthusiasm.

Chief among these scholars was William Tyndale (ca. 1494–1536). His proposal around 1522 to translate the Bible into English was rejected by Cuthbert Tunstall, the bishop of London. Tunstall was one of the first to recognize the danger of printing to the old faith. He is reputed to have said "we must root out printing or printing will root out us" (Brigdon 1992: 157). Tunstall's insight was not unique. "Bishop Nix of Norwich is alleged to have said, with reference to Tyndale's New Testament, 'it will undo us all.' " And from the other side, "John Foxe attributed the success of the Reformation . . . to the fact that 'God had opened the press to preach'." Within a year after the accession of Edward VI presses and publications increased markedly in London (Loades 1992: 57–8).

Tyndale went to Hamburg and Wittenberg, and then to Antwerp. In 1535 he was betrayed to the imperial authorities, arrested, strangled, and burned at the stake. Tyndale was a linguistic genius who, it was said, could speak fluently in Hebrew, Greek, Latin, Italian, Spanish, English, and French. From his time in Germany and his translations of Luther, it is obvious that he also knew German. Tyndale never returned to England, but his translation and publishing work were supported by large subsidies from English merchants. This connection became explicit in the latter years of his life when his refuge in Antwerp was in the English house of the Merchant Adventurers there.

Tyndale's translations of the Bible were extremely influential and have continued to influence English Bible translations up to the present. His New Testament printed in 1525 and revised in successive years flooded into England, to the anger and frustration of Tunstall and More. Just as Luther had pointed out in the first of the Ninety-Five Theses that the sacrament of penance rested on a mistranslation of the Greek, so too did Tyndale translate the Greek *metanoeite* by "repent" instead of the Vulgate's "do penance" (*poenitentiam agite*). Likewise, just as Luther consistently used "congregation" or "community" instead of "church," so Tyndale translated the Greek *ekklesia* as "congregation." The Catholic establishment was further undermined by Tyndale's translation of the Greek *presbyteros* as "elder" rather than as "priest." Once again we are reminded of the description of the Reformation as a "language event," for the laity were given the Bible not only in their language but in a text that did not even mention priests and the church! The impact of Tyndale's work is reflected in the words of Edward Fox, bishop of Hereford, addressed to his fellow bishops: "Make not yourselves the laughing-stock of the world; light is sprung up, and is scattering all the clouds. The lay people know the Scriptures better than many of us" (Dickens 1991: 95).

Along with biblical translation Tyndale also made Luther available in English (Cargill Thompson 1979). Since Luther's writings were banned, Tyndale's translations did not present them as the works of Luther. This was not plagiarism but both the better part of valor and clever marketing – Catholics could read and be inspired by Luther's celebrated *Preface to Romans* without knowing it was by the arch-heretic. Tyndale not only included this piece in his New Testament but also published it separately. He also translated and incorporated many of the other prefaces from Luther's Bible. Thomas More, in spite of his great erudition, never realized this. The further irony is that these prefaces appeared in the so-called Matthew Bible "issued by royal permission and even publicly read in church by and to people who would have been shocked to think they were listening to the authentic word of Martin Luther" (Rupp 1966: 50; Hall 1979: 115).

Miles Coverdale (1488–1568), initially an Augustinian friar at Cambridge influenced by Barnes, worked with Tyndale on the translation of the Old Testament, and was responsible for the first complete English translation of the Bible (1535). Largely through the influence of Thomas Cromwell (ca. 1485–1540), Henry's vicar general of the English Church, and archbishop Thomas Cranmer (1489–1556), the king was persuaded to put the Bible in all the churches. This was a step that could not be retracted.

Even Henry VIII's Catholic reaction of his last years could not halt the Protestant advance. The religious phraseology in middle-class wills of the time indicates the decline of saint worship and the advance of Protestant convictions (Dickens 1991: 214–15; Brigdon 1992: 380–92, 411–16, 483–6, 628–32; Duffy 1992: ch. 15 is not convinced). In particular, the 1530 will of William Tracy was an inspiration to evangelical circles where it circulated in mansucript copies. It was soon printed in Antwerp with a commentary. In November 1530 Tracy's will was convicted of heresy, and since Tracy was dead and therefore could not repent, his body was exhumed and burned as the corpse of a heretic. Tracy had written a "Lutheran" will: "I commit myself to God and his mercy, believing, without any doubt or mistrust, that by his grace and the merits of Jesus Christ, and by the virtues of his passion and of his resurrection, I have and shall have remission of all my sins and resurrection of my body and soul" (Haigh 1993: 70 argues this is unique).

Protestant convictions were present even in the court and among the tutors of Henry's son, Edward VI. With the death of Henry in 1547, the English Reformation had a period of six years for development under Edward VI and his advisors. During this time Cranmer presented the English people with his prayer books (the first in 1549, the second in 1552), the latter of which was a distinctly Protestant expression of worship and theology more Swiss than German.

The above sketch of Protestant influences and development in England cannot of course be divorced from the energetic reign of

Henry VIII (1491–1547) who became king in 1509. His father, Henry VII, had victoriously concluded the English civil war, the War of the Roses, and established the Tudor dynasty. Like his father, Henry VIII took his Catholicism very seriously and in 1521 published a tract against Luther titled *Assertio Septem Sacramentorum* ("Assertion of the Seven Sacraments," probably ghost-written) for which Pope Leo X awarded Henry the title "Defender of the Faith." Henry's defense of the seven sacraments not only indicates his life-long zealousness for the Catholic faith, in particular the doctrine of transubstantiation, but also reminds us once again of the centrality of this issue to Reformation controversies. Henry also saw in Luther's priesthood of all believers a threat to authority, civil as well as ecclesiastical. Of course it was not so long before Henry's blast against Luther seemed all too ironic as Henry attacked the papacy and divorced Catherine (marriage being one of the sacraments he had recently defended). His *Assertion of the Seven Sacraments* also proved an embarrassment to his later efforts to ally with the German Lutherans.

The King's Great Matter

Henry's break with Rome was not theological but personal and political. There are indications that Henry was a sexual athlete, but perhaps no more so than other monarchs. Henry VII was concerned to provide stability, prestige, and power to the fledgling Tudor house. He pursued this through long diplomatic wrangling for an alliance with Spain that was cemented by the marriage of Catherine of Aragon to his first son, Arthur. But five months after the marriage, the young Arthur died. In order not to lose his new connection to one of the oldest and most powerful houses of Europe, Henry immediately proposed that his second son, Henry (later Henry VIII), marry the young widow. Since Leviticus 18: 6–18 prohibited marriages within close relationships, a special papal dispensation for the marriage of Henry and Catherine was obtained from Pope Julius II.

Henry and Catherine were married in 1509. Of Catherine's numerous pregnancies only one child survived, Mary Tudor, born in 1516. By 1525, the queen was forty and there appeared no hope for further children. In the meantime Henry was involved with a variety of mistresses, and then became infatuated with Anne Boleyn, one of the ladies at court and sister to one of his earlier mistresses. It has been argued that his growing desire to be rid of Catherine and to remarry was motivated not just by his intense attraction to Anne Boleyn, but primarily by concern for the stability of the Tudor reign and England itself. He needed a son to succeed him in order to avoid the spectre of civil war over the succession, and the many problems foreseen if his daughter succeeded him. The only previous attempt to pass the English crown to a woman, Mathilda, the daughter of Henry I (d. 1135) had resulted in a ruinous civil war lasting 19 years.

Henry appealed to Pope Clement VII to annull his marriage with Catherine on the biblical basis that it was invalid to marry a deceased brother's widow (Leviticus 20: 21: "If a man takes his brother's wife, it is impiety; he has uncovered his brother's nakedness, they shall be childless"). This appeal put the pope in an extremely difficult situation. Doctrinally it would be awkward, to say the least, for the pope to grant Henry's request because that would impugn the decision of a prior pope to allow the marriage and thereby raise the question of papal fallibility, already sharply put by Luther. More to the point, perhaps, in explaining the pope's hesitation, was that at this time (1527, just asfter the sack of Rome) the pope was the virtual prisoner in Rome of the Emperor Charles V, Catherine's nephew.

Henry's rage at Cardinal Wolsey for failing to persuade the pope to his cause led to Wolsey's downfall. Wolsey himself recognized the truth in the adage of the times: *quia indignatio principis mors est* ("for the wrath of the king is death" – Proverbs 16: 14). At the end Wolsey ruefully reflected: "But if I had served God as diligently as I had done the King, he would not have given me over in my grey hairs" (Cavendish 1964: 141, 183). In 1529 Thomas More (1478–1535) replaced Wolsey as Lord Chancellor.

Thomas Cromwell (ca. 1485–1540), who gained the favor of the king in spite of having been in the service of Wolsey, followed the suggestion of Thomas Cranmer, and finally achieved the king's desire by appealing to the universities of England and Europe for a decision on the marriage case. Cromwell also suggested that the crown displace the pope as head of the church in England. The English court granted the dispensation for Henry's annulment in 1533. The pope responded by annulling the annulment and excommunicating Henry. In turn, Henry replied in 1534 with the Act of Supremacy which appointed the king and his successors "the only Supreme Head on earth of the Church of England . . . [including] full power and authority . . . to visit, repress, redress, reform, order, correct, restrain, and amend all . . . heresies" (Bray 1994: 114). Henry's severance of the English church from the papacy and subjugation of it to the crown in parliament depended on something more than his desire for divorce: the growth of antipapal and Erastian political opinion. Erastianism, named after the

Swiss theologian Thomas Erastus (1524–83), posits the authority of the state over the church, including subjecting excommunication to state approval. The medieval forerunner of Erastianism was Marsiglio of Padua (ca. 1275–1342), whose argument for the subordination of the church to the state (*Defensor pacis*, 1324) was a treasure trove of texts for the propagandists supporting Henry VIII (Dickens 1991: 106–08).

This decisive break of the English church from Rome was accompanied by a loyalty oath to the king. Thomas More lost his head in 1535 for refusing to sign it. More, so often popularly portrayed as the warm and courageous humanist, defender of Erasmus, and dreamer of perfect societies (in his *Utopia*), was an "intransigent champion of Catholic orthodoxy" for whom "the heretic's death at the stake was of little moment, because he was already destined for the fire eternal." During More's two and a half years as chancellor he fought against the availability of Scripture and worked to eradicate heresy, that is, heretics (Brigdon 1992: 179–81; Haigh 1993: 67). More's famous silence before the Act of Supremacy is revealing of his thought. One answer would jeopardize his conscience; the other answer would jeopardize his life. Since to court death when it could be avoided was the sin of suicide, he kept silent. This was neither consent nor provable treasonous dissent; but it was an irritation to the king, who granted More permanent silence. More went to his death with dignity and humor. Approaching the rickety scaffold, More said to his guard: "I pray you, Master Lieutenant, see me safe up and, for my coming down, let me shift for myself." And to the axeman, he said: "Pluck up thy spirits, man, and be not afraid to do thine office. My neck is very short. Take heed therefore thou strike not awry, for saving of thine honesty" (Roper 1964: 254). Decapitation is not as easy as the movies suggest. It was not unusual for unskilled executioners to need two or more strokes to accomplish their job, as, for example, with Mary Queen of Scots.

The Act of Supremacy was a constitutional break from papal authority, not an introduction of Protestantism. Thus while Henry utilized to his advantage the anticlerical, especially the antipapal, sentiments of his people, he reaffirmed Catholic dogma in the Statute of Six Articles in 1539 (Bray 1994: 222–32). The Six Articles maintained transubstantiation, communion of one kind for the laity, clerical celibacy, sanctity of monastic vows, necessity of auricular confession, and private masses; and declared the denial of any of these to be heresy. As mentioned above, this was a penal act with the death penalty for denying transubstantiation.

Henry further consolidated his position as head of the English church by suppressing first the smaller and then the larger monasteries in 1536 and 1539. The dissolution of the monasteries, which sadly led to the destruction of so much art and architecture, effectively eliminated the last refuge of papism (monasticism did not spring back during Mary's reign), and thus to some degree smoothed the way for Protestant development. Furthermore, it enriched the king's treasury and by selling the monastic lands to wealthy laity it ensured lay self-interest against future reintroduction of monasticism.

Passions, Politics, and Piety

While Henry's passions have provided raw material for movies, few historians would rely on them to explain the conception of the English Reformation. Henry's divorce "did not alone cause the Reformation; it did not even, if we like, play any large part in bringing about a movement which rested on national feeling and the scandal of a corrupt Church; but without it there would still have been no Reformation because the powerful intercession of the crown would have been against it and not for it" (Elton 1969: 114). Thus Henry's wives and their children have a legitimate place in the story of the development of English Protestantism.

On 25 January 1533, Henry secretly married Anne Boleyn (ca. 1501–36), now pregnant with Elizabeth who would be born in September. It was, of course, crucial to Henry that his expected heir be born legitimate. In March the statute restraining appeals to Rome was passed, and this made possible Henry's divorce from Catherine. Anne was crowned queen on 1 June 1533, to the anger of many English-women and the open snub of Thomas More who did not attend (Brigdon 1992: 211). More realized the danger of refusing to endorse the king's action by not attending the coronation, but conscience was as important to him as it was to Luther. In responding to the bishops' request he attend, More paraphrased the classic tale of the ruler's dilemma of what to do with a virgin convicted of a capital crime when it was against the law to execute a virgin. A councilor solved the ruler's perplexity with the advice: "Let her first be deflowered and then after may she be devoured" (Roper 1964: 229–30). More could accept his death but not the "deflowering" of conscience he saw occurring to so many all around him.

Anne was not merely the catalyst for Henry's break from Rome, but – it has long been argued – an advocate for evangelical views with Henry and at court. Her family had sheltered and supported Thomas Cranmer who became archbishop of Canterbury, and she herself promoted Protestant bishops. Some of her chaplains became future Protestant leaders in England, including Matthew Parker, archbishop of Canterbury under her daughter Elizabeth. Numerous anecdotes from the time indicate her patronage of evangelical clergy, refugees, and booksellers as well as her enthusiasm for French and English Bibles (Brigdon 1992: 221–3; Orth 1993: 424–5). Unfortunately for Anne, Henry's passion rapidly waned as their child was a girl, and future pregnancies ended in miscarriages. As long as Catherine lived, Anne was secure as queen since the repudiation of her marriage would imply the validity of the marriage to Catherine. Catherine died in January 1536. On 17 May Cranmer declared Anne's marriage void, and on 19 May she was beheaded on charges of adultery. Her guilt or innocence of these charges remains a disputed question.

On 30 May Henry married Jane Seymour, a lady of the court. In October, Henry at last had a son – Edward – whose birth cost his mother's life. It is of interest for the course of the Reformation in both France and Scotland that after the defeat of James V of Scotland at Solway Moss (1542), Henry proposed that Mary Stuart wed Edward. The Scots however preferred alliance with England's enemy France, and she was betrothed to the dauphin, Francis II of France.

Henry next married Anne of Cleves, on 6 January 1540 at the prompting of Cromwell to establish a political alliance with the duchy of Cleves against the emperor and on the basis of an all too flattering portrait of her painted by Holbein. When she arrived in England Henry was immediately displeased with both her and Cromwell. By the end of June, Henry had divorced her, and Cromwell was on the way to the scaffold for this and other advice the king did not like. In August 1540 Henry married Catherine Howard. She seems to have lacked discretion about the court, and her adultery was the cause for her beheading in February 1542 on the charge of treason. Catherine Parr, the king's last wife whom he married in June 1543, had the good sense to remain in both his political and marital beds and thus outlived him. Henry himself died on 27 January 1547, and the Tudor succession according to earlier legislation and the king's will passed to his children Edward, Mary, and Elizabeth, in that order.

Edward VI and Protestant Progress

Edward VI came to the throne at the age of nine; always sickly, he died in 1553. Under Edward, or more accurately his advisors, the Reformation was established in England. His uncle, Edward Seymour, earl of

Hertford, appointed lord protector and duke of Somerset, immediately ended all persecution of Protestants and led the parliament in repealing most of the treason and heresy laws, including the Six Articles. This in turn not only stimulated the return of those Protestants who had fled under Henry VIII but also attracted continental reformers, most of whom were of Zwinglian persuasion. Such prominent reformers as Martin Bucer of Strasbourg and Peter Martyr Vermigli of Italy were invited, respectively, to Cambridge and Oxford universities. Their students later played important roles during Elizabeth's reign.

Lutheran influences in England, long despised by Henry VIII, were already waning by this time due to a variety of political, personal, and theological factors including the failure of Anglo-German alliance and the repeated frustrating of Melanchthon's visits to England. Theologically, the English Reformers were developing an understanding of the eucharist, perhaps influenced by earlier Lollard criticisms of medieval Catholicism, that was more sympathetic to Zwinglian than Lutheran convictions (MacCulloch 1992: 171–4). "The Anglican Church did not follow any single Continental model, but the two men who exercised the greatest influence, partly though Cranmer and partly direct to other Englishmen, were Heinrich Bullinger and Martin Bucer" (Loades 1992: 71).

It was Martin Bucer's opposition to the Augsburg Interim (1548) that led to his banishment from Strasbourg and acceptance of Cranmer's invitation to Cambridge where he became regius professor in 1549. Here he contributed his irenic theological acumen (recall his earlier efforts to bridge the gap between Lutherans and Zwinglians with the Wittenberg concord) to the revising of the Book of Common Prayer, the touchstone of Anglican identity up to the present. Bucer's vision of the permeation of the Christian faith through the whole of society found final expression in his *De Regno Christi* ("On the Kingdom of Christ"). This was a program for reform of the church and the renewal of society, including social welfare for the poor. Bucer's death in February 1551 precluded his potential contribution toward an Anglo-continental Protestantism. Edward VI died two years later, and the consequent exile of Protestants to centers of Calvinist influence led upon their return to a more radical understanding of Reformation than Bucer's. The extent of Bucer's influence in England is currently under re-examination (Wright 1993: 2: 523–32; Hall 1994: 144–60).

The architect of English Protestantism, however, was Henry's archbishop of Canterbury, Thomas Cranmer, whose Protestant orientation found significant expression under Edward. Clerical marriage now flourished. Cranmer himself had been secretly married since 1532 to Margaret Osiander, niece of the German Lutheran theologian, Andreas Osiander. This was before Cranmer was recalled by Henry from the continent to be archbishop of Canterbury, after which Margaret was kept so discreetly in the background that the legend arose that Cranmer carried her about in a box. Cranmer's first Prayer Book of 1549 was revised in 1552. This Book of Common Prayer set the tone of an English Protestantism that avoided extremes in doctrine and liturgy, but excluded the ambiguities which had allowed Catholics to worship according to the 1549 edition. The eucharist was now presented in Swiss memorial terms (Bray 1994: 271–6; Brooks 1965; Nijenhuis 1972: 1–22). Likewise in 1553, Cranmer produced a statement of faith for the English church that represented a compromise between the Lutheran and Calvinist theologies. These Forty-Two Articles were the foundation for the later Thirty-Nine Articles that defined the Church of England under Elizabeth I, and continue to inform the Anglican church today (Bray 1994: 284–311).

Catholic bishops were replaced by Protestants, some of whom, like John Hooper (1495–1555) at Gloucester, were proto-puritans and others, like John Knox, more radical Protestants. Cranmer's third major project after revision of the Prayer Book and the Forty-Two Articles was the revision of canon law. The *Reformatio legum ecclesiasticarum* (1552) was designed to replace the medieval Catholic basis of society with Reformed discipline, the third "mark" of the church after true doctrine and right use of the sacraments (Spalding 1992). The death of Edward in 1553 prevented its enactment. The reform of the English church moved rapidly; perhaps too rapidly, for it depended upon the continuing health of Edward which was never very good.

The anxiety that Protestant reforms would be undone after Edward's death by the ascent of Mary Tudor, a staunch Catholic, to the throne, led Edward and Somerset's successor, John Dudley, the duke of Northumberland, to conspire to exclude Mary from the succession on the grounds that she was illegitimate as the daughter of Catherine. In her stead they proposed Lady Jane Grey (1537–54), the Protestant grandniece of Henry VIII and daughter-in-law of Northumberland. Unfortunately for the innocent, youthful Jane Grey, this plan ran aground on the loyalty of the English to the Tudor succession. Queen for a day, or more precisely nine days, this plot cost her and the leadership of Edwardian Protestantism – Hooper, Coverdale, Latimer, Cranmer, and Ridley – their lives. Knox fled to the continent and ended up in Geneva where he bided his time for a fiery return.

Mary Tudor and Protestant Regress

The accession of Mary Tudor to the English throne severely threatened the English Reformation. Yet, ironically, Mary's overwhelming concern for the Roman Catholic faith served to strengthen the Protestant cause. By her marriage to Philip of Spain she identified Catholicism with that unpopular foreign power; by her reliance upon her cousin Reginald Cardinal Pole and his efforts to introduce the Counter-Reformation, she became more unpopular; by attempting to restore monastic lands to the church, she alienated the landed class which had bought them; by persecuting Protestant leaders without proceeding to eradicate Protestantism itself, she created an army of martyrs celebrated in John Foxe's influential *Acts and Monuments*; and by the exile of some 800 leading Protestants to Frankfurt, Geneva, and Strasbourg, she created an army of zealous Protestants trained in continental Protestantism eager to return and recapture England for the evangelical faith.

Mary Tudor reigned only five years (1553–8), but her brief reign left an indelible antagonism in English minds toward all things Catholic and Spanish. The daughter of Catherine of Aragon, she was reared Catholic, and from a purely nontheological perspective had to be Catholic in order to be the legitimate heir to the throne. She became queen because she was Henry's daughter and the English were loyal to the Tudor crown. But she failed to understand this, and the consequences were disastrous. Ironically, Mary's personal traits were the most attractive of all the Tudors. She was personally gentle, and inclined to mercy and generosity; remarkable traits in light of the treatment of her mother and herself by her father and brother. Her failings consisted primarily of her obsession with her Catholicism and her Spanish descent. Initially welcomed by her people, she died hated by nearly all.

From Mary's perspective, her vocation was to save her people from mortal sin by restoring them to papal obedience. She chose to accomplish this by a foreign policy that allied England with Spain. The Habsburg emperor Charles V was more than willing to help, and decided that his son, Philip II of Spain, should do his bit for the empire and Catholicism by marrying Mary and bringing England into the Habsburg orbit. The English were not at all pleased, for although they were by no means wedded to the recent Edwardian turn to Protestantism, they hated foreign intervention and still retained a residual dislike of papal and clerical rule. Thus as Mary's plans advanced, she and her counselors were always sniffing conspiracy and rebellion in the air. In fact, in the first months of 1554 Sir Thomas Wyatt led a rebellion of some 3,000 men into London. They were overcome and the leaders executed. Elizabeth Tudor, whom Mary regarded as "the little bastard," almost suffered the same fate, but was instead imprisoned in the Tower.

Since parliament balked at Mary's plans to restore Catholicism, she proceeded, ironically, to use her father's break from Rome to restore Rome to England. She acted as supreme head of the church to remove Protestant clergy from their churches, usually on the grounds that they had broken the vow of celibacy. The mass was restored, and with the return of Cardinal Pole the old heresy laws were reinstated accompanied with ferocious new treason laws. Parliament at last agreed to repeal all the antipapal and anti-Roman legislation passed since the days of Henry. Thereby a legal basis was provided for the Marian persecutions.

Ironically, the Spaniards, including Philip II and Charles V, were against persecution for policy reasons. But Mary and Cardinal Pole, perhaps sincerely believing that they were saving English souls from damnation, inspired heresy trials that led to the burnings of nearly 300 dissenters, who of course became martyrs for the Protestant faith. Nearly all of these Protestants went to their death for denying the mass (Brigdon 1992: 608–12). Bishops Ridley and Latimer were burned at the same place and time – Ridley undergoing a long agony because his pile burned slowly in the dampness. Archbishop Cranmer was forced to watch the burning of his friends and fellow Protestants. Cranmer himself went through a series of recantations before his own ordeal. At the end he died – to the shock and displeasure of his persecutors – not as a recanted heretic but as a repentant evangelical, steadily holding his hand that had signed recantations in the fire until he collapsed and died. His enemies found something in the ashes which they claimed was Cranmer's heart that could not burn because of its wickedness.

In September 1555 Philip returned to Spain, leaving Mary childless and disconsolate. War between Spain and France broke out, and Mary in providing assistance to Philip ended up losing Calais, the last remnant of England's medieval empire on the continent. From a practical point of view Calais was no loss, for it had been expensive to maintain and served no purpose to the English. But from a symbolic point of view, its loss was a blow to English pride and eroded the last vestiges of loyalty to Mary. In November 1558, Mary died. Cardinal Pole died 12 hours later. With their deaths the Catholic reaction was over. Mary had succeeded in destroying the two things most dear to her – the old religion and the Spanish alliance. Elizabeth learned from her sister's failure.

Elizabeth I and the *Via Media*

The reign of Elizabeth Tudor (1558–1603) may well be described as a 45-year love affair between the queen and the English, for it was a rare correspondence of purpose and program between a monarch and a people. Under Elizabeth, England turned Protestant, became a leading nation of Europe, won a world empire, and experienced a cultural renaissance (Spitz 1971: 523).

Elizabeth came to the throne at the age of twenty-five, already wise beyond her years. Just as Mary had to be Catholic in order to be a legitimate ruler, so Elizabeth had to be Protestant as she was the daughter of Anne Boleyn. Her diplomatic skill, evident in all she did, was at times tested by the pressure on her to marry for the sake of the realm, a pressure exerted not only by various lovers but by parliament as well. Eric XIV of Sweden in his search for an ally outside the Baltic area unsuccessfully proposed marriage. Her brother-in-law, Philip II, offered his services, but Elizabeth was too smart to repeat Mary's mistake. And the Valois princes, Henry of Anjou and Francis of Alençon, also tried their hands at a marriage alliance. Her passionate lover, Robert Dudley, Earl of Leicester, was not only spoiled and undependable, but was surrounded by public scandal that included the death of his wife under mysterious circumstances. Elizabeth was strongly attracted to him but ruled her heart with her head, putting her reign above her personal feelings.

Elizabeth could speak French, Latin, and Italian, and was equally skilled in double-talk. Thus she was able not only to keep many ambitious men living in hope and in her service, but also to control the factions in her court and countryside. Likewise in international politics she needed allies to forestall the economic isolation of England and to counter the growing French influence in Scotland. The constant difficulty of diplomacy was that national interest and religious conviction did not always coincide. Elizabeth stressed theology and confessional unity in her dealings with the German Protestant princes, but although her envoys said she accepted the Augsburg confession, she did not sign it. "It is in principle hard to tell if Elizabeth's diplomacy was motivated by 'True Faith', i.e. from idealistic defence of Protestantism, or from secular motives, which might be characterized as in the

'National Interest' " (Kouri 1987: 427). To Protestants, the "virgin queen" was a heroic Judith; to Catholics she was a Jezebel, a servant of infamy, and the refuge of evil men.

Elizabeth's closest advisors were always Protestants, and nearly always more Protestant than she. William Cecil, later Lord Burghley, was a moderate Protestant who served first as secretary of state and then as treasurer for nearly all of Elizabeth's reign. Her secretary of state from 1573 to 1590, Sir Francis Walsingham, followed a policy of active support for Protestants on the continent, especially the Dutch Reformed and the French Huguenots. He was also energetic in ferreting out Roman Catholic plots against Elizabeth, and developed an elaborate counter-espionage system directed particularly against the Spanish and the Jesuits.

Elizabeth sought a "middle way" between the religious extremes that not only wracked England but were erupting in wars of religion on the continent. Her pursuit of moderation was intended to provide England the peace necessary for development after the Edwardian and Marian upheavals. She knew by both experience and observation the dangers inherent in rapid religious change. She claimed she would rather hear a thousand masses than be guilty of millions of crimes done by some who suppressed masses. Thus Elizabeth held both Catholics and radical Protestants in check by fostering an Anglican settlement in doctrine and discipline. This is what prompted John Knox to observe that Elizabeth was "neither good Protestant nor yet resolute papist" (Spitz 1971: 525). Perhaps Knox knew of ministers like the vicar of Bray who kept his living through all the changes from Henry VIII to Elizabeth I. When accused of being an "unconstant changeling," Aleyn of Bray responded: "Not so, for I have always kept my principle, which is this, to live and die the vicar of Bray" (Pallier 1977: 35).

The *via media* addressed both the conservative Catholic majority and the urban Protestant minority through expressions each could read in their own way. The retention of Catholic vestments and liturgy allowed the traditional, illiterate person to experience Anglican worship much as he or she had experienced Catholic worship. At the same time, the use of English instead of Latin allowed the literate Protestant to hear a Reformation message in the sermons and prayers set within a Reformed theology framed by the Thirty-Nine Articles. The language of the eucharist was "a masterpiece of social engineering" that suggested a real presence to conservatives and a memorial communion à la Zurich to Protestants. The communicant would hear the words: "'The body of our Lord Jesus Christ, which was given for thee, preserve thy body unto everlasting life' (1549). 'Take and eat this in remembrance that Christ died for thee, and feed on him in thy heart by faith with thanksgiving' (1552)" (MacCulloch 1990: 30).

Elizabeth appointed Matthew Parker, a moderate, as archbishop of Canterbury. Parker was consecrated archbishop by three former bishops who had been expelled by Mary; thus the Anglican church retained apostolic succession. Parker had been a follower of Martin Bucer, was married, and knew well many of the Marian exiles who were now returning to England. It was from these Marian exiles that Elizabeth had to choose most of her bishops. They were of course more radical in religion than Elizabeth.

It was parliament that guaranteed the success of the queen's policy. In April 1559 parliament passed the Act of Supremacy that recognized the queen as head of the English church. All royal officials, judges, and the clergy had to take a loyalty oath acknowledging the supremacy of the crown over the church on pain of losing their office. Elizabeth, however, sensitive to the male chauvinism of the age which precluded a woman filling a priestly or ecclesiastical function, took the title "Supreme Governor" rather than "Supreme Head." To uphold the authority of any foreign prince or prelate was high treason, punishable by death. Mary's Catholic legislation was rescinded, and Edward VI's second Book of Common Prayer was reintroduced with some modifications. The retention by the Prayer Book of images, crucifixes, and vestments perhaps made it more palatable to Catholics but offended the more radical Protestants. Those clergy who refused to conform were replaced so that eventually appointees amenable to Elizabeth filled the ecclesiastical sees.

The second parliament of 1563 reaffirmed the Act of Uniformity and passed measures for its strict enforcement. The Forty-Two Articles were revised to the Thirty-Nine Articles. Elizabeth herself was involved in this revision. The articles were designed to accommodate the major evangelical theologies by denying transubstantiation on the one hand and Zwinglian symbolism on the other hand, while remaining open to the range of Lutheran and Calvinist interpretations. The Scriptures were declared the source and norm of faith, and the creeds were accepted because they may be proved by Scripture. General or ecumenical councils were declared not infallible in themselves. The article on predestination was presented in a masterfully ambiguous way.

This "Elizabethan Settlement" offended the more radical Protestants who desired to purify the church of all Roman Catholic vestiges. Those Protestants who remained within the Church of England while advocating removal of Catholic ceremonies and forms (vestments, sign of the cross, saints' days, etc.) came to be known as Puritans. Controversy over the use of vestments began already with the episcopal consecration of John Hooper during Edward's reign. The controversy, triggered by Hooper's rejection of vestments as "popish rags," focused on the theological status of *adiaphora*, or "indifferent matters." Hooper did not deny the possibility of *adiaphora*, but argued their tendency to become normative over time. If such things as vestments "be kept in the Church as things indifferent, at length they will be maintained as things necessary" (Steinmetz 1971: 148). At issue in the seemingly trivial "Vestiarian controversy" in the 1560s was the suggestion of the continuation of a priestly order symbolized by separate clerical dress within the Reformed church. This bitter controversy lasted into the seventeenth century (Collinson 1967: 60–72).

The term "puritan" has come to mean many things to many people, and even historically it is difficult to give precise definition to the label. Disparate expressions at least had in common the concern to purify the church from unscriptural practices and forms. The returning Marian exiles desired to replace Elizabeth's *via media* by the church rigorously normed by Scripture which they had witnessed in Zurich and Geneva. "The Puritans did not take the attitude that what is not forbidden is permitted. They adhered to the far more stringent principle that what is not commanded is forbidden" (Steinmetz 1971: 145). Theodore Beza, Calvin's successor and professor at the Geneva Academy, claimed apostolic warrant for the principle that "nothing at all should be added to the simplicity of the apostolic church." Among Beza's audience were the Englishmen Thomas Cartwright and Walter Travers and the Scot Andrew Melville (Collinson 1967: 110–11). The Puritans were the epitomy of literate Protestantism and were consequently influential at the court and in the universities where "they formed the front line against the Counter-Reformation" (Loades 1992: 59). The Puritans, by the way, should not be thought of in terms of later "Victorian" morality; they were not "puritanical" in the word's popular senses of "moralistic" and "prudish."

Those Protestants who rejected episcopal church polity and argued for clerical equality were called Presbyterians. And those who wanted all religious authority to be in local hands came to be called Congregationalists, Separatists, or Independents. It was the Presbyterians who above all adhered to Calvin's views in theology, discipline, and the Genevan model of the church truly reformed. Their greatest impact was in the 1570s and 1580s, but the Calvinist antipathy to royal supremacy restricted their influence. Some Puritans became increasingly radicalized to the point of separation from the establishment. The most well-known of these leaders was Robert Browne. He so symbolized the movement that Separatists were also called "Brownists." After finding refuge in the Netherlands in 1582 he published his celebrated tract *Reformation without Tarrying for Any*. The theme is reminiscent of Karlstadt's understanding of reform, and it is of interest that while Browne himself returned to uniformity, some of his followers moved to espouse positions on free will and believer's baptism which suggest affinities with Dutch Anabaptism (MacCulloch 1990: 157–61; Pater 1984a: ch. 9).

The first systematic statement of Anglicanism was presented by John Jewel (1522–71), consecrated bishop of Salisbury in 1560, in his *Apology for the Anglican Church* published in 1562. Jewel's person and work were influential upon one of the poor boys he patronized, Richard Hooker (ca. 1554–1600) who became the apologist par excellence for the Elizabethan settlement of 1559. Hooker's masterful *Treatise on the Laws of Ecclesiastical Polity* places him among the most important theologians of the English church. In response to the Puritan conviction that whatever was not expressly commanded in Scripture was unlawful, he elaborated a theory of ecclesiastical and civil law resting upon reason and natural law that was influential upon future political writers such as John Locke (1632–1704).

Another important Elizabethan was John Foxe (1516–1587) who under Mary had been a religious refugee in Strasbourg, Frankfurt, and Basle. His history of Christian persecutions was first written in Latin and published in Strasbourg in 1554. An English translation in 1563 was titled *Acts and Monuments of Matters Happening in the Church*, and is commonly known as "Foxe's Book of Martyrs." Officially approved by the Elizabethan bishops, this work went through four editions in Foxe's lifetime. The book praised the heroism and endurance of Protestant martyrs under Mary and papist tyranny, and soon ranked next to the Bible in popularity. It is here we read that when the fire was lit under the Protestant martyrs, Ridley and Latimer, Latimer said: "Be of good cheer, Ridley; and play the man. We shall this day, by God's grace, light up such a candle in England, as, I trust, will never be put out." Foxe's crimson martyrology helped to create a specifically Protestant anti-Roman Catholic consciousness that blended with the nationalistic sentiment of the Protestant English-speaking world.

Although by the end of Elizabeth's reign Roman Catholics were a small minority of mainly conservative upper nobility in England, the years from 1569 to the destruction of the Spanish Armada in 1588 were filled with perceptions of a Catholic menace. A Catholic uprising in 1569 in the north, instigated by the duke of Norfolk to advance the cause of Mary Stuart, was quickly put down. Perceptions of internal and external conspiracies to overthrow the crown were stimulated by the papal bull *Regnans in excelsis* excommunicating and deposing Elizabeth in 1570, the Ridolfi plot discovered in 1571, and the St Bartholomew's Day massacre in 1572. The last of these raised the spectre of an international conspiracy to destroy Protestantism throughout Europe. After 1575 there was growing concern that Roman Catholic priests sent from Douai (the English seminary in the Spanish Netherlands founded in 1568 by the Oxford exile William Allen) and Jesuits sent from the English College in Rome were an international fifth column for the elimination of Elizabeth. Pope Pius V made it clear that his power extended over all nations and that since Elizabeth was a slave of vice, a usurper of the pope's office, and a "Calvinist," she was cut off from the body of Christ and all subjects were absolved from oaths of allegiance to her. Rejection of royal supremacy was now an act of treason. It was the menace of Spanish invasion in 1587 that led Elizabeth finally and reluctantly to execute her cousin Mary Stuart who had been under house arrest for 19 years.

Elizabeth's course between the extremes of Catholicism and Calvinism was politically motivated because the former denied her legitimacy and the latter abolished the episcopacy that she believed supported monarchy. As her successor, James I, succinctly put it: "No bishop, no king." But she was not without religious sensibility herself. In her youth she had translated Marguerite d'Angoulême's *Mirror of a Sinful Soul*, and was appreciative of the liturgy. She held that as long as her subjects openly observed the laws of the land, their consciences should not be examined. When she banished the Jesuits in 1585, one of her motives was to temper public outrage against foreign conspiracies and thereby to minimize public attacks upon English Catholics. Like her father, Elizabeth determined the course of the Reformation in England in light of the dominant Tudor concern for royal supremacy. This concern necessitated denial of the ultramontane papacy, and shaped the course of events up to the Act of Toleration in 1689.

Mary Stuart (1542–1587) and the Reformation in Scotland

As in England, the earliest evangelical ideas in Scotland came from Luther via scholars trained in Germany, such as Patrick Hamilton who was burned as a heretic in 1528, and from those acquainted with Paris, where Luther's ideas were current by 1519. Again, as in England, merchants played a significant role in transmitting ideas; German and Scottish traders trafficked in Lutheran teachings and books as well as merchandise. But by the mid-1540s Swiss Reformed expressions of the gospel were taking the place of those from German Lutheranism. It is natural to assume that the prime source of Calvinist theology and ecclesiology influencing Scotland came directly from Geneva. After all, John Knox (ca. 1513–72), one of the Scottish Reformation leaders, had glowingly expressed his experience of the Genevan reform as "the most perfect school of Christ." However, the case can be made that the undoubted influence of Calvin upon Knox was "refracted through the prism of French Protestant experience" (Reid 1994: 197). The Scottish–French connection extended back to the thirteenth century and had been reaffirmed on the eve of the Reformation through the marriage of James V to Mary of Guise. The French crown employed Scottish mercenary archers. French monastic orders had daughter houses in Scotland. Scottish scholars taught in French universities. Knox himself was fluent in French, and preached in the Reformed churches in France. Also, the national church organization in France, in contrast to the city organization of Geneva, was more amenable to the Scottish situation. Finally, there is the circumstantial argument that the Scots confession and discipline bears close affinity to that of the French Huguenots. In its own way the royal connection between Scotland and France is important for the Scottish Reformation.

The Tudor struggle for royal supremacy is exemplified in the story of Mary Stuart, queen of Scotland. Mary was the daughter of James V (Stuart), king of Scotland. James's mother was Margaret Tudor, daughter of Henry VII and sister of Henry VIII. James's wife, the mother of Mary, was Mary of Lorraine from the powerful and very conservative French Guise family. These dynastic relationships suggest the threat Mary Stuart posed to the reign of Elizabeth.

When the English defeated the Scots at the battle of Solway Moss in 1542, Henry VIII attempted to cement Scotland to England by arranging a marriage between Edward and the infant Mary Stuart. Not surprisingly, this was rejected. In 1548 Mary was sent to France, the traditional enemy of England, where she was to be married to the dauphin, soon to become Francis II. When Francis died in 1560, the queen mother, Catherine de' Medici, did not want the rivalry of Mary whose relationship to the duke of Guise and his brother, the powerful cardinal of Lorraine, gave her too much power. The Guises themselves were in favor of Mary returning to Scotland to take up her crown because they believed she could also claim the throne of England and thus restore Catholicism there. In the meantime, a number of Scottish lords, together with John Knox, who had returned to Scotland in 1559, rose up and expelled the French from Scotland.

Unwelcome in France and suspect in Scotland, Mary Stuart returned to Scotland to take up her crown. She created partisans then, and does so even now among historians. Of her, the English historian G. R. Elton (1969: 279) wrote:

> It remains impossible so to speak about Mary Queen of Scots that all are satisfied; she had to the utmost the Stuart ability of attaching men's loyalties to herself despite the most outrageous and the most foolish of deeds. Of her famous beauty her surviving portraits provide little evidence. She was passionate, wilful, intelligent, given to violent moods of exaltation and depression, and entirely without common sense – one might say, entirely without moral sense. It was too much to expect that this young woman, reminder of the recently overthrown French domination and ardently catholic, should bring peace to the land.

Mary's immediate concern was not religion but dynastic politics. The Cardinal of Lorraine had even suggested she turn Protestant in order to achieve her claim to the English throne. And, indeed, for a while she was conciliatory towards the Protestants, a stance no doubt difficult in light of the tactless preaching Knox directed at her. This was the man who had called her mother, Mary of Guise, who was regent when Mary lived in France, an "unruly cow saddled by mistake." Knox expressed from the pulpit the Scottish outrage that Mary imported the "idolatrous mass" even if only for her court when he said that "one Mass was more fearful than if ten thousand armed enemies were landed in any part of the realm." No doubt Knox's hatred of all things French and Catholic was increased by his 19 months as a French galley slave after the defeat of the Scottish uprising at St Andrews in 1547. But Knox's opposition to Mary Stuart included also the fact that she was a woman. In his 1558 Genevan writing, *First Blast Against the Monstrous Regiment of Women*, Knox had declared that to "promote a woman to have rule above any realm is repugnant to nature, contumely to God, a thing most contrarious to His revealed will and approved ordinance, and finally it is the subversion of good order, of all equity and justice" (Spitz 1971: 465). Knox's target was the unholy trinity of Marys: Mary Tudor in England, Mary of Guise in Scotland, and Mary Stuart in France, all of whom represent the false church of Rome. Like other Reformed theologians, Knox blended the Old and New Testaments to create a vision of church and society as the theocratic new Israel. Apart from Knox's misogynism, he viewed the three Marys as Catholic tyrants, i.e. as idolatrous rulers, who must be actively resisted and deposed on pain of sin and the wrath of God against the whole community. Echoing Thomas Müntzer and the Münsterites, Knox suggests that the religious duty to revolt is incumbent on all true Christians. It is said that timing is everything. Unfortunately for Knox, his blast against Mary appeared at the beginning of Elizabeth's reign and made him persona non grata in England.

In 1564 Mary moved both to mollify the Scots' distaste for the rule of a woman and to strengthen her claim to the English throne. She married Henry Stuart, Lord Darnley and a grandson of Mary Stuart's own Tudor grandmother. Furthermore, since Lord Darnley had been born on English soil, as Mary Stuart had not, English law enabled him to inherit England. Even better for Mary, she fell madly in love with this strikingly handsome man whose contemptible character was not yet evident to her.

Soon after the marriage it became apparent that Darnley was unsuited not only for rule but even for normal human relationships. Alienated from her husband, Mary began to put her trust in her secretary, an Italian named David Riccio. Whether or not their relationship was innocent, Darnley became enraged with jealousy and with a gang broke into the queen's chamber and stabbed Riccio to death. Mary, then pregnant with her son, James, resolved to be avenged. In February 1567, Mary took her then ill husband to the house of Kirk o' Field near Edinburgh. She managed to be conveniently away when the house was blown up and Darnley, who survived the explosion, was murdered.

The conspiracy to kill Darnley was led by the Protestant James Bothwell, who took Mary to Dunbar where they lived together until he was divorced and they could be married in a Protestant rite in May. Catholic Europe was horrified, and the Scots were thoroughly fed up with a murderous and adulterous queen tainted with Catholicism. In June she was imprisoned in Loch Leven and forced to abdicate in favor of her son. Bothwell, himself not noted for constancy, deserted her and fled to Denmark. Although she managed to escape Loch Leven, she was unable to regain her crown. She fled to England and appealed to Elizabeth for help against the "rebels."

Mary Stuart thus put Elizabeth in an untenable position that even she could not temporize about indefinitely. Obviously, regicide was frowned on by all monarchs of the time. Restoration of Mary to her throne would alienate Scottish allies, but not to restore her would provide a focus for Catholic disaffection in England, as well as alienate other monarchs who regardless of religion did not wish to see people depose rulers. Elizabeth put Mary under house – rather, castle – arrest, until finally in 1586 the Elizabethan secret service produced documents that implicated Mary in a plot against the queen. Mary, Queen of Scots, was beheaded on 1 February 1587. She went to her death with great courage; holding her crucifix high and dressed in the red of martyrdom, she prayed for her enemies, mercy for Elizabeth, and grace for England. Her dynastic ambition was realized by her son, James VI of Scotland, who on the death of Elizabeth became James I of England.

Suggestions for Further Reading

Gerald Bray, ed., *Documents of the English Reformation*, Minneapolis: Fortress, 1994

Susan Brigdon, *London and the Reformation*, Oxford: Clarendon Press, 1992

Patrick Collinson, *The Elizabethan Puritan Movement*, Berkeley: University of California Press, 1967

Ian B. Cowan, *The Scottish Reformation: Church and Society in Sixteenth Century Scotland*, New York: St Martin's, 1982

A. G. Dickens, *The English Reformation*, 2nd edn, University Park: Pennsylvania State University Press, 1991

Eamon Duffy, *The Stripping of the Altars: Traditional Religion in England 1400–1580*, New Haven: Yale University Press, 1992

Christopher Haigh, *English Reformations: Religion, Politics, and Society under the Tudors*, Oxford: Clarendon Press, 1993

David Loades, *Revolution in Religion: The English Reformation 1530–1570*, Cardiff: University of Wales Press, 1992

Rosemary O'Day, *The Debate on the English Reformation*, London: Methuen, 1986

J. J. Scarisbrick, *The Reformation and the English People*, Oxford: Oxford University Press, 1984

14

Catholic Renewal and the Counter-Reformation

Men must be changed by religion, not religion by men.

Giles of Viterbo to the fifth Lateran council, 3 May 1512

Despite Pope Leo X's initial dismissal of the Reformation as nothing more than a drunken brawl among German monks, there was a growing realization even in the papacy that renewal and reform of the church could not be lightly brushed aside. Indeed, the rapidity of the reform movements throughout Europe raised apocalyptic visions in more than one curial mind. Pope Clement VII, who suffered the trauma of the sack of Rome in 1527, had a medal struck that depicted Christ bound to a column with the inscription *Post multa, plurima restant* – "After many things, even more remain." And just before his death, he commissioned Michelangelo to portray the last judgment on the front wall of the Sistine Chapel (Spitz 1971: 469).

Late Medieval Renewal Movements

It is important to recall here our earlier historiographical comments regarding the terms Catholic Reformation and Counter-Reformation. The Catholic renewal movement was not merely a reaction, a Counter-Reformation, to the Reformation. Before Luther there was already sharp criticism of the church that may be illustrated by the Italian proverb that the person who goes to Rome will lose his or her faith, and by the acrostic for Rome, *R[adix] O[mnium] M[alorum] A[varitia]*: "love of money is the root of all evil." As Giles of Viterbo proclaimed to Pope Julius II and the some 100 or so prelates assembled for the opening of the fifth Lateran council (1512–17): "Unless by this Council or by some other means we place a limit on our morals, unless we force our greedy desire for human things, the source of evils, to yield to the love of divine things, it is all over with Christendom" (Olin 1990: 57).

Giles's appeal for personal renewal as the key to reform and renewal of the church was characteristic of the Catholic reform efforts both before and after Luther. "Catholic spirituality at this time was highly individualistic and activist . . . The stress was on the individual's interior religious experience – on private prayer and meditation, self-discipline, personal sanctification and spiritual growth" (Olin 1990: 11). The late English Roman Catholic historian H. O. Evennett (1965: 61) emphasized the individualism of the Catholic reform movement. "What unites the various forms of Counter-Reformation spirituality can be said, I think, to be the stress on the individual's relation to God, . . . whose first object was not to 'reform the Church' . . . but to order their own lives to the doing of God's will and the bringing of benefit to their neighbor." Also: "It was exacting, in that it demanded continuous heroic effort at prayer and self-control and self-improvement and good works. . . . It closely linked active good works and self-improvement, and assumed the placing of a high value on the former in the sight of God for Justification" (Evennett 1970: 41). Individual saints became the norm in place of the collective of saints of the Middle Ages. The great individual saints, led by Ignatius of Loyola, John of the Cross, and Teresa of Avila, came to the fore even in the cosmos of village religiosity. These modern saints show a new way to God and to human perfection in personal and solitary discipleship (Schilling 1994: 21–2). It is of interest that what the early Catholic renewal movement perceived as the virtue to be inculcated and developed appeared to Luther as the very thing that needed reform. As argued earlier, to Luther the only gospel response to a failed piety of achievement was not its intensification but its abolition. Like ships passing in the night, Luther hammered at theological reform and Roman Catholic reformers hammered at ethical renewal. Catholic reformers, including the Jesuits, were convinced "that the primary means of healing the religious division was to instill in Catholics the desire for a more devout life" (O'Malley 1993: 278).

One of the most notorious and charismatic of the preachers who attempted to instill a more devout life was the Dominican prior, Girolamo Savonarola (1452–98), whose efforts to reform Florence in particular and the church in general led to conflict with the Borgia Pope Alexander VI and to the scaffold in 1498. Equally austere but more constructive was the Spanish Franciscan cardinal and chancellor of Castile, Francisco Ximénes de Cisneros. In synods in 1497 and 1498 he provided programs for disciplined renewal of the clergy, and in 1499 he was planning the development of what would become the University of Alcalá where from the outset Greek and Hebrew were taught. The scholars he gathered here contributed to the great Polyglot Bible. This Complutensian (from the Latin for Alcalá) Polyglot Bible was begun in 1502 and completed in 1517. The Old Testament has the Hebrew, Latin Vulgate, and Greek Septuagint with interlinear Latin in parallel columns. The Pentateuch included a Chaldee paraphrase in Hebrew characters. The Greek New Testament was the first ever printed (1514), though actual publication was delayed until 1522, perhaps due to the privilege granted Erasmus's Greek New Testament (1516).

In Italy lay spirituality found expression in the confraternities or societies known as oratories, especially the Genoese and Roman Oratories of Divine Love. Their focus was works of charity. The Geneose Oratory, founded in 1497, was inspired by St Catherine of Genoa's hospital work. The Roman Oratory, founded prior to 1517, included a number of men who became prominent Catholic reformers and influenced others such as Guillaume Briçonnet, the bishop of Meaux. New religious orders of the time included the Theatines and Capuchins. The former was founded in 1524 by among others Gian Pietro Caraffa, the future Pope Paul IV, as a community for priests. The Capuchin order, so-called because of its square hood (*cappuccio*), was founded in 1525 as a more faithful expression of the Franciscan Rule. The Capuchins grew rapidly in both size and popularity through their preaching and care for the sick and poor. Their stress on Scripture and preaching led to tensions not only with the Observant Franciscans but also with the Counter-Reformation. In 1542 their vicar general, Bernadino Ochino, one of the great preachers of Italy, fled the Inquisition to Geneva and Calvinism. His friend Peter Martyr Vermigli, the Augustinian prior at Lucca, did likewise.

Those concerned about the renewal of the church included not only leading humanists such as Erasmus but also cardinals such as Gian Matteo Giberti (1495–1543), who as bishop of Verona strove to upgrade the education and morality of his clergy, sponsored a printing press that issued editions of the Greek fathers, and developed a platform for the restoration of church discipline that was influential upon the council of Trent.

But, as is all too often the case, these early renewal efforts were too little and too late to forestall the Reformation. For example, the Emperor Maximilian had called for a reforming council in 1509; but he was outmaneuvered by Pope Julius II, who held the Lateran council in 1512 that reaffirmed the full power of the pope, condemned conciliarism, and denounced the tendency toward independence of the national churches. Furthermore, the gravity of the church's situation was not fully grasped by Rome until Leo's death in 1521. The cardinals then elected a Dutch cardinal of spotless reputation, Adrian Floriszoon of Utrecht (1459–1523), as Pope Adrian VI.

Adrian VI had studied with the Brethren of the Common Life and taught theology at Louvain, where he had received a doctorate in 1492. He was a friend of Erasmus, tutor of the young Charles V, and had been a bishop and inquisitor in Spain. An earnest and zealous reformer, he moved quickly after his election toward his goals of checking Protestantism, reconciling European princes, and reforming the curia. His slowness in reforming the curia has been attributed to his discovery – one that other curial reformers after him would also make – that reform of the curial sale of offices and benefices threatened to bankrupt the papacy and disrupt ambitions linked to the papacy as the principal patron of Italians (Jedin 1957: I, 209; Hallman 1985: 168). He frankly confessed that corruption had begun at the top, and vowed to begin the renewal of the church by the reform of the papacy. His challenge was *purga Romam purgatur mundus*, "to cleanse Rome in order to cleanse the world" (Iserloh et al. 1986: 460). Addressing the German diet in January 1523, Adrian wrote:

> Concerning ourselves you may promise that we will do everything so that first this See, from whom this evil powerfully progressed, will be reformed, so that even as corruption came from there into all lower parts, likewise from there healing and reform may emanate. . . . No one should be astonished, if we will not correct all error and abuse at once. The disease is too long established and not simple, but varied and complex. (Hillerbrand 1964: 429; Olin 1992: 118–27)

But the times were against Adrian. The Italians looked down on him for his rude Latin and lack of Renaissance sophistication. Elected in January 1522, he died in September 1523. His epitaph read: "Alas! How the power of even a most righteous man depends upon the times in which he happens to live!" (Spitz 1971: 470).

Adrian was succeeded by another Medici, a cousin to Leo X, who took the title Clement VII. He was personally of blameless character, but instead of devoting himself to official duties he was an easygoing, urbane patron of the arts. His inability to deal with Henry VIII's drive to divorce Catherine was characteristic of his ineffective efforts to conciliate all parties. He sent the moderate Cardinal Campeggio to the diet of Nuremberg in 1524 with the offer to the Lutherans of "wine and women," i.e. communion with both wine and bread and clerical marriage, without realizing how deep the doctrinal divisions had already become. In 1532 he consented to call the ecumenical council the Protestants had been requesting for the last twelve years, but died in 1534 without convoking it.

The next pope, Alexander Farnese, Pope Paul III, was a typical Renaissance prelate. He immediately made two of his teenage grand-sons cardinals in order, as he put it, to provide for his old age. He did encourage dialogue with Protestants such as Melanchthon and Bucer, and made a number of humanists cardinals. In 1536 he proclaimed that the long-desired council would meet in Mantua in May 1537. In preparation for this council he appointed a commission of nine cardinals to prepare a report for reforming the church. After two months of solid work, this commission issued the report *Consilium de emendanda ecclesia* ("Advice Concerning the Reform of the Church," 1537) which scored the abuses of nepotism, simony, pluralism of benefices, absenteeism, clerical immorality, and venality. With courage and boldness the report focused the blame for all these abuses on exaggerated papal power: "Flatterers have led some Popes to imagine that their will is law." The distinguished committee, including the cardinals Contarini, Carafa, Sadoleto, and Pole, and bishops Fregoso, Aleander, and Giberti as well as abbot Cortese and Badia, the Master of the Sacred Palace, was convinced that renewal of the church and the restoration of the primacy of pastoral ministry were contingent upon radical reform of the curia (Jedin 1957: I, 424–6; Olin 1992: 182–97; Gleason 1981: 81–100).

The fundamental issue was the management – or rather, mismanage-ment – of church property. The ancient trilogy of simony, pluralism of benefices, and nepotism had corrupted church leadership. The commis-sion perceived that the leaders of the church regarded it as their own corporation for profit rather than an institution responsible for the souls of the faithful. Their solution was not an innovative reform, but rather increased discipline and adherence to the laws of the church (Hallman 1985: 2; Gleason 1981: 56).

When the Protestants got hold of the report it only confirmed and substantiated their criticisms of the church. Furthermore, the commis-sion's emphasis on *moral* reform of the church indicated that they were unable to come to grips with Luther's explicit call for *theological* reform. Luther himself published a German translation of the report with a sarcastic preface and ironic glosses in the margins (*LW* 34: 233–67).

Nevertheless, there were Roman Catholic theologians who not only understood but even shared some of the religious concerns of Luther. In Italy these Catholics constituted a movement stretching from around 1512 into the 1560s that is often termed "Italian evangelism." They were concerned for reform of the church through reform of the individual. The vehicle for such reform is the biblical Word of God, shaped theologically by the doctrine of justification by faith. Hence these Catholic evangelicals were called already in the 1520s *spirituali* in contrast to *carnali* or *mondani* (Gleason 1993: 300). Their ideas were rooted in pre-Reformation biblical perspectives but also strengthened by Reformation debates. It is striking that at least for a time during the pontificate of Paul III, exponents of evangelism reached into the curia itself.

Scholars have not reached an agreed-upon definition of evangelism, but it has been described as an effort to adapt the insights of Luther and then also Calvin to Catholic praxis (Fenlon 1972: 21; Gleason 1978: 20–1; Marcocchi 1988; Schutte 1977). This effort to retain outward ecclesiastical structures while infusing Catholic doctrine with the ideas of Luther, Calvin, Bucer, and others found its most significant literary expression in the anonymous *Beneficio di Cristo* (1543). Gleason (1978: 10–12, 16) suggests that the *Beneficio* was strongly influenced by the 1539 edition of Calvin's *Institutes* and affirmed the doctrine of justification by faith. Thus, had the *spirituali* movement carried the day, the Italian Catholic church might have become Calvinist.

It is now clear that the doctrine of justification had many adherents in Italy, in some cases leading to the formation of Lutheran communities (Olson 1993), in others leading to the flight of prominent Catholic reformers such as Ochino and Vermigli to openly embrace Calvinism, but basically even in its curial expression being unable to influence the papacy. Why did this fundamental Protestant conviction bear so little fruit in Italy? One answer, expressed bitterly at the time, is that the Catholic evangelical elite in the curia had a failure of nerve and/or sold out to the establishment. They, unlike lower-class and lay dissenters who remained faithful and suffered for it, put their economic security above their consciences and were co-opted by positions and benefices as rewards for conformity. Gleason (1993: 305) thinks this explanation, while having some historical legitimacy, is too reductionistic. "The supposition that an entire highly educated, religiously and morally serious group like the *spirituali* simply caved in when its economic status was threatened, and accepted the *status quo*, is too simplistic. . . . They stopped short not on account of cowardice, but out of conviction, because they still believed in the possibility of joining their revitalized personal and biblical Christianity with reformed Catholic church structures and a spiritual pope at their apex."

The theology of the *spirituali* defies easy generalization, but it seems that, unlike their Protestant brethren, they could not or did not draw the logical conclusion that theological reform led to institutional reform. We are reminded here of the first sharp exchange of the Reformation between Luther and Prierias on the issue of the theology of grace alone and ecclesiastical authority. The *spirituali* somehow believed it was possible to ensure the former by strengthening the latter. Their desire to have both made them and their theology suspect to the establishment that was now mounting a Counter-Reformation.

An outstanding example of these so-called mediating theologians was Gasparo Contarini (1483–1542), whose conversion experience to salvation by faith has been likened to Luther's (Jedin 1957: I, 167; Gleason 1981: 21–33). Contarini had been present at the diet of Worms in his capacity as Venetian ambassador to the imperial court. Later (1528–30) he was ambassador to the papal court in Rome. There his deep piety and his diplomatic ability to negotiate and compromise differences led to his elevation to the cardinalate (1535) while still a layman. He sought to reconcile Protestant and Catholic differences, and advocated an ecumenical council to heal the divisions in the church. He and his Lutheran counterpart, Melanchthon, did reach agreement on some significant theological issues such as justification at the Regensburg colloquy in 1541. But their mutual efforts were rejected by both sides as compromises at the expense of the truth. With the death of Contarini, the liberal Catholic reform movement also suffered a mortal blow prior to the council of Trent.

One thing after another prompted the postponement of the council, and in 1542 war broke out again between Charles V and Francis I. The council, which we shall treat separately below, did not actually convene until 1545 – 25 years after Luther's first calls for a council. Paul III died in 1549. After the brief reigns of Julius III and Marcellus II, Cardinal Caraffa (1476–1559), now an outspoken critic of the evangelism movement he once shared, became Pope Paul IV in 1555.

The Index and the Inquisition

Paul IV is sometimes termed the first of the Counter-Reformation popes for his dogmatic rigidity and his determination to eliminate Protestantism. It was during the pontificate of Paul IV that the Catholic renewal movement centered on repression and earned the label Counter-Reformation. Two of its tools were the Index of Prohibited Books and the Inquisition.

Lists of prohibited books had been circulated since 1521, mainly by the theological faculties of Paris and Louvain. It became clear to Paul IV that effective thought control included burning not only authors but also their writings. The operative principle was that heresy is an infectious disease "transmitted above all by the printing presses from one part of Christendom to another" (Gleason 1978: 14). Thus it was Paul IV who promoted a complete list of heretical works to be universally prohibited. This *Index librorum prohibitorum* was first published in 1559 by the congregation of the Inquisition under Paul IV. It was modified in 1564 by the council of Trent. The list proscribed not only heretical Protestant works but also humanist classics thought to be injurious to morals, such as Boccaccio's *Decameron*. Even the works of Erasmus, who had once been offered a cardinal's hat, were forbidden and then later published in bowdlerized versions. In marked departure from the reception of Erasmus in other countries, Italy rejected him as a "Lutheran" heretic. The great majority of editions of the Bible and the church fathers were also prohibited or allowed only with written permission from bishops and inquisitors. The Jesuit Peter Canisius wrote from Germany that the Index was "intolerable" and a "scandal." The contemporary Jesuit scholar, John O'Malley (1993: 314) labels the Index "one of the most fanatical documents of even that fanatical pontificate."

In 1571, Pius V established a special congregation of the Index whose duties were transferred to the Holy Office (now titled the Congregation for the Doctrine of the Faith; the Index itself was abolished in 1966). The censorship activities of the Holy Office undoubtedly had a dampening effect upon culture and the spread of ideas in Catholic countries. Some recent scholars, however, have modified the older view that the Index had a devastating effect; it was less an "iron curtain" than a large mesh net. The Counter-Reformation was clearly not "an age of free cultural exchange," but neither was it a time of "cultural death" (Tedeschi 1991: 273–319, 321, 335, 338, 345). There are, of course, arguments to the contrary. Gleason (1981: 103) points out that the *Beneficio* was so successfully suppressed that an Italian copy was not discovered until the mid-nineteenth century. And Menchi (1993: 13) states that tridentine and post-tridentine repression of heretics "affected religious dissent in Italy like the lava on Pompeii in the year 79. The philo-Protestant movement was suffocated in its fermentation phase."

The Inquisition, juridical persecution of heresy by special ecclesiastical courts, has roots going back to the thirteenth-century proceedings against the Catharist heresy when the church secured the assistance of the secular powers. Although the ideal of the crusade had waned in fifteenth-century Europe, the *Reconquista* – the expulsion of all Muslims – was still a religious and political goal in the Iberian peninsula. The last

Islamic stronghold was overcome when Grenada was taken by Castile and Aragon in 1492. The all-too-common image of the Inquisition continues to center on Spain with dramatic images of burning heretics against dark skies and grim Grand Inquisitors as forerunners of the CIA and KGB ferreting out innocent victims to satisfy their paranoia and/or lust for power. There is no doubt that the Spanish Inquisition did inspire terror; but this terror was due less to the severity of punishment than to its publicity. "Most secular European legal systems punished their prisoners more severely than the Inquisition, but none pronounced its judgments more theatrically or perpetuated the memory of its condemnations more assiduously" (Monter 1990: xiii). The impressive force of the Inquisition rested on the public, authoritarian exploitation of the society's profoundly embedded fear of public shame. "In a society where public shame, *la vergüenza*, was itself a major form of punishment, the Inquisition carried the act of punishment almost to the level of art. The ultimate purpose of the general public *auto* [*de fe*] was clearly to instill salutary fear" both by proclamation of sentence and imposition of the *sanbenitos*, a penitential garment. After the expiration of the sentence or the death of the heretic this garment was hung in the major church of the heretic's city as a permanent reminder to the community of his or her heresy (Monter 1990: 57–58). Those of us living in tabloid cultures where public figures regularly blather their personal lives probably have difficulty fully grasping the power of this type of social control.

Since the Inquisition continues to be notorious in the popular mind for its secrecy and reputed use of torture, a brief word about both is in order. It is true that the Inquisition successfully maintained remarkable secrecy concerning denunciations and trials. The inquisitors themselves believed that the impenetrable secrecy of their work enabled them to avoid corruption and make unbiased investigations. Practical reasons for this secrecy included protection of the witnesses for the prosecution and the reputation of the accused. The latter could very well be found innocent, and therefore should not have the stigma of public arrest and inquiry attached to him or her.

The use of torture by the Inquisition must be seen in context. "When judging the Spanish Inquisition, we must recall that the quality of justice in Spanish secular courts had an extremely poor reputation. The most distinguished modern historian of penal procedure in Habsburg Spain concluded that the only rational response of a person threatened with arrest on criminal charges was to flee as far and as fast as possible" (Monter 1990: 74). In contrast to the secular courts, the Inquisition was a model of moderation and due process (Tedeschi 1991: 8).

The Holy Office was sceptical about the validity of confession obtained by torture, and did not employ torture as a matter of course. The age, sex, and physical condition of the accused might also preclude the use of torture. Confessions obtained by torture were not considered valid until ratified by the defendant 24 hours later outside the torture chamber. The judicial torture itself customarily was suspension of the victim by a rope and pulley, with arms bound behind the back. Supposedly the maximum length of suspension was an hour. According to one account, the torture should be moderate so that "the victim is preserved, if innocent, to enjoy his freedom, and if guilty, to receive his just punishment" (Tedeschi 1991: 145; Kamen 1985: 161–77).

The Spanish Inquisition was closely tied to the state, one of whose concerns was to acquire prisoners to man its galleys. It is of interest that the galleys were such a living hell that secular prisoners condemned to the galleys would sometimes confess to religious crimes in order to be tried by the Inquisition and perhaps receive a different punishment. In 1478 the pope granted the Spanish sovereigns the right to set up and direct the Inquisition. Inquisitors had power over all religious orders and (after 1531) even over bishops. It has been suggested that the militant orthodoxy and fanatical spirit of the Spanish church was due to the centuries of combat with Islam. But perhaps more to the point was the use of the Inquisition as a tool of social control against outsiders. This helps to account for its popularity in Spain, for it was directed not merely at Protestants, i.e. heretics, but against "alien" elements in the social body such as French immigrants and homosexuals (Monter 1990: 321–5). Ferdinand and Isabella established powerful institutional controls against any form of deviation. By 1508 Cardinal Ximénez had not only strengthened the Spanish hierarchy by a kind of rigid moral rearmament, but had himself served as Grand Inquisitor. By the 1530s the Inquisition was directed against "Erasmians" and "Lutherans."

Even before becoming pope, Caraffa (Paul IV) had been favorably impressed by the Spanish Inquisition's effectiveness and suggested that it be introduced in Italy. Paul III, fearing popular hostility, was less than enthusiastic about the idea, but reluctantly allowed Caraffa to introduce the Inquisition since moderate reform efforts were failing to curb the growth of Protestantism. Indeed, the establishment of the Roman Inquisition has been attributed to the collapse of negotiations at the Regensburg colloquy in 1541, and to the "panic in central Italy about the infiltration of Protestantism" associated with the apostasies of the well-known Ochino and Vermigli (O'Malley 1993: 311; Jedin 1957: I, 446–7). Caraffa was so eager to begin that he set up interrogation chambers in his own house, and exclaimed: "If our own father were a heretic, we would carry the faggots to burn him!" On another occasion he stated: "No man is to lower himself by showing toleration toward any sort of heretic, least of all a Calvinist!" (Spitz 1971: 477).

So the Roman tribunal was organized. The judges were the customary Dominicans who were subordinated to six cardinals appointed by the pope to serve as inquisitors general. One of these men was Cardinal Caraffa. On 21 July 1542, with the bull *Licet ab initio*, Paul III formally sanctioned the Roman Inquisition and extended its authority to all Christendom. It was an effective instrument so long as the monarch cooperated with it.

There has not been a comprehensive treatment of the Roman Inquisition due to the inaccessibility of sources, although Carlo Ginzburg (1982, 1985) has provided popular narratives through the use of local sources. Contemporary scholarship that has sought to revise the worst stereotypes associated with the Inquisition also notes its problems. Tedeschi (1991: 10–11, 23) pointedly remarks that this legal institution was "in practice, if not in theory . . . at the mercy of one man, the pope. During the pontificate of that zealous persecutor, Paul IV (1555–9), due process was placed under an almost unbearable strain, and the Church during his reign did fall into the grip of a witchhunting mentality. . . . Although many of his excesses disappeared with him there is no doubt that they must be counted among the factors contributing to the unfavorable reputation which the Holy Office has endured for centuries." A Roman mob celebrated Paul IV's death by sacking and burning the records of the Inquisition and liberating its prisoners.

The Inquisition was the defensive weapon of the Counter-Reformation; a more effective, offensive weapon of the Counter-Reformation was the new order of the Jesuits.

Loyola and the Society of Jesus

In his person, Ignatius Loyola (1491–1556) was the embodiment of both the Catholic and the Counter-Reformation. That said, it should be noted that the common attribution of an anti-Protestant motivation to Loyola for the founding of the Jesuits is misleading. Without Luther and Calvin there would still have been a Loyola. Loyola's and his colleagues' motivation was not to reform the church but "to help souls." "Although the Society of Jesus would have had a much different history, it would have come into being even if the Reformation had not happened, and it cannot be defined primarily in relationship to it."

Indeed, it may well be that Loyola never read anything by the major Reformers (O'Malley 1993: 16–18, 321, 280).

The youngest of 12 children born to a Basque family of noble lineage, Loyola was trained from his youth in the ideals of the nobility. Although he was much taken by the romances of chivalry, his life as a courtier was less than edifying. While it may be too harsh to characterize his life in courts and barracks as dissolute, it is not too extreme to say that his life took an abrupt about-face as the result of his volunteering to help defend the city of Pamplona against an advancing French army. At the siege of Pamplona in 1521 during the first of the Habsburg–Valois wars, a cannonball broke Loyola's right leg and wounded his left. His leg was set by a doctor of the victorious French army, and he was taken back to the family castle to recuperate. There, doctors found that the leg had been badly set and Loyola insisted that the leg be rebroken, reset, and a protruding bone sawed off! The ensuing discomfort and nine months of convalescence gave Loyola occasion for reflection about his life. His physical pain was compounded by his anguish at realizing that his crippling wounds also had crippled his knightly ambitions. Influenced by the reading available to him in the castle, a translation of Ludolf of Saxony's *Life of Christ* and *Flowers of the Saints*, Loyola came to the conviction that God wanted him to become a spiritual knight. Loyola's shattered chivalric ambitions found a new outlet: the defense of the church.

Military imagery has often been used to describe the self-understanding and mission of Loyola and his followers, but this is misleading if understood in a modern sense. The Jesuit Formula or "rule" describes a member of the Society "as a soldier of God beneath the banner of the cross," but in medieval parlance *militare Deo* was a synonym for a member of a religious order.

In March 1522, on the feast of the Annunciation of the Virgin Mary at Montserrat near Barcelona, Loyola offered his sword to the service of Mary, exchanged clothes with a beggar, and, as he put it, clothed himself "with the armor of Christ." His intention to set out on a pilgrimage to Jerusalem was frustrated by an outbreak of the plague, and he remained for most of the year in ascetic retreat at the nearby cave of Manresa. It was during this period of intense prayer, extreme mortification, and rigorous introspection that he developed the basis for his later famous and influential *Spiritual Exercises*. Although not published until 1548, this guide for developing conformity to God's will was already in use in 1527.

The *Spiritual Exercises* are a four-part series of meditations and rules designed to strengthen and discipline the person's will to conform to and serve the will of God. The first part of the discipline is a systematic consideration of sin and its consequences. The second part presents the significance of the life and kingdom of Christ. The third part focuses on the passion story; and the fourth part culminates the exercise by meditation on the risen and glorified Christ. The original intention was that the *Exercises* extend over four weeks. Through his exceptional insights into religious psychology, Loyola created a discipline whereby he and his followers could direct themselves through progressive resolutions to detest sin, join the ranks of God's disciples, test and confirm their commitment, and actuate their wills towards the pursuit of perfection. This systematic reasoning and meditation included daily self-examination that focused upon cultivating a single virtue or attacking a single sinful inclination. This allowed one problem area after another to be conquered in the intended process for reform of the person's life.

In contrast to Luther, Loyola perceived the problem of the church not as doctrinal aberration but as personal aberration from the teaching and tradition of the institution. The key to reform of the church, then, for Loyola was the reform of individuals. And the reform of individuals was to take place through the mastery of the person's will. By complete self-mastery, the person could avoid extremes in the pursuits of service to God and salvation of self and others. This orientation combined the Renaissance conception and esteem of the individual personality with the late medieval intentionality of the mystics for the perfection of the soul, which in Loyola's mind meant submission to Christ and the church in the person of the pope.

From Manresa, Loyola set out in 1523 for Jerusalem to convert the Muslims, but discovered in the process that his intentions needed a solid educational foundation. Thus at thirty years of age he returned to Barcelona and enrolled in a school for boys. He then went on to the University of Alcalá where the first group of followers gathered around him. Ironically, he was here suspected of heresy and twice imprisoned by the Spanish Inquisition. Acquitted, he went on to study at Paris in 1528 after a brief sojourn at Salamanca.

In Paris (1528–35), Loyola earned his Master's degree. Here he also laid the foundations for the Society of Jesus, the Jesuits, with some of his companions including Diego Lainez, who was to be the next general of the order, Alfonso Salmerón, and Francis Xavier, the great missionary to the Far East. With an oath reminiscent of the medieval Spanish crusades, they swore to dedicate themselves to go to the Holy Land to convert the Muslims. In 1537 Loyola and his companions met in Venice, were consecrated priests, and prepared to set out for

Figure 14.1 "Ignatius of Loyola," by Claude Mellan, ca. 1640, showing Loyola receiving his vision at La Storta on the outskirts of Rome. God's voice from heaven says: "I will be propitious to you in Rome."
Source: © Elke Walford, Hamburger Kunsthalle.

Jerusalem. These plans were foiled by war between Venice and the Turks, and so they decided to "seek their Jerusalem in Rome." The life of service to the church that Loyola and his small group of companions envisaged was sanctioned by Pope Paul III in 1540.

As the last major medieval monastic order, the Society of Jesus was a distinct development that embodied Loyola's unique perspective on monasticism. The older monastic ideals of contemplation and with-drawal from the world were replaced by Loyola's emphasis upon action in the world. Whereas the classic Benedictine Rule contributed stability to the religious life by locating it within the walls of a cloister, the Jesuit emphasis was on mobility for the sake of ministry wherever needed in the world. Thus Loyola's trusted assistant, Jerónimo Nadal (1507–80) continually reiterated: "We are not monks . . . The world is our house" (O'Malley 1993: 68).

The emphasis upon the active life required well-educated priests, which in turn led to the well-known long and rigorous training that candidates for the Society went through. This extra training was to interiorize monastic discipline because the Jesuits were not to be isolated in a monastery, but rather active in the world in mission and evangelism. Another distinctive element of the Society of Jesus was that the candidate took not only the three regular vows of poverty, chastity, and obedience, but also a fourth vow: a special vow of obedience to the pope. It is this special fourth vow of obedience to the pope which starkly highlights Loyola's distance from Luther on reform. To Loyola, the church was the hierarchical church. The authoritarian character of Loyola's understanding of personal relation-ship to the church is expressed in this vow to go without question or delay wherever the pope orders for the work of the church. In this sense the fourth vow intends to express apostolic ministry to the world to be facilitated by the papacy rather than vice versa. That is, the fourth vow is not "to the pope" but about mission and ministry.

The most famous – or infamous as the case may be – section of the *Exercises* is that titled "Rules for Thinking with the Church." The celebrated thirteenth rule of the *Spiritual Exercises* reads: "If we wish to proceed securely in all things, we must hold fast to the following principle: What seems to me white, I will believe black, if the hierarchical church so defines. For I must be convinced that in Christ our Lord, the bridegroom, and in his spouse, the church, only one Spirit holds sway, which governs and rules for the salvation of souls" (McNally 1967: 249). This is a jarring and extremely distasteful profession for generations still hungover from the modern cocktail of autonomy mixed of part Enlightenment philosophy and part commer-cially generated self-absorption. People in the sixteenth century, however, still believed in reality outside themselves – they might differ vociferously over mediation of the *extra nos* through Scripture or church, but they did not doubt it. In fact, such competition is only possible when opposing parties understand themselves to be within the same general framework. A soccer match requires opponents to accept the basic rules and meet in the same stadium. Thus the "Rules for Thinking with the Church" reflect their sixteenth-century Catholic context, and express Loyola's own orthodoxy *vis-à-vis* "the Lutherans," *alumbrados* (Spanish spirituals considered suspect by the Inquisition), and other heretics of the day. Loyola's understanding of reform has been understood as the epitome of the papalism soon to be defined by the council of Trent, but this understanding needs also to be tempered with the Jesuit understanding of mission (the fourth vow), which could lead to resistance to various papal directives.

In response to the Reformation, the Jesuits sought to extirpate heresy and win Protestants back to Rome by means of political influence and effective education. Jesuit political influence grew as members of the order gained access to the courts of Europe as confessors to influential persons. In this way they were effective in inducing political rulers to suppress Protestantism. The Jesuits also placed great emphasis upon education that promoted both advanced learning and strong devotion to the authority of the church. Loyola himself founded grammar schools and both the Roman College (the Gregorianum) and the German College in Rome, the latter serving as a model for papal seminaries in Germany in the 1570s and 1580s. The educational ventures not only opened a new era of formal education in Roman Catholicism, but also positively engaged the Jesuit community with their cultural contexts in a way that has gained them renown down to the present. The Jesuits also established missions in India, Malaya, Africa, Ethiopia, Brazil, Japan, and China. These missions were remarkable expressions of theological flexibility in shedding western cultural baggage and striving to inculturate the Christian faith in Asian culture. The mission to Ming China by the Italian Jesuit Matteo Ricci is exemplary of this (Spence 1984). By Loyola's death in 1556 the order included over 1,000 members, and by 1626 there were about 15,000 Jesuits throughout the world and some 440 colleges.

The Council of Trent, 1545–1563

Loyola's understanding of reform animated the council of Trent both in its spirit of individual renewal as the key to church renewal and in the fact that members of the Society of Jesus played key roles in the council as papal theologians. The council, as did Loyola himself, illustrated the twin concerns of the Catholic church: self-renewal and opposition to what it regarded as Protestant heresy. The program of the council was to reform the Christian faith, restore Christian morality, and reunite all

Christian peoples. The council was convoked in 1545 in a theoretically still united Christendom; it closed in 1563 with a Christendom rent by divisions that still affect world Christianity today.

The council of Trent, sometimes regarded as the most important council since the council of Nicea (325), definitively ended medieval hopes for conciliarism. Indeed, Trent was so influential upon the mind-set of modern Roman Catholicism that until Vatican II (1962–5) this church was known as the "tridentine" (from the Latin for Trent) church. It is with the council of Trent that the intrinsic contradiction of linking the specific "Roman" and the universal "Catholic" in the name "Roman Catholicism" received meaning as a denominational term in contrast to the varieties of Protestant churches. Following the adjournment of the council of Trent there was not another ecumenical council for 300 years and Vatican I (1869–70), which concluded one of the problem areas Trent did not resolve – papal authority and infallibility. The other problem area not treated by Trent, the person of Mary, was defined by papal decrees in 1854 (the doctrine of the immaculate conception: from conception Mary was free from original sin) and 1950 (the doctrine of the assumption: upon her death Mary was assumed bodily into heaven).

The council of Trent itself was convoked only reluctantly after numerous delays. Papal reluctance to agree to an ecumenical council was rooted in political and theological concerns. The conciliar movement of the fifteenth century had strongly challenged papal authority when it tried to place the pope under the authority of councils. And Luther's call for a free, Christian council meant a council free of papal domination, with the Scriptures rather than tradition as the norm – a demand that the pope obviously found offensive. The long delay in convening this council was also related to the desire of every party to have the council meet in its own territory in order to better control it. The town of Trent in northern Italy was finally chosen because it was technically on German soil and therefore appeased the emperor. Political events also influenced the fact that the council did not actually meet for the whole period, 1545–63, but in three distinct assemblies: 1545–7, 1551–2, and 1561–3.

The council opened on 13 December 1545 in the midst of commercial scalpers whose inflated prices for lodging and food (the price of wine increased 30 percent!) expressed their delight at the presence of such an august gathering. Initial attendance at the council was low and included only three legates, one cardinal, four archbishops, twenty-one bishops, and five generals of orders. Most participants were Italians, although there were enough Spanish clergy, sensitive to the emperor's wishes, to provide difficulty for the curia. On the initial crucial issues of voting and agenda it was decided that voting would be by individuals, and that dogmatic and disciplinary reform issues would be treated concurrently. The voting decision was a specific departure from the practice of the fifteenth-century councils which had voted by nations. This gave the papacy a distinct advantage since Italians at the council outnumbered participants from other nations.

Some of the council fathers favored far-reaching reforms of the church and conciliation with the Protestants. However, the Jesuit papal theologians, Salmerón and Lainez, effectively countered this desire both through their influence as theological advisors and as preachers at the council.

Although the council did not condemn Luther in a formal, judicial sense, the doctrinal decisions of the council were clearly intended to counter the Reformation understanding of the gospel. Against the Reformation watchword of "Scripture alone," the fourth session (April 1546) decided that the apostolic traditions must be accepted with the same reverence as Scripture: "This truth and discipline are contained in the written books *and* the unwritten traditions" (Schaff 1919: II, 80; emphasis added). The repudiation of *sola Scriptura* raised the controversial theological issue of whether Scripture and tradition are two equal sources of revelation. The significance of Trent's decision is that the *Magisterium*, the teaching authority of the Roman church, is the final interpreter of tradition and thus of Scripture. "No one, relying on his own skill, shall, – in matters of faith, and of morals pertaining to the edification of the structure of Christian doctrine, – wresting the sacred Scripture to his own senses, presume to interpret the said sacred Scripture contrary to that sense which holy mother church, – whose it is to judge the true sense and interpretation of the holy Scriptures, – hath held and doth hold" (Schaff 1919: II, 83). This decision was complemented by decreeing Jerome's Vulgate (old Latin) edition of the Bible as normative for dogmatic proofs.

In response to the Reformation watchword of "grace alone," the council affirmed the role of human cooperation with grace for salvation. The sixth session, meeting in January 1547, set forth the Catholic teaching on justification in 16 doctrinal chapters and 33 canons condemning errors. It is of interest that in affirming the free human cooperation with God's grace in salvation, the council used the very proof text of Zechariah 1: 3 ("Return to me, . . . and I will return to you") that Luther had identified as a support of salvation by human activity in his 1516 *Disputation Against Scholastic Theology* (Schaff 1919: II, 92; *LW* 31: 10–11).

There were extended efforts during this session to introduce under the leadership of the Augustinian general, Girolamo Seripando (1493–1563), the theory or doctrine of double justification. This theological position, already attempted to no avail at the colloquy of Regensburg (1541) by Contarini, strove to bring together the Lutheran and Roman Catholic concerns about justification in such a way that they would no longer be church-dividing. Seripando's point was that the received tradition did not provide the means to resolve the tension between doctrine and piety. It was crucial to Seripando to be able to affirm *both* that the Christian life is a life actually transformed by the gift of Christ, *and* that no matter how "good" the works issuing from this transformed life, salvation depends not on our works but on God's forgiveness given in Christ. The theological bottom line is that "it is on God's mercy alone that the Christian relies" (McCue 1984: 40, 55).

Seripando and those who supported him at Trent sought to overcome the tension between piety as Christian praxis and scholastic theology. He was strongly opposed by the Jesuit, Diego Lainez, who in a three-hour speech so refuted Seripando that the latter was compelled to defend his own orthodoxy. One of the many objections to the doctrine of double justification was that it dismissed the possibility of human merit for salvation. The more Augustinian view of justification in personal relational terms was rejected by the council fathers for the Aristotelian scholastic view of justification as the infusion of grace as a substance, and hence the intrinsic or ontological righteousness of the justified person (Maxcey 1979).

In response to the Reformation emphasis upon baptism and the Lord's Supper as the two sacraments of the Christian faith, the seventh session of the council reaffirmed the seven sacraments of baptism, confirmation, eucharist, penance, extreme unction, holy orders, and matrimony. These sacraments are objectively efficacious, i.e. they effect grace by virtue of their administration (*ex opere operato*). "If anyone saith, that by the said sacraments of the New Law grace is not conferred through the act performed, but that faith alone in the divine promise suffices for the obtaining of grace: let him be anathema" (Schaff 1919: II, 121). With regard to the Protestant communion with both bread and wine, Trent approved the custom of communicating under one species (i.e. the bread) and declared that this custom has the force of law (Schaff 1919: II, 173). In the thirteenth session (1551), the council reaffirmed the doctrine of transubstantiation.

Emperor Charles V was by now disturbed that the council was ignoring his demands for thoroughgoing reform, and was passing

decrees that would imperil his concern for Protestant–Catholic reconciliation. In order to avoid imperial pressure on the council, Pope Paul
III took advantage of the presence of a few cases of typhus in Trent to
induce the majority of prelates to move the council to Bologna in
March 1547. Charles made it clear that he thought this was an illegal
move, and he proceeded to try to settle the religious controversies in
Germany on his own through the Augsburg Interim of 1548. Paul III
died in 1549.

In 1551 Pope Julius III recalled the council to Trent. Protestant
delegates arrived in January of 1552, but they were obviously too late to
have any influence on the decrees already formulated against the central
concerns of the Reformers. A Protestant military rally against Charles
led to Catholic fears that the Protestants would invade Trent, hence this
second assembly was suspended.

The third assembly of the council of Trent (1561–3) met under the
skillful diplomacy of Pope Pius IV. By this time, all hope of conciliat-
ing the Protestants had evaporated. This assembly took the earlier
dogmatic decrees for granted and thereby avoided battles over whether
it was a legitimate continuation of the first two assemblies. The bitter
debates of this period revolved around reform proposals, especially the
obligatory residence of bishops in their sees. Tendencies by the
Spanish, the French, and the imperialists to decentralize the church and
thus diminish the powers of the papacy were overcome by skillful
diplomacy that won the monarchs over to the pope's position. The
basis for the ultramontanism (the centralization of authority and
influence in the papacy) that culminated in the declaration of papal
infallibility in 1870 was thus established. The council itself became a
means for renewed rejection of conciliarism by this papal triumph.
Although no decree described the power and functions of the papacy,
the council submitted the decrees to the pope for his confirmation. On
26 January 1564 the pope issued the bull *Benedictus Deus* confirming the
canons and decrees of the council of Trent. The bull stated that the pope
alone had the right to interpret them.

While the council of Trent failed to achieve all its goals of reformation of the faith, restoration of morality, and reunion of all Christians,
it certainly restored spirit and energy to the Roman church. The
decades following the council witnessed renewed theological scholarship and education, moral reform, and spiritual growth as Catholicism
responded to Protestantism. Disciplinary decrees of the council stimulated biblical preaching and the establishment of seminaries to provide
an educated clergy for pastoral work. A variety of moral reforms were

also carried out with regard to clerical celibacy and chastity, and the residency and faithfulness of bishops.

The Catholic reform movement was essentially personal. The church was to be transformed by transforming its members; and its members were to be transformed by a transformed elite leadership. The emphasis upon personal, spiritual renewal was the emphasis of both tridentine reforms and Loyola's Jesuits. But the renewal of prayer, penance, and spiritual and corporal works of mercy, as important as it was, neglected liturgical reform. The heroic stature of individuals such as Loyola could not substitute for the centrality of public, corporate worship that Luther and other Protestant reformers had recovered. While liturgical reform and hymnody were crucial to the Protestant reformers, the Catholic reformers remained liturgically indifferent. Late sixteenth-century Catholic worship still preserved the highly clerical complexion it had received in the Middle Ages. Of course, Catholic worship did not lack festival, drama, and artistry, but the corporate biblical emphases revived by Luther, Zwingli, Calvin, and other Protestant reformers remained in the shadows. "Historians of liturgy and spirituality have generally argued that for our period there seems to have been a definite abandonment of the official corporate life of the Church as the ordinary vehicle for the faith-life of the believer. What replaced it is called 'spirituality' " (Rasmussen 1988: 281).

The spirituality of Catholic reform was the ascetic, subjective, and personal piety exemplified by such athletes of mysticism as Teresa of Avila (d. 1582) and John of the Cross (d. 1591), and their baroque artistic expressions exemplified by Bernini's striking sculpture "St Teresa in Ecstasy" (1646) and the paintings "Christ on the Cross" and "Resurrection" by El Greco (d. 1614). Indeed, it may be argued that baroque art expressed the triumphalism of the tridentine Counter-Reformation for in its form it manifested control over seemingly turbulent forces, and in its content it focused on the emphases of the Counter-Reformation: Mary, the saints, Corpus Christi processions, and regnant popes with the keys of St Peter. As in these expressions of tridentine spirituality, "the cult of the Eucharist soon became an anti-Protestant affirmation and thus characteristic of the 'counter' aspect of Catholic Reform. At the same time, it was rooted in the medieval desire for visualization, 'the gaze that saves.' Exposition and benediction with the exposed Sacrament developed into an elaborate ritual of 'perpetual' adoration, cemented into The 'Forty Hours' (*Quarant'ore*)" (Rasmussen 1988: 282).

These were all activities, according to the Catholic scholar of the Counter-Reformation, Evennett (1970: 31–2), "in which active striving

after self-control and the acquisition of virtues would be vital; in which
zeal for good works of mercy and charity, and labour for the salvation
of souls, were to predominate: a spirituality which was to reflect the
bustle of energy and determination of sixteenth-century man, feeling at
last that he had a power over himself and over things, to be applied, in
the Counter-Reformation, for the greater glory of God and the revival
of his Church." More succinctly put: "The counter-reformation doctrine of Christian struggle . . . announced that Man – even in the face of
his almighty Creator – carried, to some extent, his own fate in his own
hands" (Evennett 1970: 36). This was precisely the doctrine Luther had
striven to overcome. "But the Tridentine Reform was no mere
restoration of the Middle Ages. In almost all its manifestations it
displayed anti-Reformation characteristics" (Iserloh et al. 1986: 510).

Suggestions for Further Reading

H. Outram Evennett, *The Spirit of the Counter-Reformation*, ed. with a postscript by
  John Bossy, Notre Dame: University of Notre Dame Press, 1970
Elizabeth G. Gleason, ed. and tr., *Reform Thought in Sixteenth-Century Italy*, Chico:
  Scholars, 1981
Hubert Jedin, *A History of the Council of Trent*, 2 vols, St Louis: B. Herder, 1957
W. W. Meissner, SJ, *Ignatius of Loyola: The Psychology of a Saint*, New Haven: Yale
  University Press, 1992
William Monter, *Frontiers of Heresy: The Spanish Inquisition from the Basque Lands to
  Sicily*, Cambridge: Cambridge University Press, 1990
John C. Olin, *Catholic Reform: From Cardinal Ximenes to the Council of Trent 1495–1563*,
  New York: Fordham University Press, 1990
John W. O'Malley, SJ, ed., *Catholicism in Early Modern History: A Guide to Research*, St
  Louis: Center for Reformation Research, 1988
John W. O'Malley, SJ, *The First Jesuits*, Cambridge, MA: Harvard University Press,
  1993
John Tedeschi, *The Prosecution of Heresy: Collected Studies on the Inquisition in Early
  Modern Italy*, Binghamton: Medieval and Renaissance Texts and Studies, 1991

15

Legacies of the Reformations

Listening from the distance of centuries across the death chasms and howling kingdoms of decay, it is not easy to catch everything.

Thomas Carlyle (1795–1881)

One of the consequences of the Reformations in general and the council of Trent in particular was the splintering of western Christendom. Some of the legacies of this fragmentation of the medieval *corpus Christianum* were almost immediately apparent with, for example, the rise of confessionalization, while the catalytic action of others, such as theological pluralism, were long-term influences. In one way or another, however, the legacies of the Reformations have affected every aspect of modern life and thought. Description and analysis of these legacies already fills more library shelves than most of us can manage. Therefore in the guise of a conclusion I shall only suggest some of the Reformations' legacies in the areas of confessionalization, politics and the right of resistance, culture in general, women, the "other," and ecumenism.

Confessionalization

One of the most obvious consequences of the Reformations was the division of the medieval Catholic church into a number of churches. The process by which these various communities established their own identities is known as confessionalization. In recent German scholarship the term "confessionalization" has become a paradigm of societal history. Confessionalization "designates the fragmentation of the unitary Christendom (*Christianitas latina*) of the Middle Ages into at least three confessional churches – Lutheran, Calvinistic or 'Reformed,' and post-tridentine Roman Catholic. Each formed a highly organized system, which tended to monopolize the world view with respect to the individual, the state, and society, and which laid down strictly formulated norms in politics and morals" (Schilling 1986: 22; 1992: ch. 5). The Protestant communities began to develop their own cultural and social identities informed by both their specific theologies and their hostilities to each other as well as to the old faith. Catholicism, now properly delimited by the adjective "Roman," did likewise. The late medieval intramural attempts to reform the church became extramural exercises in self-definition. In this process the fluidity of Reformation beginnings rigidified as the edifice complexes of each community structured an identity over against the others.

The decisions of the council of Trent on justification, Scripture, and the sacraments made so definitive the divisions that had arisen in the Reformation that hopes for a reunited Christian church would not begin flickering again until the ecumenical movement of the twentieth century. By the conclusion of the council of Trent, there was a second generation of reformers whose memories of the "one, holy, catholic, and apostolic church" had receded behind the vivid present impressions of the martyrs and confessors of their own particular communities. Loyalty to the "fathers" of the church now came increasingly to mean loyalty to the confessions of faith of the previous generation. Conversations between and even among the churches consisted largely of mutual condemnations and anathemas. The intensity and rancor of these theological and ecclesiastical conflicts is reflected in Philip Melanchthon's sigh on his deathbed that finally he was being delivered from the *rabies theologorum* – the "madness of the theologians." This "madness" contributed to the atrocities of the Thirty Years War (1618–48).

The competitiveness of the churches led to a kind of siege mentality. Protestant theologians became so involved in constructing theological systems to protect their churches and to wall off alternatives that the late sixteenth and early seventeenth centuries came to be known as the period of Protestant orthodoxy or Protestant scholasticism. Both Lutherans and Calvinists developed theories of verbal and plenary inspiration to safeguard the sole authority of Scripture against the Roman Catholic use of tradition on the one hand and the dissidents' use of experience and "inner light" on the other hand. The Reformers' original understanding of faith as trust and confidence in God's promise shifted in the heat of battle to understanding faith in terms of intellectual assent to correct doctrine. The resulting highly rationalized schemata of salvation are exemplified by the chart of election and reprobation drawn up by the Elizabethan Puritan, William Perkins (1558–1602) (Hinson 1976: ch. 7; Muller 1978), and the strict Calvinism formulated at the synod of Dort (1618–19) in the Netherlands. The latter is sometimes referred to as the "Tulip synod" because its decrees may be arranged to spell the flower for which Holland is famed: *T*otal depravity, *U*nconditional election, *L*imited atonement, *I*rresistible grace, *P*erseverance of the saints.

A rationalistic and creed-bound Protestantism and Catholicism contributed politically to the developments of the consolidation of the early modern state and its concomitant imposition of social discipline, and intellectually to the rationalism, Deism, and Pietism that fed the Enlightenment of the eighteenth and nineteenth centuries. The medieval aspiration for a Christian society, the *corpus Christianum*, fragmented into the aspirations of the different confessional groups. Without a unitary sacred ideal for the integration of society and without the means and will to enforce a particular confessional ideal for all Europe, toleration became a path to social peace and the eventual secularization of society. The displacement of a unified sacred society by confessional communities also had psychological and ethical consequences.

> Translated in psychological terms, it meant the internalization of discipline, based on decorum and piety, and the suppression, or at least, the redirection of violence and anger. . . . Described variously as "the civilizing process," or "social disciplining," the transformation of social norms expressed itself also in the spread of bourgeois values, epitomized by the emphasis on learning and self-quest, and by the simultaneous praise of family life and more rigid definition of its sexual boundaries. (Hsia 1989: 184)

Politics

The Reformations introduced into western culture the problem of pluralism – religious, social, and cultural. Since the modern world is still struggling with this legacy in its classrooms and courtrooms, and on its streets and battlefields, it should not be surprising that the people of the sixteenth century found it exceedingly difficult to live with alternative and competing commitments. This was compounded by a universal fear of anarchy and social disorder (Ozment 1985: 22–7). The first response by all parties was to compel conformity. But religious commitments are not easily swayed by laws and force. In some cases Protestant triumphalism contributed to the development of a "chosen nation" syndrome. England's overcoming of the threats of the Spanish Armada (1588) and the failure of the recusant (English Catholic

Figure 15.1 "Liberae Religionis Typus," ca. 1590. This anti-Lutheran "Triumphal Procession" of "free religion" reverses the Protestant caricature of Catholics as destroyers of the peace and ravagers of the land. Here Luther and Calvin, on the lead horses, pull at mismatched pace the wagon of "free religion" which brings in its train destruction, cruelty, rebellion, poverty, and the degeneration of morality and authority. These consequences are depicted in the right background. On the wagon are two masked devils with opened Bibles in their hands. They proclaim with fanfare that anyone can read the Bible as they like and can despise the authority of the ancient church. The four naked devils on the wagon's corners call for the rejection of religion and for social chaos. The three virtues of piety, peace, and justice flee the anarchy of "free religion." This cartoon is a kind of reversal of Karlstadt's "Wagon Cartoon" (see figure 3.3).
Source: Bibliothèque Nationale, Paris.

rejection of the Anglican church) conspiracy to blow up the Houses of Parliament and the king (the Gunpowder Plot, 1605) were interpreted in terms of God's election and blessing of the nation. This messianic sense of being a chosen nation was carried into the new world and contributed to the nascent identity of the United States as a "city set on a hill" with a "manifest destiny," characteristics which continue to exert political influence.

Another response to political pluralism was to assert the rights of the individual conscience. In various ways, Luther's statement to the emperor at the diet of Worms in 1521 has had political echoes ever since: "My conscience is captive to the Word of God. I cannot and will not retract anything, for it is neither safe nor right to go against conscience. I cannot do otherwise, here I stand, may God help me, Amen" (*LW* 32: 112–13). Later Luther was equally adamant in defending the freedom of faith against both the theological right (the pope) and left (Karlstadt and Müntzer): "I will constrain no man by force, for faith must come freely without compulsion" (*LW* 51: 77; see *LW* 45: 108). Passive resistance was not confined to Protestants but was common to all those who differed on religion with their rulers, such as Catholics in Elizabethan England.

If a ruling authority is in the wrong, Luther supported conscientious objection. "What if a prince is in the wrong? Are his people to follow him then too? Answer: No, for it is no one's duty to do wrong; we must obey God (who desires the right) rather than men [Acts 5: 29]" (*LW* 45: 125). Soon Lutheran jurists and theologians were developing constitutional and theological arguments for the resistance of lesser magistrates to the emperor's coercion of the faith of his subjects. Protestant political resistance was first defended in the Lutheran Magdeburg confession (1550–1) which in turn directly influenced French Calvinist political thought. Huguenot arguments for a constitutionalism that limited royal power and defended individual conscience were advanced by François Hotman's *Franco-Gallia* (1573), Theodore Beza's *Right of Magistrates* (1574), and Philippe du Plessis-Mornay's more radical *Vindication Against Tyrants* (1579) which authorized individual rebellion on the explicitly religious grounds that God may "raise up new liberators" outside the constitutional framework. In England, John Poynet's *A Short Treatise of Politic Power* (1556), the first break with the English conception of passive obedience, was also influenced by Luther and the Magdeburg confession (Schulze 1985: 209; Hildebrandt 1980; Höss 1963; Skinner 1980). The authority of kings became relative before God, the King of kings. Protestant arguments for resistance to tyranny continued to ferment political change in the eighteenth-century American and French revolutions. These arguments "provided significant ingredients of the constitutionalism that was such an important part of those ideologies. Traces of these sixteenth-century ideas even survive into the twentieth century. They were used in the midcentury struggle against modern totalitarianisms. They are with us still" (Kingdon 1988: 219). That Luther's theological exposition of the duty of political resistance to unjust government is not merely of historical interest is seen in its use in the Norwegian and German resistance to Nazism. In the lapidary phrase of Luther and later of Dietrich Bonhoeffer: "If the coachdriver is drunk, we have to put a spoke in the wheel" (see Duchrow 1987: 34, ch. 3; De Grouchy 1988: 124–30; Berggrav 1951: 300–19; Siemon-Netto 1995).

But the Reformation legacy to politics was not merely rooted in the defense of conscience against compulsion. Many of the doctrinal positions of the Reformation contributed to the rise of a democratic ethos. This point should not be taken anachronistically, for the Renaissance had reinforced centuries of political thought which viewed "democracy" as undisciplined and unprincipled mob rule subject to self-serving demagogues (Kingdon 1973: 187). Nevertheless, Luther's translation of the Bible and his emphasis upon universal education to facilitate reading it, a path followed by other Reformers as well, was a step toward depriving the elite of exclusive control over words as well as the Word. The doctrine of the priesthood of all the baptized proclaimed that the ordained priest or minister is distinguished from all other Christians only by office. For Luther the church is no longer a hierarchical institution but a community of believers in which "no one is for himself, but extends himself among others in love." Thus he translated *ecclesia* not as "church" (*Kirche*) but as "community" (*Gemeinde*), "congregation" (*Gemeine*), and "assembly" (*Versammlung*). And his 1523 pamphlet, *The Right and Power of a Christian Congregation or Community to Judge All Teaching and to Call, Appoint, and Dismiss Teachers, Established and Proved from Scripture*, has been viewed as "a 'whopping endorsement' of *communal* equality and autonomy" (Ozment 1985: 9). The Calvinist idea of the church as a covenanted community contributed to the idea of social contract. These antihierarchical, leveling processes were corrosive of political as well as ecclesiastical structures. In the words of William Tyndale: "As good is the prayer of a cobbler as of a cardinal, and of a butcher as of a bishop; and the blessing of a baker that knoweth the truth is as good as the blessing of our most holy father the pope" (Richardson 1994: 29). Religious egalitarianism could lead to social and political egalitarianism. Politically, the Reformers' goal was the social experience of communion. As John Knox declared: "Take from us the freedom of assemblies and [you] take from us the evangel" (Spitz 1971: 552).

As suggestive as many of these theological motifs are in relation to modern political developments, it is important to remember both that the confessional period coincided with absolutism and that particular confessions cannot be simply equated with political developments. "There is no simple correlation between a particular confession and a political form. Recent research has shown that we need to rethink traditional associations of the Counter-Reformation with the absolutist state, Lutheranism with political conformity, and Calvinism with democratic republicanism" (Hsia 1989: 53; Schilling 1986: 21).

Culture

The Reformation touched every aspect of culture: work, economics, art, literature, and music. The doctrine of justification by grace alone through faith alone released energy for this world that had hitherto been devoted to achieving the next world. With their new ethos of vocation or calling, the Reformers undercut the medieval dualism of sacred and secular work. In the medieval world only the religious (priests, monks, nuns) had a sacred vocation or calling from God. Those who worked in the secular world were understood by all to be on a lower and less God-pleasing plane. In contrast, the Reformers emphasized that whatever a person did in the world that served the neighbor and helped build up the human community was pleasing to God. All mundane tasks from changing diapers to changing laws were imbued with religious significance, not because human works are salvatory but because God intends neighbors to be served. As Luther once explained his own ministry: "A cow does not get to heaven by giving milk, but that is what she is made for" (Bainton 1957: 299).

The Reformations and Women

Nowhere was this understanding of vocation applied more explosively to medieval life than in the area of sex and marriage. According to Ozment (1980: 381): "No institutional change brought about by the Reformation was more visible, responsive to late medieval pleas for reform, and conducive to new social attitudes than the marriage of Protestant clergy. Nor was there another point in the Protestant program where theology and practice corresponded more success-fully." The Reformers vigorously criticized the Roman church's imposition of celibacy upon priests, monks, and nuns, not only because it was viewed as a good work contributing to salvation but because men and women were thereby removed from service to the neighbor, the divine order of marriage and family was contravened, and the created goodness of sexuality was denied. To Luther and Calvin, marriage was not just the legitimation of sexual fulfillment through procreation but above all the context for creating a new awareness of human community with all its pains and joys. So Luther declared: "Marriage does not only consist of sleeping with a woman – anybody can do that – but of keeping house and bringing up children" (*LW* 54: 441). Those who followed Luther saw in marriage not only a new, joyous appreciation for sexual relations, but also a new respect for women as companions. Luther could not imagine life without women: "The home, cities, economic life, and government would virtually disappear. Men can't do without women. Even if it were possible for men to beget and bear children, they still couldn't do without women" (*LW* 54: 161). For Luther this included the intelligence, piety, and ethics of women.

On the other hand, it would take a very narrow focus indeed to overlook the medieval patriarchalism and sexism, and even misogynism, which continued to find expression in the Reformations. On this subject as well as others which jar contemporary consciousness, it is important that we are not anachronistic. "All of Europe, probably including most women, consistently esteemed women less than men, and the Reformation articulated but did not bring about a marked change in this attitude" (Karant-Nunn 1989: 40). Thus the Spanish humanist, Juan Luis Vives, was in favor of educating women so long as they remained silent. "Considering that women are, 'by nature, sick animals,' Vives concluded that 'much more important than having learned and well-spoken women is having good and honest ones.' " And, in his late sixteenth-century portrayal of the perfect wife, *La perfecta casada*, Fray Luis de León posited that "women are created as an afterthought of God, as only a helper and comfort to men, and are loaded with the constant need to atone since 'from women came the beginning of sin, and by her we all die' " (Costa 1989: 90).

Such misogynist views were not limited to Catholics. Among the Calvinists, John Knox is notorious for his "blast" against women rulers, even though his mother-in-law was instrumental in his theological development (Healey 1994; Frankfurter 1987). Calvin himself believed the government of women "utterly at variance with the legitimate order of nature, . . . to be counted among the judgments with which God visits us" (Duke et al. 1992: 40). Yet this same Calvin carried on extensive correspondence with noblewomen concerned for reform, and was open theologically if not practically to the ordination of women as pastors in the church (Douglass 1985; Thompson 1992). The most extreme misogynist treatment of women must be that of the enforced polygamy at Münster. Yet it has been suggested that along with the desire for male control, this practice was a kind of asceticism that viewed sex solely for increasing the tribe of the elect (Marr 1987: 353). The Anabaptists thus in general shared traditional Catholicism's negative valuation of human sexuality and rejected the magisterial Reformers' positive appreciation of sexual relations as the gift of God's creation. Furthermore, the Anabaptist emphasis on the purity of the church obligated wives and husbands to shun apostate spouses. "In practical terms, Anabaptist women were equal only in martyrdom" (Wiesner 1988: 153).

A frequently asked question is whether the Reformation made any difference for women. Was the Reformation a help or a hindrance to women? The answers usually revolve around the elements sketched above as well as the loss of female saints, especially those associated with childbirth, and the closing of the monastic option for women, thus narrowing their life-choices to spouse and mother. The more recent introduction of gender studies allows another approach to the issue. "Gender" broadens the subject beyond the Reformation's effects on men and women *per se* to its effect on societal determinations of what it means to be male or female. "Unlike biological sex, gender is socially constructed and varies from society to society and over time" (Wiesner 1992: 159).

One example is Luther's effort to redefine what his society thought appropriate for male and female behavior. Medieval society and theology provided considerable sanction to prostitution and civic brothels. Aquinas justified the need for prostitutes by analogy to a cesspit for a palace. They functioned to purify a town which without them would soon become corrupt. The church tolerated prostitution because its gender values denigrated sex and also assumed that male lust was an anarchic, uncontrollable force which if not provided an outlet would pollute the town's respectable women. Since the marital age rose to about twenty-two to twenty-five, so that a youth could master a trade and become able to earn a living before marriage, public brothels for the unmarried were thought to prevent the greater evils of adultery and rape.

The response of Luther and his colleagues was not moralistic but rather an attack on their culture's gender presupposition concerning males. Their point was that the cure (the brothel) is worse than the disease (male sexual desire). In his 1520 *Address to the Christian Nobility*, Luther laments the toleration of brothels. He is aware of their rationale, but "should not the government which is temporal and also Christian, realize that such evil cannot be prevented by that kind of heathenish practice?" (*LW* 44: 214–15). Luther's consistent effort to redefine the gender issue is evident in his lectures on Genesis toward the end of his life: "The example concerning the houses of ill fame which are tolerated in the large cities does not deserve to be discussed; for it is clearly in conflict with the Law of God, . . . It is silly for them to suppose that outcroppings of debauchery and adultery are reduced by this means. . . . Lust is increased rather than cured by this means, . . ." (*LW* 3: 259; Ozment 1983: 56). That these perspectives were not without some impact is indicated by events in Zwickau. Syphilis was present in the town already in 1497, but the brothel was not shut down until 1526. "Venereal disease itself did not drive them to close the brothel. The Reformation did" (Karant-Nunn 1982: 24). Luther and those who followed him attempted to redefine their culture's understanding of male gender from uncontrollable impulse to social responsibility.

Toleration and the "Other"

Toleration was not the long suit of the Reformations. "Among the convictions of the age and of its law the belief that death by execution in its more horrible forms was a proper reward for those who denied the ultimate and basic loyalties stood firmly entrenched. . . . Of course, one may hold various views of the truth of Christ's Church on earth, and people did. But one needs to recognize that all the representatives of those various views agreed upon the need for an ultimate sanction" (Elton 1977: 206–7). There were, to be sure, the exceptions who proved the rule, such as Castellio and a few French advocates for religious freedom, as well as those Spiritualists who based ecumenism on religious experience. Sebastian Franck exemplifies the latter when he says: "I have my brothers among the Turks, Papists, Jews and all peoples. Not that they are Turks, Jews, Papists and Sectaries or will remain so; in the evening they will be called into the vineyard and given the same wage as we" (Edwards 1988: v).

Similarly, the medieval legend of the three rings related in Bocaccio's *Decameron* advocated tolerance. The legend relates how a great lord declared his heir would be known by possession of his precious ring. Before his death he had exact copies made of his ring which he gave to his three sons, each of whom believed himself the heir. In 1599,

Menocchio related this story to his inquisitor with the moral that God had given his law to Christians, Turks, and Jews. Each believes it is *the* heir, but we cannot tell which one is the right one. Menocchio therefore advocated tolerance be extended also to heretics. The consequence was his execution by order of the Holy Office (Ginzburg 1982: 49–51).

Apart from exceptions such as Franck, the Turks were widely feared not only as the "other" but as the forces of Antichrist whose advance into southern and central Europe was a spiritual as well as a military threat. The irony, of course, is that the Turkish military threat to the Empire preoccupied so much of Charles V's time and resources that he was unable to proceed vigorously against the Reformation. Thus from a purely political perspective, Luther might have seen the Turks as an ally against the papacy. But Luther's primary concern was theology not politics, and therefore he saw the Turks in particular as the rod of God's wrath against a sinful Empire, and Islam in general as the enemy of God since Mohammed denies Christ is the Son of God and Savior of the world. It is of interest that Luther rejected the calls for a crusade against the Turks on the same basis that he rejected the religious sanctions for violence advocated by Müntzer: the gospel may not be advanced nor protected by force. Armed conflict against the Turk can only be waged by Christians who repent of their sin and are led by the constituted authority of the emperor (*LW* 46: 155–205). But, for Luther, the Turkish threat was primarily the religious issue of Islam's challenge to the Christian faith. Luther therefore used his influence to make possible Theodore Bibliander's 1542 translation of the Koran on the grounds that it could be refuted only if one knew it. Unlike the medieval interpreters of Islam, Raymond Lull and Nicholas of Cusa, Luther did not view Islam as a kind of "anonymous Christianity" or a Christian sect. For Luther there could be no interreligious dialogue with an "other" who did not acknowledge Jesus Christ as the Redeemer of humankind (Kandler 1993: 8). "As with the Jews, he [Luther] was concerned not about converting the Turks, whom he believed obdurate, but about informing Christians" (Brecht 1993: 354). The Reformations' view of Christian–Islamic conflict as an eschatological confrontation between God and Satan continues to have detrimental influence among some modern Protestant groups.

The most neuralgic subject of the relation of the Reformations to the "other" is the treatment of the Jews. Christian hostility to Jews was not, of course, *sui generis* in the Reformation but has a long, sordid history that extends back to the New Testament and the early church. By the eve of the Reformations the Jews were not only seen as rejected

by God for denying Jesus and crucifying him, but were also blamed for
the plague, accused of ritual murder of Christian youths and profana-
tion of the eucharistic host, suspected of plots to destroy Christendom,
and widely resented for economic reasons (Robinson 1992: 9–22).
These myths, legends, and resentments found iconographic expression
that reflected and concretized prejudice. The fourth Lateran council
(1215) required Jews to wear yellow badges (tragically revived in the
Nazi era) for easy identification and thereby social separation. Already
in the eleventh century sculptural personifications of synagogue and
church, still present in the gothic cathedrals of Europe, contrasted a
divinely rejected Judaism as a blindfolded, downcast woman dropping
the biblical tablets of the Law with the victorious church as a clear-
sighted, crowned woman, banner flying from one hand and a chalice in
the other (Edwards 1988: 22; Mellinkoff 1993: 1: 48–9). The most
demeaning iconography depicted the long-popular association of Jews
with excrement. Thus the thirteenth-century *Judensau* image depicting
Jews sucking at the teats of a sow included by the fifteenth century the
additional depiction of Jews at the animal's rear eating and drinking
excrement (Mellinkoff 1993: I, 108; II, pl. IV. 24).

The power of such visual images affected conduct. Jews were
slaughtered thousands at a time in pogroms, and were expelled
wholesale from England (1290), France (1306), Spain (1492), and
Portugal (1497). "In 1555, Paul IV created the Roman ghetto and began
to enforce some of the most stringent restrictions on the Jews' freedom
in all of Italy and to countenance judicial atrocities against them in the
papal state" (O'Malley 1993: 188). However, the antecedent for
modern racial antisemitism may well be the pure blood laws instituted
by the Spanish Inquisition which "maintained that degenerate Jewish
blood was impervious to baptism and grace. . . . Jewishness, then, was
not a statement of faith or even a series of ethnic practices but a
biological consideration" (Friedman 1987: 16).

What is surprising in light of this tradition is Luther's initial
departure from the medieval anti-Jewish legacy. In his 1523 tract *That
Jesus Christ Was Born a Jew*, he emphasized that God has honored the
Jews above all peoples and that therefore Christians should treat Jews in
a brotherly manner (*LW* 45: 200–1). Furthermore, in contrast to the
medieval canonical prohibition of Christian–Jewish marriage, Luther
wrote:

> Just as I may eat, drink, sleep, walk, ride with, buy from, speak to, and
> deal with a heathen, Jew, Turk, or heretic, so I may also marry and
> continue in wedlock with him. Pay no attention to the precepts of those

Figure 15.2 (a) This early fourteenth-century sandstone relief of the *Judensau* is on the southeast corner under the eave of the Wittenberg parish church. Luther referred to this in his later diatribes against the Jews. (b) The counterpoint to this and a memorial to the horrible events of the Holocaust was placed at the base of this church wall in 1988. The German text reads: "God's true name / the reviled Schem-Hamphoras / which Jews before Christians / held inexpressibly holy / perished in six million Jews / under a sign of the cross."
Source: Carter Lindberg.

fools who forbid it. You will find plenty of Christians – and indeed the greater part of them – who are worse in their secret belief than any Jew, heathen, Turk, or heretic. A heathen is just as much a man or a woman – God's good creation – as St Paul, St Peter, and St Lucy, not to speak of a slack and spurious Christian. (*LW* 45: 25)

Thus Luther's follower, Urbanus Rhegius (1489–1541), advocated an enlightened toleration of Jews as fellow citizens (Hendrix 1990).

Tragically and shamefully, Luther by the end of his life raged against the Jews and advised destruction of their homes, synagogues, and books as well as prohibition of Jewish civil rights. In light of Nazi use of these later anti-Jewish writings it is important to emphasize that Luther as well as other evangelical and Roman Catholic writers must be seen in their historical context (Oberman 1984; Lindberg 1994; Rowan 1985; Nijenhuis 1972: 38–72), and, more importantly, that Luther's animus toward the Jews was theological not racist. "Luther identified a Jew by his religious beliefs, not by his race. (Identification of a Jew by his race is, in any case, a concept foreign to the sixteenth century.) If a Jew converted to Christianity, he became a fellow brother or sister in Christ. For racial anti-Semitism religious belief is largely irrelevant" (Edwards 1983: 139). Nevertheless, "hostile statements by Renaissance and Reformation figures are very likely to seem even more terrible today, against the backcloth of Auschwitz than when they were originally delivered" (Edwards 1988: 51–2).

The Reformations encountered the "other" not only at home but also abroad. Jesuit missionaries were active in China and Japan, and initiated the first steps toward what is now called "inculturation" (Moran 1993; Witek 1988). They wore local dress and followed local customs. Francis Xavier (1506–52), an original member of the Jesuits, through his travels to India, Japan, and China became sensitized to the issues involved in introducing the Christian faith to non-western cultures. His work was advanced in the next generation by Matteo Ricci (1552–1610; Spence 1984). "In Brazil Jesuits took courageous stands against the abuses of slave raids and evoked great wonderment from the natives as word sped through the jungles that among the Portuguese there were some who defended them" (O'Malley 1993: 78). The most renowned opponent to Spanish exploitation of Native Americans is Bartolomé de Las Casas (1474–1566). This Spanish Dominican opposed and exposed both in America and in the Spanish court the atrocities of the Spanish settlers. He advanced his cause through his books *The Brief Account of the Destruction of the Indies* (1552) and *In Defense of the Indians* (ca. 1550). Sadly, Las Casas stood nearly alone in his arguments for a non-

Eurocentric vision of the world and equity for all (Friede and Keen 1971; Hanke 1974).

In contrast to the sixteenth-century missionary activity of Roman Catholics, Protestant missions are usually dated from the seventeenth-century evangelization of Native Americans by the Puritans. There was, however, a short-lived Genevan mission to Brazil in the mid-sixteenth century that apparently had Calvin's support. And the Swedish Lutheran pastor Johan Campanius ministered to the Delaware Indians from 1643 to 1648. His translation of Luther's Small Catechism into Lenni-Lenape "is the first attempt by a European to reduce a North American Indian language to writing" (Skarsten 1988: 59).

Economics, Education, and Science

Perhaps the point where the Reformers' proclamation of vocation has received the most attention in the modern world is where religion and economics intersect. Since the publication of Max Weber's *The Protestant Ethic and the Spirit of Capitalism* it has been popular to associate capitalism with Calvinism. The so-called "Weber thesis" is that Calvinist theology so stressed predestination that anxious believers began to seek signs of their divine election in worldly success such as business. In response to this popular conception of Weber's contribution to theories of modernization (see Schilling 1992: 240, 305, 356–7; Green 1959; Eisenstadt 1968), it should be noted that the profit economy or early forms of capitalism clearly antedated the Reformation, and that Calvin did not associate material success with the individual's standing before God. Calvin's understanding of predestination and providence was not individualistic but communal and world-historical. The doctrine of predestination is an affirmation that despite evil and suffering the ultimate destiny of the world and history rests in the good and infallible hands of God.

Because Calvin's theology was communal not individualistic, he could perceive riches as a divine blessing not in terms of endorsement of the individual's standing before God but rather as God's blessing to be shared with the whole community. Conversely, poverty is an expression of the wrath of God not toward the individual but toward the whole community for sin and thus to be borne by the whole community in support of the poor. The "blame the victim/praise the achiever" ideology of modern times is a secularized and individualized kind of covenant theology which associates worldly failure or success with moral virtue. The biblical answer to this form of "Deuteronomic history" which attributes failure and poverty to intrinsic character flaws and success to moral achievement is the Book of Job. Job is the idealized picture of the person who fulfills the covenant with God, yet nevertheless suffers terribly. His friends, convinced that goodness brings rewards and sin incurs punishments, can only tell him he must have sinned. With friends like that, who needs enemies! The Reformation answer of Luther and Calvin is to recall that God himself suffered, and hence Christians also should not expect that faith promises a rose garden. Already in 1518 at the Heidelberg disputation Luther had asserted that faith and worldly success were not equivalent, and attacked all claims to the contrary as "theologies of glory."

In the realm of economics Luther and Calvin vigorously attacked capitalism as unrestrained greed and called for government control of capitalism. On the other hand, Luther, Zwingli, and Calvin all contributed to the development of modern social welfare. Urban and state welfare programs were instituted sensitive to structural causes of un- and underemployment, and to the necessity for job training and civic responsibility for preventing as well as alleviating poverty.

The Reformation doctrines of justification and vocation also had an impact upon the development of education and the sciences. Building upon the contributions of the humanists, the Reformers stressed education as the resource for preparing persons for service to the whole community. As mentioned earlier, the Reformers liberated the Word and therefore also words from captivity to the elite. If there is to be a priesthood of all believers, then all – including women – should be able to read. It may be that literacy enhanced the self-esteem of women, but that consequence was also perceived as dangerous to the male status quo. Thus Henry VIII attempted – unsuccessfully – to prohibit the Bible to women. It was not accidental that universal literacy was first achieved in Scotland and the Protestant areas of Germany. As Melanchthon declared, "the ultimate end which confronts us is not private virtue alone but the interest of the public weal." And by 1560 Knox and his colleagues had drawn up a vision for a national system of education in Scotland.

But it may be argued that Luther's greatest contribution was not just his tracts on such practical subjects as that towns should establish schools and public libraries and that parents should make sure that their children go to school, but rather his initiation of a new way of thinking. In our time it has become fashionable to call a major change in thinking a "paradigm shift." Luther's thorough rejection of Aristotle and classical "authorities" is no less than a paradigm shift from medieval epistemology based on deduction from textual authorities to an epistemology of induction and experience. Physics was liberated from metaphysics. In his theological context, Luther stated: "It is not by understanding, reading, or speculation that one becomes a theologian, but through living, dying, and being damned" (*WA* 5: 163). Less dramatically, he also said: "None of the arts can be learned without practice. What kind of physician would that be who stayed in school all the time? When he finally puts his medicine to use and deals more and more with nature, he will come to see that he hasn't as yet mastered the art" (*LW* 54: 50–1). This shift from deduction to induction was recognized by contemporaries who called the maverick physician Paracelsus (1493–1541) "the Luther of the physicians." The point was that Paracelsus shared Luther's view of authority. Similarly, the English thinker Francis Bacon (1561–1626) compared Aristotle to Antichrist and indicted Greek philosophers for conjuring scientific knowledge out of their heads instead of seeking it in nature. The suspicion of metaphysics led to the foundation of modern rationalism in the work of René Descartes (1596–1650) with evidence and mathematics as the keys to interpreting the world in terms of mechanical regularity.

Institutionally Luther and Melanchthon were instrumental in the development of the medical faculty at the University of Wittenberg. On the personal side, Luther's son, Paul, became a respected physician. And Melanchthon's son-in-law Casper Peucer (1525–1602) was a physician as well as a theologian. By the seventeenth century, the University of Wittenberg had a renowned medical faculty. The turn away from the old authorities was evident in the important contributions of Salomon Alberti (1540–1600) in anatomical studies and the contributions of other colleagues to botany.

Ironically, the theological controversies after the death of Luther also contributed to the development of science. For example, Johann Kepler (1571–1630) was not accepted for ordained ministry because his theology of the Lord's Supper was not regarded as orthodox. He then became an assistant to the Danish Lutheran astronomer Tycho Brahe (1546–1601). In spite of his disappointment over rejection for the ministry, Kepler wrote in his first publication, "I wanted to become a theologian. For a long time I was restless. Now, however, observe how through my efforts, God is being celebrated in astronomy." Kepler went on to influence Newton and contribute to the triumph of the Copernican over the Ptolemaic theory of planetary motion.

Similarly, the Royal Society of London focused on scientific studies because they were free from both dogmatism and skepticism. Yet Kepler spoke for many of his scientific colleagues when he described scientists as "thinking God's thoughts after him." By and large these were religious men zealous to discover and admire the works of God in nature.

Literature and the Arts

From the beginning of the Reformation, historiography played an important role. Luther used history to argue that the papacy of his day was an aberration from the early church, martyrologists such as John Foxe used history selectively to present their case for the truth and witness of Protestantism, and the dissidents argued that the entire church had fallen when it became the establishment under Constantine in the fourth century. The first comprehensive history of the church arose in this context. In 13 volumes the "Magdeburg Centuries" under the general editorship of the Lutheran theologian Matthew Flacius (1520–75) covered the first 13 centuries of the church from the viewpoint that the pope was the Antichrist whose empire of the Roman Church had constantly opposed the work of God. The Catholic response was the equally biased *Ecclesiastical Annals* by Caesar Baronius (1538–1607), which appeared in numerous volumes between 1588 and 1607. Although these histories were designed to make history serve their respective theologies, they did stimulate the development of historical criticism.

National literatures were influenced by their respective great Reformers. There are too many major contributions to even list them here, other than to mention the Elizabethan dramatist William Shakespeare (1564–1616), whose literary brilliance and insight into human life remains unequaled. Behind much of the literary outpouring stimulated by the Reformations was the vernacular Bible. It "worked as a midwife to bring forth a whole great literature. It enabled a tinker of Bedford to write *The Pilgrim's Progress*. In an age when Milton could believe that God had chosen his Englishmen to perform his special tasks, it was the Bible which nerved the arm of Oliver Cromwell and fortified the spirit of the pioneers in New England" (Dickens 1991: 157). Vernacular Bibles were also significant in the norming of languages. The Luther Bible continues to be published in Germany, and the King James Bible (1611) commissioned by James I at the Hampton Court conference in 1604 has influenced English language and expressions up to today.

In art and music the sacramentally oriented Reformations stimulated compositions that continue to enrich modern life. All the Protestant

Reformers worked to make the liturgy accessible to the people, but not all complemented the liturgy with art and music as glorious gifts of God. Luther's anti-iconoclastic theology is evident in his appreciation of art and its contribution to faith and politics (Hofmann 1983; Zapalac 1990). Luther also put music in service of the gospel through an extensive hymnody which intended involvement of the whole congregation. He frequently affirmed that "next to the Word of God, music deserves the highest praise" (*LW* 53: 323). By the end of the century some 4,000 Protestant hymns had been written. Many of Luther's hymns continue to be well known and sung today, especially "A Mighty Fortress Is Our God," and the chorales which informed later works by Bach. Indeed, by the time of Buxtehude and Bach the Lutheran tradition of musical worship "had blossomed into a rich musical, liturgical, and spiritual experience, with a wide range of congregational, choral, vocal, organ, and instrumental music" (Leaver 1990: 157; *TRE* 18: 602–29). That Bach's own musical work was rooted in Luther's theology and the Lutheran liturgy is evident not only from his annotations in his two sets of Luther's collected works but also in his use of Lutheran motifs. The well-known Reformation themes of justification by faith alone, law and gospel, and the theology of the cross echo through Bach's works in both music and words (Chafe 1985; Lee 1985).

This was not the case in the Zwinglian and Calvinist Reformations. In Zurich Zwingli, assuming that music distracted from worship and that worship should be a purified service of the Word alone, banned all forms of chant, and in 1524 closed all the organs (Garside 1966: 44). Bern followed suit. We have already seen the contributions of Clement Marot and Calvin himself to the development of psalmody and the Huguenot Psalter. But organ and instrumental music was also prohibited in the Genevan churches. In this the Swiss Reformed were consistent with their iconoclastic orientation toward art in general. In contrast to the Lutheran and Catholic sacramental conviction that the finite is capable of the infinite, the Reformed effort to eliminate all forms of idolatry was informed by a sacramental theology that denied the "real presence," and therefore strictly limited art to the secular realm (Irwin 1993: 28). As Karlstadt had argued for the abolition of images, so Calvin too asserted the validity of the Old Testament prohibition of images. The use of images always leads to idolatry. "Therefore it remains that only those things are to be sculptured or painted which the eyes are capable of seeing: let not God's majesty, which is far above the perception of the eyes, be debased through unseemly representations" (McNeill and Battles 1960: I, 112). The Genevan churches were to be

completely free of images. Iconoclasm reflected both the earlier humanist critique of the externalization of religion and a rejection of the medieval desire for visualization, "the gaze that saves," which had led to adoration of relics and the host rather than participation in the Lord's Supper. There was also the ethical motive that it is better to support the poor than to decorate the church. Erasmus wrote: "How many dedicate candles to the Virgin and Mother of God, even in mid-day when it serves no purpose? How few dedicate themselves equally to a life of chastity, modesty, and love to spiritual things?" (Hofmann 1983: 8; Wandel 1995). The Calvinist emphasis that true decoration of the church consists in the moderation, piety, and virtues of reformed lives rather than costly materials had the effect of "moralizing beauty" (*TRE* 20: 282). It is claimed that the Reformation "decisively advanced the secularization of Western art: theoretically by its desacralization, and practically by reduction of its churchly function" (*TRE* 20: 284).

The council of Trent also expressed concern about idolatrous misuse of art, and sought to reduce "lasciviousness" in art. The most notorious case of this concern for decorum was the painting over of nudity in Michelangelo's great "Judgment of the World." Nevertheless, Roman Catholicism retained the conviction that images may move the heart to recall the preached Word of God.

Back to the Future:
The Reformations and Modernity

The relationship of the Reformations to modernity has been a controversial subject for some time, and raises numerous questions concerning interpretations of both periods. Historians critical of the past hegemony of intellectual and theological interpretations reject simple claims of Reformation patrimony of the modern age. The Reformation

---

Figure 15.3 "The Law and the Gospel" or "Allegory of Law and Grace" by the Wittenberg artist Lucas Cranach the Elder, ca. 1530, is one of the most complete artistic renderings of Luther's theology. On the left the devil, death, and the Law of Moses drive Adam toward hell. On the right John the Baptist points Adam to the crucified Christ, the lamb bearing the sins of the world. The picture connects the fate of humanity and the event of Christ as presented in central biblical passages supplied in the margins. This depiction was repeated on numerous Lutheran altars, Bibles, and elsewhere.
Source: Photo Eberhard Renno, Weimar Schlossmuseum.

Figure 15.4 "The Light of the Gospel Rekindled by the Reformers," ca. 1630. Triumphalist depictions of the Reformation often presented Luther in such outstanding roles as evangelist, saint, paragon of virtue, and even the law-giving Moses. This Dutch broadside is exceptional in presenting a harmonious union of the significant European Reformers and their forerunners Wyclif and Hus in a scene that alludes to Christ's Last Supper in the circle of his disciples. In the place of Christ is the "trinity" of Luther with open Bible, Calvin, and the Italian Calvinist, Hieronymous Zanchi. Opposite them in the place of Judas are a cardinal, a devil, the pope, and a monk who represent the fourfold form of Catholic false faith. The blazing candle set on the Bible signifies the true divine light brought into the open by the Reformers (Matthew 5: 15). The assembled Reformers are seen as the preservers, spreaders, and also the martyrs of the divine light of true faith in contrast to their Catholic opponents, servants of darkness, who attempt to blow out the candle.
Source: Kunstsammlungen der Veste Coburg.

is to be understood for its own sake and not (mis-)used for contemporary historical and religious speculation. This is an important warning against "Whiggish" interpretations of the Reformation which view it as the initiation of inevitable progress toward the triumph of truth. "The Reformation remains, in the first instance, the Reformation, and its relationship to modern times is misleading. Historians have a need for modesty" (Nipperdey 1987: 539).

Yet it needs to be said that if historical study includes the purpose of freeing us "from the dead hand of history," then our study of the past entails more than antiquarianism. "When we have finished bewailing the greed, folly and fanaticism of the sixteenth century, the Reformation still stands in mountainous bulk across the landscapes of western Christianity. It concerned significant issues which still live to perplex and divide us" (Dickens 1991: 394–5). There is among historians an increasing willingness to affirm that the Reformation was a turning point with great significance for universal history beyond its religious concerns. This significance has been described in terms of desacralization and deritualization which in the critique of institutions and hierarchies provided space for individual self-determination, the internalization of discipline, and "the civilizing process" (Hsia 1989: 183; Rublack 1993; Blaschke 1993: 511). The prophetic critique of all efforts to ascribe ultimacy to the penultimate was not a force for the past but rather set free intellectual, social, and political impulses toward modernization (Schilling 1992: ch. 7) which brought forth new forms of thought and political–social life. To borrow a concept from modern medicine, the religious, political, and social forces interplayed together like a syndrome to create the specific effects of their interrelationship (Schilling 1988: 86).

Luther certainly did not set out to modernize society, to initiate the modern period, nor even to set off a social revolution. The modern period was already underway when Luther was engaged with his religious struggle to find a merciful God. But it was Luther's religious discovery that righteousness before God is received not achieved which cleared away the obstacles which had till then still prevented the complete breakthrough of the modern world (Blaschke 1993: 520).

This suggests, if I may be allowed some antics with semantics, the relevance of irrelevance. Unlike his contemporaries concerned with fine-tuning the engines of their society so that it would run better, Luther and his fellow-Reformers came to the conclusion that the issue was not running better but running in the right direction. This conclusion was derived from their study of the sources of their society rather than its goals and achievements. We are obviously far removed from the sixteenth century, but also remarkably close to some of the same issues. We too live in a culture rooted in a piety of achievement no less debilitating for all that it is secular instead of religious. The modern concern for the salvation of the economy is no less consuming than the medieval concern for the economy of salvation; and contemporary cathedrals of capitalism and other ideologies require no fewer "good works" than those of the Middle Ages. Study of the distant world of the Reformations thus provides that horizon which offers a perspective on the present. "It questions the self-assurance of our modern existence. For just because it is remote does not mean that it is necessarily totally outdated" (Nipperdey 1987: 535).

Of course the Reformation era was not a golden age; those who hanker for the good old days often are not fully aware of what life then entailed. Yet forgetfulness of the past contributes to incomprehension of the present. Two brief examples may suffice here. Modern Westerners cannot seem to grasp that anything beyond economics and politics could motivate contemporary acts of terrorism or the internal and international policies of other cultures. We have forgotten that our own forefathers quite willingly killed and accepted death on the basis of religious commitments. We ignore religious dynamics at our own peril. Within our own culture we have elevated individual rights to the point of privatism and the erosion of the common good of the whole community. Thus we think of discipline such as that exercised by the Geneva Consistory as punitive social control. At the same time we wonder about the alienation and the breakdown of social relations in our large cities which stems from anomie. We have forgotten that communities where an eye was kept on everyone else's business had the constructive goal of serving and caring for the whole community (see Kingdon 1993b: 679; 1994: 34).

Awareness of the Reformations' contributions to the development of our world both helps us understand how we got this way and provides a critical horizon for evaluation of the results.

Suggestions for Further Reading

Jane Dempsey Douglass, *Women, Freedom and Calvin*, Philadelphia: Westminster, 1985

John Edwards, *The Jews in Christian Europe 1400–1700*, London: Routledge, 1988

R. Po-Chia Hsia, *Social Discipline in the Reformation: Central Europe 1550–1750*, London: Routledge, 1989

Joyce Irwin, "Society and the Sexes," in Steven Ozment, ed., *Reformation Europe: A Guide to Research*, 343–59, St Louis: Center for Reformation Research, 1982

Sherrin Marshall, ed., *Women in Reformation and Counter-Reformation Europe: Public and Private Worlds*, Bloomington: Indiana University Press, 1989

Kathryn Norberg, "The Counter Reformation and Women: Religious and Lay," in John W. O'Malley, SJ, ed., *Catholicism in Early Modern History: A Guide to Research*, 133–46, St Louis: Center for Reformation Research, 1988

Heiko A. Oberman, *The Roots of Anti-Semitism in the Age of the Renaissance and Reformation*, Philadelphia: Fortress, 1984

Steven Ozment, *When Fathers Ruled: Family Life in Reformation Europe*, Cambridge, MA: Harvard University Press, 1983

Heinz Schilling, *Civic Calvinism in Northwestern Germany and the Netherlands: Sixteenth to Nineteenth Centuries*, Kirksville: Sixteenth Century Journal Publishers, 1991

Heinz Schilling, *Religion, Political Culture and the Emergence of Early Modern Society: Essays in German and Dutch History*, Leiden: E. J. Brill, 1992

Merry Wiesner, "Studies of Women, The Family, and Gender," in William S. Maltby, ed., *Reformation Europe: A Guide to Research*, II, 159–87, St Louis: Center for Reformation Research, 1992

Chronology

1294–1303	Pope Boniface VIII: bull *Unam sanctam* (1302): "submission . . . to the bishop of Rome is altogether necessary for salvation."
1309–77	Papacy in Avignon ("Babylonian captivity of the church")
ca. 1320–84	John Wyclif (rejected overlordship of pope, demanded an independent English national church, propounded sole authority of Scripture)
1324	Marsiglio of Padua's *Defensor pacis* ("Defender of the Peace")
1337–1453	Hundred Years War between France and England, after which England retained only Calais of its former vast French possessions
1348	University of Prague founded
1348–52	Plague throughout Europe ("Black Death")
1356	Golden Bull (election law: king to be promoted to emperor; restricted to seven electors; excluded papacy)
1365	University of Vienna founded
1370–1415	Jan Hus (applied Wyclif's ideas to Czech church reform and national goals; executed in 1415 at council of Constance)
1378–1415	Western schism between popes in Rome and Avignon
1379	University of Erfurt founded
1381	English Peasants' Revolt led by Wat Tyler and John Ball
ca. 1405–57	Lorenzo Valla, Italian humanist (exposed "Donation of Constantine" as forgery)
1409	Council of Pisa, resulting in three popes
1409	University of Leipzig founded
1414–18	Council of Constance: schism ended; decreed regular meetings of councils and conciliar authority over pope; Hus burned
1419–36	Hussite wars; pope and emperor reject Hussite demands for free preaching, cup to laity, clerical poverty, and role of secular courts *vis-à-vis* church
1431–49	Council of Basle: Prague compact offered cup to laity; division of council and move to Ferrara; council of Ferrara–Florence (1437–39): proposed union with Greek church not realized

1438	Pragmatic sanction of Bourges: "Gallican" liberties for French church
1438–1806	Emperors from House of Habsburg
1439	*Reformatio Sigismundi* (anonymous reform tract: strong critique of secular and ecclesiastical abuses)
ca. 1450	Invention of printing with movable metal type (Gutenberg); scholastic controversies between *via antiqua* (Thomism and Scotism) and *via moderna* (Occamism)
1452–1519	Leonardo da Vinci
1453	Fall of Constantinople
1455–85	English Wars of the Roses: House of Lancaster (red rose) vs House of York (white rose); decimation of higher nobility; led to founding of House of Tudor by Henry VII
1455–1522	Johann Reuchlin (German humanist)
1456	Start of political protests against clerical abuses: *Gravamina* of German nation
1458–64	Pope Pius II
1466–1536	Erasmus of Rotterdam, "Prince" of European humanists
1471–1528	Albrecht Dürer
1473–1543	Nicholas Copernicus
1474–1566	Bartolomé de Las Casas
1475–1564	Michelangelo
ca. 1480–1541	Andreas Bodenstein von Karlstadt
1481–	Inquisition in Spain (against Waldensians, Cathari, Jews, and Moors)
1483–1546	Martin Luther
1484–1531	Ulrich Zwingli
1486–1525	Elector Frederick the Wise of Saxony
ca. 1489–1525	Thomas Müntzer
1489–1556	Thomas More
ca. 1491–1556	Ignatius Loyala
1492	End of Arab rule in Spain; discovery of America by Columbus; expulsion of Jews from Spain
1492–1503	Pope Alexander VI (Rodrigo Borgia)
1493	"New world" divided between Spain and Portugal
1493–1519	Maximilian I, Holy Roman Emperor
1496–1561	Menno Simons
1497	Expulsion of Jews from Portugal
1498	Burning of Florentine Dominican preacher of repentance, Savonarola (b. 1452)
1500–58	Emperor Charles V
1502	University of Wittenberg founded
1503–13	Pope Julius II: pope as territorial prince comparable in life

	and practice to secular princes; indulgence (1507) for building of St Peter's in Rome
1506	Start of new construction of St Peter's
1509–47	Henry VIII; wives: Catherine of Aragon, mother of Mary, 1509–33; Anne Boleyn, mother of Elizabeth I, 1533–6; Jane Seymour, mother of Edward VI, 1536–7; Anne of Cleves, Jan. 1540–June 1540; Catherine Howard, 1540–2; Catherine Parr, 1543– (outlived Henry)
1509–64	John Calvin
1512–17	Fifth Lateran council: condemnation of conciliarism
1513–21	Pope Leo X
1515	Thomas Wolsey (ca. 1475–1530), cardinal and English chancellor, papal legate
1515–47	Francis I of France
1516	Concordat of Bologna between Francis I of France and Pope Leo X: French national church established
1517	Luther's "Ninety-Five Theses"
1519	Leipzig debate with Eck; election of Charles V as king of Germany, crowned emperor in 1520; start of Spanish conquest of Mexico
1520	Luther's Reformation manifestos: *Address to the Christian Nobility of the German Nation*, *Babylonian Captivity of the Church*, *The Freedom of a Christian*, and *Treatise on Good Works*; papal bull threatening excommunication; *Exsurge Domine*; burning of papal bull and canon law in Wittenberg
1521	Philip Melanchthon's *Loci communes*, the first Reformation systematic theology; Luther's excommunication by Leo X; diet of Worms and edict of Worms; Luther taken into protective custody at the Wartburg Castle; *Assertion of the Seven Sacraments* by Henry VIII against Luther; reception of title "Defender of the Faith" from Pope Leo X
1521–2	Wittenberg disturbances
1521–6	First Habsburg–Valois War
1522	Reformation in Zurich; Turkish conquest of Rhodes
1522–3	Pope Adrian VI
1523	Knights' Revolt in Germany
1523–34	Pope Clement VII
1524–6	Peasants' War in Germany
1525	Disputation in Zurich on baptism; first believer's baptism in Zurich
1526	First Zurich council mandate of capital punishment against the Anabaptists; University of Marburg (first Protestant university) founded; battle of Mohács; Ludwig II of Hungary, defeated and killed by Turks, succeeded by Ferdinand of Austria

1526–9	Second Habsburg–Valois War
1527	Mantz executed by drowning in Zurich; Schleitheim Articles; sack of Rome by imperial troops
1528–42	Bugenhagen's church orders for reform of churches and schools
1529	Luther's Small and Large Catechisms; in England, Wolsey replaced as chancellor by Sir Thomas More; "protestation" of the evangelical estates at the diet of Speyer; Turkish siege of Vienna; Marburg colloquy
1530	Charles V crowned emperor at Bologna; diet of Augsburg: Augsburg confession and confutation
1531	Formation of the Schmalkaldic League for Protestant defense; death of Zwingli at second battle of Kappel
1532	Resignation of Thomas More; Reformation in Geneva
1534	Act of Supremacy in England
1534–5	Anabaptist kingdom in Münster
1535	Execution of More and Fisher
1536	Suppression of the smaller English monasteries; execution of Anne Boleyn; publication of Tyndale's translation of the Bible; Wittenberg concord; Reformation in Denmark and Norway; first edition of Calvin's *Institutes of the Christian Religion*
1536–8	Third Habsburg–Valois War; Calvin's first stay in Geneva
1538–41	Calvin in Strasbourg
1539	Suppression of the large English monasteries; Statute of the Six Articles
1540	Execution of Cromwell; Pope Paul III's sanction of the Society of Jesus
1540–1	Religious colloquies aimed at overcoming confessional division in the Empire: colloquy of Worms (Granvelle, Eck, Melanchthon, Calvin) without result, transferred to Regensburg
1541	Death of Karlstadt in Basle; Calvin returns to Geneva
1542–4	Fourth Habsburg–Valois War; ends with Peace of Crépy
1542	Ireland made a kingdom; war with Scotland and defeat of James V at Solway Moss; Roman Inquisition
1545–7	First session of the council of Trent
1546	Death of Luther
1546–7	Schmalkaldic War; defeat of Protestants at Mühlberg
1547	Death of Francis I; succeeded by Henry II; "*Chambre ardente*" established against heresy; death of Henry VIII
1547–53	Reign of Edward VI in England; repeal of the Six Articles (1547)
1548–52	The Augsburg Interim: Imperial formula of compromise to

	be valid until a conciliar decision; rejected by the Protestant estates
1549	*Consensus Tigurinus* (Zurich consensus) in Switzerland; first Prayer Book in England
1550	Magdeburg confession
1551	Forty-two Articles (Cranmer)
1551–2	Second session of the council of Trent
1553	Burning of Michael Servetus in Geneva; second Prayer Book in England
1553–8	Reign of Mary Tudor; restoration of Catholic bishops; execution of Lady Jane Grey
1554	Marriage of Mary Tudor and Philip of Spain
1555	Calvin's final victory in Geneva; diet of Augsburg; the Augsburg confession (1530) recognized along with the Catholic faith as legal in the Empire; Religious Peace of Augsburg (*cuius regio, eius religio*)
1556	Emperor Charles V resigns his office in favor of his brother Ferdinand
1557	England joins Spain in war against France; Calvinist preaching in Poland
1558	Death of Charles V (21 September)
1558–1603	Reign of Elizabeth Tudor in England: repeal of Mary's Catholic legislation; re-enactment of Henry VIII's Acts of Supremacy and Uniformity
1559	Final edition of Calvin's *Institutes*; founding of Geneva Academy; death of Henry II of France; first Index of Prohibited Books
1560	Death of Melanchthon; Amboise conspiracy; death of Francis II, succeeded by Charles IX with Catherine de' Medici as regent; first edict of toleration in France; Catholic renewal in Milan under Cardinal Charles Borromeo (1538–1584)
1561	Colloquy of Poissy; Mary Stuart returns to Scotland; Belgic confession
1561–3	Third session of the council of Trent
1562	First French War of Religion; massacre of Huguenots at Vassy by duke of Guise; French settlement in Florida
1562–98	Wars of Religion in France
1563	Peace of Amboise ends first War of Religion; Huguenots receive limited toleration
1564	Death of Calvin
1564–1616	William Shakespeare
1564–1642	Galileo
1566	Roman Catechism
1567	Mary Stuart abdicates in favor of her son James VI;

	Spanish occupation of the Netherlands
1568	Second French War of Religion ends and third begins
1568–1648	Netherlands struggle for liberation against Spain
1570	Peace of Saint-Germain ends third War of Religion
1571–1630	Johann Kepler
1572	St Bartholomew's Day massacre; fourth War of Religion begins
1573	End of fourth War of Religion; Henry, duke of Anjou, elected king of Poland; Francis Hotman, *Francogallia*
1574	Death of Charles IX, succeeded by duke of Anjou, Henry III; fifth War of Religion
1575	Union of Protestants and *politiques* in France
1576	Henry of Navarre declares for Protestant cause; toleration granted; formation of Catholic Holy League
1577	Sixth civil war in France begins and ends; alliance of England with the Netherlands
1580	Seventh civil war in France
1582	Gregorian reform of calendar; Ricci in China; death of Teresa of Avila
1584	Death of duke of Anjou makes Henry of Navarre heir to French throne
1585	Spain allies with French Catholic League; Pope Sixtus V excommunicates Henry of Navarre
1586	Sir Francis Drake's expedition to the West Indies
1587	Henry of Navarre defeats royal army; League plots in Paris; execution of Mary Stuart
1588	"Day of Barricades" drives Henry III from Paris; Henry assassinates the Catholic League leaders, duke of Guise and cardinal of Guise; English destruction of the Spanish Armada
1589	Assassination of Henry III; Henry of Navarre begins Bourbon dynasty
1590	Henry IV lays siege to Paris; duke of Mayenne sets up rival government
1592	English army supports Navarre in Normandy
1593	Henry of Navarre converts to Catholicism
1594	Henry enters Paris; grants toleration to Huguenots
1595	Assassination attempt on Henry IV; France declares war on Spain; Clement VII receives Henry back into Roman church and recognizes him as king of France
1596	France allies with England and Netherlands against Spain
1596–1650	René Descartes
1598	Peace between France and Spain; edict of Nantes grants toleration and liberties to Huguenots
1603	Death of Elizabeth I

1603–25	Reign of James VI (of Scotland), I (of England); personal union of England and Scotland
1605	Gunpowder Plot to blow up Houses of Parliament in England; death of Beza
1606–69	Rembrandt
1608–74	John Milton
1610	Assassination of Henry IV, succeeded by Louis XIII with Marie de' Medici as regent
1611	Completion of English Bible translation (King James version)
1618–19	Synod of Dort in Netherlands
1618–48	Thirty Years War
1620	Voyage of *Mayflower*; pilgrims in Massachusetts
1633	Galileo renounces Copernican theory before the Inquisition
1636	Harvard University founded
1642–9	English civil wars

Genealogies

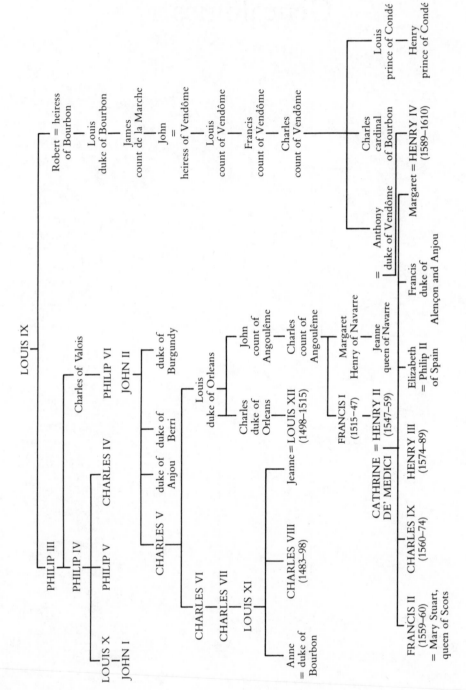

The Houses of Valois and Bourbon, to 1610

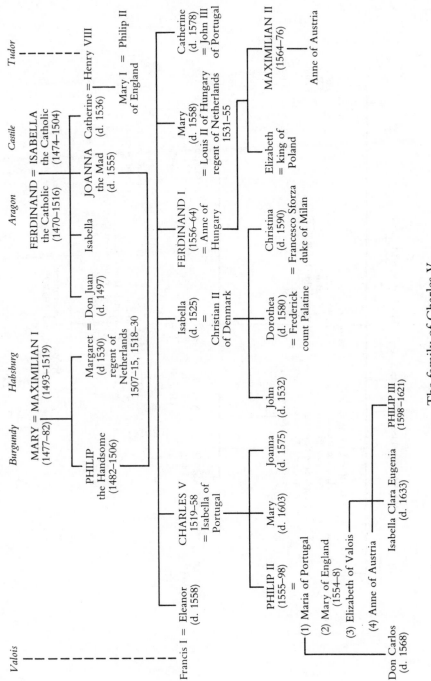

The family of Charles V

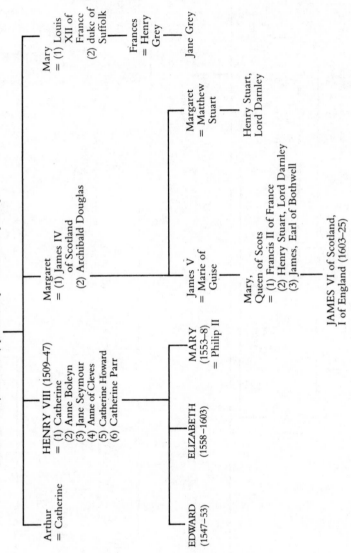

HENRY VII (1485–1509) [Lancaster] = Elizabeth [York]

Arthur
= Catherine

HENRY VIII (1509–47)
= (1) Catherine
  (2) Anne Boleyn
  (3) Jane Seymour
  (4) Anne of Cleves
  (5) Catherine Howard
  (6) Catherine Parr

EDWARD
(1547–53)

ELIZABETH
(1558–1603)

MARY
(1553–8)
= Philip II

Margaret
= (1) James IV
      of Scotland
  (2) Archibald Douglas

James V
= Marie of
  Guise

Mary,
Queen of Scots
= (1) Francis II of France
  (2) Henry Stuart, Lord Darnley
  (3) James, Earl of Bothwell

JAMES VI of Scotland,
I of England (1603–25)

Margaret
= Matthew
  Stuart

Henry Stuart,
Lord Darnley

Mary
= (1) Louis
      XII of
      France
  (2) duke of
      Suffolk

Frances
= Henry
  Grey

Jane Grey

The English crown, 1485–1603

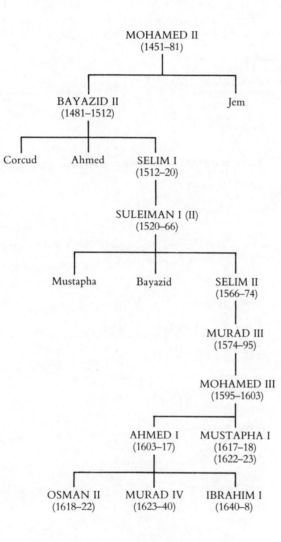

Ottoman sultans, 1451–1648

Alexander VI (Borgia), 1492–1503
Pius III, 1503
Julius II (della Rovere), 1503–13
Leo X (Medici), 1513–21
Hadrian VI (Dedel), 1522–3
Clement VII (Medici), 1523–34
Paul III (Farnese), 1534–49
Julius III (del Monte), 1550–5
Marcellus II (Cervini), 1555
Paul IV (Caraffa), 1555–9
Pius IV (Medici)*, 1559–64
Pius (Ghislieri), 1566–72
Gregor XIII (Boncompagni), 1572–85
Sixtus V (Peretti), 1585–90
Urban VII (Castagna), 1590
Gregory XIV (Spondrato), 1590–1
Innocent IX (Fachinetti), 1591
Clement VIII (Aldobrandini), 1592–1605

*Not related to the Florentine Medici popes, Leo X and Clement VII.

Popes, 1492–1605

Maps

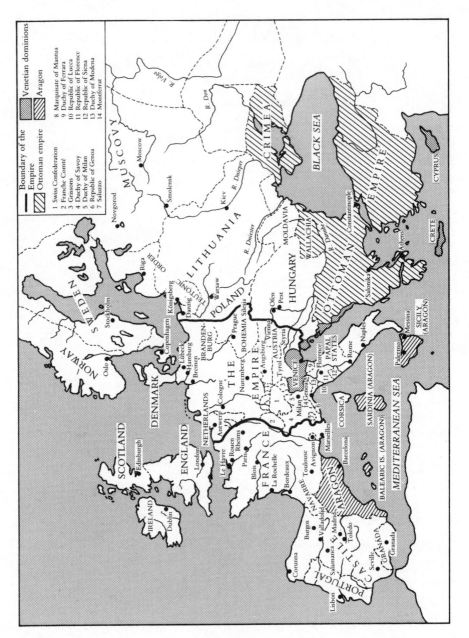

Europe about 1500

Boundary of the
Empire
Ottoman empire

Venetian dominions

Aragon

1 Swiss Confederation
2 Franche Comté
3 Grissons
4 Duchy of Savoy
5 Duchy of Milan
6 Republic of Genoa
7 Saluzzo

8 Marquisate of Mantua
9 Duchy of Ferrara
10 Republic of Lucca
11 Republic of Florence
12 Republic of Siena
13 Duchy of Modena
14 Montferrat

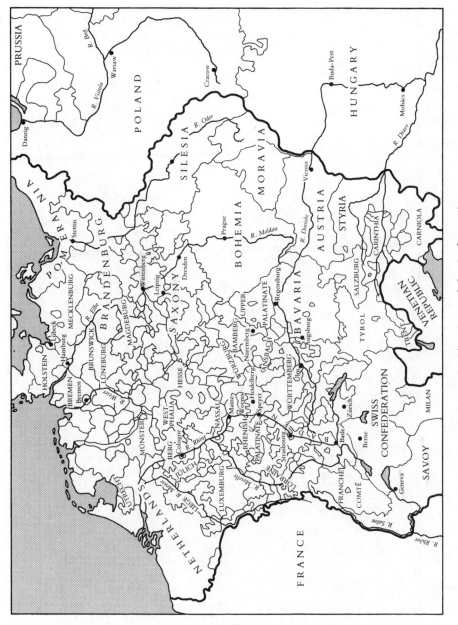

Germany at the time of the Reformation

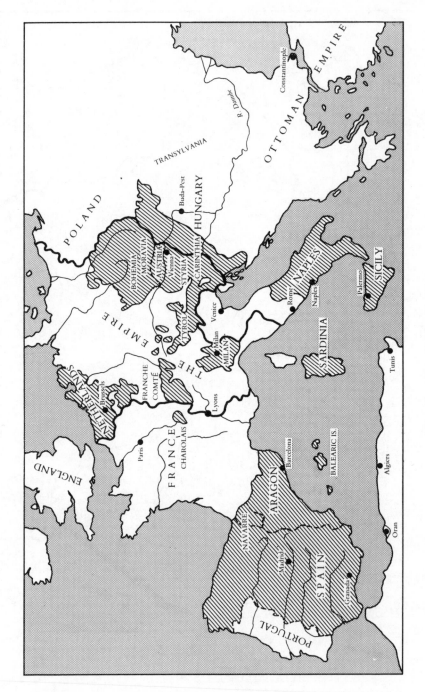

The Empire of Charles V

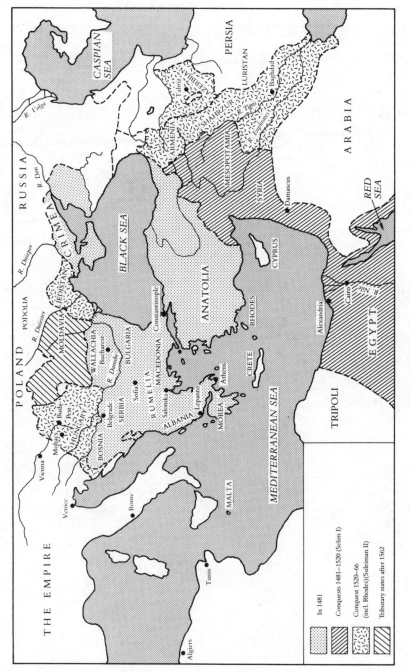

THE EMPIRE

POLAND

RUSSIA

PODOLIA

R. Dnieper

R. Dniester

R. Volga

R. Don

CASPIAN SEA

CRIMEA

PERSIA

Tabriz

AZERBIJAN

ARMENIA

SHAHRZUR

LURISTAN

Baghdad

R. Tigris

R. Euphrates

MESOPOTAMIA

MOLDAVIA

WALLACHIA

Bucharest

R. Danube

BLACK SEA

ANATOLIA

SYRIA

Damascus

ARABIA

RED SEA

Vienna

Buda

Pest

Mohács

HUNGARY

Belgrade

BOSNIA

SERBIA

Sofia

BULGARIA

Constantinople

RUMELIA

MACEDONIA

Salonika

ALBANIA

Lepanto

MOREA

Athens

CRETE

RHODES

CYPRUS

Cairo

R. Nile

Alexandria

EGYPT

Venice

Rome

MEDITERRANEAN SEA

MALTA

TRIPOLI

Tunis

Algiers

In 1481

Conquests 1481–1520 (Selim I)

Conquest 1520–66
(incl. Rhodes)(Suleiman II)

Tributary states after 1562

The Ottoman Empire

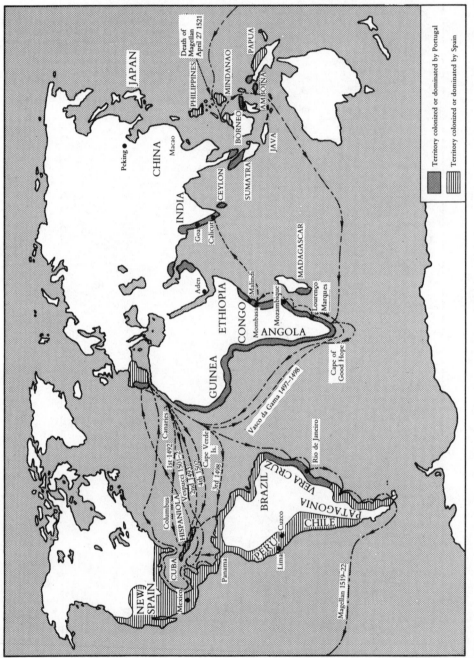

The Portuguese and Spanish overseas empires

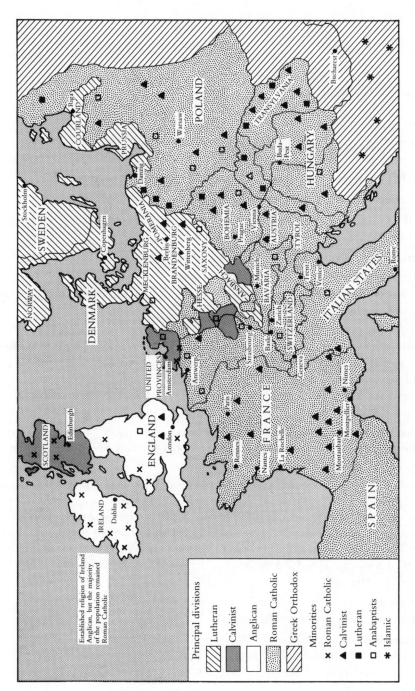

Religious divisions in Europe about 1600

Principal divisions

Lutheran
Calvinist
Anglican
Roman Catholic
Greek Orthodox

Minorities

× Roman Catholic
▲ Calvinist
■ Lutheran
□ Anabaptists
✳ Islamic

Established religion of Ireland Anglican, but the majority of the population remained Roman Catholic

NORWAY
SWEDEN   Stockholm
DENMARK   Copenhagen
SCOTLAND   Edinburgh
IRELAND   Dublin
ENGLAND   London
UNITED PROVINCES   Amsterdam
Antwerp
FRANCE   Paris
Nantes   La Rochelle
Rennes
Montauban   Montpellier   Nîmes
SPAIN
PRUSSIA   Riga
COURLAND
POLAND   Warsaw   Danzig
MECKLENBURG   POMERANIA
BRANDENBURG   Berlin   Wittenberg
SAXONY
HESSE
BOHEMIA   Prague
AUSTRIA   Vienna
BAVARIA   Munich
TYROL
SWITZERLAND   Basle   Zürich   Geneva
Strasbourg
SANXONY
TRANSYLVANIA
HUNGARY   Buda Pest
Bucharest
ITALIAN STATES   Rome   Venice

Glossary

adiaphora "Matters of indifference" in faith and practice because they are neither banned nor mandated by Scripture.

attrition Repentance for sins out of fear of God's punishment.

benefice An endowed church office.

bull From Latin *bulla*, seal; a written papal mandate with his seal attesting to its seriousness.

canon law The legislation which governs the faith, morals, and organization of the church.

celibacy Unmarried state required of western clergy and religious since the twelfth century; rejected by the Reformers.

communicatio idiomatum The interchange of properties. Advanced by Cyril of Alexandria (d. 444) among others during christological controversies; posits that although the human and divine natures of Christ are separate, the attributes of one may be predicated of the other due to their union in the one person of Christ. The formula came to the fore in the eucharistic controversies of the Reformation.

conciliarism The doctrine that the supreme authority in the church is vested in a general or ecumenical council; promoted at the councils of Constance (1414–14) and Basle (1431–49).

council A formal church assembly convened to regulate matters of faith and discipline. A provincial council is a meeting of bishops with their archbishop; a diocesan synod is a meeting of a bishop with the clergy of his diocese; an ecumenical or general council is a meeting of all bishops of the church under the leadership of the pope or the emperor. The decrees of an ecumenical council confirmed by the pope possess the highest authority in the church (*see* conciliarism).

concupiscence The enjoyment of temporal goods which should only be used; sensuality unchecked by reason; sin.

confession (1) Private or public acknowledgement of sin. (2) Public profession of the principles of faith ascribed to by adherents before public authorities, e.g. the Augsburg confession.

contrition Repentance for sins out of love for God.

cuius regio, eius religio "Whose [the prince's] rule, his [the prince's] religion": the formula used to describe the Religious Peace of Augsburg (1555) by which rulers were permitted to decide whether their land would be Roman Catholic or Lutheran.

Donatism A fourth-century schismatic renewal movement in north Africa which stressed the holiness of the church to extent that the validity of Word and sacraments were made contingent upon the moral purity of the priest. That is, the message was dependent upon the messenger.

eucharist "Thanksgiving" in Greek; the name for the central act of worship also termed communion, Lord's Supper, and mass. The association of the term mass with eucharistic sacrifice of the Roman Catholic church prompted its eventual discontinuance by Protestants.

ex opere operantis The efficacy of the sacraments related to the receiver's subjective disposition. The orthodox interpetation posits that a proper disposition provides grace beyond that received *ex opere operato*. The heretical interpretation posits proper disposition is necessary for the validity of the sacrament (*see* Donatism).

ex opere operato Sacramental validity is due to the performance of the rite; posits the objective validity of the sacraments apart from the subjective atitudes of the priest or the recipient.

facere quod in se est To do one's very best; to do all that is within one's natural power unaided by grace; to love God above all things and thereby acquire the initial infusion of grace.

icon A sacred image or picture of Christ or a saint.

iconoclasm the destruction of icons.

indulgence The Roman Catholic church's remission of the temporal penalty due after the forgiveness of sin; a commutation of imposed penance.

liturgy The original Greek term literally means "the work of the people." In its general sense, liturgy refers to the church's prescribed services of worship; specifically it refers to the eucharist as the chief service of worship.

millenarianism The belief in a thousand-year reign of blessedness; see Revelation 20.

penance One of the seven sacraments of the Roman Catholic church which consists of confession, absolution, and penance. From the Latin *poena*, punishment, penance also refers to the ascetic practices intended to control and eradicate sinful passions as well as acts of atonement for sins.

religious As a noun, a general term for any person bound to monastic life by vows (poverty, chastity, obedience): monk, canon, friar, nun.

simony The buying or selling of church offices; term derived from Simon the Magician (Acts 8: 18–24).

transubstantiation The doctrine advanced by the fourth Lateran council (1215) that the whole substance of the bread and the wine in the eucharist is converted into the whole substance of the body and blood of Christ.

ultramontanism   Literally "beyond the mountains": refers to the centralization of authority and influence in the papacy as opposed to national or diocesan independence.

via antiqua, via moderna   Terms signifying allegiance to the "old way" of the theology of the high Middle Ages (Thomism) and the "new way" of the theology of the late Middle Ages (Nominalism, Occamism).

Vulgate   The Latin translation of the Bible largely deriving from Jerome (d. 420), declared the only authentic and definitive text of the Bible by Pope Sixtus V in 1590.

Appendix:
Aids to Reformation Studies

Orientation to the Field

James E. Bradley and Richard A. Muller, *Church History: An Introduction to Research, Reference Works, and Methods*, Grand Rapids: Eerdmans, 1995.

Norman F. Cantor, *Inventing the Middle Ages: The Lives, Works, and Ideas of the Great Medievalists of the Twentieth Century*, New York: William Morrow, 1991.

A. G. Dickens and John M. Tonkin, *The Reformation in Historical Thought*, Cambridge, MA: Harvard University Press, 1985.

Dictionaries and Encyclopedias

F. L. Cross and E. A. Livingstone, eds, *The Oxford Dictionary of the Christian Church*, Oxford: Oxford University Press, 1984.

Enzyklopädie Deutscher Geschichte, Munich: Oldenbourg. For those with reading ability in German this excellent series presents major interpretive perspectives and research work with comprehensive bibliographies. The following volumes are pertinent to Reformation studies: Peter Blickle, *Unruhen in der ständischen Gesellschaft 1300–1800* (1988); Hans-Jürgen Goertz, *Religiöse Bewegungen in der Frühen Neuzeit* (1993); Heinz Schilling, *Die Stadt in der Frühen Neuzeit* (1993); Heinrich Richard Schmidt, *Konfessionalisierung im 16. Jahrhundert* (1992).

Hans J. Hillerbrand, ed., *Encyclopedia of the Reformation*, 4 vols, New York: Oxford University Press, 1995.

G. Krause and G. Müller, gen. eds, *Theologische Realenzyklopädie*, Berlin: Walter de Gruyter, 1977–. NB: Although in German, the articles of this excellent reference work include multilingual bibliographies..

J. R. Strayer, ed., *Dictionary of the Middle Ages*, 13 vols, New York, 1983.

Surveys of the Reformation

John Bossy, *Christianity in the West 1400–1700*, Oxford: Oxford University Press, 1985.

Thomas Brady, Heiko A. Oberman, and James Tracy, eds, *Handbook of European History 1400–1600*, 2 vols, Leiden: E. J. Brill, 1994.

Euan Cameron, *The European Reformation*, Oxford: Clarendon Press, 1991.

G. R. Elton, ed., *The Reformation 1520–1559*, 2nd edn (New Cambridge Modern History, II), Cambridge: Cambridge University Press, 1990.

Hans J. Hillerbrand, *The Reformation: A Narrative History Related by Contemporary Observers and Participants*, New York: Harper & Row, 1964.

Erwin Iserloh, Joseph Glatzik, and Hubert Jedin, *Reformation and Counter Reformation* (History of the Church, ed. Hubert Jedin and John Dolan, V), New York: Crossroad, 1986.

Alister McGrath, *Reformation Thought: An Introduction*, 2nd edn, Oxford: Blackwell, 1993. Useful appendices; glossary of theological and historical terms; primary sources in English translation; standard abbreviations and references; Reformation bibliographies; chronology.

Steven Ozment, *The Age of Reform 1250–1550*, New Haven: Yale University Press, 1980.

R. W. Scribner, *The German Reformation*, Atlantic Highlands: Humanities, 1986.

Lewis W. Spitz, *The Protestant Reformation 1517–1559*, New York: Harper & Row, 1985.

Bibliographies and Guides to Research

Archive for Reformation History: Literature Review. An annual supplement containing annotated multilingual review of recent research.

Kenneth Hagen, ed., *Luther Digest: An Annual Abridgement of Luther Studies*, Fort Wayne: Luther Academy, 1993.

Hans J. Hillerbrand, ed., *A Bibliography of Anabaptism 1520–1630*, Elkhart: Institute of Mennonite Studies, 1962.

Hans J. Hillerbrand, ed., *A Bibliography of Anabaptism, 1520–1630: A Sequel 1962–1974*, St Louis: Center for Reformation Research, 1975.

Lutherjahrbuch. An annual which contains an excellent extensive multilingual bibliographical section.

William S. Maltby, ed., *Reformation Europe: A Guide to Research*, St Louis: Center for Reformation Research, 1992.

John W. O'Malley, SJ, ed., *Catholicism in Early Modern History: A Guide to Research*, St Louis: Center for Reformation Research, 1988.

Steven Ozment, ed., *Reformation Europe: A Guide to Research*, St Louis: Center for Reformation Research, 1982.

Chronological Tables, Charts and Maps

Kurt Aland, *Kirchengeschichte in Zeittafeln und Überblicken*, Gütersloh: Gerd Mohn, 1984.

C. Anderson, *Augsburg Historical Atlas of Christianity in the Middle Ages and Reformation*, Minneapolis: Augsburg, 1967.

Bernard Grun, *The Timetables of History*, New York, 1975.

Kurt Dietrich Schmidt and Gerhard Ruhbach, *Chronologische Tabellen zur Kirchengeschichte*, 5th edn, Göttingen: Vandenhoeck & Ruprecht, 1986.

Robert Walton, *Chronological and Background Charts of Church History*, Grand Rapids: Zondervan, 1986.

Pertinent Journals

Archive for Reformation History
Catholic Historical Review
Church History
Journal of Ecclesiastical History
Lutherjahrbuch
Lutheran Quarterly
Mennonite Quarterly Review
Revue d'histoire ecclesiastique
Sixteenth Century Journal
Theologische Literaturzeitung
Zeitschrift für Kirchengeschichte

Collected Studies of Reformers

Richard L. DeMolen, ed., *Leaders of the Reformation*, Selinsgrove: Susquehanna University Press, 1984.

Timothy George, *Theology of the Reformers*, Nashville: Broadman, 1988.

B. A. Gerrish, *Reformers in Profile: Advocates of Reform 1300–1600*, Philadelphia: Fortress, 1967.

Hans-Jürgen Goertz, ed., *Profiles of Radical Reformers: Biographical Sketches from Thomas Müntzer to Paracelsus*, Kitchener: Herald, 1982.

Heiko A. Oberman, *Forerunners of the Reformation: The Shape of Late Medieval Thought Illustrated by Key Documents*, New York: Holt, Rinehart & Winston, 1966.

Jill Raitt, ed., *Shapers of Religious Traditions in Germany, Switzerland, and Poland, 1560–1600*, New Haven: Yale University Press, 1981.

David C. Steinmetz, *Reformers in the Wings*, Philadelphia: Fortress, 1971.

Bibliography

Abray 1985: Lorna Jane Abray, *The People's Reformation: Magistrates, Clergy, and Commons in Strasbourg, 1500–1598*. Ithaca: Cornell University Press.

Aland 1965: Kurt Aland, *Martin Luther's 95 Theses*. St Louis: Concordia.

Altmann 1992: Walter Altmann, *Luther and Liberation: A Latin American Perspective*. Minneapolis: Fortress.

Anderson 1968: Charles S. Anderson, "Robert Barnes on Luther," in Pelikan 1968, 35–66.

Armstrong 1991: Brian G. Armstrong, "The Pastoral Office in Calvin and Pierre du Moulin," in Spijker 1991, 157–67.

Assion 1971/2: Peter Assion, "Matthias Hütlin und sein Gaunerbüchlein, der 'Liber vagatorum'," in *Alemannisches Jahrbuch*, 74–92.

Aston 1984: Margaret Aston, *Lollards and Reformers: Images and Literacy in Late Medieval Religion*. London: Hambledon.

Bagchi 1991: David V. N. Bagchi, *Luther's Earliest Opponents: Catholic Controversialists 1518–1525*. Minneapolis: Fortress Press.

Bainton 1941: Roland Bainton, "The Left Wing of the Reformation," *Journal of Religion* 21, 124–34.

Bainton 1951: Roland Bainton, *The Travail of Religious Liberty: Nine Biographical Studies*. Philadelphia: Westminster.

Bainton 1957: Roland Bainton, *Here I Stand: A Life of Martin Luther*. New York: Mentor.

Bainton 1960: Roland Bainton, *Hunted Heretic: The Life and Death of Michael Servetus 1511–1553*. Boston: Beacon.

Bainton 1965: Roland Bainton, ed. *Concerning Heretics, Whether they are to be persecuted . . .* New York: Octagon.

Baker 1979: Derek Baker, ed., *Reform and Reformation: England and the Contintent c.1500–c.1750*, Oxford: Blackwell.

Baker 1980: J. Wayne Baker, *Heinrich Bullinger and the Covenant: The Other Reformed Tradition*. Athens: Ohio University Press.

Baker 1988: J. Wayne Baker, "Calvin's Discipline and the Early Reformed Tradition: Bullinger and Calvin," in Schnucker 1988, 107–19.

Bakhuizen 1965: J. N. Bakhuizen van den Brink, "Ratramn's Eucharistic Doctrine and its Influence in the Sixteenth Century," in G. J. Cuming, ed., *Studies in Church History*, II, 54–77, London: Nelson.

Balke 1981: Willem Balke, *Calvin and the Anabaptist Radicals*. Grand Rapids: Eerdmans.

Barge 1968: Hermann Barge, *Andreas Bodenstein von Karlstadt*, 2 vols. Leipzig: Brandstetter, 1905; repr. Nieuwkoop: De Graaf, 1968.

Bayer 1990: Oswald Bayer,"Luther's Ethics as Pastoral Care," *LQ* 4, 125–42.

Baylor 1991: Michael G. Baylor, ed. and tr., *The Radical Reformation*. Cambridge: Cambridge University Press.

Bekenntnisschriften 1963: *Bekenntnisschriften der evangelisch-lutherischen Kirche*, 5th edn, Göttingen: Vandenhoeck & Ruprecht.

Benert 1988: Richard Benert, "Lutheran Resistance Theory and the Imperial Constitution," *LQ* 2, 185–207.

Berger 1969: Peter Berger, *The Sacred Canopy: Elements of a Sociological Theory of Religion*. Garden City: Doubleday Anchor.

Berger and Luckmann 1967: Peter Berger and Thomas Luckmann, *The Social Construction of Reality: A Treatise in the Sociology of Knowledge*. Garden City: Doubleday Anchor.

Berggrav 1951: Eivand Berggrav, *Man and State*. Philadelphia: Muhlenberg.

Berthoud 1973: Gabrielle Berthoud, *Antoine Marcourt: Réformateur et Pamphlétaire du "Livres des Marchans" aux Placards 1534*. Geneva: Droz.

Blaisdell 1982: Charmarie Jenkins Blaisdell, "Calvin's Letters to Women: The Courting of Ladies in High Places," *SCJ* 13, 67–84.

Blaschke 1993: Karlheinz Blaschke, "Reformation und Modernisierung," in Hans R. Guggisberg and Gottfried Krodel, eds, *Die Reformation in Deutschland und Europa: Interpretationen und Debatten*, 511–20. Gütersloh: Gütersloher Verlagshaus.

Blickle 1981: Peter Blickle, *The Revolution of 1525: The German Peasants' War from a New Perspective*. Baltimore: Johns Hopkins University Press.

Blickle 1982: Peter Blickle, *Die Reformation im Reich*. Stuttgart: Ulmer.

Blickle 1992: Peter Blickle, *Communal Reformation: The Quest for Salvation in Sixteenth-Century Germany*. Atlantic Highlands: Humanities.

Blickle et al.1985: Peter Blickle et al., *Zwingli und Europa*. Zurich: Vandenhoeck & Ruprecht.

Bluhm 1965: Heinz Bluhm, *Martin Luther, Creative Translator*. St Louis: Concordia.

Bluhm, 1983: Heinz Bluhm, "Luther's German Bible," in Brooks 1983, 177–94.

Boockmann 1987: Hartmut Boockmann, *Stauferzeit und spätes Mittelalter: Deutschland 1215–1517*. Berlin: Siedler.

Bornkamm 1970: Heinrich Bornkamm, *Luther im Spiegel der deutschen Geistesgeschichte*, Göttingen: Vandenhoeck & Ruprecht.

Bornkamm 1983: Heinrich Bornkamm, *Luther in Mid-Career, 1520–1530*. Philadelphia: Fortress Press.

Bossy 1983: John Bossy, "The Mass as a Social Institution 1200–1700," *PP* 100, 29–61.

Bossy 1985: John Bossy, *Christianity in the West 1400–1700*. Oxford: Oxford University Press.

Bouwsma 1980: William J. Bouwsma, "Anxiety and the Formation of Early Modern Culture," in Barbara C. Malament, ed., *After the Reformation: Essays in Honor of J. H. Hexter*, 215–46. University Park: University of Pennsylvania Press.

Bouwsma 1988: William J. Bouwsma, *John Calvin: A Sixteenth-Century Portrait*. New York: Oxford University Press.

Brady 1978: Thomas A. Brady, Jr, *Ruling Class, Regime and Reformation at Strasbourg 1520–1555*. Leiden: E. J. Brill.

Brady 1979: Thomas A. Brady, Jr, " 'The Social History of the Reformation' between 'Romantic Idealism' and 'Sociologism': A Reply," in Wolfgang Mommsen, et al., *The Urban Classes, The Nobility and the Reformation: Studies in the Social History of the Reformation in England and Germany*, 40–3. Stuttgart: Klett-Cotta.

Brady 1982: Thomas A. Brady, Jr, "Social History," in Ozment 1982, 161–81.

Brady 1985: Thomas A. Brady, Jr, review of Spitz 1985, *SCJ* 16, 410–12.

Brady 1987: Thomas A. Brady, Jr, "From Sacral Community to the Common Man: Reflections on German Reformation Studies," *Central European History* 20, 229–45.

Braudel 1972: Fernand Braudel, "History and the Social Sciences," in Peter Burke, ed., *Economy and Society in Early Modern Europe*, 11–42. New York: Harper & Row.

Bräuer and Junghans 1989: Siegfried Bräuer and Helmar Junghans, eds, *Der Theologe Thomas Müntzer: Untersuchungen zu seiner Entwicklung und Lehre*. Berlin: Evangelische Verlagsanstalt.

Bray 1994: Gerald Bray, ed., *Documents of the English Reformation*. Minneapolis: Fortress.

Brecht 1985: Martin Brecht, *Martin Luther*, I: *His Road to Reformation 1483–1521*. Minneapolis: Fortress.

Brecht 1990: Martin Brecht, *Martin Luther*, II: *Shaping and Defining the Reformation 1521–1532*. Minneapolis: Fortress.

Brecht 1993: Martin Brecht, *Martin Luther*, III: *The Preservation of the Church 1532–1546*. Minneapolis: Fortress.

Brigdon 1992: Susan Brigdon, *London and the Reformation*. Oxford: Clarendon.

Bromily 1953: G. W. Bromily, tr., *Zwingli and Bullinger*. (Library of Christian Classics, 24). Philadelphia: Westminster.

Brooks 1965: Peter Newman Brooks, *Thomas Cranmer's Doctrine of the Eucharist*. London: Macmillan.

Brooks 1983: Peter Newman Brooks, ed., *Seven-Headed Luther: Essays in Commemoration of a Quincentenary 1483–1983*. Oxford: Clarendon.

Brown 1959: Norman O. Brown, *Life Against Death: The Psychoanalytic Meaning of History*. New York: Vintage.

Brown 1975: Peter Brown, *Augustine of Hippo: A Biography*. Berkeley: University of California Press.

Bubenheimer 1977: Ulrich Bubenheimer, *Consonantia Theologiae et Iurispruden-tiae: Andreas Bodenstein von Karlstadt als Theologe und Jurist zwischen Scholastik und Reformation*. Tübingen: J. C. B. Mohr (Paul Siebeck).

Bubenheimer 1981a: Ulrich Bubenheimer, "Andreas Bodenstein von Karl-stadt," in Martin Greschat, ed., *Gestalten der Kirchengeschichte: Die Reforma-tionszeit*, 105–16. Stuttgart: Kohlhammer.

Bubenheimer 1981b: Ulrich Bubenheimer, "Gelassenheit und Ablösung: Eine psychohistorische Studie über Andreas Bodenstein von Karlstadt und seinen Konflikt mit Martin Luther," *ZKG* 92, 250–68.

Bubenheimer 1989: Ulrich Bubenheimer, *Thomas Müntzer: Herkunft und Bildung*. Leiden: E. J. Brill.

Bubenheimer 1991: Ulrich Bubenheimer, "Andreas Bodenstein genannt Karl-stadt (1486–1541)," in Alfred Wendehorst, ed., *Fränkische Lebensbilder*, XIV, 47–64. Neustadt/Aisch: Degener & Co.

Buck and Zophy 1972: L. P. Buck and J. W. Zophy, eds, *The Social History of the Reformation*. Columbus: Ohio State University Press.

Bujnoch 1988: Josef Bujnoch, ed. and tr., *Die Hussiten: Die Chronik des Laurentius von Brezová 1414–1421*. Graz: Verlag Styria.

Burgess 1980: Joseph A. Burgess, ed., *The Role of the Augsburg Confession: Catholic and Lutheran Views*. Philadelphia: Fortress.

Büsser 1968: Fritz Büsser, *Das katholische Zwinglibild: Von der Reformation bis zur Gegenwart*. Zurich.

Büsser 1989: Fritz Büsser, "Zwingli the Exegete: A Contribution to the 450th Anniversary of the Death of Erasmus," in McKee and Armstrong 1989: 175–96.

Cameron 1991: Euan Cameron, *The European Reformation*. Oxford: Claren-don.

Cantor 1991: Norman F. Cantor, *Inventing the Middle Ages: The Lives, Works, and Ideas of the Great Medievalists of the Twentieth Century*. New York: William Morrow.

Cargill Thompson 1979: W. D. J. Cargill Thompson, "The Two Regiments: The Continental Setting of William Tyndal's Political Thought," in Baker 1979, 17–33.

Castellio 1975: Sebastian Castellio, *Advice to a Desolate France*. Shepherdstown: Patmos.

Cavendish 1964: George Cavendish, "The Life and Death of Cardinal Wolsey," in Sylvester and Harding 1964, 3–193.

Chafe 1985: Eric T. Chafe, "Luther's Analogy of Faith in Bach's Church Music," *Dialogue* 24, 96–101.

Chatellier 1989: Louis Chatellier, *The Europe of the Devout: The Catholic Reformation and the Formation of a New Society*. Cambridge: Cambridge University Press/Paris: Éditions de la Maison des Sciences de l'Homme.

Chiffoleau 1980: Jacques Chiffoleau, *La Comptabilité de l'Au-delà: Les Hommes, la Mort et la Religion dans la Région d'Avignon à la Fin du Moyen Age (vers 1320–1480)*. Rome: École Française de Rome.

Chrisman 1982: Miriam U. Chrisman, *Lay Culture, Learned Culture: Books and Social Change in Strasbourg 1480–1599*. New Haven: Yale University Press.

Clebsch 1964: William A. Clebsch, *England's Earliest Protestants 1520–1535*. New Haven: Yale University Press.

Coats 1994: Catherine Randall Coats, "Reactivating Textual Traces: Martyrs, Memory, and the Self in Theodore Beza's *Icones* (1581)," in Graham 1994, 19–28.

Cochrane 1966: Arthur C. Cochrane, ed., *Reformed Confessions of the Sixteenth Century*. Philadelphia: Westminster.

Cohn 1961: Norman Cohn, *The Pursuit of the Millennium: Revolutionary Messianism in Medieval and Reformation Europe*. New York: Harper Torchbooks.

Collinson 1967: Patrick Collinson, *The Elizabethan Puritan Movement*. Berkeley: University of California Press.

Cosgrove 1993: Richard A. Cosgrove, "English Anticlericalism: A Programmatic Assessment," in Dykema and Oberman 1993, 569–81.

Costa 1989: Milagros Ortega Costa, "Spanish Women in the Reformation," in Marshall 1989, 89–119.

Courvoisier 1963: Jacques Courvoisier, *Zwingli: A Reformed Theologian*. Richmond: John Knox.

Crew 1978: Phyllis Mack Crew, *Calvinist Preaching and Iconoclasm in the Netherlands 1544–1569*. Cambridge: Cambridge University Press.

Davis 1977: Kenneth R. Davis, "The Origins of Anabaptism: Ascetic and Charismatic Elements Exemplifying Continuity and Discontinuity," in Lienhard 1977, 27–41.

Davis 1974: Natalie Zemon Davis, "Some Tasks and Themes in the Study of Popular Religion," in Charles Trinkaus and Heiko A. Oberman, eds, *The Pursuit of Holiness in Late Medieval and Renaissance Religion*, 307–36. Leiden: E. J. Brill.

Davis 1976: Natalie Zemon Davis, *Society and Culture in Early Modern France*. Stanford: Stanford University Press.

De Grouchy 1988: John De Grouchy, ed., *Dietrich Bonhoeffer: Witness to Jesus Christ*. San Francisco: Collins.

Delumeau 1984: Jean Delumeau, *Le Péché et la Peur: La culpabilisation en Occident XIIIᵉ–XVIIIᵉ siècle*. Paris: Fayard.

Delumeau 1989: Jean Delumeau, *Rassurer et protéger: le sentiment de sécurité dans l'Occident d'autrefois*. Paris: Fayard.

DeMolen 1984: Richard L. DeMolen, ed., *Leaders of the Reformation*. Selinsgrove: Susquehanna University Press.

Deppermann 1987: Klaus Deppermann, *Melchior Hoffmann: Social Unrest and Apocalyptic Visions in the Age of the Reformation*. Edinburgh: T. & T. Clark.

Deppermann et al. 1975: Klaus Deppermann, Werner Packull, and James Stayer, "From Monogenesis to Polygenesis: The Historical Discussion of Anabaptist Origins," *MQR* 49, 83–121.

Derschowitz 1991: Alan Derschowitz, *Chutzpah*. Boston: Little, Brown.

Dickens 1974: A. G. Dickens, *The German Nation and Martin Luther*. New York: Harper & Row.

Dickens 1982: A. G. Dickens, *Reformation Studies*. London: Hambledon.

Dickens 1987: A. G. Dickens, "The Shape of Anti-clericalism and the English Reformation," in Kouri and Scott 1987, 379–410.

Dickens 1991: A. G. Dickens, *The English Reformation*, 2nd edn. University Park: University of Pennsylvania Press.

Dickens and Tonkin 1985: A. G. Dickens and John M. Tonkin, *The Reformation in Historical Thought*. Cambridge, MA: Harvard University Press.

Diefendorf 1991: Barbara Diefendorf, *Beneath the Cross: Catholics and Huguenots in Sixteenth-Century Paris*. New York: Oxford University Press.

Douglass 1985: Jane Dempsey Douglas, *Women, Freedom, and Calvin*. Philadelphia: Westminster.

Douglass 1993: Jane Dempsey Douglas, "A Report on Anticlericalism in Three French Women Writers 1404–1549," in Dykema and Oberman 1993, 243–56.

Dowey 1994: Edward A. Dowey, Jr, *The Knowledge of God in Calvin's Theology*, expanded edn. Grand Rapids: Eerdmans.

Duchrow 1987: Ulrich Duchrow, *Global Economy: A Confessional Issue for the Churches?* Geneva: World Council of Churches.

Duffy 1992: Eamon Duffy, *The Stripping of the Altars: Traditional Religion in England 1400–1580*. New Haven: Yale University Press.

Duke, 1992: Alastair Duke, "The Netherlands," in Pettegree 1992, 142–65.

Duke et al. 1992: Alastair Duke, G. Lewis, and A. Pettegree, eds and trs, *Calvinism in Europe 1540–1610: A Collection of Documents*. Manchester: Manchester University Press.

Dykema and Oberman 1993: Peter A. Dykema and Heiko A. Oberman, eds, *Anticlericalism in Late Medieval and Early Modern Europe*. Leiden: E. J. Brill.

Ebeling 1970: Gerhard Ebeling, *Luther: An Introduction to his Thought*. Philadelphia: Fortress.

Edwards 1988: John Edwards, *The Jews in Christian Europe 1400–1700*. London: Routledge.

Edwards 1975: Mark U. Edwards, Jr, *Luther and the False Brethren*. Stanford: Stanford University Press.

Edwards 1983: Mark U. Edwards, Jr, *Luther's Last Battles: Politics and Polemics 1531–46*. Ithaca: Cornell University Press.

Edwards 1994: Mark U. Edwards, Jr, *Printing, Propaganda, and Martin Luther*. Berkeley: University of California Press.

Eire 1986: Carlos M. N. Eire, *War Against the Idols: the Reformation of Worship from Erasmus to Calvin*. Cambridge: Cambridge University Press.

Eisenstadt 1968: S. N. Eisenstadt, ed., *The Protestant Ethic and Modernization: A Comparative View*. New York: Basic.

Eisenstein 1979: Elizabeth L. Eisenstein, *The Printing Press as an Agent of Change: Communications and Cultural Transformations in Early Modern Europe*. Cambridge: Cambridge University Press.

Elton 1966: G. R. Elton, *Reformation Europe 1517–1559*. New York: Harper & Row.

Elton 1967: G. R. Elton, *The Practice of History*. New York: Thomas Crowell.

Elton 1969: G. R. Elton, *England Under the Tudors*. London: Methuen.

Elton 1977: Geoffrey R. Elton, "Thomas Cromwell Redivivus," *ARG* 68, 192–208.

Elton 1990: G. R. Elton, ed., *The Reformation 1520–1559*, 2nd edn (*New Cambridge Modern History, II*). Cambridge: Cambridge University Press.

Erasmus 1968: *The* Julius Exclusus *of Erasmus*, tr. Paul Pascal; int. and notes J. Kelley Sowards. Bloomington: Indiana University Press.

Erikson 1958: Erik H. Erikson, *Young Man Luther: A Study in Psychoanalysis and History*. New York: Norton.

Evennett 1965: H. Outram Evennett, "The Counter–Reformation," in Hurstfield 1965, 58–71.

Evennett 1970: H. Outram Evennett, *The Spirit of the Counter–Reformation*, ed. with postscript John Bossy. Notre Dame: University of Notre Dame Press.

Fenlon 1971: Dermot Fenlon, *Heresy and Obedience in Tridentine Italy: Cardinal Pole and the Counter Reformation*. Cambridge: Cambridge University Press.

Fichtner 1989: Paula Fichtner, *Protestantism and Primogeniture in Early Modern Germany*. New Haven: Yale University Press.

Fischer 1983: Robert H. Fischer, "Doctor Martin Luther, Churchman. A Theologian's Viewpoint," in Brooks 1983, 77–103.

Fischer 1982: Wolfram Fischer, *Armut in der Geschichte*. Göttingen: Vandenhoeck & Ruprecht.

Ferguson 1948: Wallace K. Ferguson, *The Renaissance in Historical Thought: Five Centuries of Interpretation*. Cambridge, MA: Houghton Mifflin.

Frankfurter 1987: A. Daniel Frankfurter, "Elizabeth Bowes and John Knox: A Woman and Reformation Theology," *CH* 56, 333–47.

Friede and Keen 1971: Juan Friede and Benjamin Keen, eds, *Bartolomé de Las Casas in History: Towards an Understanding of the Man and His Work*. Dekalb: Northern Illinois University Press.

Friedman 1987: Jerome Friedman, "Jewish Conversion, the Spanish Pure Blood Laws and Reformation: A Revisionist View of Racial and Religious Antisemitism," *SCJ* 18, 3–30.

Furcha 1985: E. J. Furcha, ed., *Huldrych Zwingli, 1484–1531: A Legacy of Radical Reform*. Montreal: McGill University Press.

Gäbler 1983: Ulrich Gäbler, *Huldrych Zwingli: Eine Einführung in sein Leben und sein Werk*. Munich: C. H. Beck. Eng. trans. *Huldrych Zwingli: His Life and Work*. Philadelphia: Fortress, 1986.

Gadamer 1975: Hans-Georg Gadamer, *Truth and Method*, New York: Continuum.

Galpern 1974: A. N. Galpern, "Late Medieval Piety in Sixteenth–Century Champagne," in Charles Trinkaus and Heiko A. Oberman, eds, *The Pursuit of Holiness in Late Medieval and Renaissance Religion*, 141–76. Leiden: E. J. Brill.

Garnett, 1994. George Garnett, ed. and tr., *Vindiciae, Contra Tyrannos.* Cambridge: Cambridge University Press.

Garside 1966: Charles Garside, *Zwingli and the Arts.* New Haven: Yale University Press.

Geisser et al. 1982: Hans Friedrich Geisser et al., *Weder Ketzer noch Heiliger: Luthers Bedeutung für den Ökumenischen Dialog.* Regensburg: Pustet.

George 1988: Timothy George, *Theology of the Reformers.* Nashville: Broadman.

George 1990: Timothy George, ed., *John Calvin and the Church: A Prism of Reform.* Louisville: Westminster/John Knox.

Gerrish 1967a: B. A. Gerrish, ed., *Reformers in Profile: Advocates of Reform 1300–1600.* Philadelphia: Fortress.

Gerrish 1967b: B. A. Gerrish, "John Calvin," in Gerrish 1967a, 142–64.

Gerrish 1968: B. A. Gerrish, "John Calvin on Luther," in Pelikan 1968, 67–96.

Gerrish 1992: Brian A. Gerrish, "The Lord's Supper in the Reformed Confessions," in Donald K. McKim, ed., *Major Themes in the Reformed Tradition,* 245–58. Grand Rapids: Eerdmans.

Gerrish 1993: B. A. Gerrish, *Grace and Gratitude: The Eucharistic Theology of John Calvin.* Minneapolis: Fortress.

Ginzburg 1982: Carlo Ginzburg, *The Cheese and the Worms: The Cosmos of a Sixteenth-Century Miller.* New York: Penguin.

Ginzburg 1985: Carlo Ginzburg, *Night Battles: Witchcraft and Agrarian Cults in the Sixteenth and Seventeenth Centuries.* New York: Penguin.

Gleason 1978: Elizabeth G. Gleason, "On the Nature of Sixteenth-Century Italian Evangelism: Scholarship, 1953–1978," *SCJ* 9, 3–25.

Gleason 1981: Elizabeth G. Gleason, ed. and tr., *Reform Thought in Sixteenth-Century Italy.* Chico: Scholars.

Gleason 1993: Elizabeth G. Gleason, "Sixteenth-Century Italian Spirituality and the Papacy," in Dykema and Oberman 1993, 299–307.

Goertz 1967: Hans-Jürgen Goertz, *Innere und Äussere Ordnung in der Theologie Thomas Müntzers.* Leiden: E. J. Brill.

Goertz 1982: Hans-Jürgen Goertz, ed., *Profiles of Radical Reformers: Biographical Sketches from Thomas Müntzer to Paracelsus.* Kitchener: Herald.

Goertz 1987: Hans-Jürgen Goertz, *Pfaffenhass und gross Geschrei: Die reformatorischen Bewegungen in Deutschland 1517–1529.* Munich: C. H. Beck.

Goertz 1988: Hans-Jürgen Goertz, *Die Täufer: Geschichte und Deutung.* Berlin: Evangelische Verlagsanstalt.

Goertz 1993a: Hans-Jürgen Goertz, *Religiöse Bewegungen in der frühen Neuzeit.* Munich: Oldenbourg.

Goertz 1993b: Hans-Jürgen Goertz, *Thomas Müntzer: Apocalyptic Mystic and Revolutionary.* Edinburgh: T. & T. Clark.

Graham 1994: W. Fred Graham, ed., *Later Calvinism: International Perspectives.* Kirksville: Sixteenth Century Publishers.

Grane 1987: Leif Grane, *The Augsburg Confession: A Commentary.* Minneapolis: Augsburg.

Grane 1994: Leif Grane, *Martinus Noster: Luther in the German Reform Movement 1518–1521*. Mainz: Zabern.

Graus 1969: Frantisek Graus, "Das Spätmittelalter als Krisenzeit: Ein Literaturbericht als Zwischenbilanz," *Mediaevalia Bohemica* (Supplement 1), Prague.

Graus 1971: Frantisek Graus, "The Crisis of the Middle Ages and the Hussites," in Ozment 1971, 76–103.

Graus 1993: Frantisek Graus, "The Church and its Critics in Time of Crisis," in Dykema and Oberman 1993, 65–81.

Gray 1983: Janet Gray, "The Origin of the Word Huguenot," *SCJ* 14, 349–59.

Green 1959: Robert W. Green, ed., *Protestantism and Capitalism: The Weber Thesis and its Critics*. Lexington: D. C. Heath.

Greengrass 1987: Mark Greengrass, *The French Reformation*. Oxford: Blackwell.

Grell 1994: Ole Peter Grell, "Merchants and Ministers: The Foundations of International Calvinism," in Pettegree et al. 1994, 254–73.

Greyerz 1985: Kaspar von Greyerz, "Stadt und Reformation: Stand und Aufgaben der Forschung," *ARG* 76, 6–63.

Grimm 1973: Harold J. Grimm, *The Reformation Era 1500–1650*. New York: Macmillan.

Gritsch 1983: Eric W. Gritsch, *Martin – God's Court Jester: Luther in Retrospect*. Philadelphia: Fortress.

Gritsch 1989: Eric W. Gritsch, Thomas Müntzer: A Tragedy of Errors. Minneapolis: Fortress.

Gritsch 1990: Eric W. Gritsch, "Joseph Lortz's Luther: Appreciation and Critique," *ARG* 81, 32–49.

Gritsch and Jenson 1976: Eric W. Gritsch and Robert W. Jenson, *Lutheranism: The Theological Movement and Its Confessional Writings*. Philadelphia: Fortress.

Grossmann 1975: Maria Grossmann, *Humanism in Wittenberg 1485–1517*. Nieuwkoop: B. De Graaf.

Guggisberg and Krodel 1993: Hans R. Guggisberg and Gottfried Krodel, eds, *The Reformation in Germany and Europe: Interpretations and Issues*. (*ARG* special volume). Gütersloh: Gütersloher Verlagshaus.

Hagen 1974: Kenneth Hagen, *A Theology of Testament in the Young Luther: The Lectures on Hebrews*. Leiden: E. J. Brill.

Haigh 1987: Christopher Haigh, ed., *The English Reformation Revised*. Cambridge: Cambridge University Press.

Haigh 1993: Christopher Haigh, *English Reformations: Religion, Politics, and Society under the Tudors*. Oxford: Clarendon.

Haile 1980: H. G. Haile, *Luther: An Experiment in Biography*. Princeton: Princeton University Press.

Hall 1979: Basil Hall, "The Early Rise and Gradual Decline of Lutheranism in England (1520–1600)," in Baker 1979, 103–31.

Hall 1994: Basil Hall, "Martin Bucer in England," in Wright 1994, 144–60.

Hallman 1985: Barbara Hallmann, *Italian Cardinals, Reform, and the Church as Property*. Berkeley: University of California Press.

Hamm 1988: Berndt Hamm, *Zwinglis Reformation der Freiheit*. Neukirchen-Vluyn: Neukirchener Verlag.

Hanawalt and Lindberg 1994: Emily Albu Hanawalt and Carter Lindberg, eds, *Through the Eye of a Needle: Judeo-Christian Roots of Social Welfare*. Kirksville: Thomas Jefferson University Press.

Hanke 1974: Lewis Hanke, *All Mankind is One: A Study of the Disputation between Bartolomé de Las Casas and Juan Ginés de Sepúlveda in 1550 on the Intellectual and Religious Capacity of the American Indians*. Dekalb: Northern Illinois University Press.

Hauschild 1981: Wolf-Dieter Hauschild, *Lübecker Kirchenordnung von Johannes Bugenhagen 1531*. Lübeck: Schmidt-Römhild. Asterisked references in the text indicate primary text; non-asterisked references indicate Hauschild's commentary.

Headley 1987: John M. Headley, "The Reformation as Crisis in the Understanding of Tradition," *ARG* 78, 5–23.

Healey 1994: Robert M. Healey, "Waiting for Deborah: John Knox and Four Ruling Queens," *SCJ* 25, 371–86.

Hendrix 1981: Scott Hendrix, *Luther and the Papacy: Stages in a Reformation Conflict*. Philadelphia: Fortress.

Hendrix 1990: Scott Hendrix, "Toleration of the Jews in the German Reformation: Urbanus Rhegius and Braunschweig (1535–1540)," *ARG* 81, 189–215.

Hendrix 1993: Scott Hendrix, "Considering the Clergy's Side: A Multilateral View of Anticlericalism," in Dykema and Oberman, 1993, 449–59.

Hendrix 1994: Scott Hendrix, "Loyalty, Piety, or Opportunism: German Princes and the Reformation," *Journal of Interdisciplinary History* 25 (Autumn 1994), 211–24.

Héritier 1967: Jean Héritier, "The Massacre of St Bartholomew: Reason of State and Ideological Conflict," in Salmon, 1967, 48–53.

Hertzsch 1957: Erich Hertzsch, ed., *Karlstadts Schriften aus den Jahren 1523–25*, 2 vols. Halle [Saale]: Niemeyer.

Higman 1984: Francis Higman, "Les traductions françaises de Luther, 1524–1550," in J-F. Gilmont, ed., *Palaestra typographica*, 11–56, Aubel: Geson.

Higman 1992: Francis Higman, *La Diffusion de la Réforme en France 1520–1565*. Geneva: Labor et Fides.

Hildebrandt 1980: Esther Hildebrandt, "The Magdeburg Bekenntnis on a Possible Link between German and English Resistance Theory in the Sixteenth Century," *ARG* 71, 227–53.

Hillerbrand 1964: Hans J. Hillerbrand, ed., *The Reformation: A Narrative History Related by Contemporary Observers and Participants*. New York: Harper & Row.

Hillerbrand 1986: Hans J. Hillerbrand, ed., *Radical Tendencies in the Reformation: Divergent Perspectives*. Kirksville: Sixteenth Century Journal Publishers.

Hillerbrand 1993: Hans J. Hillerbrand, " 'The Radical Reformation': Reflections on the Occasion of an Anniversary," *MQR* 67, 408–20.

Hinson 1976: Edward Hinson, ed., *Introduction to Puritan Theology: A Reader*. Grand Rapids: Baker Book House.

Hofmann 1983: Werner Hofmann, ed., *Luther und die Folgen für die Kunst*. Munich: Prestel-Verlag.

Hofstadter 1968: Richard Hofstadter, *The Progressive Historians*. New York: Knopf.

Holborn 1961: Hajo Holborn, *A History of Modern Germany: The Reformation*. New York: Knopf.

Höss 1963: Irmgard Höss, "Zur Genesis der Widerstandslehre Bezas," *ARG* 54, 198–214.

Hsia 1987: R. Po-Chia Hsia, "The Myth of the Commune: Recent Historiography on City and Reformation in Germany," *Central European History* 20, 203–15.

Hsia 1988: R. Po-Chia Hsia, ed., *The German People and the Reformation*. Ithaca: Cornell University Press.

Hsia 1989: R. Po-Chia Hsia, *Social Discipline in the Reformation: Central Europe 1550–1750*. London: Routledge.

Hudson 1988: Anne Hudson, *The Premature Reformation: Wycliffite Texts and Lollard History*. Oxford: Clarendon.

Hughes 1966: Philip E. Hughes, *The Register of the Company of Pastors in the Time of Calvin*. Grand Rapids: Eerdmans.

Hughes 1984: Philip E. Hughes, *Lefèvre: Pioneer of Ecclesiastical Renewal in France*. Grand Rapids: Eerdmans.

Huizinga 1956: Johan Huizinga, *The Waning of the Middle Ages: A Study of the Forms of Life, Thought and Art in France and the Netherlands in the Dawn of the Renaissance*. Garden City: Doubleday Anchor.

Hurstfield 1965: Joel Hurstfield, ed., *The Reformation Crisis*. London: Edward Arnold.

Irwin 1993: Joyce L. Irwin, *Neither Voice nor Heart Alone: German Lutheran Theology of Music in the Age of the Baroque*. New York: Peter Lang.

Iserloh 1968: Erwin Iserloh, *The Theses Were Not Posted: Luther Between Reform and Reformation*, tr. Jared Wicks, SJ. Boston: Beacon.

Iserloh et al. 1986: Erwin Iserloh, Joseph Glazik and Hubert Jedin, eds, *Reformation and Counter Reformation* (*History of the Church*, ed. Hubert Jedin and John Dolan, V). New York: Crossroad.

Ishida 1984: Yoshiro Ishida, "Luther the Pastor," in Lindberg 1984, 27–37.

Jackson 1972: Samuel Macauley Jackson, ed., *Ulrich Zwingli (1484–1531): Selected Works*. Philadelphia: University of Pennsylvania Press (repr.; first publ. 1901).

Jackson 1987: Samuel Macauley Jackson, ed., *Ulrich Zwingli: Early Writings*. Durham: Labyrinth (repr.; first publ. 1912).

Janz 1982: Denis Janz, *Three Reformation Catechisms: Catholic, Anabaptist, Lutheran*. New York/Toronto: Edwin Mellon.

Jedin 1957: Hubert Jedin, *A History of the Council of Trent*, 2 vols. St Louis: B. Herder.

Jedin 1973: Hubert Jedin, "Katholische Reformation oder Gegenreformation?," in Ernst Walter Zeeden, ed., *Gegenreformation (Wege der Forschung,* CCCXI), 46–81. Darmstadt: Wissenschaftliches Buchgesellschaft.

Johnson 1977: Roger Johnson, ed., *Psychohistory and Religion: The Case of Young Man Luther*. Philadelphia: Fortress.

Junghans 1983: Helmar Junghans, ed., *Leben und Werk Martin Luthers von 1526 bis 1546: Festgabe zu seinen 500. Geburtstag*, 2 vols. Berlin: Evangelische Verlagsanstalt.

Junghans 1984: Helmar Junghans, *Der junge Luther und die Humanisten*. Weimar: Hermann Böhlaus Nachfolger.

Jütte 1988: Robert Jütte, *Abbild und soziale Wirklichkeit des Bettler- und Gaunertums zu Beginn der Neuzeit*. Cologne: Böhlau.

Jütte 1994: Robert Jütte, *Poverty and Deviance in Early Modern Europe*. Cambridge: Cambridge University Press.

Kamen 1985: Henry Kamen, *Inquisition and Society in Spain in the Sixteenth and Seventeenth Centuries*. Bloomington: Indiana University Press.

Kandler 1993: Karl-Hermann Kandler, "Luther und der Koran," *Luther* 64, 3–9.

Karant-Nunn 1982: Susan Karant-Nunn, "Continuity and Change: Some Aspects of the Reformation on the Women of Zwickau," *SCJ* 13, 17–42.

Karant-Nunn 1989: Susan Karant-Nunn, "The Women of the Saxon Silver Mines," in Marshall 1989, 29–46.

Kaplan, 1994. Benjamin Kaplan, " 'Remnants of the Papal Yoke': Apathy and Opposition in the Dutch Reformation," *SCJ* 25 (1994), 653–69.

Karlstadt 1522: *Von Abtuhung der Bilder und das keyn Bedtler unther den Christen seyn sollen*, ed. Hans Lietzmann. Bonn: *Kleine Texte*, no. 74.

Karlstadt 1980: *Andreas Bodenstein von Karlstadt: 500-Jahr-Feier. Festschrift der Stadt Karlstadt zum Jubiläumsjahr 1980*. Karlstadt.

Kidd 1941: B. J. Kidd, ed., *Documents Illustrative of the History of the Church*. New York: Macmillan.

Kingdon 1956: Robert M. Kingdon, *Geneva and the Coming of the Wars of Religion in France, 1555–1563*. Geneva: Droz.

Kingdon 1967: Robert M. Kingdon, *Geneva and the Consolidation of the French Protestant Movement, 1564–1572*. Geneva: Droz.

Kingdon 1972: Robert M. Kingdon, "The Control of Morals in Calvin's Geneva," in Buck and Zophy 1972, 3–16.

Kingdon 1973: Robert M. Kingdon, "Calvinism and Democracy," in John H. Bratt, ed., *The Heritage of John Calvin*, 172–92, Grand Rapids: Eerdmans.

Kingdon 1974: Robert M. Kingdon, ed., *Transition and Revolution: Problems and Issues of European Renaissance and Reformation History*. Minneapolis: Burgess.

Kingdon 1988: Robert M. Kingdon, *Myths about the St Bartholomew's Day Massacres, 1572–1576*. Cambridge, MA: Harvard University Press.

Kingdon 1991: Robert M. Kingdon, "Popular Reactions to the Debate between Bolsec and Calvin," in Spijker 1991, 138–45.

Kingdon 1993a: Robert M. Kingdon, "Social Control and Political Control in Calvin's Geneva," in Guggisberg and Krodel 1993, 521–32.

Kingdon 1993b: Robert M. Kingdon, "Calvinist Discipline in the Old World and the New," in Guggisberg and Krodel, 1993, 665–79.

Kingdon 1994: Robert M. Kingdon, "The Geneva Consistory in the Time of Calvin," in Pettegree et al. 1994, 21–34.

Kittelson 1976: James M. Kittelson, "Humanism and the Reformation in Germany," *Central European History* 9, 303–22.

Kittelson 1982: James Kittelson, "Successes and Failures in the German Reformation: The Report from Strasbourg," *ARG* 73, 153–74.

Kittelson 1985: James Kittelson, "Visitations and Popular Religious Culture: Further Reports from Strasbourg," in Kyle C. Sessions and Phillip N. Bebb, eds, *Pietas et Societas: New Trends in Reformation Social History. Essays in Memory of Harold J. Grimm*, 89–101. Kirksville: Sixteenth Century Journal Publishers.

Kittelson 1986: James M. Kittelson, *Luther the Reformer: The Story of the Man and His Career*. Minneapolis: Augsburg.

Klaasen 1981: Walter Klaasen, ed., *Anabaptism in Outline: Selected Primary Sources*. Waterloo: Herald.

Klaasen 1993: Walter Klaasen, "From the Pillars of Hercules to the Gates of Alexander: George H. Williams and The Radical Reformation," *MQR* 67, 421–28.

Koenigsberger 1990: H. G. Koenigsberger, "The Empire of Charles V in Europe," in Elton 1990, 339–76.

Koenigsberger 1994: H. G. Koenigsberger, "The Politics of Philip II," in Malcolm Thorp and Arthur J. Slavin, eds, *Politics, Religion and Diplomacy in Early Modern Europe: Essays in Honor of De Lamar Jensen*, 171–89. Kirksville: Sixteenth Century Journal Publishers.

Kolb 1987: Robert Kolb, *For All the Saints: Changing Perceptions of Martyrdom and Sainthood in the Lutheran Reformation*. Macon: Mercer University Press.

Kouri 1987: E. I. Kouri, "For True Faith or National Interest? Queen Elizabeth I and the Protestant Powers," in Kouri and Scott 1987, 411–36.

Kouri and Scott 1987: E. I. Kouri and Tom Scott, eds, *Politics and Society in Reformation Europe: Essays for Sir Geoffrey Elton on his Sixty-Fifth Birthday*. New York: St Martin's.

Krieger and Lienhard 1993: Christian Krieger and Marc Lienhard, eds, *Martin Bucer and Sixteenth-Century Europe*, 2 vols. Leiden: E. J. Brill.

Laube 1983: Adolf Laube, ed., *Flugschriften der frühen Reformationsbewegung*, 2 vols. Vaduz: Topos.

Laube 1986: Adolf Laube, "Radicalism as a Research Problem in the History of the Early Reformation," in Hillerbrand 1986, 9–23.

Le Goff 1981: Jacques Le Goff, *La naissance du Purgatoire*. Paris: Gallimard.

Le Goff 1988: Jacques Le Goff, *Medieval Civilization 400–1500*. Oxford: Blackwell.

Leaver 1990: Robin Leaver, "Lutheran Vespers as a Context for Music," in Paul Walker, ed., *Church, Stage, and Studio: Music and Its Contexts in Seventeenth-Century Germany*, 143–61. Ann Arbor: UMI Research Press.

Lee 1985: Robert E. A. Lee, "Bach's Living Music of Death," *Dialogue* 24, 102–6.

Leff 1971: Gordon Leff, *History and Social Theory*. New York: Doubleday Anchor.

Leith 1989: John H. Leith, *John Calvin's Doctrine of the Christian Life*. Louisville: Westminster/John Knox.

Lesnick 1989: Daniel Lesnick, *Preaching in Medieval Florence: The Social World of Franciscan and Dominican Spirituality*. Athens: University of Georgia Press.

Lienhard 1977: Marc Lienhard, ed., *The Origins and Characteristics of Anabaptism/Les Débuts et les characteristiques de l'Anabaptisme*. The Hague: Nijhoff.

Lietzmann 1912: Hans Lietzmann, ed., *Johannes Bugenhagens Braunschweiger Kirchenordnung 1528*. Bonn: Marcus & Weber.

Lindberg 1972: Carter Lindberg, "Prierias and his Significance for Luther's Development," *SCJ* 3, 45–64.

Lindberg 1977: Carter Lindberg, " 'There Should Be No Beggars Among Christians': Karlstadt, Luther, and the Origins of Protestant Poor Relief," *CH* 46, 313–34.

Lindberg 1979: Carter Lindberg, "Karlstadt's *Dialogue* on the Lord's Supper," *MQR* 53, 35–77.

Lindberg 1983: Carter Lindberg, *The Third Reformation? Charismatic Movements and the Lutheran Tradition*. Macon: Mercer University Press.

Lindberg 1984: Carter Lindberg, ed., *Piety, Politics, and Ethics: Reformation Studies in Honor of George Wolfgang Forell*. Kirksville: Sixteenth Century Journal Publishers.

Lindberg 1993: Carter Lindberg, *Beyond Charity: Reformation Initiatives for the Poor*. Minneapolis: Fortress.

Lindberg 1994: Carter Lindberg, "Tainted Greatness: Luther's Attitudes toward Judaism and their Historical Reception," in Nancy Harrowitz, ed., *Tainted Greatness: Antisemitism and Cultural Heroes*, 15–35. Philadelphia: Temple University Press.

Little 1978: Lester K. Little, *Religious Poverty and the Profit Economy in Medieval Europe*. Ithaca: Cornell University Press.

Little 1988: Lester K. Little, *Liberty, Charity, Fraternity: Lay Religious Confraternities at Bergamo in the Age of the Commune*. Northampton: Smith College.

Little 1994: Lester K. Little, "Religion, the Profit Economy, and Saint Francis," in Hanawalt and Lindberg 1994, 147–63.

Loades 1992: David Loades, *Revolution in Religion: The English Reformation 1530–1570*. Cardiff: University of Wales Press.

Locher 1979: Gottfried Locher, *Die Zwinglische Reformation im Rahmen der europäischen Kirchengeschichte*. Göttingen: Vandenhoeck & Ruprecht.

Loewenich 1963: Walther von Loewenich, *Luther und der Neuprotestantismus*. Witten: Luther Verlag.

Loewenich 1976: Walther von Loewenich, *Luther's Theology of the Cross*. Minneapolis: Augsburg.

Lohse 1986: Bernhard Lohse, *Martin Luther: An Introduction to his Life and Work*. Philadelphia: Fortress.

Lohse 1991: Bernhard Lohse, *Thomas Müntzer in neuer Sicht: Müntzer im Licht der neueren Forschung und die Frage nach dem Ansatz seiner Theologie*. Göttingen: Vandenhoeck & Ruprecht.

Lortz 1968: Joseph Lortz, *The Reformation in Germany*. London/New York: Herder & Herder.

Lortz 1970: Joseph Lortz, "The Basic Elements of Luther's Intellectual Style," in Jared Wicks, SJ, ed., *Catholic Scholars' Dialogue with Luther*, 3–33. Chicago: Loyola University Press.

Lowenthal 1985: David Lowenthal, *The Past is a Foreign Country*. Cambridge: Cambridge University Press.

Lukens 1990: Michael B. Lukens, "Lortz's View of the Reformation and the Crisis of the True Church," *ARG* 81, 20–31.

Lutz 1986: Heinrich Lutz, "Europa in der Krise – Sozialgeschichtliche und religionssoziologische Analyse der Wende vom 15. zum 16. Jahrhundert," in Susanne Heine, ed., *Europa in der Krise der Neuzeit: Martin Luther: Wandel und Wirkung seines Bildes*, 11–26. Vienna: Böhlau.

McCue 1984: James F. McCue, "Double Justification at the Council of Trent: Piety and Theology in Sixteenth Century Roman Catholicism," in Lindberg 1984, 39–56.

MacCulloch 1990: Diarmaid MacCulloch, *The Later Reformation in England 1547–1603*. New York: St Martin's.

MacCulloch 1992: Diarmaid MacCulloch, "England," in Pettegree 1992, 166–87.

McGrath 1985: Alister E. McGrath, *Luther's Theology of the Cross*. Oxford: Blackwell.

McGrath 1993: Alister E. McGrath, *Reformation Thought: An Introduction*, 2nd edn. Oxford: Blackwell.

McKay et al. 1988: John McKay, Bennett Hill and John Buckler, eds, *A History of World Societies*, 2nd edn, I. Boston: Houghton Mifflin.

McKee 1984: Elsie Anne McKee, *John Calvin on the Diaconate and Liturgical Almsgiving*. Geneva: Droz.

McKee and Armstrong 1989: Elsie Anne McKee and Brian G. Armstrong, eds, *Probing the Reformed Tradition: Historical Studies in Honor of Edward A. Dowey, Jr.* Louisville: Westminster/John Knox.

McLaughlin 1986a: R. Emmet McLaughlin, "Schwenckfeld and the South German Eucharistic Controversy, 1526–1529," in Peter C. Erb, ed.,

Schwenckfeld and Early Schwenckfeldianism, 181–210. Pennsburg: Schwenck-felder Library.

McLaughlin 1986b: R. Emmet McLaughlin, *Casper Schwenkfeld: Reluctant Radical. His Life to 1540*. New Haven: Yale University Press.

McNally 1967: Robert McNally, SJ, "Ignatius Loyola," in Gerrish 1967, 232–56.

McNeill 1967: John T. McNeill, *The History and Character of Calvinism*. New York: Oxford University Press.

McNeill and Battles 1960: John T. McNeill, ed., and Ford Lewis Battles, tr., *Calvin: Institutes of the Christian Religion*, Library of Christian Classics, XX–XXI. Philadelphia: Westminster.

McNeill 1976: William H. McNeill, *Plagues and Peoples*. Garden City: Anchor.

Maltby 1992: William S. Maltby, ed., *Reformation Europe: A Guide to Research*, II. St Louis: Center for Reformation Research.

Manns and Meyer 1984: Peter Manns and Harding Meyer, eds, *Luther's Ecumenical Significance*. Philadelphia/New York: Fortress/Paulist.

Manschreck 1965: Clyde Manschreck, ed., *A History of Christianity*, II. Englewood Cliffs: Prentice-Hall.

Mansfield 1979: Bruce Mansfield, *Phoenix of his Age: Interpretations of Erasmus, c. 1550–1750*. Toronto: University of Toronto Press.

Mansfield 1992: Bruce Mansfield, *Man on his Own: Interpretations of Erasmus, c. 1750–1920*. Buffalo: University of Toronto Press.

Marcocchi 1988: Massimo Marcocchi, "Spirituality in the Sixteenth and Seventeenth Centuries," in O'Malley 1988, 163–92.

Marcus 1973: Jacob R. Marcus, *The Jew in the Medieval World. A Source Book: 315–1791*. New York: Atheneum.

Marnef, 1994. Guido Marnef, "The Changing Face of Calvinism in Antwerp, 1555–1585," in Pettegree et al. 1994, 143–59.

Marr 1987: M. Lucille Marr, "Anabaptist Women of the North: Peers in Faith, Subordinates in Marriage," *MQR* 61, 347–62.

Marshall 1989: Sherrin Marshall, ed., *Women in Reformation and Counter-Reformation Europe: Public and Private Worlds*. Bloomington: Indiana University Press.

Matheson 1988: Peter Matheson, ed. and tr., *The Collected Works of Thomas Müntzer*. Edinburgh: T. & T. Clark.

Maxcey 1979: Carl E. Maxcey, "Double Justice, Diego Laynez and the Council of Trent," *CH* 48, 269–78.

Meissner 1992: W. W. Meissner, SJ, *Ignatius of Loyola: The Psychology of a Saint*. New Haven: Yale University Press.

Mellinkoff 1993: Ruth Mellinkoff, *Signs of Otherness in Northern European Art*, 2 vols. Berkeley: University of California Press.

Menchi 1993: Silvia Seidel Menchi, *Erasmus als Ketzer: Reformation und Inquisition im Italien des 16. Jahrhunderts*. Leiden: E. J. Brill.

Meyer 1965: Hans Meyer, SJ, *Luther und die Messe*. Paderborn: Bonifacius Verlag.

Moeller 1971: Bernd Moeller, "Piety in Germany around 1500," in Ozment 1971, 50–75.

Moeller 1977: Bernd Moeller, *Deutschland im Zeitalter der Reformation*. Göttingen: Vandenhoeck & Ruprecht.

Moeller 1979: Bernd Moeller, "Stadt und Buch: Bemerkungen zur Struktur der reformatorischen Bewegung in Deutschland," in Wolfgang J. Mommsen, ed., *Stadtbürgertum und Adel in der Reformation: Studien zur Sozialgeschichte du Reformation in England und Deutschland*, 25–39. Stuttgart: Klett-Cotta.

Moeller 1982: Bernd Moeller, *Imperial Cities and the Reformation: Three Essays*, ed. and trans. H. C. Erik Midelfort and Mark U. Edwards, Jr. Durham: Labyrinth. (First publ. 1972.)

Moeller 1987: Bernd Moeller, "Luther in Europe: His Works in Translation 1517–1546," in Kouri and Scott 1987, 235–51.

Mollat 1986: Michel Mollat, *The Poor in the Middle Ages: An Essay in Social History*, tr. Arthur Goldhammer. New Haven: Yale University Press.

Monter 1967: William Monter, *Calvin's Geneva*. New York: Wiley.

Monter 1990: William Monter, *Frontiers of Heresy: The Spanish Inquisition from the Basque Lands to Sicily*. Cambridge: Cambridge University Press.

Moran 1993: J. F. Moran, *The Japanese and the Jesuits: Alesandro Valignano in Sixteenth-Century Japan*. London: Routledge.

Muller 1978: Richard A. Muller, "Perkins' *A Golden Chaine*: Predestinarian System or Schematized *Ordo Salutis*?," *SCJ* 9, 69–81.

Murray 1974: Alexander Murray, "Religion Among the Poor in Thirteenth-Century France," *Traditio* 30, 285–324.

Naphy 1994: William G. Naphy, *Calvin and the Consolidation of the Genevan Reformation*. Manchester: Manchester University Press.

Neuser 1994: Wilhelm Neuser, ed., *Calvinus Sacrae Scripturae Professor: Calvin as Confessor of Holy Scripture*. Grand Rapids: Eerdmans.

Nicholls 1988: David Nicholls, "The Theatre of Martyrdom in the French Reformation," *PP* 121, 49–73.

Nicholls 1992: David Nicholls, "France," in Pettegree 1992, 120–41.

Niesel 1956: Wilhelm Niesel, *The Theology of Calvin*. Philadelphia: Westminster.

Nijenhuis 1972: W. Nijenhuis, *Ecclesia Reformata: Studies on the Reformation*. Leiden: E. J. Brill.

Nipperdey 1987: Thomas Nipperdey, "The Reformation and the Modern World," in Kouri and Scott 1987, 535–52.

Nischan 1994: Bodo Nischan, "Confessionalism and Absolutism: The Case of Brandenburg," in Pettegree et al. 1994, 181–204.

Nugent 1974: Donald Nugent, *Ecumenism in the Age of the Reformation: The Colloquy of Poissy*. Cambridge, MA: Harvard University Press.

Nygren 1948: Anders Nygren, "The Role of the Self-Evident in History," *Journal of Religion* 29, 235–41.

Oberman 1963: Heiko A. Oberman, *The Harvest of Medieval Theology: Gabriel Biel and Late Medieval Nominalism*. Cambridge, MA: Harvard University Press.

Oberman 1966: Heiko A. Oberman, *Forerunners of the Reformation: The Shape of Late Medieval Thought Illustrated by Key Documents*. New York: Holt, Rinehart & Winston.

Oberman 1973: Heiko A. Oberman, "The Shape of Late Medieval Thought: The Birthpangs of the Modern Era," *ARG* 64, 13–33.

Oberman 1984: Heiko A. Oberman, *The Roots of Anti-Semitism in the Age of the Renaissance and Reformation*. Philadelphia: Fortress.

Oberman 1986: Heiko A. Oberman, *The Dawn of the Reformation: Essays in Late Medieval and Early Reformation Thought*. Edinburgh: T. & T. Clark.

Oberman 1988: Heiko A. Oberman, "Teufelsdreck: Eschatology and Scatology in the 'Old' Luther," *SCJ* 19, 435–50.

Oberman 1989a: Heiko A. Oberman, "Die Gelehrten die Verkehrten: Popular Response to Learned Culture in the Renaissance and Reformation," in Ozment 1989, 43–62.

Oberman 1989b: Heiko A. Oberman, *Luther: Man between God and the Devil*. New Haven: Yale University Press.

Oberman 1992: Heiko A. Oberman, "*Europa afflicta*: The Reformation of the Refugees," *ARG* 83, 91–111.

Oberman 1994: Heiko A. Oberman, "*Initia Calvini*: The Matrix of Calvin's Reformation," in Neuser 1994, 113–54.

O'Connell 1974: Marvin R. O'Connell, *The Counter-Reformation 1560–1610*. New York: Harper Torchbooks.

O'Day 1986: Rosemary O'Day, *The Debate on the English Reformation*. London: Methuen.

Olin 1966: John C. Olin, ed., *John Calvin and Jacopo Sadoleto: A Reformation Debate*. New York: Harper Torchbooks.

Olin 1990: John C. Olin, *Catholic Reform: From Cardinal Ximenes to the Council of Trent 1495–1563*. New York: Fordham University Press.

Olin 1992: John C. Olin, *The Catholic Reformation: Savonarola to Ignatius Loyola*. New York: Fordham University Press.

Olson 1989: Jeannine Olson, *Calvin and Social Welfare: Deacons and the "Bourse française"*. Selinsgrove: Susquehanna University Press.

Olson 1972: Oliver K. Olson, "Theology of Revolution: Magdeburg, 1550–1551," *SCJ* 3, 56–79.

Olson 1981: Oliver K. Olson, "Matthius Flacius Illyricus 1520–1575," in Raitt 1981, 1–17.

Olson 1993: Oliver K. Olson, "Baldo Lupetino, Venetian Martyr," *LQ* 7, 6–18.

O'Malley 1988: John W. O'Malley, SJ, ed., *Catholicism in Early Modern History: A Guide to Research*. St Louis: Center for Reformation Research.

O'Malley 1991: John W. O'Malley SJ, "Was Ignatius Loyola a Church Reformer? How to Look at Early Modern Catholicism," *CHR* 77, 177–93.

O'Malley 1993: John W. O'Malley SJ, *The First Jesuits*. Cambridge, MA: Harvard University Press.

Orth 1993: Myra D. Orth, "Radical Beauty: Marguerite de Navarre's Illuminated Protestant Catechism and Confession," *SCJ* 24, 383–425.

Osborne 1963: John Osborne, *Luther*. New York: Signet.

Oyer 1977: John Oyer, "The Influence of Jacob Strauss on the Anabaptists: A Problem in Historical Methodology," in Lienhard 1977, 62–82.

Ozment 1971: Steven Ozment, ed., *The Reformation in Medieval Perspective*. Chicago: Quadrangle.

Ozment 1973: Steven Ozment, *Mysticism and Dissent: Religious Ideology and Social Protest in the Sixteenth Century*. New Haven: Yale University Press.

Ozment 1975: Steven Ozment, *The Reformation in the Cities: The Appeal of Protestantism to Sixteenth-Century Germany and Switzerland*. New Haven: Yale University Press.

Ozment 1979: Steven Ozment, "Pamphlets as a Source: Comments on Bernd Moeller's 'Stadt und Buch'," in Wolfgang J. Mommsen, ed., *Stadtbürgertum und Adel in der Reformation: Studien zur Struktur der Reformation in England und Deutschland*, 24–8. Stuttgart: Klett-Cotta.

Ozment 1980: Steven Ozment, *The Age of Reform 1250–1550*. New Haven: Yale University Press.

Ozment 1982: Steven Ozment, ed., *Reformation Europe: A Guide to Research*. St Louis: Center for Reformation Research.

Ozment 1983: Steven Ozment, *When Fathers Ruled: Family Life in Reformation Europe*. Cambridge, MA: Harvard University Press.

Ozment 1985: Steven Ozment, "Luther's Political Legacy," in James F. Harris, ed., *German–American Interrelations: Heritage and Challenge*, 7–40. Tübingen: Tübingen University Press.

Ozment 1989: Steven Ozment, ed., *Religion and Culture in the Renaissance and Reformation*. Kirksville: Sixteenth Century Journal Publishers.

Ozment 1992: Steven Ozment, *Protestants: The Birth of a Revolution*. New York: Doubleday.

Packull 1977: Werner Packull, *Mysticism and the Early South German–Austrian Anabaptist Movement 1525–1531*. Scottdale: Herald.

Pallier 1977: D. M. Pallier, "Popular Reactions to the Reformation during the Years of Uncertainty 1530–1570," in Felicity Heal and Rosemary O'Day, eds, *Church and Society in England: Henry VIII to James I*, 35–56. London: Macmillan.

Panofsky 1955: E. Panofsky, *The Life and Art of Albrecht Dürer*. Princeton: Princeton University Press.

Parker 1993: Charles H. Parker, "French Calvinists as the Children of Israel: An Old Testament Self-Consciousness in Jean Crespin's *Histoire des Martyrs* before the Wars of Religion," *SCJ* 24, 227–48.

Parker 1963: T. M. Parker, *The English Reformation to 1558*. London: Oxford University Press.

Pater 1984a: Calvin A. Pater, *Karlstadt as the Father of the Baptist Movements: The Emergence of Lay Protestantism*. Toronto: University of Toronto Press.

Pater 1984b: Calvin A. Pater, "Lay Religion in the Program of Andreas Rudolff-Bodenstein von Karlstadt," in DeMolen 1984, 99–133.

Pauck 1959: Wilhelm Pauck, ed., *Melanchthon and Bucer*. (Library of Christian Classics, 19.) Philadelphia: Westminster.

Payne 1970: John B. Payne, *Erasmus: His Theology of the Sacraments*. Richmond: John Knox.

Pelikan 1964: Jaroslav Pelikan, *Obedient Rebels: Catholic Substance and Protestant Principle in Luther's Reformation*. New York: Harper & Row.

Pelikan 1968: Jaroslav Pelikan, ed., *Interpreters of Luther: Essays in Honor of Wilhelm Pauck*. Philadelphia: Fortress.

Pelikan 1971: Jaroslav Pelikan, *Historical Theology: Continuity and Change in Christian Doctrine*. London: Hutchinson.

Pelikan 1984: Jaroslav Pelikan, *The Christian Tradition*, IV: *Reformation of Church and Dogma 1300–1700*. Chicago: University of Chicago Press.

Pettegree 1992: Andrew Pettegree, ed., *The Early Reformation in Europe*. Cambridge: Cambridge University Press.

Pettegree 1994: Andrew Pettegree, "Coming to Terms with Victory: The Upbuilding of a Calvinist Church in Holland, 1572–1590," in Pettegree et al. 1994, 160–80.

Pettegree et al. 1994: Andrew Pettegree, Alastair Duke and Gillian Lewis, eds, *Calvinism in Europe 1540–1620*. Cambridge: Cambridge University Press.

Postel 1980: Rainer Postel, "Sozialgeschichtliche Folgewirkungen der Reformation in Hamburg," in Wenzel Lohff, ed., *450 Jahre Reformation in Hamburg. Eine Festschrift*, 63–84. Hamburg: Agentur des Rauhen Hauses.

Potter 1976: G. R. Potter, *Zwingli*. Cambridge: Cambridge University Press.

Powicke 1965: Maurice Powicke, *The Reformation in England*. London: Oxford University Press, repr; first publ. 1941.

Prestwich 1985: Menna Prestwich, *International Calvinism 1541–1715*. Oxford: Clarendon.

Preus 1974: James S. Preus, *Carlstadt's "Ordinaciones" and Luther's Liberty: A Study of the Wittenberg Movement 1521–22*. Cambridge, MA: Harvard University Press.

Raitt 1981: Jill Raitt, ed., *Shapers of Religious Traditions in Germany, Switzerland, and Poland, 1560–1600*. New Haven: Yale University Press.

Ranum 1980: Orest Ranum, "The French Ritual of Tyrannicide in the Late Sixteenth Century," *SCJ* 11, 63–81.

Rasmussen 1988: Niels Krogh Rasmussen, OP, "Liturgy and Liturgical Arts," in O'Malley 1988, 273–97.

Reid 1971: W. Stanford Reid, "The Battle Hymns of the Lord: Calvinist Psalmody of the Sixteenth Century," *SCJ* 2, 36–54.

Reid 1982: W. Stanford Reid, ed., *John Calvin: His Influence in the Western World*. Grand Rapids: Zondervan.

Reid 1994: W. Stanford Reid, "Reformation in France and Scotland: A Case Study in Sixteenth-Century Communication," in Graham 1994, 195–214.

Rempel 1993: John D. Rempel, *The Lord's Supper in Anabaptism: A Study in the Christology of Balthasar Hubmaier, Pilgram Marpeck, and Dirk Philips*. Waterloo: Herald.

Repgen 1987: Konrad Repgen, "What is a 'Religious War'?," in Kouri and Scott 1987, 311–28.

Richardson 1994: Anne Richardson, "William Tyndale and the Bill of Rights," in John A. R. Dick and Anne Richardson, eds, *William Tyndale and the Law*, 11–29. Kirksville: Sixteenth Century Journal Publishers.

Ridley 1966: Jasper Ridley, *Thomas Cranmer*. Oxford: Clarendon.

Rilliet 1964: Jean Rilliet, *Zwingli: Third Man of the Reformation*. Philadelphia: Westminster.

Robinson 1992: John Hughes Robinson, *John Calvin and the Jews*. New York: Peter Lang.

Roelker 1968: Nancy Lyman Roelker, *Queen of Navarre: Jeanne d'Albret 1528–1572*. Cambridge, MA: Harvard University Press.

Roelker 1972a: Nancy Lyman Roelker, "The Appeal of Calvinism to French Noble Women in the Sixteenth Century," *Journal of Interdisciplinary History* 2, 391–418.

Roelker 1972b: Nancy Lyman Roelker, "The Role of Noblewomen in the French Reformation," *ARG* 63, 168–95.

Roper 1989: Lyndal Roper, *The Holy Household: Women and Morals in Reformation Augsburg*. Oxford: Clarendon.

Roper 1964: William Roper, "The Life of Sir Thomas More," in Sylvester and Harding 1964, 195–254.

Rorem 1988: Paul Rorem, "Calvin and Bullinger on the Lord's Supper," *LQ* 2–3, 155–84, 357–89.

Rorem 1994: Paul Rorem, "The *Consensus Tigurinus* (1549): Did Calvin Compromise?," in Neuser 1994, 72–90.

Rörig 1967: Fritz Rörig, *The Medieval Town*. Berkeley: University of California Press.

Rosenthal 1972: Joel Rosenthal, *The Purchase of Paradise: Gift-Giving and Aristocracy 1307–1485*. London: Routledge & Kegan Paul.

Rowen and Harline 1994: Herbert H. Rowen and Craig E. Harline, "The Birth of the Dutch Nation," in Malcolm R. Thorp and Arthur J. Slavin, eds, *Politics, Religion and Diplomacy in Early Modern Europe: Essays in Honor of Delamar Jensen*, 67–81. Kirksville: Sixteenth Century Journal Publishers.

Rowan 1985: Steven Rowan, "Luther, Bucer and Eck on the Jews," *SCJ* 16, 75–90.

Rubin 1991: Miri Rubin, *Corpus Christi: The Eucharist in Late Medieval Culture*. Cambridge: Cambridge University Press.

Rublack 1988: Hans-Christoph Rublack, "The Song of Contz Anahans: Communication and Revolt in Nördlingen, 1525," in Hsia 1988, 102–20.

Rublack 1993: Hans-Christoph Rublack, "Reformation und Moderne: Soziologische, theologische und historische Ansichten," in Guggisberg and Krodel 1993, 17–38.

Rupp 1953: Gordon Rupp, *The Righteousness of God: Luther Studies*. New York: Philosophical Library.

Rupp 1966: Gordon Rupp, *Studies in the Making of the English Protestant Tradition*. Cambridge: Cambridge University Press.

Rupp 1969: Gordon Rupp, *Patterns of Reformation*. Philadelphia: Fortress.

Salmon 1967: J. H. M. Salmon, ed., *The French Wars of Religion: How Important Were the Religious Factors?* Lexington: D. C. Heath.

Scarisbrick 1984: J. J. Scarisbrick, *The Reformation and the English People*. Oxford: Oxford University Press.

Schaff 1919: Philip Schaff, ed., *The Creeds of Christendom*, 3 vols. New York: Harper & Brothers.

Scharfenberg 1986: Joachim Scharfenberg, "Martin Luther in psychohistorischer Sicht," in Susanne Heine, ed., *Europa in der Krise der Neuzeit*, 113–28. Vienna: Böhlau.

Scharffenorth 1982: Gerta Scharffenorth, *Den Glauben ins Leben ziehen . . . : Studien zu Luthers Theologie*. Munich: Chr. Kaiser.

Scharffenorth 1983: Gerta Scharffenorth, *Becoming Friends in Christ: The Relationship between Man and Woman as Seen by Luther*. Geneva: Lutheran World Federation.

Schilling 1986: Heinz Schilling, "The Reformation and the Rise of the Early Modern State," in Tracy 1986, 21–30.

Schilling 1988: Heinz Schilling, *Aufbruch und Krise: Deutschland 1517–1648*. Berlin: Siedler.

Schilling 1991: Heinz Schilling, *Civic Calvinism in Northwestern Germany and the Netherlands*. Kirksville: Sixteenth Century Journal Publishers.

Schilling 1992: Heinz Schilling, *Religion, Political Culture and the Emergence of Early Modern Society: Essays in German and Dutch History*. Leiden: E. J. Brill.

Schilling 1994: Heinz Schilling, "Luther, Loyola, Calvin und die europäische Neuzeit," *ARG* 85, 5–31.

Schmidt 1992: Heinrich Richard Schmidt, *Konfessionalisierung im 16. Jahrhundert*. Munich: Oldenbourg.

Schnucker 1988: Robert V. Schnucker, ed., *Calviniana: Ideas and Influence of Jean Calvin*. Kirksville: Sixteenth Century Journal Publishers.

Schoenberger 1977: Cynthia Grant Schoenberger, "The Development of the Lutheran Theory of Resistance: 1523–1530," *SCJ* 8, 61–76.

Schultze 1985: Winfried Schultze, "Zwingli, Lutherisches Widerstandsdenken, monomachischer Widerstand," in Peter Blickle, Andreas Lindt and Alfred Schindler, eds, *Zwingli und Europe*, 199–216. Zurich: Vandenhoeck & Ruprecht.

Schutte 1977: Anne Jacobson Schutte, *Pier Paolo Vergerio: The Making of an Italian Reformer*. Geneva: Droz.

Schwiebert 1950: E. G. Schwiebert, *Luther and his Times: The Reformation from a New Perspective*. St Louis: Concordia.

Scott 1989: Tom Scott, *Thomas Müntzer: Theology and Revolution in the German Reformation*. New York: St Martin's.

Scott and Scribner 1991: Tom Scott and Bob Scribner, eds, *The German Peasants' War: A History in Documents*. Atlantic Highlands: Humanities.

Scribner 1981: R. W. Scribner, *For the Sake of Simple Folk: Popular Propaganda for the German Reformation*. Cambridge: Cambridge University Press.

Scribner 1986: R. W. Scribner, *The German Reformation*. Atlantic Highlands: Humanities.

Scribner 1987: R. W. Scribner, *Popular Culture and Popular Movements in Reformation Germany*. London: Hambledon.

Scribner 1990: R. W. Scribner, "Politics and the Institutionalization of Reform in Germany," in Elton 1990, 172–97.

Scribner 1993: Bob Scribner, "Anticlericalism and the Cities," in Dykema and Oberman 1993, 147–66.

Scribner and Benecke 1979: Bob Scribner and Gerhard Benecke, eds, *The German Peasant War of 1525 – New Viewpoints*. London: Allen & Unwin.

Seaver 1982: Paul Seaver, "The English Reformation," in Ozment 1982, 271–96.

Séguenny 1987: André Séguenny, *The Christology of Caspar Schwenkfeld: Spirit and Flesh in the Process of Life Transformation*. Lewiston: Edwin Mellen.

Selinger 1984: Suzanne Selinger, *Calvin Against Himself: An Inquiry in Intellectual History*. Hamden: Archon.

Shirer 1960: William Shirer, *The Rise and Fall of the Third Reich*. New York: Simon & Schuster.

Sider 1974: Ronald J. Sider, *Andreas Bodenstein von Karlstadt: The Development of His Thought 1517–1525*. Leiden: E. J. Brill.

Sider 1978: Ronald J. Sider, ed., *Karlstadt's Battle with Luther: Documents in a Liberal–Radical Debate*. Philadelphia: Fortress.

Siemon-Netto 1995: Uwe Siemon-Netto, *The Fabricated Luther: The Rise and Fall of the Shirer Myth*. St Louis: Concordia.

Skarsten 1988: Trygve Skarsten, "Johan Campanius, Pastor in New Sweden,"*LQ* 2, 47–87.

Skinner 1980: Quentin Skinner, "The Origins of the Calvinist Theory of Revolution," in Barbara C, Malament, ed., *After the Reformation: Essays in Honor of J. H. Hexter*, 309–30. University Park: University of Pennsylvania Press.

Southern 1970: R. W. Southern, *Western Society and the Church in the Middle Ages*. Baltimore: Penguin.

Southern 1974: R. W. Southern, *The Making of the Middle Ages*. New Haven: Yale University Press.

Spalding 1992: James C. Spalding, ed. and tr., *The Reformation of the Ecclesiastical Laws of England, 1552*. Kirksville: Sixteenth Century Journal Publishers.

Spence 1984: Jonathon D. Spence, *The Memory Palace of Matteo Ricci*. New York: Viking Penguin.

Spijker 1991: Willem van't Spijker, ed., *Calvin: Erbe und Auftrag. Festschrift für Wilhelm Neuser zu seinem 65. Geburtstag*. Kampen: Kok Pharos.

Spijker 1993: Willem van't Spijker, "Bucer and Calvin," in Krieger and Lienhard 1993, I, 461–70.

Spijker 1994: Willem van't Spijker, "Bucer's Influence on Calvin: Church and Community," in Wright 1994, 32–44.

Spitz 1962: Lewis W. Spitz, ed., *The Reformation: Material or Spiritual?* Boston: D. C. Heath.

Spitz 1971: Lewis W. Spitz, *The Renaissance and Reformation Movements*. Chicago: Rand McNally.

Spitz 1985: Lewis W. Spitz, *The Protestant Reformation 1517–1559*. New York: Harper & Row.

Spruyt, 1991. Bart J. Spruyt, "Listrius *lutherizans*: His *Epistola theologica adversus Dominicanos Suollenses* (1520)" in *SCJ* 22, 727–51.

Stauffer 1967: Richard Stauffer, *Luther as Seen by Catholics*. Richmond: John Knox.

Stayer 1972: James M. Stayer, *Anabaptists and the Sword*. Lawrence: Coronado.

Stayer 1980/1: James Stayer, "Polygamy as 'Inner-Worldly Asceticism': Conceptions of Marriage in the Radical Reformation," *Documenta Anabaptistica Neerlandica* 12–13 (1980–1).

Stayer, 1990: James M. Stayer, "The Anabaptists and the Sects," in Elton 1990, 118–43.

Stayer 1991: James M. Stayer, *The German Peasants' War and Anabaptist Community of Goods*. Montreal: McGill-Queen's University Press.

Stayer and Packull 1980: James M. Stayer and Werner O. Packull, eds, *The Anabaptists and Thomas Müntzer*. Dubuque/Toronto: Kendall/Hunt.

Steinmetz 1971: David C. Steinmetz, *Reformers in the Wings*. Philadelphia: Fortress.

Steinmetz 1976: David C. Steinmetz, "The Necessity of the Past," *Theology Today* 33, 168–76.

Steinmetz 1986: David C. Steinmetz, *Luther in Context*. Bloomington: Indiana University Press.

Steinmetz 1990: David C. Steinmetz, "Calvin and his Lutheran Critics," *LQ* 4, 179–94.

Stephens 1986: W. P. Stephens, *The Theology of Huldrych Zwingli*. Oxford: Clarendon.

Stephens 1992: W. P. Stephens, *Zwingli: An Introduction to his Thought*. Oxford: Clarendon.

Stock 1982: Ursala Stock, *Die Bedeutung der Sakramente in Luthers Sermonen von 1519*. Leiden: E. J. Brill.

Strauss 1963: Gerald Strauss, *Historian in an Age of Crisis: The Life and Work of Johannes Aventinus 1477–1534*. Cambridge, MA: Harvard University Press.

Strauss 1971: Gerald Strauss, ed. and tr., *Manifestations of Discontent in Germany on the Eve of the Reformation*. Bloomington: Indiana University Press.

Strauss 1978: Gerald Strauss, *Luther's House of Learning: Indoctrination of the Young in the German Reformation*. Baltimore/ London: Johns Hopkins University Press.

Strohm 1989: Theodor Strohm, " 'Theologie der Diakonie' in der Perspektive der Reformation," in Paul Philippi and Theodor Strohm, eds, *Theologie der Diakonie*, 175–208. Heidelberg: Heidelberger Verlagsanstalt.

Sunshine 1994: Glenn S. Sunshine, "Reformed Theology and the Origins of Synodal Polity: Calvin, Beza and the Gallican Confession," in Graham 1994, 141–58.

Sutherland 1967: N. M. Sutherland, "Calvin's Idealism and Indecision," in Salmon 1967, 14–24.

Sutherland 1978: N. M. Sutherland, "Catherine de Medici: The Legend of the Wicked Italian Queen," *SCJ* 9, 45–56.

Sutherland 1980: N. M. Sutherland, *The Huguenot Struggle for Recognition*. New Haven: Yale University Press.

Sylvester and Harding 1964: Richard S. Sylvester and Davis P. Harding, eds, *Two Early Tudor Lives*. New Haven: Yale University Press.

Tappert 1959: Theodore Tappert, ed., *The Book of Concord: The Confessions of the Evangelical Lutheran Church*. Philadelphia: Muhlenberg.

Tedeschi 1991: John Tedeschi, *The Prosecution of Heresy: Collected Studies on the Inquisition in Early Modern Italy*. Binghamton: Medieval and Renaissance Texts and Studies.

Tentler 1977: Thomas N. Tentler, *Sin and Confession on the Eve of the Reformation*. Princeton: Princeton University Press.

Thompson 1992: John Lee Thompson, *John Calvin and the Daughters of Sarah: Women in Regular and Exceptional Roles in the Exegesis of Calvin, His Predecessors, and His Contemporaries*. Geneva: Droz.

Tillich 1960: Paul Tillich, *The Protestant Era*. Chicago: Phoenix.

Tjernagel 1965: Neelak Tjernagel, *Henry VIII and the Lutherans: A Study in Anglo-Lutheran Relations from 1521 to 1547*. St Louis: Concordia.

Torrance 1994: James B. Torrance, "The Concept of Federal Theology: Was Calvin a Federal Theologian?," in Neuser 1994, 15–40.

Tracy 1986: James D. Tracy, ed., *Luther and the Modern State in Germany*. Kirksville: Sixteenth Century Journal Publishers.

Tracy, 1993. James D. Tracy, "Public Church, *Gemeente Christi*, or *Volkskerk*: Holland's Reformed Church in Civil and Ecclesiastical Perspective, 1572–1592," in Guggisberg and Krodel 1993, 487–510.

Vogt 1867: Karl A. T. Vogt, *Johannes Bugenhagen Pomeranus. Leben und ausgewählte Schriften*. Elberfeld: R. L. Friedrichs.

Walker 1969: Williston Walker, *John Calvin: The Organiser of Reformed Protestantism (1509–1564)*. New York: Schocken.

Walton 1967: Robert C. Walton, *Zwingli's Theocracy*. Toronto: University of Toronto Press.

Walton 1984: Robert C. Walton, "Zwingli: Founding Father of the Reformed Churches," in DeMolen 1984, 69–98.

Wandel 1990: Lee Palmer Wandel, *Always Among Us: Images of the Poor in Zwingli's Zurich*. Cambridge: Cambridge University Press.

Wandel 1995: Lee Palmer Wandel, *Voracious Idols and Violent Hands: Iconoclasm in Reformation Zurich, Strasbourg, and Basel*. Cambridge: Cambridge University Press.

Watanabe 1994: Nobuo Watanabe, "Calvin's Second Catechism: Its Predecessors and its Environment," in Neuser 1994, 224–32.

Wendel 1963: François Wendel, *Calvin: Origins and Development of His Religious Thought*. New York: Harper & Row.

Wicks 1970: Jared Wicks, SJ, ed., *Catholic Scholars' Dialogue with Luther*, Chicago: Loyola University Press.

Wicks 1978: Jared Wicks, SJ, *Cajetan Responds: A Reader in Reformation Controversy*. Washington, DC: Catholic University of America Press.

Wiedermann 1983: Gotthelf Wiedermann, "Cochlaeus as a Polemicist," in Brooks 1983, 195–205.

Wiesner 1988: Merry Wiesner, "Women's Response to the Reformation," in Hsia 1988, 148–171.

Wiesner 1992: Merry Wiesner, "Studies of Women, The Family, and Gender," in Maltby 1992, 159–87.

Wiley 1990: David N. Wiley, "The Church as the Elect in the Theology of Calvin," in George 1990, 96–117.

Wilken 1972: Robert Wilken, *The Myth of Christian Beginnings: History's Impact on Belief.* New York: Doubleday Anchor.

Wilks 1963: Michael Wilks, *The Problem of Sovereignty in the Later Middle Ages*. London: Cambridge University Press.

Williams 1992: George H. Williams, *The Radical Reformation*, 3rd edn. Kirksville: Sixteenth Century Journal Publishers.

Williams and Mergal 1957: George Williams and Angel Mergal, eds, *Spiritual and Anabaptist Writers*. (Library of Christian Classics, 25.) Philadelphia: Westminster.

Willis-Watkins 1989: David Willis-Watkins, "Calvin's Prophetic Reinterpretation of Kingship," in McKee and Armstrong 1989, 116–34.

Witek 1988: John W. Witek, SJ, "From India to Japan: European Missionary Expansion, 1500–1650," in O'Malley 1988, 193–210.

Wohlfeil and Goertz 1980: Rainer Wohlfeil and Hans-Jürgen Goertz, *Gewissensfreiheit als Bedingungen der Neuzeit. Fragen an der Speyerer Protestation von 1529*. Göttingen: Vandenhoeck & Ruprecht.

Wolfe 1993: Michael Wolfe, *The Conversion of Henri IV: Politics, Power, and Religious Belief in Early Modern France*. Cambridge, MA: Harvard University Press.

Wolgast 1985: Eike Wolgast, "Reform, Reformation," in Otto Brunner et al., eds, *Geschichtliche Grundbegriffe. Historisches Lexikon zur politisch-sozialen Sprache in Deutschland*, V, 313–60. Stuttgart: Klett-Cotta.

Wright 1993: D. F. Wright, "Martin Bucer and England – and Scotland," in Krieger and Lienhard 1993, II, 523–32.

Wright 1994: D. F. Wright, ed., *Martin Bucer: Reforming Church and Community*. Cambridge: Cambridge University Press.

Wuthnow 1989: Robert Wuthnow, *Communities of Discourse. Ideology and Social Structure in the Reformation, the Enlightenment, and European Socialism*. Cambridge, MA: Harvard University Press.

Zapalac 1990: Kristin E. S. Zapalac, *"In His Image and Likeness": Political Iconography and Religious Change in Regensburg, 1500–1600*. Ithaca: Cornell University Press.

Zeeden 1973: Ernst Walter Zeeden, ed., *Gegenreformation*. Darmstadt: Wissenschaftliches Buchgesellschaft.

Ziegler 1969: Philip Ziegler, *The Black Death*. London: Penguin.

Zuck 1975: Lowell H. Zuck, ed., *Christianity and Revolution: Radical Christian Testimonies 1520–1650*. Philadelphia: Temple University Press.

Index